FORMAL ONTOLOGY IN INFORMATION SYSTEMS

Frontiers in Artificial Intelligence and Applications

FAIA covers all aspects of theoretical and applied artificial intelligence research in the form of monographs, doctoral dissertations, textbooks, handbooks and proceedings volumes. The FAIA series contains several sub-series, including "Information Modelling and Knowledge Bases" and "Knowledge-Based Intelligent Engineering Systems". It also includes the biennial ECAI, the European Conference on Artificial Intelligence, proceedings volumes, and other ECCAI – the European Coordinating Committee on Artificial Intelligence – sponsored publications. An editorial panel of internationally well-known scholars is appointed to provide a high quality selection.

Series Editors:
J. Breuker, R. Dieng-Kuntz, N. Guarino, J.N. Kok, J. Liu, R. López de Mántaras,
R. Mizoguchi, M. Musen and N. Zhong

Volume 150

Recently published in this series

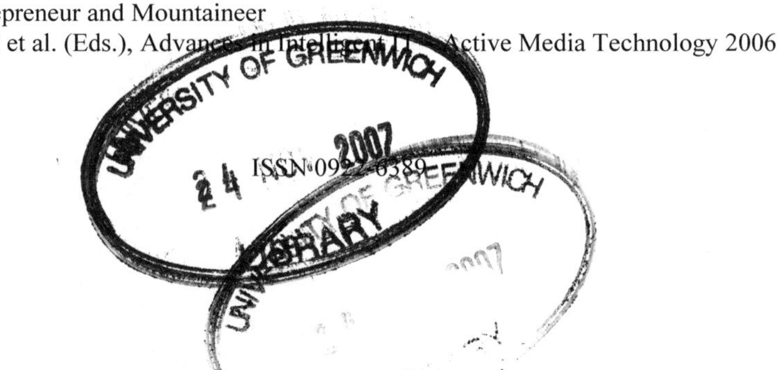

ISSN 0922-6389

Formal Ontology in Information Systems

Proceedings of the Fourth International Conference (FOIS 2006)

Edited by

Brandon Bennett

School of Computing, University of Leeds, UK

and

Christiane Fellbaum

Department of Psychology, Princeton University, New Jersey, USA

IOS
Press

Amsterdam • Berlin • Oxford • Tokyo • Washington, DC

ISBN 1-58603-685-8
Library of Congress Control Number: 2006934681

Publisher
IOS Press
Nieuwe Hemweg 6B
1013 BG Amsterdam
Netherlands
fax: +31 20 687 0019
e-mail: order@iospress.nl

Distributor in the UK and Ireland
Gazelle Books Services Ltd.
White Cross Mills
Hightown
Lancaster LA1 4XS
United Kingdom
fax: +44 1524 63232
e-mail: sales@gazellebooks.co.uk

Distributor in the USA and Canada
IOS Press, Inc.
4502 Rachael Manor Drive
Fairfax, VA 22032
USA
fax: +1 703 323 3668
e-mail: iosbooks@iospress.com

Formal Ontology in Information Systems
B. Bennett and C. Fellbaum (Eds.)
IOS Press, 2006

Preface

Since ancient times, ontology, the analysis and categorisation of what exists, has been fundamental to philosophical enquiry. But, until recently, ontology has been seen as an abstract, purely theoretical discipline, far removed from the practical applications of science. However, with the increasing use of sophisticated computerised information systems, solving problems of an ontological nature is now key to the effective use of technologies supporting a wide range of human activities. The ship of Theseus and the tail of Tibbles the cat are no longer merely amusing puzzles. We employ databases and software applications to deal with everything from ships and ship building to anatomy and amputations. When we design a computer to take stock of a ship yard or check that all goes well at the veterinary hospital, we need to ensure that our system operates in a consistent and reliable way even when manipulating information that involves subtle issues of semantics and identity. So, whereas ontologists may once have shied away from practical problems, now the practicalities of achieving cohesion in an information-based society demand that attention must be paid to ontology.

Researchers in such areas as artificial intelligence, formal and computational linguistics, biomedical informatics, conceptual modeling, knowledge engineering and information retrieval have come to realise that a solid foundation for their research calls for serious work in ontology, understood as a general theory of the types of entities and relations that make up their respective domains of inquiry. In all these areas, attention is now being focused on the content of information rather than on just the formats and languages used to represent information. The clearest example of this development is provided by the many initiatives growing up around the project of the Semantic Web. And, as the need for integrating research in these different fields arises, so does the realisation that strong principles for building well-founded ontologies might provide significant advantages over ad hoc, case-based solutions. The tools of *formal ontology* address precisely these needs, but a real effort is required in order to apply such philosophical tools to the domain of information systems. Reciprocally, research in the information sciences raises specific ontological questions which call for further philosophical investigations.

The purpose of FOIS is to provide a forum for genuine interdisciplinary exchange in the spirit of a unified effort towards solving the problems of ontology, with an eye to both theoretical issues and concrete applications. In our call for papers, we asked for contributions reporting work in a wide range of areas, all of which are important to the development of formal ontologies:

Foundational Issues:

- Kinds of entity: particulars vs. universals, continuants vs. occurrents, abstracta vs. concreta, dependent vs. independent, natural vs. artificial

- Formal relations: parthood, identity, connection, dependence, constitution, subsumption, instantiation
- Vagueness and granularity
- Identity and change
- Formal comparison among ontologies
- Ontology of physical reality (matter, space, time, motion, ...)
- Ontology of biological reality (genes, proteins, cells, organisms, ...)
- Ontology of mental reality (mental attitudes, emotions, ...)
- Ontology of social reality (institutions, organizations, norms, social relationships, artistic expressions, ...)
- Ontology of the information society (information, communication, meaning negotiation, ...)
- Ontology and natural language semantics, ontology and cognition, ontology and epistemology, semiotics

Methodologies and Applications:

- Top-level *vs.* application ontologies
- Role of reference ontologies; Ontology integration and alignment
- Ontology-driven information systems design
- Requirements engineering
- Knowledge engineering
- Knowledge management and organization
- Knowledge representation; Qualitative modeling
- Computational lexica; Terminology
- Information retrieval; Question-answering
- Semantic web; Web services; Grid computing
- Domain-specific ontologies, especially for: Linguistics, Geography, Law, Library science, Biomedical science, E-business, Enterprise integration

Out of the 76 papers submitted to FOIS-06, 29 were secected by the Programme Committee, with the help of a number of extra reviewers (listed in the following section on Conference Organisation). With few exceptions, all papers have been refereed by three experts. On behalf of the Organising Committee, we would like to thank the members of the Program Committee and additional reviewers for their careful work and constructive suggestions, which have helped us to produce a very high quality conference programme. We are also extremely grateful to the two invited speakers, Doug Lenat and Antony Galton, for enthusiastically agreeing to speak at FOIS. Finally, we would like to thank the Conference Chair, Nicola Guarino, the Local Chair, Bill Andersen, the Publicity Chair, Leo Obrst, the Website Administrator, Sira Greco, and Allan Third for help with editing the camera ready copy. The hard work and good will of all these people have contributed to the success of FOIS-06.

Brandon Bennett
Christiane Fellbaum

Conference Organisation

Organising Committee

Conference Chair
Nicola Guarino — Laboratory for Applied Ontology, ISTC-CNR, Trento, Italy

Programme Chairs
Brandon Bennett — School of Computing, University of Leeds, UK
Christiane Fellbaum — Cognitive Science Laboratory, Princeton University, USA; Berlin Brandenburg Academy of Sciences and Humanities, Berlin, Germany

Local Chair
Bill Andersen — Ontology Works, USA

Publicity Chair
Leo Obrst — The MITRE Corporation, USA

Website Maintenance
Sira Greco — Laboratory for Applied Ontology, ISTC-CNR, Trento, Italy

Programme Committee

Bill Andersen — Ontology Works, USA
Nicholas Asher — Department of Philosophy, University of Texas at Austin, USA
Nathalie Aussenac-Gilles — Research Institute for Computer Science, CNRS, Toulouse, France
John Bateman — Department of Applied English Linguistics, University of Bremen, Germany
Brandon Bennett — School of Computing, University of Leeds, UK
Stefano Borgo — Laboratory for Applied Ontology, ISTC-CNR, Italy
Joost Breuker — Leibniz Center for Law, University of Amsterdam, The Netherlands
Roberto Casati — Jean Nicod Institute, CNRS, Paris, France
Werner Ceusters — New York State Center of Excellence in Bioinformatics and Life Sciences, SUNY at Buffalo
Anthony Cohn — School of Computing, University of Leeds, UK
Matteo Cristani — University of Verona, Italy
Ernest Davis — Department of Computer Science, New York University, USA

Martin Dörr	Institute of Computer Science, FORTH, Heraklion, Greece
Carola Eschenbach	Department for Informatics, University of Hamburg, Germany
Jérôme Euzenat	INRIA Rhône-Alpes, France
Christiane Fellbaum	Cognitive Science Laboratory, Princeton University, USA and Berlin Brandenburg Academy of Sciences and Humanities, Berlin, Germany
Antony Galton	School of Engineering, Computer Science and Mathematics, University of Exeter, UK
Aldo Gangemi	Laboratory for Applied Ontology, ISTC-CNR, Roma, Italy
Pierdaniele Giaretta	Department of Philosophy, University of Verona, Italy
Michael Gruninger	University of Toronto, Canada
Nicola Guarino	Laboratory for Applied Ontology, ISTC-CNR, Trento, Italy
Udo Hahn	Jena University, Germany
Jerry Hobbs	University of Southern California, USA
Eduard Hovy	University of Southern California, USA
Ingvar Johansson	Institute for Formal Ontology and Medical Information Science, University of Saarland, Germany
Werner Kuhn	IFGI, Muenster
Fritz Lehmann	USA
Alessandro Lenci	University of Pisa, Italy
Leonardo Lesmo	Department of Informatica, University of Torino, Italy
Bernardo Magnini	Centre for Scientific and Technological Research, ITC-irst, Trento, Italy
David Mark	Department of Geography, State University of New York, Buffalo, USA
William McCarthy	Department of Accounting & Information Systems, Michigan State University, USA
Chris Menzel	Department of Philosophy, Texas A&M University, USA
Simon Milton	Department of Information Systems, University of Melbourne, Australia
Philippe Muller	Research Institute for Computer Science, University of Toulouse III, France
John Mylopoulos	Department of Computer Science, University of Toronto, Canada
Leo Obrst	The MITRE Corporation, USA
Barbara Partee	University of Massachusetts, USA
Massimo Poesio	Department of Computer Science, University of Essex, UK
Ian Pratt-Hartmann	Department of Computer Science, University of Manchester, UK
James Pustejovsky	Department of Computer Science, Brandeis University, USA
David Randell	Imperial College London, UK
Robert Rynasiewicz	Johns Hopkins University, USA

Contents

7. Maintaining and Exploiting Ontologies

Invited Talks

Formal Ontology in Information Systems
B. Bennett and C. Fellbaum (Eds.)
IOS Press, 2006

Problems of Scale in Building, Maintaining and Using Very Large Formal Ontologies

Doug LENAT
Cycorp, USA

Abstract. Though Cyc is a formal ontology, the process of building it, over the past 22 years, has been a passionately empirical process. We have had several surprises along the way, some of them scientific, some engineering, and some sociological. For instance, the requirement to represent arbitrary pieces of commonsense knowledge led us, in the mid-1980's, against our intuitions, to move to an increasingly expressive formal representation language. By 1990, we had to admit that the dream of a "Final Encyclopedia" of correct knowledge was a chimera, and what we needed to focus on was a tapestry of locally-consistent "micro-theories" containing contextualized knowledge. Since then, we have begun to work out the fine structure of these micro-theories, their important attributes and ways in which they related to each other, and to appreciate the surprising complexity of the calculi required to formally reason across them. We have also experienced a tipping-point, methodologically, over the past few years, as the ontology has grown large enough to serve as an inductive bias for further knowledge acquisition. I.e., Cyc increasingly actively helps with its own continuing expansion, and by now almost all the activity going on at Cycorp is related to semi-automatic learning from corpora (including the Web) of text and structured sources, whereas as recently as three years ago the majority of the activity here was a cadre of ontological engineers manually writing more axioms to expand the Cyc Knowledge Base. We've also developed and used — and in most cases discarded — a series of interfaces, training paradigms, and so on, as the ontology has grown. In the talk, I shall survey what we used, and when, and why we moved on. Most of the reasons have to do with the ontology outgrowing the tools, or increasing variety among the types of users and ontological engineers. Finally, I will discuss some of our ongoing research efforts, and ongoing interface efforts, which are becoming increasingly intermingled — and why that is perhaps inevitable.

Keywords. Ontology Design, Ontology Maintenance

Formal Ontology in Information Systems
B. Bennett and C. Fellbaum (Eds.)
IOS Press, 2006

On What Goes On:
The Ontology of Processes and Events

Antony GALTON

*School of Engineering, Computer Science, and Mathematics,
University of Exeter, Exeter, UK*

Abstract. The purpose of this talk is to advocate a particular way of thinking about processes and their relationship to objects and events. The point of view put forward is unorthodox in that it regards processes as being in some ways more closely akin to objects than to events, specifically with regard to their relationship to the directly experienced world and their capacity for undergoing change over time. A consequence of this is that the traditional distinction between continuants and occurrents becomes overshadowed by a more prominent distinction, that between the world of direct experience (made up of, *inter alia*, objects and processes) and the world of historical record (made up of events). In conclusion, a number of remarks are offered concerning the implications of this shift of viewpoint for formal ontology.

Keywords. Process, Event, Continuant, Occurrent, Experiential, Historical

Nowadays, we all acknowledge that ontology is not just about objects: the world we live in, and which we set ourselves to describe, is a world of constant change, and we will never do justice to that world unless we fashion our ontological tools in such a way as to accommodate the fact of this change. That much, perhaps, is uncontentious; the difficulties begin when we seriously confront the question of how this is to be done.

The changes that we see in the world include processes and events: in the course of this talk I shall try to put across a particular view as to how these two kinds of item are related. I do not advocate this as a uniquely correct view: doubtless different ways of describing these things are appropriate to different circumstances. But I do advocate it as a point of view which may be fruitful, particularly as a means to sorting out various confusions which talk of objects, processes and events is prone to.

An immediate question to confront is whether processes and events should be treated as entities in their own right, i.e., as 'first-class citizens' of the ontology, or whether they should be relegated to the status of *attributes* of physical objects, the latter being treated as the only first-class entities. Historically, attitudes to ontology have varied from extreme parsimony (e.g., the idea, most frequently associated with Bertrand Russell, that the only first-class entities are 'sense data') to extreme promiscuity (the term is due to Jerry Hobbs [4]) by which first-class status can be accorded even to such seemingly nebulous entities as the intensity of of a man's belief that his wife might possibly have deceived him.

Processes and events are surely not *that* nebulous, but there is no doubt that a good case could be made for regarding them as somehow less fully-fledged members of the ontology than the material objects whose changes they comprise. This is an issue which I do not wish to become entangled with here: and indeed, I believe it is perfectly legitimate to embark on a discussion of the ontology of these things prior to establishing their status in this sense. After all, a substantial part of the business of ontology is *taxonomic* — establishing classifications and hierarchies which encapsulate the relationships amongst the various concepts we employ, and if we have good reason to classify attributes of entities as well as the entities themselves then it seems that such attributes should also be grist to the ontologist's mill. In short, we can embark on the ontological enterprise before establishing the precise logical status of what we are classifying.

I shall therefore have no qualms about at least according an honorary first-class status to processes and events, in order to discuss how they should be classified, and how they are related to each other and to other kinds of entities. Thus from now on I shall take it for granted that processes and events are legitimate objects of ontological enquiry, and indeed shall seek to argue that they are *necessary* objects of ontological enquiry, that an ontology that has no place for them is *ipso facto* incomplete.

At the present time, in the formal ontology community, a natural starting point from which to launch a discussion of processes and events is the philosophical distinction between continuants and occurrences. This has been encapsulated in the distinction between SNAP and SPAN ontologies that has been advocated by Barry Smith and his collaborators. In the words of Grenon and Smith [3], 'a good ontology must be capable of accounting for spatial reality both synchronically (as it exists at a time) and diachronically (as it unfolds through time)', these two tasks being assigned to SNAP and SPAN ontologies respectively — thus what is proposed is not a single ontology but rather a coordinated ensemble of ontologies of these two different kinds.

The inhabitants of a SNAP ontology are continuants, that is, 'entities that have continuous existence and a capacity to endure ... through time even while undergoing different sorts of changes', while the inhabitants of the SPAN ontology are occurrents, that is, 'processes, events, activities, changes'. The elements of a SNAP ontology include 'all continuants existing at some given instant of time', and of course the designation SNAP is suggested by the idea of a *snapshot*, a complete picture of the universe at an instant. A SPAN ontology, by contrast, of necessity spans a succession of instants, and specifically contains those entities whose nature encompasses such spans.

I want to consider more closely the invocation of 'instants' here. One generally conceives of an instant as a part of time that has no duration, and within which no change can occur. A superficially attractive picture of time has it that the 'flow' of time arises from the 'stitching together' of innumerable durationless instants. This is the picture implicit in the conventional mathematical representation of a time interval as a set of instants the form

$$[t_1, t_2] = \{t \in \mathbb{R} : t_1 \leq t \leq t_2\}.$$

However useful this may be as an abstraction for certain technical purposes (and of course, in the mathematical context that gave rise to it, this picture is a beautiful and significant achievement), it seems to me that as an account of what time really is it is fundamentally incoherent. The essence of time is surely tightly bound up with change, but the mathematical picture contains no change, only a static ensemble of individually static snapshots.

Consider a man walking. What do we see if we observe him at an instant? (A real snapshot, i.e., a photograph, is a crude approximation to this, but of course the snapshots of the SNAP ontology are fully three-dimensional and encompass the whole universe at the times they represent.) We might suppose that whereas we see the man, we do not see the walking: that is, while the man is wholly present in the snapshot, he is there motionless, and the best we can say is that his posture at that instant is characteristic of the sequence of postures assumed by a walking man — in other words, we may *infer*, with some plausibility, that he is walking, but cannot see the walking because it is not actually present in the snapshot. But, so the argument might go, if no single SNAP ontology contains walking, then a world which contains walking cannot solely comprise SNAP ontologies, and we are led to invoke the SPAN ontology to put the walking in.

While this may seem persuasive, we must not lose sight of the fact that the instantaneous snapshot is an idealisation. I believe that it arises as a conflation of two separate things: on the one hand, static representations such as photographs, and on the other hand, our idea of the present as the temporal location of our immediate experience. What the snapshot shows is precisely what was present at the time that it was taken.

But the present of our experience is nothing like a snapshot. What we experience is a *dynamic* world, not a static one. In the photograph we can only *infer* that the man is walking; in our actual present experience, looking at the man himself, we can *see* him walking. We perceive motion and change directly, just as we perceive shapes and colours. (Some change is admittedly either too slow or two fast for us to perceive directly — just as some shapes are too large or too small and some colours too bright or too dim.) Indeed, we perceive *processes* directly, for walking is not just motion, it is a particular structured kind of motion, a process: processes are present in the world right now.

Moreover, like objects, processes can change: the walking can get faster, or change direction, or become limping. All around us processes undergo changes: the rattling in the car becomes louder, or changes rhythm, or may stop, only to start again later. The flow of the river becomes turbulent; the wind veers to the north-west.

In all these respects, processes seem to contrast with events. There are, admittedly, many different ways of understanding the terms 'process' and 'event', and hence correspondingly different ways or portraying the relationship between them. Some authors regard processes as a subclass of events; other authors have it the other way round; others still treat them as two disjoint subclasses of some broader category such as 'occurrences', 'situations', or 'eventualities'. Here I wish to advocate a particular understanding of the term 'event' by which the contrast between process and event is brought out with maximal clarity. I believe this is justified because in real language we hardly ever use the two terms interchangeably; indeed, in the dictionaries I have consulted, neither term figures at all in the definition of the other.

Some events are *durative*, that is, they take time to occur; such events are as it were *made of* processes. Durative events are to processes as physical objects are to matter: this has often been noted and was stated in very nearly this form by Emmon Bach [1]. Just as there is an obvious distinction between 'table' (a kind of physical object) and 'wood' (a type of matter, of which a table might be made), so there is an analogous distinction between 'battle' (a kind of event) and 'fighting' (a kind of process, of which a battle might consist). And just as some physical objects have complex constitution, being made of components of different kinds of stuff, so an event may involve a number of different processes (e.g., a journey might involve driving, flying, walking, and travelling by train).

A different kind of event is *punctual*. In idealisation, such an event takes no time at all to occur, it is instantaneous. In reality this is generally sensitive to granularity. The paradigmatic punctual event is the onset of motion, when a physical body starts moving.

If at each moment the body is either at rest or in motion, then the transition between rest and motion cannot be other than instantaneous, since there can be no time at which the body is neither at rest nor in motion. But in the case of an extended body, if the motion is initiated by an impact on one side of it, it will take some admittedly very brief time before the motion is communicated to the far side, so the transition from the body's being wholly at rest to its being wholly in motion cannot be literally instantaneous. But these sorts of consideration are rather irrelevant to the point at issue, which is that if an event is defined as the initiation of some process then it is thereby being conceptualised as, in idealisation, instantaneous. As such it is a rather different kind of event from those which are conceptualised as durative, since it cannot be said to be made of process-stuff in the way that they are.

The world does not consists of objects *and* stuff: to describe a part of the world as an object is to describe a portion of stuff in a particular way. When I refer to a table (which happens to be, say, of wood), I am referring to a certain quantity of wood, but I am not referring to it *as* wood, but rather as an artefact constructed for the purpose of supporting smaller objects at a convenient height above floor level. This is an entirely familiar point (one might think of the four 'causes' of Aristotle here). Equally, if I refer to a journey from London to Paris I am describing an event in terms of what is accomplished by it, i.e., the transition between a situation in which someone, or something, is located in London, to a situation in which it is in Paris; but in referring to a particular journey of this type I am thereby implicitly referring to its constituent processes — which might involve various combinations of driving, flying, sailing, or travelling by train.

The relationship between processes and events is not all one-way: processes can also be defined in terms of events. This happens, for example, if I say, in answer to the question what I am doing right now, that I am going to the station. There is no such process as 'going': but if someone goes to the station, that is an event, and to say that I am now going to the station is to say that some process constitutive of an event of that type is currently going on. We can abbreviate this by saying that the *event* is going on, but strictly speaking the event is not something that can be said to exist from moment to moment in this way, rather it is something that, once it has happened, we can retrospectively ascribe to the time interval over which it occurred. Thus 'I am going to the station' describes a process in terms of the event that will have occurred if the process continues to the point at which my goal in initiating it is realised.

Another way in which processes can be defined in terms of events is through repetition. Many processes are of this kind: there is a process which we describe as 'hammering' which consists of repeated occurrences of the event of striking one hammer-blow. Many processes, on analysis, can be seen as being of this type, even if the way we describe them does not explicitly draw attention to this fact — e.g., walking consists of taking a succession of steps, each one of which is a discrete event (itself consisting of the process of swinging one of the legs forward while the other leg is in contact with the ground).

This draws attention to a key feature of processes which makes them clearly distinct from events: processes are *open-ended*, whereas events are closed. An event is a discrete chunk of history: it has a beginning and an end (or, in the case of truly instantaneous events, the 'chunk' becomes a 'sliver' and the end coincides with the beginning). A process is not like that: a process goes on from moment to moment, and in principle can continue going on. (Of course, there may be extraneous factors which prevent it from doing so: a falling process necessarily terminates when the falling object hits the ground — and the closed chunk of falling which thereby has occurred is an event, i.e., a fall.) One way of expressing this is to say that processes and events occupy time differently: an event is a piece of history, a process can be experienced now.

This distinction is in turn related to another one which has often been noted, particularly in the linguistics literature: processes are homogeneous, but events are not. This is usually explained as follows: if a process goes on over some time interval, then it goes on over each subinterval of that interval, whereas if an event occurs over that interval, then it does not occur over any of the proper subintervals. To illustrate: if I bake a cake over the interval between 2 p.m. and 3 p.m., then it is not true that I bake a cake over any lesser subinterval; but if it rains (a process) throughout that interval then it rains from 2 p.m. to 2.10 p.m., and from 2.10 p.m. to 2.20 p.m., etc. If you believe in instants, then you could say that it rains at each instant within the interval from 2 p.m. to 3 p.m.; more concretely, we could say that at any time during that interval, you would have experienced rain. This is generally subject to a caveat about granularity, e.g., it is claimed that walking does not occur over any subinterval shorter than the time to take one step, but I am inclined to be sceptical about this — the process 'smears' out over the whole interval, so that I can say that *right now*, in the experiential present, there is a walking process.

The fact that a process is present at each moment that it goes on, whereas an event is rather associated in a unitary way with a whole interval, is intimately connected with the fact that processes, but not events, can be the direct objects of experience, present in the dynamic snapshots which we have conceived in contrast to the more conventional, but unrealistic, notion of a static snapshot. In this respect processes are almost more like continuants than occurrents: like ordinary physical objects, they are present from moment to moment, they can be experienced directly, they undergo change. Contrast this with events: an event occupies an interval — go to a subinterval and you only capture part of the event; events can usually not be experienced directly, rather you experience the constituent processes and when the event is over you can synthesise these experiences into a whole which by then is part of history, not direct experience (so there is nothing to stop you from *remembering* an event: memory, unlike experience, has room for extended intervals); and events cannot meaningfully be said to undergo change, they just happen (whenever we speak as if an event changes, in fact we are talking about a constituent process — e.g., if I say the battle is getting fiercer, I mean that the battling process, i.e., the fighting, is getting fiercer).

We can summarise the distinction between processes and events under two headings — how processes *differ from* events, and how they are *related to* events.

First, from the above discussion, processes differ from events in the following ways:

- Processes can be experienced directly.
- Processes can undergo change.
- Processes are open-ended.
- Processes are homogeneous.

Events lack all of these properties.

Second, events and processes are intimately related: each can be described in terms of some relationship it bears to the other. In particular:

- An event can be described in terms of its constituent processes ("He had a swim").

- An event can be described in terms of a process that is initiated or terminated by it ("He began/stopped swimming").
- A process can be described in terms of an event of which it is a constituent ("He is swimming a length").
- A process can be described as the open-ended repetition of an event ("He is swimming lengths")

These relationships suggest the possibility of an *algebra* of processes and events, in which constituency, initiation, termination, and repetition figure as operators for converting process terms to event terms and vice versa. This is close in spirit to work that has been done both in linguistics and in AI.

Perhaps none of this sufficiently emphasises the great difference in character between processes and events, and to bring this out we should return to the SNAP/SPAN dichotomy and re-examine it in the light of the above conclusions. The first two properties of processes — that they can be experienced directly, and that they can undergo change — are shared with objects (by which I mean, essentially, continuants) but not with events. While not going so far as to suggest that processes *are* continuants (though I *have* suggested this, in [2]), it does seem to me that these properties place them more on the side of SNAP than of SPAN. A snapshot of the world which is more akin to the experiential present — in other words, a dynamic snapshot rather than a static one — must contain processes as well as objects.

This seems to me to call into question the usefulness of the traditional distinction between continuants and occurrents. A more apposite distinction is between the dynamic world that can be the object of immediate experience (the 'now'), and the historical record that emerges as a static synthesis of a succession of such dynamic snapshots. Processes, with objects, belong in the former; events belong in the latter. Thus, in comparison with the SNAP/SPAN picture, processes have *swapped sides*: in the new picture that I am advocating, processes belong with objects amongst the changeable, dynamic contents of the world, rather than with events, which are essentially static *faits accomplis* belonging to the historical overview that spans the constantly changing succession of dynamic snapshots.

What are the implications of all this for formal ontology? There are implications for classification, and implications for logical representation and inference.

As regards classification, I would suggest that the contents of our ontology should be organised, at the top-level, as follows:

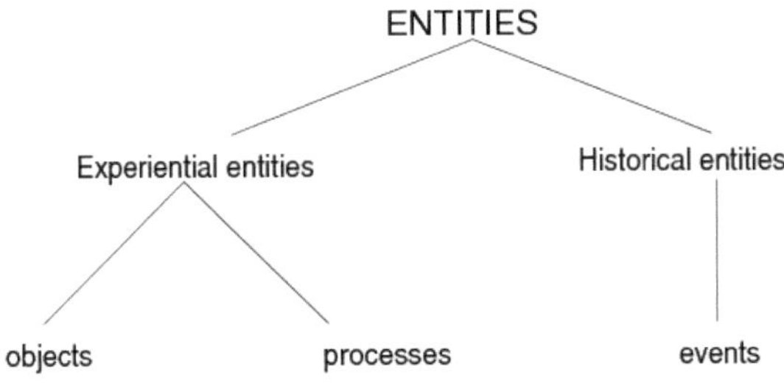

I have said nothing here about how processes are to be distinguished from objects, and it seems to me that one of the attractive features of this scheme is precisely that it makes much more plausible the notion, which many people find tempting, that ordinary objects strictly speaking *are* processes. Potentially, this could lead to a view of the world that is process-oriented in a more than usually thoroughgoing way — to the world-views espoused by, for example, Bergson and Whitehead. Such views have enjoyed something of a revival in recent times, witness the papers collected in [6]. But even if we stop short of this, we are still in a much better position to approach a phenomenon such as a river, which seems to be delicately poised between being on the one hand an object and on the other hand a process. And of course, on closer examination many things we call objects become much more process-like; this is particularly true of living objects. On the view I am advocating, we can accommodate this quite easily without having to countenance bizarre notions such as the identification of objects with events. (Of course, if a human being is identified with a complex process then when the human dies, and the process terminates, an event has been completed which is made of that process. But this event is a human life, not a human being.)

The second set of implications for formal ontology concerns the logical representation of objects, processes, and events. In particular, since processes can undergo change, they must resemble objects in being the bearers of time-variable attributes. An obvious way to accomplish this formally is to allow both objects and processes to participate in predications of the form $P(a, t)$, where a is a term denoting either an object or a process (in short, an experiential entity), and the formula ascribes property P to that entity at time t. Another formula might withhold that same property from the same entity at some other time, as $\neg P(a, t')$, thereby allowing us to express change in the object or process a. Amongst the properties that can be expressed by different predicates P here, a particularly important one is $Exists$, which can be used to specify the lifetime of an object or process:

$$\forall t(Exists(a, t) \leftrightarrow In(t, lifetime(a))),$$

where $In(t, i)$ says that time t falls within interval i.

Predications of this sort should be unavailable for events; as already noted, events occupy time in a quite different way from processes, and if e is a term representing an event (here I mean an event token rather than a type), all we can say about it, as far as time is concerned, is that it occurs over some particular interval i, i.e., $time(e) = i$.

These formal fragments are related to each other as follows. If a process a has lifetime i, then there is an event, $life(a)$ which is precisely the life of that process and which occurs on the interval i, and hence we can put

$$time(life(a)) = lifetime(a).$$

What is the difference between the process a and the event $life(a)$? The process a is something that exists at certain times; it can be the direct object of experience for someone present at any of those times; its properties may be different at different times. At any time that the process exists (i.e., is in operation) it is in principle open for the process to continue existing at subsequent times. Only when it comes to an end (i.e., ceases to exist) can we then synthesise the entire history of a into the event $life(a)$. Much of this can still be said in the case where a is not a process but an object, further reinforcing the alignment of processes with objects rather than events.

As stated at the outset, the view I have tried to put across in this talk is not claimed to be in any sense uniquely correct. It is a view that I found myself compelled to adopt initially as a result of following through the consequences of the observation that occurrents, as traditionally understood, while they can *be* changes, cannot themselves undergo change. With the observation that processes clearly can change, the view of processes as traditional occurrence is quickly undermined.

I offer the experiential/historical dichotomy to the ontological community as perhaps providing a more congenial setting in which to develop detailed taxonomies of the dynamic aspects of the world. Indeed, the dichotomy is hardly new: the terminology of 'experiential' vs 'historical' I have taken from the linguist John Lyons, who used it in the context of a discussion of verb aspect nearly thirty years ago [5]. Although I have made some initial attempts to work out some of the details of my proposal in a formal way, these are not yet ready for dissemination.

References

[1]　Emmon Bach. The algebra of events. *Linguistics and Philosophy*, 9:5–16, 1986.

[2]　Antony P. Galton. Processes as continuants. In James Pustejovsky and Peter Revesz, editors, *13th International Symposium on Temporal Representation and Reasoning (TIME 2006)*, page 187. IEEE Computer Society, 2006.

[3]　Pierre Grenon and Barry Smith. SNAP and SPAN: Towards dynamic spatial ontology. *Spatial Cognition and Computation*, 4(1):69–104, 2004.

[4]　Jerry R. Hobbs. Ontological promiscuity. In *Proceedings of the 23rd Annual Meeting of the Association for Computational Linguistics, Chicago 1985*, pages 61–69, 1985.

[5]　J. Lyons. *Semantics*. Cambridge University Press, Cambridge, 1977. 2 volumes.

[6]　J. Seibt, editor. *Process Theories: Crossdisciplinary Studies in Dynamic Categories*. Kluwer Academic Publishers, 2003.

1. Foundations and Methodology

Formal Ontology in Information Systems
B. Bennett and C. Fellbaum (Eds.)
IOS Press, 2006

Against Idiosyncrasy in Ontology Development

Barry SMITH[*]
*Department of Philosophy and National Center for Ontological Research,
University at Buffalo, USA and Institute for Formal Ontology and Medical Information
Science, Saarbrücken, Germany*

Abstract. The world of ontology development is full of mysteries. Recently, ISO Standard 15926 ("Lifecycle Integration of Process Plant Data Including Oil and Gas Production Facilities"), a data model initially designed to support the integration and handover of large engineering artefacts, has been proposed by its principal custodian for general use as an upper level ontology. As we shall discover, ISO 15926 is, when examined in light of this proposal, marked by a series of quite astonishing defects, which may however provide general lessons for the developers of ontologies in the future.

Keywords. Upper-level ontology, data models for the oil and gas industry, ISO.

What Happens When Data Models and Ontologies are Confused

Ontologies are, in one respect at least, comparable to telephone networks: they are designed to support exchange of information. The value of an ontology therefore depends, at least in part, on the quality of the network for shared communication which it provides, and on the number of users who agree to adopt this common network. This means that it depends also on the existence of a straightforward learning path for new users, and of clear and easily accessible documentation.

Before proposing an ontology for a given domain, accordingly, its custodians have a duty to maximize the likelihood that it will provide for the needs of maximally large numbers of potential users. This duty is all the more palpable where the ontology in question is advanced as an *upper-level ontology*, which is to say: an ontology that is designed for general adoption, as in the case of ISO Standard 15926 ("Lifecycle Integration of Process Plant Data Including Oil and Gas Production Facilities"), which is now being advanced as an upper-level ontological framework for 'integrating diverse information systems' and 'integrating [and] analyzing mid-level ontologies' without restriction.[1]

I do not address here the question whether ISO 15926 is able to meet the specific data management needs of the community for which it was built. When examined in light of its potential use as an upper-level ontology, however, it is no less clear that ISO 15926 is marked by a series of defects, of a type which are, sadly, all too familiar in the ontology domain. Many of these defects flow from the terminological confusions

---

[*] Corresponding author: Barry Smith, Department of Philosophy, 130 Park Hall, University at Buffalo, NY 14260, USA; E-mail: phismith@buffalo.edu.

which arise when the authors of an ontology do not take account of the fact that expressions such as 'instance', 'entity', 'object', 'represent', etc., are used in different ways by different (database, programmer, general user) communities. Others flow from the employment of philosophical and logical tools and theories which, although perhaps of some interest in their own right, are so counterintuitive from the perspective of the general users of ontologies as to constitute serious obstacles to learnability and accessibility. Yet others flow from simple use-mention confusions, where entities in reality are confused with their names or 'representations'. Because these and related defects are still so common in ontology development work, I have used ISO 15926 as a source of examples of the characteristic ways in which ontology developers can go wrong. My goal is thus not one of mere criticism; rather, it is to draw out certain general principles which a good ontology should satisfy if it is to even reach the starting gate to be considered for adoption in the future, paying special attention to the role of ontologies in supporting the exchange of information. I have, surely, misunderstood many things in my attempts to come to grips with what I still see as the dark mysteries of ISO 15926; but even this provides evidence in favor of our first general principle:

1. **The principle of intelligibility**: an ontology that is advocated for general use should be understandable to those familiar with ontology development work who are willing to invest a reasonable amount of effort in mastering its documentation.

The major part of ISO 15926 is copyrighted by the International Organization for Standardization, from where it can be purchased, at a not inconsiderable sum, as a pdf file.[2] This brings us to a further general lesson, which we can formulate as follows:

2. **The principle of openness:** An ontology should be open and available to be used by all potential users without any constraint, other than (1) its origin must be acknowledged and (2) it should not to be altered and subsequently redistributed except under a new name.[3] In addition the ontology should be (3) explained in ways which make its content intelligible to human beings, and (4) implemented in ways which make this content accessible to computers.

This principle implies not only that an ontology, if it is recommended for general use, should be in the public domain, but that the ontology should be marked by openness also in the wider sense that its features should be explained in clear, simple English, extended, where necessary, with technical terms.

In a domain like ontology, as is already clear for independent reasons, adoption by ISO does not guarantee that an artifact satisfies all the requirements which might reasonably be placed on an international standard.[4] Indeed the attempt to enforce adoption of an ontology by taking the route of ISO standardization may bring costs: it makes it harder to correct errors; it often involves the making of less than ideal compromises, turning on the fact that adoption by ISO requires compatibility with prior ISO standards, many of which are – particularly in the informatics area – low in quality.

Use the Tried and Tested

Of the 201 terms included in the ISO 15926 upper-level ontology, 88 are of the form 'class of X'. 'Class' itself is defined as follows:

DEFINITION: A <class> is a <thing> that is an understanding of the nature of things and that divides things into those which are members of the class and those which are not according to one or more criteria.

(We note that terms are included in ISO 15926 definitions sometimes with, and sometimes without, angle brackets. The significance of this practice is not explained in the publicly available documentation.)

The definition tells us that a class is a thing that is an *understanding of the nature of things*. While we are not told what 'understandings' are, we are provided with some helpful examples of the use of 'class', for example: 'Centrifugal pump is a <class>'.

The logic which is proposed by ISO 15926 to govern its classes is, astonishingly not the Zermelo-Fraenkel or some other well-understood standard set theory, but rather a highly specialized variant thereof (the theory of so-called 'non-well-founded sets') devised by mathematician-philosophers for the purposes of logical modeling of certain non-terminating computational processes.[5] The principal mark of this theory is that it allows sets to contain themselves, thereby generating infinitely descending chains of the form:

$$\ldots \in A \in A \in A \in A \in A \in A \in A \in A \in A \in A \in A \in A.$$

With this proposal, which is analogous to proposing the use of some particularly esoteric version of the mathematics of quantum field theory for the purposes of balancing a checkbook, ISO 15926 flouts:

3. **The principle of simple tools:** An ontology is an artifact created to support exchange of information, for example across disciplinary boundaries; it is not the place to try out the latest new bits of mathematics you read about last week.

Perhaps non-well-founded set theory is being invoked because the developers of ISO 15926 thought that it was necessary in order to make sense of assertions such as "Class is a member of Class". Yet other, much simpler, and more familiar, languages, such as Common Logic,[6] which have the advantage that they are also used by other ontology developers, permit such statements to be made while providing a conventional semantics.

Don't Reinvent the Wheel

ISO 15926 complicates its theory of classes still further by allowing classes with both actual and possible members: 'Although there is only one <class> that has no members, there can be a <class> that has no members in the actual world, but which does have members in other possible worlds.' Only one such class? Or also several? And does *it* really exist? Or is it only such that it *can* exist? Sadly, nothing like a modal logic is supplied by ISO 15926, in spite of the fact that a number of standard treatments of these matters already exist and are used by other ontologies. Rather it develops its own theory of actuality and possibility on the fly, thereby flouting:

4. **The principle of re-using available resources:** if an ontology deals in a systematic way with entities or operators which are dealt with perfectly well already in some recognized resource used also by other ontology developers, then it should utilize this recognized resource.

We see another contravention of principle 4. in the treatment of terms like 'class_of_relationship_with_related_end_1', which is defined as follows (you will need to read this twice):

> DEFINITION: A <class_of_relationship_with_related_end_1> is a <class_of_relationship> where a particular <thing> is related in the <class_of_relationship>, rather than the members of a <class>. The related <thing> plays the <role_and_domain> indicated by the class_of_end_1 attribute.

There is a perfectly good theory of relations, ranges, domains, ordered pairs, and of the transitivity, symmetry, etc. of relations, which is part of standard set theory. But because this resource was apparently ignored by the developers of ISO 15926, the result is gobbledygook, which no one (or at least: no one outside the oil and gas industry data-modeling community) would ordinarily feel the need to use, and definitions which no ordinary person would be in a position to understand.

Matters are made worse by the fact that some of the definitions are associated with terms with well-established meanings. That old terminological habits die hard is, unfortunately, a lesson still all too seldom taken account of in ontology development. It implies:

5. **The principle of terminological moderation:** Stay as close as possible to the terms already used by your intended audience and to their already established meanings. Use only terms for which either (1) there is a reasonable expectation that intended users of the ontology will have a need for them, or (2) such terms are required to fill gaps in the ontology in order to create a complete hierarchy.

6. **The principle of intelligible definitions**:[7] Use definitions which are both (1) humanly intelligible (to avoid error in human use and maintenance) and (2) formally specifiable (as far as possible in such a way as to support one or other standard type of software).

A Rose is a Rose

The publicly accessible portions of the ISO 15926 documentation[8] consist on the one hand of a list of terms together with definitions, and on the other hand of a set of diagrams. Neither the terms, nor the definitions, nor the diagrams are marked by a high degree of intelligibility.

Consider the sample term 'class_of_cause_of_beginning_of_class_of_individual', for which we are provided with the following:

> DEFINITION: A <class_of_cause_of_beginning_of_class_of_individual> is a <class_of_relationship> that indicates that a member of a <class_of_activity> causes the beginning of a member of a <class_of_individual>.

Note the characteristic confusion of use and mention here. It is not, as the definition implies, the *class* which 'indicates', but rather (as common sense would suggest) the corresponding *term*. (This problem is only made worse by the fact that it is not clear from its documentation whether ISO 15926 makes a distinction between a term and its referent.)

The term 'class_of_cause_of_beginning_of_class_of_individual' itself indicates further that we are to focus here on the *causes of beginnings of classes*. Yet the definition (in its strange, roundabout way) seems to be about the causes of the beginnings of *individuals* (it is about the members of the class of individuals). This is fortunate, because under the entry for 'class' we are told that classes do not have beginnings, so that there could not literally *be* a 'class_of_cause_of_beginning_of_class_of_individual'. By 'beginning_of_class_of_individual', therefore, ISO 15926 in fact means: *beginning of individual.* Its authors were accordingly not adhering to:

7.	**The principle of terminological coherence:** for any expression 'E' in an ontology, 'E' means E.

From this it follows immediately that each expression in an ontology should have the same meaning on every occasion of use.

The requirement of univocity[9] would normally, and for good reason, be regarded as a trivial constraint on the sensible use of language. Departures therefrom lead to a variety of familiar types of confusion and contribute much to the fact that (as will become all too painfully clear in what follows) the documentation of ISO 15296 will be unintelligible to almost all conceivable users of an upper-level ontology.[10]

One implication of the principle of terminological coherence is that an ontology should construct its complex terms in such a way that their constituent parts preserve their ordinary meanings. This principle is violated almost everywhere in the ISO 15926 documentation; thus for example the expression 'individual' is very often used (in order to save space?) to mean, not: *individual*, but rather: *possible individual.* The term 'class_of_individual' is defined as 'a class whose members are instances of <possible_individual>'. The term 'possible individual' itself is defined, oddly, as meaning 'thing that exists in space and time'.

Respect Compositionality

The most conspicuous puzzle raised by the treatment of many 'class_of_X' terms in ISO 15926 (as also of the many 'class_of_class_of_X' terms) turns on the very fact that these terms are included at all. For if classes or sets are needed, and if one needs to iterate the 'class of' (or 'set of') operator, then one will surely do this by means of some general facility, rather than by giving names in *ad hoc* fashion to just those 81 'class of' or 'class of class of' terms one thinks one needs. (This is another application of the principle of re-use of available resources.)

In addition to 'class_of_cause_of_beginning_of_class_of_individual', ISO 15926 includes many other 'class_of X' entries for which the underlying 'X' term is itself, for whatever reason, missing from the ontology:

class_of_composite_material	class_of_molecule
class_of_compound	class_of_number
class_of_dimension_for_shape	class_of_organism
class_of_feature	class_of_organization
class_of_feature_whole_part	class_of_particulate_material
class_of_functional_object	class_of_person
class_of_inanimate_physical_object	class_of_property_space
class_of_indirect_connection	class_of_relationship_with_related_end_1
class_of_individual	class_of_relationship_with_related_end_2
class_of_information_object	class_of_relationship_with_signature
class_of_information_presentation	class_of_representation_translation

class_of_information_representation   class_of_scale_conversion

class_of_isomorphic_functional_mapping   class_of_sub_atomic_particle

Thus while we have 'class_of_organism' and 'class_of_person' in the ontology, we do not also have 'organism' and 'person'. Why not? Are there no *persons* in the world of the ISO 15926 ontology (which was developed by the oil and gas industries, we will remember, 'to support the integration and handover of large engineering artefacts')? More importantly still, is it appropriate to leave out 'person' and 'organism' in an *upper-level* ontology, when 'stream' and 'representation of Gregorian date and UTC time' are included?

These problems arise because the developers of ISO 15926 were not adhering to:

8.   **The principle of compositional term construction:** if an ontology uses in a systematic way terms of the form '*a* † *b*' (where '†' stands in for some term-binding operator like 'of' or 'with') then it should include also the corresponding *a* and *b* terms (or they should link to treatments of the latter in some other standard ontology).

The arguments for this principle are, I hope, clear. Not only does it contribute to intelligibility (users will more readily understand what '*a* of *b*' or '*a* with *b*' means if they are first of all provided with elucidations of the meanings of '*a*' and '*b*'); it helps also to ensure completeness of the ontology (and in a way that also simplifies the business of error checking) – as contrasted with the mystifying randomness in term selection by which the ISO 15926 ontology is currently marked.

Exploit Recursion

In addition to the 'class of' terms in the ontology, we are also provided with an odd list of 'class of class of' terms:

class_of_class_of_composition   class_of_class_of_relationship

class_of_class_of_definition   class_of_class_of_relationship_with_signature

class_of_class_of_description   class_of_class_of_representation

class_of_class_of_identification   class_of_class_of_representation_translation

class_of_class_of_individual   class_of_class_of_responsibility_for_

class_of_class_of_information_   representation

   representation   class_of_class_of_usage_of_representation

Again, I could find no rationale for including just these items in the list rather than others. It is however worth noting that two of them, namely 'class_of_class_of_composition' and 'class_of_class_of_representation' have no corresponding 'class of' term in the ontology, though the first of these contains a reference to such a term in its definition:

> DEFINITION: A <class_of_class_of_composition> is a <class_of_class_of_ relationship> whose members are instances of <class_of_composition>. It indicates that a member of a member of the class_of_class_of_part is a part of a member of an instance of the class_of_class_of_whole,

which yields a nice gallimaufry of use-mention confusions in the provided

EXAMPLE: Toxicity description is a class_of_class_of_part of a material data sheet, where the description "has carcinogenic components" is a class_of_part on the Mogas Material Safety Data Sheet, and copy #5 of the Mogas Material Safety Data Sheet has "has carcinogenic components" as a part.

From this we learn that a description is a class (what, then, are the *members* of a description?); the rest of the example text departs too far from grammatical English to make sense.

Don't Confuse Types and Instances

It is a widespread problem with almost all contemporary work on ontologies and terminologies that inadequate attention is paid to the distinction between types (kinds, universals) and instances (individuals, particulars). Thus for example we find in the ANSI standard for controlled vocabularies[11] that the same relation of part to whole is asserted to obtain both between what are called 'general concepts', for example *brain* and *central nervous system*, and between what are called 'specific instances', for example *Toronto* and *Ontario*, thereby entrenching as part of an international standard what is in fact a well-documented confusion.[12,13]

In the same confused vein, ISO 15926 defines 'class of information object' to mean: 'a <class_of_arranged_individual> whose members are members of zero or more <class_of_information_representation> and of zero or more <class_of_ information_presentation>', informing us that '[u]sually, it is a physical_object (like a paper document) that is classified as a <class_of_information_object> ... Newspaper is a <class_of_information_object>.'

Why do we have 'a paper document ... is classified as a <class_of_information_ object>' rather than the seemingly more sensible: a paper document is classified as an information_object'?

9.　**The principle of types and instances:** An ontology should clearly mark whether given expressions are referring to types (universals, kinds, generals) or to instances (particulars, tokens, individuals).

What is meant by 'Newspaper is a <class_of_information_object>' is of course something like: *newspaper is_a information object*, or in other words: *the type newspaper is_a_subtype_of the type information_object* – something which can be said also, and more directly, and using English grammar, as follows: *a newspaper is an information object*.

Don't Confuse Mass Nouns and Count Nouns

ISO 15926 defines 'class_of_compound' to mean: 'a <class_of_arranged_individual> whose members consist of arrangements of molecules of the same or different types, bound together by intermolecular forces'. We are told that '[t]his includes both mixtures and alloys ... Water, sulphuric acid, sand, limestone, and steel can be represented by instances of <class_of_compound>.' What we are not told is whether it is some given *portion* of water or rather the corresponding substance-*type* which is an instance of this class.

If the former, should not the ontology, given its purpose, provide (or better: refer to, or link to) a serviceable theory of portions and masses of stuff (and indeed a link to some ontology of liquids[14])? Instead ISO 15926 has developed its own theory of portions and masses, which are called 'batches', and which satisfy axioms like:

> A Batch is a type of Material.
> All Batches are Materials.
> All Equipments are Materials.
> Each Material must be either a Batch or an Equipment – but not both.

Avoid Circularity

Like all good top-level ontologies, our "Integration of life-cycle data for oil and gas production facilities" ontology contains its own tiny, hand-crafted ontology of mathematics, constructed out of terms such as 'class_of_number', which is defined as meaning: 'a <class_of_class> whose members are members of <arithmetic_number>'; and 'integer_number' for which we are provided with the helpful:

> DEFINITION: An <integer_number> is an <arithmetic_number> that is an integer number.

The latter reminds us also of:

10. **The principle of non-circularity**: a good ontology should recognize the distinction between defined and primitive terms; it should avoid circular definitions; and, *a fortiorissimo*, it should avoid HL7-style nonsense-definitions of the forms: '*an a is the b of an a*', or: '*an a is an a which is b*'.

Leaving aside certain very special contexts,[15] circular definitions provide benefits neither to human beings nor to machines. They arise because ontology developers, who have not realized that not all terms in an ontology can be defined, are seeking a spurious completeness.

Don't Use Plural Nouns with Singular Verbs

ISO 15926 comes also with its own home-built geometry, as for example in:

> DEFINITION: A <class_of_dimension_for_shape> is a <class_of_class_of_relationship> that indicates that members of the class_of_shape have a dimension that is a member of the class_of_dimension.

We are told in elucidation that 'Specifying that members of the "class of circle" have members of "class of diameter" is an instance of <class_of_dimension_for_shape>.' This is (I think) a roundabout way of saying: circles have diameters.

Note that 'class of circle' and 'class of diameter' are themselves not included in the ontology, and neither is the term 'dimension_**for**_shape'. There is however a term 'dimension_**of**_shape', defined as 'a <class_of_class_of_relationship> that indicates that members of the <shape_dimension> are dimensions of the <shape> members'. Life is made even harder by the fact that the example text provided for the above definition – 'The sets of 10m lines that are diameters of 10m circles is an example of <dimension_of_shape>' – conforms only loosely to the rules of English grammar. In particular, it reflects a departure from:

11. **The principle of singular nouns:** the terms of an ontology should be formulated in the singular, and the ontology's documentation should pay careful attention to the distinction between singular and plural nouns and to the requirement of noun-verb agreement.

Combine Terms Coherently

The chaotic switching around in the use of 'of' and 'for' in the geometric corner of ISO 15926 reminds us of another general lesson:[16]

12. **The principle of coherence in the use of generic term-building operators:** If an ontology uses in a systematic way terms of the form 'a † b' (where '†', again, stands in for 'with', 'without', 'of', etc.), then it should specify clearly the syntax of '†', provide a statement of what expressions of the form 'a † b' mean in terms of the meanings of 'a' and 'b', and use each such form in the same way throughout.

An analogous principle applies of course also to unary operators such as 'class of'. In several places ISO 15926 has pairs of terms 'X' and 'class of X', which are such that the definition of the former stands in no obvious relation to the definition the latter (in a way which would create serious obstacles, were the ontology ever to reach the point where it was required to support automatic reasoning). Thus for example we have, in addition to the pair 'dimension_of_shape' and 'class_of_dimension_for_shape', also the pair 'shape_dimension' and 'class_of_shape_dimension'. The last two terms are defined, in seeming independence of each other, as follows:

DEFINITION: A <shape_dimension> is a <class_of_class_of_individual> that is a set of <individual_dimension> that define an aspect of a shape.

DEFINITION: A <class_of_shape_dimension> is a <class_of_class> that is a dimension of a <class_of_shape>.

Similarly we have the two terms 'responsibility_for_representation' and 'class_of_ responsibility_for_representation', which are defined as follows:

DEFINITION: A <responsibility_for_representation> is a <relationship> that indicates that the controller <possible_individual> administers the controlled <representation_of_thing>.

DEFINITION: A <class_of_responsibility_for_representation> is a <class_of_ relationship> whose members indicate that a <possible_individual> (usually an organization) deems that members of the pattern can be used as representations of the represented thing.

In each such case, in a properly constructed ontology, the 'class of' term would be introduced, not by means of its own special definition, but rather in the obvious recursive way, bringing (again) obvious benefits of formal coherence along the way.

Check Your Work for Errors

Note the use in the above definitions of problematic expressions such as 'indicate', 'deems', 'usually', and so forth, a pattern which is illustrated also in ISO 15926's own miniature theory of mereology, which contains definitions like:

> DEFINITION: A <feature_whole_part> is an <arrangement_of_individual> that indicates that the part is a non-separable, contiguous part of the whole.

The general lesson here is:

13. **The principle of non-subjective definitions**: when formulating definitions avoid the use of phrases like 'which may ...', 'that indicates ...', '... characterize ...', 'an aspect of ...' which invite subjective interpretation.

For another example of the problem which this principle is designed to prevent, consider the ISO 15926 term 'class_of_relationship_with_signature', which is defined as: 'a <class_of_relationship> that may have a <role_and_domain> specified for each end'. Is a <class_of_relationship> which does *not* have a <role_and_domain> specified for each 'end' also a class_of_relationship_with_signature? In every case? Only in some cases?

> ISO 15926 comes also with its own miniature theory of physics:

> DEFINITION: A <class_of_sub_atomic_particle> is a <class_of_arranged_individual> whose members are constituent particles of atoms.

> EXAMPLE: Proton, electron, meson, neutron, positron, muon, quark, and neutrino can be represented by instances of <class_of_sub_atomic_particle>

whereby:

> DEFINITION: An <arranged_individual> is a <possible_individual> that has parts that play distinct roles with respect to the whole. The qualities of an <arranged_individual> are distinct from the qualities of its parts.

What are the *parts* of a neutrino? What distinct *roles* do they play? What roles do quarks play in the integration and handover of large engineering artefacts?

> DEFINITION: A <class_of_feature_whole_part> is a <class_of_arrangement_of_individual> whose members are instances of <feature_whole_part>.

> EXAMPLE Thermowells have stems, and tables have tops are examples of <class_of_feature_whole_part>.

The two just-mentioned definitions tell us that the entities which serve as wholes in instances (?) of <feature_whole_part> should be non-separable; yet the *examples* include tables (wholes) and tops (parts), where surely many tops *are* separable. So what does 'non-separable' mean? And how does its use here relate to its use in the definition of 'composite material', where we are told that fibreglass and carbon fibre consist of 'separable compounds'?

Don't Confuse Definitions with Comments

14. **The principle of non-redundant definitions**: do not include clauses in definitions which contribute nothing to the application of the definition.

This principle is violated for example in:

> DEFINITION: An <event> is a <possible_individual> with zero extent in time. An <event> is the temporal boundary of one or more <possible_individual>s, although there may be no knowledge of these <possible_individual>s.

> DEFINITION: A <possible_individual> is: a <thing> that exists in space and time. This includes:
>
> – things where any of the space-time dimensions are vanishingly small,
> – those that are either all space for any time, or all time and any space,
> – the entirety of all space-time,
> – things that actually exist, or have existed,
> – things that are fictional or conjectured and possibly exist in the past, present or future,
> – temporal parts (states) of other individuals,
> – things that have a specific position, but zero extent in one or more dimensions, such as points, lines, and surfaces.
>
> In this context existence is based upon being imaginable within some consistent logic, including actual, hypothetical, planned, expected, or required individuals.

Question: are things which look like small flies from a distance actual or possible individuals?

> DEFINITION: An <actual_individual> is a <possible_individual> that is a part of the space-time continuum that we inhabit. It exists in the present, past, or future of our universe, as opposed to some imagined universe.

Question: what is the difference between 'being part of the space-time continuum that we inhabit' (= being actual) and 'existing in space and time' (= being possible)? Why are fictional things included in the list of entities which exist in space and time? Is this because 'space' and 'time' themselves refer to possible space and possible time? If so, then are actual individuals themselves more properly to be conceived as entities which exist in possible, or in actual, space-time? Note how the confusions here stem from contravention of the principle of term coherence. If '*A*' does not mean: *A*, but rather: *possible A*, then '*possible A*' itself means something like: *possible possible A*, and so on, *ad exasperandum*.

Conclusion: ISO 15926 Is Not An Ontology

We can come closer to an understanding of ISO 15926 if we consider its treatment of qualities, such as length or temperature or color; or of roles, such as the status of someone in an organisation. ISO 15926 does not recognize entities of these sorts. It deals with the color or length of an entity X, rather, by talking about X's relationships to strings or number-representations. My suspicion is that something similar applies to all the entries in ISO 15926. If this is so, of course, then we do not have here anything which could properly be described as an ontology. Rather, we have the equivalent of a coding scheme, rather like the Standard Algebraic Notation for Chess. The latter is, to be sure (unlike ISO 15926), elegant and efficient. But it is not an ontology of chess.

Acknowledgements

This work was funded in part by the National Institutes of Health through the NIH Roadmap for Medical Research, Grant 1 U 54 HG004028. Thanks are due also to the Alexander von Humboldt and Volkswagen Foundations, to Bill Andersen, and, last but not least, to Matthew West.

References

[1]   M. West, "ISO 15926 – Integration of Lifecycle Data", Presentation at Upper Ontology Summit, National Institute of Standards and Technology (NIST), Gaithersberg, MD, March 15, 2006, http://ontolog.cim3.net/file/work/UpperOntologySummit/UO-Summit-Meeting_20050315/UOS--west_20060315.ppt (last visited April 23, 2006).

[2]   *ISO Store: Browse, Search and Purchase ISO Standards*: http://www.iso.org/iso/en/ (last visited April 23, 2006).

[3]   http://obofoundry/org/. Last accessed July 1, 2006.

[4]   B. Smith, W. Ceusters and R. Temmerman, "Wüsteria", Medical Informatics Europe (MIE 2005), Geneva, *Stud Health Technol Inform.* 2005;116:647–652.

[5]   P. Aczel. *Non-well-founded sets*, CSLI Lecture Notes 14, Stanford: Center for the Study of Language and Information, 1988.

[6]   Common Logic Standard, http://cl.tamu.edu (last visited April 23, 2006).

[7]   J. Köhler, K. Munn, A. Rüegg, A. Skusa, B. Smith, "Quality Control for Terms and Definitions in Ontologies and Taxonomies", *BMC* Bioinformatic, s2006, 7:212.

[8]   ISO/FDIS 15926-2 - Lifecycle integration of process plant data including oil and gas production facilities: Data model: EXPRESS and EXPRESS-G listing: http://www.tc184-sc4.org/wg3ndocs/wg3n1328/lifecycle_integration_schema.html (last visited April 23, 2006).

[9]   B. Smith, J. Köhler and A. Kumar "On the application of formal principles to life science data: A case study in the Gene Ontology", *Data Integration in the Life Sciences* (DILS 2004), 79-94.

[10] B. Smith and W. Ceusters, "HL7 RIM: An Incoherent Standard", *Medical Informatics Europe 2006*, in press.

[11] ANSI/NISO Z39.19-2005, "Guidelines for the Construction, Format, and Management of Monolingual Controlled Vocabularies", http://www.niso.org/standards/resources/Z39-19-2005.pdf.

[12] B. Smith, et al., "Relations in Biomedical Ontologies", *Genome Biology* (2005), 6 (5), R46.

[13] M. Donnelly, T. Bittner and C. Rosse, "A Formal Theory for Spatial Representation and Reasoning in Biomedical Ontologies", *Artificial Intelligence in Medicine*, Vol. 36, Nr. 1, 2006, 1–27.

[14] P. Hayes, "Naive Physics 1: Ontology for Liquids", in: J. Hobbs and R. Moore. (eds.) *Formal Theories of the Commonsense World*, Norwood, N.J.: Ablex Pubs, 1985, 71–107.

[15] A. Gupta and N. Belnap, *The Revision Theory of Truth*, Cambridge MA: MIT Press, 1993.

[16] C. J. Mungall, "Obol: Integrating Language and Meaning in Bio-Ontologies", *Comparative and Functional Genomics*, 2004, 5(7):509-520.

Formal Ontology in Information Systems
B. Bennett and C. Fellbaum (Eds.)
IOS Press, 2006

Distinctions Produce a Taxonomic Lattice: Are These the Units of Mentalese?

Andrew U. FRANK

Institute for Geoinformation and Cartography, TU Vienna, Austria

Abstract. Ontologies describe a conceptualization of a part of the world relevant to some application. What are the units of conceptualizations? Current ontologies often equate concepts with words from natural languages. Words are certainly not the smallest units of conceptualization, neither are the sets of synonyms of WordNet or other linguistically justified units. I suggest to take distinctions as basic units and to construct concepts from them whereas other approaches start with concepts and discover properties that distinguish them. Distinctions separate concepts and produce a taxonomic lattice, which contains the named concepts together with other potential conceptual units. The taxa are organized in a superclass/subclass (better supertaxa/subtaxa) relation and for any two taxa there is always a single least common supertaxon. Algorithms to maintain such a taxonomic structure and methods to combine different taxonomies are shown, using a four valued (relevance) logic as introduced by Belnap [1]. The novel aspect of the method is that distinctions that are only meaningful in the context of other distinctions restrict the lattice of concepts to the meaningful subset.

The approach is restricted to the *is_a* relation between classes; it relates to Formal Concept Analysis, but replaces the "formal attributes" with (necessary) distinctions and uses a four-valued logic. It stresses the focus of recent ontological studies like DOLCE or WonderWeb on qualities; it is expected that distinctions as introduced here for the *is_a* hierarchy influence the mereological aspects of an ontology (i.e., the *part_of* relation) and connect to Gibson's affordances [2] and contribute to the classification of operations.

Keywords. Ontology, Taxonomy, Qualities, Lattice.

Introduction

Words from natural language or sets of synonyms are often used in ontologies as the conceptual building block. Gärdenfors has already pointed out that concepts depend on context and "we constantly *learn* new concepts and *adjust* old ones in the light of new experiences" (Gärdenfors [3], 102, emphasis by Gärdenfors). The conflict between the fluidity of concepts and the rigidity of ontological knowledge acquisition results in the observed difficulties with building ontologies and it is difficult to integrate ontologies or similar artifacts like database schemas.

Distinctions between concepts could be the building blocks for the 'language of thought' (Fodor [4]). Following Pinker, Gärdenfors, Lakoff and many others (Lakoff [5]; Pinker [6]; Gärdenfors [3]), our concepts of the world are not arbitrary but reflect the physical, bodily, and social constraints of the world: we make the differences that are meaningful for operations we want to carry out and notice distinctions that are relevant for our lives. Distinctions create intensional and extensional sets of entities and differentiate between concepts. They serve as building blocks to construct taxonomies and help with knowledge acquisition.

This paper concentrates on taxonomies, what Masolo et al. [7] have called lightweight ontologies. In a taxonomy constructed from necessary distinctions, the deduction of sub- and superclass (*is_a*) relations is immediate and algorithm for knowledge acquisition and integration use database operations and do not require logical inferences. The integration of two independently elaborated ontologies requires only the identification of the distinctions—of which there are much less than class concepts; additional identification of common taxa strengthen the integration.

The paper is structured as follows: the next section clarifies the terminology used, linking the work to the DOLCE/WonderWeb terminology. Section 3 discusses briefly the difference between linguistically justified conceptual units and the finer grained concepts addressed here. Section 4 shows how distinctions lead to lattices of concepts and gives the examples used in the paper. The fifth section collects the formal definitions and properties of the taxonomic lattice of distinctions. Section 6 shows how new concepts are added to such a taxonomic lattice and how such lattices can be integrated. Section 7 introduces rules to restrict the application of distinctions and excludes impossible combinations. Section 8 shows some results from a prototypical implementation and section 9 lists future work, especially the connection to mereology and dynamic ontologies with operations.

1. Terminology

It is amazing that the field of ontological studies that pretend to clarify the meaning of words is itself entangled in a confusing terminology. From different terminologies I mostly follow the WonderWeb definitions [7]. The word *concept* will be used to describe a unit in the mental realm, something in our mind; whereas *kind* describes collections of things in the world that have some commonality (I avoid the often used term *category* to avoid confusion with mathematical category theory (Asperti and Longo [8]; Krötzsch, Hitzler et al. [9])). The terms *type* and *classes* are used to describe extensional and intensional sets of representations; classes considered only in an *is_a* relationship will be called *taxa* (singular *taxon*). The term *distinction* describes the difference between the individuals in two taxa, based on the observation of a single quality.

Individuals (for example, my dog Fido) are often called object or entities and described sometimes by proper nouns (whereas classes are described by sortals). Individuals have *qualities,* "within a certain ontology, we assume that these qualities belong to a finite set of *quality types*" ([7], 16, emphasis in the text). The basic qualities are observable (weight, color, etc.) but other qualities are culturally constructed (Searle [10]). Properties are (unary) universals; I see them as functions that applied at a specific time to a specific individual result in a value from a *quality space* [3] (the *quale* in DOLCE (Gangemi, Guarino et al. [11]; Masolo, Borgo et al. [7])). I will use the term *word* for linguistic units and *symbol* for the representations in a formal system.

2. Linguistics as a Start for Ontology?

Linguists have studied the vocabulary, the lexicon of languages extensively. Their efforts to understand the semantics of words have often provided starting points for ontologists:

2.1. Words

Words in a natural language are recognizable signs (tokens). They stand for the equivalence class of utterances, written signs, etc., they are *invariant under representations*—written or spoken in different forms and in most languages subject to grammatical transformations (e.g., the addition of a terminal 's' to form a plural in English). The abstract word "dog", which we find in a dictionary entry, describes the equivalence class of all representations of the word.

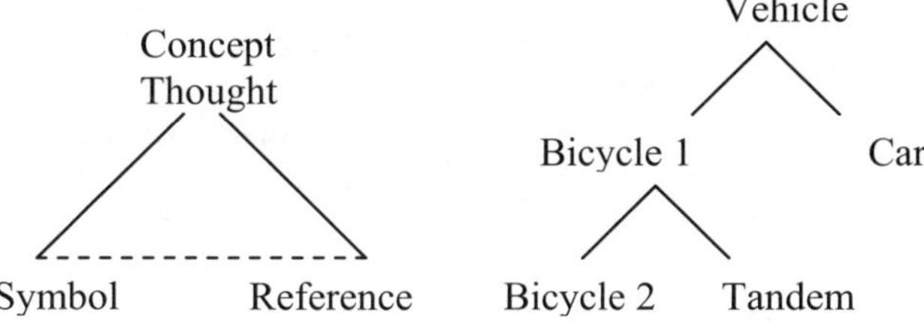

Figure 1. The semiotic triangle   **Figure 2.** The taxonomy for context 1 and 2

In the semiotic triangle (**Figure 1**) (Eco [12]) the relation between symbol and referent is not direct but indirect through the concept in the human mind. The relationship is influenced by prototype effects and family resemblance (Rosch [13]; Pinker [6]; Gärdenfors [3]).

It is accepted that multiple concepts are associated with a single word. Linguists separate homonymy, two words sounding or written the same but with different meaning, and polysemy, the same word having different meanings. The same words in natural languages often stand for a class and a related super-class, depending on the context. Consider first a legal text in which permitted action for different kinds of vehicles are discussed—*bicycles* are separated from *cars*. The second text describes an encounter of a group of people "there were three bicycles and one tandem". *bicycle₁* (from the legal context) is the superordinate of *bicycle₂* (from the second text) (**Figure 2**). In general, the lexicon is not sufficient to mark all the distinctions between concepts; natural language is economical and reuses a combination of words to achieve finer subdivisions.

2.2. Synset

WordNet (Fellbaum [14]) introduced sets of synonyms (synsets), which group words, such that, in a fixed context, the words in a synset can be exchanged against each other. Many research contributions—including papers by myself—have equated synset with conceptual unit and used WordNet as a start for an ontology. WordNet provides a finer and more structured division of meaning than ordinary dictionary entries. In particular,

WordNet has a hierarchical hypernym/hyponym structure that is often used to demonstrate ontological processing.

Nevertheless, synsets are not likely the finest grained conceptual units, because they do not translate from one language to another language; they are language specific (EuroWordnet project). Assuming that conceptual units are language specific (but otherwise context invariant) would push the ill-famed Whorfian hypothesis (Carroll [15]) into a new field.

3. Taxonomy as a Set of Distinctions

Consider a set of concepts arranged as a taxonomy. The taxonomy consists of a set of taxa [9]. These taxa are considered different from each other, they are distinct. In this paper, I consider the taxa and the taxonomy as constructed from a set of distinctions, with the interpretation that all individuals in a taxon have a particular value for the quality related to the distinction. A distinction is related to a particular type of qualities that map from individuals to a small set of values. For example, cars are distinct from bicycles as they are motorized and bicycles not; cars have for the distinction *motorized* the value *True*, bicycles the value *False*. Every taxon in a taxonomy is different from any other by at least one distinction value, the set of distinction is an intensional definition of the taxonomy (Priss [16]).

A taxonomy organizes the taxa in an *is_a* relation, which corresponds to a subset relation between the set of individuals classified in these taxa. If *S* is a subtaxon of *A* then every individual that is an element of *S* is also member of *A*, every (necessary) distinction that individuals of *A* have is shared by individuals of *S*. The discussion here is in terms of the taxa and not in terms of individuals (this is different from DOLCE, BOF, and similar ontologies); the reference to individuals is only a motivation for the formalization. The discussion is limited to *is_a* relations between taxa and I leave the connections with mereology and operations in a dynamic ontology for future work.

Example: Classify vehicles, first by a *land/water* distinction, and then separate bicycles from cars by having a motor or not, and use the same distinction for water vehicles, separating rowboats from steamships (**Figure 3**). Note that we have a word *vessel* to describe water vehicles, but no corresponding term seems to exist for land vehicles. This taxonomy makes sense if we have only to distinguish between these concepts (*bicycle*, *car*, *rowboat*, and *steamship*). To distinguish between *n* taxa at least $log_2\ n$ binary distinctions are necessary; in this sense the taxonomy in **Figure 3** is minimal.

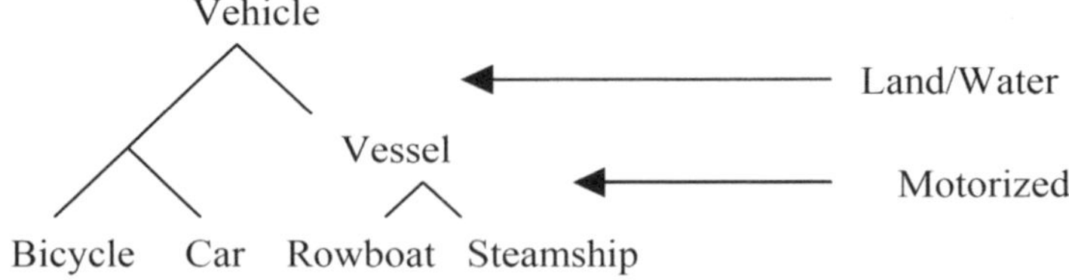

Figure 3. The taxa produced by the distinctions "Land_Water" and "Motorized"

3.1. Boolean and multi-valued distinctions

In general, the property that distinguishes the two taxa are not Boolean values: any (small) set of distinct values can serve. For bicycles, one could ask for number of seats (1,2,3), for vehicles the environment in which they operate (Land, Water, Air). Without loss of generality, the discussion concentrates on Boolean distinctions (in subsection 5.1 treatment of non-Boolean distinctions is shown). In the following diagrams I will annotate the taxa with the distinctions without showing the values not to overload the diagrams. Diagrams are shown as semi-lattices without the trivial bottom element.

3.2. Impediments of hierarchical taxonomies

Current ontologies discuss mostly hierarchical taxonomies, but many systems accept heterarchies, (e.g., OWL). Organizing words in a strict hierarchy (i.e., a structure in which each element has exactly one superordinate) leads (1) to the question of selecting a unique starting point (or several ones) and then (2) to setting the order in which distinctions are applied. WordNet, for example, has selected a small number of unique beginners for the hierarchies—there were 25 for nouns (Miller [17], 29) and some additional ones for verbs etc. DOLCE classifies a material object by the distinctions Particular, Endurant, PhysicalEndurant (in this order) ([7], 14). The selection of unique beginners and the order of distinctions influences the structure of the ontology and hinders integration of ontologies that have different unique beginners or use different order. Classifying the taxa from **Figure 3** by first splitting in motorized or not and then in land/water would be equally good for other purposes like regulating the need for a permit to conduct a motorized vehicle on land or water (**Figure 4**); note that no node in this taxonomy describes *vessel*!

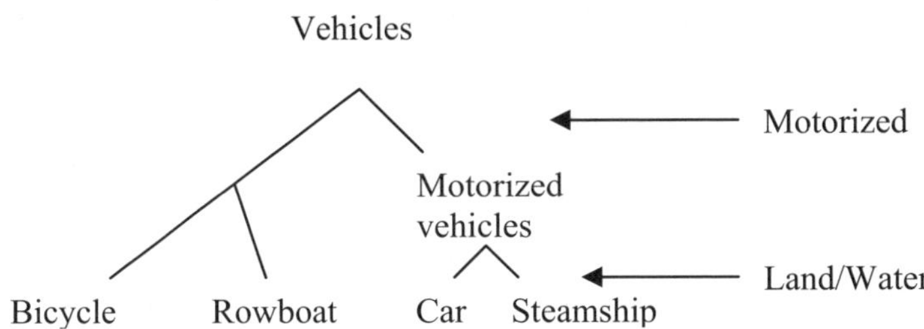

Figure 4. An alternative taxonomy to Figure 1

The extensive debate on inheritance in the object-oriented software community has shown that modeling human conceptualizations in a hierarchy introduces artifacts. Distinctions can be applied in any order and produce a heterarchy, specifically a semi-lattice. This structure represents not only the concepts introduced and named by the user, but also the different supertaxa (land vehicle, motorized vehicle, etc.), which may be meaningful in some related context and are useful when merging different ontologies.

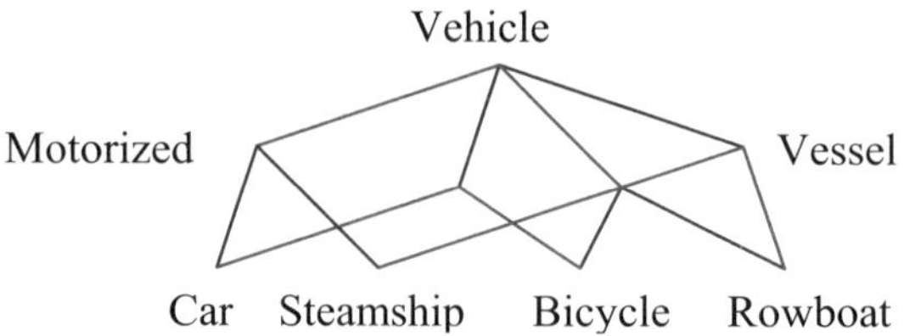

Figure 5. Merging the taxonomy from Figure 1 and 4 to form a semi-lattice

3.3. Dependencies between distinctions

Some distinctions are often not applicable if not another distinction has a particular value. For example, if we distinguish between a taxon of physical objects and one of non-physical ideas, then a distinction *motorized* applies only to the subtaxa of physical objects. Representing such dependencies as rules reveals the intended semantics of distinctions of the taxonomy.

3.4. Difference to Formal Concept Analysis

Formal Concept Analysis (Wille [18]; Priss [16]) was developed to deduce automatically higher level concepts from a description of individuals with quality values. The result of the analysis are concepts that generalize the knowledge found in the individual cases. The taxonomic lattice of concepts is organizing taxa that are defined by distinctions, not simple values (for example, values of distinctions describe regions that partition the quality space). Nevertheless, some of the results from Formal Concept Analysis are directly applicable to the taxonomic lattice, as will be seen in the next section (Burmeister [19]).

4. Formalization of a Taxonomy

A taxonomy consists of distinctions (d_j) and taxa (A_i). Distinctions map from a taxon to a set of distinction values from a domain $D : d_j :: A \rightarrow 2^D$; the cardinality of D is small and 2^D denotes the usual powerset over D. The taxa are characterized by a set of values for the distinctions. Without loss of generality, I start the discussion with Boolean distinction ($D = \{True. False\}$). The formalization here can be seen as a subset of description logic (Brachman and Levesque [20]).

A taxon is described by two sets of Boolean distinctions: the set of the affirmed and the set of negated distinctions, where each distinction appears at most once, either in the affirmed or in the negated set; the intersection of the affirmed and negated set is empty. Between two taxa, a partial order $<$ is defined, extending the ordinary subset relation to the pair of sets; note that the supertaxon has the smaller set of distinction and the subtaxon the larger!

$$\forall a : aff(a) \cap neg(a) = \varnothing$$

$$a \subset b \Leftrightarrow aff(a) \supset aff(b) \wedge neg(a) \supset neg(b)$$

$$a \wedge b = (aff(a) \cap aff(b), neg(a) \cap neg(b))$$

$$a \vee b = (\mathit{aff}(a) \cup \mathit{aff}(b), \mathit{neg}(a) \cup \mathit{neg}(b))$$

The distinction defines a lattice with a top taxon *everything* that has no distinctions and a bottom taxon *nothing*. For any two taxa a unique, least supertaxon exists, called the *join* ($\wedge$) and a largest subtaxon, called the *meet* ($\vee$). The *join* is computed as the intersections of the affirmed and the negated distinctions. The *meet* of two taxa is the union of the affirmed and negated distinctions and if any distinction is in both resulting sets, then the result is *undefined* represented by the *nothing* taxon.

The interpretation of *join* is 'the smallest taxon that includes both of the given taxa'—for example, the *join* of *rowboat* and *Bicycle* is *non-motorized vehicle*. The interpretation of *meet* is 'the largest taxon that has all the qualities of the two given ones'; for example, the *meet* of *motorized vehicle* and *vessel* is *steamship* (**Figure 5**). This construction of a Boolean lattice is an application of Belnap's four-valued logic [1], with the values, {*A, not A, A or not A* (indifferent), *A and not A* (undefined)} (**Figure 6**). It is used in relevant logics and increasingly applied to problems of information science.

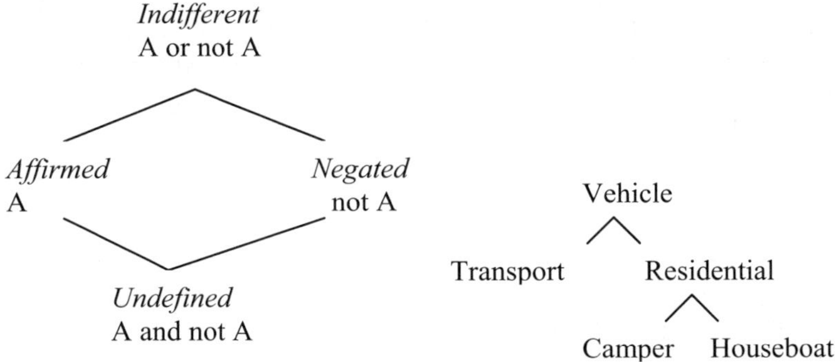

Figure 6. Belnap's four valued logic   **Figure 7.** A taxonomy for campers and houseboats

4.1. Multi-valued distinction

For distinctions that have multiple values, a taxon is characterized by the set of the values the distinction can take, interpreted as 'every individual in this taxon will have one of these values'. The *join* is the union of the values for this distinction in both taxa and the *meet* is the intersection of these values; an empty set of values for a distinction represents *undefined* and the set of all values for the distinction the value *indifferent*.

Example: Extend the distinction *Land/Water* to *Habitat* with the values {*Land, Water, Air*}; then the taxon *Steamship* is described by {*Motorized = {True}, Habitat = {Water}}*. The taxon *Seaplane* is described by {*Motorized = {True}, Habitat = {Water, Air}}*. The *join* of *seaplane* with *car {Motorized = {True}, Habitat = {Land}}* gives *MotorVehicle {Motorized = {True}, Habitat = {Land, Water, Air} = indifferent}*.

4.2. Named taxa

All taxa in a taxonomic lattice are created by the set of distinctions and need not be stored; one could say that they are virtual. Some taxa are of particular interest to the ontologist and are associated with a descriptive label and a natural language gloss to indicate the intention. Only these named taxa are stored with the affirmed and negated set of distinctions. Typically diagrams of ontologies show only these named taxa, but the construction of all taxa in the taxonomic lattice makes *join* and *meet* operations produce a super- and subtaxon in all cases (but these are not necessarily one of the named taxa!) and helps with the maintenance and integration of taxonomies.

5. Operations to Manage a Taxonomic Lattice of Distinctions

5.1. Add or delete named taxa that can be expressed with the given set of distinctions

Adding a named taxon to a taxonomic lattice without introducing a new distinction is just adding the label and the gloss to the taxon, because potentially all taxa that can be constructed from the given distinctions are already in the taxonomic lattice. Practically speaking, one checks that not another named taxon with the same values for the distinction has been added before. This allows to detect if a taxon is added twice with different terminology or to identify distinctions that must be added to differentiate two otherwise not differentiable taxa. Example: name the taxon *Wheeler {Motorized, Land}* to complement the taxon *Vessel* in **Figure 3**. Deleting a named taxon from the lattice is just removing the name—the potential taxa remains in the lattice as a combination of distinctions.

5.2. Add a taxon and a new distinction

To add a distinction to a taxonomic lattice is only changing the potential taxa but stored taxa need not be changed—the existing taxa all receive the value *indifferent* for the new distinction. The new distinction can be added to existing named taxa; for example: a new distinction *isResidence* is added (see **Figure 7**) and the taxa *HouseBoat* and *Camper* can be distinguished.

5.3. Split at taxon with a new distinction

Consider the case where an existing taxon should be split in two. For example in **Figure 8** we want to introduce a taxon *Dieselboat* to contrast with *Steamship* in the taxonomy of **Figure 3**. For this we have to introduce a new distinction *SteamEngine* and mark the existing taxon *Steamship* with this as an affirmed distinction (and propagate this to all subtaxa of *Steamship*!). The taxa *Dieselboat* and *Motorboat* can be named.

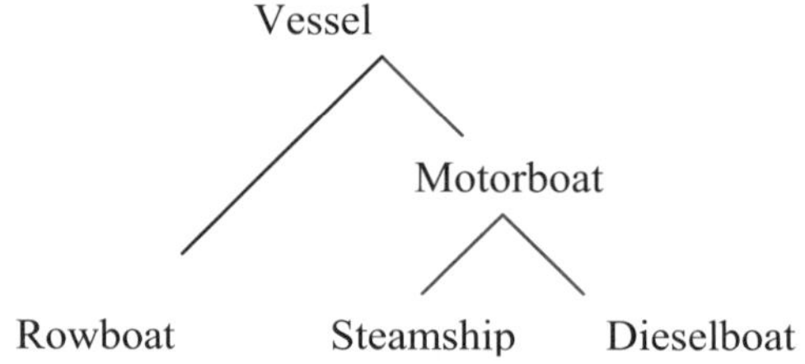

Figure 8. Taxonomy with distinction *steamEngine*

The general procedure for adding a new distinction is: first, identify the sibling of the new taxon and decide on the distinction (**Figure 9**). Second, add the distinction to the two sibling taxa, once affirmed, once negated (and propagate to the subtaxa of the existing taxon). This produces automatically a new supertaxon (the *join* of the sibling and the new taxon).

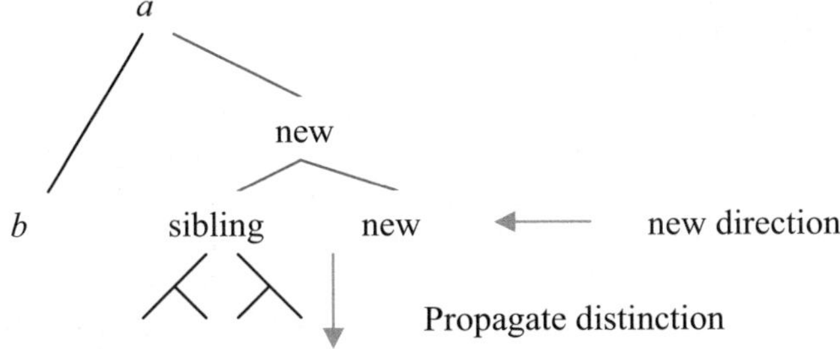

Figure 9. General approach to addition

5.4. Merging two taxonomies

Two taxonomies *A, B*, with different distinctions can be combined. Taxa that lack a value for a distinction acquire the default value *indifferent* for this distinction. The resulting taxonomic lattices are much larger but the named taxa remain distinct and keep their characterization by the set of affirmed and negated distinctions (note that taxa are defined as set of distinction values—thus even if the intentions for two concepts are the same, if the taxa are defined by different distinctions, they are considered different). This is possible because the named concepts represent only a small part of the lattice of concepts. The result, however, is a combination without any interaction between the taxonomies. For any combination of taxa from taxonomy *A* and taxonomy *B* the *join* and the *meet* are top (everything) and bottom (nothing)—no new information is generated.

More useful is the combination of taxonomies where at least some distinctions are the same or can be identified. Then the combination of the two lattices shows the interaction between the concepts. Example: Merging the ontology of vehicles of **Figure 3** and **Figure 7** gives a lattice with the distinctions *Land/Water* (shared), *Residential,* and *Motorized.* Relationships between the taxa are established; for example, the *join* from *Houseboat* and *Steamboat* is *Vessel*; the *meet* of *Residence* and *LandVehicle* is *Camper.* These relations are based only on the identified distinctions and result automatically without any changes in the description of the named taxa (except for adding the default value *indifferent* for distinctions that were not originally used).

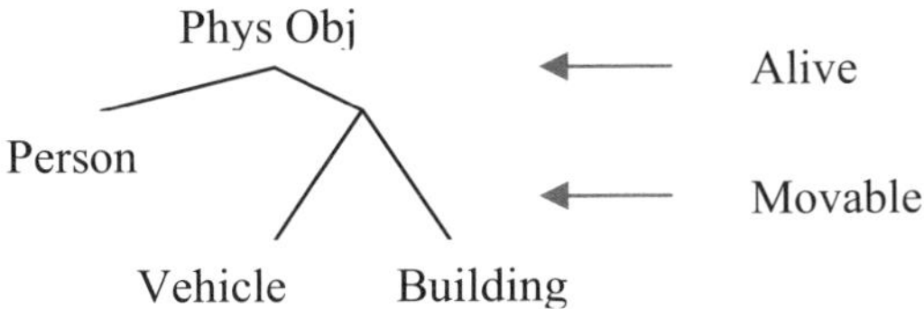

Figure 10. A taxonomy with distinctions alive and movable

Even more integration is achieved when not only distinctions are identified but also named concepts. This is especially important, if the top level distinctions differed between the two ontologies. Assume that the ontology of **Figure 3** is merged with

Figure 10. Then the distinctions for *Vessel* in **Figure 10** must be added to the distinctions of *Vessel* in **Figure 3** (and reverse) before the two taxonomies are merged by identifying the distinctions.

5.5. Preserving initial taxonomies

Merging taxonomies to make database interoperable leads to a new taxonomy but the relations to the original taxonomies *A* and *B* must be preserved. The concept lattice spans the space of all combinations of distinctions. It is therefore possible to maintain in it the original taxa together with taxa that result from mergers or updates. Changed taxa are given new names and operations to determine sub- and supertaxa can be restricted such that they give the same results as before the merger. It is only necessary to restrict the operations to consider only the distinction available originally in the taxonomy and to select—among the taxa that become equal by this restriction—the ones that are most general.

6. Reduction in the Size of the Taxonomic Lattice

Certain distinctions are only meaningful when other distinctions have specific values. For example, only physical objects have weight—a distinction of objects lighter or heavier than water is only meaningful for physical objects, not for immaterial objects. Adding rules to express these dependencies reduces the size of the lattice by the following interpretation (formulated for the case of Boolean distinctions, but generalizable):

> *Rule: (aff, neg) -> {distinction}*

If the affirmed and negated distinctions are not present in a taxon then only the values indifferent or undefined are possible; distinct values (*A, not A*) are mapped to undefined. This prunes the lattice from impossible taxa, e.g., a rule: *{physObj}* -> *{color}* excludes a taxon for *green ideas* because color is restricted as a distinction to physical objects. The rules express the intended semantics of distinctions and serve to communicate these intentions among the ontologist working on a taxonomy and warn the ontologist when attempting to enter taxa with inconsistent distinctions.

These rules do not apply when computing the *join* because if a distinction is justified in both taxa from which we calculate the *join*, then it is also justified in the intersection of the two. Neither do they apply when computing the *meet*, because if a distinction is present in one of the two then it is also justified in the union.

7. Prototype

Software to demonstrate this approach has been implemented in Haskell (Peyton Jones, Hughes et al. [21]) and a set of concepts were entered, separated taxonomies merged and the result interrogated. The operations manage sets of distinctions and use straight forward representations and operations on sets. The most complex operations compute set intersections for the small sets of distinctions! Taxa accumulate distinctions downwards; the number of distinctions is less than or equal to the depth of the taxonomic lattice. In general, a taxonomic lattice with n distinctions has at most $3^n + 1$ element.

The prototype produces supporting information for the ontologist about sub- and supertaxa to a given set of distinctions and warns if a taxon with the same set of distinctions as another already existing one is about to be entered. More advanced tools from Formal Concept Analysis may be applied in the future.

8. Conclusion

The formalization is strictly speaking about tokens that are interpreted as distinctions and taxa and for which we establish a small set of rules and relations that respect the interpretation. I assume that the simplicity of the proposed formalization comes from the explicit introduction of the distinctions between taxa instead of inferring these from other types of description of the taxonomy. It seems that describing taxa by giving their distinguishing qualities is not more difficult to alternative methods used in, say, Protégé.

The flexibility in adding new distinctions as a situation requires, the connection between distinction and bodily interactions with the environment and the simplicity of the deduction suggest further investigation whether a definition of fine-grained and adaptable concepts based on distinction corresponds to some aspects of human mental concepts. The formalization shown here gives hints to possible test cases.

8.1. Future work

The application of a fuzzy four-valued logic (Straccia [22]) to taxonomies should be studied to understand how it can contribute to represent prototype effects in taxonomies [13]. The mapping between different subsets of a taxonomy may be useful to discuss metaphorical usage, e.g., *heavy thoughts*, *green ideas*, and *flying proposals* correspond to comparable taxa that are just different in one distinction (physical vs. immaterial object).

The work presented here is restricted to taxonomies (*is_a* relation). A promising connection is to mereology (*part_of* relation). It is known that certain qualities carry over from the whole to the parts: if a car is a physical object, then each part of it is a physical object. Other qualities do not carry from whole to part: if a cat is *alive* then the parts of the cat (tail, leg, etc.) are not *alive*—or perhaps alive in different, restricted sense. Further, one must inquire how to express distinctions that are expressed as equivalence classes, e.g., a definition of biological taxa as 'interbreeding'.

Considering taxonomies of processes with related entities of different types, e.g., "Tom is cutting a loaf of bread with a knife", can be seen as connecting different taxa: person, bread, and knife. Generalization of processes by removing distinctions from the taxa involved can thus be described: Tom is cutting foodstuff with a tool > Tom is separating foodstuff > An agent is moving material. This gives a finer order relation to operations than currently available and shows how to relate taxonomies and processes in a dynamic ontology (Frank [23]).

Acknowledgements

I am grateful for comments from Werner Kuhn and Stella Frank, who have helped me to improve the presentation. I appreciated the suggestions and constructive critique by the reviewers that were useful for preparing the final text.

References

[1]   Belnap, N. D. (1977). A Useful Four-Valued Logic. Modern uses of multiple-valued logic. G. Epstein and J. M. Dunn. Dordrecht, NL, Reidel: 5--37.
[2]   Gibson, J. (1979). The Ecological Approach to Visual Perception. Hillsdale, NJ, Erlbaum.
[3]   Gärdenfors, P. (2000). Conceptual Spaces, MIT Press.
[4]   Fodor, J. A. (1984). "Precis of The Modularity of Mind." Behavioral and Brain Sciences 8: 1-5.
[5]   Lakoff, G. (1987). Women, Fire, and Dangerous Things: What Categories Reveal About the Mind. Chicago, IL, University of Chicago Press.
[6]   Pinker, S. (1999). Words and Rules, Basic Books.
[7]   Masolo, C., S. Borgo, et al. (2003). WonderWeb Deliverable D18 (Ontology Library). Trento, Italy, Laboratory For Apüplied Ontology - ISTC-CNR: 247.
[8]   Asperti, A. and G. Longo (1991). Categories, Types and Structures - An Introduction to Category Theory for the Working Computer Scientist. Cambridge, Mass., The MIT Press.
[9]   Krötzsch, M., P. Hitzler, et al. (2005). Category Theory in Ontology Research: Concrete Gain from an Abstract Approach. Karlsruhe, Germany, Institut AIFB, Universität Karlsruhe: 6.
[10] Searle, J. R., Ed. (1995). The Construction of Social Reality. New York, The Free Press.
[11] Gangemi, A., N. Guarino, et al. (2002). Sweetening Ontologies with DOLCE. EKAW 2002.
[12] Eco, U. (1977). Zeichen - Einfuehrung in einen Begriff und seine Geschichte. Frankfurt a. Main, Edition Suhrkamp.
[13] Rosch, E. (1973). On the Internal Structure of Perceptual and Semantic Categories. Cognitive Development and the Acquisition of Language. T. E. Moore. New York, Academic Press.
[14] Fellbaum, C., Ed. (1998). WordNet: An Electronic Lexical Database. Language, Speech, and Communication. Cambridge, Mass., The MIT Press.
[15] Carroll, J. B. (1956). Language, Thought and Reality - Selected Writing of Benjamin Lee Whorf. Cambridge, Mass., The MIT Press.
[16] Priss, U. (to appear). "Formal Concept Analysis in Information Science." Annual Review of Information Science and Technology 40: 22.
[17] Miller, G. A. (1998). Nouns in WordNet. WordNet An Electronicd Lexical Database. C. Fellbaum. London, England, MIT Press: 23-46.
[18] Wille, R. (2000). Boolean Concept Logic. Conceptual Structures: Logical, Linguistic and Computational Issues. B. Ganter and G. Mineau. Berlin-Heidelberg-New York, Springer. LNAI 1867: 317-331.
[19] Burmeister, P. (2003). Formal Concept Analysis with ConImp: Introduction to the Basic Features. Darmstadt, Germany, TU-Darmstadt: 50.
[20] Brachman, R. J. and H. J. Levesque, Eds. (1985). Readings in Knowledge Representaion. Los Altos, California, Morgan Kaufmann.
[21] Peyton Jones, S., J. Hughes, et al. (1999). "Haskell 98: A Non-Strict, Purely Functional Language." from http://www.haskell.org/onlinereport/.
[22] Straccia, U. (1997). A Four-Valued Fuzzy Propositional Logic. 15th International Joint Conference on Artificial Intelligence, Nagoya, Japan, Proceedings of IJCAI-97.
[23] Frank, A. (2006). Distinctions - A Common Base for a Taxonomic Calculus for Objects and Actions. Vienna, Institute for Geoinformation and Cartography.

Formal Ontology in Information Systems
B. Bennett and C. Fellbaum (Eds.)
IOS Press, 2006

39

Nontological Engineering

Wacław KUŚNIERCZYK[†]
Department of Information and Computer Science
Norwegian University of Science and Technology

Abstract. This article reflects an ongoing effort to systematize the use of terms applied by philosophers and computer scientists in the context of ontology and ontological engineering. We show that a common reference terminology is needed to connect terms in representational artifacts to what they mean ontologically. Without such a reference, statements in and about knowledge representation languages will be ambiguous, both as between various languages and within a single language.

We identify problems common to a number of knowledge representation languages used to formalize ontologies. We show that a reference terminology can be used to disambiguate the meanings of some, and to reveal ontological problems in other, evidently confused, statements in and about different representation languages. Our final conclusion is not that our proposed terminology is the ultimate one to serve as a common reference; rather, we argue that it is necessary to have such a standard with well-defined terms linked to an axiomatized theory, if unambiguous cross-paradigm and cross-language communication is to be achieved.

Keywords. Knowledge representation, ontological engineering, ontology, terminology.

1. Introduction

Ontology, as a branch of philosophy occupied with the study of being, has a long history; ontological questions, such as *What exists?* and *What is existence?*, were disputed by ancient philosophers even before Plato and Aristotle laid the groundworks of ontology — the philosophical discipline — in its modern shape. On the other hand, ontologies, as artifacts for expressing and exchanging knowledge about portions of reality with the rigor of a formal and computer-understandable language, are a relatively recent invention. [1] There is currently an explosion of efforts in development, publishing, merging and applying ontologies; it has been fuelled mostly by the rapid increase, both in number and size, of public online data, information and knowledge sources with diverse structures and incompatible languages (the 'database tower of Babel' problem) that call for a principled approach to semantic integration. This explosion, in turn, has created a broad niche for ontological research and ontological engineering. [2]

[†]Correspondence: Department of Information and Computer Science, Norwegian University of Science and Technology (NTNU), Sem Sælands vei 7–9, 7027 Trondheim, Norway; E-mail: waku@idi.ntnu.no

Ontologies flourish in just about every imaginable corner of our scientific and non-scientific activity; this is especially visible in the natural sciences, e.g., under the umbrella of Open Biomedical Ontologies[1] (OBO). But while one of the principal goals behind the effort of constructing ontologies is to enable both a human user and an automated reasoner to access and comprehend multiple databases without being forced to investigate their implementational details, the cure seems often to be no better than the disease: the ontologies themselves are modeled in various paradigms, represented in different languages and stored in custom-made databases. Consequentially, the promised benefit may easily become outbalanced by the burden of having to parse, interpret and match multiple heterogeneous ontologies (the 'ontology tower of Babel' problem?). OBO ontologies, for example, employ quite different concepts, methods and techniques in the modeling of their domains, despite a common syntactic commitment.[2]

Our goal in this article is threefold: to provide evidence that there is a load of confusion in what ontological engineers say; to support the claim that it is essential to state precisely, in ontological terms, what it is that one attempts to create a representation of; to argue that it may be reasonable to start with a simplified account of existence in order to provide ontological engineers with a common reference for the purpose of disambiguation, and then extend this base to satisfy the expectations of both philosophers and computer scientists.

The rest of the article is organized as follows. In Sec. 2 we argue that the relation between ontlogical engineering artifacts and reality is often unclear, and provide examples of confusing uses of terms such as 'ontology' and 'concept'. In Sec. 3 the reference terminology proposed by Smith et al. [3] is refined and extended. Section 4 shows possible applications of the terminology. Finally, in Sec. 5 we summarize our work.

2. Nontological Engineering

The ideal team of experts who set off to create an ontology of a particular domain consists, at the very least, of domain experts, knowledge modellers (usually computer scientists), and those with expertise in philosophical ontology. Yet given that formal ontology [1] is just one of many branches of philosophy, and that the subject-matter of virtually any science and industry may be the object of ontological engineering, philosophical ontologists will likely be greatly outnumbered by ontological engineers. The scale and diversity of the attempts to fill up the ontology niche emphasizes the need for a sound, understandable and reusable basis for this discipline. An attempt to systematize the foundations should be based on consent rather than on competition, and must be thorough. An account of these foundations should, to best serve the ontology engineering world, be easily understandable, but by no means oversimplified or confused; it should allow for a shared understanding of how different ontological engineering paradigms may be used to model the same reality.

Two recently published books seem to be intended as a reference for those who seek such an account. One of them, the *Handbook on Ontologies* [4] *"demonstrates standards that have been created recently; it surveys methods that have been developed and it shows how to bring both into practice of ontology infrastructures and applications that are the best of their kind.*" The other, *Ontological Engineering*, [5] "*presents the major issues of ontological engineering and describes the most outstanding ontologies currently available.*" Unfortunately, a closer look at the books reveals a number of problems, of which poor use of English, redundant introduction of terms, inconsistent citation schemes and hardly readable figures are perhaps not the most serious, but certainly interfere with a reader's understanding. Both books were written, by and large, by computer scientists for computer scientists, to provide guidance through the world of ontologies; yet the result of the authors' effort may be no less confusing than what they attempt to disambiguate.

After having presented a number of conflicting definitions of what an *ontology* is (see below), the authors of *Ontological Engineering* conclude: "*We can say that as there is consensus among the ontology community, no one can get confused about its usage* [of the term 'ontology']." But the actual situation seems to be quite the opposite: there is much confusion as to what an ontology (a representational artifact) is, what it is that its components represent, and what the principles for building an ontology are. In his discussion of principles for the design of ontologies, Gruber says that "*ontological commitment is based on consistent use of vocabulary.*" [6] Ontologies are built to provide consistent vocabularies for different domains. But is there any commitment to a consistent vocabulary in the community of ontological engineers? In the following two sections we provide evidence that the answer to this question is no. *Quis custodiet ipsos custodes?*

2.1. Ontologies of Ontologies?

In philosophy, ontology is a systematic account of being; [7] it is the *existence in reality* which is the subject of study and description. In computer science, the term 'ontology' seems to have been given a number of different, conflicting meanings; compare the following few statements involving this term:

A specification of a representational vocabulary for a shared domain of discourse — definitions of classes, relations, functions, and other objects — is called an ontology. [8]

An ontology is a set of logical axioms designed to account for the intended meaning of a vocabulary. [9]

Ontologies can be used to provide a concrete specification of term names and term meanings. (. . .) An ontology is a specification of the conceptualization of a term. [10]

An ontology is a hierarchically structured set of terms for describing a domain that can be used as a skeletal foundation for a knowledge base. [11]

Ontologies are quintessentially content theories, because their main contribution is to identify specific classes of objects and relations that exist in some domain. [12]

"An ontology is a formal specification of a shared conceptualization". [8] (. . .) Conceptualization means an abstract model of some aspect of the world, taking the form of a definition of the properties of important concepts and relationships. [13]

Ontology languages allow users to write explicit, formal conceptualizations of domain models. [14]

Ontologies are explicit representations of agents' commitments to a model of the relevant world. (. . .) Ontologies are specific, high-level models of knowledge underlying

> all things, concepts, and phenomena. (...) Generally, an ontology is a metamodel describing how to build models. [15]
> An ontology is not just a representation — in a computer — of [a] domain. [16]

Three issues are in focus in these characterizations of an ontology as a representational artifact: *what* the domain of an ontology is, *how* an ontology represents that domain, and the *purpose* of the representation. Although the issue of how to represent knowledge has been debated for decades, there is little consensus on what structure is essential for a representational artifact to be called an ontology; see, e.g., Lassila and McGuinness [10] or Studer et al. [16] for more discussion. Furthermore, it has only recently been pointed out that it is often unclear what it is that the subject matter of an ontology encompasses: specific individuals, or rather general patterns in a domain; our knowledge about them — or the *lack* of such knowledge — or even terms in that very same ontology. [17,18] The definitions above clearly illustrate this uncertainty: is an ontology an abstract model of a domain, a conceptualization of such a model, or a specification of such a conceptualization? What is the domain represented by a specification of a conceptualization of a domain model?

In Sec. 3.2 we propose to define what an ontology is in terms of what it is that the ontology represents, irrespectively of the expressivity of the underlying representation language and the actual structural complexity of the artifact. The issue seems, superficially, to be purely terminological; however, as it is argued in, e.g., Smith and colleagues' *Wüsteria*, [19] dire consequences follow if it is not made perfectly clear what the represented domains are: whether a term in an ontology represents an entity in reality, a belief about an entity, an act of observation of an entity, a documentation of an observation or belief, a belief about an observation, etc. Where communities of ontology developers do not share a single coherent view on these matters, the result is a confusion. But even if the problem were purely terminological, one motivation for building and using ontologies is to standardize vocabularies — why should we not speak in standard terms about these very standardization efforts themselves?

2.2. Classes of Classes?

The problem of imprecise definitions of the term 'ontology' is reflected in the equally untidy use of terms for an ontology's components and the corresponding elements of the domain. Compare the following statements:

> A concept is a meaning. [20] The most basic concepts in a domain should correspond to classes that are the roots of various taxonomic trees. [21] Concepts are terminological descriptions of classes of individuals. [22] Concepts represent classes of objects. [5] Just as in the object-oriented paradigm, there are two fundamental types of concepts in KM: *instances* (individuals) and *classes* (types of individuals). [23] [Concepts] can be concrete (like a patient) or abstract ((...) a prototypic patient). [24]
> Classes represent concepts, which are taken in a broad sense. [5] A class is a set of entities. Each of the entities in a class is said to be an instance of the class. An entity can be an instance of multiple classes, which are called its types. A class can be an instance of a class. [25] The class *rdfs:Class* defines the class of all classes. [5] A class

has an intensional meaning (the underlying concept) which is related but not equal to its class extension. [26]
Instances are used to represent elements or individuals in an ontology. (...) Individuals represent instances of classes. (...) Individuals represent instances of concepts. [5] Individuals are assertional, and are considered instances of concepts. [22]

One apparent, purely terminological, confusion arises from the fact that some authors use the term 'classes' to denote the elements of reality represented with what they call 'concepts', thus reserving the latter term for denoting elements of a representation, while others do the reverse; the same can be said about the terms 'instance' and 'individual'. However, statements such as "a class can be an instance of a class" reveal again the problem of uncertainty as to *what* is being represented, signalized earlier in Sec. 2.2: the (in)distinction between the representing and the represented. The issue is not merely one of incoherent nomenclature: it is not clear whether a class of all classes, and those classes themselves, are elements of the represented domain, elements of a formal representation of the domain, or, perhaps, elements of a representation of a mental imagination of the domain. The similarly confusion-loaded use of the term 'concept' has been earlier discussed by, e.g., Grenon [27] and Smith [18].

3. A Reference Terminology

In a recent paper, Smith et al. [3] propose a simplified systematization of terminology used in biomedical ontology research; according to their view, reality is composed of entities, which may be instances, universals, and classes, among others. Instances stand in various relations to each other; universals are abstractions of, and are instantiated by, instances; collections are roughly equivalent to sets of instances. On the side of a representation of reality, there are simple representational units such as terms, and complex representational units such as ontologies and inventories. We adopt this simplified view here; we will insist on a clear terminological distinction between the elements of reality and the components of its representations. Terms such as 'concept' and 'class' should be, consistently within each context of use, mapped onto precise definitions, such as those that we will refer to here.

In the next two sections we propose a terminology for speaking of what can be found in *reality* (Sec. 3.1) and for the types of structural elements from which a *representational artifact* may be built (Sec. 3.2). Our aim is to encourage the use of a vocabulary that allows for a clear distinction of the elements of an ontology from the elements of its domain.

3.1. Reality

Entities and reality. Everything that exists is an *entity*; the totality of all entities forms *reality*.[3] Whenever we speak of only some of the entities in reality, we speak of a *partition* of reality, or a *domain*. Similarly to [3], but with some terminological modifications, we distinguish the following *categories* of entities (we refer to the axiomatization of these categories as presented by Bittner et al. [28]):

Abstract entities. *Abstraction* is a process of treating one or more entities as if they were identical by appealing to what they have in common, while leaving out (abstracting from) what they do not have in common.[4] An *abstract* entity is, in this sense, one that shares with those other entities from which it is generated by abstraction only those properties that all of them share; it is an *abstraction* of those entities, which are its *instances*. Bittner et al. [28] show one way to axiomatize a theory of those abstract entities which, according to the realist standpoint, can be identified with universals.[5]

Related to, but distinct from abstraction is *generalization*. An abstract entity *generalizes* another abstract entity if all instances of the latter are also instances of the former. The latter is said to *specialize* the former.[6]

Particulars. A *particular* is an entity that is not an abstract entity; particulars cannot be instantiated — nothing can be said to be an instance of a particular. Particulars, though, can be (are) instances of abstract entities. In [28], particulars are called, and axoimatized as, *individuals*.[7]

Collections. Any number of arbitrary entities can be gathered together to form a *collection*; a collection is thus defined by the totality of the entities that it *includes*. The entities that form a collection are *members* of that collection.[8] The members of a collection are *not* its instances, and the collection is *not* an abstraction of its members; the collection does not have to make any claim as to its members' characteristics, or to how they stand to each other. Bittner et al. [28] treat collections as if they were of a category distinct from that of abstract entities and particulars; this is not the only view on collections, however — Smith, for example, argues that collections are particulars.[9] In any case, collections are distinct from abstract entities, in the sense introduced above.

A collection that includes all, and only those, entities that are instances of a certain abstract entity (at a particular time instant), is the *extension* of that entity (at that time instant). For each abstract entity there may be formed, by gathering all its instances, a collection that is this entity's extension; but not every collection is an extension of an abstract entity. A collection that contains all, but not only, those entities that are members of another collection, *subsumes* (but does not *contain*) the other collection; the former is *not* a generalization of the latter. We refer to [28] for a detailed discussion and formalization of collections and the temporal issues of relations between collections, abstractions and particulars; note, however, that collections are treated there as sets in the mathematical sense, while we would like to understand the term 'collection' more generally, to cover also multisets and the like.

The term *class* is sometimes used with the meaning we gave to *collection*; it is also used in other senses, however — for example, to denote abstract entities, or to denote *both* abstractions and collections. Here it will be treated exclusively as a synonym of *collection*.[10]

Relations. The term 'relation' is pervasively used in ontological engineering to denote both what holds between two abstract entities and what holds between two particulars (instantiation of an abstract entity by a particular is sometimes seen as a relation as well); however, these types of relations should not be confused. In [29,3] Smith et al. distinguish relations that hold between abstract entities (*abstract entity-level*, AL, relations), relations that hold between particulars (*particular-level*, PL, relations), and relations that hold between a particular and an abstract entity (PAL). Bittner et al. extend this scheme and, in addition, distinguish relations that hold between collections (*collection-level*, CL), relations that hold between a particular and a collection (PCL), and relations that hold between a collection and an abstract entity (CAL). [28] Examples of such relations are: generalization and specialization (AL), individual parthood (PL), instantiation and exemplification (PAL), subsumption and partonomic inclusion (CL), membership (PCL), and extension (CAL).

Since abstract entities are abstractions of particulars, it is tempting to see abstract entity-level relations as abstractions of particular-level relations; however, according to the view that relations are not entities of yet another category of being,[11] [30] this should be seen as no more than a (perhaps useful) analogy. Using this analogy, abstract entity-level relations specify different patterns of the corresponding particular-level relations; for example, an AL part-whole relation between two abstract entities can be understood as a constraint that dictates that its PL counterpart holds between each instance of the first abstraction and some instances of the second abstraction, and possibly, but not necessarily, *vice versa*. (Bittner et al. discuss three versions of the relation of partonomic inclusion of universals; see also [31].)

3.2. Representation

Of the representational artifacts described by Smith et al. [3], both representational units (atomic artifacts) and representational structures (compound artifacts) are needed. The former are atomic in the sense that they represent individual entities in reality (or relations — but see above),[12] the latter are composed of the former and represent partitions of reality. [32] All representational artifacts themselves are *particulars* in reality, usually in a partition distinct from that represented. Top-level or upper-level ontologies, such as Sowa's top-level ontology [33] or SUO [34], attempt to capture categories rather than abstract entities etc., and will thus not be proper ontologies in the sense of the term we propose below, since categories themselves are not abstract entities in reality. Knowledge-representation ontologies, such as Gruber's Frame Ontology [8], on the other hand, are ontologies in our sense, since they represent what is general in reality.

Terms. *Terms* are units representing particulars, abstract entities, collections, and relations. Most knowledge representation languages distinguish between terms representing particulars and terms representing abstract entities. Collections, however, are treated either as particulars (and represented as 'instance' terms, instantiating 'collection classes'), or are confused with abstract entities (and represented as 'class' terms). Even if we adopt the former view (collections are particulars) rather than that of collections being entities of a distinct category (as in [28]), we suggest to clearly distinguish the representation of collections from the representation of particulars (or: from the representation of *other* particulars). Relations are usually represented as special relation-terms, called *relations, roles* or *properties*.

Structures. Smith et al. [3] distinguish three types of representational structures: *ontologies, terminologies* and *inventories*; we refer to that article for a detailed introduction. Such representational structures are different in that they are composed of terms representing entities of distinct categories in reality: abstract entities, collections (but see above),[13] and particulars, respectively. (The criterion for a representational artifact to be called an 'ontology' is thus not its formal structure and complexity of the underlying representation language, but rather what it is that is represented by its terms.) Note that terms for relations such as instantiation, membership and extension that bridge different representational structures are not elements of any such structure (e.g., the term representing instantiation is neither an element of an ontology, nor of an inventory). Each representational structure may be hierarchical, i.e., its terms may be partially ordered; in the case of ontologies and terminologies, generalization and subsumption, respectively, are typically chosen as partial order relations forming the hierarchical backbone. Additional representational structures may be needed, for example, if it is desired to organize relations (relation terms) into a hierarchy. Note that such a 'relation ontology' is not an ontology in the sense defined, since its elements do not represent abstract entities in reality.

For clarity, it might be better to call the elements of a representational artifact 'class-terms' (terms representing classes), 'concept-terms', 'instance-terms', etc., rather than 'classes', 'concepts', 'instances', respectively. The latter should be reserved for referring to the elements of the represented domain.

4. Appplication of the Reference Terminology

The statements quoted in Sec. 2 may be confusing, especially if presented side by side; mapping onto the reference terminology may disambiguate some of these expressions, but some are harder to interpret. In the following, we discuss examples of both situations. For each quoted statement or a sequence of statements (in italics) we suggest a clearer statement using our terminology (in plain roman), or point out that no unambiguous mapping to this terminology is possible.

Nomenclatural Disambiguation.   Where direct mapping reveals valid ontological statements, we say that the expressions are *nomenclaturally disambiguated*. The following examples illustrate nomenclatural disambiguation:

Concepts represent classes of objects. Classes represent concepts.
Terms in an ontology (abstract entity-terms) represent abstract entities in a domain.

A concept is a meaning.
The entity represented by a term is the term's meaning. Note that some authors use the term 'concept' to refer not only to the category of abstract entities or collections (classes), but also to the category of particulars (e.g., [23]) or to relations (e.g., [35]).

Concepts can be concrete or abstract.
Terms represent particulars or abstract entities in a domain; terms in an inventory (particular-terms) represent the former; terms in an ontology represent the latter.

Instances are used to represent elements or individuals in an ontology.
Terms in an inventory represent particulars in a domain.

Concept taxonomies are created through generalization relationships between classes.
Hierarchical organization of terms in an ontology (or in a terminology) reflects gen-

eralization (or subsumption) that holds between abstract entities (or between collections) in the represented domain.

Ontological Ambiguity. In some cases an attempt at translation reveals ontologically dubious statements. Not all such statements can be repaired in an obvious way. Consider the following quotations:

> *The class 'Class' defines the class of all classes. The class 'Class' is an instance of the class 'Class'.*

The *class of all classes* may denote the category of collections (or the category of abstract entities); since every term in a terminology (or in an ontology) represents a collection (or an abstract entity) in reality, there is no need for explicitly representing these categories. To explicitly represent categories, we need terms that are not elements of an ontology or of a terminology, but of a separate representational structure — a *categoriology*, say. The *class 'Class'* is thus a term in a categoriology and represents the category of collections (or of abstract entities), but the category is *not* a particular, an it is *not* an instance of itself, or of an abstract entity.

> *A class represents a collection of resources.* (1) *Classes are themselves resources.* (2) *The collection of all classes is itself a class.* (3) *The class extension of a class is the set of members of the class.* (4) *A class may be a member of its own class extension.* (5) [36]

These few statements are an almost contiguous fragment of a single publication. Resources "may be physical objects, abstract concepts, in fact anything that has identity." [36] Classes are abstract entities (4), representational elements (1), and collections (3). A class has members, but the set of those members is not the class itself, but rather the class's extension (4). The extension of the collection of all classes is then the set of all classes, and the collection (a class, 3) is both a member of itself and of its own extension. (There is hardly any reasonable reading of this text.)

5. Conclusions and Discussion

In this article we show that the ontology engineering society is far from speaking a common standardized language while talking about their efforts in building shared vocabularies. Our main concern is that semantic integration of information stored in multiple resources, which is one of the main motivations for building ontologies, may fail due to problems with mapping terms in different ontologies. Inconsistent nomenclature is only a lesser part of the problem; it is the imprecision of meaning that may be a real obstacle. Not only are terms such as *class* and *concept* used interchangeably, not only do they often refer to each other in their definitions, rendering such definitions virtually meaningless, but also the intended meaning of these terms is not always clear. If individual ontological engineers, independently of their idiosyncratic naming conventions, represent the same entities in reality as if they were of different ontological categories, then there may be no sound mapping between terms in the ontologies they build.

Drawing on the results of earlier work by Smith and colleagues (e.g., [28,3,29,31]), we present a refined version of the terminology that they propose, and show that it is possible to reconcile a number of superficially conflicting statements, while in other cases we reveal that there is no ontologically clear meaning is given to expressions in and about knowledge representation languages. The terminology is intended to play to various knowledge representation formalisms a role analogous to that which the Inter Lingual Index and Language Independent Modules of EuroWordNet [37] play to its language-specific wordnets.

Our examples show not only that it is possible to recover from ontological ambiguities, but also that it is essential to be able to refer to an understanding of reality, an ability that automated reasoners have not gained yet. If ontologies, intended to enable automated agents to link various resources, fail to do their job because of their incompatible representations of reality, then higher-level ontologies added on top of the existing ones with the intention of enabling the agents to match the lower-level ontologies are likely to fail due to the very same problem.

The presented work is by no means finalized. Whenever there is a need for standardization, there is a need for a broad discussion; we hope to have, with this article, motivated such a discussion.

Endnotes

[1] Open Biomedical Ontologies, http://obo.sourceforge.net

[2] http://obofoundry.org presents a collaborative attempt to resolve these problems.

[3] We take the term *reality* to collectively refer to everything that exists, including any imagination and representation of some part of reality. The interpretation of what *everything* and *exists* mean is left to the reader's intuition; we take a realist stand here, as opposed to, e.g., idealism or anti-realism.

[4] Compare to, for example, the definition of abstraction given by Michalski in [38]: "Abstraction reduces the amount of detail in a description of a given reference set."

[5] If abstract entities are understood as *universals* (that exist outside space and time, independent of and prior to their instances, as in some sort of Platonic realism, or are multiply located in space and time, existing only within particulars, as Aristotle claimed), then what we represent are universals. If abstract entities are understood as *concepts* (that exist only in our minds as mental images or ideas, or as discriminative abilities of cognitive agents), then it is these concepts we represent — but these concepts are then no reflection of universals.

[6] Compare to, for example, the definition of generalization given by Michalski in [38] (with minor modifications): "Generalization generates a description that characterizes a larger reference set than the reference set of the original description."

[7] The term 'individual' is closely related, and often treated as synonymous, to 'particular'; however, it is sometimes used with the slightly different meaning of 'that which is numerically single', referring also to abstract entities.

[8] In [28], collections can have only particulars as members; further extensions are possible, though, but may easily lead to problems, and thus deserve a thorough discussion, one that we cannot include here.

[9] Private conversation. See also [32].

[10] Despite the risk of confusion, we find it convenient to use the term *class*: while 'subcollection of a collection' sounds odd, 'subclass of a collection' is hardly any better. To speak of 'subclasses of classes', we need 'classes'.

[11] We will not pursue this issue here. In some representation formalisms (e.g., description logics [39], OWL-DL [14]) relations are regarded as neither abstractions nor particulars, while in others (e.g., RDF [36] or CreekL [35]) they are treated as what is understood as classes there.

[12] Atomic artifacts may be compound in the sense of the corresponding elements of the underlying representation language (e.g., frames with slots with facets).

[13] The neologism *classology* might be more appropriate here. The term *taxonomy* is often used with the meaning of a structure with hierarchically organized elements — which

neither necessary nor sufficient to recognize an artifact as an ontology or a terminology. Note that all representational structures discussed here are in fact built of terms.

Acknowledgements

The author thanks Barry Smith for motivation and support, Jörg Cassens for friendly remarks, and the anonymous reviewers for criticism and helpful comments.

References

[1]   B. Smith. *Blackwell Guide to the Philosophy of Computing and Information*, chapter Ontology, pages 155–166. Blackwell, 2003.

[2]   N. Guarino and M.A. Musen. Applied Ontology: Focusing on content. *Applied Ontology*, 1:1–5, 2005.

[3]   B. Smith, W. Kuśnierczyk, D. Schober, and W. Ceusters. Towards a coherent terminology for principles-based ontology. Submitted for publication to KRMED2006, 2006.

[4]   S. Staab and R. Studer, editors. *Handbook on Ontologies*. Springer-Verlag Berlin Heidelberg, first edition, 2004.

[5]   A. Gómez-Pérez, M. Fernández-López, and O. Corcho. *Ontological Engineering*. Advanced Information and Knowledge Processing. Springer-Verlag London Limited, first edition, 2004.

[6]   T.R. Gruber. Towards Principles for the Design of Ontologies Used for Knowledge Sharing. In N. Guarino and R. Poli, editors, *Formal Ontology in Conceptual Analysis and Knowledge Representation*, Deventer, The Netherlands, 1993. Kluwer Academic Publishers.

[7]   T. Hofweber. Logic and ontology. In Edward N. Zalta, editor, *The Stanford Encyclopedia of Philosophy*. Stanford University, Stanford, CA, winter 2003 edition, 2003.

[8]   T.R. Gruber. A translation approach to portable ontology specification. *Knowledge Acquisition*, 5(2):199–220, 1993.

[9]   N. Guarino. Formal ontology and information systems. In Nicola Guarino, editor, *Proceedings of the 1st International Conference on Formal Ontologies in Information Systems, FOIS'98, Trento, Italy*, pages 3– 15. IOS Press, 1998.

[10] O. Lassila and D. McGuinness. The role of frame-based representation on the Semantic Web. KSL-01-02. Technical report, Knowledge Systems Laboratory, Stanford University, Stanford, California, 2001.

[11] B. Swartout, P. Ramesh, K. Knight, and T. Russ. Toward distributed use of large-scale ontologies. In A. Farquhar, M. Gruninger, A. Gómez-Pérez, M. Uschold, and P. van der Vet, editors, *AAAI'97 Symposium on Ontological Engineering, Stanford University, California, USA*, pages 138–148, 1997.

[12] B. Chandrasekaran, J.R. Josephson, and V.R. Benjamins. What are ontologies, and why do we need them? *IEEE Intelligent Systems*, 14:20–26, 1999.

[13] F. Baader, I. Horrocks, and U. Sattler. *Handbook on Ontologies*, chapter Description Logics, pages 3–28. Springer-Verlag Berlin Heidelberg, 2004.

[14] G. Antoniou and F. van Harmelen. *Handbook on Ontolgies*, chapter Web Ontology Language: OWL, pages 67–92. Springer-Verlag Berlin Heidelberg, 2004.

[15] V. Devedžić. Understanding ontological engineering. *Communications of the ACM*, 45(4ve):136–144, 2002.

[16] R. Studer, V.R. Benjamins, and D. Fensel. Knowledge engineering: Principles and methods. *Data Knowledge Engineering*, 25(1-2):161–197, 1998.

[17] O. Bodenreider, B. Smith, and A. Burgun. The ontology-epistemology divide: A case study in medical terminology. In Achille Varzi and Laure Vieu, editors, *Proceedings of the International Conference on Formal Ontology and Information Systems, FOIS2004*, 2004.

[18] B. Smith. Beyond concepts: Ontology as reality representation. In Achille Varzi and Laure Vieu, editors, *Proceedings of the International Conference on Formal Ontology and Information Systems, FOIS2004*, 2004.

[19] B. Smith, W. Ceusters, and R. Temmerman. Wüsteria. In *Proceedings of Medical Informatics Europe*, 2005.

[20] *UMLS Knowledge Sources Documentation*, February Release 2006AA edition, 2006.

[21] M.K. Smith, C. Welty, and D. McGuinness. *OWL Web Ontology Language guide. W3C Recommendation 10 February 2004*, 2004.

[22] C. Welty. The ontological nature of subject taxonomies. In Nicola Guarino, editor, *Proceedings of the 1998 International Conference on Formal Ontology in Information Systems (FOIS'98)*. IOS Press, 1998.

[23] P. Clark and B. Porter. *KM - The Knowledge Machine 2.0 Users Manual*.

[24] E. Plaza and J.L. Arcos. *Overview of Noῦς v. 1.0. Draft*. Institut d'Investigació en Intelligencia Artificial.

[25] V.K. Chaudhri, A. Farquhar, R. Fikes, P.D. Karp, and J.P. Rice. *Open Knowledge Base Connectivity 2.0.3*, 1998.

[26] S. Bechhofer, F. van Harmelen, J. Hendler, I. Horrocks, D. McGuinness, P.F. Patel-Schneider, and L.A. Stein. *OWL Web Ontology Language reference. W3C Recommendation 10 February 2004*, 2004.

[27] P. Grenon. Knowledge management from the ontological standpoint. In *Proceedings of the WM2003 Workshop on Knowledge Management and Philosophy*, 2003.

[28] T. Bittner, M. Donnelly, and B. Smith. Individuals, universals, collections: On the foundational relations of ontology. In Achille Varzi and Laure Vieu, editors, *Formal Ontology and Information Systems. Proceedings of the Third International Conference (FOIS 2004)*, pages 37–48. IOS Press, 2004.

[29] B. Smith, W. Ceusters, B. Klagges, J. Köhler, A. Kumar, J. Lomax, C. Mungall, F. Neuhaus, A.L. Rector, and C. Rosse. Relations in biomedical ontologies. *Genome Biology*, 6:R46, 2005.

[30] B. Smith. *Experience and Analysis*, chapter Against Fantology, pages 153–170. HPT & ÖBV, Vienna, 2005.

[31] B. Smith and C. Rosse. The role of foundational relations in the alignment of biomedical ontologies. In M. Fieschi et al., editors, *Proceedings of MedInfo 2004*, pages 444–448. IOS Press, Amsterdam, 2004.

[32] B. Smith and T. Bittner. A theory of granular partitions, 2001.

[33] J.F. Sowa. *Knowledge Representation: Logical, Philosophical, and Computational Foundations*. Brooks Cole publishing Co., Pacific Grove, California, 1999.

[34] R.A. Pease and I. Niles. IEEE Standard Upper Ontology: A progress report. *Knowledge Engineering Review*, 17(1):65–70, 2002.

[35] A. Aamodt. *A Knowledge Intensive, Integrated Approach to Problem Solving and Sustained Learning*. PhD thesis, Norwegian University of Science and Technology, 1991.

[36] B. McBride. *Handbook on Ontologies*, chapter The Resource Description Framework (RDF) and its Vocabulary Description Language RDFS, pages 67–93. Springer-Verlag Berlin Heidelberg, 2004.

[37] P. Vossen, W. Peters, and J. Gonzalo. Towards a universal index of meaning. In *Proceedings of the ACL-99 Siglex workshop, University of Maryland*, 1999.

[38] R.S. Michalski. *Machine Learning: A Multistrategy Approach*, volume IV, chapter Inferential Theory of Learning: Developing Foundations for Multistrategy Learning, pages 3–61. Morgan Kaufmann Publishers, 1994.

[39] F. Baader, D. Calvanese, D. McGuiness, D. Nardi, and P. Patel-Schneider, editors. *The Description Logic Handbook*. Cambridge University Press, 2003.

Formal Ontology in Information Systems
B. Bennett and C. Fellbaum (Eds.)
IOS Press, 2006

51

Towards Foundational Semantics

Ontological Semantics Revisited

Philipp CIMIANO [a,1] and Uwe REYLE [b]

[a] *Institute AIFB, University of Karlsruhe*
[b] *IMS, University of Stuttgart*

Abstract. In line with Nirenburg and Raskin's paradigm of ontological semantics, we adhere to the basic tenet that natural language semantics needs to be captured with respect to an explicitly formalized ontology. Many researchers in computational semantics, however, have neglected the ontological aspects of meaning representation, and even more have neglected aspects of meaning representation related to domain-independent ontologies, i.e. foundational or upper-level ontologies. In this paper we argue for a stronger integration of foundational ontologies in computational semantics. We show that relying on foundational ontologies can, on the one hand, lead to a clean separation between domain-specific and domain-independent components of natural language processing systems. On the other hand, we show how the interplay between foundational, domain ontologies and lexical semantics resources can elegantly account for disambiguation as well as allow to draw non-trivial inferences. Further, a temporal theory compliant with the foundational ontology is absolutely necessary for supporting temporal reasoning in natural language understanding.

Keywords. NL semantics, ontologies, foundational ontologies, lexical resources

1. Introduction

In the computational linguistics community, on the one hand, huge manual efforts have been and are still being devoted to developing large lexical semantic resources such as WordNet[2], FrameNet[3] or PropBank[4]. WordNet is in essence a lexical database linking words to their meanings, FrameNet basically provides case frames and their roles for situations and events occurring in the world, and the aim of PropBank is to provide argument structures for verbs, nouns etc. In the Semantic Web and Knowledge Engineering communities, on the other hand, a lot of effort has been spent on developing foundational [16] or general ontologies [12,19], domain ontologies[5] and ontology languages [21]. While the above mentioned lexical resources are widely used within natural language processing, neither ontologies nor their interplay with the above mentioned lexical resources have received much attention. Within computational semantics, for example,

---

[1] The first author acknowledges financial support from the BMBF project SmartWeb, funded by the German Ministry of Research, as well as the projects SEKT and X-Media funded by the European Union.
[2] http://wordnet.princeton.edu/
[3] http://framenet.icsi.berkeley.edu/
[4] http://www.cis.upenn.edu/~mpalmer/project_pages/ACE.htm
[5] See for example the DAML ontology library at http://www.daml.org/ontologies/

a large body of work has addressed the construction of logical form (LF) from natural language input. However, aspects of meaning related to domain theories or ontologies have been neglected to a large extent. For the interpretation of the logical form, a logical theory or ontology axiomatizing the meaning of the symbols used is nevertheless crucial.

In line with Nirenburg and Raskin's *Ontological Semantics* framework, we thus adhere to the basic tenet that natural language semantics needs to be captured with respect to an explicitly formalized ontology. Further, we argue for a novel direction in computational semantics, i.e. what we will call *foundational semantics*. Foundational semantics differs from ontological semantics in that it is concerned with identifying that abstract meaning layer which remains constant across domains and applications. In this respect our approach differs crucially from the ontological semantics framework of Nirenburg and Raskin, who are not concerned with domain-independent aspects of meaning.

From a theoretical point of view, foundational semantics aims at identifying the core components of the domain-independent meaning layer as well as to clarify their interplay, thus contributing to the understanding of the principles of semantic construction. From a practical point of view, the commitment to the principles of foundational semantics is expected to have a clear impact on the engineering of natural language processing systems, allowing to modularize their design and foster their adaption to new domains by clearly separating domain-specific from domain-independent components. When using a foundational ontology, the meaning of (question) pronouns, prepositions, adverbs and other closed-class words can in fact be captured in a domain-independent manner, thus fostering the reuse of such a domain-independent lexicon across domains and applications. Talking about foundational semantics is thus in our view tantamount to talking about domain-independent meaning representation. The core ingredients of foundational semantics are thus, on the one hand, a foundational ontology allowing to express elementary things about the world, but also linguistic components such as a lexical ontology, linking language to the world (e.g. WordNet) as well as lexical semantic resources such as FrameNet or PropBank, providing case frames with their corresponding roles as well as subcategorization structures for verbs, adjectives, nouns etc.

In this paper we provide a first step towards clarifying how the different components of foundational semantics interact with each other, but also with domain-specific ontologies to construct a logical form which is interpretable with respect to the logical theories or ontologies in question. We focus in this paper in particular on the role that foundational ontologies can play in meaning construction and we show how the different resources interplay together for the purposes of lexical disambiguation and reasoning. The novelty of our paper lies exactly in its exploratory nature as it is, to our knowledge, the first paper devoted to exploring the relation between foundational ontologies and natural language semantics.

As we will need to get concrete, we need to use one specific foundational ontology. For pragmatic reasons, we will commit to the DOLCE foundational ontology. However, this choice does not reflect any ontological commitment from our side. With respect to what will be said in this paper, any foundational ontology can be reused as long as it is reasonably axiomatized. In what follows we give a brief overview of DOLCE, which will be necessary for the understanding of the remainder of this paper. Further, in Section 3 we discuss how the meaning of closed-class words can be specified with respect to the foundational ontology, and in Section 4 we show how the different resources interplay for the purposes of disambiguation and reasoning. Finally, in Section 5 we discuss the importance of temporal reasoning for natural language understanding before discussing some related work and concluding.

2. Foundational Ontologies - DOLCE

Recently, there has been considerable research on foundational ontologies, especially in the context of the Semantic Web (compare [16]). One of the envisioned scenarios in the Semantic Web is that computer agents are able to understand content as well as to negotiate with other agents autonomously. A successful negotiation, however, presupposes that both parties agree on the meaning of the issues under consideration and to which they legally commit. Therefore, it is an absolute must that meaning is formalized in a reasonably unambiguous way. To address these needs, foundational ontologies have become interesting in the context of the Semantic Web initiative as their aim is to provide such a (reasonably) unambiguous axiomatization of meaning independently of a certain domain. Foundational ontologies are typically also called *general* or *upper level* ontologies. The crucial characteristics of a foundational ontology are (compare [16]): (i) strong axiomatization, (ii) explicit ontological commitment, and (iii) minimality. The first point, strong axiomatization, directly relates to the need for the unambiguous specification of meaning necessary for allowing a sound negotiation between agents. Strong axiomatization contrasts with many so called *light-weight* ontologies developed nowadays, mainly consisting of a taxonomy, thus leaving a lot of margin for interpretation of the concepts. Explicit ontological commitment means that the foundational ontology should make its basic design choices explicit. Such design choices typically reflect basic logico-philosophical choices related to the representation of time, space, modality etc. Finally, minimality means that a foundational ontology should commit to as few ontological choices as possible to allow for a wide use and applicability.

A more or less recent example for a foundational ontology is the Descriptive Ontology for Linguistic and Cognitive Engineering (DOLCE), which has been developed by the Laboratory of Applied Ontology in the context of the WonderWeb project (compare [16]). As the name suggests, DOLCE has a strong cognitive bias in the sense that it does not aim at representing the world as it is with respect to logico-philosophical considerations, but as it is perceived by humans. It is certainly out of the scope of this paper to discuss the basic ontological commitments of DOLCE with respect to time and space. The interested reader should consult [16]. The basic class hierarchy adopted in DOLCE is depicted in Figure 1. A crucial distinction in DOLCE is the one between *perdurants* and *endurants*. Endurants are entities which exist in time (bound to a certain interval) and undergo change in shape, parts etc. Examples are persons, cars, theories, etc. Perdurants are entities which happen in time, e.g. events such as a party, a concert. All entities have *qualities* such as color, shape, size, etc. as well as concrete *quale*, i.e. values of these qualities at a certain time point. Qualities are related to their quales through the predicate $ql(q, t)$. In particular, DOLCE also distinguishes between spatial and temporal quale, i.e ql_{SL} and ql_{TL}.

Further, DOLCE also provides fundamental relations between perdurants, such as temporal overlap, which is defined as follows:

$$x \bigcirc_T y \leftrightarrow \exists t, t' (ql_T(t, x) \wedge ql_T(t', y) \wedge O(t, t'))$$

Overlap is defined in terms of the atomic predicate parthood, i.e.

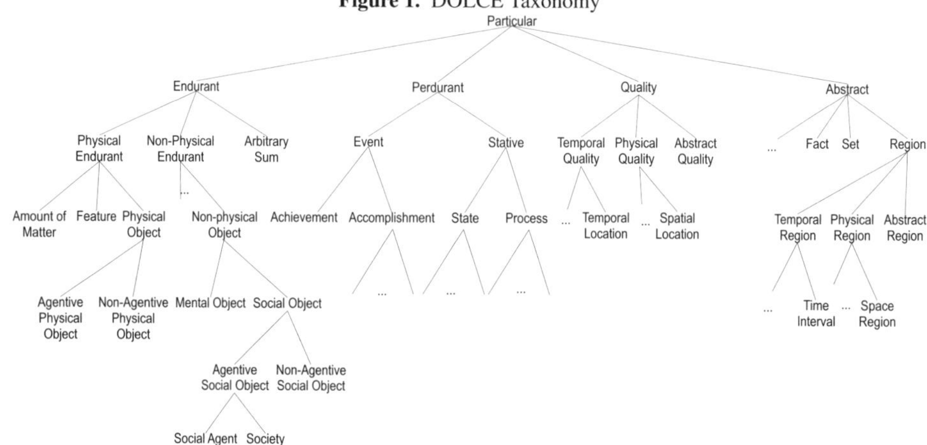

Figure 1. DOLCE Taxonomy

$$O(x, y) \leftrightarrow \exists z (P(z, x) \wedge P(z, y))$$

Further, a very useful property is homogeneity, it is defined as follows in DOLCE:

$$HOM(\Phi) \leftrightarrow \Phi \sqsubseteq PD \wedge \Box \forall x, y(\Phi(x) \wedge P_T(y, x) \rightarrow \Phi(y))$$

i.e. a homogeneous property holds for all its temporal parts. Hereby, $\Phi \sqsubseteq PD$ essentially states that Φ is subsumed by PD^6, i.e. Φ is a kind of perdurant (see [16] for details). DOLCE also provides predicates for expressing temporal inclusion between entities which have temporal quales (denoted by $\subseteq_T$) and spatio-temporal inclusion between entities which have spatial quales, i.e., $\subseteq_{ST}$.

Finally, for the purposes of this paper we will assume a temporal order between temporal regions. However, we will not make assumptions about whether this order should be a partial or a total one. There exist different possibilities to axiomatize a temporal order $\leq_T$ between temporal regions. However, we will not discuss any further the different possibilities for defining such a temporal order. A standard choice would for example be an interval-based temporal logic such as presented in [1] or [13].

3. Domain Independence

As argued in the introduction, a clean separation between domain-specific and domain independent meaning is very desirable to foster the reuse of a system across domains. In this section we discuss how the meanings of certain closed-class words with constant meaning across domains can be specified with respect to a foundational ontology. We discuss this using a question answering system as an example.

In question answering systems, wh-pronouns such as *which*, *what*, *where*, *who* or *when* have a constant meaning across domains. The same holds for temporal and locative

---

[6]In this paper we use the description logic notation $\sqsubseteq$ to denote subsumption. Further we use the signs $\sqcup$ and $\sqcap$ to denote concept union and intersection, respectively. We assume this notation as an abbreviation of the corresponding first-order formulas given in [3].

prepositions such as *in, at, after,* etc. It would be thus desirable to capture the meaning of these words with respect to a foundational ontology such as DOLCE. To illustrate our proposal, let us consider the following example questions to a natural language interface:

- Who killed John F. Kennedy?
- Where was John F. Kennedy murdered?
- When was John F. Kennedy murdered?
- Who was murdered on November 22, 1963?
- Who was murdered in Dallas?
- Which american president was murdered after Kennedy was killed?

Here, the wh-pronouns and prepositions would have the meaning specified in Figure 2. There, APO stands for *Agentive Physical Object*, S for *Space Region* and TR for *Temporal Region*.

As syntactical backbone we build on Logical Description Grammars (LDG) [18], a lexicalized formalism inspired by Lexicalized Tree Adjoining Grammars (LTAG) [14], in which the basic syntactic units are so called elementary trees representing extended lexical projections of words which encapsulate logical arguments. Nodes in these elementary trees are marked positively or negatively and parsing boils down to identifying positively and negatively nodes of compatible syntactic categories, respecting precedence and dominance in the tree. Negatively marked nodes hereby typically correspond to argument positions which need to be filled with lexical content provided by positively marked nodes. The root node of the elementary trees for the wh-pronouns in Figure 2 are thus marked positively. The semantics is specified using the lambda calculus and constructed en par with the identification of nodes. The lambda expressions are thus composed with each other by means of functional application as specified by the elementary trees yielding an overall interpretation of a sentence (or question) as a result (see [5] for a detailed description of the use of the lambda calculus for semantic construction). In our notation, the lambda expression constituting the semantics of a node is given under it and refer to the semantics of other nodes below in the tree.

Semantically, wh-pronouns behave like a determiner in the sense that they typically combine with a property to yield a complete formula. Prepositions behave differently in the sense that they combine with a determiner phrase (dp) and a verb phrase (vp_2) to yield a further verb phrase (vp_1) the semantics of which is – in essence – the result of attaching the temporal or spatial condition imposed by the preposition to the event variable of vp_2. Note here that the temporal and spatial conditions imposed by the preposition are specified with respect to DOLCE predicates. It is also important to mention that the different meanings of *in* (spatial vs. temporal) pose different constraints on the dp, i.e. they require a temporal region (TR) or spatial region (S), respectively. The extension of LDG allowing to pose type constraints on the nodes as well as the corresponding notation (specifying the exact types after the node with a colon ':' or the subsuming type with '$\leq$') were already introduced in [7].

Here '?x' is a question operator which specifies which variables are bound within the logical query. Our example questions would thus be interpreted as the following formal queries to a knowledge base:

1. $?x\ (APO(x) \wedge \exists e\ kill(e, x, JFK))$
2. $?x\ (S(x) \wedge \exists e\ (ql_{SL}(e, x) \wedge murdered(e, JFK) \wedge EV(e)))$
3. $?x\ (TR(x) \wedge \exists e\ (ql_{TL}(e, x) \wedge murdered(e, JFK) \wedge EV(e)))$

Figure 2. Semantics of wh-pronouns and prepositions specified w.r.t. DOLCE

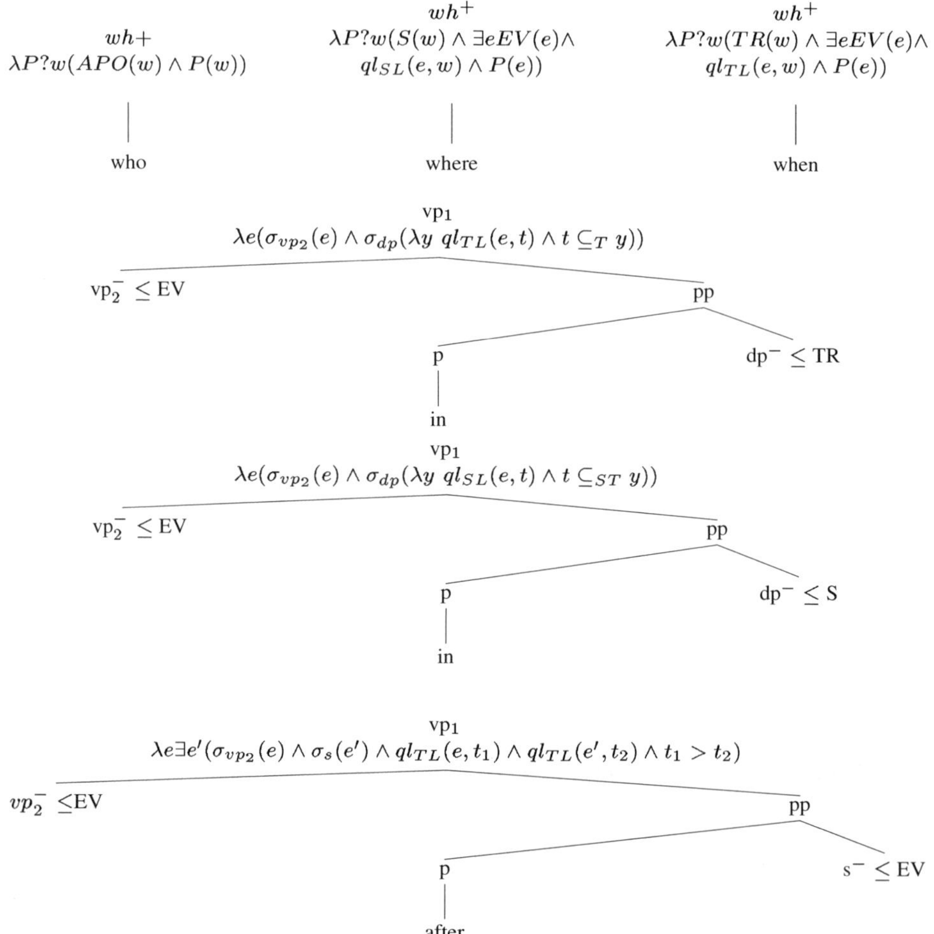

4. $?x \; (APO(x) \wedge \exists e \; (murdered(e,x) \wedge ql_{TL}(e,t) \wedge t \subseteq_T t' \wedge$
$month(t',11) \wedge day(t',22) \wedge year(t',1963)))$

5. $?x \; (APO(x) \wedge \exists e \; (murdered(e,x) \wedge ql_{SL}(e,t) \wedge t \subseteq_{ST} Dallas))$

6. $?x \; (president(x,USA) \wedge \exists e,e' \; (murdered(e,x) \wedge ql_{TL}(e,t_1) \wedge$
$killed(e',JFK) \wedge ql_{TL}(e',t_2) \wedge t_1 >_T t_2))$

We have thus shown how the meaning of wh-pronouns as well as spatial and temporal prepositions can be captured with respect to a foundational ontology and thus reused across domains.

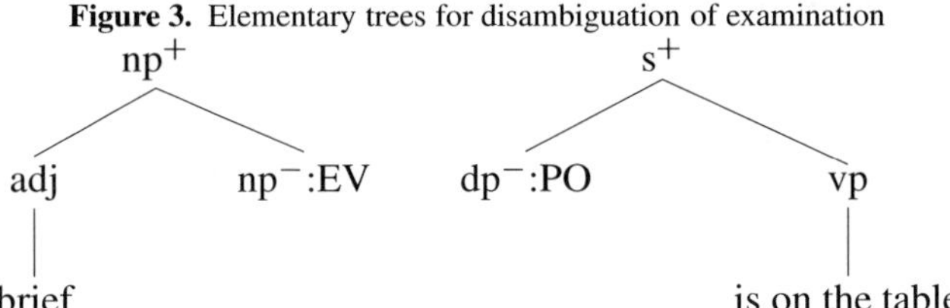

Figure 3. Elementary trees for disambiguation of examination

4. Interplay of Resources

Having shown how the meaning of closed-class words can be captured with respect to a foundational ontology, we turn to the issue of describing the interplay of different resources, i.e. foundational ontologies, domain ontologies, case frames and selectional restrictions specified with respect to the ontologies for the purpose of disambiguation. Further, we also show how this interplay can also yield non-trivial inferences as a result, provided that domain-specific knowledge is considered.

4.1. Lexical Disambiguation

Selectional restrictions of verbs pose type constraints on their potential arguments and have thus a natural application in the disambiguation of the meaning of verbs as well as of their arguments. They are naturally expressed in terms of concept hierarchies, where the realm of relevant concepts ranges from domain-specific ones to those found in upper-level ontologies. In case the different meanings of a word correspond to different foundational categories, it even suffices to directly represent selectional restrictions with respect to categories such as provided by DOLCE.

Take, for example, a nominalization like *examination*, which is ambiguous between an event reading and a physical object reading. Combinations with verbal phrases or adjectives may disambiguate the noun depending on the concept the verbal phrase or adjective selects. An adjective like *brief* will identify the event reading and a verbal phrase like *being on the table* the physical object reading. The lexicon entry for the adjective *brief* and the representation of the verbal phrase *is on the table* would look as in Figure 3, where the ontological selectional restriction w.r.t. DOLCE on a node is given after the colon.

Using these entries, we could thus clearly distinguish between the event and object reading of examination in these contexts. In other cases, these distinctions are more subtle as is the case of the verb *to force* which has, for example, a *compel-* and a *break_open-* reading. The latter one requires the object to be of type physical object (PO), and not ANIMATE.

Following Dowty ([8]) we assume that the participants of an event are given by thematic roles. Thematic roles are functions from perdurants to entities that are implicated in these perdurants. The thematic roles that we will consider in this paper are AGENT,[7] CAUSER, THEME, and INSTR. Their values are constrained by the following set of axioms, in which θ ranges over thematic roles and the DOLCE participation relation PC states that x is involved in the occurrence of y.

---

[7]We use AGENT to include agents that are not necessarily capable of intentions.

$$\theta(e, x) \rightarrow PO(x) \wedge PD(e) \wedge PC(x, e)$$

Thus, thematic roles are specializations of the participation relation PC of DOLCE. We assume that the thematic roles are mutually exclusive (without stating the corresponding axioms explicitly here).

A further and more interesting set of axioms that involves thematic roles deals with ontological constraints that are determined for each thematic role by the type of perdurant the verb denotes, i.e. with the verb's selectional restrictions. Suppose that e is a perdurant denoted by a verb like *force* with its two meanings, *compel* and *break_open*, then that meaning is selected in context for which the corresponding implication is fulfilled:

$$compel(e) \wedge AGENT(e, x) \wedge THEME(e, y) \rightarrow$$

$$Human(x) \wedge Human(y)$$

$$break\_open(e) \wedge AGENT(e, x) \wedge THEME(e, y) \rightarrow$$

$$Human(x) \wedge (PO \sqcap \neg ANIMATE)(y)$$

The formulation of selectional restrictions on thematic roles thus leads to disambiguation of verbal meanings.

Prepositions are typically also ambiguous. *With*-pps are for example ambiguous between an instrumental reading as in (1.a), a co-agentive reading as in (1.b) and a noun-modifying reading. The corresponding elementary trees for the different readings of *with* we consider are shown in Figure 4. Now let us consider the following examples:

(1)   a.   The doctor cured Peter with penicillin.
           b.   The doctor cured Peter with the internist.

Let us assume that an instrumental reading in a cure event poses the constraint that the instrument in question is either an Amount of Matter (M), Light, Heat or some Process (PRO), i.e.

$$cure(e) \wedge INSTR(e, x) \wedge \neg Human(x) \rightarrow (M \sqcup Light \sqcup Heat \sqcup PRO)(x)$$

This allows us to interpret the penicillin as the instrument of curing, but not the internist, which requires a co-agentive interpretation. This shows how the correct meaning of prepositions can be selected as a byproduct of fulfilling the logical conditions imposed by thematic roles.

4.2. Inferencing

To see how verb meanings, logical conditions on their thematic roles and ontological knowledge interact with each other to yield non-trivial inferences, let us consider the sentence:

(2)   The doctor cured Peter with Belladonna.

World knowledge about Belladonna says that it contains the toxic substance Atropine. Further, Atropine leads to poisoning if ingested in a quantity of more than 3 mg for adults and 1 mg for children, i.e.

$$(3) \quad \forall x \ (Belladonna(x) \rightarrow M(x) \land \exists s \ contains(x,s) \land Atropine(s))$$

$$\forall e,a,b \ (ingest(e,a,b) \land \exists y \ (age(a,y) \land y \geq 18) \land$$

$$\exists s,m \ (contains(b,s) \land Atropine(s) \land mass(s,m) \land m \geq 3mg)$$

$$(4) \quad \rightarrow poisoned(Res(e),a))$$

$$\forall e,a,b \ (ingested(e,a,b) \land \exists y \ age(a,y) \land y < 18 \land$$

$$\exists m,s \ (contains(b,s) \land Atropine(s) \land mass(s,m) \land m \geq 1mg)$$

$$(5) \quad \rightarrow poisoned(Res(e),a))$$

where $Res(e)$ denotes the resultative state of an event e. The core of the meaning of *cure* is a change of state, e, of the organism or organ, y, from being affected by some disease, z, to the state s of not being affected. This event may be represented by means of the BEC(come) operator as $BEC(e, \lambda s \neg SUFFER\_FROM(s,y,z))$, i.e.

$$cure(e) \land AGENT(e,x) \land THEME(e,y) \land$$

$$Human(x) \land (BodyPart \sqcup Organism)(x) \rightarrow$$

$$\exists ec,e,e',z \ (CAUSE(ec,e',e) \land AGENT(e',x) \land$$

$$(6) \quad BEC(e, \lambda s \neg SUFFER\_FROM(s,y,z)))$$

The meaning of the $BEC(e, \lambda s \ P(s))$ operator essentially is that the event e brings about a state s in which the condition P holds. For a more detailed description of the BEC(ome) operator, the interested reader is referred to Dowty [9].

If a substance is the instrument or agent of a curing event, then it is either ingested, inhaled, injected or applied to the skin, i.e.

$$\forall e,a,p,m \ (cure(e,a,p) \land INSTR(e,m) \land M(m) \rightarrow$$

$$\exists e' \ e' \subseteq_T e \land (ingest(e',p,m) \lor inhale(e',p,m) \lor$$

$$injectedInto(e',m,p) \lor appliedToSkinOf(e',m,p)))$$

Further, assuming that being poisoned yields a contradiction with the resultative state of cure as well as assuming that Peter is an adult and ingested the Belladonna, we could derive that he was treated with a dose of Belladonna below 3mg, as otherwise he would have been poisoned. This shows how additional conditions on thematic roles and world knowledge can lead to non-trivial inferences.

5. Temporal Reasoning

To demonstrate how important temporal reasoning is for natural language understanding, let us discuss the following contrastive examples already discussed in [2], [11] and recently in [6]:

a. John arrived at the oasis. The camels <u>are</u> standing under the palms.
b. John arrived at the oasis. The camels <u>were</u> standing under the palms.

     P. Cimiano and U. Reyle / Towards Foundational Semantics

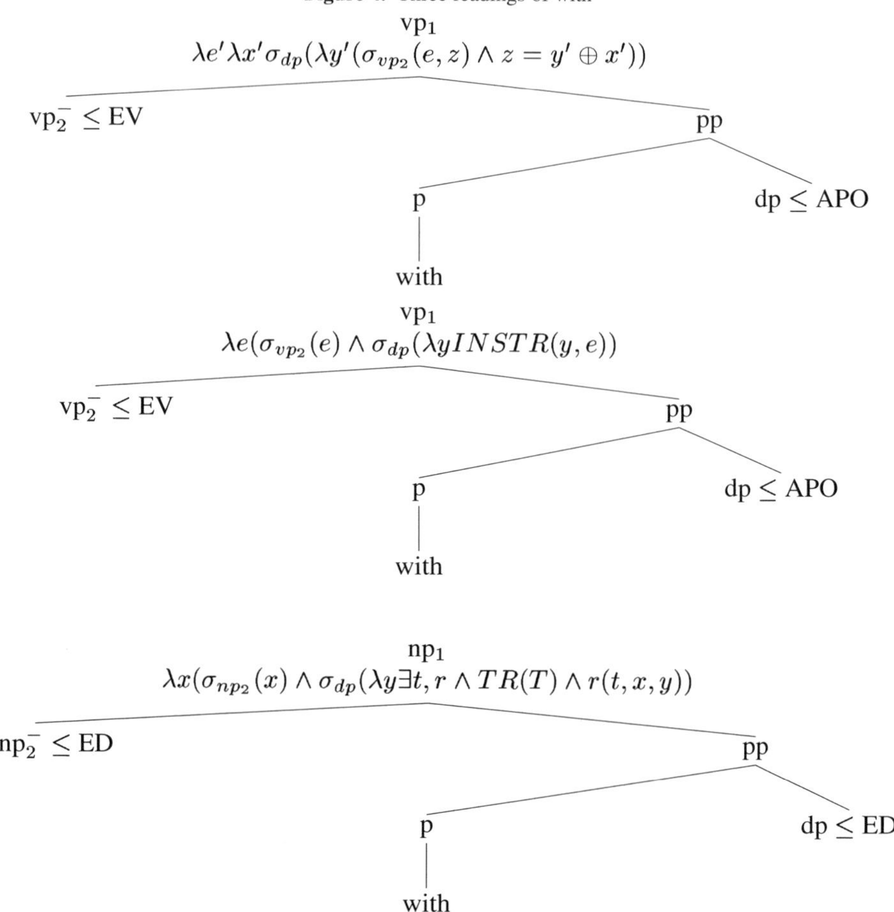

Figure 4. Three readings of with

While in the first case it is possible to interpret the camels as the means of transport by which John arrived, in the second discourse this interpretation is not possible due to the use of the imperfect *were standing* (compare [11,6]). The reason which is typically assumed is that the standing e' temporally overlaps with the arrival e, i.e. $e \bigcirc_T e'$ in terms of DOLCE, thus leading to a contradiction. It is definitely not the issue of this paper to explain what linguistic conditions lead exactly to pose that e and e' overlap (see [15] for a discussion of the temporal implications of imperfect vs. the simple past). Interesting for our purposes is the event structure as well as spatio-temporal consequences of *arrive* and *stand*. First of all, we will assume the following logical representation of sentence b):

$$\exists e, e', j, o, c, p \ arrive\_at(e) \wedge AGENT(e, j) \wedge john(j)$$

$$THEME(e, o) \wedge event(e) \wedge oasis(o) \wedge camels(c) \wedge$$

$$under(e', c, p) \wedge state(e') \wedge palms(p) \wedge e \bigcirc_T e'$$

Further, arriving implies a preparatory traveling phase which is part of the nucleus of arrive, and traveling implies a means of transport spatio-temporally correlated with the traveler:

$$\forall e, a, o \; (arrive\_at(e) \wedge AGENT(e, a) \wedge THEME(e, o) \rightarrow \exists e'$$

$$(travel\_to(e') \wedge AGENT(e', a) \wedge THEME(e', o) \wedge e' \in prep(e)))$$

$$\forall e, a \; (travel\_to(e) \wedge AGENT(e, a) \rightarrow \exists m$$

$$(MeansOfTransport(m) \wedge loc(e, m) = loc(e, a)))$$

And loc is functional, i.e. $\forall e, a, b, c \; (loc(e, a) = b \wedge loc(e, a) = c \rightarrow b = c)$.

With respect to our example, it is thus the case that the following holds for the preparatory traveling phase e': $loc(e', j) \neq o$ and thus $loc(e', c) \neq o$ (assuming that the camels are the mode of transport). Assuming that HOM(loc) this should be the case for any temporal part of the preparatory phase.

Overlapping an event also implies overlapping its preparatory phase:

$$\forall e, e', e'' \; (e \bigcirc_T e' \wedge e'' \in prep(e') \rightarrow e \bigcirc_T e'')$$

This means that the standing in which $loc(e, c) = o$ holds overlaps with the preparatory phase in which $loc(e', c) \neq o$ holds, yielding a logical inconsistency due to homogeneity and the functional definition of loc.

6. Related Work and Conclusion

We discuss in this section the work of Nirenburg and Raskin [17], Bateman [4], as well as Fillmore et al. [10].

The ontological semantics framework of Nirenburg and Raskin shares many aspects with our proposal of foundational semantics. First, both approaches share the commitment to an explicitly represented ontology. Second, Nirenburg and Raskin are also concerned with the specification of selectional restrictions for disambiguation purposes. However, they are not concerned with separating domain-specific from domain-independent meaning representation.

Bateman has also considered upper-level ontologies for natural language processing, in particular in the context of generation tasks. The Penmann Upper Model is in fact an upper-level ontology built on the basis of linguistic concepts. Defining concepts on a linguistic basis in fact eases the generation of natural language to express theses concepts. It remains unclear, however, if the Penmann Upper Model is also suitable for natural language understanding purposes.

In the context of the FrameNet project, the aim of Fillmore et al. is to provide case frame semantics for verbs, specifying their core and non-core roles for application within text understanding [10]. However, FrameNet does not specify additional logical conditions which a frame element or slot needs to fulfill as in our approach. We have shown that specifying such conditions is necessary to rule out inconsistent readings as well as to support inferencing. Recently, Scheffczyk et al. have also discussed how to link FrameNet to existing general ontologies [20].

Summarizing, we have argued in this paper for the benefits of using a foundational ontology such as DOLCE for the purpose of capturing natural language semantics. We have in particular shown how foundational ontologies can (i) foster reusability of a system across domains, (ii) play an important role in disambiguation, (iii) provide a basis to draw non-trivial inferences as well as (iv) support temporal reasoning for NLP applications. From the perspective of our foundational semantics proposal, we have provided a first step towards clarifying its ingredients and examining their interplay.

References

[1] J. Allen and G. Ferguson. Actions and events in temporal logic. *Journal of Logic Computation*, 4(5):531–579, 1994.

[2] N. Asher and A. Lascarides. Bridging. *Journal of Semantics*, 15, 1999.

[3] F. Baader, D. Calvanese, D. McGuiness, D. Nardi, and P. Patel-Schneider, editors. *The Description Logic Handbook*. Cambridge University Press, 2003.

[4] John A. Bateman. Upper modeling: organizing knowledge for natural language processing. In *5th. International Workshop on Natural Language Generation, 3-6 June 1990*, 1990.

[5] P. Blackburn and J. Bos. *Representation and Inference for Natural Language – A First Course in Computational Semantics*. CSLI Publications, 2005.

[6] P. Cimiano. Ingredients of a first-order account of bridging. In *Proceedings of the 5th International Workshop on Inference in Computational Semantics (ICOS-5)*, 2006.

[7] P. Cimiano and U. Reyle. Ontology-based semantic construction, underspecification and disambiguation. In *Proceedings of the Prospects and Advances in the Syntax-Semantic Interface Workshop*, pages 33–38, 2003.

[8] D. Dowty. On the semantic content of the notion of "thematic role". In G. Chierchia, B. Partee, and R. Turner, editors, *Properties, Types, and Meanings*, volume 2, pages 69–129. Kluwer Academic Publishers, 1989.

[9] D.R. Dowty. *Word Meaning and Montague Grammar*. Dordrecht, 1979.

[10] C.J. Fillmore and C.F. Baker. Frame semantics for text understanding. In *Proceedings of the NAACL Workshop on WordNet and Other Lexical Resources*, 2001.

[11] C. Gardent and K. Konrad. Interpreting definites using model generation. *Journal of Language and Computation*, 1(2):193–209, 2000.

[12] R.V. Guha and D.B. Lenat. CYC: A midterm report. *AI Magazine*, 11(3):32–59, 1990.

[13] J.R. Hobbs and F. Pan. An ontology of time for the semantic web. *ACM Transactions on Asian Language Information Processing (TALIP)*, 3(1):66–85, 2004.

[14] A.K. Joshi and Y. Schabes. Tree-adjoining grammars. In *Handbook of Formal Languages*, volume 3, pages 69–124. Springer, 1997.

[15] H. Kamp and U. Reyle. *From Discourse to Logic*. Kluwer, 1993.

[16] C. Masolo, S. Borgo, A. Gangemi, N. Guarino, and A. Oltramari. Ontology library (final). WonderWeb deliverable D18.

[17] M. McShane, S. Nirenburg, and S. Beale. An implemented, integrative approach to ontology-based NLP and interlingua. Technical report, Institute for Language and Information Technologies, University of Maryland, Baltimore County, March 2005.

[18] Reinhard Muskens. Talking about trees and truth-conditions. *Journal of Logic, Language and Information*, 10(4):417–455, 2001.

[19] I. Niles and A. Pease. Towards a standard upper ontology. In *Proceedings of the 2nd International Conference on Formal Ontology in Information Systems (FOIS)*, pages 17–19, 2001.

[20] J. Scheffczyk, C.F. Baker, and S. Narayanan. Ontology-based reasoning about lexical resources. In *Proceedings of the OntoLex Workshop at the 5th International Conference on Lexical Resources and Evaluation (LREC)*, 2006.

[21] S. Staab and R. Studer, editors. *Handbook on Ontologies*. International Handbooks on Information Systems. Springer, 2004.

2. Space and Mereology

Formal Ontology in Information Systems
B. Bennett and C. Fellbaum (Eds.)
IOS Press, 2006

A theory of granular parthood based on qualitative cardinality and size measures

Thomas BITTNER[1,2,3,4] and Maureen DONNELLY[1,3]
[1]*Department of Philosophy,* [2]*Department of Geography*
[3]*New York State Center of Excellence in Bioinformatics and Life Sciences*
[4]*National Center for Geographic Information and Analysis*
State University of New York at Buffalo

Abstract. We present a theory of granular parthood based on qualitative cardinality and size measures. Using standard mereological relations and qualitative, context-dependent relations such as *roughly the same size*, we define a granular parthood relation and distinguish different ways in which a collection of smaller objects may sum to a larger object. At one extreme, an object x may be a mereological sum of a large collection p where the members of p are all negligible in size with respect to x (e.g., x is a human body and p is the collection of its molecules). At the other extreme, x may be a mereological sum of a collection q none of whose members are negligible in size with respect to x (e.g., x is again a human body and p is the collection consisting of its head, neck, torso, and limbs).

We cannot give precise quantitative definitions for relations such as *roughly the same size* or *negligible in size with respect to* since these are, even within a fixed context, vague relations. The primary focus in the formal theory presented in this paper is on the context-independent logical properties of these qualitative cardinality and size relations and their interaction with mereological relations. In developing our formal theory, we draw upon work on order of magnitude reasoning.

Keywords. Qualitative reasoning, vagueness, context, formal ontology

1. Introduction

There have been some interesting recent proposals for developing theories of parthood which take into account aspects of granularity, scale, and context [1,15,14]. The importance of taking into account granularity and scale in bio-medical ontologies has been emphasized, for example, in [9,13,16,12]. It is the aim of this paper to contribute to this work by presenting an axiomatic theory of granular parthood and scale based on qualitative cardinality and size relations, such as *roughly the same size*. For the development of the axiomatic theory we draw on work on order of magnitude reasoning by Raiman, Mavrovouniotis *et al*, and Dague [11,10,5,4].

That the interpretation of expressions like 'roughly the same size' is context dependent is widely acknowledged [6,8,17,3]. However, there are different strategies for dealing with this context-dependence. Van Deemter [17], for example, explicitly represents context in the object-language of his theory. In this paper, we deal with context-dependence in a more indirect way: context is represented abstractly in numerical parameters which determine the canonical interpretations of the qualitative size and cardinality relations of the formal theory. This allows us to focus in the theory only on context-independent logical properties of the qualitative relations.

Obviously we cannot, even in a given context, specify precisely what is meant by, e.g, *roughly the same size* since this is, even once the context is fixed, a vague relation. Although the canonical models use precise numerical parameters for fixing the interpretation of the qualitative size and relations, it is not expected that precise numerical parameters fixed in an actual practical contexts. At best, we associate contexts demanding high precision with a different range of numerical parameters than contexts requiring only loose precision. Since the logical properties of the relations of our theory are valid over a range of numerical parameters, the formal theory can be used for reasoning even where relations such as *roughly the same size* lack precise numerical definitions.

The remainder of this paper is structured as follows: we start by presenting an axiomatic theory of finite collections and relative cardinality. We then extend the theory by introducing parthood and relative size relations among the objects in the collections.

We present the formal theory in a sorted first-order predicate logic with identity. We use the letters w, x, y, z as variables ranging over objects and p, q, r as variables ranging over collections of objects. All quantification is restricted to a single sort. Leading universal quantifiers are generally omitted and restrictions on quantification are to be understood by the conventions on variable usage.

2. Collections

We use $\in$ for the member-of relation between objects and collections. Collections are finite sets of two or more objects.

We require: every collection has two or more members (AC1); two collections are identical if and only if they have the same members (AC2); if x and y are distinct objects, there is a collection consisting of just x and y (AC3).

$$AC1\ (\exists x)(\exists y)(x \in p \wedge y \in p \wedge x \neq y)$$
$$AC2\ p = q \leftrightarrow (x)(x \in p \leftrightarrow x \in q)$$
$$AC3\ x \neq y \rightarrow (\exists p)(x \in p \wedge y \in p \wedge (z)(z \in p \rightarrow z = x \vee z = y))$$

We define union, intersection, and difference relations between collections. It follows from AC2 that unions, intersections, and differences of collections are unique whenever they exist. r is the union of p and q if and only if x is a member and p or x is a member of q ($D_\cup$). r is the intersection of p and q if and only if x is a member of r if and only if x is a member of p and x is a member of q ($D_\cup$). r is the difference of q in p if and only if x is a member of r if and only if x is a member of p and x is not a member of q ($D_\setminus$).

$$D_\cup \quad \cup pqr \equiv (x)(x \in r \leftrightarrow (x \in p \vee x \in q))$$
$$D_\cap \quad \cap pqr \equiv (x)(x \in r \leftrightarrow (x \in p \wedge x \in q))$$
$$D_\setminus \quad \setminus pqr \equiv (x)(x \in r \leftrightarrow (x \in p \wedge x \notin q))$$

We require: the union of two collections always exists (AC4); if p and q share at least two members, then the intersection of p and q exists (AC5); if p has at least two members that are not members of q, then the difference of q in p exists (AC6).

$AC4\ (\exists r)\cup pqr$

$AC5\ (\exists x)(\exists y)(x \neq y \wedge x \in p \wedge y \in p \wedge x \in q \wedge y \in q) \rightarrow (\exists r)\cap pqr$

$AC6\ (\exists x)(\exists y)(x \neq y \wedge x \in p \wedge y \in p \wedge x \notin q \wedge y \notin q)) \rightarrow (\exists r)\setminus pqr$

Axioms AC1-AC6 ensure that collections behave roughly like sets with at least two members. We introduce the term $p \cup q$ for the union of p and q.

p is a *sub-collection* of q ($p \subseteq q$) if and only if every member of p is also a member of q ($D_\subseteq$). p is a *proper sub-collection* of q ($p \subset q$) if and only if p is a sub-collection of q and p and q are not identical ($D_\subset$).

$$D_\subseteq\ p \subseteq q \equiv (x)(x \in p \rightarrow x \in q) \qquad\qquad D_\subset\ p \subset q \equiv p \subseteq q \wedge p \neq q$$

We can prove that $\subseteq$ is reflexive, antisymmetric, and transitive.

Collection r is *symmetric with respect to* collections p and q if and only if any member of r is member of p if and only if it is a member of q (D_{Sym_C}).

$$D_{Sym_C}\ Sym_C\ rpq \equiv (x)(x \in r \rightarrow (x \in p \leftrightarrow x \in q))$$

On the intended interpretation, collection r is symmetric with respect to p and q whenever the standard set-theoretic intersection of r and p is identical to the standard set-theoretic intersection of r and q. For example, the collection $C_1 = \{1,2,3,4,5\}$ is symmetric with respect to $C_2 = \{4,5,10,20,30\}$ and $C_3 = \{-5,-4,4,5,10\}$. But C_2 is not symmetric with respect to C_1 and C_2.

We use $[p]$ in the meta-language to refer to the number of members of p. Notice that if, as intended, p ranges over finite sets with at least two members, $[p]$ must be a natural number greater than one. In the formal theory, we introduce an equivalence relation $\asymp$ between collections where the intended interpretation of $p \asymp q$ is: p and q have the same cardinality ($[p] = [q]$). We require that: $\asymp$ is reflexive, symmetric, and transitive (AC7-9); if p is a sub-collection of q and p and q have the same cardinality then p and q are identical (AC10); if r is symmetric with respect to p and q then p and q have the same cardinality if and only if the union of p and r has the same cardinality as the union of q and r (AC11) ; for all collections p and q there is a collection r such that either (i) r and p have the same cardinality and r is a sub-collection of q or (ii) r and q have the same cardinality and r is a sub-collection of p (AC12); if there is a sub-collection of q that has the same cardinality as p and there is a sub-collection of p that has the same cardinality as q then p and q have the same cardinality (AC13).

$AC7\ \ p \asymp p$

$AC8\ \ p \asymp q \rightarrow q \asymp p$

$AC9\ \ p \asymp q \wedge q \asymp r \rightarrow p \asymp r$

$AC10\ p \subseteq q \wedge p \asymp q \rightarrow p = q$

$AC11\ Sym_C\ rpq \rightarrow (p \asymp q \leftrightarrow (p \cup r) \asymp (q \cup r))$

$AC12\ (\exists r)[(r \asymp p \wedge r \subseteq q) \vee (r \asymp q \wedge r \subseteq p)]$

$AC13\ (\exists r_1)(r_1 \asymp p \wedge r_1 \subseteq q) \wedge (\exists r_2)(r_2 \asymp q \wedge r_2 \subseteq p) \rightarrow p \asymp q$

We can prove: if p is a proper sub-collection of q and q has the same cardinality as r then p and r have different cardinalities (TC1); if s_1 is the difference of r in p and s_2 is the difference of r in q and r is symmetric with respect to p and q then p and q have the same cardinality if and only if s_1 and s_2 have the same cardinality (TC2).

$$TC1\ (p \subset q \wedge q \asymp r) \to \neg p \asymp r$$
$$TC2\ \backslash prs_1 \wedge\ \backslash qrs_2 \wedge Sym_C\ rpq \to (p \asymp q \leftrightarrow s_1 \asymp s_2)$$

The cardinality of p is *less than or equal* to the cardinality of q if and only if there is a sub-collection r of q that has the same cardinality as p ($D_\leq$). On the intended interpretation, $p \leq q$ holds if and only if $[p]$ is less than or equal to to $[q]$. The cardinality of p is *less than* the cardinality of q if and only if the cardinality of p is less than or equal to the cardinality of q and p and q do not have the same cardinality($D_<$).

$$D_\leq\ p \leq q \equiv (\exists r)(r \asymp p \wedge r \subseteq q) \qquad D_<\ p < q \equiv p \leq q \wedge \neg p \asymp q$$

We can prove: if p is a sub-collection of q, then the cardinality of p is less than or equal to the cardinality of q (TC3); if p is a proper sub-collection of q, then the cardinality of p is less than the cardinality of q (TC4); for any collections p and q, the cardinality of p is less than or equal to the cardinality of q or the cardinality of q is less than or equal to the cardinality of p (TC5); $\leq$ is reflexive (TC6); if the cardinality of p is less than or equal to the cardinality of q and cardinality of q is less than or equal to the cardinality of p, then p and q have the same cardinality (TC7); $\leq$ is transitive (TC8); $<$ is transitive (TC9); $<$ is asymmetric (TC10); if the cardinality of p is less than or equal to the cardinality of q and q and r have the same cardinality, then the cardinality of p is less than or equal to the cardinality of r (TC11); if r and p have the same cardinality and the cardinality of p is less than or equal to the cardinality of q then the cardinality of r is less than or equal to the cardinality of p (TC12).

$$TC3\ p \subseteq q \to p \leq q \qquad\qquad TC8\ \ p \leq q \wedge q \leq r \to p \leq r$$
$$TC4\ p \subset q \to p < q \qquad\qquad TC9\ \ p < q \wedge q < r \to p < r$$
$$TC5\ p \leq q \vee q \leq p \qquad\qquad TC10\ p < q \to \neg q < p$$
$$TC6\ p \leq p \qquad\qquad\qquad\quad TC11\ p \leq q \wedge q \asymp r \to p \leq r$$
$$TC7\ p \leq q \wedge q \leq p \to p \asymp q \qquad TC12\ r \asymp p \wedge p \leq q \to r \leq q$$

3. Close and negligible cardinalites of collections

In this section we formalize the binary relations between collections: *close-to* (in cardinality) and *negligible with respect to*. Let ϵ be a parameter such that $0 < \epsilon < 0.5$. On the intended interpretation, p is close to q if and only if $1/(1 + \epsilon) \leq [p]/[q] \leq 1 + \epsilon$. p is negligible with respect to q if and only if $[p]/[q]$ is smaller than $\epsilon/(1 + \epsilon)$.

Consider Figure 1. Values for the cardinality of p range along the positive horizontal axis and values for the cardinality of q range along the positive vertical axis. If p and q have the same cardinality then $([p], [q])$ represents a point on the dotted line. If $1/(1 + \epsilon) \leq [p]/[q] \leq 1+\epsilon$ (i.e., p is close to q), then $([p], [q])$ represents a point lying within the area delimited by the dashed lines. If $[p]/[q]$ is smaller than $\epsilon/(1+\epsilon)$ (i.e., p is negligible with respect to q), then $([p], [q])$ represents a point lying between the positive vertical axis and the solid diagonal line.

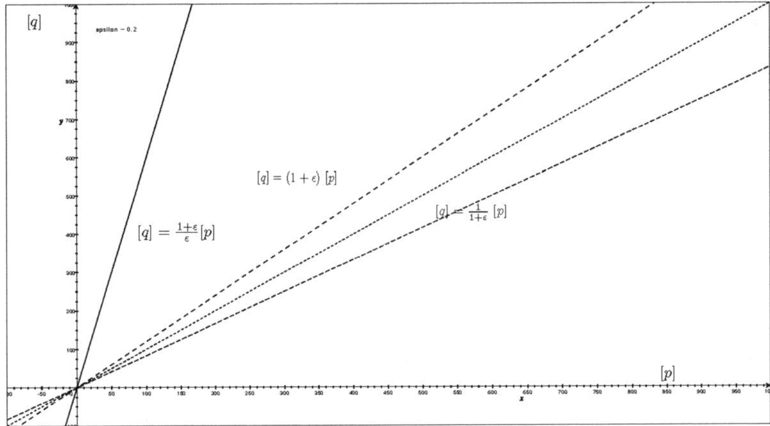

Figure 1. Graph for $\epsilon = 0.2$

Now consider a fixed collection q and imagine that different values of ϵ are appropriate for different contexts. The smaller the value of ϵ, the smaller the value of $|[p] - [q]|$ must be for p to count as close to q and the smaller $[p]$ must be for p to count as negligible with respect to q. To picture this situation graphically: the smaller the value of ϵ, the narrower the corridor between the dashed diagonal lines in Figure 1 and also the narrower the corridor between the solid diagonal line and the positive vertical axis. Consider Table 1. If $\epsilon = 0.2$ and q has cardinality 100, then collections with cardinalities between 84 and 120 count as close to q and collections with less than 17 members count as negligible with respect to q. By contrast, if $\epsilon = 0.01$ and q has cardinality 100, then $[p]$ must equal 100 or 101 for p to count as close to q and no collection has a cardinality small enough to count as negligible with respect to q.

ϵ	$[q]$	$p \simeq q$	$p \ll q$
0.7	100	$58.8 \leq [p] \leq 170$	$[p] < 41.146$
0.2	100	$83.3 \leq [p] \leq 120$	$[p] < 16.666$
0.1	100	$9.9 \leq [p] \leq 110$	$[p] < 9.0909$
0.01	100	$99.009 \leq [p] \leq 101$	$[p] < 0.99$

Table 1. The parameter ϵ determines which collections are close and which collections are negligible with respect to other collections.

The choice of a value of ϵ between 0 and 0.5 is determined by the level of precision assumed in a particular context. For example, one would chose a larger value of ϵ in a context where the goal is to represent the general functions of the human organ systems than in contexts where the goal is to represent precise analyses of particular blood samples. An important advantage of the presented theory is that the axioms are valid for all choices of ϵ between 0 and 0.5.

Axioms for 'close to'. In the axiomatic theory, we represent *close to* as a relation $\simeq$ between collections, where $p \simeq q$ is interpreted as: $1/(1 + \epsilon) \leq [p]/[q] \leq 1 + \epsilon$. We require: $\simeq$ is reflexive (AC14) and symmetric (AC15); if r is symmetric with respect to p and q and p is close to q, then $p \cup r$ is close to $q \cup r$ (AC16); if p is close to q and the cardinality of r is greater than or equal to that of p and less than or equal to that of q, then p is close to r and q is close to r (AC17).

$$AC14\ p \simeq p$$
$$AC15\ p \simeq q \rightarrow q \simeq p$$
$$AC16\ Sym_C\ rpq \wedge p \simeq q \rightarrow (p \cup r) \simeq (q \cup r)$$
$$AC17\ p \simeq q \wedge p \leq r \wedge r \leq q \rightarrow (p \simeq r \wedge q \simeq r)$$

Notice that unlike [11] and [5] we do not require $\simeq$ to be transitive. In many of the intended models of our theory, it is possible to find collections $r_1, \ldots, r_n$ such that $p \simeq r_1, r_1 \simeq r_2, \ldots$ and $r_n \simeq q$ and but NOT $p \simeq q$. Hence, adding a transitivity axiom for $\simeq$ would give rise to a version of the Sorites paradox [7,17].

If the cardinalities of p and q are the same and q is close to r, then p is close to r (TC13); if p is close to q and the cardinalities of q and r are the same, then p is close to r (TC14); if the cardinalities of p and q are the same, then p is close to q (TC15).

$$TC13\ p \asymp q \wedge q \simeq r \rightarrow p \simeq r$$
$$TC14\ p \simeq q \wedge q \asymp r \rightarrow p \simeq r$$

$$TC15\ p \asymp q \rightarrow p \simeq q$$

Notice that the axioms for $\simeq$ are significantly weaker than the axioms for $\asymp$. $\simeq$ is not an equivalence relation; a collection may be close to one of its proper sub-collections; for disjoint collections p and q, there may be some collection r such that the union of p and r is close to the union of q and r even though p is not close to q.

Definition of 'negligible'. Let p and q be collections. p is *negligible with respect to q* if and only if there exist r and s such that (i) p and r have the same cardinality, (ii) r is a sub-collection of q, (iii) s is the difference of r in q and (iii) s is close to q $(D_{\ll})$.

$$D_{\ll}\ p \ll q \equiv (\exists r)(\exists s)(r \asymp p \wedge r \subseteq q \wedge \setminus qrs \wedge s \simeq q)$$

When $\simeq$ is interpreted so that $s \simeq q$ holds if and only if $1/(1 + \epsilon) \leq [s]/[q] \leq 1 + \epsilon$, then $p \ll q$ holds if and only if $[p]/[q]$ is smaller than $\epsilon/(1 + \epsilon)$. We require that if p is negligible with respect to q and the cardinality of q is less than or equal to the cardinality of r, then p is negligible with respect to r (AC18).

$$AC18\ p \ll q \wedge q \leq r \rightarrow p \ll r$$

We can prove: if p is negligible with respect to q, then the cardinality of p is smaller than the cardinality of q (TC16); if the cardinality of p is less than or equal to the cardinality of q and q is negligible with respect to r, then p is negligible with respect to r (TC17); if p is a sub-collection of q and q is negligible with respect to r, then p is negligible with respect to r (TC18); if p is negligible with respect to q and q a sub-collection of r, then p is negligible with respect to r (TC19); $\ll$ is transitive (TC20).

$$TC16\ p \ll q \rightarrow p < q$$
$$TC17\ p \leq q \wedge q \ll r \rightarrow p \ll r$$

$$TC18\ p \subseteq q \wedge q \ll r \rightarrow p \ll r$$
$$TC19\ p \ll q \wedge q \subseteq r \rightarrow p \ll r$$
$$TC20\ p \ll q \wedge q \ll r \rightarrow p \ll r$$

Definition of 'large'. p is *large* if and only if some other collection is negligible with respect to p (D_{Lg}). When $\simeq$ is interpreted so that $p \simeq q$ holds if and only if $1/(1 + \epsilon) \leq [p]/[q] \leq 1 + \epsilon$, p is large if and only if $[p] > (2 + 2\epsilon)/\epsilon$. For example, if $\epsilon = 0.01$, then collections of cardinality greater than 202 are large.

$$D_{Lg} \; Lg \; p \equiv (\exists q)(q \ll p)$$

We can prove: super-collections of large collections are large (TC21); sub-collections of non-large collections are non-large (TC22).

$$TC21 \; Lg \; p \wedge p \subseteq q \rightarrow Lg \; q \qquad\qquad TC22 \; p \subseteq q \wedge \neg Lg \; q \rightarrow \neg Lg \; p$$

4. The mereology of objects

We introduce the primitive binary relation P, where Pxy is interpreted as: object x is part of object y.

We define: x *overlaps* y if and only if there is an object z such that z is part of both x and y (D_O); x is a *proper part* of y if and only if x is part of y and y is not part of x (D_{PP}); z is a *difference* of y in x if and only if any object w overlaps z if and only if w overlaps some part of x and that does not overlap y (D_-); z is a *sum* of x and y if and only if any object w overlaps z if and only if w overlaps x or y (D_+); z is a *sum* of collection p, $z\sigma p$, if and only if any object overlaps z just in case it overlaps a member of p (D_σ). We also say in this case that z is a *p-sum*.

$$
\begin{aligned}
&D_O && O \; xy \equiv (\exists z)(P \; zx \wedge P \; zy) \\
&D_{PP} && PP \; xy \equiv P \; xy \wedge \neg P \; yx \\
&D_- && - \; xyz \equiv (w)(O \; wz \leftrightarrow (\exists w_1)(P \; w_1 x \wedge \neg O \; w_1 y \wedge O \; w_1 w)) \\
&D_+ && + \; xyz \equiv (w)(O \; wz \leftrightarrow (O \; wx \vee O \; wy)) \\
&D_\sigma && z\sigma p \equiv (w)(O \; wz \leftrightarrow (\exists x)(x \in p \wedge O \; xw))
\end{aligned}
$$

We have the usual axioms of reflexivity (AP1) and transitivity (AP2). We also require that if x is not a part of y then there is a difference of y in x (AP3) and that there is a binary sum of any two objects (AP4).

$$
\begin{aligned}
&AP1 \; P \; xx && AP3 \; \neg P \; xy \rightarrow (\exists z)(- \; xyz) \\
&AP2 \; P \; xy \wedge P \; yz \rightarrow P \; xz && AP4 \; (\exists z)(+ \; xyz)
\end{aligned}
$$

We can prove: if everything that overlaps x overlaps y then x is part of y (TP1); if x is a p-sum, then every member of p is part of x (TP2); if x is a p-sum, y is a q-sum, and p is a sub-collection of q then x is part of y (TP3).

$$
\begin{aligned}
&TP1 \; (z)(O \; zx \rightarrow O \; zy) \rightarrow P \; xy \\
&TP2 \; x \in p \wedge y\sigma p \rightarrow P \; xy
\end{aligned}
\qquad\qquad TP3 \; x\sigma p \wedge y\sigma q \wedge p \subseteq q \rightarrow P \; xy
$$

A collection p is *discrete* if and only if distinct members of p do not overlap (D_D).

$$D_D \; D\,p \equiv (x)(y)(x \in p \wedge y \in p \wedge O\,xy \to x = y)$$

We say that object z is a *discrete sum* of the collection p, $z\Delta p$, if and only if p is discrete and z is a p sum (D_Δ). We can prove that if x is a discrete p-sum then the members of p are proper parts of x (TP4).

$$D_\Delta \; z\Delta p \equiv D\,p \wedge z\sigma p \qquad\qquad TP4 \; x\Delta p \wedge y \in p \to PP\,yx$$

We define that z is *mereologically symmetric* with respect to x and y if and only if for every object w that is part of z: w is part of x if and only if w is part of y (D_{Sym_P}).

$$D_{Sym_P} \; Sym_P\,zxy \equiv (w)(P\,wz \to (P\,wx \leftrightarrow P\,wy))$$

5. Relative size of objects and granular parthood

Exactly the same size. We use $\|x\|$ in the meta-language to refer to the exact volume size of object x. x and y have *exactly the same size* if and only if $\|x\| = \|y\|$. In the formal theory we introduce the *same size* relation $\sim$ where, on the intended interpretation, $x \sim y$ holds if and only if $\|x\| = \|y\|$. We require: if x is part of y and y is part of x, then x and y are the same size (AP5); $\sim$ is symmetric (AP6); $\sim$ is transitive (AP7); if x is part of y and x and y have the same size then y is part of x (AP8); if w_1 is a sum of x and z and w_2 is a sum of y and z and z is symmetric with respect to x and y then: x and y have the same size if and only if w_1 has the same size as w_2 (AP9).

$$AP5 \; P\,xy \wedge P\,yx \to x \sim y$$
$$AP6 \; x \sim y \to y \sim x$$
$$AP7 \; x \sim y \wedge y \sim z \to x \sim z$$
$$AP8 \; P\,xy \wedge x \sim y \to P\,yx$$
$$AP9 \; +xzw_1 \wedge \; +yzw_2 \wedge Sym_P\,zxy \to (x \sim y \leftrightarrow w_1 \sim w_2)$$

We can prove: $\sim$ is reflexive (TP5); if x is a proper part of y and y has the same size as z or if x has the same size as y and y is a proper part of z, then x and z are different sizes (TP6); if w_1 is a difference of z in x and w_2 is a difference of z in y and z is symmetric with respect to x and y, then x and y have the same size if and only if w_1 and w_2 have the same size (TP7).[1]

$$TP5 \; x \sim x$$
$$TP6 \; [(PP\,xy \wedge y \sim z) \vee (x \sim y \wedge PP\,yz)] \to \neg x \sim z$$
$$TP7 \; -xzw_1 \wedge \; -yzw_2 \wedge Sym_P\,zxy \to (x \sim y \leftrightarrow w_1 \sim w_2))$$

---

[1] Notice that we do not introduce a total size ordering on objects analogous to the $\leq$ ordering on collections. This is because we do not want to commit to the assumption that for any two objects x and y, either x has a part of exactly the same size as y or y has a part of exactly the same size as x.

Roughly the same size and granular parthood. We introduce the relations *roughly the same size* ($\approx$) and *granular parthood* ($\lll$) between objects, which are roughly analogous to the relations *close to* and *negligible with respect to* on collections. Let ω be a parameter such that $0 < \omega < 0.5$. On the intended interpretation, x is *roughly same size as* y if and only if $1/(1 + \omega) \leq \|x\|/\|y\| \leq 1 + \omega$. x is a *granular part* of y (i.e., a part of y of negligible size) if and only if x is part of y and $\|x\|/\|y\|$ is less than $\omega/(1 + \omega)$.

The parameter ω determines which objects are roughly the same size and which of an object's parts are negligible in size with respect to it. This corresponds to the way in which the parameter ϵ determines which cardinalities are close and which cardinalities negligible with respect to others. As with ϵ, the value of ω can vary according to context. The axioms of our theory are valid for all choices of ω between 0 and 0.5.

Consider Table 2. If HB is a human body of average volume 70 liter and HH is HB's heart of average volume 0.3 liter, then HH is a granular part of HB for choices of ω larger than 0.0043. HB's cells (average size $400 * 10^{-15}$) are granular parts of HB for all choices of ω listed in the table.

ω	$HB \simeq y$	$y \preceq HB$	$y \lll HB$
0.2	$58.333 \leq \|y\| \leq 84$	$11.666 \leq \|y\| \leq 70$	$\|y\| < 11.666$
0.1	$63.636 \leq \|y\| \leq 77$	$6.363 \leq \|y\| \leq 70$	$\|y\| < 6.363$
0.01	$69.307 \leq \|y\| \leq 70.7$	$0.693 \leq \|y\| \leq 70$	$\|y\| < 0.693$
0.001	$69.93 \leq \|y\| \leq 70.07$	$0.0699 \leq \|y\| \leq 70$	$\|y\| < 0.0699$

Table 2. The parameter ω determines which objects are roughly the same size and which of an object's parts are granular parts. Average volume in liters: human body (HB) = 70 liter, human heart (HH) = 0.3 liter, average cell (HC) = $400 * 10^{-15}$ liter.

Axioms for $\approx$. We require: $\approx$ is reflexive (AP10); $\approx$ is symmetric (AP11); if w_1 is a sum of x and z and w_2 is a sum of y and z and z is symmetric with respect to x and y and x and y are roughly the same size, then w_1 and w_2 are the roughly the same size (AP12); if x and y are roughly the same size and y and z are the same size, then x and z are roughly the same size (AP13); if x and y are roughly the same size and x is a part of z and z is a part of y, then z and x, as well as z and y, are roughly the same size (AP14).

$$AP10\ x \approx x$$
$$AP11\ x \approx y \rightarrow y \approx x$$
$$AP12\ +xzw_1 \wedge\ +yzw_2 \wedge Sym_P\ zxy \wedge x \approx y \rightarrow w_1 \approx w_2$$
$$AP13\ x \approx y \wedge y \sim z \rightarrow x \approx z$$
$$AP14\ x \approx y \wedge P\ xz \wedge P\ zy \rightarrow (z \approx x \wedge z \approx y)$$

We can prove: x and y are the same size and y and z are roughly the same size, then x and z are roughly the same size (TP8); if x and y are the same size, then x and y are roughly the same size (TP9).

$$TP8\ x \sim y \wedge y \approx z \rightarrow x \approx z \qquad\qquad TP9\ x \sim y \rightarrow x \approx y$$

For reasons analogous to those discussed in the context of $\simeq$ we do not require $\approx$ to be transitive.

Granular and non-granular parthood. x is a *granular part* of y (i.e., x is a part of y whose size is negligible with respect to y) if and only if x is a proper part of y and any difference of x in y has roughly the same size as y $(D_{\lll})$.[2]

$$D_{\lll}\ x \lll y \equiv PP\ xy \wedge (z)(-\ yxz \to z \approx y)$$

As discussed above, on the intended interpretation $x \lll y$ holds if and only if $\|x\|/\|y\| < \omega/(1+\omega)$. Consider Table 2. For $\omega = 0.01$, if x is a human body of size 70 liter, then any part y of x with $\|y\| < 0.693$ liter is a granular part of x.

We can prove: $\lll$ is asymmetric (TP10) and transitive (TP11); if x is part of y and y is a granular part of z then x is granular part of z (TP12); if x is a granular part of y and y is part of z then x is granular part of z (TP13).

$$TP10\ x \lll y \to \neg y \lll x \qquad\qquad TP12\ P\ xy \wedge y \lll z \to x \lll z$$
$$TP11\ x \lll y \wedge y \lll z \to x \lll z \qquad TP13\ x \lll y \wedge P\ yz \to x \lll z$$

x is a *non-granular part* of y if and only if x is part of y and x is not a granular part of y $(D_{\preceq})$. It follows immediately that non-granular parthood is reflexive.

$$D_{\preceq}\ x \preceq y \equiv P\ xy \wedge \neg x \lll y$$

On the intended interpretation, $x \preceq y$ holds if and only if x is part of y and $\|x\|/\|y\| \geq \omega/(1+\omega)$.

x and y are of the same *scale with respect to* z if and only if x and y are both non-granular parts of z $(D_{\cong})$

$$D_{\cong}\ x \cong_z y \equiv x \preceq z \wedge y \preceq z$$

On the intended interpretation, $x \cong_z y$ holds if and only if x and y are parts of z, $\|x\|/\|z\| \geq \omega/(1+\omega)$, and $\|y\|/\|z\| \geq \omega/(1+\omega)$. Consider Table 2. For $\omega = 0.001$, an average-sized human heart and an average sized human leg are of the same scale with respect to the 70 liter human body of which both are parts.

6. Aggregates and scale

We require: if x is a p-sum and all members of p are granular parts of x, then p is large (AA1); if x is a discrete p-sum and all members of p are of non-granular parts of x, then p is not large (AA2).

$$AA1\ x\sigma p \wedge (y)(y \in p \to y \lll x) \to Lg\ p$$
$$AA2\ x\Delta p \wedge (y)(y \in p \to y \preceq x) \to \neg Lg\ p$$

It follows from (AA1) that if x is part of y and x is roughly the same size as y, then x is a non-granular part of y (TA1).

---

[2]Notice that we do not define a relation 'of negligible size with respect to' for arbitrary, possibly disjoint objects analogous to $\lll$ on collections. This because we do not want to commit to the general thesis that any object x has a part of that is roughly the same size as any smaller object.

$$TA1 \; P \; xy \wedge x \approx y \to x \preceq y$$

Object x is a p-*assembly* if and only if x is a discrete p-sum and all members of p are non-granular parts of x (D_{Ass}). Object x is a p-*aggregate* if and only if x is a discrete p-sum and all members of p are granular parts of $x(D_{Ag})$.

$$D_{Ass} \; Ass \; xp \equiv x\Delta p \wedge (y)(y \in p \to y \preceq x)$$
$$D_{Ag} \; Ag \; xp \equiv x\Delta p \wedge (y)(y \in p \to y \lll x)$$

For example, my liver is an aggregate of liver cells in contexts with ω larger than $5.7143 * 10^{-13}$ and ϵ larger than $1.143 * 10^{-12}$ ($\|$my liver$\| = 0.7$ liter, $\|$an average cell$\| = 400 * 10^{-15}$ liter). My body is an assembly of the collection of my major body parts (my torso, my head, my neck, my left arm, my left leg, …) in contexts with $\omega < 0.01$ and $\epsilon < 0.02$ ($\|$my neck$\| = 0.7$ liter and $\|$my body$\| = 70$ liter).

We can prove: if x is a p-assembly then p is not large (TA2); if x is a p-aggregate, then p is large (TA3); if x is a p-assembly and y and z are members of p, then y and z are of the same x-scale (TA4).

$$TA2 \; Ass \; xp \to \neg Lg \; p$$
$$TA3 \; Ag \; xp \to Lg \; p$$

$$TA4 \; Ass \; xp \wedge y \in p \wedge z \in p \to y \cong_x z$$

7. Conclusions

We have presented an axiomatic theory of size and granular parthood. The theory is based on the formal characterization of the primitive relations: member of ($\in$) (between objects and collections); same-cardinality-as ($\asymp$) and close-to-in-cardinality ($\simeq$) (between collections); part-of (P), exactly-the-same-size ($\sim$) and roughly-the-same-size ($\approx$) (between objects). In our theory, we are able to formally distinguish between: i) large and non-large collections, ii) the granular and non-granular parts of a given object, and iii) assemblies and aggregates. We thereby extend existing work on mereology, context, and order of magnitude reasoning.

Our theory has a number of limitations: (1) It does not take into account time. Hence we cannot do justice to the fact that most objects most objects gain and lose parts over times. Moreover, there is a critical distinction between gaining or losing granular parts and gaining or losing non-granular parts. Only in rare contexts does it matter whether a human body loses cells, but the loss of a limb or an organ is always a significant event. In [2], we develop a time-dependent mereology. We are currently working on a combined theory of parthood, change, and scale.

(2) We focus in this paper exclusively on similarity in cardinality and size, leaving aside similarity in type. However, there are critical distinctions between homogeneous aggregates (p-aggregates where all members of p are of the same type) and heterogeneous aggregates (p-aggregates where members of p are of different types) [2]. By combining the work in this paper with a theory of types or universals, we can distinguish between different sorts of homogeneous and heterogenous aggregates.

References

[1]   B. Bennett. Physical objects, identity and vagueness. In D. Fensel, Deborah McGuinness, and Mary-Anne Williams, editors, *Principles of Knowledge Representation and Reasoning: Proceedings of the Eighth International Conference (KR2002)*, San Francisco, CA, 2002. Morgan Kaufmann.

[2]   T. Bittner and M. Donnelly. A temporal mereology for distinguishing between integral objects and portions of stuff. Technical report, SUNY Buffalo, Department of Philosophy, 2006.

[3]   T. Bittner and B. Smith. Vague reference and approximating judgments. *Spatial Cognition and Computation*, 3(2):137–156, 2003.

[4]   P. Dague. Numeric reasoning with relative orders of magnitude. In *Proceedings of the National Conference on Artificial Intelligence*, pages 541–547, 1993.

[5]   P. Dague. Symbolic reasoning with relative orders of magnitude. In *Proc. 13th Intl. Joint Conference on Artificial Intelligence*, pages 1509–1515. Morgan Kaufmann, 1993.

[6]   Michael Dummett. Wang's paradox. *Synthese*, 30:301–324, 1975.

[7]   D. Hyde. Sorites paradox. In *Stanford Encyclopedia of Philosoph*. 1996.

[8]   R. Keefe. Context, vagueness and the sorites. In J.C. Beall, editor, *Liars and Heaps*. Oxford University Press, 2003.

[9]   A. Kumar, B. Smith, and D. Novotny. Biomedical informatics and granularity. *Functional and Comparative Genomics*, 5:501–508, 2004.

[10]   M. Mavrovouniotis and G. Stephanopoulos. Formal order-of-magnitude reasoning in process engineering. *Computers and Chemical Engineering*, 12:867–881, 1988.

[11]   O. Raiman. Order of magnitude reasoning. *Artificial Intelligence*, 51:11–38, 1991.

[12]   A. Rector, J. Rogers, and T. Bittner. Granularity scale & collectivity: When size does and doesn't matter. *Journal of Bioinformatics*, 2005.

[13]   A. Rector, J. Rogers, A. Roberts, and C. Wroe. Scale and context: Issues in ontologies to link health- and bio-informatics. In *Proceedings of the AMIA 2002 Anual Symposium*, pages 642–646, 2002.

[14]   H.R. Schmidtke. Aggregations and constituents: geometric specification of multi-granular objects. *Journal of Visual Languages & Computing*, 16(4):289–309, 2005.

[15]   H.R. Schmidtke. Granularity as a parameter of context. In A.K. Dey, D.B. Leake B.N. Kokinov, and R.M. Turner, editors, *Modelling and Using Context*, pages 450–463. Springer, 2005.

[16]   B. Smith, W. Ceusters, B. Klagges, J. Köhler, A. Kumar, J. Lomax, C. Mungall, F. Neuhaus, A. Rector, and C. Rosse. Relations in biomedical ontologies. *Gnome Biology*, 6(5):r46, 2005.

[17]   K. van Deemter. The sorites fallacy and the context-dependence of vague predicates. In M. Kanazawa, C. Pinon, and H. de Swart, editors, *Quantifiers, Deduction, and Context*, pages 59–86. CSLI Publications, Stanford, CA, 1995.

Formal Ontology in Information Systems
B. Bennett and C. Fellbaum (Eds.)
IOS Press, 2006

Spatial Dimensionality as a Classification Criterion for Qualities

Florian PROBST [1], Martin ESPETER
Institute for Geoinformatics, University of Münster, Germany

Abstract. We discuss how the spatial extent of physical endurants influences the conceptualization of their spatial qualities. Comparing the spatial dimensionality of a physical endurant with the spatial dimensionality of its qualities leads to an interesting formal ontological question. Should a spatial quality be conceptualized as having a value range instead of a single value when its bearer has a higher spatial dimensionality? For example, the one-dimensional *depth* quality can be conceptualized as having a value range when it is assigned to the three-dimensional water body of a lake. In terms of the foundational ontology DOLCE, the "value" of a quality, sometimes called quale, is located at an atomic region at a certain time. Allowing a value range at a time is to model qualities as being located at non-atomic regions at a time. That might be philosophically debatable, yet, this modeling approach enables the development of information discovery systems that can cope with ontologically imprecise user queries and can assist the user in defining ontologically precise quality specifications. This brings formal ontology closer to practical applications.
The investigation is based on the foundational ontology DOLCE and introduces a classification for spatial qualities based on their spatial dimensionality.

Keywords. formal ontology, spatial feature, geospatial ontology engineering

Introduction

In the context of open and distributed information sources, successful discovery of an information source requires a precise description of the offered information and a precise formulation of a query. Formal ontology has proven a useful basis to enable precise descriptions. One can expect that professional ontology engineers take the burden of providing semantic annotations for information sources offered via the web that are consistent with a foundational ontology[2]. But can one expect an information requester to be able to formulate queries that are consistent with a foundational ontology? Natural language leaves a substantial range of ambiguity in the meanings of words denoting qualities. This has proven to be efficient and powerful in direct human communication but turned out to be the central drawback when no direct dialog for

---

[1] Corresponding Author: Florian Probst, Robert-Koch-Str. 26-28, 48149 Münster, Germany; E-mail: f.probst@uni-muenster.de

[2] We employed DOLCE as foundational ontology for the investigations presented here. http://www.loa-cnr.it/DOLCE.html

agreeing on the meaning of the used symbols is possible. One can observe that (geospatial) questions which appear valid when stated in natural language cannot be aligned consistently to the foundational ontology DOLCE [1]. For example, "What is the depth of Lake Constance?" The emerging problem with quality specification is as follows.

According to DOLCE, a quality can have only one quale (value) at a certain time. In this sense, stating that a lake has a depth quality implies that the lake has only one depth "value" at a time. This is problematic since one can conceptualize the water body as having a single depth quality whose depth values increase from zero (at the lake shore) to a maximum depth value. In other words, the *depth* quality's quale changes in time as well as in space. Yet, the change in space is limited to the space region occupied by the lake's water body.

We present an approach that takes spatial dimensionality as central criterion for classifying qualities of physical endurants. In this context, two contradicting modeling possibilities arise.

1. A quality can be conceptualized as having a quale located at a non-atomic quality region when the quality is inherent in an entity with a higher spatial dimensionality. In other words, the quality has a "value range". For example, the depth of a lake.

2. An entity with spatial dimensionality n is modeled with an infinite number of qualities with dimensionality $<$ n, each quality having a single value. For example, a lake (3D) has infinitely many depth qualities (1D), each with a single quale (value).

In this paper, we make a case for possibility 1). Allowing a quality to be located at a non-atomic quality region may be debatable from a philosophical point of view, but it allows the user in the process of discovering suitable information sources to enter the discovery process with a rather imprecise question. It is important that systems are able to accept such imprecise queries and assist to turn them into precise queries. We assume that users tend to take the context of their query as obvious or even as the only possible context, thus they tend to neglect the need for a precise quality specification. While driving a truck, the question, "What is the height of the tunnel?" seems to refer obviously to the *minimum height* quality.

We show that dimensionality plays a crucial role in the way we assign spatial qualities to physical objects. The results contribute to the development of semantic reference systems as introduced in [2].

The remainder of the paper is organized as follows. The background section introduces the notions of physical endurant, feature, quality, quality space and quale as well as our assumptions about physical space and spatial dimensionality.

We introduce our view on how endurants extend in physical space and emphasize in this context the importance of spatial features and their spatial dimensionality. We provide an axiomatization of spatial qualities and their extent in space. We then discuss the consequences, when a spatial feature and its *spatial extent* quality have a different dimensionality, thus are located at non-identical space regions. We conclude by discussing the benefits of this quality specification approach for the discovery process of information sources.

Background

Our work is based on the foundational ontology DOLCE [1]. The following section introduces the categories relevant for our purposes. Furthermore, we briefly introduce our assumptions regarding physical space.

Physical Endurants

The main characteristics of a physical endurant are its location in space, its complete presence at a certain time and its participation in some perdurant, which is sometimes called temporal entity. Any physical endurant has some direct physical quality apart from having a spatial location. It can be a part of some other physical endurant as well as having other physical endurants as part. DOLCE provides three subcategories of physical endurant: Amount of Matter, Physical Objects and Features. Since features are relevant for our purposes here, they are briefly introduced.

The main characteristic of a feature is its one-sided generic dependence ([1] axiom Ad 70) on its host, which means that the host can exist without the feature but not vice versa. For some *spatial* features however, we assume that even *mutual generic dependence* applies. Examples for such features are *body* or *surface*. They are essential parts of their hosts. For example, an apple has a feature *apple surface* and the apple cannot exist without it. The feature's constituting amount of matter can be changed, e.g. the apple can shrivel, yet there is still a surface.

The most important distinction between feature and quality is that qualities are the only entities that can be directly observed or measured. A feature does have physical qualities. The *surface* feature has an *area* quality. The *area* quality can be measured in contrast to the *surface* which cannot be measured. It is important to note that the qualities of a feature indirectly characterize the feature's host. Fore example, the *volume* quality of an apple's *body* characterizes the apple.

A feature can be part of another physical endurant as well as having another feature as part. In contrast, qualities inhere in other entities, they can be neither part of an entity nor have parts.

Quality, Quality Space and Quale

Qualities are seen as the basic entities we can perceive or measure, for example shapes, colours, weights or lengths [1]. Every physical endurant comes with certain qualities, which exist as long as the endurant exists. DOLCE defines a strict distinction between a quality (e.g., the colour of a specific rose), and its "value" (e.g., a particular shade of red).

The "value" of a quality is understood as atomic quality region and is called a quale. Quality regions are abstract entities. Currently, DOLCE requires that a quality can be located at exactly one quale at a time. Over time however, the quale can change. Together, the regions at which the qualities of a certain quality type are located form the quality space of that quality type. As described in [3], the general idea is that for each perceivable or conceivable quality a region in at least one associated quality space exists.

Assumptions about Physical Space

Since we aim to provide a classification of qualities based on their extent in physical space, we briefly introduce our assumptions about physical space. Several ontology projects that attempt to account for physical space are summarized in [4].
We assume that a three dimensional physical space exists. We assume all physical endurants to be *in* this physical space. In DOLCE, the *spatial location* quality is the central spatial quality accounting for *being located* in physical space. We understand this quality in a Newtonian sense as identifying the region in physical space that a physical object occupies. In this sense, the *spatial location* quality identifies its absolute position in space.

In this investigation, we take physical space *to be* a quality space with three orthogonal *location* dimensions. This has the side effect that physical space as such is understood as an abstract entity. We assume that within this three dimensional physical space, regions with lower dimensions can exist. See definitions (1-3) below.

A potential misunderstanding is that the quality space for *spatial location* accounts directly for the *volume, shape, area* or *length* qualities of an entity. This holds only indirectly. An entity which has a *volume* or an *area* quality does necessarily have a *spatial location* quality, yet *volume* and *location* qualities are distinct qualities.

More generally, a quality space for spatial location requires a spatial reference system in order to turn the absolute locations in space into comparable and measurable space regions. This is inline with Kuhn and Raubal [5], proposing that spatial reference systems are special kinds of semantic reference systems.

Physical Endurants and Their Spatial Qualities

After introducing physical endurants, qualities, their associated quality spaces and the assumptions about physical space, we now discuss the spatial qualities of physical endurants.

Being in Space versus Extending in Space

Being in space and *being extended* in space are often understood as synonym. In our approach, it is important to distinguish between both. In DOLCE, *being in space* is reflected in the *spatial location* quality that any physical endurant necessarily entertains. The quality space of the *spatial location* quality directly refers to physical space; physical space *is* the quality space of the spatial location quality. In other words, any physical endurant has a spatial location quality that has as "value" the space region it occupies. We assume this quality to be the most central spatial quality since it is a prerequisite for an entity to be in space. But how to describe *being in space* more precisely? Here, the spatial qualities *extent* and *figure (shape)* come into play. The distinction between *being in* space and *being extended* becomes apparent when taking physical endurants into account whose *spatial location* qualities are located at atomic regions in space. Casati et al. [6] indicate that a theory of spatial representation should account for the fact that the different types of spatial entities bear different types of relations to space. The corner of a desk top, the midpoint of a desk edge or the balance point of a desk surface are examples for physical endurants which are in space, yet which do not extend in space, since they do not entertain qualities like *volume, area* or *length*. Here, we depart from the assumptions made in Asher and Vieu [7] and Borgo et al. [8], that the entities we deal with in space do necessarily extend in three dimensions. We assume that surfaces, edges or corners *do* play a role in our every day interactions in space and that it is exactly their lower dimensional spatial extent that plays a crucial role in the way we assign spatial qualities (indirectly) to physical objects. We see some support for this assumption in the approach to deal with boundaries presented by Casati and Varzi [9].

Spatial Features and Spatial Qualities

A prominent argument why the spatial qualities *extension* and *shape* are most central is given by Kant [10, p. 17]: "Thus, if I take away from our representation of a body all that the understanding thinks as belonging to it, as substance, force, divisibility, etc., and also whatever belongs to sensation, as impenetrability, hardness, color, etc.; yet there is still something left us from this empirical intuition, namely, extension and shape."

We assume that Kant's notion of *body* refers here to what we will define as spatial feature. In our approach, we restrict *spatial extension* qualities and *shape* qualities to inhere exclusively in spatial features. This in turn leaves physical objects to entertain spatial qualities only indirectly via the spatial features that they necessarily have.

We propose the category SPATIAL FEATURE as a direct sub-category to FEATURE with four sub-categories: 1D-FEATURE, 2D-FEATURE, 3D-FEATURE AND EXTESNION-LESS FEATURES (Fig. 1). All spatial features do necessarily have a host that is a physical object.

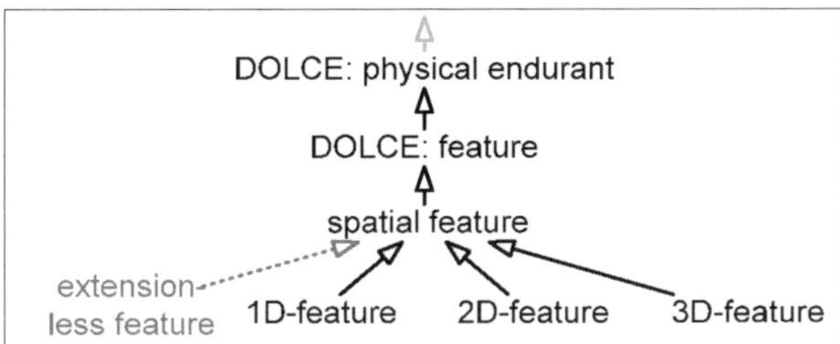

Fig. 1. Proposed sub categories of FEATURE. DOLCE is intentionally not restricted to a certain dimensionality of space. To be practically applicable in geospatial application we introduce three feature types classified according to their dimensionality. The position of extension-less-features is debatable.

3D-Features. The feature *body* is conceptualized as extending in all three dimensions of physical space. In other words, its *spatial location* quality is located at a space region that extends in all three spatial dimensions of physical space. All features whose spatial location quality is located at a 3D region are individuals of the category 3D-Features.

2D-Features. The feature surface is conceptualized as extending only in two spatial dimensions. For example, an apple's surface has a two-dimensional extent since the space region at which its *spatial location* quality is located extends only along two of the three spatial dimensions. Still, the surface's two-dimensional region is part of the three-dimensional physical space. In contrast, the apple's peel is a physical object and as such located at a three dimensional region.

1D-Features. Features with a *spatial location quality* that is located at a region that extends only along one of the three spatial dimensions belong to the category 1D-FEATURE. For example, a tabletop can have edges.

Extension-less Feature. Finally, a feature that is located in physical space but does not extend in physical space is an extension-less feature. Being located in physical space but at the same time being extension-less means to have an *atomic* spatial location quality in either a 1D-, 2D-, or 3D-region. In this sense, extension-less features are special kinds of the above defined feature types. Apart from the *spatial location* quality, an extension-less feature has consequently no *spatial extent* qualities like a *volume, area* or *shape*. For this reason, we can observe extension-less features only indirectly via features which extend in space. The category of extension-less features requires further investigation.

Types of Space Regions
The *spatial location* quality is located in a quality region that accounts directly for a region in physical space. The region *is-a* space region.

We assume three types of physical space regions that are distinguished according to their number of spatial dimensions: 1D-, 2D-, and 3D- space regions.

$$1\text{D-S}(x) \vee 2\text{D-S}(x) \vee 3\text{D-S}(x) \rightarrow S(x) \tag{1}$$
(from DOLCE [1]: S :: space region)

We can imagine that an individual of each of these region types can shrink to an atomic extent. This leaves us with three kinds of atomic space regions. Only an extension-less (0D) feature can be located at such atomic regions. We leave the discussion about extension-less features open. The focus is on features that are located in non-atomic regions with one, two or three dimensions.

In the following, we introduce the relations *is-spatial-location-quality* and *is-spatial-location-quale*, which we require for defining spatial feature (4). A spatial feature is a feature which has a spatial location quality which in turn can be located at either a 1D-, a 2D,- or a 3D-spatial region. The fact that a spatial feature can be located at any space region type differentiates it form a physical object.

"x is a spatial location quality of y"

$$\text{slqt}(x,y) \triangleq \text{qt}(x,y) \wedge SL(x) \wedge (SF(y) \vee SQ(y)) \tag{2}$$
(from DOLCE [1]: SL:: spatial location (quality)[3]; qt:: is-quality-of (Ad38). The characterizations of the predicates SF (spatial feature) and SQ (spatial quality) are given in (4) and (5).)

"x is a spatial location quale of y (at time t)"

$$\text{slql}(x,y,t) \triangleq \text{ql}(x,y,t) \wedge (1\text{D-S}(x) \vee 2\text{D-S}(x) \vee 3\text{D-S}(x)) \wedge SL(y) \tag{3}$$
(from [1]: ql:: is-quale-of (Ad 58))

Spatial Feature

$$\begin{aligned}
SF(z) \rightarrow &\ F(z) \wedge (\exists y\ (\text{slqt}(y,z)) \\
&\wedge \exists x,t\ (\text{slql}(x,y,t)\ ) \wedge (1\text{D-S}(x) \vee 2\text{D-S}(x) \vee 3\text{D-S}(x))
\end{aligned} \tag{4}$$
(from [1]: F::Feature)

---

[3] For better readability we would prefer the label SLQ over SL to indicate that spatial location is a quality, but we keep the notation introduced in DOLCE [1].

A spatial feature has a spatial location quality that has its quale in a one-, two- or three-dimensional region of physical space (1D-S; 2D-S; 3D-S).

Dimensionality of Spatial Qualities

The previous section introduced spatial features. Relevant for our classification of features is their *spatial location* quality that accounts for *being in space,* or more precisely, that accounts for the dimensionality of the space region in which the *spatial location* quality is located.

Additionally to that spatial quality essential for any physical endurant, we introduce the categories SHAPE QUALITY and SPATIAL EXTENT QUALITY. Fig. 2 shows three sub-categories of SPATIAL QUALITY.

According to DOLCE, any physical quality has the same location in physical space as its bearer [1, axiom Dd37], and is called a spatial quale. We do not follow this approach here. In DOLCE, a *depth* quality would have the same spatial location as the lake it inheres in. For our purposes we need the possibility to state that the location quale of a quality is either identical with the location quale of its bearer or that it is a lower dimensional part of its bearer's location quale (8). This requires that any spatial quality itself has an individual *spatial location* quality, independently of the *location quality* of its bearer.

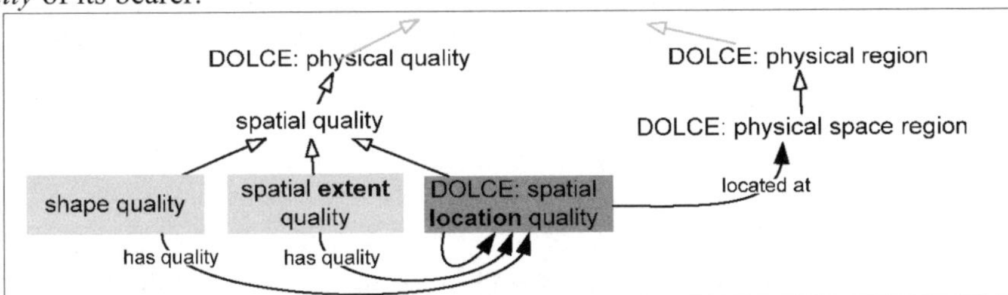

Fig. 2. Proposed extension of the category SPATIAL QUALITY. Note, any *spatial extent* quality and any *shape* quality themselves have a *spatial location* quality that in turn is located at a region in physical space.

Spatial Quality

$$SQ(z) \rightarrow PQ(z) \wedge \exists y \, (slq\mathbf{t}(y,z)) \tag{5}$$
(from DOLCE [1]: PQ :: Physical Quality)

We define a spatial quality (SQ) as a physical quality (PQ) which, at any time it exists, has a spatial location quality (SL). *Spatial extent* qualities (SEQ) can have spatial location qualities that are located at 1D-, 2D-, or 3D-space regions. This is axiomatized in the relation *is-spatial-location-quality-of* (2). As Casati and Varzi [9, p.123] state, "regions are those things that are located at themselves". This allows to categorize *spatial location* qualities as *spatial* qualities. We do not provide formalizations for *shape* qualities since they are not in the scope of this paper.

Spatial Extent Quality

$$SEQ(z) \rightarrow SQ(z) \tag{6}$$

"x is a spatial extent quality of y"

$$\text{seqt}(x,y) \triangleq \text{SEQ}(x) \wedge \text{SF}(y) \tag{7}$$

Spatial features and *spatial extent* qualities are related via the *is-spatial-extent-quality-of* relation (seqt). Both, *spatial extent* qualities and features can entertain *spatial location* qualities (2) these in turn can be located at any of the previously defined space regions (1),(3).

In Fig. 3, the three proposed sub-categories of SPATIAL EXTENT QUALITY are depicted. The individual *spatial extent* qualities are categorized according to the region type to which the regions of their *spatial location* quality belong. A *spatial extent* quality that has a *spatial location* quality that is located at a 3D-space region is categorized as *3D-spatial extent* quality.

At this point, we draw the attention to a possible source of confusion. Central to a quality is that it is an *observable entity*. This is reflected by the fact that is has a quale (*Ausprägung*). The quale is a region in the quality's quality space. According to DOLCE, a quale is an abstract particular. In turn, a quality is understood as an entity which itself can have qualities.

It is important to distinguish between the direct quale of a quality and the qualia of its qualities. Direct and indirect qualia are located in different quality spaces. In the case of *spatial extent* qualities, the quality has a direct quale for a spatial extent, e.g. a volume, an area or an elongation. Additionally, any *spatial extent* quality has a *location* quality. The *location* quality has its quale in the quality space corresponding to physical space.

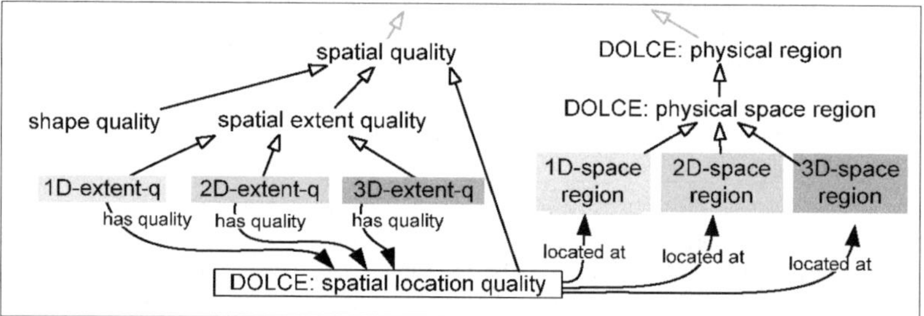

Fig. 3. Any *spatial extent* quality does itself have a *spatial location* quality. The *spatial location* quality of a *spatial extent* quality is located in a 1D-, 2D-, or 3D-space region. (All statements made above for *spatial extent* quality do apply in analogy for *shape* quality, too. Yet, they are omitted for readability.)

Non-Atomic Quality Regions

In the previous sections, we introduced the spatial dimensionality of features and spatial qualities. We continue by discussing the possible consequences arising when a spatial feature and its *spatial extent* quality entertain *spatial location* qualities that are located in space regions of different types.

The mereological relations between the physical space region at which the *spatial extent* quality is located and the physical space region at which the spatial feature is located are at the core of the investigations presented here. We identify the following relations between the space region of a feature and the space region of its *spatial extent* quality.

"x is a **lower dimensional part** of y" In order to distinguish the dimensionality of a spatial extent quality and the dimensionality of its bearer, the type of space region at which their location qualities are located need to be compared. If a space region is located in another space region and if this space region has a lower dimensionality than the space region in which it is located, the following relation applies:

$$ldp(x, y) \triangleq PP(x,y) \land$$
$$((1D\text{-}S(x) \land (2D\text{-}S(y) \lor 3D\text{-}S(y))) \lor (2D\text{-}S(x) \land 3D\text{-}S(y))) \tag{8}$$
(from DOLCE [1]: PP:: proper part (Dd14))

"v is an **atomic-quale-quality** of w". A feature and its spatial extent qualities each are located at a spatial region. If the space regions are identical, then the spatial extent qualities each have an atomic quale. Such an atomic quale can be approximated with a single value, e.g. $2km^3$. This relation applies for example between a water body and its volume quality:

$$aqlqt(v,w) \triangleq seqt(v,w) \land \forall y,y'((slqt(y,v) \land slqt(y',w))$$
$$\land \forall t (\forall x,x'(slql(x,y,t) \land slql(x',y',t)))) \rightarrow x \square x' \tag{9}$$
(from DOLCE : $P(x,y) \land P(y,x) \rightarrow x = y$ (Ad6), P :: Parthood)

"v is a **non-atomic-quale-quality** of (spatial feature) w" If the region at which the spatial extent quality's **spatial location quality** is located is a lower dimensional part of the region at which the spatial feature's **spatial location quality** is located, then the spatial extent quality has a **non atomic quale**. This relation applies for example between a water body and its depth quality. This relation is depicted in the lower part of Fig 5. The relations are labelled "q-location of depth quality" and "q-location of feature":

$$naqlqt(v,w) \triangleq seqt(v,w) \land \forall y,y'(slqt(y,v) \land slqt(y',w))$$
$$\land \forall t (\forall x,x'(slql(x,y,t) \land slql(x',y',t))) \rightarrow ldp(x, x') \tag{10}$$

These definitions entail: If a quality is conceptualized to be inherent in a feature that occupies a higher dimensional space region, then the spatial location of the quality is not exactly defined. It can "move" within the region of the feature. A 1D-space region has one degree of freedom within a 2D-space region, and two degrees of freedom within a 3D-space region. Fig. 4 shows an example for a depth quality inherent in the feature *water body* of river. In the example, the *depth* quality is conceptualized as 1D quality, thus its *spatial location* quality is located at a 1D-space region. The *depth* quality has two degrees of freedom within the 3D-space region occupied by the water body.

Thus, it is impossible to locate a *spatial extent* quality at an atomic region (assign a single value to it) if the dimensionality of its *location* quality differs from that of the feature it inheres in. In other words, the quale of a quality with a lower dimensionality does not only vary in time but also in space. Such a quality takes a range of possible values at a time. It is located at a non-atomic region in its quality space.

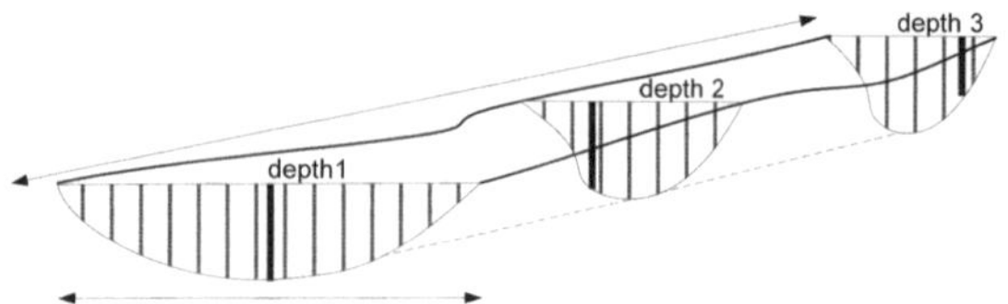

Fig. 4. Example: The water body of a stream is located at a 3D space region. If a *depth* quality is assigned to it, then the 1D space region of the quality has two degrees of freedom within the region of the water body. Exemplarily, three possible locations are depicted.

In the context of information sources dealing with observations and measurements, it appears essential to make sure that the observed quality, e.g. the *depth* of a river is located at an atomic region of its quality space. This requires that qualities with lower dimensionality than their bearers are further specified. This can be achieved in two ways.

1. The spatial location of the quality is defined exactly. In the river example, this is achieved when the water level *at a certain location* is measured. The depth quality is further specified as the depth quality at a certain location and a certain time.

2. The quality is defined to take an atomic quale that takes a clearly identifiable location in the quality space at a certain time. In the river example, this could be the *maximum depth*, the average depth, or any other quale that can be singled out of the range of possible atomic-regions at which the quality can be located.

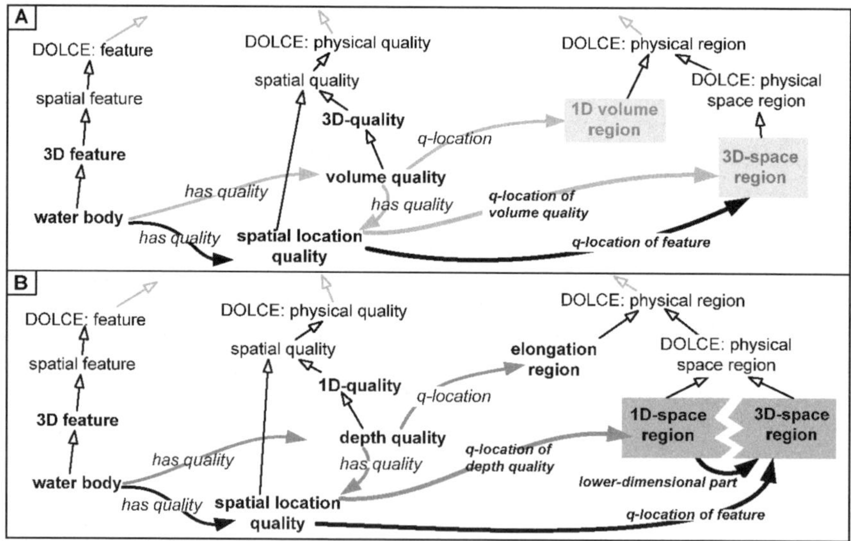

Fig. 5. A: The *volume* quality of a water body has exactly one "value" (quale). The region to which the volume quality refers has no degree of freedom, since it is identical with the space region the water body occupies. **B:** The *depth* quality has a "value range" since the *depth* quality's *spatial location* quality is located in a space region that has two degrees of freedom within the space region of the water body.

Summary and Conclusion

To enable successful discovery of geospatial information sources providing observation results, the first step is to specify precisely the qualities for which observation results are provided and in which physical endurants the quality is inherent.

We presented a first cut at an ontology for spatial qualities based on the foundational ontology DOLCE. Central to our approach is the spatial dimensionality of spatial qualities. This implies that a spatial quality itself has a spatial location quality, and thus a location in physical space. In our approach, a *spatial extent* quality has a direct location in its associated quality space as well as an indirect location in physical space via its *spatial location* quality. For example, the *spatial extent* quality *volume* is located directly in its one-dimensional quality space for volume as well as indirectly in a three-dimensional region in the quality space accounting for physical space.

In order to talk about dimensionality we introduced the categories 1D-SPACE REGION, 2D- SPACE REGION, and 3D- SPACE REGION as subcategories of SPACE REGION, as well as four subcategories for SPATIAL FEATURE (4), where the individuals are classified according to their spatial dimensionality.

A consequence of our approach is that a spatial feature and its *spatial extent* quality both have an individual *spatial location* quality. Central to our approach is that the space regions (spatial qualia) of these two *spatial location* qualities can be

- **identical.** In this case, the relation ***atomic-quale-quality-of*** (9) holds between the feature and its *spatial extent* quality. It indicates that the quality has a single "value" at a time. For example, the volume of a lake has exactly one value at a time.
- **different**. In this case, the relation ***non-atomic-quale-quality-of*** (10) holds between the *spatial extent* quality and its feature. It indicates that the quality has a value range at a certain time. For example, the depth of a lake has a value range at a time.

In the context of information source discovery, discovery systems that implement ontology based-search according to our approach will allow the information requester to start her search with basic level concepts [11]. For example, assume a user interested in observation results of depth qualities of lakes in a certain region. An information discovery system will allow the user to start his search with the notions depth and lake. Since the depth quality is a one-dimensional quality (see Fig. 5) and the water body of the lake is a three-dimensional spatial feature, the spatial location quale of quality and feature are not identical. Thus, the relation defined in (10) holds, indicating that the *depth* quality has a value range at a certain time. At this point, the information discovery system informs the user that she can request only value *ranges* for this combination of quality type and feature type. It is possible that the user implicitly assumed that the notion "lake depth" always refers to the *maximum depth* quality. Information discovery systems based on our approach would enforce to state these assumptions explicitly, e.g. the user has to choose the qualities for which it is possible to return a single observation value, such as the *maximum* depth quality.

In addition to that, our approach allows to specify variances, or any other quality characterizing the *value range* of a quality. The variance accounts for the way in which the "values" of a quality vary. Variance is a quality frequently used in geospatial applications, thus it is important that the underlying ontology can account for it. Variance qualities are only possible if lower dimensional spatial qualities are conceptualized to inhere in higher dimensional spatial features.

Future Work

Spatial extent qualities like height or volume are often assigned as direct qualities to physical objects. In this paper, we proposed that only spatial features should have *spatial extent* qualities. One could further require that only amounts of matter, which constitute physical objects, can have physical qualities like temperature, mass or color. Temporal qualities in turn are direct qualities of perdurants in which a physical object participates. A physical object may play a certain role. Yet, it is the role, which entertains abstract qualities like monetary or historical value. This raises the question: Which direct qualities can be assigned to a physical object?

This investigation was focused on qualities understood as unary characteristics of entities. Further investigations are required to incorporate other kinds of observable entities into the approach, for example binary characteristics such as *directions* or *distances* between spatial entities.

Acknowledgements

Discussions with Krzysztof Janowicz, Eva Klien, Claudio Masolo, Stefano Borgo, Michael Lutz and Werner Kuhn have greatly influenced the ideas presented here. The work has been supported by the German Research Foundation (DFG) grant KU 1368/4-1 (Semantic Reference Systems) and the SWING project (IST-FP6-26514).

References

[1] Masolo, C., Borgo, S., Gangemi, A., Guarino, N., Oltramari, A. *WonderWeb Deliverable D18, Ontology Library (final)*. http://wonderweb.semanticweb.org/deliverables/documents/D18.pdf

[2] Kuhn, W.: *Semantic Reference Systems*. International Journal of Geographical Information Science 17 (2003) 405-409

[3] Guizzardi, G.: Ontological Foundations for Structural Conceptual Models. Enschede, Netherlands (2005)

[4] Bateman, J., Farrar, S.: *Towards a generic foundation for spatial ontology*. In: Proc. Formal Ontology in Information Systems (2004)

[5] Kuhn, W., Raubal, M.: *Implementing Semantic Reference Systems*. In: Proc. AGILE 2003 - 6th AGILE Conference on Geographic Information Science (2003) 63-72

[6] Casati, R., Smith, B., Varzi, A.: *Ontological Tools for Geographic Representation*. In: N. Guarino, (ed.) Formal Ontology in Information Systems. ISO Press (1998) 77-85

[7] Asher, N., Vieu, L.: *Towards a Geometry of Common Sense: A Semantics and a Complete Axiomatization of Mereotopology*. In: Proc. 14th International Joint Conference on Artificial Intelligence (1995) 846-852

[8] Borgo, S., Guarino, N., Masolo, C.: *A Pointless Theory of Space Based On Strong Connection and Congruence*. Principles of Knowledge Representation and Reasoning (1996)

[9] Casati, R., Varzi, A. C.: Parts and Places. The Structures of Spatial Representation. MIT Press, Cambridge, MA (1999)

[10] Kant, I.: Critique of Pure Reason (translation: F. Max Müller). The MacMillan Company, London (1896)

[11] Rosch, E.: *Principles of Categorization*. In: E. Rosch and B. Lloyd, (eds.): Cognition and Categorization. Lawrence Erlbaum Associates (1978) 27-48

Formal Ontology in Information Systems
B. Bennett and C. Fellbaum (Eds.)
IOS Press, 2006

The Image as Spatial Region: Location and Adjacency within the Radiological Image

James M. FIELDING [a,b,1], Dirk MARWEDE [a,c]

[a] *Institute for Formal Ontology and Medical Information Science, Saarland University, Germany*
[b] *Centre for the Study of Pragmatism and Analytic Philosophy, University of Paris I, France*
[c] *Department of Diagnostic Radiology, Leipzig University Hospital, Germany*

Abstract. Biomedical ontologies define entities and relations in order to represent knowledge in the biomedical domain. In this paper we concentrate on the domain of medical imaging. In previous work, we analyzed a representative sample of computed tomography reports in order to determine to which entities and relations the terms used in such reports refer (with regard to the Foundational Model of Anatomy (FMA) and the recently published Open Biomedical Ontology (OBO) Relation Ontology, respectively) in order to construct an imaging ontology for electronic reporting in radiology. In this paper we expand the role of two OBO relations in particular, as they may be applied to radiological image information: the relations **located_in** and **adjacent_to**. Defining these relations in terms of the basic topological relations of Region Connection Calculus (RCC), we show how the qualitative description of image feature locations in radiological reporting may be formalized for reasoning.

Keywords. Biomedical Ontology, Radiology, Imaging, Qualitative Spatial Reasoning.

1. Introduction

In previous work [1], we analyzed a sample of typical CT reports to determine the entities and relations referred to there (with regard to the Foundational Model of Anatomy (FMA) [2], and the OBO Relation Ontology [3], respectively). On the basis of this work, and the ontological principles of Basic Formal Ontology (BFO) [4], we created a prototype application ontology, called RadIO [5], for the electronic management of radiological reporting, capable of integrating the RSNA's RadLex lexicon [6] with the canonical anatomical knowledge of the FMA. In this application ontology, we supplemented the OBO relations with a set of radiology-specific relations for ascribing image features like *shape*, *morphology*, *size* and *signal* to the entities appearing in these images. However, since these relations were generally hold between entities and their atomic properties, the reasoning capability afforded was minimal at best. In what follows, we return to the domain of medical imaging, adapting the OBO relations of **located_in** and **adjacent_to** to the two-dimensional realm of the

---

[1] Corresponding Author: James Fielding, IFOMIS, Universität des Saarlandes, Postfach 151150, D-66041 Saarbrücken, Germany; Email: matthew.fielding@ifomis.uni-saarland.de.

radiological image, in order to demonstrate how these relations may afford a significantly greater degree of reasoning in the imaging domain.

1.1. Clinical Radiology

Radiology departments nowadays are highly computerized environments. Apart from the image acquisition process, images are reconstructed after acquisition (post-processing techniques), stored in huge database repositories (or PACS, picture archiving communication systems), and distributed within networks which allow the images to be displayed on dedicated workstations to the radiologists or clinicians in remote locations. Radiologists interpret these images and dictate a report of their findings, in recent times via speech recognition software. These reports are then stored in radiological information systems (RIS) as free-text. In general, little is known about the terminology used by radiologists, and consequently (despite the fact that these reports serve as the basis for the communication of diagnostic results across practitioners), the management of radiology reports has not been significantly affected by IT tools such as ontologies [7].

1.2. Biomedical Ontologies

Today, the word 'ontology' enjoys two different meanings. In the context of knowledge representation, *ontology* is frequently used to describe concepts modeled in a specific domain and the relations which are supposed to exist between those concepts. In the context of philosophy, *ontology* is concerned with the types of entities existing in reality and with the relations that exist between these types and their corresponding instances. From this philosophical point of view, the representation of entities and relations in reality is not restricted to the definition of the concepts used by experts in a specific domain. These definitions employ a terminology specific to the domain in question, which only hinders the understanding of these concepts from a view outside of that domain, and thus the interoperability of the resultant ontology when interfaced with ontologies from other neighbouring domains. In order to realize interoperability, these various domain-specific application ontologies require a reference, according to the principles of which they are standardized; for example, the FMA, which may be commonly applied across the various biomedical subdomains that require recourse to anatomical knowledge. This distinction between *application* and *reference ontologies* applies not only to entity types, but to relations as well. One major obstacle to the interoperability of currently existing ontologies is that, to date, no standard set of formal ontological relations has been universally accepted. Within the Open Biological Ontology framework (OBO), however, a set of top-level ontological relations has recently been published to address this problem. These relations give ontology researchers the tools required for the development and integration of biomedical ontologies: clear definitions for a set of relations commonly applicable throughout the biomedical domain.

2. Ontological Foundations of the Medical Imaging Domain

2.1 Types and Instances

The term 'type' is here used to refer to what in the knowledge representation community is occasionally expressed under the heading of 'concept' or 'class' and what in the philosophical literature are called 'universals' or 'kinds'. A type is that which is general in reality. By contrast, instances are those things that are particular individuals. Instances exist in time and space and relate to each other in a variety of instance-level relations. The type *abdomen* is a universal in the biomedical domain; an instance of this type is the particular abdomen of a particular patient at a particular time and place. Similarly, the type *image of abdomen* is a universal in the biomedical imaging domain; an instance of this type is a concrete image that can be viewed and described in its particular reality.

2.2. Continuants and Perdurants

Continuants and processes are two sorts of entities that relate in different ways to time [4]. Continuants are those entities that continue through time, wholly present at each moment of their existence. Examples of biomedical continuants are entities such as organs, cells, and medical devices, as well as their properties. Examples of biomedical image continuants are static images of the lung, or liver, etc, but also the particular properties present in these images such as colour patches, or image shadows. Processes, on the other hand, are those sorts of entities that are never fully present at any one moment in time, but instead unfold themselves in successive phases or temporal parts. Entities such as these, which perdure through time, are events such as the heart's pumping of blood, a surgery session, or the many processes by which an image of the human body is attained, such as the application of x-rays. In our current work, we deal only with static images, although in principle, such an analysis could extend to dynamic video as well.

2.3. Fiat and Bona Fide Entities

Not all the boundaries between entities in reality correspond to some absolute determinable location, such as the boundary between one's teeth, between the lungs and mediastinum, or between one kidney and another. In biomedical reality, the boundaries between many entities and regions do not always correspond to any genuine qualitative or numeric change; as Germany and France have been divided from one another by political agreement, so too have the exact boundaries between the right pulmonary artery and truncus pulmonaris, for example, been established by the convention of medical practitioners. With entities of this sort, given any particular region at some arbitrarily small level of granularity, it may not be possible to determine whether this region belongs to one entity or the other; however, (like Germany and France) this does not mean that there exists no real boundary between them. Following [8], we call entities and boundaries of the first type *bona fide*, and entities and boundaries of the second type *fiat*.

2.4. The Radiological Notion of 'Finding'

The assertions made by a radiologist when reporting, for example 'normal liver,' signify that the liver in an image *appears to be* normal. This is particularly important to note since not all pathologies are susceptible to all imaging techniques at all times (cancer on the cellular level, for example), and a liver that appears normal in an image may not in fact be so. The ways bodily entities appear on the image depend on the imaging technique applied, and the right technique must be applied to return the proper results; a lung imaged with magnetic resonance (MRI), for example, appears differently than the same lung imaged with a computed tomography (CT). In the context of reporting imaging observations, radiologists have introduced the notion of *finding* for any appearance that is not considered normal. In radiological practice, a *finding* can range from simple features like *density* or *shape* to highly interpretative diagnoses like *pneumonia* or *malignant neoplastic tumour* [9]. Independently of how radiologists look at body entities projected on an image, or what techniques are employed, it is necessary to make the distinction between these two domains of reality explicit: the domain of the body and the domain of the image.

2.5. Image Entities

The ontological category of *image entity* is our solution to this distinction. Image entities, like all other entities, are divided according to the type/instance (i.e. universal/particular) and continuant/perdurant (i.e. static/dynamic) distinctions. Similarly, they are susceptible to both *bona fide* and *fiat* boundaries. In our radiological image ontology, we distinguish three image entity types: *anatomical image entity*, *pathological image entity*, and *visual feature*.

Anatomical Image Entity. Most terms found in radiology reports referred to the appearance of anatomical entities. These terms include those referring to the appearance of *bona fide* anatomical entities, i.e. those entities physically delimited by the object itself, like anatomical structures such as organs and some organ parts (e.g. lung, or left lung), anatomical spaces (e.g. thoracic cavity, perirenal space), and body substances (e.g. blood). Also included are terms that refer to the appearance of *fiat* entities, i.e. entities which reflect human demarcation, such as some organ parts (e.g. liver segment) and body regions (e.g. upper abdomen). The anatomical image entities of this category are images of those types of entities typically represented in canonical anatomy ontologies such as the FMA.

Pathological Image Entities. The non-anatomical image entities referred to in radiology reports are of two sorts: 1. the appearance of pathological structures and spaces, and 2. the appearance of biomedical artifacts such as medical devices and implants. Of the pathological sort, are terms referring to the appearance of pathological structures (e.g. tumour), substances (e.g. pleura effusion), and spaces (e.g. bulla). The corporeal entities that correspond to the image entities in this category are those typically represented within disease classification systems like SNOMED-CT [10] or the International Classification of Diseases (ICD) [11].

Image Features. Image features are visual properties of anatomical and pathological image entities that further qualify them. Terms such as 'round,' 'large,' or 'dense,' are used by radiologists to describe the various visual characteristics of entities as they appear in the image. It is on the basis of these features that a radiologist interprets an image and asserts whether it indicates a normal or pathological condition.

3. OBO and RCC Relations Applied to the Radiological Image

In our previous work, we have shown that a number of radiology-specific relations can be provided (in particular, the relations **has_shape**, **has_size**, **has_composition**, **has_coordinate**, and **has_signal**). However, since these relations are generally used solely for ascribing atomic properties to image entities, their reasoning capacity is severely limited. Despite this limited reasoning capacity however, applying the OBO relations of **located_in** and **adjacent_to** to the imaging domain, we may define these relations in terms of the basic set of definitions of Region Connection Calculus (see, for example, [12]). These definitions may subsequently be used for reasoning about the specific location and orientation of 2D image entities.

3.1. OBO Primitive Relations

Not all relations can be defined, for otherwise we risk infinite regress. Hence, some relations have been declared as primitive in the OBO framework; these relations are domain-neutral, and as far as possible, self-explanatory. This category includes relations such as **has_part, has_participant**, **has_agent,** and **derives_from**, among others. The two primitive OBO relations most frequently found in the reports we examined are **located_in** and **adjacent_to**. In the radiological domain, these relations are most frequently used to relate pathological image entities to the anatomical image entities that serve as their 'host,' and thus form a large portion of the information required by radiologists.

The relation of **located_in** is formulated in the OBO framework as follows:

> c **located_in** r **at** t: a primitive relation between a continuant instance and a spatial region which it exactly occupies at a time.

As stated in the OBO documentation, this relation thus 'reflects the fact that each continuant is at any given time associated with exactly one spatial region, namely its exact location,' though this may subsequently be expanded to include location relations holding between two continuant instances or two spatial region instances. As with the OBO framework, we have adapted this basic location relation to hold between spatial regions located within each other; however, in our adaptation this relation holds independently of time, as the image is in fact a "snap-shot" and does not change relative to this time.

The relation of **adjacent_to** is formulated in the OBO framework as follows:

> c **adjacent_to** c_i **at** t: a primitive relation of proximity between two disjoint continuants at a time.

Adapting these relations to the biomedical imaging domain allows us to define a set of more specific relations that fall under these as subtypes. For example, the image of the lumen of the right pulmonary artery in a radiograph such as a CT-scan (see

Image 1) forms an extended space, which passes out of the space of mediastinum and into the space of the right lung. Defining a set of more specific location relations, allows us, for example, to specify the exact location of the thrombus referred to above in relation to either the mediastinum or the right lung, or both.

3.2. RCC Basics

RCC is based on a single primitive: the 'connection' relation (C). At its most basic level, this relation is reflexive and symmetric, formalized as follows:

$\forall x C(x,x)$ — reflexivity: all spatial entities are connected to themselves

$\forall x,y C(x,y) \rightarrow C(y,x)$ — symmetry: if x is connected to y, then y is connected to x

Additional relations that may hold between two regions may be defined in terms of C using the following simple set of definitions:

$DCxy = def. -C(x,y)$	x is disconnected from y
$Pxy = def. \forall z[C(z,x) \rightarrow C(z,y)]$	x is part of y
$Pixy = def. Pyx$	Inverse of Pxy
$PPxy = def. P(x,y) \& -P(y,x)$	x is a proper part of y
$EQxy = def. P(x,y) \& P(y,x)$	x coincides with y
$Oxy = def. \exists z[P(z,x) \& P(z,y)]$	x overlaps with y
$DRxy = def. -O(x,y)$	x is discrete from y
$POxy = def. O(x,y) \& -P(x,y) \& -P(y,x)$	x partially overlaps y
$ECxy = def. C(x,y) \& -O(x,y)$	x externally connects with y
$TPPxy = def. PP(x,y) \& \exists z[EC(z,x) \& EC(z,y)]$	x is a tangential PP of y
$TPPixy = def. TPPyx$	Inverse of $TPPxy$
$NTPPxy = def. PP(x,y) \& -\exists z[EC(z,x) \& EC(z,y)]$	x is a non-tangential PP of y
$NTPPixy = def. NTPPyx$	Inverse of $NTPPxy$

This set of definitions provides the foundation for what is known as the 'RRC-8' set, comprising PO, TPP, NTPP, EQ, TPPi, NTPPi, EC, and DC (cf. Fig. 1). As these relations provide a basic foundation for reasoning about spatial regions, we focus our efforts here. Subsequent work will involve expanding this set to include more complex relations, and validating the utility of these formalisms for the imaging domain.

The upper part of Figure 1 shows the subsumption lattice of possible relations holding between pairs of regions, all of which are definable purely in term of C; these lines connect the set of more restrictive relations (lower) to more inclusive ones (higher). For example, two regions standing in the mid-level relationship DR (i.e. are discrete from each other) can stand in either of the two more expressive, lower-level relations EC or DC (i.e. external connection or disconnection). The middle part of Figure 1 shows the standard graphic representation for each of these relations defined for two regions, *a* and *b*.

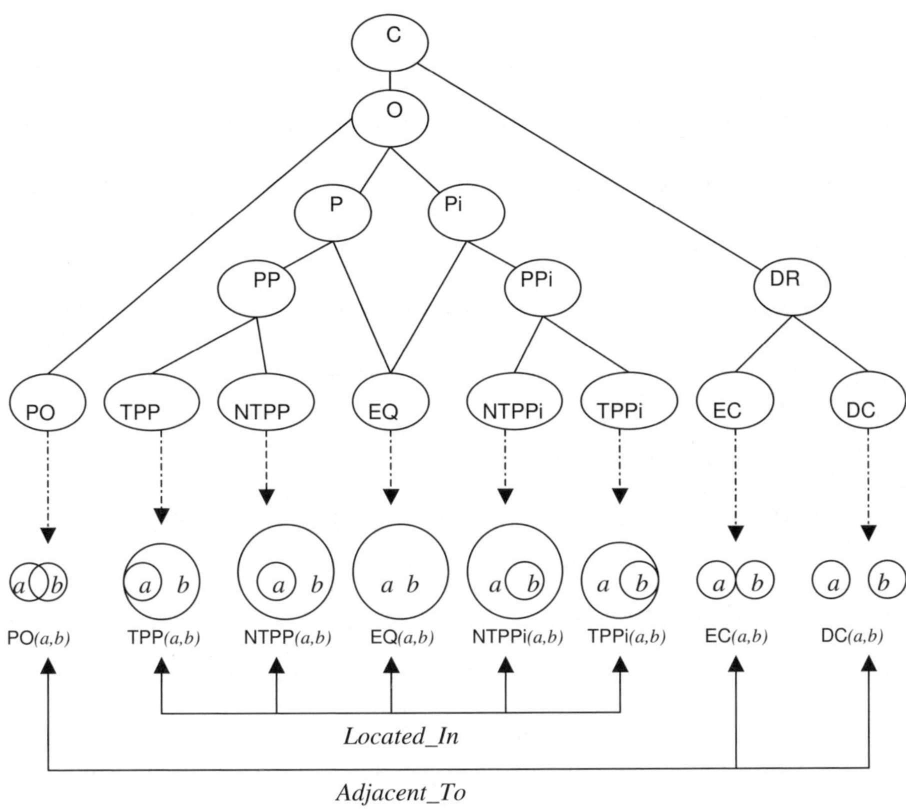

Figure 1. Subsumption hierarchy with graphic interpretations of the basic RCC-8 relations and OBO alignments

3.3. RadIO-Varieties of the **Located_In** and **Adjacent_To** Relations

The bottom part of Figure 1 shows the relationship classes of our adaptation of the RCC relations to the OBO relations of **located_in** and **adjacent_to**; we call these relations 'RadIO-varieties' to highlight the fact that these are not anatomical in the strict sense of the word, but apply only to the spatial regions of the image and not to the anatomical entities themselves. (A tumour, located in the right lung, for example, could never be defined as a part of the right lung, but the spatial region occupied by the tumour in an image would be a proper part of the spatial region occupied by the image of the right lung.) In our radiological adaptation of the basic RCC-8 relations, TPP, NTPP, NTPPi (the inverse of NTPP) and TPPi (the inverse of TPP) belong to RadIO specifications of the **located_in** relation, and the relations of PO, EC, and DC belong to the RadIO specifications of the **adjacent_to** relation. While these RadIO specifications do not themselves play any role in the ontology's spatial reasoning (this is properly left to the RCC relations), they do provide a platform for integrating applications that have need or spatial reasoning (such as RadIO) with other applications also conforming to the OBO standard that do not (and thus still have recourse to the OBO location and adjacency relation).

These specifications require that we adapt the basic OBO location relations to reflect the specific ontological structures of the two-dimensional image entities which are our concern here. For instance, because all image entities are of a homogeneous structure no matter what they represent (even hollow spaces such as the lungs are as solid as any other anatomical image entity, ontologically, it is only their signal values that differ), our radiological version of the location relation holds not between a continuant entity and a spatial region which it occupies (as the definition above states), but rather between one continuant image entity and another, so that:

> An image entity c is **RadIO_located_in** another image entity c_I, when the RCC parthood relation holds between the spatial region r, exactly occupied by the continuant image entity c, and the spatial region r_I, exactly occupied by c_I, independently of time.

We formalize this relation as follows:

> c **RadIO_located_in** c_I =*def.* $\exists r, r_I$ (c **located_in** r & c_I **located_in** r_I & $P(r,r_I)$)

While the **adjacent_to** relation (as holding between continuant entities of all sorts) can be imported into the two-dimensional realm of the radiological image quite naturally, we still need to account for a few of the fundamental differences implied in the imaging domain. First, the OBO relation of adjacency states above that two continuants standing in this relation are disjoint; while this definition holds for continuant image entities as well, it is somewhat different for the spatial regions which they occupy. Since spatial image regions are created by projecting three-dimensional entities upon a two-dimensional surface, the spatial regions of properly disjoint entities may in fact overlap in the image (i.e., share a part), although they do not do so in reality. To account for this, we are required to generalize the notion of adjacency to include those cases where overlapping of spatial region occurs in the image, so that:

> An image entity c is **RadIO_adjacent_to** another image entity c_I, when the RCC parthood relation holds between neither of the regions r or r_I, exactly occupied by c and c_I, and c is adjacent to c_I or r and r_I overlap (i.e. there is a third region r_2 which stands in the RCC parthood relation to both r and r_I), independently of time.

We formalize this relation as follows:

> c **RadIO_adjacent_to** c_I =*def.* $\exists r, r_I$(c **located_in** r & c_I **located_in** r_I & - $(P(r,r_I)$ v $Pi(r,r_I))$ & c **adjacent_to** c_I v $PO(r,r_I)))$

In addition, note that the definition of the OBO **adjacent_to** relation states that adjacency is 'a relation of proximity' and (since this relation is primitive) there are no criteria for determining exactly how proximal two entities must be in order to satisfy this relation. Thus, where the location relations in the **RadIO_located_in** come more or less for free, the definition governing the **RadIO_adjacent_to** intrinsically requires that the OBO adjacency relation already holds (unless PO holds, as we have defined this relation). The OBO adjacency does we indeed come for free in the case of the RCC relation of external connection (what connects, but does not overlap, must be adjacent), and as we have seen we can expand our radiological definition of adjacency to include overlap; however, we cannot infer adjacency from the RCC relation of disconnection. Two disconnected regions may or may not be adjacent, and this can only be determined by the examining radiologist based on entities in question, the normal position in which they stand, and the context under which the examination was performed. We qualify this relation therefore with the following disjunction:

$$c \textbf{ RadIO\_adjacent\_to } c_1 \equiv \exists r, r_1 \, ((c \textbf{ located\_in } r \ \& \ c_1 \textbf{ located\_in } r_1) \ \& \ ((\text{PO}(r,r_1) \lor \text{EC}(r,r_1) \lor (\text{DC}(r,r_1) \ \& \ c \textbf{ adjacent\_to } c_1))))$$

Providing RCC-varieties of the adjacency relation proved slightly more difficult than the location relation, mainly due to ambiguity in the type of language we use to ascribe adjacency, which could be used to describe an image entity's orientation with or without connection (perhaps a thin membrane or other anatomical boundary separates them), and in some cases, with a partial overlap, where the regions remain distinct enough so as not to be 'located in' exactly, but are situated in a proximate space. For a formalism defined in terms of 'connection,' these details hold a heavy ontological weight: therefore, attributing adjacency in our application ontology, a radiologist will be required to specify which of these important distinctions holds.

3.4. Reasoning with RCC and Radiological Images

The main reasoning mechanism used by RCC is the composition table, containing information about the transitive closure of RCC relation pairs. The composition table for RCC-8 is shown in Table 1. Given three spatial regions, $a, b,$ and $c,$ and two RCC relations, R_1 and $R_2,$ such that $R_1(a,b)$ and $R_2(b,c)$ holds, the composition table can be used to determine $R_3,$ the set of RCC relationships that may hold between regions a and $c.$ In cases where several alternative relationships might hold, the composition table entry represents a disjunction of these relations.

$R_1(x,y)$ \ $R_2(y,z)$	DC	EC	PO	TPP	NTPP	TPPi	NTPPi	EQ
DC	no info	DR, PO, PP	DR, PO, PP	DR, PO, PP	DR, PO, PP	DC	DC	DC
EC	DR, PO, PPi	DR, PO, TPP, TPPi	DR, PO, PP	EC, PO, PP	PO, PP	DR	DC	EC
PO	DR, PO, PPi	DR, PO, PPi	no info	PO, PP	PO, PP	DR, PO, PPi	DR, PO, PPi	PO
TPP	DC	DR	DR, PO, PP	PP	NTPP	DR, PO, TPP, TPPi	DR, PO, PPi	TPP
NTPP	DC	DC	DR, PO, PP	NTPP	NTPP	DR, PO, PP	no info	NTPP
TPPi	DR, PO, PPi	EC, PO, PPi	PO, PPi	PO, TPP, TPPi	PO,PP	PPi	NTPPi	TPPi
NTPPi	DR, PO, PPi	PO, PPi	PO, PPi	PO, PPi	O	NTPPi	NTPPi	NTPPi
EQ	DC	EC	PO	TPP	NTPP	TPPi	NTPPi	EQ

Table 1. RCC-8 Relational Composition Table

4. Informed Reporting via the Imaging Domain Ontology

Reporting on anatomical image entities can be performed by evaluating an anatomical image entity as normal, or by describing visual features and pathological image entities located in these anatomical image entities and interpreting those observations. In this section, we take a typical example from the biomedical imaging domain. We demonstrate how the location and orientation of the image entities contained there may be qualitatively described by radiologists and how these may subsequently be used for spatial reasoning concerning the entities involved.

4.1. Example: Acute Pulmonary Embolism

Image 1 is one of a series of CT image slices taken from the thorax, a few centimeters above the heart. A typical free-text report documenting these findings, might read something like:

> Central subtotal thromboembolism with a large thrombus located in the right pulmonary artery and the left lower lobe artery extending through almost the full diameter of the vessels. Bilateral pleural effusion, predominantly on the right side. Degenerative change of the thoracic spine.

1	Truncus pulmonalis
2	Aorta ascendens
3	Aorta descendens
4	Right Lung
5	Left Lung
6	Right pulmonary artery
7	Thrombus in the right pulmonary artery.
8	Thrombus in the left lower lobe pulmonary artery.
9	Pleural effusion
10	Thoracic vertebral body.

Table 2. Continuant image entities of Image 1.

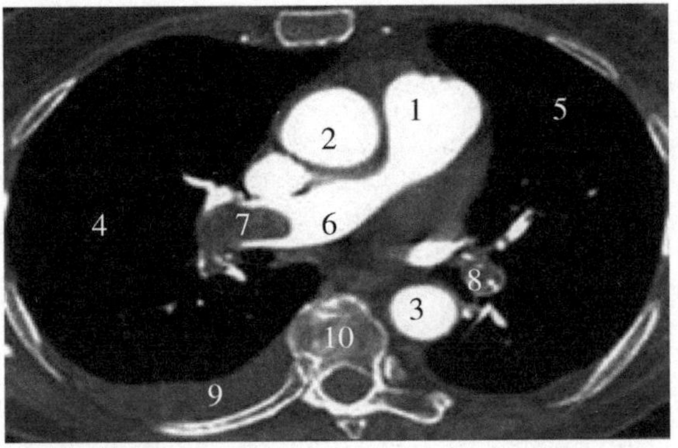

Image 1. CT-Scan of the thorax showing the pulmonary arteries with embolism

In our ontology-based report manager, the radiologist, having specified that a thrombus is located in the right pulmonary artery, would be given a series of more specific RCC-variety location relations to choose from (namely, PP, PPi, TPP, TPPi, NTPP, or NTPPi), further specifying the exact location of the thrombus with regard to the right pulmonary artery, at which point, the examining radiologist would in this case select TPP (tangential proper part). This statement would be formalized as follow:

TTP(*thrombus, right pulmonary artery*)

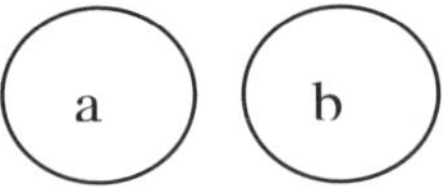

Since the right pulmonary artery extends beyond the boundaries of the mediastinum into the right lung however, we may determine the location of this thrombus more specifically with regard to the lungs. Given that:

PO(*right pulmonary artery, right lung*)

From the RCC-8 composition table, we can infer that one of the following relations will hold:

i)   DR(*thrombus right lung*), or
ii) PO(*thrombus, right lung*), or
iii) PP(*thrombus, right lung*).

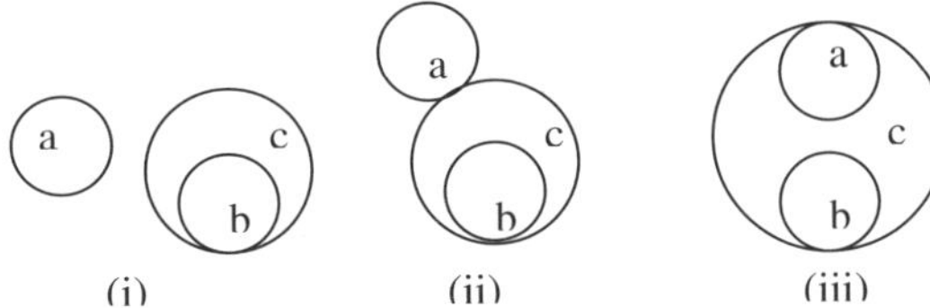

In other words, the thrombus is either *discrete from, partially overlapping with,* or *a proper part of,* the right lung. At this point, the radiologist will be given this selection of possible relations for further specifying the exact location of the thrombus in regard to the right lung – in this case, *partial overlap* – because some part of the thrombus is located in the region of the lung and some part in the region of the mediastinum, which distinguishes the location of this thrombus from that of the thrombus located in the left lower lobe artery, which is a proper part (i.e. completely contained within the region) of the left lung.

5. Conclusion

This paper presents the foundations for developing a robust theory of qualitative spatial location appropriate for reasoning with information about radiographic images. We have shown how the image may be divided up into discrete image entities (anatomical and pathological image entities), and a set of qualitative RCC-based spatial relations that may hold between these entities (connection, parthood, overlap, etc.). The RCC relations are additionally grouped around a pair of primitive OBO relations, **located_in** and **adjacent_to**. Adopting the RCC framework for reasoning with these relations and entities allows us to determine additional information about the location and orientation of these entities, information which may not be explicitly provided by radiologists when annotating images in their reports, expanding the scope of our application ontology and the type of information that may be contained therein. Grouping these RCC relations around standard OBO relations provides a platform for integrating applications which require spatial reasoning (like RadIO, presented in part here) with those that do not, while contradicting the principles of neither.

Acknowledgements

The present paper was written under the auspices of the Wolfgang Paul Program of the Alexander von Humboldt Foundation, the Network of Excellence in Semantic Interoperability and Data Mining in Biomedicine of the European Union, and the project Forms of Life sponsored by the Volkswagen Foundation.

References

[1]   Marwede D, Fielding JM, Smith B. Entities and Relations in Medical Imaging: An Analysis of Computed Tomography Reporting. Forthcoming.
[2]   Rosse C, Mejino JL, Jr. A Reference Ontology for Biomedical Informatics: the Foundational Model of Anatomy 5. *Journal of Biomedical Informatics* 2003 Dec; 36(6):478-500.
[3]   Smith B, Ceusters W, Klagges B, Kohler J, Kumar A, Lomax J, Mungall CJ, Neuhaus F, Rector A, Rosse C. Relations in Biomedical Ontologies. *Gnome Biology*, 2005.
[4]   Grenon P, Smith B, Goldberg L. Biodynamic Ontology: Applying BFO in the Biomedical Domain. *Studies in Health, Technology, Information* 2004; 1002:20-38.
[5]   Marwede D, Fielding JM. RadIO: A Prototype Application Ontology for Radiology Reporting Tasks. Forthcoming.
[6]   http://mirc.rsna.org/radlex/services
[7]   Langlotz CP. Automatic Structuring of Radiology Reports: Harbinger of a Second Information Revolution in Radiology 6. *Radiology* 2002 Jul; 224(1):5-7.
[8]   Smith B. Fiat Objects. *Topoi: International Review of Philosophy* 2001; 20(2):131-148.
[9]   Bell DS, Pattison-Gordon E, Greenes RA. Experiments in Concept Modeling for Radiographic Image Reports. *Journal of the American Medical Informatics Association*, 1994; 1(3): 249-62.
[10]   Spackman K. SNOMED RT and SNOMED CT. Promise of an international clinical terminology. *MD Computing* 2000 Nov; 17(6): 29.
[11]   Parman CC. ICD-10-CM. *Journal of Oncology Management* 2004 Jan;13(1):8.
[12]   Gotts NM, Gooday JM, Cohn AG. A Connection Based Approach to Common-Sense Topological Description and Reasoning. *Monist* 1996; 79(1): 51-75.

3. Ontology in Biology and Biochemistry

Formal Ontology in Information Systems
B. Bennett and C. Fellbaum (Eds.)
IOS Press, 2006

From GENIA to BIOTOP

Towards a Top-Level Ontology for Biology

Stefan SCHULZ [a,1], Elena BEISSWANGER [b], Udo HAHN [b], Joachim WERMTER [b], Anand KUMAR [c], Holger STENZHORN [c]

[a] *Department of Medical Informatics, Freiburg University Hospital, Germany*
[b] *Jena University Language and Information Engineering (JULIE) Lab, Germany*
[c] *Institute for Formal Ontology and Medical Information Science (IFOMIS), Saarbrücken, Germany*

Abstract. The increasing need for advanced ontology-based knowledge management in the life sciences is generally being acknowledged but, up until now, the development of biological ontologies lacks adherence to foundational principles of ontology design. This is particularly true of so-called upper-level ontologies such as the GENIA ontology which covers biological continuants and has mainly been devised for corpus annotation in a text mining context. As an alternative, we introduce BIOTOP, an upper ontology of physical continuants in the domain of biology, with a coverage similar to the GENIA ontology. We report on design specifications and modeling decisions for BIOTOP which are based upon formal ontology principles. As a major desideratum, these continuants are described in terms of necessary and sufficient conditions. We accomplished this goal for 85 out of the 146 existing GENIA classes. We use OWL-DL as a formal knowledge representation language and may thus use a terminological reasoner for classification in order to check and maintain consistency during the ontology engineering phase.

Keywords. Bio-Ontologies, Upper-Level Ontologies, OWL-DL

1. Introduction

The rapid increase of scientific knowledge in the life sciences has created an enormous need for advanced knowledge management in this field. As a consequence, many efforts have been devoted to develop description languages to help structure the knowledge of this domain. Whereas cell biology and genomics have only marginally been covered by the traditional clinical vocabularies (such as the roughly 100 sources made available by the Unified Medical Language System (UMLS) [17]), the development of the Gene Ontology [7] and, more generally, the Open Biomedical Ontologies (OBO) framework [13] have put the case of ontology development at the very top of their task agenda.

As with the UMLS, each OBO ontology is independently developed and provides a partial, highly focused view on biology and medicine, fueled by the specific interests of various ontology designers. OBO includes at present (July 2006) 58 ontologies covering

---

[1]Corresponding Author: Stefan Schulz, Department of Medical Informatics, Freiburg University Hospital, Stefan-Meier-Strasse 26, 79104 Freiburg, Germany; E-mail: stschulz@uni-freiburg.de.

cell types and components, the anatomy and development of several organisms (plants and animals), chemical entities, biological pathways and processes, molecular functions and others. The OBO ontologies, up until now, adhere to a rather simple design pattern: Nodes (called terms) are organized in directed acyclic graphs (DAGs) with labeled edges (relations) such as *Is_A*, *Part_Of*, *Develops_From* and others.

Most of the OBO ontologies were created in a completely informal and ad-hoc fashion which is likely to create conflicting and contradictory interpretations. For example, in the statement *A Part_Of B* (with *A* and *B* being OBO terms which we consider as referring to universals), the assertion that "some instances of A are part of some instances of B" is quite different from the assertion that "all instances of A are part of some instance of B" or that "all instances of B have and instance of A as part" [23,18]. A proposal has recently been made to provide consistent and unambiguous formal definitions of the relational expressions that ontologies in OBO [21] should adhere to.

The necessity of a generalized upper-level to support the interoperability between different domain ontologies and to enforce the consistency in the process of ontology construction and maintenance has been advocated by many researchers though this goal still has not been realized so far. Whilst several proposals for general-purpose upper ontologies exist (e.g., DOLCE [6] and BFO [22]) and are already subject to vivid discussions, this issue is not really on the radar in the biology domain.

Whereas BIO-BFO [8] and Simple Bio Upper Ontology [15] are sketched without any concrete application context, the GENIA upper ontology is most commonly used for the semantic annotation of texts by the biological text mining community. According to its designers, GENIA

> "is intended to be a formal model of cell signaling reactions in human. It is to be used as a basis of thesauri and semantic dictionaries for natural language processing applications such as information retrieval and filtering, information extraction, document and term classification and categorization. Another use of the GENIA ontology is to provide the basis for an integrated view of multiple databases. [24]"

The GENIA ontology limits itself to a set of highly general upper-level categories and is restricted to biological continuants. It contains 45 terms (called "classes") which are arranged in a tree-wise fashion at a maximum depth of 6 nodes. Besides the taxonomic relation *Is_A* it does not contain any further relations or definitory axioms. Instead, so-called "scope notes" informally phrase the meaning of the single classes as natural language statements [24]. As said above, the predominant application of the GENIA ontology targets semantic annotation of named entities in biological literature abstracts [14].

In this paper we propose a common upper ontology for biology and adopt the GENIA ontology as the starting point for its development. Taking different traditions of ontology development into account we define a set of best-practice principles and use them for a critique of the GENIA ontology as well as the subsequent design of a new upper ontology of biological continuants. The newly designed ontology is intended to facilitate the interoperability between existing biomedical ontologies, e.g., the Gene Ontology, ChEBI, the Mouse Ontology and other OBO ontologies, but also medical ontologies such as the Foundational Model of Anatomy (FMA) and SNOMED CT. Due to precisely defined axioms this newly created ontology has the potential to be more rigorous, consistent and valid than its precursors.

2. Methodology

2.1. Different Traditions of Ontology Design

One may distinguish three fundamentally different approaches to ontology design due to different traditions, interests and purposes. These different approaches still give rise to misunderstandings and often fruitless discussions. We refer to them as (i) the lexical-cognitivist, (ii) the philosophical-realist, and (iii) the computer science approach.

2.2. The Lexical-Cognitivist Approach to Ontology Design

Natural language constitutes the primary means of communication between domain experts, as used in scientific publications, textbooks, glossaries and dictionaries. The abstraction from word meanings is therefore the most natural way domain experts, such as biologists, chemists or physicians (generally lacking in-depth knowledge in philosophy, logics and computer science) tend to organize their domains of interest. Related to the methodologies developed by lexicographers and librarians, this approach is also supported by the cognitive science community which is more interested in describing the mental representation of reality rather than in the mind-independent reality itself. Prototypical features of concepts (as the entities of thought) therefore guide the enterprise of ontology construction. Evidence for this language and cognition centered view is the preference of the words "terms" or "concepts" for describing the nodes in an ontology, as well as the restriction to inter-concept relations which depict semantic association (of what "normally" has a good degree of plausibility) rather than subscribing to strict formal properties of the relational statements being used. A discussion of semantic underspecifications of concept-to-concept relationships is often regarded as some kind of sophistry. This position is also backed by philosophical positions which dispute the accessibility of a mind-independent reality.

2.3. The Philosophical-Realist Approach to Ontology Design

Regardless of inter-philosophical divergences (which are often difficult to communicate to the outside world), philosophers who dedicate themselves to formal ontologies generally build upon a millenary tradition of metaphysics and logics. Their endeavor of exactly describing entities of being in their essence generally requires a rich inventory of logical constructs. For many purposes, first-order logics is considered as insufficient for adequately describing reality. The claim of describing reality by logical statements is most decidedly raised by the Aristotelian tradition. Accordingly, classifying the world's entities in terms of their genera and differentiae is adopted as a fundamental guideline for the design of formal ontologies.

2.4. The Computer Science Approach to Ontology Design

Computer science has borrowed the term "ontology" from philosophy, using it preferably in the hitherto non-existent plural form. Here, ontologies are mainly conceived as computable abstractions of certain domains of interest, mainly driven by concrete application requirements. Traditionally, only little emphasis has been put on upper ontologies which has somewhat changed with the advent of the Semantic Web. However, the view prevails that different ontologies represent different and, unfortunately, partly incompatible views of a given reality. Rather than focusing on upper ontologies, computer science ontologists tend to feel more challenged by the tasks of semantic mediation and brokerage. Another contrast to purely philosophical ontologists is the strong focus on computability. Therefore, higher-order logics and even full first-order logics are commonly discarded due to their high computational costs. The attempt of describing more tractable subsets of logic was one of the major driving forces of developing description logics [1].

2.5. Principles of Ontology Building and Critique

A reasonable starting point for the ontological analysis of the biological upper-level is given by the following principles [5]: (i) select a set of foundational relations, (ii) define the ground axioms for these relations, (iii) establish constraints across the basic relations, (iv) define a set of formal properties induced by these formal relations, (v) introduce the basic categories and classify the relevant kinds of domain entities accordingly, and, finally, (vi) elicit the dependencies and interrelations among the basic categories. In our case, most of these basic categories are borrowed from the upper ontologies BFO [22] and DOLCE [6] enriched by principles introduced by Rector *et al.* [16]. Accordingly, we adopt the generally accepted, mutually exclusive divisions between universals and particulars on the one hand, and between continuants and occurrents on the other. Particulars (individuals) are the concrete and countable entities in the world (e.g., "my hand") whereas universals are entities which are instantiated by particulars (e.g., "hand"[2]). Orthogonal to this dichotomy, a fundamental distinction between continuants and occurrents is also commonly introduced. The GENIA ontology has no explicit category for occurrents[3] and hence its focus is put on the representation of continuants.

Furthermore we subscribe to the canonical relations[4] recently adopted by OBO [21]: **Instance_of** relates an individual entity to a certain class. *Is_A* relates two classes in terms of taxonomic subsumption. The relation **part_of** and its inverse **has_part** relate individuals in terms of parthood.[5] Furthermore, **derives_from** holds between an individual which was either identical or part of another individual at some instant in time. Finally, **has_function** and its inverse **inheres** hold between individual material entities (such as molecules) and their inherent (biological) functions. As a subcategory of dependent continuants we introduce here the important notion of *biological function*. Although function is not addressed directly by the current state of the GENIA ontology, it will prove necessary for a complete definitory framework of GENIA classes.

---

[2]In the context of this paper the term *universal* will be considered synonymous with the terms *class* and *type*. We refrain from the use of the term *concept* due to its multiple, partly contradictory senses. Our distinction between universals and particulars is made explicit by strict naming conventions: names of universals use *Upper Case* initials, while names of particulars are written in *lower case* letters.

[3]In practice, annotators have been using the residual category "other" for tagging occurrents.

[4]We use the following naming conventions: Relations in which one or more individuals are involved are expressed by means of **bold face expressions and lower case initials**. Relations involving classes only come with *Upper Case Initials and Italic Fonts*.

[5]We understand parthood as proper parthood in the sense of formal mereology [20], i.e., a transitive, irreflexive and asymmetric relation.

2.6. Analysis and Reconstruction of GENIA

Our approach to design a new ontology covering the existing GENIA classes rests on the following steps:

1. We analyze each GENIA "scope note" in terms of its definitory value, both under an intensional (i.e., the definition) and an extensional (i.e., the subordinate classes) point of view. We hereby focus on how the linguistic expressions contain sufficient information to delimit the meaning of the associated term and the extension of the class it refers to.

2. Under the assumption of the current GENIA ontology being a taxonomy we analyze it with regard to proper classification principles. Keeping in mind that a major purpose of GENIA is to unambiguously assign exactly one semantic label to each text entity under scrutiny, this requires a mono-hierarchical classification tree with pair-wise disjoint and exhaustive classes at each classificatory level.

3. We logically redefine the classes, exploiting both the associated scope notes and canonical biological knowledge. As we are aware of the fact that a comprehensive ontological account often requires a highly expressive language, we do not a priori impose any restriction on that language. However, wherever computationally expensive formalizations result, we transform them into a simplified representation using OWL-DL, according to the preferences of the computer science approach to ontology implementation. The expressivity problems can most likely be solved by integrating rules through the Semantic Web Rule Language (SWRL) [11] in our BIOTOP implementation. This framework built on top of OWL-DL allows to combine class definitions with rules and, by doing so, makes it feasible to express complex facts that cannot be expressed using class definitions alone. A caveat is that the rules must be applied carefully to avoid excessive computational costs. If applied with care, however, they can certainly improve the existing coverage of the domain. Hence, their use will be investigated as a future step in the development of BIOTOP.

4. A major requirement rarely met by any existing biological ontology is the introduction of true definitions. This means that both the necessary (i.e., getting from a class to its conditions) and the sufficient conditions (i.e., getting from the conditions to a specific class) for class membership which need to be described. The latter is one of the main requirements in order to fully exploit the inferential power of description logic reasoners such as RACER [10]. Machine reasoning is then used for checking the logical consistency of the ontology. Any inconsistency found will then require additional change iterations. We expect that abstraction from full first-order logic will lead to a loss of expressivity which we intend to counterbalance by the introduction of auxiliary constructs.

5. The interfaces to existing ontologies such as the Gene Ontology, CHEBI, etc. are identified. Besides this, the new ontology should exhibit a sufficient granularity and coverage to support a mapping to the classes of the GENIA ontologies without ambiguities. This would meet the requirements of the text mining community for which GENIA has evolved as a kind of a quasi standard.

3. Analysis of GENIA

3.1. Analysis of Scope Notes

A general impression of the scope notes is that besides cursory hints to related terms, they do not contain sufficient definitory information. A reason for this may be that the annotators using GENIA were too familiar with these terms and hence believed that no additional information was required. Summarizing some of the typical shortcomings, Table 1 reveals that only a quarter of all classes are fully defined by their scope note. Half of the GENIA classes are incompletely described by just enumerating their subclasses or listing examples. Yet another quarter does not even have a scope note.

3.2. Analysis of GENIA's Ontological Structure

A formally correct taxonomic classification is done on the basis of the ontological nature of the entities. Classes in an ontology stand for universals (or logical expressions denoting universals), whilst instances correspond to entities which cannot be instantiated [5]. Whereas it is straightforward to assume classes such as organism, cell, individual DNA (desoxyribonucleic acid) molecule to be instantiated by concrete entities (e.g., "this individual cell under this microscope"), we also observed numerous oddities which arise with regard to other classes such as source, cell type, tissue, protein family or group. identified the following kinds of classes which require deeper ontological inquiry.

3.2.1. Source and Substance

The division between "Source" and (chemical) "Substance" constitutes the uppermost partition of the GENIA ontology. Whereas "Substance" refers to chemical substances involved in biochemical reactions, "Sources" are defined as "biological locations where substances are found and their reactions take place". They are subdivided into natural (such as organism, cell) and artificial sources (such as cell line). As much as it may be acceptable that for specific purposes biological objects are not distinguished from the space they occupy, biological location can hardly be accepted as a suitable upper-level distinction. For example, "Natural Source" subsumes different kinds of entities (cell, cell component) which also occur in artificial sources, e.g., cell lines. Our suggestion is therefore to treat "Source" as a role and not as top-level class.

Feature	Occurrences	Class	Scope Note
No Definition	11	Carbohydrate	
Examples Only	18	Amino Acid Monomer	An amino acid monomer, e.g., tyr, ser
Partial Definition	2	Artificial Sources	Cultured, immortalized or otherwise artificially processed sources
Full Definition	10	Domain or Region of Protein	A tertiary structure that is supposed to have a particular function, e.g., SH2
Enumeration of Subclasses	4	Organism	Organisms include multi- and mono-cell organisms

Table 1. Analysis of GENIA scope notes

3.2.2. Cell Type

"Cell Type" occurs as a sibling of "Organism" and "Tissue" and is vaguely described in the corresponding scope note as "a cell type, e.g., T-lymphocyte, T-cell, astrocyte, fibroblast". Here the question arises whether the attribute "type" is merely a notational flavor or conveys an additional meaning, e.g., a metaproperty instantiated by universals instead of individuals [5]. An instance of "Cell Type" would therefore not be an individual cell but rather a universal such as "Fibroblast" or "Leukocyte". But in turn this argument would equally justify the creation of classes such as "Tissue Type" or "Organism Type". In any case, such classes would specialize the class "Natural Source" since sources are defined as biological locations and a "Cell Type" is definitely not a biological location. Hence we suggest to ignore the meta-level reading and read "Cell Type" as "Cell".

3.2.3. Family or Group

A similar problem can be found with classes labeled "Family or Group" (in the DNA, RNA and Protein branch) defined by GENIA as "a family or a group of proteins, e.g., STATs[6]". Such a class definition addresses the need of a reference to instances of a human-made classification scheme for proteins rather than to instances of biological classes. That again, would correspond to a meta-class reading leading to conflicts with the parent classes "Protein" and "Substance". We may argue that such classification schemes follow biological functions, locations and other roles (e.g., structure proteins, enzymes, or transport proteins) and because of this an account for this phenomenon by a separate branch of the ontology (e.g., "Role", "Function", "Entity of Classification") would be required.

3.2.4. Other

Residual categories, although repeatedly criticized [3,2], are characteristic for classification systems since they allow for an exhaustive, non-overlapping coverage of a given domain even for those entities which do not fall into the properly defined categories. GENIA's use of residual categories (e.g., "Other Natural Source", "Other Organic Compound") is however quite inconsistent because residual categories are only present in some partitions but missing in others (e.g., "Natural Source"). Although residual classes are ontologically irrelevant (i.e., their instances lack a common property), they can nevertheless be formalized as the logical complement to the union of their siblings. However, they may be misused for classifying those instances which are simply underspecified due to missing information and hence degrade the quality of classification.

3.2.5. Masses, Aggregates and Collectives

Many kinds of biological and chemical entities occur as collectives of uniform objects (e.g., cell collections or H_2O molecules). More complex aggregations of cells and intracellular matrices are present in biological tissues. A prototypical example is "Tissue", described in GENIA as "a tissue, e.g., peripheral blood, lymphoid tissue, vascular endothelium". That is not a proper definition but merely an enumeration of possible subclasses. For instance, "Tissue" in a biological context denotes an aggregate of cells and intracellular substances. Due to this fact it is not clear what exactly is an instance of

---

[6]Signal Transducers and Activators of Transcription

"Tissue". The main difficulty here is to make a clear commitment to the referents of such mass or collection terms. In principle, there are good arguments to refer to either (i) the totality of the mass/collective (e.g., all red blood cells (RBCs) in an organism), (ii) any portion of it (e.g., the RBCs in a lab sample) or (iii) the minimal constituent (e.g., a single RBC). So far there is no biological ontology which sufficiently accounts for the distinction between single objects and collectives.

4. Design of the BIOTOP Ontology

The design of BIOTOP (Biological Top-Level) was done by two of the authors with good knowledge in description logics as well as molecular biology. For ontology engineering, we used the Protégé ontology editor [12] supported by the RACER terminological reasoner [10] for consistency checking. This framework required a restriction to the OWL-DL language specification. BIOTOP contains a total of 146 classes (85 fully defined), 12 relations and 171 restrictions. The ontology successfully classifies on a middle-end laptop computer in about four minutes. It is available for download from `http://morphine.coling.uni-freiburg.de/~schulz/BioTop/BioTop.html`. In the course of engineering the BIOTOP ontology, several design decisions were taken which we discuss next.

4.1. Relations

In addition to the class-level taxonomy-building *Is_A* relation, we introduced the mereological relations **proper_part_of** and **has_proper_part** which relate individuals. Although the OBO relations proposal prefers the reflexive reading (e.g., "my body is part of itself") [21], we adopt the irreflexive variant for two reasons. Firstly, reflexivity is counterintuitive in biology since the common language use of 'part' excludes identity. Secondly the OWL-DL language specification does not support reflexive relations. Just as proposed by Simons [20], taking **proper_part_of** as a primitive is just a matter of convention. The relations **proper_part_of** and **has_proper_part** are subrelations of **located_in** and **location_of**, respectively [21]. The refining criteria for distinguishing **proper_part_of** from **located_in** are complex and discussed in [19]. Two subrelation pairs of **has_proper_part** were introduced, *viz.* **has_grain** and **grain_of** (according to [16]) as well as **component_of** and **has_component**, respectively, both relations being intransitive. The relation **has_grain** allows for the definition of collectives (i.e., amounts of cells, molecules, etc.) in terms of their constituent objects. The relation **has_component** relates compounds to their constituent components. An example for this is the relation between a protein chain and its constituent amino acid monomers. The criterion for the assignment of this subrelation is based on the notion of a partition: all parts related by **has_component** are mutually non-overlapping and sum up to the whole entity. We can formally deduce this relation from **has_proper_part** as follows (using $\sum$ for the mereological sum [25] and the RCC relations **po** for proper spatial overlap and **dc** for spatial disconnection [4]):

$$\textbf{has\_component}_P(a, b_0) \leftrightarrow \tag{1}$$

$$\exists a, b_0, ..., b_n : \bigcap_{\nu=0}^{n} \textbf{has\_proper\_part}(a, b_\nu) \cap \left[\bigcap_{\nu=0}^{n-1} \bigcap_{\mu=\nu+1}^{n} \neg\textbf{po}(b_\nu, b_\mu) \right] \cap \sum_{\nu=0}^{n} b_\nu = a$$

The relation **has_grain** can be formalized in a similar way:

$$\textbf{has\_grain}(a, b_0) \leftrightarrow \exists a, b_0, ..., b_n : \bigcap_{\nu=0}^{n} \textbf{instance\_of}(b_\nu, B) \cap \qquad (2)$$

$$\bigcap_{\nu=0}^{n} \textbf{has\_proper\_part}(a, b_\nu) \cap \left[\bigcap_{\nu=0}^{n-1} \bigcap_{\mu=\nu+1}^{n} \textbf{dc}(b_\nu, b_\mu) \right] \cap \sum_{\nu=0}^{n} b_\nu = a$$

Whereas a compound's sortal identity depends on the exact sum of its components, a collective identity does not. If one removes a single blood cell from a given blood sample then the type of the sample still remains the same. But if a nucleotide is removed from a gene sequence then it instantiates a different type. Another criterion is that grains unlike components are not spatially connected. However, this requires a clear-cut conceptualization of connection. Another difference between grains and components can be found in the relation between components and compounds depending on a partition (see subscript P in formula 1). There may be different ways to dissect an entity into compounds. Consider a human skeleton which is normally partitioned into its 206 bones. A more coarse-grained partition (e.g., considering skull and pelvis single components), however, is also possible. Also, a DNA sequence can be partitioned either into nucleotides or into tri-nucleotide units called codons with each coding for a single amino acid. Finally, the arrangement of components is fundamentally relevant to the nature of the compound, whereas the arrangement of grains is irrelevant for the collective. (This issue is not considered in the above formula.)

Since it is not possible to directly translate the above formula into OWL-DL, these considerations need to be added via primitive classes. Future versions of the BIOTOP ontology may discard those primitive classes and instead apply SWRL rules at this point.

4.2. Collectives

The introduction of collectives as classes of their own, in contrast to their constituent objects, is justified by the ontological difference between these two kinds of entities and the referential ambiguity which can commonly be observed in texts. From a cognitive point of view, a distinction between masses and collectives is plausible, since humans perceive them in a different way and therefore use different language constructs (e.g., "some blood", "du sang", "Blut" vs. "erythrocytes", "des érythrocytes", "Erythrozyten"). This is the reason why DOLCE makes an ontological distinction between "Collection" and "Amount of Matter". We consider such a distinction arguable since is depends on the scale of granularity and type distinction. Due to the atomicity of matter, actually any amount of matter can be described as a collective of particles. We even refrain from an upper distinction between collectives and count entities because any material continuant can be regarded as a collection of elementary particles.

4.3. New Classes

In order to (at least partly) fulfill our objective of describing ontology classes in terms of full definitions, we introduced additional classes, many of which are only textually addressed in the GENIA scope notes. An example of this is the class "Particle". It was originally meant to represent the classical notion of molecule or atom as constituent of matter. As a property of such a class we required that it should not be homomerous, i.e., no part of a particle itself should be a particle. Classifying the ontology under this constraint immediately led to a series of inconsistencies. A closer analysis of chemical entities revealed that it is indeed highly problematic to classify chemical entities in terms of unity [9]. Whereas at the level of small molecules this could still be accounted for by additional subdivisions (e.g., amino acid molecule vs. amino acid residue) this is nearly impossible for the domain of macromolecules in which several flavors of chemical bonds (i.e., hydrogen bonds, polar bonds and ionic bonds) are responsible for a broad and continuous range of cohesive forces. We therefore dropped the notion of a whole and consequently the requirement of non-homomerity for particles.

A further example of a newly introduced class is "Heterocyclic Base" which is used for the definition of "Nucleotide". Compared to other ontologies, the number of fully defined classes (i.e., definitions in terms of both necessary and sufficient attributes) is quite high. Interestingly, there are no such definitory statements in any of the current OBO ontologies.

4.4. Rearranged Classes

Some classes in the original GENIA ontology are misleading. For instance, "Amino Acid" subsumes any compound which contains amino acids though the term is regularily used for amino acid monomers. Hence we introduced the classes "Amino Acid Monomer" and "Amino Acid Polymer" in order to avoid confusion. Generally, there seems to be a major confusion in the domain concerning monomers, polymers and subdivisions of polymers. The prototypical example for this is DNA. According to the GENIA ontology, the term DNA refers to one or more of

1. a DNA monomer constituted by a base, desoxyribose and a phospate residue;
2. one polymer constituted by DNA monomers, bound together by covalent bonds;
3. two complementary strands of DNA polymers (cf. 2), joined by hydrogen bonds;
4. any subdivision of item 2 or 3, provided it is made up of more than one DNA monomer.

In BIOTOP we therefore made a sortal distinction between DNA monomer (according to item 1), full DNA (according to item 2) and DNA which corresponds to item 4. Double strands are considered to be of different types.

4.5. New Branches

As already pointed out, the "Family or Group" categories from the original GENIA ontology are improperly arranged in the hierarchy. In GENIA these categories were included to denote terms such as "enzyme" or "membrane protein". In a statement such as "the enzyme E", "enzyme" refers to a biological function whereas "E" refers to an amount of molecules. What is meant here is that "E" exercises the function "enzyme". In order to account for this peculiarity we introduced an additional branch named "Non-Physical Continuant" which subsumes "Biological Function" together with "Biological Location". Just as in the GENIA ontology, BIOTOP does not elaborate on biological processes, events, or actions. In the current version it only contains one single class named "Occurrent". An enhancement towards a more detailed description of this kind of entities will constitute an important issue of future work.

4.6. Mapping to GENIA

In order to guarantee downward compatibility, the original GENIA ontology was added as an additional layer, in a separate step. To this end, all terminal GENIA nodes (i.e., those which are used for semantic annotation) were added as jointly exclusive classes and linked to the BIOTOP classes by *Is_A* relations. Consistency is assured by applying the terminological reasoner.

4.7. Interfacing with Other Ontologies

Several BIOTOP classes can be used as links to other existing ontologies. For example, "(Bio)Molecular Function", "Cellular Component" and "Biological Process" provide links to the homonymous branches of the Gene Ontology. The same can be applied to the CHEBI ontology. "Molecular Function$_{BioTop}$" interfaces with "Biological Role$_{ChEBI}$", "Atom$_{BioTop}$" and "Compound$_{BioTop}$" with "Molecular Entities$_{ChEBI}$" and "Subatomic Particles$_{BioTop}$" with "Elementary Particles$_{ChEBI}$". "Organism$_{BioTop}$", "Tissue$_{BioTop}$" and "Body Part$_{BioTop}$" can finally be linked to species-specific OBO ontologies, to the Foundational Model of Anatomy (FMA) and to clinical terminologies.

5. Discussion and Conclusion

In this paper we introduced design principles and modeling decisions for the biological top-level ontology BIOTOP which is based on the GENIA ontology/annotation vocabulary as a semantic glue for connecting existing biomedical ontologies. BIOTOP has been devised as a rather expressive model which makes use of the full range of OWL-DL constructs. Future applications of BIOTOP will include the provision of semantically precise classes to improve the quality of semantically annotated corpora (while keeping downward compatibility to GENIA) and the assurance the consistency of biological ontologies in the further development of OBO and clinical terminologies. The latter goal may be partially impaired by the high computing demands of BIOTOP as a consequence of its expressiveness. We also plan to augment the current purely OWL-DL based implementation with SWRL rules. By doing so we believe to overcome the still existing expressivity gaps (stemming from the insufficient OWL-DL constructs) and hence to achieve better domain coverage. Necessary further steps will be BIOTOP's enhancement in the domain of biological functions and processes and the (semi-automatic) generation of natural language definitions in order to facilitate its usage and to assure its adequacy.

Acknowledgments. This research was supported by the European Network of Excellence "Semantic Mining" (NoE 507505). The second, third, and fourth author were additionally funded by the BOOTStrep project under grant FP6-028099, both within the EC's 6th Framework Programme.

References

[1]   F. Baader, D. Calvanese, D. L. McGuinness, D. Nardi, and P. F. Patel-Schneider, editors. *The Description Logic Handbook. Theory, Implementation, and Applications.* Cambridge, U.K.: Cambridge University Press, 2003.

[2]   O. Bodenreider, B. Smith, and A. Burgun. The ontology-epistemology divide: A case study in medical terminology. In Achille C. Varzi and Laure Vieu, editors, *Proceedings of FOIS 2004*, pages 185–195.

[3]   J. J. Cimino. Auditing the Unified Medical Language System with semantic methods. *Journal of the American Medical Informatics Association*, 5(1):41–45, 1998.

[4]   A. G. Cohn. Formalising bio-spatial knowledge. In Chris Welty and Barry Smith, editors, *Proceedings of FOIS 2001*, pages 198–209.

[5]   A. Gangemi, N. Guarino, C. Masolo, and A. Oltramari. Understanding top-level ontological distinctions. In *Proceedings of the IJCAI-01 Workshop on Ontologies and Information Sharing*, pages 26–33, 2001.

[6]   A. Gangemi, N. Guarino, C. Masolo, A. Oltramari, and L. Schneider. Sweetening ontologies with dolce. In *Proceedings of EKAW 2002*, pages 166–181.

[7]   Gene Ontology Consortium. Creating the Gene Ontology resource: Design and implementation. *Genome Research*, 11(8):1425–1433, 2001.

[8]   P. Grenon, B. Smith, and L. Goldberg. Biodynamic ontology: Applying BFO in the biomedical domain. In *Ontologies in Medicine*, number 102 in Studies in Health Technology and Informatics, pages 20–38, 2004.

[9]   N. Guarino and C. A. Welty. Identity, unity, and individuality: Towards a formal toolkit for ontological analysis. In *Proceedings of ECAI 2000*, pages 219–223.

[10] V. Haarslev and R. Möller. RACER: A core inference engine for the Semantic Web. In *Proceedings of the 2nd International Workshop on Evaluation of Ontology-based Tools, Located at ISWC 2003*, pages 27–36, 2003.

[11] I. Horrocks, P. F. Patel-Schneider, H. Boley, S. Tabet, B. Grosof, and M. Dean. SWRL: A Semantic Web Rule Language Combining OWL and RuleML, 2004. `[http://www.w3.org/Submission/SWRL]` Last accessed: May 5th, 2006.

[12] N. Fridman Noy, R. W. Fergerson, and M. A. Musen. The knowledge model of PROTEGE-2000: Combining interoperability and flexibility. In *Proceedings of EKAW 2000*, pages 17–32.

[13] OBO. Open Biological Ontologies (obo), 2005. `[http://obo.sourceforge.net]` Last accessed June 26th, 2005.

[14] T. Ohta, Y. Tateisi, and J.-D. Kim. The GENIA corpus: An annotated research abstract corpus in molecular biology domain. In *HLT 2002 – Proceedings of the 2nd International Conference on Human Language Technology Research*, pages 82–86.

[15] A. Rector, R. Stevens, and J. Rogers. Simple bio upper ontology, 2006. `[http://www.cs.man.ac.uk/~rector/ontologies/simple-top-bio]` Last accessed: May 5th, 2006.

[16] A. L. Rector, J. Rogers, and T. Bittner. Granularity, scale and collectivity: When size does and does not matter. *Journal of Biomedical Informatics*, 39(3):333–349, 2006.

[17] UMLS. *Unified Medical Language System.* Bethesda, MD: National Library of Medicine, 2005.

[18] S. Schulz and U. Hahn. Parthood as spatial inclusion: Evidence from biomedical conceptualizations. In *Proceedings KR 2004*, pages 55–63.

[19] S. Schulz, A. Kumar, and T. Bittner. Biomedical ontologies: What *part-of* is and isn't. *Journal of Biomedical Informatics*, 39(3):350–361, 2006.

[20] P. Simons. *Parts: A Study in Ontology.* Oxford: Clarendon Press, 1987.

[21] B. Smith, W. Ceusters, B. Klagges, J. Köhler, A. Kumar, J. Lomax, C. Mungall, F. Neuhaus, A. L. Rector, and C. Rosse. Relations in biomedical ontologies. *Genome Biology*, 6(5):R46 (1:15), 2005.

[22] B. Smith and P. Grenon. The cornucopia of formal-ontological relations. *Dialectica*, 58(3):279–296, 2004.

[23] B. Smith, J. Williams, and S. Schulze-Kremer. The ontology of the Gene Ontology. In *Proceedings of the 2003 Annual Symposium of the American Medical Informatics Association*, pages 609–613, 2003.

[24] Tsujii Laboratory. Genia project home page, 2003. `[www-tsujii.is.s.u-tokyo.ac.jp/GENIA]` Last accessed: May 5th, 2006.

[25] A. C. Varzi. Mereology. In Edward N. Zalta, editor, *Stanford Encyclopedia of Philosophy*. Stanford: The Metaphysics Research Lab, 2003. `[plato.stanford.edu]` Last accessed: May 5th, 2006.

Formal Ontology in Information Systems
B. Bennett and C. Fellbaum (Eds.)
IOS Press, 2006

Modular Ontology Design Using Canonical Building Blocks in the Biochemistry Domain

Christopher J. THOMAS[1], Amit P. SHETH[1] and William S. YORK[2]

[1] LSDIS Lab, Department of Computer Science, University of Georgia
[2] Complex Carbohydrate Research Center (CCRC), University of Georgia
Athens, Georgia, USA
{cthomas, amit}@cs.uga.edu, will@ccrc.uga.edu

Abstract

The field of BioInformatics has become a major venue for the development and application of computational ontologies. Ranging from controlled vocabularies to annotation of experimental data to reasoning tasks, BioOntologies are advancing to form a comprehensive knowledge foundation in this field. With the Glycomics Ontology (GlycO), we are aiming at providing both a sufficiently large knowledge base and a schema that allows classification of and reasoning about the concepts we expect to encounter in the glycoproteomics field. The schema exploits the expressiveness of OWL-DL to place restrictions on relationships, thus making it suitable to be used as a means to classify new instance data. On the instance level, the knowledge is modularized to address granularity issues regularly found in ontology design. Larger structures are semantically composed from smaller canonical building blocks. The information needed to populate the knowledge base is automatically extracted from several partially overlapping sources. In order to avoid multiple entries, transformation and disambiguation techniques are applied. An intelligent search is then used to identify the individual building blocks that model the larger chemical structures. To ensure ontological soundness, GlycO has been annotated with OntoClean properties and evaluated with respect to those. In order to facilitate its use in conjunction with other biomedical Ontologies, GlycO has been checked for NCBO compliance and has been submitted to the OBO website

1. Introduction

The field of BioInformatics has seen a dramatic increase of available ontologies for many of the life sciences domains. The Ontologies in the OBO project [17], especially the Gene Ontology (GO) [6] with its comprehensive schema and thousands of instances, take leading roles. As a broad lexicon or dictionary, GO serves one of the major purposes of ontologies: facilitating agreement. However, it is not designed for extensive computational use, so the amount of machine-accessible knowledge is limited. Only two types of relationships between the different entities in the ontology are formalized, *is_a* and *part_of*. Other relationships can only be simulated by reification of new terms that are then used in the *is_a* and *part_of* hierarchies [22].

An ontology that provides rich, machine accessible relationships must be formalized. Knowledge modeling languages such as KIF [7], RDF [13] or the W3C-recommended Ontology Web Language OWL [11] allow such formalizations with different expressiveness. OWL in its three flavors Lite, DL and Full promises to be a good compromise between expressiveness and computational complexity on the one hand and versatility and simplicity on the other.

In the context of the "BioInformatics for Glycan Expression" core of the NCRR Integrated Resource for Biomedical Glycomics project, a suite of web-accessible ontologies has been developed for the glycoproteomics domain. The goal of this suite is to have a basis for description, annotation and reasoning, such that every step from experimental setup over experimental conduct and analysis to acquisition of hypotheses and theories can be formalized. This paper focuses on issues related to representation, expressiveness, granularity and instance population in the development of the Glycan Structure Ontology GlycO.

Glycans are complex carbohydrate structures, which play key roles in the development and maintenance of living cells. Glycans are built from simpler monosaccharide residues (such as mannose and glucose), which constitute the nodes of tree structures with edges that are comprised of chemical bonds between the residues. The synthesis of these glycans in organisms is an intricate process that can be modeled as a collection of biosynthetic pathways. At each step in such a pathway, an enzyme-catalyzed reaction 'adds' a new residue as a leaf to an existing structure or 'moves' a whole sub-tree to a different parent. It is well established that alongside genes and proteins, glycans play a major role in cell functions.

The aim of glycoproteomics is to understand cellular processes that are mediated by the interaction of proteins, the genes that encode them, and the glycans that are attached to their surfaces. Our goal in developing GlycO has been to assess the extent to which knowledge in this domain can be logically formalized to facilitate the discovery and specification of relationships between the glycan structures, their metabolism, and their functions. Among the challenges faced were those of a limited expressiveness of the chosen OWL-DL standard, and mereological issues of granularity.

The main contributions of this work include:

- Creating a more meaningful domain model by
  - Building a schema that captures the richness of the domain using expressive language, esp. restrictions
  - Supporting modeling of molecular structures that are important for domain scientists
  - Rigorously modeling with canonical instances used as building blocks
- Populating the ontology by extracting and disambiguating instance information from multiple heterogeneous sources
- Allowing for more meaningful queries by formalizing knowledge that is usually inferred in database models
- Addressing granularity issues

Following this introduction, section 2 will describe the conceptualization and formalization of the glycoproteomics domain in GlycO. section 3 will detail the sources and algorithms used for the automatic population, while section 4 will evaluate GlycO and discuss the impact it can have on biochemical applications. Section 5 finally concludes the paper.

2. Ontology Design

2.1   General Considerations

The rules of syntax alone cannot determine the meaning of the statements expressed by the words in that syntax. A fundamental aspect of ontology development is the capture of semantics in a formal syntax, i.e., the unambiguous formalization of statements or states of affairs. Representation of meaning using first order logic is limited to stating that an object has certain properties and relationships with other objects. Even generalizing these properties to sets or classes of objects bears problems [22]. It is necessary to find a balance between the unambiguous representation of objects including their relationships and any attempt to capture the infinitude of relationships present in the world.

We therefore are limited to modeling very specific problems that require a finite amount of representation. The critical objects and their relationships must be identified and then formalized so that machines can infer new or implicit knowledge from the given information. Despite the identified fact that syntax incompletely determines semantics, in cases of restricted domains the actual words and their order in a statement can correspond quite directly to the meaning of it. Hence, if we know the rules that govern the syntax as well as the context, the words and their syntactical structure often suffice to determine their meaning.

Collections of biological entities, such as genes, proteins and carbohydrates, are assumed to have a syntactic structure, much like natural language. For example, we assume that the structure of the genome directly or indirectly encodes the structure of the entire organism. By knowing the syntactic and semantic rules that govern gene structure, we can assign meanings to DNA strings and substrings, *i.e.*, identify genes and the protein sequences they encode. Of course, this is not always a trivial task, but provided the genes themselves (and not their environmental context) constitute the information basis, we can gain a large amount of knowledge by studying gene syntax and semantics. We make a similar simplifying assumption for glycans, which clearly influence cellular properties. Ideally, we can capture the correspondence between a glycoprotein's biological properties and the presence of specific glycan structures at specific locations on the protein's surface.

Developing a highly expressive formal ontology for a comparatively narrow field of research requires the constant interaction between domain experts and knowledge engineers. The modeling of knowledge calls for a profound understanding of a domain. The domain expert must fully participate in ontology development and understand the formalisms used for specifying the conceptualization of the domain. Conversely, the knowledge engineer must analyze the ontology to avoid ontological fallacies in modeling. The Ontoclean methodology [9] explains how concepts should be classified on a meta-level according to distinctions like rigid versus non-rigid concepts, entities versus roles, etc. The knowledge engineer must have enough domain knowledge to apply these distinctions to the ontology.

Although GlycO is focused on the glycoproteomics domain, it is critical that it is sufficiently comprehensive to invoke important concepts in the related disciplines of proteomics and genomics. By providing links to other ontologies that describe the fields closely related to glycoproteomics, it allows for scientific discovery of complex or unknown relationships across research fields. Because it is assumed that the ontology will be used for such discovery, it needed to be strongly restricted to clearly distinguish the asserted concepts by semantically modeling the subtle differences in glycan structure that modulate their biological functions. Only then a correct identification of discovered concepts and relationships can be achieved. GlycO is meant to be more than a controlled vocabulary; its intention is to be used for reasoning in scientific analysis and discovery.

2.2   Schema Design

Initially, the glycoproteomics domain was broadly analyzed, terms were collected, and the way these terms are used by scientists was examined. It turns out that the informal usage of the *is_a* relationship, as in "a glycan is a carbohydrate", implies a hierarchy of concepts with multiple inheritances. We wanted to keep the "colloquial" use of the biochemistry terminology consistent with the ontology, while also adding more distinguishing descriptions in the form of named relationships and their restrictions. There are many ways of classifying monosaccharide residues, which are the building blocks of glycans. For example, it is possible (and equally valid) to classify them according to the number of carbon atoms in the monosaccharide or as a structural variant. That is, a -D-Glc*p* residue can be identified amongst other criteria as both a hexosyl residue (with 6 carbons) and an aldosyl residue (embodying the aldo- structural variant). We account for all of these properties by allowing a particular monosaccharide residue to inherit from several super classes. Whether this directed acyclic graph is explicitly asserted or subsequently inferred is secondary. For example, the absolute configuration D and subsumption by the superclass *residue* are necessary and sufficient properties of the class D-*residue*. A reasoner will automatically subsume any *residue* class that has the absolute configuration D under the class D-*residue*. A hierarchy with multiple inheritance will almost always automatically arise when a more sophisticated logical description of classes is used alongside restricting conditions. For this reason, criticism of multiple inheritance, as in [23] seems impractical to us.

The first level of abstraction contains the three classes "*Chemical Entity*", "*Chemical Property*" and "*Reaction*". This is an appropriate starting point in that upper level ontologies such as SUMO distinguish between "Object", "Attribute" and "Process". The Gene Ontology uses *cellular_component*, *biological_process* and *molecular_function* on the first level of abstraction. The analog to *molecular_function* is in our case defined in the functional ontology *EnzyO [4]*, which describes enzymes and their functions. This compliance with standard classifications facilitates the integration of GlycO with other ontologies. From there, a finely grained class hierarchy is defined (see Figure 1 for a selection of the first 4 levels of the GlycO hierarchy).

The relationship hierarchy in GlycO is built with respect to emerging standards in the biomedical domain. The OBO relationship ontology [17][22] is used as a starting point and more refined named relationships are added. See Figure 2 for a part of the GlycO relationship hierarchy.

With 14 levels, GlycO has a deeper hierarchy than many other domain ontologies. This finely grained class design is essential for the purposes of evaluating experimental results using the knowledge stored in the ontology. Small differences in the glycan structure might affect the kind of interactions an individual glycan or members of a class of glycans have with other objects in the ontology.

The hierarchy of concepts is one aspect of semantics captured in an ontology, but the addition of other relationships is required to realize an expressive model. A concept by itself might be useful for a human observer, but only by understanding it within a context of other concepts. Scientists infer related concepts according to their background knowledge. For machines, this background knowledge needs to be stated explicitly. The authors of [23] raised the issue that the biomedical ontology MGED contained too many named relationships that impede the computational use of the ontology. We disagree with this assessment of ontology design. A large number of named relationship increases the semantic value of an ontology [21], if these relationships are well defined. We address the dilemma of generality versus computational complexity by making use of a relationship hierarchy, modeling the relationships from more general down to more specific. Upper level relationships are e.g. *has_part* or *affects* and their inverses. Inheriting lower level relationships restrict domains and ranges of the upper level relationships. For example, *has_carbohydrate_residue* is essentially a *has_part* relationship, but its domain is restricted to *glycan* and its range is restricted to *carbohydrate_residue*. If the ontology is to be merged or aligned, an alignment algorithm will be able to map this relationship to a more general relationship in a different ontology that does not explicitly formalize the specific *has_carbohydrate_residue* relationship.

As the name indicates, a class hierarchy provides a means of classification. Together with relationships and restrictions it specifies what can possibly exist within the realm that is described. Classes themselves exist only in a very abstract sense. The instances in the ontology are meant to provide a representation of the things that actually exist in the domain of interest.

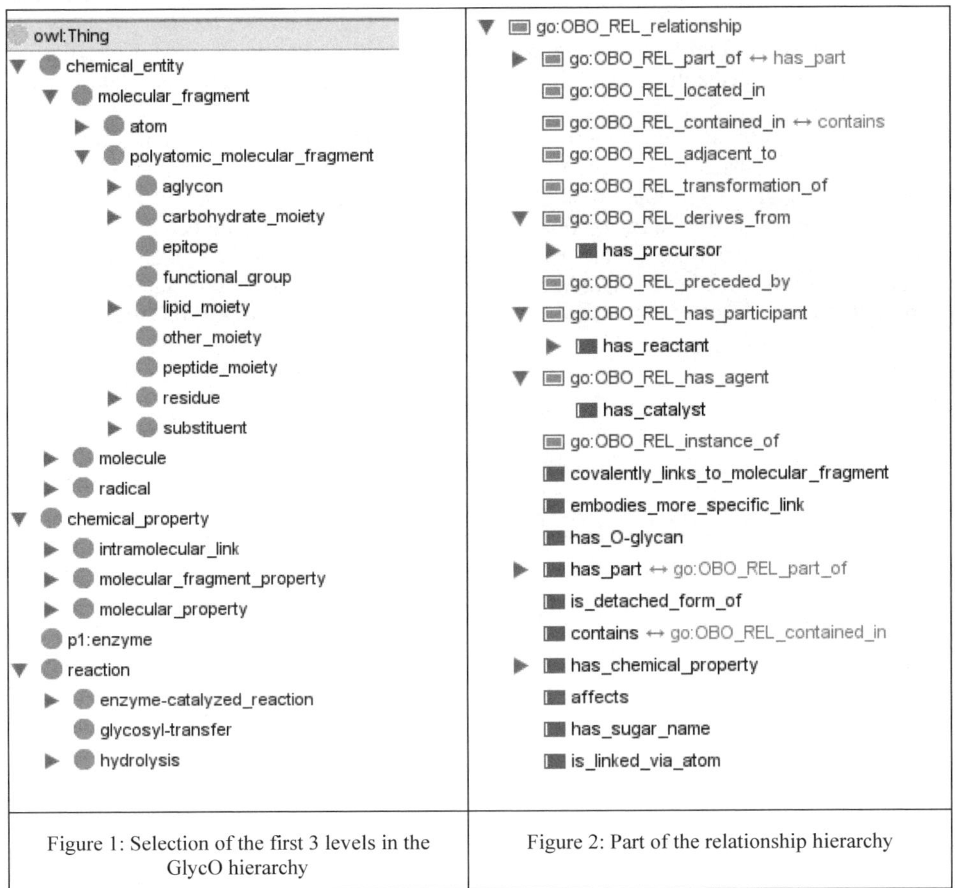

Figure 1: Selection of the first 3 levels in the GlycO hierarchy	Figure 2: Part of the relationship hierarchy

2.3   Canonical Instances

The problem of deciding where to make the cut between classes and instances and what to consider as an instance is well known in ontology design [16]. Even though *OntoClean* [9] describes some fallacies that can occur when making wrong choices for classes vs. instances, it is usually seen as an arbitrary, domain- or task-dependent choice. There is no rigorous formal methodology behind these choices.

Noy and McGuinness [16] give a good example for the wine ontology in which the designer has to decide whether the type of wine or the single bottle are of particular interest to the users of the ontology.

By analogy, an ontology in the glycan domain could describe individual glycan molecules. With 10^{15} (or more) chemically identical glycan molecules in a purified laboratory sample, this would be a tedious and useless endeavor. It makes much more sense to describe archetypal glycan molecules. Within the context of GlycO, it is not very useful to have a simple, mostly textual description of the glycan structure, as in most carbohydrate databases. To describe the complex structural features of glycans, each glycan is composed of several building block instances that model the monosaccharide residues. Each residue instance is richly described by the sub-tree it terminates and by additional properties that define how it is chemically linked to the next residue in the glycan. We chose this level of granularity for our description because these individual features can be associated with the physiological properties of the glycan and the cellular machinery involved in its biosynthesis, catabolism, recognition, etc.

For the current version, which focuses on the N-glycans subclass, this is accomplished by defining a tree structure of canonical residue entities that subsumes most N-glycans. That is, almost all of the known N-glycan structures can be completely specified by choosing a subset of the nodes of this tree. This subset forms a connected subtree that includes the root residue. This tree (known as GlycoTree) has been previously described [25], and we have formalized that structure as a collection of interconnected, canonical residue instances in GlycO. See Figure 3 for an image of GlycoTree.

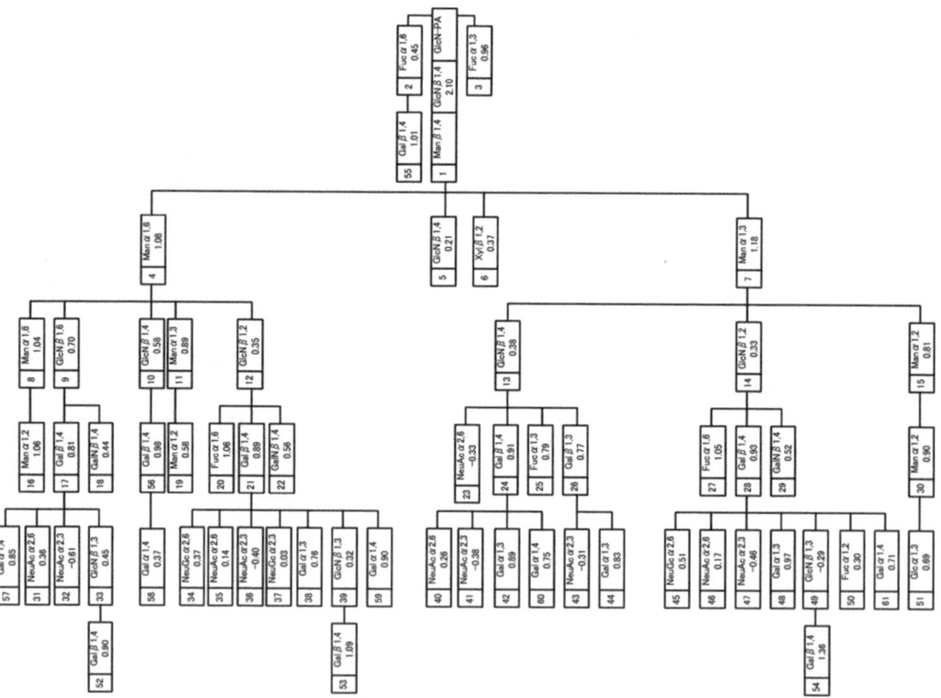

Figure 3: The GlycoTree structure that subsumes most known N-Glycans, as depicted in [25]

In spite of its practicality, the use of canonical residues to describe glycan structures evoked some ontological problems. If a glycan instance is chosen as a representative for all real glycans that have this structure, can we also let a residue instance that appears in many glycan instances, be at that same level of abstraction? The key question here was in our case to which extent an instance is determined by its context. In particular, the issue was whether it was ontologically justifiable to have each residue instance determined only by its chemical structure and the residue to which it is linked in the glycan. From a purely structural point of view this was justified with the GlycoTree structure elaborated by Takahashi and Kato [25]. Practically, it is justified by the reduction in the number of residue instances that results when different glycans can "reuse" the same residue in the same position. We believe that we can also semantically justify this decision because it reflects the way glycans are synthesized along their metabolic pathways, where enzyme-catalyzed reactions 'add' new residues as leaves to the existing glycan tree structures or 'move' the entire glycan to a protein. A specific type of residue is added in a reaction catalyzed by a specific enzyme at a specific position in the precursor glycan. We know that, for example, a mannose residue in position 1 is functionally different from a mannose residue in position 4. What remains to be demonstrated is whether residues in the same position in different glycans can be mapped to a particular function or participation in a metabolic pathway. This assumption is naturally underlying the current implementation. The chosen design can help determining whether this assumption is valid or not, because it is easily falsifiable on a case-by-case basis. We can easily establish sets of glycans that contain the same canonical residue instance and query whether the members of the set have common biological functions or are part of the same metabolic pathway.

Another issue of granularity is deciding which granular partitions of the world are represented [1]. Even in the molecular context of GlycO, different levels of granularity arise, especially when it comes to the representation of chemical linkage. Conceptually, larger molecular fragments are linked together, for example in glycans that attach to proteins. However, the actual link is naturally between two atoms. Intermediate links can also be asserted, such as the link between the glycan root residue and the amino acid in the protein that it attaches to. This issue was resolved by allowing chemical links to embody all these links recursively. The link is promoted from a simple relationship to a first class object that is defined by the two objects it links and by a more refined link.

Furthermore, atoms are parts of molecular fragments, which in turn are parts of molecules. This is an example of a partition into bona-fide versus fiat objects [1]. Molecules exist as wholes independently of other objects Molecular fragments describe functional partitions, even though they actually exist as such for extremely short amounts of time during chemical reactions, and should thus rather be seen as fiat objects.

3. Populating the Ontology

3.1　　General Considerations

Creating ontologies is usually costly. In addition to a schema design, the actual domain knowledge in form of instances needs to be gathered, conceptualized and formalized. CYC [14] and GO are examples of ontologies that require high maintenance, due to the need for manual curation. This is not an issue in ontologies that only describe a schema to be used for database integration or as vocabularies. But since instance descriptions in GlycO are very different from those found in databases, ways to automate this process needed to be found. The objective in the development of GlycO was to have an expressive and restrictive schema that allows automatic and hence less expensive maintenance, given that semi-structured and reliable information is available for its population.

3.2   Populating GlycO from trusted sources

With CarbBank [3], KEGG [12] and SweetDB [15], several databases exist that contain trusted and up-to-date information about glycan structures. Even though CarbBank was discontinued, its content is of high quality and it is still used as a reference in other databases.

The GlycO schema specifies more complex relationships than these databases. A large number of properties not specified in their schema can be computationally inferred from the information given in the databases and are then explicitly added to the glycan description in the ontology. Hence we use these sources to populate the ontology with carbohydrate instances, alongside other sources for the population of gene and protein information. We assume that while each of the databases can contain incorrect entries, it is less likely that all three have the same incorrect entry. For this reason we extracted information from all these databases and compared this information during the population. To gather the data, the Semagix Freedom toolkit[20] was used that facilitates extraction of information from semi-structured websites and converts it to a structured representation that can be exported as XML or RDF or accessed via an API.

3.3   An Intelligent Population Algorithm

A structured representation of data does not necessarily guarantee its usefulness. Since the information was extracted from different sources, it has to be disambiguated to avoid having differently named copies of the same structure. As mentioned above, a simple textual description of structures is not suitable for our purposes and would only give an RDF encoding of already existing databases. In order to disambiguate the potential instances, the textual description of the structure was converted into the internal GlycoTree representation. This was performed using a multi-step process in which ambiguity is progressively removed as more meaningful representations are generated.

Conventionally, glycans are represented in the so-called IUPAC format, which is a two-dimensional textual representation that visually reflects the inherent tree structure and is easily comprehended by the human eye. Unfortunately, this representation is not unique. A web service is provided[1] that converts this representation into the structurally unambiguous LInear Notation for Unique description of Carbohydrate Sequences (LINUCS) [2]. Since this conversion is purely based on structure, it does not disambiguate different naming conventions for the substructures of the complex carbohydrate, the monosaccharide residues. For this purpose, another conversion is used that transforms the LINUCS representation into the XML-based GLYcan Data Exchange (GLYDE) format [19], which semantically disambiguates the different naming conventions of monosaccharide residues. XML has an inherent tree structure and GLYDE uses this fact. A child monosaccharide residue in a glycan is simply represented as a child node in the XML representation. This makes it relatively easy to perform tree operations on this representation. (See Figure 4 for the population workflow)

In the GlycoTree model each monosaccharide residue is defined by its type, its linkage and its position in the GlycoTree. Because of its canonical representation, the root node

---

[1] http://www.glycosciences.de/tools/linucs/

of a glycan can potentially be the root node of any sub tree of the GlycoTree. The population algorithm identifies and assigns the sub tree that corresponds to a particular glycan that is to be instantiated in the ontology. This is done by looking for sub tree isomorphisms. Several efficient sub tree isomorphism algorithms are available [18]. In our case, because of comparable small glycan structures, a depth-first search was sufficient. Additionally, the glycan constitutes a complete sub tree isomorphism; i.e. there cannot be a node in the glycan representation that is not part of the larger tree, nor can there be merely a homomorphism such that edges in the GlycoTree would need to be contracted to accommodate the glycan structure. If no isomorphism can be found, new GlycoTree nodes are generated automatically to complete the ontology. Here as well a report is generated so the domain expert can verify the correctness. New tree nodes can be inappropriately generated as a result of an incorrect structural description or classification of the glycan in the database. We identified several incorrect glycan descriptions by checking all new nodes that were generated during the population process. As only a few new nodes were generated, this is much easier than checking the entire set of glycan instances for errors.

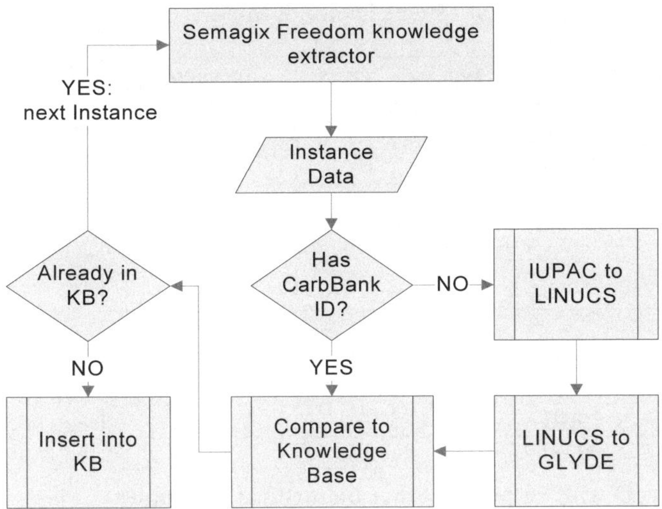

Figure 4: GlycO population workflow

The population algorithm will also be used to automatically build minimal trees for other glycan subclasses, such as O-glycans and glycolipids, which have not been classified entirely in such a tree structure. In [10] such tree structures are built, but only cover 61.2% of the known carbohydrate structures.

The set of GlycoTree nodes that represent a particular glycan can be easily compared to another set of nodes that represents a different glycan instance in the ontology. Two glycans are the same if and only if their tree node sets are identical. This method of disambiguation proved to be the more robust than other criteria, such as a common identifier, which is unreliable because every database uses proprietary accession numbers. Although all of the databases that were used as trusted sources make reference to CarbBank identifiers, CarbBank is no longer actively curated and these databases contain glycans that do not have a CarbBank ID.

4. Evaluation

It is difficult to measure the quality of an ontology. Guarino [8] proposed an evaluation based on precision and recall with respect to a reference conceptualization. This of course requires a formal conceptualization that applies to the same domain. With respect to the OntoClean ontology, for example, such a formal evaluation can show whether certain meta-properties of concepts are correctly assigned in the ontology. We rigorously modeled the GlycO ontology according to this meta-methodology. Another dimension for evaluation are structural metrics that assign numerical values to criteria such as depth, breadth, fan-outness, etc. [5][26]. These metrics are useful especially in large ontologies to get an idea of their structural character. Of course, none of these metrics can really tell us how useful an ontology will be and how well it models its domain. Table 1 shows the results of comparing GlycO to other biomedical ontologies using these metrics. Instance information is not taken into consideration. GlycO shows the highest connectivity, indicating a rich set of well defined and logically restricted relationships. The average number of sub terms gives an indication of the fan-out, but also the depth of GlycO. In a comparable fan-out measure, when siblings are counted, the number of siblings ranges between 1 and 15 with an average of 6.

Ontology	*No. of Terms*	*Avg. sub- terms*	*Connectivity*
GlycO	**324**	**2.5**	**1.7**
ProPreO	**244**	**3.2**	**1.1**
MGED	228	5.1	0.33
Biological Imaging methods	260	5.2	1.0
Protein-protein interaction	195	4.6	1.1
Physico-chemical process	550	2.7	1.3
BRENDA	2,222	3.3	1.2
Human disease	19,137	5.5	1.0
GO	200,002	4.1	1.4

Table 1: Evaluation of GlycO with respect to other biomedical ontologies

Pathways can be queried using GlycO, even though they are not explicitly defined the way they are in some databases. A pathway is essentially a sequence of reactions that lead from one chemical compound to another. The advantage of our representation is, that any path between compounds can be shown, by traversing relationships, even if these compounds are not explicitly assigned to a specific pathway, given that all the reactions that are involved are formalized in the ontology. This makes the representation of pathways in the ontology more flexible than that in many databases. Figure 5 shows the GlycO representation of some steps in the N-Glycan biosynthesis pathway.

Another application that requires sophisticated algorithms on databases is described in [10]. The different glycan trees that the authors identify are inherently encoded in the canonical residues and links and can thus easily be queried as well as visualized.

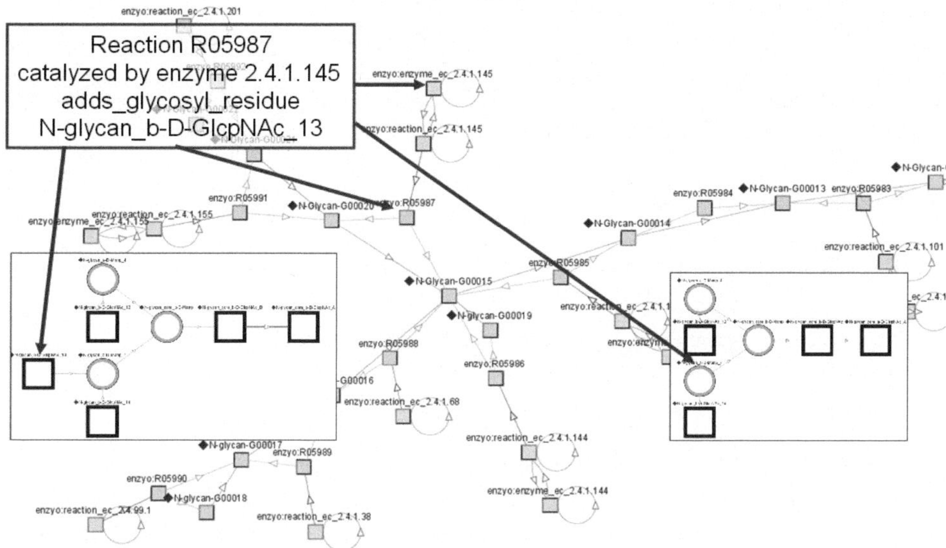

Figure 5: A part of the N-Glycan biosynthesis pathway as encoded in GlycO. For better visibility, only few relationship types are visualized. N-glycan_b-D-GlcpNAc_13 is the beta-D-GlcpNAc residue number 13 as enumerated in the GlycoTree model.

5. Conclusion

GlycO is not only a vocabulary or a schema meant for database integration, but provides a rich description of the knowledge in the glycoproteomics domain, semantically describing interactions and functions of structures and their substructures as well as their synthesis.

By semantically modeling the structure of molecules with reusable canonical instances, we can evaluate the hypothesis that larger structures exhibit properties and functions that can partially be inferred from the knowledge of the properties and functions of their substructures. The GlycO schema allows a glycan structure to be represented as more than the sum of its parts, paving the way for the identification of the molecular basis for emergent properties. To our knowledge is GlycO the first ontology that models its domain in such detail as described. The formalization of this knowledge allows immediate access to information that so far is only available through specialized tools and algorithms that work on the textual representation in the various biochemistry databases. It was shown that with a sufficiently rich schema alongside trusted sources, automatic extraction, modeling and classification of high-quality instance data is possible.

In the context of this modeling, mereological problems were encountered and addressed. By promoting some of the relationships in the ontology to first class objects, recursive definitions of these relationships allow their expression on different levels of granularity.

6. Acknowledgement

This work is part of the Integrated Technology Resource for Biomedical Glycomics (5 P41 RR18502-02), funded by the National Institutes of Health National Center for Research Resources. Donation by Semagix of its Freedom platform for semantic application development is also acknowledged.

References

[1]   Bittner T, Smith B. *A theory of granular partitions*. Foun dations of Geographic Information Science, M Duckham et al. (eds.). London: Taylor & Francis, 2003: 117-151.

[2]   Bohne-Lang A.; Lang E.; Forster T.; von der Lieth CW. *LINUCS: linear notation for unique description of carbohydrate sequences*. Carbohydr Res. 336:1-11, 2001.

[3]   Doubet, S. and Albersheim, P. *CarbBank*. Glycobiology, 2, 1992

[4]   EnzyO. lsdis.cs.uga.edu/projects/glycomics/enzyo/

[5]   Gangemi, A.; Catenacci, C.; Ciaramita, M.; Lehmann, J. *A theoretical framework for ontology evaluation and validation*. Proceedings of the 2nd Italian Semantic Web Workshop, Trento, Italy, 2005.

[6]   Gene Ontology Consortium. *Gene Ontology: Tool for the Unification of Biology*. Nature Genetics, 25:25-29, 2000.

[7]   Genesereth, M. R., and Fikes, R. E. Knowledge Interchange Format, Version 3.0 Reference Manual. Technical Report Logic-92-1, Computer Science Department, Stanford University, 1992

[8]   Guarino, N. *Toward a formal evaluation of ontology quality*. IEEE Intelligent Systems, 19(4), 2004

[9]   Guarino, N. and Welty, C. *Evaluating Ontological Decisions with OntoClean*, Comm. ACM, 45(2), 2002, pp. 61–65.

[10] Hashimoto, K., Kawano, S., Okuno, Y., and Kanehisa, M. *Global Tree of Known Carbohydrate Structures to Analyze Biosynthetic Pathways*. 15th International Conference on Genome Informatics (GIW2004), December 2004.

[11] Horrocks, I.; Patel-Schneider, P.F. and van Harmelen, F. *From SHIQ and RDF to OWL: the making of a Web Ontology Language*, Journal of Web Semantics 1(1): 7-26 (2003)

[12] Kanehisa, M. and Goto, S. *KEGG: Kyoto Encyclopedia of Genes and Genomes*, Nucleic Acids Research, 2000, Vol. 28(1)

[13] Klyne, G and Carroll, J. Resource Description Framework (RDF): Concepts and abstract syntax. http://www.w3.org/TR/2004/REC-rdf-concepts-20040210/ (2004)

[14] Lenat, D. and Guha, R.V. *Building Large Knowledge-Based Systems*: Representation and Inference in the Cyc Project, Addison-Wesley. 1990.

[15] Loß, A.; Bunsmann, P.; Bohne, A.; Loß, A.; Schwarzer, E.; Lang, E. and Von der Lieth, C.-W. *SWEET-DB: an attempt to create annotated data collections for carbohydrates*, Nucleic Acids Research, 2002, Vol 30(1)

[16] Noy, N.F. and McGuinness, D.L. *Ontology Development 101: A Guide to Creating Your First Ontology*. Knowledge Systems Laboratory, 2001

[17] OBO: Open Biomedical Ontologies. http://obo.sourceforge.net

[18] Raymond, J.W. and Willett, P. *Maximum common subgraph isomorphism algorithms for the matching of chemical structures*, Journal of Computer-Aided Molecular Design, 16(7), 2002.

[19] Sahoo, S.S.; Thomas, C.J. Sheth, A.P.; Henson, C; York, W.S. *GLYDE - An expressive XML standard for the representation of glycan structure.* Carbohydrate Research, 340(18), 2005

[20] Sheth, A.; Bertram, C.; Avant, D.; Hammond, B.; Kochut, K.; Warke, Y. *Managing Semantic Content for the Web*, IEEE Internet Computing, July/August 2002.

[21] Sheth, A.P.; Arpinar, I.B. and Kashyap, V. *Relationships at the Heart of Semantic Web: Modeling, Discovering, and Exploiting Complex Semantic Relationships*, in Enhancing the Power of the Internet: Studies in Fuzziness and Soft Computing, M. Nikravesh, L. A. Zadeh, B. Azvine, R.R. Yager (Eds), Springer-Verlag, 63-94, 2004

[22] Smith, B.; Ceusters, Werner; Klagges, B.R.E.; Köhler, J; Kumar, A.; Lomax, J.; Mungall, C.; Neuhaus, F.; Rector, A.L. ; Rosse, C. *Relations in Biomedical Ontologies.* Genome Biology, 6, 2005

[23] Soldatova, L.N. and King, R.D. *Are the current ontologies in biology good ontologies?* Nature Biotechnology 23, 2005

[24] SUMO: http://ontology.teknowledge.com/

[25] Takahashi, N. and Kato, K. *GlycoTree*, Trends in Glycoscience and Glycotechnology, 15, 2003.

[26] Samir Tartir, I. Budak Arpinar, Michael Moore, Amit Sheth, Boanerges Aleman-Meza. *OntoQA: Metric-Based Ontology Quality Analysis*, IEEE ICDM 2005 Workshop on Knowledge Acquisition from Distributed, Autonomous, Semantically Heterogeneous Data and Knowledge Sources. Houston, Texas, November 27, 2005

Formal Ontology in Information Systems
B. Bennett and C. Fellbaum (Eds.)
IOS Press, 2006

What is a Biological Function?

Patricia DIAZ-HERRERA
Department of Philosophy, University at Buffalo, Buffalo, NY 14260 USA
pd7@buffalo.edu

Abstract. This paper examines the concepts *biological function* (BF) and *functioning* as they are used in recent work on formal ontology and its applications in the biomedical domain. My purpose is not to offer an entirely new definition of BF. My objectives are: (1) to find out the basic features of BF mentioned in the reviewed articles; (2) to make more explicit the description of BF already present in those articles by relating it to an ontological category system; and (3) to emphasize the distinction between three cases of predication involving BFs, a distinction that should be taken into account when designing an information system. Hopefully, the results will make a contribution to the goal of providing a general, objective description of biological functions.

Keywords. Biological function, functioning, neo-Aristotelian ontology, real definition, ontological square, dispositional predication, occurrent predication.

Introduction

The concept of biological function is fundamental for the philosophy of biology and medicine: biologists describe the role of traits in certain organisms using functional language, and the notions of health and disease have been defined by means of the notion of biomedical normality, which includes functional terms [2,3]. Likewise, the clarification of the notion of biological function is fundamental for the information systems subfield dealing with formal representations in biomedicine. The general goals of philosophic ontology and its relationship to information systems ontology are discussed in [15]. One of the contributions the philosophical ontologist can make is to provide a description grounded in reality, *i.e.* an objective description of the structure of a certain domain. The philosophical ontologist attempts to discover truths about a certain domain of objects, in this case the biological domain. The philosophical ontologist seeks to produce real definitions, descriptions of the essence of an object, and not only stipulations of the meaning of a term in a certain context. A related task of ontology in information science is to support the classification of entities by identifying the ontological category to which they belong.

The need of objective descriptions and ontological categorizations has been gradually recognized by the information systems community, since those descriptions and categorizations can help to solve practical problems such as database integration. Smith and Welty [13] expressed the link between philosophical ontology and information systems as follows:

The knowledge engineer, conceptual modeler, or domain modeler realizes the need for declarative representations which should have as much generality as possible to ensure reusability but would at the same time *correspond to the things and processes they are supposed to represent.* (…) the very lack of grounding in external reality is precisely what created the problems (…) of legacy *system integration.* How can we make older systems with different conceptual models but overlapping semantics work together, if not by referring to the common world to which they all relate? [13; pp iv-v]

This paper examines the concepts *biological function* (BF) and *functioning* as they are used in recent work on formal ontology and its applications in the biomedical domain. In the articles Johansson [4], Johansson, Smith and Tsikolia [5], Smith and Grenon [11], and Smith, Munn, and Papakin [12], biological functions are characterized in slightly different ways. My purpose is not to offer an entirely new definition of BF. My objectives are: (1) to find out the basic features of BF mentioned in the reviewed articles; (2) to make more explicit the descriptions of BF and functioning already present in those articles by relating them to an ontological category system; and (3) to emphasize the distinction between three cases of predication involving BFs, a distinction that should be taken into account when designing an information system and classifying data in the biomedical field. Hopefully, the results will make a contribution to the goal of providing both general and objective descriptions of biological functions.

It is common to distinguish two major approaches to defining biological functions with several variants [14, 3]. The first major approach began with Robert Cummins' theory and is called the 'Causal-role' analysis of function (CR-function). The second approach, endorsed by authors such as L. Wright or Ruth G. Millikan [7] is called the 'etiological' or 'evolutionary' analysis of function (E-function). A critical account of L. Wright is given in [1].

The articles that I examine can be grouped as the "neo-Aristotelian" approach because they assume both a neo-Aristotelian ontology and a neo-Aristotelian theory of definition. The neo-Aristotelian-function (NA-function) can be fully assimilated neither to CR-function nor to E-function. The NA-function analysis attempts to capture the non-explanatory elements of functional language and is non-reductive in the sense that it admits universals. The NA-analysis provides an ontological account of BF, covering aspects that are not emphasized by the other major approaches.

Though the goal of each of the examined articles is not to provide a technical definition of BF, it is important for the project of applying formal ontology in the biomedical domain to assume, through its different developments, one and the same concept of BF. In the first section of the paper, I present four NA-function characterizations and explain their implications in order to answer the following questions: Which are the necessary and sufficient conditions that appear in all those characterizations? Do they provide the tightest possible description of BF?

In the second section, I state a description of BF and a description of functioning based on the conditions established in the articles reviewed. In the final section, I apply the ontological square proposed by Neuhaus, Grenon and Smith [8] and E. J. Lowe [6] in order to make the ontological content of the definitions more explicit, and to distinguish between three cases of predication involving BFs. This is a non-formal application of the four category ontology that has not been done before as far as I know.

1. Characterizations of BF and Functioning

1.1 Real definitions

The characterizations found in the texts reviewed are intended to be characterizations of BF *per se*, i.e. of a mind-independent entity which is an "objective feature of the world" [5; p4].

It is common to distinguish between real definitions and stipulations. Real definitions are definitions *de re*, *i.e.*, definitions that attempt to provide the essence of mind-independent entities. They state the necessary and sufficient conditions for being a certain kind of thing. A real definition is expressed by a sentence that specifies the conditions that must be satisfied for something to be an entity of a given sort. Ontology is concerned with real definitions. (The relevance of the Aristotelian theory of definition to the task of ontology is discussed in [10])

By contrast, stipulations are definitions *de dicto*, *i.e.* definitions of terms. A stipulation is expressed in a sentence whose predicate specifies the necessary and sufficient conditions for the correct use of a certain term, namely, the subject of that sentence. A stipulation is always conventional: it tells us what to understand by a certain term in a certain context. A stipulation does not attempt to provide the essence of the *definiendum*; it characterizes a linguistic entity, not a non-linguistic entity.

A real definition attempts to provide the essence of a non-linguistic entity, i.e. the properties which an entity of a certain kind must possess and cannot lack. The ontologist must not look for stipulations but for real definitions. The description I propose in section 2.1 below seeks to be a step towards a real definition.

I present the characterizations of BF and functioning found in the articles reviewed in order to identify the necessary and sufficient conditions they propose and to examine whether they provide a description which is not too broad or too narrow. As I mentioned, those articles have different goals and are not concerned specifically with providing a strict definition of BF, but this does not mean that we should not attempt to clarify the notions they assume.

1.2 Functioning as a four-dimensional shape: Johansson [4]

After pointing out that functional statements are relational and often teleological, Johansson recalls two main philosophical accounts of functions: a) the reductive accounts, according to which function talk is eliminable in favor of causal talk involving the notion of natural selection; b) the non-reductive accounts, according to which a function consists in a causal process together with a socially assigned purpose. In his view, there is a third sense of 'function': this term denotes a kind of four dimensional shape or process shape. Johansson argues that function concepts can be ordered on scales, in a similar way as other measurable properties are ordered. The notion of perfect functioning is like a standard unit; it is not a teleological notion. The concept of function that he proposes intends to be non-Darwinian, non-anthropomorphic and non-causal.

When a functional entity is functioning, it participates in a process. The functional entity is a tri-dimensional body that retains its identity through property changes. In other words, this body is an enduring entity without temporal parts. It has a shape-with-size and a hardness that make the process possible. The process in which that entity is involved, e.g. a certain movement, unfolds through its successive temporal parts. The existence of the process depends on the body. Thus, the body is not only a property bearer, but also a process bearer.

The functioning is, then, a process that, when represented in an abstract space, has three spatial and one temporal dimension, thus constituting "a specific four-dimensional shape bounded by a specific time interval." [4; p3][1]

According to Johansson, the functioning of the heart is an instance of a process shape. He claims that the realization of the process shape "(i) (…) is a necessary condition of the heart's functioning, (ii) it can be analyzed independently of any causal process in which it is involved; and (iii) it does not necessarily have an assigned purpose." [4; p5]

The process shape is neither a cause nor an effect, "it is, just, a *shape*" [4]. It can be described independently from concrete objects that exemplify it. In itself, a process shape is neither a causal, nor a teleological process, nor a mixture of them. Therefore, "*at least part of what makes true* a statement such as 'The function of the screwdriver is to fasten and extract screws' is both non-causal and non-teleological" [4]. This article focuses on the functioning rather than the function itself. The function itself is conceived as a disposition that, when actualized, is an instance of the process shape:

> A cylinder piston at rest in an engine at rest still has its function. But, what about a piston in a broken cylinder, or a piston on a shelf in a warehouse? In my opinion, both have the dispositional property of being able to be in the state of functioning, too. But this is of no crucial importance for my analysis. The important thing is that (…) even a piston taken out of all functional contexts can still be imagined as performing the movement which it performs when functioning (…) [4; p4].

Besides these characterizations, the functioning of the heart is said to exist only as a relation or "a relational process between at least two other spatiotemporal entities of highly determinate sorts."[4] That is, "in order to perform its function, a heart has to be related to a body…". [4] Johansson appears to have in mind a three-place relation: 'The heart pumps blood to the body' would be symbolized as: *Pabc*, where *Pxyz* = *x* pumps *y* to *z*; *a* = the heart; *b* = blood; *c* = body.

From this, it can be *inferred* that BF is a dispositional property of an organ of being able to be in the state of functioning. However, if we tried to construct a definition of BF with only those elements, that "definition" would not be informative because it would be circular: the *definiendum* is included in the *definiens*. It can be paraphrased as follows: BF is an organ's capacity of functioning. We can ask, then, what is functioning?

The functioning of an organ is characterized in two ways, as

(a) an instance of a four-dimensional shape or process shape, and

(b) a relational process between at least two other spatiotemporal entities.

These characterizations cannot be considered as strict definitions of functioning. Johansson does not claim that he has provided strict definitions. What he holds is that "the functional statement 'The function of the heart is to pump blood' is then *made true*

---

[1] Page numbers for [4] correspond to the online version. In the following quotes, the italics are mine.

in part by an entity that is both non-causal and non-teleological". [4] In other words, he considers that he has established only necessary conditions of functioning.

Each (a) and (b) are necessary conditions of the functioning of an organ. Although every functioning is a four-dimensional shape, not every four-dimensional shape is a functioning. There are process shapes which are neither biological functions (e.g. the process shape of the rotating screwdriver) nor functions at all (e.g. the process shape of a glass rolling from point A to point B on a surface). The same can be said of (b): every functioning of an organ is a relational process involving at least two other spatiotemporal entities, but not vice versa.

I submit that (a) and (b) are not jointly sufficient, since there are entities which fulfill both (a) and (b) but are not functions. For instance, the rolling of a glass between two points of a surface is both an instance of a four-dimensional shape and a relational process, since the movement can only take place in relation to points on the surface.

1.3 BF as Constituent Function: Johansson, Smith and Tsikolia [5]

The authors propose a classificatory system for life sciences and medicine called 'pure functional anatomy' which is complementary to structural anatomy and pure physiology. This taxonomic system puts functions in the center and is based on the distinction between enduring entities and processes. While traditional anatomy is grounded in spatial-structural parts, pure functional anatomy is grounded in spatial-functional parts of the organism.

The authors introduce the notion of constituent function (CF), a primitive non-reductionist notion of function. CF are relational and can also be called 'component functions' or 'part-to-whole functions'. The point of departure of the proposal is the human body, which is regarded as a functional unit whose function –which is not a CF— is to preserve its own life. The human body is an organism that has the function of self-preservation, and "most bodily functions are CF, i.e., they are functions relative to this larger whole" [5; p5]. There is a first level of spatial-functional parts of the human body, namely, the main bodily systems, e.g. circulatory, respiratory, etc. In general, their function is to contribute to the preservation of the life of the whole.

A function-bearer (e.g. an organ, a system) does not have a CF in and of itself. CF is not a monadic property, i.e. an intrinsic function. Therefore, "nothing can be a CF if it is not the function of some part of a larger functional unit..." [5; p. 13], and the human body as a whole has no CF in itself.

All the bodily systems, its spatial-functional parts, and their CFs endure. They do not have temporal parts. The processes which are realizations of these functions, i.e. their functional activities or functionings, do have temporal parts. For instance, the activity of the heart has two phases which are two temporal parts.

Reductionist accounts of function assume that function talk is always explanatory. Then, it can be reduced to talk about causes, dispositions, or adaptiveness.[2] The non-reductive account of functions holds that function talk is often purely descriptive. The statement 'Entity X has a function F' is describing a relational feature of entity X.

---

[2] For instance, R. Cummins' reductive definition is: "to ascribe a function to something is to ascribe a capacity to it which is singled out by its role in an analysis of some capacity of a containing system" (quoted in [5], 22.) The authors find some similarity between Cummins' intrasystemic role analysis and their own non-reductive account. However, they do not endorse Cummins' definition because he tries to eliminate the concept of function, substituting it with a concept of "role".

The taxonomic formula of the proposal focuses on 1) spatial-functional parts existing in a human organism at an arbitrary point in time –that is, the SNAP-shot perspective, and 2) the unfolding of a given process of functioning along a certain time extension –that is, the SPAN perspective. Thus, the taxonomic formula expresses both spatial-functional parthood relations (SNAP formula) and temporal parts of functionings (SPAN formula) as follows:

SNAP formula:
In the functional unit A,
one function of the spatial part and functional subunit B of A is
to V in relation to X, Y, Z,…;

SPAN formula:
This function (V) has in its functioning as temporal parts
the phases P_1 to P_n.

Is the taxonomic formula a definition of biological function? No, or at least not directly, because the formula uses the concept of CF, but its purpose is not to determine the conditions of a function *qua* function. Its purpose is, as far as I can see, to describe the general structure of the processes called 'functionings'. It describes what it is for a subunit of a given whole *to have a certain function*, from the structural and the processual perspectives. Hence, it does not precisely define what it is, in general, *to be a function*. Nevertheless, since the function (V) is "depicted by verb phrases" [5] we can infer that a function is a capacity of an organ or system to perform a certain activity involving other organs or systems.

The article contains the following characterizations:

1. A CF is the function of some part of a larger functional unit.
2. BF is a relational feature of an entity that belongs to a larger whole.
3. The function of the constituent parts are defined in relation to the function of the whole to which they belong, e.g. the function of the human body is to preserve its life, and the most general CF of the main bodily systems is to contribute to preserve the life of the whole.
4. BF is an enduring entity.
5. A functioning is a process which is a realization of a BF.

From (1) and (2) it follows that biological functions are CFs. But (1) does not tell us what a function is in itself. (2) tells us that a biological function is a relational property of an organ or bodily system, but that is just a generic characteristic shared by other relational properties that can be predicated of the parts of an organism. (3) states a property of CF, but in this context it is unclear whether it is a necessary or a sufficient condition. Note that it seems that CFs are relational in two senses: a) because they are part-to-whole functions, i.e. the organ or system has a function only in relation to the function of a larger functional unit, and b) because they involve several entities, which can be larger units or not, for those entities can belong to "every possible level along any given taxonomic path". [5]

A generic condition for being a BF is stated in (4). And (5) might be said to express generic and specific conditions of 'functioning', but it relies on the notion of

BF, which is unclear. Below, I will consider whether this definition is the tightest possible or not.

Implicit in the taxonomic formula is the following characterization: BF is a disposition or capacity of an organ or system to perform a certain activity involving other organs or systems. This is more clearly stated in the next articles.

1.4 Biological Function as a SNAP, dependent entity: Smith and Grenon [11]

The authors present typologies of formal-ontological relations, defined as "relations that can obtain between entities of distinct ontologies" [11; p9].[3] Formal relations traverse and glue the SNAP-SPAN perspectives. Each ontology is an inventory of beings, which are linked together by formal relations like dependence and parthood. The SNAP perspective captures continuant or endurant entities that persist identically through time. The SPAN perspective captures occurent or perdurant entities which unfold themselves through the succession of their temporal parts.

Formal relations are constructed according to their signature, i.e. the ontologies to which the *relata* belong, the arity of the relation and its directionality.

How are functions and functionings characterized from this point of view? Which kind of formal relations are there between a functional entity, its function, and the corresponding functioning?

In order to reveal the differences between SNAP Dependent entities it is necessary to subdivide the typology given in the article [11; p5 fig. 1]. It might be that the umbrella term 'property' constitutes just one kind among other possible dependent entities. Properties can be either monadic, if they depend on one substantial entity, or relational, if they depend on more than one substantial entity. Processes, which are dependent on substantial things, can be monadic or relational. Thus, the typology of SPAN entities [11; p7 fig. 2] should also be subdivided.

Reading the typologies from bottom up we obtain these characterizations:

(1) A function is a relational property which is a kind of dependent, continuant (or endurant) entity.

(2) A functioning is a relational process which is a kind of occurrent (or perdurant) entity.

Characterizations (1) and (2) express the most general categories to which all functions and functionings belong, respectively. They are the kind of characterizations generated in a top-level ontology. In (1), the nearest genus of 'function' is 'property', and the specific difference is 'relational'. In (2), the nearest genus of 'functioning' is 'process', and the specific difference is 'relational'. However, since the authors did not intend to provide a definition of BF, the specificity of BFs and functionings is not explicit here.

The authors do not mention this explicitly, but more specific features of BFs and functionings can be construed using the types of signatures that formal relations have in the binary case. Some of the formal relations that hold between functional entities, their functions, and their corresponding functionings are *involvement* and *realization*. Those relations are necessary conditions for being either a function or a functioning. A special

---

[3] This pagination corresponds to the online version.

type of the involvement relation, i.e. *sustaining-in-being*, is a good candidate to be a sufficient condition for some BFs, since sustaining-in-being is a property peculiar to some biological functionings, which distinguishes them from other kinds of processes and functionings. Likewise, the relation of realization can also provide a sufficient condition for being a BF, since 'being realized by a bodily process' is a feature that distinguishes BF from other properties. These conditions will be considered to formulate a definition of BF in the second section.

1.5 BF as a beneficial or sustaining CF: Smith, Munn and Papakin [12]

The authors define 'bodily system' and understand the causal interaction between systems. The authors provide a framework for a formal definition of 'bodily system' and associated notions, like function and functioning.

In the section devoted to functions, the authors present many of the characteristics mentioned above. They do not consider that those characteristics are the necessary and sufficient conditions of the phenomena studied: "We cannot provide a definition of (biological) function here. Rather, we can only set forth certain general propositions which describe what is characteristic of those entities biologists call 'functions' (...)" [12; p12].[4]

One of the general propositions is:

(A) If an organism Y has a constituent part X, and if X is the bearer of a function Z, then those processes which are the realizations of the function Z are (in normal circumstances) such as to sustain the organism in existence. [12]

This is not a definition of BF, but a statement of a property some biological functionings possess, i.e. their capacity of sustaining the organism's life. It is equivalent to saying that a functioning is a realization of a CF that sustains the organism's existence. As we have seen, in this account a BF is always a CF. And the role a CF performs is determined by the function of the whole to which it belongs.

The content of proposition (A) can be rephrased in order to construct a definition of BF. This will be attempted in the next section.

Another important feature of BFs is that they "can exist even when they are not being realized". [12] This means that a BF is not only a relational property of its bearer, but also a property that can be actualized by a process or can remain as a potential feature only. Then, BFs can also be regarded as dispositions to perform a determinate activity.

2. Towards a Neo-Aristotelian definition of BF

This section integrates the information presented before in order to obtain the tightest possible description. It will be necessary to consider the conditions gathered and to assess them to determine which of them should be part of the description.

---

[4] This pagination corresponds to the online version.

2.1 Extension and intension

How can we determine the nearest genus and the specific difference of BF? The criteria to select the best possible candidates among the generic conditions are the extension and the intension of the generic concepts. By means of the extension and the intension of each concept, it is possible to draw a conceptual (Porphyrean) tree with the candidates to nearest genus and specific difference. The nearest genus has less extension than the higher genus, but its intension contains more information.

For instance, *continuant entity* is a concept with more extension than *continuant dependent entity*, but the latter concept has a richer intension than the former because its meaning is more determinate. The concept *relational property* is less extended than the other two. *Relational property* is a concept that can be subdivided: there are relational properties that are part-to-whole and relational properties that are non-part-to-whole.

Relational properties can be actualized or remain as a potentiality only. A disposition is a relational property that is not actualized, a property in the sense of a universal. Insofar as a BF remains non-actualized, its nearest genus is "dispositional, part-to-whole relational property".

We can further specify this kind of property taken into account the way in which it is actualized. How does a BF differ in this respect from other kinds of functions? Only BFs can be realized by bodily processes. Bodily processes are relational, because they depend on a plurality of substances. Not every bodily process actualizes a BF, but every BF is actualized by a bodily process. For instance, a tooth has a cavity as a result of a series of processes that occurred in the mouth and on the tooth surface. Those processes created an environment that facilitated the development of bacteria on the enamel. The physiological processes that lead to the formation of a cavity are not a BF of the tooth. The tooth does not have, as one of its BFs, the formation of cavities.

A peculiar feature of many BFs is that they contribute to sustain in being a substantial entity. Hence, one of the species of relational processes is that of the "sustainers" of a substantial entity, so to speak. However, we cannot say that necessarily, a BF of a certain organism contributes to the sustaining in being of the whole organism, as Smith, Munn and Papakin [12] argue. The reason is that there are many counterexamples to their characterization of BF as a sustaining CF. For instance, reproductive functions do not contribute to the sustaining or survival of an organism – in some cases, they even hurt the organism's survival, e.g. the asexual reproduction in unicellular organisms—, and there are malfunctions in reproduction that do not affect survival, such as infertility.[5]

Considering these facts, a BF can be described as follows:

> A *Biological Function* is dispositional, relational property of a part (e.g. an organ) of a larger unity (e.g. a bodily system) that enables that part to perform a certain activity which involves other parts, and that may contribute (directly or indirectly) to the sustaining in being of the whole organism.

---

[5] David Hershenov called my attention to these counterexamples, which are considered by Boorse [2], and to Plantinga's cases. Alvin Plantinga [9] pointed out cases in which some malfunctions keep an organism alive (e.g. a perforated aorta together with a poor heart rate can keep a person alive), whereas the proper function would kill the organism (e.g. the perforated aorta together with a normal heart rate would produce an hemorrhaging leading to death). If the concept of proper function is defined by appealing to the survival of the organism, it is subject to the same counterexamples.

Secreting saliva is a disposition of the salivating glands, which are part of the mouth and the digestive system. The function of salivation enables the process of mastication and digestion of food. These processes, in turn, contribute to the sustaining in being of the human organism.

This is an non-formal definition that can give a framework for a formal definition. The set of necessary conditions (genus) includes:

- Being a relational property, i.e. a feature dependent on a plurality of substantial entities.
- Being a relational property exemplified by an entity that is part of an organism.
- Being a dispositional property, i.e. a property that may or may not be actualized.

The set of conditions that, together with the generic conditions, establish the sufficient conditions of some BF includes:
- Being realized by a bodily process or activity that involves several entities which are part of an organism.
- Being realized by a bodily process that may sustain in being an organism.

The description of Biological Functioning is, then:

A *Biological Functioning* is a process that actualizes a dispositional, relational property of a part (e.g. an organ) of a larger unity (e.g. a bodily system) such that the process may contribute (directly or indirectly) to the sustaining in being of the whole organism.

2.2 The ontological status of BFs and functionings. Three cases of predication

In this section I apply in a non-formal way the ontological square proposed by E.J. Lowe [6] and Neuhaus, Grenon and Smith [8] to the case of BFs and functionings. The goal is to clarify the ontological status of these entities and the formal relations that hold between BFs, functionings and their bearers, and to distinguish three cases of predication involving BFs.

The ontological square represents a (neo-Aristotelian) ontology with:

a) Four basic kinds of entities: Substantial Universals or kinds, Non-Substantial Universals or properties, Individual or particular substances, and Property instances or tropes, and

b) Several formal relations between them: characterization, instantiation, exemplification, inherence, constitution, etc.

Instantiation is the relation that holds between kinds and individual substances: an individual substance is an instance of a natural kind, which is a substantial universal. For example, my heart is an instance of the natural kind *heart*. The relation between properties and tropes is also instantiation: a trope is an instance of a property, e.g. the particular hue of redness of my heart is an instance of the universal "redness". A trope inheres always in an individual substance: the particular hue of redness of my heart inheres in my heart. This means that a trope cannot exist as an independent entity.

Both kinds and properties are universals. A property specifies or characterizes a kind, that is, a property enriches the meaning of the term denoting a kind. The concept of a kind has more extension than the concept of a property, whereas the concept of a property has more intension than the concept a kind. For example, the property "having four ventricles" specifies the natural kind "heart". Finally, the relation between a property and an individual substance is exemplification, e.g. my heart exemplifies the universal "having four ventricles".

The ontological square is represented in Figure 1, which combines elements taken from [8; fig. 1] and [5; fig. 8.1].

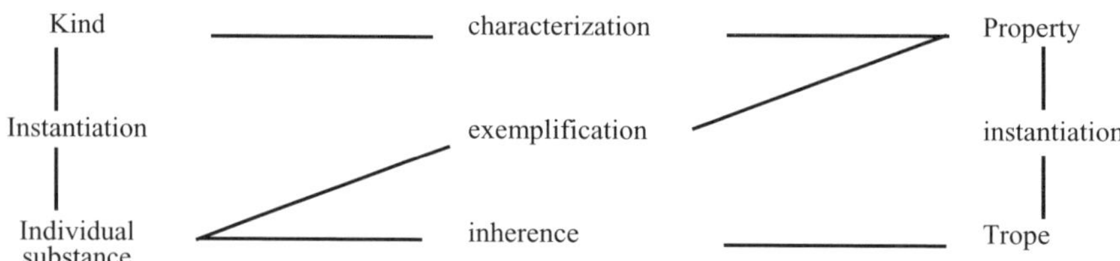

Figure 1. The Ontological Square.

The square reads as follows: an individual substance instantiates a kind; a trope inheres in an individual substance; a property characterizes a kind, etc. Taking into account the proposed definition, the ontological square for BFs is represented in Figure 2.

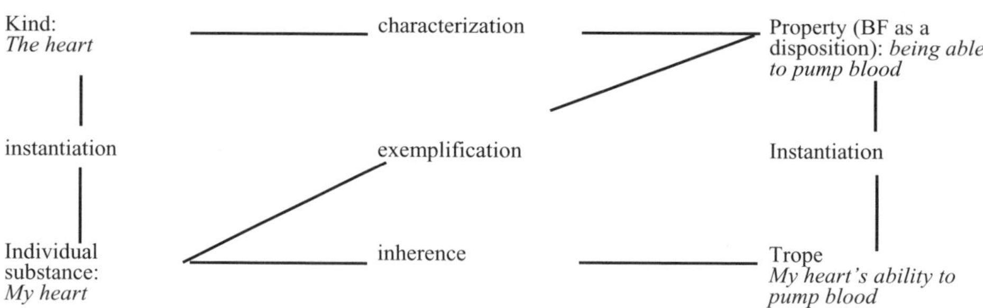

Figure 2. Ontological square of a BF.

This shows that, if we consider BF as a disposition, the relation between the bearer and BF is that of exemplification. But if we consider BF as a trope, the relation between the BF and the bearer is that of inherence. The definition of BF I proposed (section 2.1) describes BF as a property of a natural kind.

For E.J. Lowe the ontological square provides the ground of the distinction between two types of predication: the dispositional and the occurrent predication [6; p124]. The dispositional predication is exhibited in statements like 'This stuff *dissolves* in water'. The occurrent predication is exhibited in statements like 'This stuff *is dissolving* in water'.

Dispositional predications have the form '*a* instantiates a kind K which possesses *F*ness'. Occurrent predications have the form '*a* possesses a trope of *F*ness'. A dispositional sentence does not entail an occurrent sentence, for they express two different states of affairs. In the dispositional case, we describe an object's belonging to a kind which possesses some property. In the occurrent case, we describe an object's possessing a trope of some property.

We can distinguish a third case of predication: when we express a law of nature, we are using a variant of the dispositional case. Sentences like 'Water dissolves common salt' have the form '*a* kind K possesses *F*ness'. A substantial kind term is the grammatical subject in the statement of a natural law. In this case, we describe a kind's possessing a universal.

3. Concluding remarks

We can apply the dispositional/occurrent distinction to statements about BFs. We have to distinguish three cases of predication and, correspondingly, three different states of affairs that make true those predications. Table 1 summarizes these three cases.

Table 1. Three cases of predication involving BFs.

Case of predication	State of affairs expressed	Example
Law of nature	A natural kind's possessing a BF (*qua* disposition)	'The heart pumps blood.'
Dispositional predication	An object's instantiating a kind which possesses a BF (*qua* disposition)	'This heart pumps blood.'
Occurrent predication	An object's possessing a trope of a BF (i.e. a functioning).	'This heart is pumping blood.'

I have proposed a description for BF and biological functioning that attempts to integrate the essential elements found in the four articles reviewed. The three predication cases should be clearly distinguished when designing an information system involving BFs.

Acknowledgments

I would like to thank the three anonymous reviewers for their commentaries. I am grateful to David Hershenov, Ingvar Johansson and Pierre Grenon for their commentaries and corrections to earlier versions of this paper. The remaining mistakes are my responsibility. I am indebted to Marcos Jimenez and Francisco Diaz for their invaluable technical assistance. The paper was written under the auspices of the National Council for Science and Technology of Mexico (CONACYT) and the Department of Philosophy, University at Buffalo.

References

[1]   Boorse, Christopher. 1976. Wright on Functions. *Philosophical Review,* 85:70-86.
[2]   Boorse, C. 1977. Health as a Theoretical Concept. *Philosophy of Science*, 44(4), December, 542-573.
[3]   Boorse, C. 2002. A Rebuttal on Functions, in A. Ariew, R. Cummins, and M. Perlman (eds.) *Functions: New Essays in the Philosophy of Psychology and Biology.* NY: Oxford, 63-112.
[4]   Johansson, Ingvar. 2004. Functions, Function Concepts, and Scales. *The Monist* 86, 96-115.
      Online version at: < http://hem.passagen.se/ijohansson/functions1.htm >
[5]   Johansson, I., Smith, B., Tsikolia, N. *et al.* 2005. Functional Anatomy. A Taxonomic Proposal. *Acta Biotheoretica*, 53(3), 153-66.
      Online version at: < http://ontology.buffalo.edu/medo/Functional_Anatomy.pdf >
[6]   Lowe, E. J. 2006. *The Four-Category Ontology. A Metaphysical Foundation for Natural Science.* NY: Oxford University Press.
[7]   Millikan, Ruth G. 1989. In Defence of Proper Functions. *Philosophy of Science* 56(2), 288-302.
[8]   Neuhaus, F., Grenon, P. and Smith, B. Forthcoming. A Formal Theory of Substances, Qualities, and Universals, in Varzi, A. and Vieu, L. (eds.) *Proceedings of FOIS 2004.* International Conference on Formal Ontology and Information Systems, Turin, 4-6 November 2004. <http://ontology.buffalo.edu/bfo/SQU.pdf >
[9]   Plantinga, Alvin. 1993. *Warrant and Proper Function.* NY: Oxford University Press.
[10] Smith, Barry. Forthcoming. The Logic of Biological Classification and the Foundations of Biomedical Ontology, in Dag Westerstahl (ed.), *Invited Papers from the 10th International Conference in Logic Methodology and Philosophy of Science*, Oviedo, Spain, 2003. Elsevier-North-Holland. < http://ontology.buffalo.edu/bio/logic_of_classes.pdf >
[11] Smith, B. and Grenon, P. 2004. The Cornucopia of Formal-Ontological Relations. *Dialectica*, vol. 58, no. 3.
[12] Smith, B., Munn, K. and Papakin, I. 2004. Bodily Systems and the Spatial-Functional Structure of Human Body, in D. Pisanelli and M. Domenico (eds.) *Ontologies in Medicine: Proceedings of the Workshop on Medical Ontologies*. Rome, October 2003, Amsterdam: IOS Press, 39-63.
      Online version at: < http://ontology.buffalo.edu/medo/OBS.pdf >
[13] Smith B. and Welty, C. 2001. Ontology: Towards a New Synthesis. Introduction to the Second International Conference on Formal Ontology and Information Systems. *FOIS'01*, October 17-19, 2001, Ogunquit, Maine, USA: IOS Press, iii-ix.
[14] Walsh, D. M. and A. Ariew. 1999. A Taxonomy of Functions, in Buller, D. J. (ed.) *Function, Selection, and Design.* Albany: SUNY Press, 257-279.
[15] Zúñiga, G. 2001. Ontology: Its Transformation From Philosophy to Information Systems. *FOIS'01*, October 17-19, 2001, Ogunquit, Maine, USA: IOS Press, 187-197.

4. Actions and Events

Formal Ontology in Information Systems
B. Bennett and C. Fellbaum (Eds.)
IOS Press, 2006

Simultaneous Events and the "Once-Only" Effect

Haythem O. ISMAIL
German University in Cairo
Department of Computer Science
haythem.ismail@guc.edu.eg

Abstract. Some events recur, and some happen only once. Galton refers to the latter as "once-only" events [1]. In a first-order logic of events that makes a type-token distinction, the possibility of concurrent occurrences of the same event renders the characterization of the intuitive *once-onliness* not very intuitive. In particular, the paradigmatic case of the nth occurrence of a recurring event is shown to be not necessarily once-only. Counter-examples give rise to a classification of events based on the temporal relations among their occurrences. The problematic cases turn out to be those events that involve an indefinite individual; we call these *indefinitely-specified* events. We consider two options. The first is to restrict our event ontology, as has been implicitly done in most logics of events, to events that are definitely-specified. The second is to admit all sorts of events into our ontology and distinguish those that are definitely-specified from those that are not by statements in the object language. We opt for a representation of events as functional terms in the logic, and those terms denoting indefinitely-specified events seem to inevitably contain variables. Such non-ground terms turn out to be semantically problematic. To smoothly resolve these problems, we adopt Shapiro's logic of arbitrary and indefinite objects in which indefinite individuals are denoted by special terms [2]. Thus, indefinitely-specified events are naturally represented by functional terms with at least one argument denoting an indefinite individual.

Keywords. Knowledge representation, events, indefinites.

1. Introduction

Most events possibly recur. For example, birthday parties, naps, and drives to work are all recurrent events. By their very nature, some events happen only once. As far as we know, Galton [1] was the first to explicitly point out this class of events. For example, someone's first birthday, the splitting of a particular cell, someone's turning 21, or, in general, someone's doing something for the nth time, are all events that can happen only once. We shall follow Galton and call these events *once-only* events.

Once-only events are interesting to the logician, particularly a logician concerned with issues of tense and aspect. For example, an idealized conceptualization of the English perfect is as an operator that yields a permanent state [1,3]. A permanent state is one that, once it starts to hold, will persist forever. The onset of a permanent state is therefore a once-only event, and a logic of aspect should support this inference. But once-only events are not only interesting to the logician, they are also interesting to state-of-the-art information systems. For example, any scheduling system would need to make a clear distinction between recurrent and once-only events.

For a knowledge representation system to reason about once-only events, we need to accomplish two tasks:

Task 1. Sharpening our intuitions regarding which events are once-only and which are recurrent.

Task 2. Developing a formal system with sufficient expressive and inferential powers to support representing and reasoning about once-onliness.

Task 2 is a purely logical endeavor, but **Task 1** is an intellectual exercise that possibly falls outside the bounds of logic, but certainly fits within the realm of ontology. A system that accomplishes those tasks has been developed in [1], with a more thorough investigation of semantics, soundness, and completeness in [4].

However, a certain property of the two systems developed by Galton conceals some difficulties with accomplishing our two tasks. In particular, Galton's systems do not allow for simultaneous (or, more broadly, concurrent) occurrences of the same event. These systems are basically propositional tense logics extended with aspect operators and *event radicals*, which are symbols denoting event types. Thus, no event tokens are representable, and the notion of multiple simultaneous occurrences of the same event type does not even arise. In [1], and as far as event occurrence goes, only the fact that an event type occurs at some time (in the past or future) is representable. The system is silent about what that exactly means: does it mean that there is exactly one occurrence of the event at the time, or that there are possibly multiple simultaneous occurrences?[1] In [4], however, the model-theoretic semantics reveals how this is resolved. [4] identifies an event with its set of occurrences. Since Galton's ontology does not include event tokens (i.e., occurrences) as primitives, he identifies these (roughly) with the intervals over which they occur. Thus, the tacit assumption is that there can only be one occurrence of any event at any given time.

In the more recent work reported in [5] (which is not concerned with once-only events), event tokens are indeed first-class entities in the ontology denoted by terms in the logic. However, tokens are identified with pairs $\langle \eta, \mathbf{e} \rangle$, where $\mathbf{e}$ is an event type and η is an *episode* of that type. (An episode is an interval carrying with it all the history in a branching time structure.) Thus, simultaneous tokens of the same event type are still not distinguished by this system.

In this paper, I investigate problems with accomplishing **Task 1** and **Task 2** in a common sense reasoning system that makes a type-token distinction and allows for simultaneous occurrences of the same event. One question is whether we need to do this, whether there are indeed events with simultaneous occurrences. This issue, together with problems with **Task 1**, is taken on in Section 2. The rest of the paper is dedicated to different issues in accomplishing **Task 2**.

---

[1]For some, the preferred meaning may be the second. Asserting that an event occurs at a time could be thought of as an assertion about the existence of an occurrence of that event. The standard semantics of existence assertions would allow multiple occurrences of the event at the said time. But, in that case, [1] fails to correctly account for once-onliness; the best it can do is to account for events with multiple occurrences that are all simultaneous.

2. Patterns of Occurrence

2.1. Two Examples

Consider a T.V. channel correspondent reporting live from a war-torn city and delivering the following piece of troubling news.

(1) The first explosion occurred at 3 p.m.

Is the correspondent reporting a once-only event? It would seem so, given that the nth occurrence of a recurrent event is a typical example of once-onliness.[2] But this is not exactly true. For suppose that two explosions, not one, happen simultaneously, at 3 p.m. sharp. In this case, it is not clear whether the reporter is being sloppy in their choice of words, or whether the first-explosion event is, after all, not once-only. Consider the first alternative, where the reporter is assumed to have misused the phrase "first explosion". In this case, the first-explosion event is certainly once-only, but it just never took place. In particular, since two explosions happened simultaneously, then neither of them could be considered the first. In fact, all explosions reported to have taken place are pre-ordered, and one might argue that a strict linear order is needed to be able to define the nth occurrence. Although this is a reasonable analysis, it is not satisfying. In particular, the notion of a pre-order of events is not very intuitive. People would find it a little counter-intuitive to see how several explosions can occur, while a first-explosion never does. In addition, and if we take this line of thought to an extreme, since neither explosion qualifies as being *the* first-explosion, it would seem that the next explosion to occur would! The other alternative is to say that there are indeed two first-explosions and abandon the idea of the first-explosion being a once-only event. Note that the two alternatives correspond to two ways of interpreting "first explosion". On one interpretation, a first-explosion is an explosion which is strictly followed by any other possible explosions. On another interpretation, a first-explosion is one which is not strictly preceded by any other explosions. We shall come back to explosions, but consider another example.

A professor asks a deep question in the classroom and announces that the first student to come up with the correct answer will get one bonus point. After this announcement has been made, everyone in the classroom is awaiting (or busily trying to be the agent of) some event. This is the event of someone coming up with the correct answer for the first time. Is this a once-only event? It is not clear. If a particular student pronounces the correct answer, then no later pronouncements of the same answer will earn other students bonus points. Thus, we may judge the event as being once-only. But suppose that *two* students come up with the correct answer simultaneously. Who will get the bonus point? Only one of them? Neither? Or both? If only one, then which one? And what criteria will the professor use to determine which of the two simultaneous events is the first? If neither, then, at the very best, it is just unfair. If both, which is probably the common practice in such cases, then, once again, we have to give up the assumption that the nth occurrence of a recurrent event is *necessarily* once-only.[3]

---

[2]Needless to say, "first explosion" here means the first explosion in the city on the day the report is aired.

[3]Another alternative is to think of a single first-correct-answer event whose agent is a plural individual à la [6, for example]. But this analysis will be awkward in our situation, where the two students making up the purported plural individual competitively, rather than collectively, seek the correct answer.

2.2. Serials, Races, and Witnesses

The two examples discussed above reveal one thing: reasoning about once-onliness can be tricky. This is not confined to the case of the nth occurrence event, but may also be shown to apply to other cases of once-onliness. This at least complicates **Task 1** as described in Section 1. But let's explore the issue a little further and see whether some structure could be imposed on the problematic patterns of occurrence. The unproblematic pattern is that where the occurrences of an event form a strict linear order. In this case, *no* occurrences of the event are simultaneous. I will call events exhibiting this pattern *serials*.

Another pattern, represented in the above two examples, is that where multiple n^{th} occurrences are possible. In this case, *some* occurrences of the event are simultaneous. I will call events that exhibit this pattern *races*. This choice of name is intended to remind us of the prototypical case of a race, where two runners arrive at the end line simultaneously—a situation very similar to that of the second example above.

A third pattern is that where *all* occurrences of the event are necessarily simultaneous. What is an example of an event exhibiting this pattern? Recall the T.V. report on explosions, and consider the reporter uttering (2) instead of (1).

(2) The first explosion was heard at 3 p.m.

The event reported here is the *hearing* of the first explosion. This event has many occurrences, as many as there are people who have heard the explosion. Yet, the event is not recurrent; all occurrences are simultaneous, they all took place at 3 p.m.[4] There are two events involved here: an explosion and a hearing of the explosion. In general, whenever there is a *perceived event* (generally a race) and a *perception event*, all occurrences of the latter are simultaneous. I will use the term *witnesses* to refer to such perception events and any other events exhibiting the same pattern. A particularly relevant example of a witness is the event of the nth occurrence of a race.

But serials, races, and witnesses are not all there is. So far we have only considered examples of punctual events—those that could be conceived of as occurring at time points (or atomic intervals). For durative events, two more patterns are possible. Durative occurrences of the same event may overlap in time. Consider the first screening of a movie. If the movie is showing in two movie theaters, then we have two overlapping screenings. They can start (and, hence, end) at the same time, or one of them can start after the first starts but before it ends. In the first case, we have something similar to races, but for durative events. In the second case, things are are a little vague. For we might prefer to pick as the first screening the one that starts first. Yet, we may also consider both screenings to be tokens of the first-screening event, adopting the view that a second screening is one that necessarily starts after the first ends. Overlapping can also take a third form if we consider events whose occurrences are not necessarily of the same duration. In that case, the period of one occurrence could be a proper sub-period of another. (Consider the event of running around a track, where the duration of an occurrence depends on the speed of the runner.) Durative events may also be interleaved. A multi-

---

[4]For a physicist, these events are probably not simultaneous on a fine-grained conception of time, due to the speed of sound and the spatial distribution of the different hearers.

programmed operating system will concurrently run two processes by interleaving their executions. The nth process-running is again not clearly once-only.

Without loss of generality, the rest of the paper will concentrate only on races and witnesses as problematic cases for once-onliness.

2.3. Indefinitely-Specified Events

Races and witnesses are problematic cases for the once-onliness of the nth occurrence of an event. We have considered examples of each of these cases. What is an example of a serial—the unproblematic case? Here is a list:

1. The explosion of a particular bomb.
2. A particular student's coming up with the right answer.
3. A particular person's hearing the explosion of a particular bomb.
4. The screening of a particular movie in a particular movie theater.
5. The running of a particular process by an operating system.

The difference between these examples and the corresponding problematic examples, is that all individuals involved in the above serials are particular, definite individuals. A race or a witness (with respect to once-onliness) may be turned into a serial by fixing (or particularizing) all indefinite individuals it involves. This indefinite-specification of races and witnesses is the source of the difficulties they pose. Each of the simultaneous occurrences of an indefinitely-specified event (a race or a witness) is also an occurrence of a definitely-specified event (a serial). Consequently, it is also the unique occurrence of some once-only event, namely the event of the nth occurrence of the serial. (In the case of an explosion, fixing the indefinite directly yields a once-only event—that of a particular bomb exploding.)

The above discussion suggests that the class of definitely-specified events is identical to that of serials. One direction of that identity is evident: a definitely-specified event is a serial. Once all individuals involved in an event are fixed, then, at any time, there can be only one occurrence of the event. The other direction deserves some discussion. Consider the act of driving a car. At any time, there can only be one driver of a particular car. This means that the indefinitely-specified event of someone's driving of a particular car is indeed a serial. Conversely, at any time, only one car may be driven by a particular driver. Thus, the indefinitely-specified event of a particular person's driving of some indefinite car is a serial. Other examples of such indefinitely-specified serials include the reelection of an American president, someone's eating of a particular apple (but not a particular person's eating of some apple) or someone's cutting of a particular rope. It could be argued that more than one person can eat the same apple or cut the same rope. One analysis may hold that these are not examples of serials. Another analysis may allude to plural individuals [6], asserting that multiple agents *collectively* eat the apple or cut the rope.

The above examples show that there are indeed indefinitely-specified serials. But wait. Even such cases have two special features. First, that the above examples of indefinitely-specified events are serials seems to be only contingent. For one may construct possible worlds in which cars are designed such that the same car may be simultaneously driven by more than one driver, or such that a person may simultaneously drive more than one car, or such that more than one person can assume the American presidency at a given time. This is in contrast to the near-logical necessity of a definitely-specified event's being a serial. Second, one may always reduce the indefiniteness of the above serials to a very special type of indefiniteness. For example, the indefiniteness of the American president is only indirectly a person-indefiniteness, but is primarily temporal. The standard representation of "American president" is as a function of time; once you fix a time, you would definitely identify the reelected president. Fixing the indefinite time of a temporally-indefinite event yields a once-only event with the time of its unique occurrence as part of its specification. Similarly, we may think of the car driver, the apple eater, or the rope cutter as (partial) functions of time.

An important note on terminology is important at this point. A definitely-specified event is one involving only definite individuals. An indefinitely-specified event is one involving at least one non-temporal indefinite. A temporally-indefinite event is one involving only temporal indefinites.

I believe that a temporally-indefinite event is the only possible case of a non-definitely-specified serial. Let $e(x)$ be an indefinitely-specified event, where x is the indefinite. (For simplicity, I am assuming a single indefinite.) There are three cases to consider.

1. At any given time, more than one individual satisfies the restrictions on x. If a and b are two such individuals, then possible simultaneous occurrences of $e(a)$ and $e(b)$ imply that $e(x)$ is not a serial.
2. At all times, a single individual satisfies the restrictions on x. If this is a logical or a domain constraint, then the representation of the event is incorrect, since it should be definitely-specified (for example, using Russell's definite descriptor, ι). Otherwise, we are in a situation similar to case 1.
3. At any given time, a single individual satisfies the restrictions on x. This is a case of temporal indefiniteness.

We, thus, arrive at the following hypothesis.

- Serial = Definitely-specified $\cup$ Temporally-indefinite.
- Race $\cup$ Witness = Indefinitely-specified.

3. A Formal System

In this section, we investigate **Task 2**—developing a formal system for reasoning about once-onliness. Given the results of Section 2, we will need this system to distinguish serials, races, and witnesses; and to grant true once-onliness to serials. This system may easily be extended to account for overlapping occurrences, but some work is needed to include interleaved occurrences.

3.1. Semantic and Ontological Commitments

The system is intended to be integrated into the logic of states and events introduced in [7] and described in detail in [3]. This logic has been proposed in the process of developing an embodied cognitive agent based on the SNePS knowledge representation and reasoning and acting system [8,9,10].

The system to be developed here inherits two features of SNePS-based logics.

1. Terms represent anything that we can think or talk about. SNePS semantics is based on Alexius Meinong's theory of objects (see [8,11]), where terms denote objects of thought of a cognitive agent.
2. Given 1, the ontology includes objects, times, propositions, events and event occurrences, to mention only those entities that are particularly relevant to this paper. In addition, actual occurrences, possible occurrences, and incomplete occurrences are all members of the ontology.

It should be noted that SNePS-based logics are term-logics. In particular, there are no predicate symbols, only functions from tuples to proposition-denoting terms. Nevertheless, to simplify the exposition, I will assume a standard first-order logic. (But see [12] for details.)

As mentioned above, to reason about once-onliness, we need to distinguish serials. This distinction could be made at either the ontological level, or at the logical level. At the ontological level, we can opt for admitting only definitely-specified events into our ontology. This is indeed the implicit assumption of almost all logics of events in which event types are granted the status of first-class individuals.[5] In particular, this is the implicit (but possibly unintended) position taken in [1,4], where all examples of event radicals are definitely-specified. If we adopt this view, then we need not worry about once-onliness. In particular, the nth occurrence event will be once-only for all event types.

This position, however, would limit the expressivity of our logic and deprives our ontology of many events that we can think or talk about. In particular, indefinitely-specified events allow us to make general statements about big classes of events. For example, we only need to state the effects of explosions once, for a single indefinitely-specified explosion, not once for *each* definitely-specified explosion of a particular bomb.

3.2. The Logic

Sorts. We use a sorted first-order logic with equality. The following is a list of the sorts and their intended meanings.

- $\mathcal{I}$: A sort for individuals. We use the superscript i to designate variables and $0-$ary functions of this sort. When not superscripted, x, y, and z are variables of this sort. Self-explanatory small caps symbols are constants of sort $\mathcal{I}$. Examples include JOHN, MARY, BOMB12 (for a particular bomb), etc.
- $\mathcal{T}$: A sort for times. We use the superscript t to designate variables and $0-$ary functions of this sort. When not superscripted, $t, t_1, t_2, \ldots$ are variables of this sort.
- $\mathcal{C}$: A sort for event categories (or event types). We use the superscript c to designate variables and $0-$ary functions of this sort.
- $\mathcal{E}$: A sort for event tokens (or occurrences). We use the superscript e to designate variables and $0-$ary functions of this sort. When not superscripted, $e, e_1, e_2, \ldots$ are variables of this sort.
- $\mathcal{N}$: A sort for natural numbers. Familiar numerals $(1, 2, 3, \ldots)$ are constants of this sort. When not superscripted, variables i and j are of this sort.

---

[5]There are notable exceptions—Process Specification Language [13], for example.

Function and Predicate Symbols. These symbols denote typed $n-$ary functions or predicates ($n > 0$). Here is a list of some domain-independent function and predicate symbols, with their informal semantics.

- Occ: $\mathcal{N} \times \mathcal{C} \longrightarrow \mathcal{C}$, where $\mathrm{Occ}(i, c)$ is the event category of the $[\![i]\!]^{\mathrm{th}}$ occurrence of event category $[\![c]\!]$.[6]
- Cat: a predicate symbol over $\mathcal{E} \times \mathcal{C}$, where $[\![\mathrm{Cat}(e, c)]\!]$ means that event token $[\![e]\!]$ is of category $[\![c]\!]$.
- Occurs: a predicate symbol over $\mathcal{E} \times \mathcal{T}$, where $[\![\mathrm{Occurs}(e, t)]\!]$ means that event token $[\![e]\!]$ occurs at time $[\![t]\!]$.

In addition, domain-dependent function and predicate symbols will be used as we need to, with their semantics informally specified as we consider different examples. [7]

3.3. Representing Once-Onliness

With the formal machinery now at our disposal, consider how we can define serials, races, witnesses, and once-onliness.

In the following schemas, c denotes a term of sort $\mathcal{C}$.

- Serial$(c) =_{\mathrm{def}}$
  $\forall t, e_1, e_2[[\mathrm{Cat}(e_1, c) \wedge \mathrm{Cat}(e_2, c) \wedge \mathrm{Occurs}(e_1, t) \wedge \mathrm{Occurs}(e_2, t)] \Rightarrow e_1 = e_2]$
- Witness$(c) =_{\mathrm{def}}$
  $\exists t_1 \, \forall e, t_2[[\mathrm{Cat}(e, c) \wedge \mathrm{Occurs}(e, t_2)] \Rightarrow t_2 = t_1]$
- Race$(c) =_{\mathrm{def}} \neg[\mathrm{Serial}(c) \vee \mathrm{Witness}(c)]$.

Thus, an event category is a serial if no two distinct tokens occur simultaneously. An event category is a witness if there is a unique time (t_1) such that, if a token of that event occurs, it will have to occur at that time. The uniqueness of t_1 could be secured by proper axiomatization of "Occurs". A race is just the default, or unmarked, case of an event category.[8]

Let us now turn to once-onliness.

- OnceOnly$(c) =_{\mathrm{def}} \mathrm{Serial}(c) \wedge \mathrm{Witness}(c)$.

Why is the above a definition of once-onliness? To see why, note that if c is a serial, then there is a unique occurrence of c (if any) at a time t. In addition, if c is a witness, then t is the only possible time at which c may occur. Thus, c's unique occurrence at t is its only occurrence.[9] In fact, we can derive the following result, given an appropriate set of inference rules and a proper axiomatization of Occurs. (The proof is straightforward, but is omitted for limitations of space.)

---

[6] Where τ is a term, $[\![\tau]\!]$ is the denotation of τ.

[7] To simplify the exposition, I have opted for a standard first-order logic with equality. In the SNePS tradition, an equivalence relation, denoted by the predicate "Equiv", typically replaces identity ("="). This relation holds between two intensions (Meinongian objecta) if they happen to pick out the same extension. See [14] for more details.

[8] A strengthening of the logic by a necessity operator is perhaps needed to dismiss cases where an event category is only contingently a serial or a witness.

[9] On a feature-analysis account, we can think of two binary features, given by the definitions of serials and witnesses above. Think of the first ($\pm S$) as the uniqueness of occurrence at a time, and of the second ($\pm W$) as the uniqueness of the time of occurrence. These two features define a 2×2 matrix, where serials are $\langle +S, -W \rangle$, witnesses are $\langle -S, +W \rangle$, races are $\langle -S, -W \rangle$, and once-only events are $\langle +S, +W \rangle$.

- OnceOnly(c) $\Leftrightarrow$
$$\forall e_1[[\mathrm{Cat}(e_1,c) \land \exists t_1[\mathrm{Occurs}(e_1,t_1)]] \Rightarrow$$
$$\forall e_2[\,[\mathrm{Cat}(e_2,c) \land \exists t_2[\mathrm{Occurs}(e_2,t_2)]] \Rightarrow e_2 = e_1]]]$$

The complexity of the above formula stems from our admitting possible and incomplete tokens of an event category. In particular, stating something of the form $\mathrm{Cat}(e,c)$ does not mean that e actually occurs; we have to also state $\mathrm{Occurs}(e,t)$, for some t. Once-only events can have multiple possible (imagined) and incomplete tokens, but only one occurrence. Thus, the above definition states that an event category is once only if an occurrence of any of its tokens is its unique occurrence.

Recalling our suggestion in Section 2.2 that the category of the nth occurrence of an event is a witness, we may now easily derive (4), given (3).

(3) $\forall c, i[\mathrm{Witness}(\mathrm{Occ}(i,c))]$

(4) $\forall c, i[\mathrm{Serial}(c) \Rightarrow \mathrm{OnceOnly}(\mathrm{Occ}(i,c))]$

4. A Problem with Indefinites

4.1. The Problem

Given the above system, we should be able to assert of particular domain-dependent event categories that they are serials, races, witnesses, or once-only. For example, we should be able to assert that the event of some (indefinite) bomb exploding is a race. But how would we represent this indefinitely-specified event? First of all, we cannot do it using a ground term; for a ground term would certainly pick out a definitely-specified event. The obvious option is to somehow introduce an existential quantifier. For example, to state that an explosion is a race, we can use (5).

(5) $\exists x[\mathrm{Bomb}(x) \land \mathrm{Race}(\mathrm{Explode}(x))]$

But there are several problems with this representation. First, what does the term "Explode(x)" denote? Does it denote the explosion of an indefinite bomb? Or the explosion of an indefinite entity, since the restriction of x's being a bomb is not part of the term? What if x is bound by a universal quantifier, would the meaning of the term change? More importantly, the above representation is obviously incorrect. It means that there is some bomb whose explosion is a race. But this is contradictory, since the explosion of that alleged bomb is certainly a serial (in fact, a once-only event).

What we seem to be facing here is yet another problem of quantifying-in. In this case, it is quantifying into an event category predication that is causing the trouble. What we need is to somehow bring the binding quantifier and the restriction on the variable inside the scope of "Race". Unfortunately, this cannot be done in the current system.

We can, however, adopt Shapiro's logic of arbitrary and indefinite objects [2], which solves the problem in an elegant and intuitive way.

4.2. Shapiro's Logic of Arbitrary and Indefinite Objects

Shapiro's logic, $\mathcal{L}_A$, is motivated by several issues in knowledge representation for commonsense reasoning and natural language understanding. For limitations of space, these motivations will not be discussed here. Nor will the complete logic be presented in detail; the interested reader may consult [2]. Only the relevant aspects of this logic will be minimally discussed.

Among its terms, $\mathcal{L}_A$ includes what are called *quantified terms*. They come in two types:

1. If x is a variable and $\phi(x)$ is a formula containing at least one free occurrence of x, then $(any\ x)$ and $(any\ x\ \phi(x))$ are *arbitrary terms*. If A is an arbitrary term, then x is the variable of A, *any* is the determiner of A, and $\phi(x)$ is the restriction of A (and x). A denotes the arbitrary individual satisfying the restrictions in $\phi(x)$.
2. If x is a variable, $q_1, \ldots, q_n$ are variables or arbitrary terms, and $\phi(x)$ is a formula containing at least one free occurrence of x, then $(some\ x)$, $(some\ x\ \phi(x))$, $(some\ x\ (q_1, \ldots, q_n))$, and $(some\ x\ (q_1, \ldots, q_n)\ \phi(x))$ are *indefinite terms*. If I is an indefinite term, then x, *some*, and $\phi(x)$ are as for arbitrary terms (with *some* replacing *any*). $q_1, \ldots, q_n$, if included, are called the supporting variables of I and x. I denotes the indefinite individual satisfying the restrictions in $\phi(x)$, and dependent on the arbitrary individuals denoted by $q_1, \ldots, q_n$.

One of the motivations behind $\mathcal{L}_A$ is to provide a natural representation of donkey sentences. (6) is the famous donkey sentence due to [15], and (7) is its representation in $\mathcal{L}_A$.

(6) Every farmer who owns a donkey beats it.

(7) Beats($(any\ x\ \mathrm{Farmer}(x) \wedge \mathrm{Owns}(x, (some\ y\ (x)\ \mathrm{Donkey}(y))))$), y)

The arbitrary term $(any\ x\ \mathrm{Farmer}(x) \wedge \mathrm{Owns}(x, (some\ y\ (x)\ \mathrm{Donkey}(y))))$ denotes the arbitrary farmer who owns a donkey. The indefinite term $(some\ y\ (x)\ \mathrm{Donkey}(y))$ denotes the indefinite donkey that depends on the farmer x. (The inclusion of the supporting variable x maintains scoping information.) Here, due to *structure sharing*, the y that occurs as the second argument of *Beats* is the same one that occurs as the variable of the indefinite term.

4.3. Representing Indefinitely-Specified Events

We may now make use of Shapiro's indefinite terms to represent indefinitely-specified events. Going back to the example of explosions, here is a possible representation of the event category of some bomb exploding.

- $\mathrm{Explode}(some\ x\ \mathrm{Bomb}(x))$

Thus, to state that an explosion is a race, we may use (8).

(8) Race(Explode($some\ x\ \mathrm{Bomb}(x)$))

What is interesting here is that we have a rough syntactic characterization of definitely-specified events, indefinitely-specified events, and temporally-indefinite events.

- An event term is definitely-specified if it has no indefinite sub-terms.
- An event term is temporally-indefinite if the only indefinite sub-terms it has have variables of sort $\mathcal{T}$.
- An event term is indefinitely-specified if it has at least one indefinite sub-term with a variable not of sort $\mathcal{T}$.

5. Conclusions

We have examined the notion of once-only events and concluded that recognizing both event types and event tokens admits multiple simultaneous occurrences of typical cases of once-onliness. A classification of event types, distinguished by their patterns of occurrence, was shown to make the necessary distinctions between true cases of once-only events and problematic ones. The notion of indefinite specification was shown to underlie this classification. We have also shown how a logical system may account for this classification and how problems with quantifying into indefinitely-specified event terms may be resolved, using Shapiro's logic of arbitrary and indefinite objects.

6. Acknowledgements

The author thanks Stuart Shapiro and three anonymous reviewers for their comments on an earlier version of this paper.

References

[1] Antony Galton. *The Logic of Aspect*. Clarendon Press, Oxford, 1984.
[2] Stuart C. Shapiro. A logic of arbitrary and indefinite objects. In Dedier Dubois, Chris Welty, and MaryAnne Williams, editors, *Principles of Knowledge Representation and Reasoning: Proceedings of the Ninth International Conference (KR2004)*, pages 565–575. AAAI Press, 2004.
[3] Haythem O. Ismail. *Reasoning and Acting in Time*. PhD thesis, University at Buffalo, The State University of New York, 2001.
[4] Antony Galton. The logic of occurrence. In Antony Galton, editor, *Temporal Logics and Their Applications*, pages 169–196. Academic Press, 1987.
[5] Brandon Bennett and Antony Galton. A unifying semantics for time and events. *Artificial Intelligence*, 153(1–2):13–48, 2004.
[6] Godehard Link. *Algebraic Semantics in Language and Philosophy*. CSLI Publications, Stanford, CA, 1998.
[7] Haythem O. Ismail and Stuart C. Shapiro. Two problems with reasoning and acting in time. In Anthony Cohn, Fausto Giunchiglia, and Bart Selman, editors, *Principles of Knowledge Representation and Reasoning: Proceedings of the Seventh International Conference (KR 2000)*, pages 355–365, San Francisco, CA, 2000. Morgan Kaufmann.
[8] Stuart C. Shapiro and William J. Rapaport. SNePS considered as a fully intensional propositional semantic network. In N. Cercone and G. McCalla, editors, *The Knowledge Frontier*, pages 263–315. Springer-Verlag, New York, 1987.

[9] Stuart C. Shapiro. SNePS: A logic for natural language understanding and commonsense reasoning. In Łucja M. Iwańska and Stuart C. Shapiro, editors, *Natural Language Processing and Knowledge Representation: Language for Knowledge and Knowledge for Language*, pages 175–195. AAAI Press/The MIT Press, Menlo Park, CA, 2000.

[10] Stuart C. Shapiro and Haythem O. Ismail. Anchoring in a grounded layered architecture with integrated reasoning,. *Robotics and Autonomous Systems*, 43(2–3):97–108, May 2003.

[11] Stuart C. Shapiro and William J. Rapaport. Models and minds: Knowledge representation for natural-language competence. In Robert Cummins and John Pollock, editors, *Philosophy and AI: Essays at the Interface*, pages 215–259. MIT Press, Cambridge, MA, 1991.

[12] Stuart C. Shapiro. Belief spaces as sets of propositions. *Journal of Experimental and Theoretical Artificial Intelligence*, 5:225–235, 1993.

[13] Craig Schlenoff, Michael Gruninger, Florence Tissot, John Valois, Josh Lobell, and Jintae Lee. The process specification language (PSL): Overview and version 1.0 specification. Technical Report NISTIR 6459, National Institute of Standards and Technology, Gaithersburg, MD, 2000.

[14] Anthony S. Maida and Stuart C. Shapiro. Intensional concepts in propositional semantic networks. *Cognitive Science*, 6:291–330, 1982.

[15] P. T. Geach. *Reference and Generality*. Cornell University Press, Ithaca, NY, 1962.

Formal Ontology in Information Systems
B. Bennett and C. Fellbaum (Eds.)
IOS Press, 2006

155

Temporal Qualification and Change with First–Order Binary Predicates

Pierre GRENON [a,b,1]

[a] *IFOMIS, Saarland University, Germany*
[b] *Department of Philosophy, University of Geneva, Switzerland*

Abstract. Some temporal ontologies require a way of enforcing the temporal qualification of certain assertions—those about changing entities. In a knowledge representation language based on first–order logic, this is straightforwardly done by having a category of temporal regions and augmenting predicates with an additional
argument place for the time at which a given predicate holds.

Here, I address the problem of representing entities changing over time and enforcing temporal qualification in first–order languages with predicates at most binary. It is possible, I argue, using temporal entities known as perdurants (events
or processes)—towards which binary languages seem *prima facie* biased. There is
however virtually no ontological cost for an ontology which in addition to changing
entities recognizes changes, events and processes. Temporal knowledge representation therefore is not a lost cause even with languages with syntax and semantics
limited to the representation of binary relations.

Keywords. Temporal ontology, knowledge representation, languages with binary
predicates

1. Preliminaries

1.1. Temporal Qualification and Change

Atomic assertions in ontologies are of three sorts: i) an entity instantiates or belongs
to a kind, ii) a property inheres in an entity (or, synonymously, an entity exemplifies a
property), and iii) an entity is in a certain relation to an entity (or more). We can say that
there are two sorts of temporally extended entities. Those which can change over time in
some respect or another and those which can not. As illustration, consider the following:

> Plato is an adult.

> Plato is 1,80 meters tall.

> Plato likes Socrates.

and again:

---

[1]Correspondence: IFOMIS, Universität des Saarlandes, Saarbrücken, Postfach 151150, Deutschland; E-
mail: pgrenon@ifomis.uni-saarland.de.

The death of Socrates is a death from poisoning.

The death of Socrates occurs in Athens.

The lamenting of Plato occurs a few paces from the death of Socrates.

Entities such as Plato and Socrates are endurants; they endure [1]: persist in time but can change. For them, to have a property is in the general case to have it at a time (leaving aside essential and lifelong constant properties, e.g. Plato is a person, he does not know about the American continent). Entities such as the death of Socrates and the lamenting of Plato are perdurants; they perdure: persist in time through the succession of their temporal parts. For them, to have a property is to have it atemporally and to have a transient property is for these entities to have a (so–called "temporal") part which has the property atemporally. So, endurants change (they can have distinct and contradictory properties at different times) but perdurants do not change (rather they have different parts with different, possibly contradictory, properties).

The need for temporal qualification in predication is motivated by the need to account for change in entities and the correlated indexing of their properties and relations to certain times. If an entity does not change in a certain respect, then temporal qualification becomes superfluous. The mere indication of the temporal location of such an entity (the time at which it exists) suffices to indicate the time over which it has the feature in question.

1.2. Representation

Representing change in the respects listed above in endurants using temporal qualification is one of the most straightforward and natural operations in knowledge representation (KR henceforth) with languages with no or few expressive constraints. There are however distinct strategies which are not on a par with respect to their ontological character.

One strategy is to have a non temporal language (allowing for non temporally qualified, I will say "plain", assertions) and then bundle assertions in the right sort of way. There are two such main ways. The first uses a sentential operator taking a sentence and a time and which yields truths when sentences are correlated with adequate times, and falsehoods otherwise. The second builds distinct ontologies and representations for different times.

Either way, this strategy tends to give no ontological status to a category of times (time instants or regions) nor to a category of changes. It puts times in the semantics and models change as discrepancy in the truth value of an assertion over time. [2] It is not, so to speak, an ontological strategy for temporal KR. A variant of the second way adds a dedicated ontology for times and perdurants (among which changes as entities) in a modular framework whose complexity is augmented by the articulation of the two sorts of ontologies. [1]

Another strategy consists in a purely first–order (FO henceforth) logical approach in which temporally sensitive predicates have an argument place for the time at which their plain proxies obtain. Starting from a plain vocabulary, we can then enforce temporal qualification by augmenting the arity of the relevant vocabulary and having a dedicated argument place for predicates taking a time. Relations between entities then are also relations to a time. We go for instance from a plain vocabulary containing *Adult, Child, likes* to a temporal vocabulary containing: *adultAt, childAt, likesAt*. This strategy allows ontological commitment to time and, at least in principle, to change. It is moreover a strategy which can deal mono–ontologically with change, endurants, and perdurants. For this reason, this strategy and generally a KR strategy in which all can be done and referred to in a FO logical language will be taken as paradigmatic of ontological KR, and in particular, temporal KR.

The problem I wish to address here is that this strategy is not available when temporal KR is done with languages limited to predicates of arity at most two (I will say "binary languages"). Clearly, the predicate *likesAt* is ternary and not a predicate of a binary language.

1.3. Impoverished Languages

Is the issue ludicrous? It is a mere scholar exercise if our benchmark for a KR language is FO logical or allows for sentential operators. Many KR languages are as expressive as FO ones or more, e.g. KIF [3] or CycL (the language of the Cyc system [4] which allows virtually every sort of representations alluded to). In the research area of the semantic web, however, KR is done with designed computable fragments of FOL (variants of Description Logics [5]) which are binary languages. Therefore, if irreducibly ternary predicates are needed, these are outside the purview of the KR capabilities of these languages.

[6]—but virtually all semantic web related publications—is illustrative of the mode of the default options for temporal KR in binary language, if only by omission of this problem. It gives examples of what is expressible in two particular binary languages, RDFS and OWL. In particular, it says that RDFS allows to:

> – state that **Peter** is an instance of the class **Canadian**, and that his **age** has value 48.

OWL allows moreover, among other things, to:

> – state that the class **Canadian** is defined precisely as those members of the class **Person** that have **Canada** as a value of the property **Nationality**; and
> – state that **age** is functional.

The problem is that assertions with such a vocabulary *prima facie* require temporal qualification. In all generality, nationality is indexed to time and age is only functional when it is a relation between a person, a date, and an age. In both cases, the perspicuous way of representing these relations over a domain of entities—not including sentences—are through ternary predicates allowing for temporal qualification. Short of this, the sort of KR illustrated in the examples above is one done in a temporally circumscribed ontology. And it is therefore not surprising that in the context of description logic, tense logics are paradigmatic. [7]

In first analysis, this situation poses a thorny problem for the representation of bi–categorial ontologies (with both endurants and perdurants) since they require temporal qualification. The purpose of this paper is not finding a mere reduction of temporal predicates in a binary language. We know there are many ways of reducing a predicate's arity (see [8] for some examples). The objective is to find ontologically sound reductions, i.e. which do not require a modification of the ontology, and identify the theoretical underpinnings of a systematic methodology for accomplishing this feat.

In the next section, I briefly argue for the lack of straightforward ontological solutions. In section 3, I examine conditions of reducibility of ternary temporal predicates. In section 4, I describe a method for systematic reduction of these predicates. Finally, in section 5, I propose an interpretation of this method and identify its conditions of ontological soundness.

For lack of space, I sacrifice formal rigor and make no attempt to give proper semantics to the formalism used. Formalism is here both object of discussion and illustrative. I will systematically adopt intuitively helpful naming conventions which should make obvious the intended constraints on the vocabulary or its intended meaning.

2. Fiddling with Ontology

An obvious ontological solution to our problem of representation would be to introduce either relations or facts (states of affairs) as proxy entities for predicates or propositions requiring temporal qualification. It should be clear however that any such solution will constitute a major self–defeating ontological disruption when trying to remain within the boundaries of a bi–categorial ontology of endurants and perdurants. We will take for granted that in the remainder of this paper we will exclusively consider solutions which remain within these boundaries.

The theory of perdurants—more generally unchanging entities—can be couched in a binary language. That of endurants apparently requires temporal qualification of predicates and at least some ternary predicates (e.g. *is a part of at* or *is located in at*). There are two undesirable but straightforward solutions:

1. reduction of endurants to perdurants, which is obviously and precisely problematic because it is a reduction, therefore a radical change in ontology rather than a representation,
2. partial representation of the part of the theory of endurants which bears formulation in a binary language (i.e. leaving out all temporal vocabulary).

These solutions take the syntactic and semantic limitation of a language as representational limitations. But we can not just motivate a reduction on the basis that the representation of an ontology is straightforward and not that of another. It is also unclear that the apparent limitation of the language constitutes a definitive ontological bias which warrants truncating a specification.

Suppose an ontology contains: i) two disjoint categories of endurants and perdurants, ii) the theory of a primitive relation R (e.g. *parthood*) which is similar for, but adapted to, each category. It is natural to have two variants of R, R_t^3 (e.g. *partOfAt*) and R^2 (e.g. *partOf*) which are respectively a ternary relation between two endurants and a time and a binary relation between two perdurants (e.g. the axiomatizations of BFO and DOLCE in [9]).

We can ask whether R_t^3 is the same as R^2 modulo an argument for time. The question is meaningful only if about relations in intension (obviously they differ in extension). There are two ways of comparing them: i) projecting R_t^3 to its non temporal argument places (R_t^2) and compare it with R^2, ii) temporally qualifying R^2 (R^3, it holds whenever the time is a part of the time at which the two original relata co–exist) and compare it with R_t^3. In the first case, direct comparison does not suffice, we need to use a sentential operator to simulate temporal qualification over the two relations. We see easily that at best R^2, respectively R^3, is a constant version of R_t^2, respectively R_t^3.

But not all relations between endurants obtain constantly over the lifetime of their relata. That is precisely where the need for their temporal qualification comes from. So, generally, R_t^2 (respectively R_t^3) is precisely not R^2 (respectively R^3). Preserving constant relations amounts to truncature and making the other constant to reduction.

Only ontologies which deal with endurants through instantaneous (or unchanging extended) states—with plain vocabulary—can do with only one primitive, because they use a method for temporal qualification which belongs to the first strategy discussed in 1.2. For other ontologies, we need to find a reduction of temporal predicates.

3. Fiddling with Predicates I: Decompositions of Relations

Let us focus on the problem of the reduction of ternary temporal predicates in a binary language—our discussion generalizes to higher arity ones. Generally speaking, we do not find the following reduction:

$$R(x, y, z) \text{ reduces to } \phi(x, y) \wedge \chi(x, z) \wedge \psi(y, z) \tag{1}$$

That is, a ternary predicate with a temporal argument is generally not reducible to a combination of binary predicates of its arguments taken pairwise.

Consider these three facts:

Plato is born in Athens in -427.

Plato is in the Academia in -360.

The beard of Plato is white in -360.

Consider a possible representation with ternary temporal predicates:

$$bornInAt(Plato, Athens, -427) \tag{2}$$

$$isInAt(Plato, Academia, -360) \tag{3}$$

$$hasColourAt(PlatoBeard, White, -360) \tag{4}$$

And consider now the following:

$$bornIn(Plato, Athens) \wedge bornAt(Plato, -427) \wedge isAt(Athens, -427) \tag{5}$$

$$isIn(Plato, Academia) \wedge isAt(Plato, -360) \wedge isAt(Academia, -360) \tag{6}$$

$$hasColour(PlatoBeard, White) \wedge isAt(White, -360) \wedge isAt(Plato, -360) \tag{7}$$

Clearly, (2) reduces to (5). But (3) does not reduce to (6), nor (4) to (7). They do not, that is, provided Plato has not always been in the Academia or, if always there, has not only lived in -360 and that his beard has not always been white or, if always white, that he has not only had a beard in -360. Insisting that the reductions hold is making Plato and his beard in -360 entities in their own right whose existence is circumscribed to this time; it is saying that, actually, Plato and his beard are not endurants but perdurants and that the facts above are about their respective temporal parts in -360. If the equivalence held, the entities in questions would not be entities susceptible of change, but this is the sort of entity we mean to deal with, so we must reject the equivalences.

Why does (2) reduces to (5)? One answer is that it is essential to Plato that he was born in Athens in -427. But what truly makes the difference here is that he was not born somewhere else *too* nor at an other time *too*. *bornIn* and *bornAt* represent functional relations. *Athens* and -427 are both functional images of *Plato* and in that capacity *Plato* makes the link between them. *Plato* is not a relation, he is an individual but, in a way, he is relating the other entities by acting as a central node—I will say a "pivot"—in the restructuring of the fact represented by (2) and (5). This is also why the third conjunct in (5) seems superfluous (although, formally, it has to be entailed by something involving the rest of the expression).

A credible conjecture about (1) is that it applies when at least one of the relata is a pivot in the represented fact. More generally, there has to be something uniquely pointed at and which pinpoints the assertion and articulates the reduction. It is an entity which can not change in the relevant respect, just as *Plato* with respect to his place and date of birth, even if he can change in some other respect. This shows, but merely shows, in which straightforward way temporal qualification is reducible when it is superfluous. Predicates such as *bornInAt* can be regarded as shorthand, syntactic sugar, but are never ineliminable even in a language with ternary predicates.

Is it possible to find a pivot for the decomposition of *hasColourAt* into binary relations? Suppose that *PlatoBeard* continuously exists over a period Δt and that it changes colour during that time so that, for example, it is black at T_1 and white at T_2. We have:

$$hasColourAt(PlatoBeard, Black, T_1) \land hasColourAt(PlatoBeard, White, T_2) \land$$
$$\neg\, hasColourAt(PlatoBeard, Black, \Delta t) \land \neg\, hasColourAt(PlatoBeard, White, \Delta t) \tag{8}$$

We agree that the decomposition offered in (6) does not apply. The reason is that there is no particular among the related entities with functional relations to the other entities. One solution then is to add one. There is no room here to discuss general strategies as strategies depend on the particularity of an ontology, but we can illustrate one possibility. We want to avoid splitting *PlatoBeard* into temporal parts, so we approach change in colour as a succession of properties of *PlatoBeard* (it goes from black to white after all). *PlatoBeard* has at T_1 a particular quality, a colour, and this colour is throughout its existence of the kind *Black*. Although beards can change colours—they exemplify colour kinds in temporally sensitive ways—it is essential to colour particulars to be of the kind they are, e.g. the blackness of *PlatoBeard* existing at T_1 is essentially a blackness. A perspicuous representation of the first conjunct in (8) is then:

$$hasColour(PlatoBeard, Colour_1)$$

$$\land\, isAt(Colour_1, T_1) \land instanceOf(Colour_1, Black) \tag{9}$$

Changes in the colour of *PlatoBeard* are successions of its colours, each colour uniquely pinpointing the relevant fact. We thus avoid change of beard, i.e. there are no two numerically distinct beards with different colours because the colour of the beard is not essential to the beard, and Plato change, i.e. there are no two numerically distinct Plato with differently coloured beards because the colour of his beard is not essential to Plato either.

It was easy to add a colour. Starting with a universal *Black*, we instantiate blackness to a particular which is functionally related to its bearer and the time of its existence. But can we do the same for (3)? Here, there is no universal. *Plato, Academia*, and -360 are particulars and they simply do not stand in functional relations taken pairwise, and there is no way we can bring a particular by instantiating any of them. Conceiving Plato as having an instance with a functional relation to *Academia* and to -360 is treating Plato as a perdurant with temporal parts (the putative instances of Plato-universal, elements of the Plato-class, or temporal parts of the perdurant Plato serve formally the same purpose).

One indication, however, is that there is a difference between the relations used in (3) and (4). *isInAt* is so to speak the subject of a bare relation. (It maps to the most general cartesian product of subsets of the domain to which map all locational relations at a time.) On the other hand, *hasColourAt* is determinate in one of its respects, it takes only a colour in its relevant argument place, rather than an attribute of a specified kind as would a version of this relation of equal generality to *isInAt*. That sort of determination is not a property of *isInAt* which is a totally general location relation. This suggests that the contrived solution to the reduction of (4) had to do with this determination.

4. Fiddling with Predicates II: Parametrization

Any n-place predicate is rewritable as an i-place predicate for all i such that $i < n$ and preserving the same sense, i.e. allowing to represent the same state of affairs ([10] makes the point about propositional functions). Let us speak of an operation of "parameterization". There can be more than one way of parameterizing a predicate—depending in particular on the order of arguments which will be ignored here for the sake of simplicity.

Parameterization fixes a respect in which the lower arity relation obtains. Emphatically, parameterization is not generalization (neither universal nor existential) in one or more argument place. The general notation and schema for a parameterization is this, where Arg_i is an individual occurring in the i argument place in R^n:

$$\ulcorner R^{n-1} Arg_i \urcorner (x_1, \ldots, x_{i-1}, x_{i+1}, \ldots, x_n) \equiv R^n(x_1, \ldots, x_{i-1}, Arg_i, x_{i+1}, \ldots, x_n) \tag{10}$$

in contradistinction to either of the following:

$$R^{n-1} \forall_i (x_1, \ldots, x_{i-1}, x_{i+1}, \ldots, x_n) \equiv \forall y\, R^n(x_1, \ldots, x_{i-1}, y, x_{i+1}, \ldots, x_n) \tag{11}$$

$$R^{n-1} \exists_i (x_1, \ldots, x_{i-1}, x_{i+1}, \ldots, x_n) \equiv \exists y\, R^n(x_1, \ldots, x_{i-1}, y, x_{i+1}, \ldots, x_n) \tag{12}$$

A parameterization of R^n in i arguments, for $1 \leq i < n$, is called "i–partial" or simply "partial" and a parameterization in n arguments is called "total".

Let us proceed to the case of temporal predicates, ternary ones for the sake of simplicity (but the procedure generalizes to higher arity ones). Suppose then we start with a temporal predicate R^3. A typical expression using R^3 will be written:

$$R^3(Arg_1, Arg_2, Arg_3) \tag{13}$$

where the Arg_i are individuals. Modulo the order of arguments and the order of iterated parameterization, there are three one–partial, three two–partial, and one total parametrizations of R^3 as shown in table 1 yielding the rewrite of (13). Choices of

Table 1. Prototypical parameterizations of (13).

one–partial	two–partial	total
$\ulcorner R^2 Arg_1 \urcorner (Arg_2, Arg_3)$	$\ulcorner R^1 Arg_1 Arg_2 \urcorner (Arg_3)$	$\ulcorner R^0 Arg_1 Arg_2 Arg_3 \urcorner$
$\ulcorner R^2 Arg_2 \urcorner (Arg_1, Arg_3)$	$\ulcorner R^1 Arg_1 Arg_3 \urcorner (Arg_2)$	
$\ulcorner R^2 Arg_3 \urcorner (Arg_1, Arg_2)$	$\ulcorner R^1 Arg_2 Arg_3 \urcorner (Arg_1)$	

parametrizations in a binary language are: i) a binary predicate, ii) a unary predicate, and iii) a constant. The challenge is to find a suitable interpretation as, for instance, intuitively shown in table 2 and more formally as follows (D is the domain of discourse, as expected):

$\ulcorner R^2 Arg_1 \urcorner$ is a binary relation which holds—possibly *inter alia*—between Arg_2 and Arg_3.

    (13) is true *iff* $\ulcorner R^2 Arg_1 \urcorner (Arg_2, Arg_3)$ is true

        iff the ordered pair $(Arg_2; Arg_3)$ belongs to a suitable subset of DxD.

$\ulcorner R^1 Arg_1 Arg_2 \urcorner$ is a property of—possibly *inter alia*—Arg_3.

    (13) is true *iff* $\ulcorner R^1 Arg_1 Arg_2 \urcorner (Arg_3)$ is true

        iff the individual Arg_3 belongs to a suitable subset of D.

$\ulcorner R^0 Arg_1 Arg_2 Arg_3 \urcorner$, in contradistinction to both of the above, is an individual.

    (13) is true *iff* $\exists y(y = \ulcorner R^0 Arg_1 Arg_2 Arg_3 \urcorner)$ is true

        iff the individual $\ulcorner R^0 Arg_1 Arg_2 Arg_3 \urcorner$ belongs to D.

There is nothing intrinsically wrong with partial parameterizations which in fact can contribute handy shorthand to KR. Using them amounts to creating vocabulary whose use is limited to representing the content of a knowledge base (i.e. a world state) with a fixed context linked to an individual in the domain: e.g. a time, a location, or even an

Table 2. Parameterizations of (3).

one–partial	two–partial	total
platoIsInAt(Academia,-360)	*PlatoInAcademiaAt(-360)*	*PlatoInAcademiaAt-360*
isInAcademiaAt(Plato,-360)	*PlatoInAt-360(Academia)*	
isInAt-360(Plato,Academia)	*InAcademiaAt-360(Plato)*	

attribute. Maybe the historical Plato is not very exciting, but the same procedure could be used for a patient's medical records or an archaeological site. This procedure could also be used for specifying prototypical instances of a category, e.g. anatomical ones. It is more generally a way of specifying any corpus of knowledge in a domain which is marked by a central referent, e.g. the Earth for geography.

This approach might come in handy in small ontologies, but becomes quickly unmanageable in large ones recollecting variant (differently parameterized) vocabulary and dealing with endless variations (e.g. of *isInAt* such as *isInAtT1*, *isInAtT2*, ..., *socratesInAt*, *phedoInAt*, ..., *critoInAcademiaAt*, etc). (A partial solution is to subsume partial parameterizations under predicates defined as in (12). This is only a partial solution and it promotes multiple inheritance, but this is another problem.)

The fatal shortcoming of FO binary languages in this context is that they allow for no explicit account of partial parameterizations, e.g. no way of enforcing the link between the predicate *isInAt-360* and the parameter -360. If it were not for the name, which is completely irrelevant in an axiomatization, we would have no clue that the predicate represents the relation of spatial location in -360. To explicit this link, we need a ternary language and a version of (10) as abbreviating definition. Short of this, we either need a sentential operator or to extend the language in a meta–linguistic way so as to allow attribution of properties to predicates. OWL Full allows certain assertions of the second sort and so would a free logic type of KR language, e.g. SCL [11]. But, even if possible, it is still unclear whether the language—or a binary fragment thereof—could have the resource to spell out what it meant for *platoIsInAt* to be about *Plato* and what it tells about *platoIsInAt(Academia, -360)*.

The appeal of total parameterization is that its result can be interpreted as an individual, i.e. in the domain rather than as a relation or as a property. We can then legally spell out the links between the parameterization and the parameters in a binary language. It is the most commensurate to the expressive power of the binary FO language. Moreover, nothing short of total parametrization can produce an additional particular. This is because, if the result of partial parameterizations are interpreted as particulars, then the account of the situation is only partial. Or rather, it is partial until the links identifying the parameters are introduced. But that operation amounts precisely to a total parameterization. It is easy to see that it is for similar reasons that our discussion generalizes to higher arity predicates.

5. Ontological Extension, Reduction, and Soundness

5.1. Temporal Qualification and Parameterization

Let us call a parameterization in the temporal argument a "temporal parameterization". What is the link between temporal qualification and temporal parameterization? Roughly, both operations are converse. Temporal parameterization fixes the value of a temporal predicate in its temporal argument place to define a plain (lower arity) predicate. Temporal qualification is the de–parameterizing of this (temporal) value. It takes the parameter from the intension of the relation and puts it as an additional argument place in the modified extension of that relation. By abstraction over this argument place, we obtain the temporally qualified variant of the plain predicate.

Such an operation is not limited to temporal arguments. Consider ways of representing the fact that Plato is an adult in -400 and the sort of ontologies to which they naturally associate. Table 3 shows four assertions corresponding to non trivially distinct

Table 3. Plato is an adult in -400.

Ontologies	Atemporal	Temporal
Nominalist	In -400: $Adult^1(Plato)$	$adultAt(Plato,-400)$
Realist	In -400: *exemplifies(Plato,Adult)*	*exemplifiesAt(Plato,Adult,-400)*

ontologies. Atemporal ontologies recognize a category of times (temporal regions or instants), temporal ontologies do not. Realist ontologies recognize a category of universals (attributes as abstract particulars), e.g. *Adult* exemplified by Plato, but nominalist ontologies do not, as they recognize only Plato and treat exemplification as class membership. Temporal FO predicates are temporal qualifications of atemporal ones. Conversely, atemporal ones are temporal parameterizations of temporal ones (compare $Adult^1$ in an ontology indexed to the year -400 and $\ulcorner AdultAt^1\text{-}400 \urcorner$). But the same is true if we go across columns rather than rows (compare $Adult^1$ and $\ulcorner Exemplifies^1 Adult^0 \urcorner$).

We see that parameterization and qualification are not ontologically neutral operations. Both are potentially expansive ontological tools as they require introducing particulars, and these particulars could be of a kind which is not recognized by the ontology— leading to a distinct ontology. In addition, parameterization is a potentially reductive tool. For instance, it allows to dispense with a category of time or with universals. But in some cases the expansive outcome of parameterization can be neutral, namely in cases in which the added entities are of kinds which are already recognized by the ontology.

5.2. Temporal Pivot

What are we doing when we totally parameterize a multiple arity predicate? We summon an individual and we link it to the relata of the parameterized predicate by a series of binary relations. For instance, (3) is represented linking *PlatoIsInAcademiaAt-360* (renamed *A*) to *Plato*, *Academia*, and -360, respectively, e.g.:

$$who(A, Plato) \wedge where(A, Academia) \wedge when(A, -360) \tag{14}$$

We have seen that: i) a ternary temporal predicate is trivially reducible to a combination of lower arity predicates when one of the relata is a pivot (*Plato* in (2)) and ii) in some cases, we can bring in one more entity implicit so to speak in the state of affairs to act as a pivot (*Colour*$_1$ in (4)). What total parametrization allows is to do the later systematically.

The only question that remains is what sort of entity this is. And the only significant ontological question is whether this entity belongs to a category that is additional to the categories of the ontology from which we started or whether it can fit in the existing ontology. For a start, the pivot obtained through temporal parametrization is a temporal entity, it has a relation to a time. It is credible then to ask whether this is an entity which changes over time or not. If the entity is changing, we are facing the problem of its own change and of temporal qualification again, and we enter a potentially infinite regress. It is credible to think that the entity is not an endurant but a perdurant. If this interpretation is correct, then in order to represent temporal qualification and change in a binary language we need a category of perdurants, the introduction of one of its instances as pivot, and, hence, binary relations to characterize this instance. If this is all we require, we are within the boundaries of a bi–categorial mono–ontological solution represented in a binary language.

Is it, then, possible in such an ontology to find in a principled way a suitable perdurant allowing for the representation of temporally qualified assertions about endurants? Observe first that there is the adulthood of Plato, the part of his life during which he is 1,80 m, the part of his life during which he likes Socrates, the part of Peter's life during which he is Canadian, that during which he is 48, etc. The life of an endurant is the aggregate of all processes (of change and non change) in which that endurant participates—therefore a life and its parts are perdurants. [1] The answer to our question is that lives and parts thereof are pivots for temporal facts about endurants. Is this solution uniform? In particular, could we give a pivot to facts such as that Plato is a person or that he does not know about the American continent? Yes, the life of Plato.

6. Conclusion

Binary FO languages are not capable of a straightforward ontological rendering of temporal qualification and hence of change in the relevant entities. They are not however ontologically biased in the way that only entities which do not change can be represented. But they are ontologically constraining in the sense that they require a category of perdurants involving changing entities to act as pivot in the relevant temporal facts. It is hardly a significant cost for bi–categorial ontologies in which the necessary top–level category is already present and it is no cost at all when the relation between endurants and their lives is recognized. In those cases, the procedure is systematic and ontologically sound and the benefit is clearly greater than ontological reduction or truncated representation. Problems should occur for eliminatist theories which reject processes and event and, in those cases, the languages are simply unable to faithfully allow representation. Then again, fine tuning can always produce wonders.

Acknowledgements

This paper was written under the auspices of the Wolfgang Paul Program of the Alexander von Humboldt Foundation, the European Union Network of Excellence on Medical Informatics and Semantic Data Mining, and the Volkswagen Foundation under the auspices of the project "Forms of Life". I am grateful to Pierluigi Miraglia and Michael Pool for their comments.

References

[1]   P. Grenon and B. Smith, SNAP and SPAN: Towards Dynamic Geographical Ontology, *Spatial Cognition and Computation*, **4**(1) (2004), 69–103.

[2]   D.M. Gabbay, I. Hodkinson, and M. Reynolds, *Temporal Logic: Mathematical Foundation and Computational Aspects, Volume 1*, Clarendon Press, Oxford, 1994.

[3]   M.R. Genesereth, R.E. Fikes et al., *Knowledge Interchange Format Version 3 Reference Manual*, Report Logic-92-1, Stanford University Logic Group, 1992.

[4]   D. Lenat and R.V. Guha, *Building Large Knowledge-Based Systems*, Addison Wesley, 1990.

[5]   P.F. Patel–Schneider and B. Swartout, *Description Logic for Knowledge Representation System Specification from KRSS Group of Arpa Knowledge Sharing Effort*, November 1, 1993.

[6]   I. Horrocks, P.F. Patel–Schneider, and F. van Harmelen, From SHIQ and RDF to OWL: The Making of a Web Ontology Language, *Journal of Web Semantics*, **1**(1) (2003), 7–26.

[7]   A. Artale and E. Franconi, Introducing Temporal Description Logics, *TIME* (1999), 2–5.

[8]   A. Rector and N. Noy (Eds.), Defining N-ary Relations on the Semantic Web, *W3C Working Group Note*, 2006.

[9]   C. Masolo, S. Borgo, A. Gangemi, N. Guarino, and A. Oltramari, *Ontology Library (final). WonderWeb Deliverable D18*, 2003.

[10] C.I. Lewis and C.H. Langford, *Symbolic Logic*, Dover, 1959.

[11] C. Menzel and P. Hayes, SCL: A Logic Standard for Semantic Integration, in A. Doan, A. Halevey, and N. Noy (Eds.), *Semantic Integration*, CEUR Workshop Proceedings, vol. 82 (2003).

Formal Ontology in Information Systems
B. Bennett and C. Fellbaum (Eds.)
IOS Press, 2006

The Instrumental Stit
A Study of Action and Instrument

Pawel GARBACZ

The John Paul II Catholic University of Lublin
20-950 Lublin, Poland

Abstract. The focus of this paper are actions in which agents employ instruments
in order to achieve desired outcomes. I explore the ontological structure of such
actions and the semantic features of the sentences by means of which we refer to
these actions. The logical framework for this philosophical enterprise is the theory
of the so-called stit operator: . . . see to it that . . . . I modify the original formulation
in such a way that we could represent those events in which agents see to things
with the help of physical objects. As a result, I obtain a formal theory of the operator
of instrumental stit: . . . see to it that . . . with the help of . . . .

Keywords. logic of agency

Introduction

Actions are among the focal objects of study in a number of research disciplines. Although different theoretical perspectives usually lead to different research methods, one
of the unifying methodological factors is the use of logical or mathematical tools to represent actions, agents, dynamic environments, etc. Still, the majority of these formalisms
(e.g. Cohen and Levesque's logic of rational agency [2], BDI system [4], KARO framework [5]) neglect the trivial observation that it is a rule rather than an exception that
while performing actions, we use tools or instruments. We do things with things: we
write letters with pens, eat with spoons, travel by cars, etc. In short, most of our actions
are performed with the help of physical objects. This neglect is of particular importance
when we represent such action-related features as action results, agent abilities, objective
opportunities, which depend on use of tools and instruments.

The aim of the present paper is to provide a rigorous and possibly universal account
of such events. The account is also expected to define the semantic features of the action-
cum-instrument locutions. Consequently, I look for a conceptual structure that could
serve both as a formal ontology of action and as a semantic model of action-related
occurrences.

I will focus here on the relation between an agent and the outcome(s) of his actions.
My starting point is the theory of the so-called stit operators (as codified in [1]), which
seems to be particularly suitable for this purpose. The result is a logic of instrumental stit
(*i-logic*).

Actions and instruments

We perform various actions and we describe these actions in a variety of ways. Performing actions, we often use tools or instruments. Speaking about actions, we sometimes specify the means by which actions are performed. Let us consider actions executed with the help of physical objects. When an agent employs an object in such a way, the object will be called an *instrument* (for this agent).

As an informal background, I assume the definition of instrument proposed by Randall Dipert in [3]:

> [...] an instrument is an object one of whose properties has been thought by someone to be means to an end and that has been intentionally employed in this capacity. [...] To be thought as a means to an end, an object must be conceived to make a net positive causal contribution to an end. ([3], p. 24-25)

Since the relation of a human agent to its body is radically different from the relation of the agent to the instruments he uses, I assume that no part of the agent's body may become an instrument (for this agent). Besides, for the sake of simplicity, I will neglect the cases when an agent uses (a part of) another agent's body as an instrument.

Notice that Dipert's definition allows that

- an object may be an instrument for one agent and may not be an instrument for another agent (with respect to the same set of properties),
- an object may be an instrument with respect to one set of properties (for an agent) and may not be an instrument with respect to other set of properties (for the same agent),
- selecting a set of properties, an agent may in effect (inadvertently) choose more than one object provided that all objects he chooses share all selected properties.

When an agent selects a set of properties while contemplating some object as a possible instrument, I will call any such property *instrumental* (for the agent). When the agent actually employs this object in order to perform an action, the action he performs will be called *instrumental* (for him).

In order to make the abstract formalism more tangible, I will use throughout the paper Dipert's example of instrumental action described by the sentence "David killed Goliath with the help of a stone".

Deliberative stit

The theory of stit claims to provide a formal semantics for action sentences. The canonical form of such locutions, as recommended by the stit approach, is: α sees to it that φ (abbreviated as: α stit:φ); in our case: David saw it that he killed Goliath (with the help of a stone).

[1] provides us with a general account of the relation between the sentences from the first group and the sentences from the second group. The account in question consists of several theses.

1. agentiveness of stit
   α stit: φ is always agentive for α.

2. stit complement

   α stit: φ is grammatical and meaningful for any arbitrary sentence φ.
3. stit paraphrase

   φ is agentive for α just in case φ may be useful paraphrased as α stit: φ
4. stit normal form

   If a complex expression has an action-related sentence as a complement, nothing but confusion is lost if this complement is taken to be a stit sentence. (cf. [1], p. 7-15).

In this paper I ignore such action-related sentences as obligations, permissions, imperatives, etc., and the theses related thereto.

Although [1] defines four kinds of stit operator, I will use only the operator of deliberative stit (*dstit*). The informal reading of this operator is: "α dstit: φ" means that that φ is guaranteed by a present choice made by α. The formal definition for this, and other operators, is based on a structure of branching time. This structure is a pair $< Tree^B, \leqslant^B >$, where $Tree^B$ is a non-empty set of moments and $\leqslant^B$ is a partial order in $Tree^B$ that satisfies two additional conditions:[1]

$$\forall m_1, m_2 \exists m_3 (m_3 \leqslant^B m_1 \wedge m_3 \leqslant^B m_2). \tag{1}$$

$$m_1 \leqslant^B m_3 \wedge m_2 \leqslant^B m_3 \rightarrow m_1 \leqslant^B m_2 \vee m_2 \leqslant^B m_1. \tag{2}$$

[1] defines $History^B$ as the set of $\subseteq$-maximal $\leqslant^B$-chains in $Tree^B$. The elements of this set, denoted by "h", "h_1", "h_2", $\ldots$, are called histories. The set $H^B(m)$ includes all histories that contain a moment m. Two histories $h_1, h_2 \in History^B$ are said to be undivided at a moment m_1 (written: $h_1 \equiv^B_{m_1} h_2$) iff $m_1 \in h_1 \cap h_2$ and there is such a moment $m_2 \in Tree^B$ that $m_1 <^B m_2$ and $m_2 \in h_1 \cap h_2$ provided that m_1 has a $<^B$-successor.

The next element of the stit formal structure is the choice function. The function $Ch^B \; Agt \times Tree^B \rightarrow \wp(\wp(History^B))$, where Agt is a set of agents, assigns to each agent at each moment a spectrum of choices. Each such choice concerns those actions that are available for a given agent at that moment. [1] stipulates that for any moment m and any agent a, $Ch^B(a, m)$ is a partition of $H^B(m)$.

If $h \in X \in Ch^B(a, m)$, then $Ch^B(a, m, h) = X$. Two histories h_1, h_2 are said to be choice equivalent for an agent a at a moment m (written: $h_1 \equiv^B_{a,m} h_2$) iff $Ch^B(a, m, h_1) = Ch^B(a, m, h_2)$. [1] argues that no agent can choose among undivided histories.

$$h_1 \equiv^B_m h_2 \rightarrow h_1 \equiv^B_{a,m} h_2. \tag{3}$$

All agents' choices (at a given moment) are claimed to be mutually independent (cf. [1], p. 217-218). Let f_m be such function on Agt that $f_m(a) \in Ch^B(a, m)$. Then this mutual independence is secured by axiom 4.

---

[1] In order not to confuse the original theory of stit with my proposal, I put a superscript "B" (for Belnap) over each formal symbol of the former theory which has a different meaning in the latter.

$$\bigcap \{f_m(a) \ \ a \in Agt\} \neq \emptyset.^2 \tag{4}$$

In this structure we can define the satisfaction condition for the canonical form of stit locutions (see 5). As usual,

- "$\mathfrak{M}^{\mathfrak{B}}$" denotes a model for a first-order language containing stit locutions,
- "$\mathfrak{V}^{\mathfrak{B}}$" denotes a function of valuation,
- "$\mathfrak{M}^{\mathfrak{B}}, \mathfrak{V}^{\mathfrak{B}}, m, h \vDash \varphi$" abbreviates the expression "a formula φ is satisfied in a model $\mathfrak{M}^{\mathfrak{B}}$ and a valuation $\mathfrak{V}^{\mathfrak{B}}$ at a moment m and history h".

$$\mathfrak{M}^{\mathfrak{B}}, \mathfrak{V}^{\mathfrak{B}}, m, h \vDash \beta \text{ dstit } \varphi \equiv \mathfrak{V}^{\mathfrak{B}}(\beta) \in Agt \wedge \tag{5}$$

$$\wedge \forall h_1 \in Ch^B(\mathfrak{V}^{\mathfrak{B}}(\beta), m, h) \ \mathfrak{M}^{\mathfrak{B}}, \mathfrak{V}^{\mathfrak{B}}, m, h_1 \vDash \varphi \wedge$$

$$\wedge \exists h_1 \in H^B(m) \ \mathfrak{M}^{\mathfrak{B}}, \mathfrak{V}^{\mathfrak{B}}, m, h_1 \nvDash \varphi.$$

Under some simplifying assumptions, our running example could be modelled by this definition as follows. David saw to it that he killed Goliath with the help of a stone iff David is an agent and one of the choices available to David contains only such histories in which David kills Goliath with the help of a stone and another choice of David contains one history in which David does not kill Goliath with the help of a stone. The most crucial of the aforementioned assumptions has it that agents' choices are represented as sets of histories. Then, any set from a partition $Ch^B(a, m)$ is supposed to correspond to exactly one choice available for an agent a at a moment m.

From stit to instrumental stit

While expressing the agentive aspect of actions, the stit approach misrepresents their instrumental characteristics. The canonical form takes into account the agent who performs an action and the outcome of the action, but neglects the means by which the agent achieves this outcome. Disregarding the instrumental aspects of action, the stit approach misrepresents such sentences as:

1. David killed Goliath with the help of a stone.
2. David killed Goliath with the help of a spear.

It seems that the stit canonical forms of 1 and 2 would be either 3 (one for both) or 4:

3. David saw to it that he killed Goliath.
4. a. David saw to it that he killed Goliath with the help of a stone.
   b. David saw to it that he killed Goliath with the help of a spear.

If 3 is the canonical form of both 1 and 2, then 1 is semantically equivalent to 2. On the other hand, if 4 contains the canonical forms of 1 and 2, then, the semantic difference between 1 and 2 is of the same importance as the difference between 5 and 6.

---

[2] For the sake of clarity, let me explain the trivial:

- $x \in \bigcap Y \equiv \forall X \in Y x \in X,$
- $x \in \bigcup Y \equiv \exists X \in Y x \in X.$

5. David saw to it that he committed suicide.
6. David saw to it that he became a bishop.

Namely, 4a. is rendered as "x stit φ" and 4b. as "x stit ψ", where $\varphi \neq \psi$.

I intend to extend the stit theory in such a way that we could fully account for the instrumental aspect of actions. To this end, I modify the canonical form of action sentences: α sees to it that φ with the help of β (abbreviated as α stit: φ $_{\text{wth}}$ β). This form is considered here as the canonical form of locutions describing instrumental actions. The operator "... stit: ... $_{\text{wth...}}$" will be called the *operator of instrumental stit* (*istit*). Following [1] (p. 5-18), I will describe my canonical form by introducing a number of theses which informally describe the interface between the canonical form and the genuine action sentences. In this description I use two phrases: "to be agentive for" and "to be instrumental for". Informally speaking, a sentence φ is *agentive* for α iff α is an agent who performs the action described by φ or achieves the outcome described by φ. Similarly, a sentence φ is *instrumental* for α iff α is an instrument by means of which the action described by φ is performed or the outcome described by φ is achieved.

1. agentiveness of istit

   α stit: φ $_{\text{wth}}$ β is always agentive for α.
2. instrumentality of istit

   α stit: φ $_{\text{wth}}$ β is always instrumental for β.
3. istit complement

   α stit: φ $_{\text{wth}}$ β is grammatical and meaningful for any arbitrary sentence φ.
4. istit adjunct

   α stit: φ $_{\text{wth}}$ β is grammatical and meaningful for any arbitrary noun and any (grammatically well-formed) noun phrase β.
5. istit instrumental paraphrase

   φ is instrumental for β just in case φ may be usefully paraphrased as α stit: φ $_{\text{wth}}$ β, for some α.
6. istit normal form

   If a complex expression has an instrumental action-related sentence as a complement, nothing but confusion is lost if this complement is taken to be a stit sentence.

Agents, instruments, and choices in branching time

The present theory of istit modifies Belnap's theory of the deliberative stit. In [1] the basic element of the stit semantics is the structure of branching time. Any moment that constitutes this structure is said to be an instantaneous, spatially unlimited, really possible event ([1], p. 178); thus the structure of moments is not represented in the formalism. In order to speak about instrumental actions, I will represent this structure in the following way.

Let *Entity* ($e, e_1, \cdots \in Entity$) be a set of all possible entities within a given domain and let a set *Property* ($p, p_1, \cdots \in Property$) represent all of their possible properties. Both notions are to be construed fairly broadly; nonetheless, in this paper the latter set is restricted to monadic properties. Any pair $< X, D >$ will be called a *possible world* provided that $\emptyset \neq X \subseteq Entity$ and $D: Property \rightarrow \wp(Entity)$. Let *Tree* be a family of sets of possible worlds. If $e \in X$ and $< X, D > \in \bigcup Tree$, then I will say that *e exists in* a possible world $< X, D >$. If $e \in D(p)$ and $< X, D > \in \bigcup Tree$, I will say that an entity *e has a property p in* a possible world $< X, D >$. I assume that all and only entities that exist in a possible world $< X, D >$ have any properties therein.

$$< X, D > \in \bigcup Tree \rightarrow (e \in X \equiv \exists p \, e \in D(p)). \tag{6}$$

[1] has it that the truth value of any atomic sentence should be relativised to a moment and to a history because one and the same atomic sentence may be true at a given moment relative to one history and false at the same moment relative to another history. The truth value of an atomic sentence is relative both to a moment and a history when (and because) the sentence has something to do with the choice made at this moment by some agent. Since agents and their choices are causally effective parts of the world, the adequate representation of a world-stage should contain the representations of these choices. On assumption that agents' choices are, as a rule, indeterministic and mutually independent, we should model them with the help of the notion of possible world. All things considered, the simplest solution is to represent a world-stage as a set of sets of possible worlds.

I will call the elements of $Tree$ *thick world-stages*. I let $W, W_1, W_2, \ldots$, range over thick world-stages. Any thick world-stage corresponds to such representation of the world at a given moment that differentiates among different choices available to agents at this moment. If $W \in Tree$, then the elements of W, i.e. possible worlds, will be also called *thin world-stages*. I let $w, w_1, w_2, \ldots$ range over thin world-stages. If $w \in \bigcup Tree$, this is to mean that w is an adequate representation of the world at a given moment that includes an adequate representation of agents' choices. More perspicuously speaking, this thin world characterises one of the combinations of choices possible for agents at this moment.

From the intuitive point of view, my thick world-stages correspond to moments from the original theory of stit. Any thin world-stage from a thick world-stage corresponds to a choice made by some agent at the respective moment, i.e. at this thick world-stage. As a result, it is the thick world-stage and not the thin world-stage that gathers, so to speak, all the choices that are available for the agent. Furthermore, the "objective", i.e. the choice-independent, aspect of any such thin world-stage is shared by all other thin world-stages from the thick world-stage. Following the indeterministic presupposition of [1], I assume that any choice made at a given moment (i.e. thick world-stage) is causally independent from any other choice at that moment.

As for our example, different thin world-stages may represent different choices available to David at the moment, i.e. at the thick world-stage, when he chose the stone by means of which he killed Goliath. For instance,

- a thin world-stage w_1 represents David's choice of a heavy stone with blunt edges,
- a thin world-stage w_2 represents David's choice of a solid stone with sharp edges,
- a thin world-stage w_2 represents David's choice of a long wooden spear.

Believing that it is not possible that at some moment nothing exists, I assume that there are no empty thick world-stages.

$$\emptyset \notin Tree. \tag{7}$$

Let $Obj \subseteq Entity$ be a set of non-agentive physical objects. I let $o, o_1, o_2, \ldots$ range over Obj. A function $Prop{:}Obj \times \bigcup Tree \rightarrow \wp(Property)$ assigns to each physical object at a thin world stage a set of properties that this object has at this world stage (cf. definition 8). Any such set will be called a *qualitative content* of the object at the thin world-stage.

$$w =< X, D >\rightarrow Prop(o, w) = \{p \in Property \;\; o \in D(p)\}. \tag{8}$$

Because a thin world-stage from a given thick world-stage is different from any other thin world-stage from the same thick world-stage only with respect to agents' choices, all qualitative contents of physical objects in these thin world-stages are identical.

$$\forall w_1, w_2 \in W \;\; Prop(o, w_1) = Prop(o, w_2). \tag{9}$$

Then, if $w \in W$, I put $Prop(o, W){:=}Prop(o, w)$.

In general, a physical object may change its properties through time, i.e. it is possible that $Prop(o, W_1) \neq Prop(o, W_2)$ when $W_1 \neq W_2$. Still, I assume that at least one property of each object is rigid through time, i.e. throughout different thick world-stages, which assumption guarantees minimal ontological stability of physical objects. Let $Exist(o) = \{W \in Tree{:}Prop(o, W) \neq \emptyset\}$.

$$\bigcap\{Prop(o, W) \;\; W \in Exist(o)\} \neq \emptyset. \tag{10}$$

Let $Agt \subseteq Entity$ be a set of agents. $a, a_1, a_2, \ldots$ will range over agents. Since the set Obj is defined to contain non-agentive physical objects, I assume that $Agt \cap Obj = \emptyset$.

The function $Instr{:}Agt \times \bigcup Tree \rightarrow \wp(Property)$ will model agents' selections of instrumental properties. The expression "$Instr(a, w) = X$" means that at a thin world-stage w an agent a selects a set X of properties as a set of instrumental properties. When $Instr(a, w) = \emptyset$, this means that a does not select any instrumental property at w. For any thick world-stage W, the set $\{Instr(a, w) \;\; w \in W\}$ specifies all selections of instrumental properties which are possible for an agent a at W. I will refer to this set by means of the function term "$Instr(a, W)$". Notice that 7 implies that $Instr(a, W) \neq \emptyset$, for all $W \in Tree$. If $Instr(a, W) = \{\emptyset\}$, then this is to mean that an agent a is not able to make any selection whatsoever at a (thick) world-stage W.

Let us return to the running example. If the action performed by David is instrumental, then it involves an act of selection of instrumental properties. In general, David may select various groups of such properties, i.e. each choice of (instrumental) action available to him corresponds to a selection of instrumental properties. Then any set $Instr(\text{David}, w) \neq \emptyset$ contains one selection of instrumental properties contemplated by David. For instance,

- $Instr(\text{David}, w_1) = \{$being heavy, fitting David's hand, having blunt edges$\}$,
- $Instr(\text{David}, w_2) = \{$being solid, fitting David's hand, having sharp edges$\}$,
- $Instr(\text{David}, w_3) = \{$being long, being wooden, being heavy$\}$.

Let "$i(a, w)$" denote the set of all instruments selected by an agent a at a world w. I assume in this paper that selecting instrumental properties, any agent is fallible in his selection, i.e. choosing among the actual properties, he may inadvertently "add" some new properties to the properties the instrument he chooses actually possesses. Nevertheless, such error-prone agents choose at least one actual property of any physical object they select as an instrument.

$$o \in i(a, w) \equiv Instr(a, w) \cap Prop(o, w) \neq \emptyset. \tag{11}$$

I assume that each such selection is (minimally) rational, which in the present context means that if an agent a chooses an instrument by selecting some instrumental properties, then at least one physical object possesses at least some of the selected properties.

$$Instr(a, w) \neq \emptyset \rightarrow \exists o \; Instr(a, w) \cap Prop(o, w) \neq \emptyset. \tag{12}$$

Within the context of the running example, this means that David chooses a stone as an instrument when he selects at least one of the properties that the stone actually possesses. Thus, he may inadvertently choose two stones if he selects the property of fitting David's hand (cf. the above examples of David's choices).

Because any choice of any agent is, in principle, causally operative, I define in $\bigcup Tree$ (and not in $Tree$) the relation of causal order (written: $\leqslant$). Following [1], I assume that it is a partial order.

$$w \leqslant w. \tag{13}$$

$$w_1 \leqslant w_2 \wedge w_2 \leqslant w_1 \rightarrow w_1 = w_2. \tag{14}$$

$$w_1 \leqslant w_2 \wedge w_2 \leqslant w_3 \rightarrow w_1 \leqslant w_3. \tag{15}$$

Obviously, $w_1 < w_2 \equiv w_1 \leqslant w_2 \wedge w_1 \neq w_2$.

Given the informal understanding of the distinction between thin and thick world-stages, it is clear that

- no two (different) thick world-stages can share a common thin world-stage (cf. 16),
- no two thin world-stages from one thick world-stage are related by $<$ (cf. 17),
- it is not possible that one thick world-stage both causally proceeds and succeeds another thick world stage (cf. 18).

$$W_1 \neq W_2 \rightarrow W_1 \cap W_2 = \emptyset. \tag{16}$$

$$w_1, w_2 \in W \rightarrow \neg w_1 < w_2. \tag{17}$$

$$\exists w_1 \in W_1 \exists w_2 \in W_2 \; w_1 < w_2 \rightarrow \neg \exists w_1 \in W_1 \exists w_2 \in W_2 \; w_2 < w_1. \tag{18}$$

I define *History* as a set of $\subseteq$-maximal $\leqslant$-chains in $\bigcup Tree$. The elements of this set, denoted by "h", "h_1", "h_2", …, will be called *histories*. As in [1], I postulate that histories meaningfully overlap (19) and exclude backward branching of histories (20).

$$\forall w_1, w_2 \exists w_3 (w_3 \leqslant w_1 \wedge w_3 \leqslant w_2). \tag{19}$$

$$w_1 \leqslant w_3 \wedge w_2 \leqslant w_3 \rightarrow w_1 \leqslant w_2 \vee w_2 \leqslant w_1. \tag{20}$$

The symbol "$H(W)$" will denote the set of all histories that contain at least one thin world-stage that belongs to a thick world-stage W. Notice that axiom 17 entails that for any $W \in Tree$ and $h \in History$, the set $W \cap h$ is either empty or contains exactly one thin world. Subsequently, $H(W)$ contains all histories that contain exactly one thin world-stage from W. The symbol "$h(W)$" will denote the thin world-stage at which a history h intersects a world-stage W (provided that this thin world-stage exists).

I will say that two histories $h_1, h_2 \in History$ are *undivided* at a thin world stage w_1 (written: $h_1 \equiv_{w_1} h_2$) iff $w_1 \in h_1 \cap h_2$ and there is such a world-stage $w_2 \in \bigcup Tree$ that $w_1 < w_2$ and $w_2 \in h_1 \cap h_2$ provided that w_1 has a $<$-successor. I will say that two histories $h_1, h_2 \in History$ are *undivided* at a thick world stage W (written: $h_1 \equiv_W h_2$) iff for some $w \in W, h_1 \equiv_w h_2$.

The next element of the istit structure is the choice function. As before, the function $Ch{:}Agt \times Tree \rightarrow \wp(\wp(History))$ assigns to each agent at each world-stage a spectrum of available choices. As before, for each thick world-stage W, the function Ch is assumed to generate a partition of $H(W)$.

$$\emptyset \notin Ch(a, W). \tag{21}$$

$$X, Y \in Ch(a, W) \rightarrow (X \neq Y \rightarrow X \cap Y = \emptyset). \tag{22}$$

$$\bigcup Ch(a, W) = H(W). \tag{23}$$

Bearing in mind two previously mentioned assumptions, namely:

- that any thin world-stage from a given thick world-stage corresponds to a combination of all choices available to the agents (at the latter world-stage),
- that these choices are mutually independent,

I submit the following two axioms that establish a correspondence between thin world-stages and agents' choices. Let F_W be a family of all functions $f{:}Agent \rightarrow \wp(History)$ such that $f(a) \in Ch(a, W)$.

$$\forall f \in F_W \bigcap \{f(a) \quad a \in Agent\} \neq \emptyset. \tag{24}$$

$$\forall w \in W \exists f \in F_W \, (h \in \bigcap \{f(a) \quad a \in Agent\} \rightarrow h(W) = w). \tag{25}$$

24 is my counterpart of Belnap's axiom 4. Axiom 25 guarantees that every thin world-stage is a "result" of a combination of agents' possible choices (at a certain moment).

If $h \in X \in Ch(a, W)$, then I put $Ch(a, W, h){:=} X$. Two histories $h_1, h_2 \in History$ are said *choice equivalent* for an agent a at a world-stage W (written: $h_1 \equiv_{a,W} h_2$) iff $Ch(a, W, h_1) = Ch(a, W, h_2)$. Accepting arguments from [1], I assume that no agent can choose between undivided histories.

$$h_1 \equiv_w h_2 \rightarrow h_1 \equiv_{a,w} h_2. \tag{26}$$

Although in general the notion of selection, which is expressed here by the symbol "*Instr*", is conceptually independent from the notion of choice, which is expressed here by the symbol "*Ch*", choices of instrumental actions are not independent from selections of instrumental properties. The relation therebetween is fixed by axiom 28. The axiom boils down to the claim that all selections of instrumental properties within a given choice of instrumental action are identical. The symbol "$ch_i(a, W)$" is to represent a choice of instrumental action for an agent a at a world-stage W.

$$X \in ch_i(a, W) \equiv X \in Ch(a, W) \wedge \exists h \in X \; Instr(a, h(W)) \neq \emptyset. \tag{27}$$

$$h_1, h_2 \in X \in ch_i(a, W) \wedge w_1 \in h_1 \wedge w_2 \in h_2 \rightarrow \tag{28}$$

$$\rightarrow Instr(a, w_1) = Instr(a, w_2).$$

Any structure $< Entity, Property, Tree, Agt, Obj, Instr, \leqslant, Ch >$ will be called an *i-structure* if its elements satisfy the above definitions and axioms.

Language of i-logic

The *alphabet of the i-logic* is the union of the following sets:

1. a set $\mathbb{CONST}$ of individual constants: $b, b_1, b_2, \ldots$,
2. a set $\mathbb{VAR}$ of individual variables: $x, y, z, x_1, y_2, \ldots$,
3. a set $\mathbb{PRED}$ of monadic predicate letters: $A, B, C, A_1, B_1, \ldots$,
4. $\{\neg, \wedge, \square, \forall, \text{avail}, \text{instr\_for}, \text{dstit}, \text{istit}_{\text{wth}}\}$.

Given this definition, the *language of the i-logic*, denoted here by the symbol "$\mathbb{L}$", may be defined in the usual way. The expression "$\text{avail}(\beta)$" is to be read: a physical object β is available. The expression "β_1 instrument_for β_2" is to be read: a physical object β_1 is an instrument for an agent β_2. The expression "$\square\varphi$" is to be read: it is settled that φ.

Semantics

Let $\mathfrak{S} =< Entity, Property, Tree, Agt, Obj, Instr, \leqslant, Ch >$ be an i-structure. Any function $\mathfrak{I}: \mathbb{CONST} \cup \mathbb{PRED} \rightarrow Entity \cup Property$ will be called an $\mathfrak{S}$-interpretation if it satisfies the following conditions:

1. $\mathfrak{I}(\mathbb{CONST}) \subseteq Entity$,
2. $\mathfrak{I}(\mathbb{PRED}) \subseteq Property$.

The pair $< \mathfrak{S}, \mathfrak{I} >$ will be called a *model* for the i-logic.

Let $\mathfrak{M}$ be a model for the i-logic. Any function $\mathfrak{V}:\mathbb{VAR} \rightarrow Entity$ be called a *valuation* in $\mathfrak{M}$. For the sake of simplicity, I put $\mathfrak{V}(a) = \mathfrak{I}(a)$ when $a \in \mathbb{CONST}$.

Now we are in a position to define the satisfaction conditions for $\mathbb{L}$. The expression "$\mathfrak{M}, \mathfrak{V}, W, h \vDash \varphi$" abbreviates the expression "a formula φ is satisfied in a model $\mathfrak{M}$ and valuation $\mathfrak{V}$ (in $\mathfrak{M}$) at a world-stage W and history h". I assume that "$\mathfrak{M}, \mathfrak{V}, W, h \vDash \varphi$" is a well-formed expression only when the set $W \cap h$ is not empty.

$$\mathfrak{M}, \mathfrak{V}, W, h \vDash \delta(\beta) \equiv \exists w \in W \; \mathfrak{I}(\delta) \in Prop(\mathfrak{V}(\beta), w). \tag{29}$$

The following two definitions rephrase the respective definitions from [1] (see e.g. 5 above).

$$\mathfrak{M}, \mathfrak{V}, W, h_1 \vDash \Box\varphi \equiv \forall h_2 \in H(W) \; \mathfrak{M}, \mathfrak{V}, W, h_2 \vDash \varphi. \tag{30}$$

$$\mathfrak{M}, \mathfrak{V}, W, h \vDash \beta \text{ dstit } \varphi \equiv \mathfrak{V}(\beta) \in Agt \; \wedge \tag{31}$$

$$\wedge \forall h_1 \in Ch(\mathfrak{V}(\beta), W, h) \; \mathfrak{M}, \mathfrak{V}, W, h_1 \vDash \varphi \wedge \exists h_1 \in H(W) \; \mathfrak{M}, \mathfrak{V}, W, h_1 \nvDash \varphi.$$

$$\mathfrak{M}, \mathfrak{V}, W, h \vDash \text{avail}(\beta) \equiv Prop(\mathfrak{V}(\beta), h(W)) \neq \emptyset. \tag{32}$$

$$\mathfrak{M}, \mathfrak{V}, W, h \vDash \beta_1 \text{ instr\_for } \beta_2 \equiv \tag{33}$$

$$\equiv \mathfrak{V}(\beta_1) \in Obj \wedge \mathfrak{V}(\beta_2) \in Agt \wedge \mathfrak{V}(\beta_1) \in i(\mathfrak{V}(\beta_2), h(W)).$$

$$\mathfrak{M}, \mathfrak{V}, W, h \vDash \beta_1 \text{ istit } \varphi \text{ with } \beta_2 \equiv \tag{34}$$

$$\equiv \mathfrak{V}(\beta_1) \in Agt \wedge \mathfrak{V}(\beta_2) \in Obj \wedge$$

$$\wedge \forall h_1 \in Ch(\mathfrak{V}(\beta_1), W, h) \; \mathfrak{M}, \mathfrak{V}, W, h_1 \vDash \varphi \wedge \mathfrak{V}(\beta_2) \in i(\mathfrak{V}(\beta_1), h_1(W)) \wedge$$

$$\wedge \exists h_1 \in H(W) \mathfrak{M}, \mathfrak{V}, W, h_1 \nvDash \varphi \wedge \mathfrak{V}(\beta_2) \notin i(\mathfrak{V}(\beta_1), h_1(W)).$$

Definition 34 extends the above definition of dstit with two clauses related to the instrumental aspect of actions: a clause that corresponds to the positive condition of 31 and a clause that corresponds to the negative condition. The former guarantees that seeing to things with the help of instruments, agents select instrumental properties. As for the latter clause, definition 31 implies that an agent sees to it that φ only if one of his choices results in $\neg\varphi$. Likewise, definition 34 has it that an agent sees to it that φ with the help of β only if one of his possible choices does not involve any selection of instrumental properties.

According to definition 34, David saw to it that he killed Goliath with the help of a stone iff (i) David is an agent, (ii) the stone is an object, (iii) one of the choices available to David involves only such histories in which David kills Goliath and in each such history David selects that stone as an instrument, and (iv) another choice of David involves one history in which David does not kill Goliath and in which David does not select the stone at stake as an instrument.

If for all $W \in Tree$ and all $h \in History$, it is the case that for all valuations $\mathfrak{V}$ in a model $\mathfrak{M}$, $\mathfrak{M}, W, h \vDash \varphi$, then φ is said to be *valid in* a model $\mathfrak{M}$. If a formula φ is valid in all models, then it is said to be a *tautology* of the i-logic (written: $\vDash \varphi$).

Some tautologies of i-logic

$$\models x \text{ istit } A(y) \text{ }_{\text{wth } z} \rightarrow x \text{ dstit } A(y) \wedge z \text{ instr\_for } x \wedge \neg(\Box z \text{ instr\_for } x). \quad (35)$$

$$\models x \text{ instr\_for } y \rightarrow \neg(y \text{ instr\_for } z). \quad (36)$$

$$\models \text{avail}(x) \rightarrow \Box\text{avail}(x). \quad (37)$$

$$\models x \text{ instr\_for } y \rightarrow \text{avail}(x). \quad (38)$$

$$\models x \text{ instr\_for } y \wedge \neg(\Box x \text{ instr\_for } y) \rightarrow x \text{ istit } (x \text{ instr\_for } y) \text{ }_{\text{wth } y}. \quad (39)$$

$$\models \text{avail}(y) \rightarrow \neg(x \text{ istit } (\text{avail}(y))_{\text{wth } z}). \quad (40)$$

$$\models x \text{ istit } A(y) \text{ }_{\text{wth } z} \rightarrow \neg(\Box A(y)) \wedge \neg(\Box(x \text{ instr\_for } z))). \quad (41)$$

$$\models x \text{ istit } A(y) \text{ }_{\text{wth } z} \rightarrow A(y). \quad (42)$$

$$\models x \text{ istit } A(y) \text{ }_{\text{wth } z} \rightarrow x \text{ istit } (x \text{ istit } A(y) \text{ }_{\text{with } z}). \quad (43)$$

$$\models x \text{ istit } A(y_1) \text{ }_{\text{wth } z} \wedge x \text{ istit } B(y_2) \text{ }_{\text{wth } z} \rightarrow x \text{ istit } (A(y_1) \wedge B(y_2)) \text{ }_{\text{with } z}. \quad (44)$$

Further Work

One obvious extension of the above considerations is an Hilbert-style axiomatic system proved to be sound and complete with respect to the semantics for the i-logic. Another fairly natural development would be to redefine other stit operators, in particular the achievement stit, in order to elaborate other instrumental aspects of actions. Finally, one could extend the above formal framework so that one could express therein such essential factors of instrumental actions as beliefs, desires, and plans.

Acknowledgments

The research presented in this paper was funded by the Marie Curie Intra-European Fellowship schema (EIF-006550).

References

[1] Nuel Belnap, Michael Perloff, and Ming Xu. *Facing the Future: Agents and Choices in Our Indeterminist World*. Oxford University Press, Oxford, 2001.

[2] P. R. Cohen and H. J. Levesque. Intention is choice with commitment. *Artificial Inteligence*, 42:213–261, 1990.

[3] Randall Dipert. *Artifacts, Art Works and Agency*. Temple University Press, Philadelphia, 1993.

[4] Anand S. Rao and Michael P. Georgeff. Modeling rational agents within a bdi-architecture principles of knowledge representation and reasoning (kr'91). In R. Fikes and E. Sandwall, editors, *Proceedings of Knowledge Representation and Reasoning*, pages 473–484, San Mateo (CA), 1991. Morgan Kaufmann.

[5] B. van Linder, W. van der Hoek, and J. J. Meyer. Formalizing abilities and opportunities of agents. *Fundamenta Informaticae*, 34(1-2):53–101, 1998.

Formal Ontology in Information Systems
B. Bennett and C. Fellbaum (Eds.)
IOS Press, 2006

Towards an ontology of agency and action
From STIT to OntoSTIT+

Nicolas TROQUARD [a,b,c], Robert TRYPUZ [b,c] Laure VIEU [a,b]

[a] *Institut de Recherche en Informatique de Toulouse, Université Paul Sabatier & CNRS*
[b] *Laboratorio di Ontologia Applicata, ISTC, CNR, Trento*
[c] *Università di Trento*

Abstract. A variety of disciplines and research areas have separately studied the notions of action, agents and agency, but no integrated and well-developed formal ontology for them is currently available. This paper is a first attempt at bridging this gap, focusing especially on the relationship between agency and action.

The departure point is STIT logic, the most expressive among the current logics of agency. Agency is the relationship between an agent and the states of affairs it brings about, without referring to how this is done, i.e., the actions performed. Since ontological investigations are best done in a first-order framework, making explicit at the language level the domain of quantification, we first propose a first-order theory that is proved equivalent to the propositional modal logic STIT. The domain and language of this theory is then extended to cover actions, obtaining the theory we call OntoSTIT+.

Keywords. ontology of action, agency, action, logic of agency, STIT

Introduction

Action and agency are crucial notions for a variety of application domains, e.g., multiagent systems and interaction modelling, planning and robotics, law and social modelling... Accordingly, many different research areas, among which the quite rich discipline of philosophy of action, have proposed theoretical accounts. Unfortunately, these proposals are often unrelated; a correlate is that no well-developed ontology of action and agency is currently available. This paper is a first attempt at bridging this gap, focusing especially on the relationship between agency and action, mostly studied separately.

STIT logic (in short: STIT) is one of the most suitable logical systems dealing with *agency*, both in terms of expressivity and formal properties. The key idea of agency comes from Anselm around the year 1100, who argued that acting is best described by what an agent brings about or, in STIT terms, "sees to it that" is true. Agency is thus the relationship between an agent (or a group of agents) and the states of affairs it can bring about, without referring to how this is done, i.e., the actions performed. Reducing the ontological commitment is of course positive, but if one wants to reason on actions themselves, considering their preconditions, distinguishing between different ways of reaching a given state of affairs, analysing the internal structure of the action (its participants other than the agent, its way of unfolding in time) and its essential relationship with the agent's mental states, avoiding to introduce actions in the picture becomes impossible.

STIT is a propositional modal logic. Integrating agency and actions in the same framework could be done by extending STIT with some other modal operators dealing more explicitly with actions like those of PDL; this path has begun to be explored in [1]. However, with modal operators, the domains of interest and their ontological properties are not made explicit in the language but left hidden in the models. Another direction is to work directly in the more expressive framework of first-order logic, more suitable to easily formulate many properties and explore the variety of possible ontological choices.

The methodology chosen for the work presented here is therefore to first express the ontological assumptions of STIT in a first-order theory, called OntoSTIT; this is the purpose of Section 2, after a formal presentation of STIT in Section 1. Then, we propose to extend this theory by enlarging its language and its domain of interpretation to include actions proper. Section 3 is thus dedicated to discussing OntoSTIT+. Having started from a decidable modal logic, future work will examine if OntoSTIT+ is suitable as intended models of some extension of STIT that maintains good reasoning properties.

1. STIT logic

This section is a short introduction to STIT, a family of modal logics of agency [2,3]. We start with pointing out the important properties of STIT, which justifies why we have chosen it as a basis. Then we present the language and syntactic structure of this logic as well as its semantics. Doing so, we try to follow the terminology that is used by its authors, although we are aware that some terms used in STIT might be misleading; in such cases we provide clarification.

Formal properties of STIT.   STIT is not the only logic of agency, even though it enjoys formal properties that make it particularly attractive. One such property is that STIT is more expressive than two well-known logics of agency, ATL and CL [4,5]. *Alternating-time Temporal Logic* (ATL) is a direct extension of CTL [6] for multi-agent systems, introducing agents and coalitions of agents who can opt, at every state (or 'choice point'), for a particular subset of the possible courses of time [7]. Pauly's *Coalition Logic* (CL) [8] has been introduced independently in game theory to reason about what agents are able to achieve. As shown by Goranko in [9], CL corresponds to the fragment of ATL restricted to some operators. The second important property of STIT is its decidability, proven in [3, Part VI]. This fact makes STIT an appropriate tool for reasoning.

STIT language.   In this paper, we focus on the STIT variant based on the operator called Chellas's stit (*cstit*) with many agents. The language of STIT (L_{STIT}) is described as follows: $\phi \triangleq p \mid a = b \mid \neg\phi \mid \phi \wedge \phi \mid \mathbf{F}\phi \mid \mathbf{P}\phi \mid \Box\phi \mid [a\,cstit : \phi]$, where p belongs to a set of atomic propositions Atm ($p \in Atm$) and a, b are elements of set of agents Agt ($a, b \in Agt$). $\mathbf{F}$ and $\mathbf{P}$ are the standard Prior-Thomason's future and past temporal operators. $\Box$ is the historical necessity operator. $[a\,cstit : \phi]$ is the agentive operator "agent a sees to it that ϕ".

STIT Models.   Before describing the standard STIT models we need to introduce a few concepts regarding the underlying temporal structures. A *branching time frame* is a structure $\langle Mom, < \rangle$ in which Mom is a nonempty set of moments, and $<$ is a transitive and irreflexive partial order relation such that there is no backward branching and every two moments have a common lower bound. In such a branching time frame moments are ordered in a tree-like structure, where forward branching represents the *indeterminacy* of the future and the very possibility of agency, and the lack of backward branching represents the determinacy of the past.

A maximal set of linearly ordered moments from Mom is a *history*. "Intuitively, each history represents some complete temporal evolution of the world, one possible way in which things might work out" [2]. As a matter of fact, many possible courses of the world are possible, which exactly expresses the idea of indeterminacy. A given moment might be contained in several different histories. Let thus $H_m = \{h | m \in h\}$ be the set of histories passing through m, those histories in which m occurs.

A *STIT model* is a structure $\mathcal{M}$ of the form $\langle Mom, <, Agt, Choice, v \rangle$, where $\langle Mom, < \rangle$ is a branching-time frame, v is a valuation function $v : Atm \to 2^{Mom \times Hist}$, where $Hist$ is the set all histories. Agt is a non empty set of agents acting in time (all intentional components are ignored). $Choice : Agt \times Mom \to 2^{2^{Hist}}$ is a function whose values are noted $Choice_a^m$ for given agent a and moment m. $Choice_a^m$ is a partition into equivalence classes of the set of histories H_m through m.

Intuitively, the function $Choice$ represents the possible constraints that an agent is able to exercise upon the course of events at a given moment, i.e. the choices open to the agent at that moment, implicitly corresponding to his or her possible actions.[1] By choosing one choice cell, the agent can rule out the other histories that do not belong to this choice cell and that are possible at the moment of her or his choice. Formally, by choosing—or 'acting'—at m, the agent a selects a particular set of histories from $Choice_a^m$ within which the history to be realized then lies. Given a history $h \in H_m$, $Choice_a^m(h)$ represents the particular choice (set of actions) from $Choice_a^m$ containing h. Histories belonging to a particular choice cell are the *possible outcomes* that might result from performing some *underlying action*.

Choices must be effective. The choice available to an agent at a given moment should not allow a distinction between histories that do not branch at that moment. For each agent, any two histories that are undivided at m must belong to the same choice cell of the partition $Choice_a^m$.

Finally, if there are multiple agents, agents' choices must be independent and compatible. For each moment and for any possible choice of each agent a at that moment, the intersection of all the possible choices selected must contain at least one history.

Semantics.   Assuming a STIT model $\mathcal{M}$, we can define the conditions of satisfaction in $\mathcal{M}$ for STIT's formulae, starting with standard operators. In the following, m/h is an *index*, i.e., a pair consisting of a moment m in Mom of $\mathcal{M}$ and a history h from H_m, and v is the evaluation function of $\mathcal{M}$.

$$
\begin{aligned}
\mathcal{M}, m/h &\models p & &\Longleftrightarrow & & m/h \in v(p), p \in Atm. \\
\mathcal{M}, m/h &\models \neg\phi & &\Longleftrightarrow & & \mathcal{M}, m/h \not\models \phi \\
\mathcal{M}, m/h &\models \phi \wedge \psi & &\Longleftrightarrow & & \mathcal{M}, m/h \models \phi \text{ and } \mathcal{M}, m/h \models \psi \\
\mathcal{M}, m/h &\models \mathbf{P}\phi & &\Longleftrightarrow & & \text{there is some } m' \in h \text{ s.t. } m' < m \text{ and } \mathcal{M}, m'/h \models \phi \\
\mathcal{M}, m/h &\models \mathbf{F}\phi & &\Longleftrightarrow & & \text{there is some } m' \in h \text{ s.t. } m < m' \text{ and } \mathcal{M}, m'/h \models \phi
\end{aligned}
$$

Historical necessity (or settledness) at a moment m (in a history h) is defined as truth in all histories passing through m. Formally: $\mathcal{M}, m/h \models \Box\phi \iff \mathcal{M}, m/h' \models$

---

[1]There are no actions in STIT, but an action can be seen as corresponding to the choice that the proposition denoting its effects is true (now or at some future point) in a selected set of histories.

ϕ for all $h' \in H_m$. When $\Box\phi$ holds at m, p is said to be *settled true at m*. $\Diamond p$ is defined in the usual way as $\neg\Box\neg\phi$, and stands for historical possibility. The intuitive idea is that $\Box\phi$ should be true at some moment if ϕ is true at that moment no matter how the future will turn out.

The extension of a formula is given by: $|\phi|_m^{\mathcal{M}} = \{h \in H_m | \mathcal{M}, m/h \models \phi\}$. $|\phi|_m^{\mathcal{M}}$ is the set of histories h passing through moment m such that the sentence ϕ is true at m/h.

Now we are ready to define the agentive operator $[\_cstit: \_]$.[2] Let a be an agent in $\mathcal{A}gt$ and m/h an index, $\mathcal{M}, m/h \models [a\,cstit: \phi] \iff Choice_a^m(h) \subseteq |\phi|_m^{\mathcal{M}}$. A statement of the form $[a\,cstit: \phi]$, expressing the idea that the agent a sees to it that ϕ, is defined as true at an index m/h just in the case the action performed by a (the choice of a) at that index guarantees the truth of ϕ. The action might result in a variety of possible outcomes, but the statement ϕ must be true in each of them, even though the agent cannot determine which one it will be. For example, my action of *buttering the toast* leads to the state that the *toast is buttered*. This state of affair has to hold in all histories belonging to my choice cell, if I want to truly say that *I saw to it that the toast is buttered*. However many other states of affairs may hold in the histories where the *toast is buttered*. For example the *toast is buttered* may lie either in the history where *the toast is buttered and my tea is cold* or in the history where the *toast is buttered and my tea is hot* and so forth.

[3, p. 435-450] provides a sound and complete axiomatization with respect to the class of models $\mathcal{M}$ and proves its decidability.

Axiomatics.   The STIT version considered here is axiomatized as follows:

(A0) Axioms for propositional logic
(A0') Axioms for Prior-Thomason's temporal operators **P, F**
(A1) S5 axioms for both modal operators $\Box$ and $[\_cstit: \_]$
(A2) $\Box\phi \rightarrow [a\,cstit: \phi]$
(A3) Axioms for standard identity in $\mathcal{A}gt$
(AIA$_k$) $diff(a_0, ..., a_k) \wedge \Diamond[a_0\,cstit: p_0] \wedge ... \wedge \Diamond[a_k\,cstit: p_k] \rightarrow \Diamond([a_0\,cstit: p_0] \wedge ... \wedge [a_k\,cstit: p_k])$ $(k \geqslant 1)$, where:
(DA) (Distinct agents) $diff(a_0) \triangleq \top$, $\mathrm{diff}(a_0, ..., a_{n+1}) \triangleq diff(a_0, ..., a_n) \wedge a_0 \neq a_{n+1} \wedge ... \wedge a_n \neq a_{n+1}$, for any $n \geqslant 0$

and takes as rules of inference *modus ponens* and *necessitation*:

(RN) from ϕ infer $\Box\phi$

2. STIT Ontology of Agency - OntoSTIT

2.1. A modal or an ontological approach?

As explained in the beginning of last section, STIT is a quite expressive logic of agency. It has very important formal properties, and accordingly, it knows a growing influence. However, from the ontological point of view, it is not totally clear to what extent STIT captures the intuitions of agency, and how this relates to the notion of action, in particular as it is studied in the philosophy of action.

---

[2]STIT models allow the definition of many stit operators. For instance, $dstit$ (deliberative stit) and $astit$ (achievement stit) are other well-known operators in the STIT literature. Here, we focus only on $cstit$, but $dstit$ can be easily defined by means of $cstit$ and historical necessity ($[a\,dstit: \phi] \triangleq [a\,cstit: \phi] \wedge \neg\Box\phi$).

It is well known that propositional modal logic has expressivity limitations in comparison with first order logic; this is actually why it has better calculability properties. But whereas the latter enables the expression of rich theories capturing almost all intuitions, the former forces us to tie our intuitions into an at times uncomfortable suit. In this sense it is not surprising that inside the ontological community those who deal with the concept of action and agency have little or no interest in STIT Logic, as Belnap, one of the authors of STIT Logic, complained:

> *The modal logic of agency is not popular. Perhaps largely due to the influence of Davidson (see the essays in Davidson 1980 [10]), but based also on the very different work of such as Goldman 1970 [11] and Thomson 1977 [12], the dominant logical template takes an agent as a wart on the skin of an action, and takes an action as a kind of event. This 'actions as events' picture is all ontology, not modality, and indeed, in the case of Davidson, is driven by the sort of commitment to first-order logic that counts modalities as Bad. [3]*

On the other hand—the argument goes—STIT is philosophically well motivated and *"has the advantage that it permits us to postpone attempting to fashion an ontological theory, while still advancing our grasp of some important features of action..."* [3].

Although, as said earlier, is it true that the first-order framework is more adequate to ontological studies, we would like to draw a slightly different picture from Belnap's. As any representation framework, propositional modal logics do carry ontological assumptions, even though these are often hidden in properties of their models rather than explicitly stated in the language. So, even though the focus in STIT work has (deliberately) not been put on ontological questions, STIT is already in some sense an ontology of agency.

In order to clarify what are STIT's ontological assumptions and establish a base ground on which to build a richer ontology of agency and action, we will in the next sections extract those features of action captured by STIT, and make them explicit in a first-order theory proved equivalent to it, that we will call *OntoSTIT*.

2.2. From STIT to OntoSTIT

We first present the new first-order language we will be using, and then the axiomatic theory that we call OntoSTIT. Following the technique of 'T-encoded semantics' [13,14], and thanks to STIT's completeness with respect to the class of models $\mathcal{M}$ (see above), it can be shown that STIT is equivalent to OntoSTIT.

2.2.1. Language

OntoSTIT is a theory of first-order logic with identity and its language, $L_{OntoSTIT}$, is defined in a standard way. We nevertheless assume the following conventions for variables and constants symbols of $L_{OntoSTIT}$:

- Ω is the set of variables ranging on Particulars: $x_1, ..., x_n (..., s, t, x, x', x'', y, z, ...)$;
- Λ is the set of constants denoting Particulars: **a, h, m, y, z**, ...;
- Π is the set of constants denoting States of Affairs: **p, p', p''**, ...;
- Δ is the set of constants denoting (primitive) Universals: AG, MO, HT, IN, PRE, $HOLDS$, PO.

The latter predicate constants are understood as, respectively, "is an agent", "is a moment", "is a history", incidence between a moment and a history, precedence between moments, the relation such that at a moment and a history a proposition "holds", the relation such that an agent at a moment makes sure that two histories are both "possible outcomes" of its action.

The models of OntoSTIT are those of STIT, the class of models $\mathcal{M}$. The domain of quantification in which Ω is interpreted covers agents, moments and histories. Even if this is a first-order theory, we need to refer to propositions. The language contains therefore a set of constants that could be seen as denoting *reified* atomic propositions, but will simply be interpreted as states of affairs in $\mathcal{M}$. The truth of such propositions is asserted exclusively via the (meta-)predicate $HOLDS(m, h, \mathbf{p})$ which expresses the idea of STIT that the proposition $\mathbf{p}$ is true at the moment m and the history h. No Boolean or modal combination of these propositions is allowed within $HOLDS$.

2.2.2. *Characterization of primitive relations and categories; definitions*

Order on moments.   The precedence relation PRE between moments (As1) is transitive (As2) and irreflexive (As3). The linearity in the past is expressed by (As4). (As5) says that any two moments have a lower bound (historical connection).

(As1) $PRE(x, y) \rightarrow MO(x) \wedge MO(y)$[3]
(As2) $PRE(x, y) \wedge PRE(y, z) \rightarrow PRE(x, z)$
(As3) $\neg PRE(x, x)$
(As4) $PRE(x, z) \wedge PRE(y, z) \rightarrow x = y \vee PRE(x, y) \vee PRE(y, x)$
(As5) $\exists z((PRE(z, x) \vee z = x) \wedge (PRE(z, y) \vee z = y))$

Agents.   We assume that there is at least one agent (As6). Nothing more is known about agents in OntoSTIT, just as in STIT.

(As6) $\exists x AG(x)$

Moments and histories.   There is at least one moment (As7). In STIT models, a history is a set of moments and the relationship between a moment and a history is expressed by $m \in h$. In OntoSTIT language, a history is denoted by a particular individual and no set theoretical axioms are assumed. We simply express the relation between moments and histories by the relation $IN(x, y)$: "the moment x is *in* the history y" or "the history y passes through the moment x" (As8). For any moment, there is some history that passes through it (As9). (As10) is an axiom schema ensuring that when a proposition $\mathbf{p}$ holds at the moment x and the history y, x is in y.

(As7) $\exists x MO(x)$
(As8) $IN(x, y) \rightarrow MO(x) \wedge HT(y)$
(As9) $MO(x) \rightarrow \exists y IN(x, y)$
(As10) $HOLDS(x, y, \mathbf{p}) \rightarrow IN(x, y)$, for each constant $\mathbf{p}$ in Π

---

[3]Universal quantifications over whole formulas are left implicit. We make use of the standard priorities between connectives to avoid unnecessary bracketing.

Histories.   That histories denote maximally linearly ordered sets is guaranteed by axiom (As11), using a defined predicate *MLO* for maximally linearly ordered (Ds2), itself based on the defined predicate *LO(x)* for linearly ordered (Ds1). Theorem (Ts1) expresses the idea that if the same moments are in two histories then those histories are identical. The predicate UD, for undivided, can be defined: two histories x and y are undivided at moment z if and only if for some moment t later than z, it is the case that t is in x and y.

(Ds1) $LO(z) \triangleq \forall x, y(IN(x, z) \wedge IN(y, z) \rightarrow x = y \vee x < y \vee y < x)$

(Ds2) $MLO(x) \triangleq LO(x) \wedge \neg \exists y(LO(y) \wedge x \neq y \wedge \forall z(IN(z, x) \rightarrow IN(z, y)))$

(As11) $HT(x) \rightarrow MLO(x)$

(Ts1) $\forall z(IN(z, x) \leftrightarrow IN(z, y)) \leftrightarrow x = y$

(Ds3) $UD(x, y, z) \triangleq \exists t(PRE(z, t) \wedge IN(t, x) \wedge IN(t, y))$

Possible Outcome.   The predicate $PO(x, y, z, t)$, for possible outcome, expresses the intuitions that are behind the *Choice* function in STIT: at moment y, histories z and t – that pass through y (As13)[4] – are the possible outcomes of some action performed by agent x (As12) (see Figure 1). We call the histories z and t 'possible outcomes' because each of them *might* result from the action performed by the agent x at y although he cannot determine which will be the actual one. In other words, an agent by his action restricts the possible futures to those histories that are possible outcomes of his action. Note that as STIT, OntoSTIT does not explicitly model action. In other words, actions are not present as individuals in our ontology. That is why we cannot express the intuition, neither in STIT nor in OntoSTIT, that an agent performs a particular action. However this will be possible in OntoSTIT+ (see Section 3).

(As12) $PO(x, y, z, t) \rightarrow AG(x) \wedge MO(y) \wedge HT(z) \wedge HT(t)$

(As13) $PO(x, y, z, t) \rightarrow IN(y, t)$

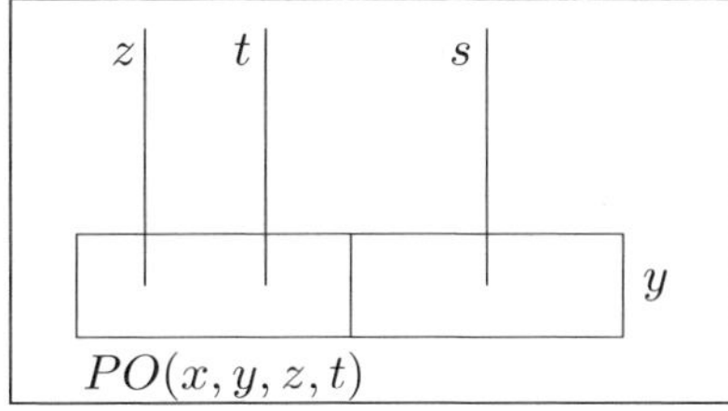

Figure 1. At the moment y, the histories z and t are the possible outcomes of some action performed by the agent x.

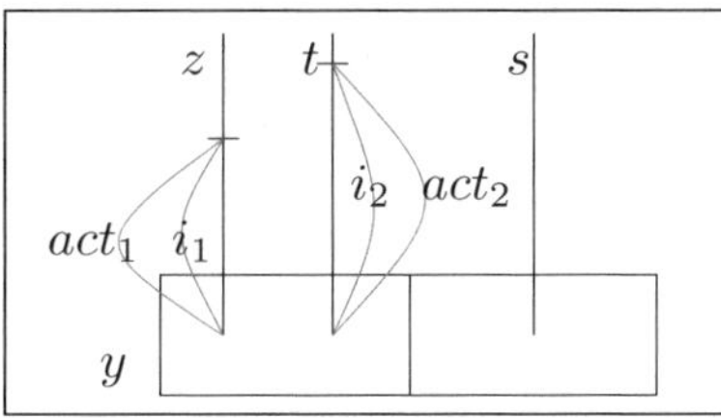

Figure 2. Action Token act_1 (act_2) Lies-On History z (t). Action Token act_1 (act_2) Runs-Through Interval i_1 (i_2).

Considering that the first two arguments are fixed, PO is an equivalence relation. It is reflexive (As14), transitive (As15) and symmetric (As16):

(As14) $IN(y, z) \rightarrow PO(x, y, z, z)$

(As15) $PO(x, y, s, t) \wedge PO(x, y, t, z) \rightarrow PO(x, y, s, z)$

(As16) $PO(x, y, z, t) \rightarrow PO(x, y, t, z)$

Axiom (As17) says that histories that are undivided at moment y are possible outcomes of the same action.

---

[4]Because of (As16), in axiom (As13) we do not need to explicitly write that also $IN(y, z)$.

(As17) $PO(x, y, t, t') \wedge UD(t', t'', y) \rightarrow PO(x, y, t, t'')$

The axiom schema (As18) expresses the independence of choices. It means that at each moment y there is at least one history t that is common to all agents' possible choices.

(As18) $PO(x_1, y, z_1, t_1) \wedge \ldots \wedge PO(x_k, y, z_k, t_k) \rightarrow \exists t(PO(x_1, y, z_1, t) \wedge \ldots \wedge PO(x_k, y, z_k, t))$ for any $k > 1$

2.2.3. Equivalence between STIT and OntoSTIT

To prove that STIT and OntoSTIT are equivalent, we use the technique of 'T-encoded semantics' [13,14], using a function $T_{\dot{x},\dot{y}}$ that enables us to translate formulae of STIT language into formulae of OntoSTIT. This is mainly routine.

Equivalence theorem
> For all ϕ in L_{STIT}, ϕ is theorem of STIT iff $\forall x \forall y T_{\dot{x},\dot{y}}(\phi, \{x\}, \{y\})$ is a theorem of OntoSTIT, with x and y being new variables, and the interpretation of $L_{OntoSTIT}$ being constrained s.t. $\omega(x) = \dot{x}$, $\omega(y) = \dot{y}$, where ω transforms variables ranging on Ω into agents, moments or histories of a STIT model $\mathcal{M}$.

2.2.4. How to express agency in OntoSTIT?

The idea of agency is expressed in OntoSTIT by two concepts: possible outcome (PO) and the predicate $HOLDS$ on effects of choice/action. This means that actions themselves are not present in our first-order theory. We can express in OntoSTIT that an agent saw to it that some state of affairs holds (e.g. *the light is off*), even though we still cannot explicitly say by means of which action he/she has done it (we cannot make sure that *the agent switched off the light* rather than *the agent unscrewed the bulb*).

Consider the instantaneous action of *switching off the light* performed by *Robert*, now. We need to be sure that in all possible outcomes of this action it is the case that the *light is off* (we assume that the actual moment is named **n** and the actual history **h**):

(Es1) $\forall h(PO(Robert, \mathbf{n}, \mathbf{h}, h) \rightarrow HOLDS(\mathbf{n}, h, \textit{Light is off}))$

What is more, we want to say that *Robert switches off the light* is true only if *the light was on* just before the action was performed:

(Es2) $\forall x PRE(x, \mathbf{n}) \rightarrow \exists y(PRE(x, y) \wedge PRE(y, \mathbf{n}) \wedge \neg HOLDS(y, \mathbf{h}, \textit{Light is off})) \wedge$
$\quad \forall h(PO(Robert, \mathbf{n}, \mathbf{h}, h) \rightarrow HOLDS(\mathbf{n}, h, \textit{Light is off}))$.

In OntoSTIT (as in STIT) we can also express the idea that an agent brought about some state of affair but he could not have done it or simply it could have happened that that state of affair does not hold. For example we say that *Robert switches off the light*, now, but also that *the light might have been still on*.

(Es3) $\forall h \ (PO(Robert, \mathbf{n}, \mathbf{h}, h) \rightarrow HOLDS(\mathbf{n}, h, \textit{Light is off})) \wedge \exists s(IN(\mathbf{n}, s) \wedge$
$\quad \neg HOLDS(\mathbf{n}, s, \textit{Light is off})$[5]

---

[5] In STIT this formula can be expressed as follows: [*Robert cstit* : *Light is off*] $\wedge \neg\Box$(*Light is off*) which is equivalent to the formula [*Robert dstit* : *Light is off*]. From now on we do not include the preconditions in formulas representing actions.

Notice that in (Es1), (Es2) and (Es3) the moment of choice, **n**, and the moment in which the effect of the action (*the light is off*) comes out, are the same. This expresses the assumption that the action of *switching off the light* is punctual or instantaneous. Instantaneity tightly binds the outcome of the action to the choice of performing that action. Nevertheless it is possible to separate the moment of choice, **n**, and the moment of appearance of the outcome, m.

Let's consider *swimming* and the specific action *Robert swims from point A to point B*. This action belongs to the group of actions that do not go beyond bodily movement.[6] In STIT, Robert's action is expressed by the sentence: *at point A, Robert sees to it that he will be in point B* which, if true, means that at the moment of the choice, when Robert is in point A, Robert is guaranteed to reach point B. This is because all actions (or rather, all choices) are successful in STIT. This seems far too strong an assumption, as in real life, agents do change their minds and actions can abort. There is thus in STIT an agentive gap between the choice and the effects.

A similar problem occurs in the case of actions that do go beyond bodily movement, as for example with *Booth's killing of Lincoln*, (Es4), by shooting him [16]:

(Es4) $\forall h(PO(Booth, \mathbf{n}, \mathbf{h}, h) \rightarrow \exists m(PRE(\mathbf{n}, m) \wedge HOLDS(m, h, Lincoln\ is\ dead)))$

(Es4) is the translation of the STIT formula: $[Booth\ cstit: \mathbf{F}(Lincoln\ is\ dead)]$. Between the moment when *Booth chooses to kill Lincoln* and the moment when *Lincoln is dead*, we have a temporal gap. And we still have the inadequate assumption in STIT that the action consisting of the sequence of events – Booth pulling the trigger, the bullet flying, the bullet entering Lincoln, Lincoln dying – is fully determined by Booth's choice. This means that between the start of the action and the moment when its effect appears, the action cannot be stopped, neither for reasons internal to the agent (which in this case is impossible if we assume the pulling the trigger is instantaneous) nor for any external forces. The temporal gap is here both an agentive and a causal gap.

STIT's assumption that actions are always successful corresponds to the fact that actions are seen *ex post acto*. It is thus in some sense deliberate that only actions that have succeeded are taken into account[7]. As we have seen there are nevertheless good reasons to take a different point of view on actions. Indeed, this is why an extension to STIT has been proposed in [17], to include the new operator "is seeing to it that".

The *ex post acto* view solves the problem of the possible gap between the choice and the action's outcome by simply assuming some kind of determinism of choice, and [17] solves it by assuming the existence of default 'strategies'. OntoSTIT obviously inherits the undesired properties of STIT. To follow more closely findings in philosophy of action, we claim that we should avoid the agentive gap by representing explicitly the persistence of the agent's choice (intention) till the end of the action. Adding the possibility to directly refer to actions is therefore an obvious solution, which moreover opens the path for yet other extensions aimed at accounting for the richness of action concept. The extension of OntoSTIT to actions is the subject of the next section.

---

[6]Searle [15] claims that no action goes beyond bodily movement. Here we do not take issue on this.

[7]The formula $[a\ cstit: \phi] \rightarrow \phi$ is theorem of STIT.

3. Towards an Ontology of Action - OntoSTIT+

In this section we show how OntoSTIT might be extended with actions, obtaining the new theory OntoSTIT+. Its intended models extend the domain of class $\mathcal{M}$ with actions and intervals. We distinguish between action tokens and their 'action courses', which are the different possible ways a single action (i.e., an action token) might unfold in time along different histories. We show at the end of this section that in OntoSTIT+, the problems just described are solved.

3.1. Language

The language of OntoSTIT+ is that of OntoSTIT extended with new universals. Let Δ_+ be the set of all explicitly introduced universal of OntoSTIT+, $\Delta_+ = \Delta \cup \{INT, ACT, Act, INI, CO, RT, LON, AGO\}$. These new predicate constants are understood as, respectively, "is an interval", "is an action token", "is an action course","a moment is in an interval", "an action course is a course of an action token", "an action course runs through an interval","an action course lies on a history" and "an agent is the agent of an action course".[8]

3.2. Characterization of categories and primitive relations; definitions

Intervals. INI relates moments and intervals (Ap1). All intervals are linearly ordered (Ap2). (Dp1) and (Dp2) define beginning and end of intervals. Any interval has a beginning and an end (Ap3). The unicity of beginning and end for each interval is guaranteed by (Dp1), (Dp2) and (Ap2). Intervals are convex (Ap4). It is worth noting that nothing prevents a beginning of an interval from being equal to its end, so degenerated intervals are possible. (Dp3) defines the relation of temporal part between an interval and a history. For each interval there is a history of which it is temporal part (Ap5). However an interval may belong to more than one history (non-unicity).

(Ap1) $INI(x, y) \rightarrow MO(x) \wedge INT(y)$
(Ap2) $INT(x) \rightarrow \forall x, y(INI(x, z) \wedge INI(y, z) \rightarrow x = y \vee PRE(x, y) \vee PRE(y, x))$
(Dp1) $BEG(x, y) \triangleq INI(x, y) \wedge \forall z(PRE(z, x) \rightarrow \neg INI(z, y))$
(Dp2) $END(x, y) \triangleq INI(x, y) \wedge \forall z(PRE(x, z) \rightarrow \neg INI(z, y))$
(Ap3) $INT(x) \rightarrow \exists y, z(BEG(y, x) \wedge END(z, x))$
(Ap4) $INT(x) \wedge INI(k, x) \wedge INI(l, x) \wedge PRE(k, y) \wedge PRE(y, l) \rightarrow INI(y, x)$
(Dp3) $TP(x, y) \triangleq \forall z(INI(z, x) \rightarrow IN(z, y))$
(Ap5) $INT(x) \rightarrow \exists y(TP(x, y))$

Actions. The relation RT binds an action course to an interval (Ap6). The time of each action course is always fixed: there is exactly one interval such that it runs through it (Ap7). The predicate $CO(x, y)$ links an action course to an action token (Ap8). For each action course there is *exactly one* action token it it is a course of (Ap9). Similarly, for each action token there is *at least one* action course which is a course of it (Ap10). (Ap11) and theorem (Tp1) say that for each action token (and all its courses) we can always find exactly one agent that is agentive for it. (Dp4 - Dp6) define the predicates: $BAct(x, y)$, $EAct(x, y)$ and $BACT(x, y)$ which should be understood respectively as "moment x is

---

[8]In a larger setting such as DOLCE, AGO would be subsumed by participation.

a beginning of action course y", "moment x is an end of action course y", and "moment x is a beginning of action token y". The unicity of beginning and end of each action course is guaranteed by the unicity of the interval of each action course (Ap7) and the unicity of beginning and end for each interval (Dp1, Dp2, Ap2). (Ap12) guarantees that all action courses of the same action token have the same starting moment, even though they may have different ends. This is why the unicity of an action token's end (that we do not define) cannot be guaranteed, whereas its beginning exists and is unique. Finally, we define the predicate $LON(x, y)$ for "the action course x lies on the history y" by: there is an interval s such that x runs through it and s is a temporal part of y (Dp7).

(Ap6) $RT(x, y) \rightarrow Act(x) \wedge INT(y)$
(Ap7) $Act(x) \rightarrow \exists! y(RT(x, y))$
(Ap8) $CO(x, y) \rightarrow Act(x) \wedge ACT(y)$
(Ap9) $Act(x) \rightarrow \exists! y(CO(x, y))$
(Ap10) $ACT(x) \rightarrow \exists y(CO(y, x))$
(Ap11) $ACT(x) \rightarrow \exists! y(AG(y) \wedge \forall z(CO(z, x) \rightarrow AGO(y, z)))$
(Tp1) $Act(x) \rightarrow \exists! y(AG(y) \wedge AGO(y, x))$
(Dp4) $BAct(x, y) \triangleq \exists s(RT(y, s) \wedge BEG(x, s))$
(Dp5) $EAct(x, y) \triangleq \exists s(RT(y, s) \wedge END(x, s))$
(Dp6) $BACT(x, y) \triangleq \exists s(CO(s, y) \wedge BAct(x, s))$
(Ap12) $CO(x, z) \wedge CO(y, z) \rightarrow \exists t(BAct(t, x) \wedge BAct(t, y))$
(Dp7) $LON(x, y) \triangleq \exists s(RT(x, s) \wedge TP(s, y))$

3.3. Agency in OntoSTIT+

Understanding PO.   To bind the intuitions that are behind *Choice/PO* within the OntoSTIT+ framework, we propose the formula (Ap13):

(Ap13) $CO(x, y) \wedge CO(z, y) \wedge AGO(u, x) \wedge BACT(w, y) \wedge LON(x, k) \wedge LON(z, l) \rightarrow$
    $PO(u, w, k, l)$,

which says that if x and z are action courses of an action token y with beginning w and agent u, then $PO(u, w, k, l)$ is underlying choice for action token y.

Filling the agentive gap.   As we have just mentioned in section 2.2.4 actions themselves are not present in OntoSTIT and we were not able to express in it that *the agent switched off the light* by explicit referring to *switching* as such. In OntoSTIT+ we can easily do it.[9] Let's represent again the example (Es1):

(Ep1) $\exists x, z(ACT(x) \wedge \textit{switching-off-the-light}(x) \wedge \forall y, h(CO(y, x) \wedge LON(y, h) \rightarrow$
    $AGO(Robert, y) \wedge BAct(z, y) \wedge EAct(z, y) \wedge HOLDS(z, h, \textit{light-is-off})))$

Now, if we (i) loosen the condition that the action is instantaneous, i.e., that the beginning and end of each action course of a specific action token are the same, and (ii) limit the requirement that the action has been successful to the actual history **h** only, we obtain a description that captures also situations like that of example (Es4):

(Ep2) $\exists x(ACT(x) \wedge \textit{killing-Lincoln}(x) \wedge \forall y, z(CO(y, x) \wedge LON(y, \mathbf{h}) \wedge EAct(z, y) \rightarrow$
    $AGO(Booth, y) \wedge HOLDS(z, \mathbf{h}, \textit{Lincoln is dead})))$

Notice that (Ep2) does not share the problems of (Es4) because the outcome of the action is linked to the action of the agent. By extending OntoSTIT on actions and intervals we solved two problems pointed out at the end of section 2.2.4.

---

[9]Here we are assuming the existence of a number of additional predicates, like *switching-off-the-light* and *killing-Lincoln*, that categorize action tokens.

4. Perspectives

In this work, we have proposed a first-order theory, OntoSTIT, that made explicit the ontological assumptions of the most expressive modal logic of agency to date, STIT. We have then showed how this framework could be extended, including actions in the domain of OntoSTIT+, to overcome some of STIT's shortcomings.

This is only a first step towards a rich theory of actions and agency. Obviously, OntoSTIT+ still needs to be extended in many directions. To deal with expected effects, which might be useful for, e.g., defining action categories, we can perhaps take inspiration from [17], specifying default actions courses. To deal more explicitly with the agent's intentions than with the simple 'possible outcomes' predicate, integrating agent's mental attitudes is a necessity. We also need to investigate how to express that different categories of actions unfold in time in different ways (aktionsart), and introduce other participants than the agent.

Before adding too many extensions, it might be interesting to take advantage of our departing point, a decidable propositional modal logic. We would thus like to study what is the decidable part of OntoSTIT+ and the possibility to transform it back into some modal logic extending directly STIT. Finally, the integration of OntoSTIT+ within a foundational ontology like DOLCE would surely bring many further insights.

References

[1]   N. Troquard and L. Vieu. Towards a logic of agency and actions with duration. In *ECAI06*, 2006.

[2]   J. F. Horty. *Agency and Deontic Logic.* Oxford University Press, 2001.

[3]   N. Belnap, M. Perloff, and M. Xu. *Facing the future: Agents and choices in our indeterminist world.* Oxford University Press, 2001.

[4]   J. Broersen, A. Herzig, and N. Troquard. From Coalition Logic to STIT. In Wiebe van der Hoek, Alessio Lomuscio, Erik de Vink, and Mike Wooldridge, editors, *Third International Workshop on Logic and Communication in Multi-Agent Systems (LCMAS 2005)*, volume 157(4) of *Electronic Notes in Theoretical Computer Science*, pp 23–35. Elsevier, 2006.

[5]   J. Broersen, A. Herzig, and N. Troquard. Embedding Alternating-time Temporal Logic in Strategic STIT Logic of Agency, 2006. Submitted.

[6]   E. M. Clarke and E. A. Emerson. Synthesis of synchronization skeletons for branching time temporal logic. *Logics of Programs Workshop*, volume131 of Lecture Notes in Computer Science, pages 52–71. Springer Verlag, 1981.

[7]   R. Alur, T. A. Henzinger, and O. Kupferman. Alternating-time Temporal Logic. In *Proceedings of the 38th Symposium on Foundations of Computer Science*, pp. 100–109. IEEE Computer Society Press, 1997.

[8]   M. Pauly. A modal logic for coalitional power in games. *Journal of Logic and Computation*, 12(1): 149 –166, 2002.

[9]   V. Goranko. Coalition games and alternating temporal logics. In *Proceedings of the 8th conference on Theoretical Aspects of Rationality and Knowledge*, pages 259–272. Morgan Kaufmann, 2001.

[10]   D. Davidson. *Essays on Actions and Events.* Clarendon Press, Oxford, 1991.

[11]   A. Goldman. *A Theory of Human Action.* Prentice-Hall, Englewood Cliffs, N. J., 1970.

[12]   J. J. Thomson. *Acts and Other Events.* Cornell University Press, Ithaca, N.Y., 1977.

[13]   M. Manzano. *Extentions of First Order Logic.* Cambridge University Press, 1996.

[14]   H. J. Ohlbach. Combining Hilbert style and semantic reasoning in a resolution framework. *CADE-15, LNAI 1421*, pages 205–219, 1998.

[15]   J. R. Searle. *Rationality in Action.* MIT Press, Cambridge Mass., 2001.

[16]   P. M. Pietroski. *Causing Actions.* Oxford University Press, 2000.

[17]   T. Müller. On the formal structure of continuous on the formal structure of continuous action. *Advances in Modal Logic*, 5:191–209, 2005.

5. General Ontological Issues

Formal Ontology in Information Systems
B. Bennett and C. Fellbaum (Eds.)
IOS Press, 2006

193

A Blueprint for a Calculator of Intensions

Alik PELMAN
University College London

Abstract. We are on Mars again – the favourite laboratory for philosophical experiments. Our host colleagues introduce us to some Martian stuff referred to as "T", and ask us to help them to identify T on other possible worlds. Or, technically speaking, we are asked to determine the *intension* of "T", i.e., what the term designates with respect to different possible worlds. Following a short series of experiments on the planet, we conclude that the intension of "T" depends upon three factors: (1) The semantic rule linked with the term, i.e., the way in which the term is designed to pick out its referent with respect to different possible worlds (e.g., as a definite description, or as a proper name, or as an actualised description etc.); (2) The properties of the referent of "T" in the actual world; and, (3) What we shall call 'the metaphysical background of the universe', i.e., what counts as a thing vs. what counts as a property of things (e.g., whether the universe is such that it contains material objects that merely happen to have their manifest properties, or whether the universe primarily contains manifest objects that merely happen to have their material constitution). As our experiments show, changing the values of any of these variables will result in a change in the reference of the term with respect to different possible worlds, viz., it will result in a change in the intension of the term. We then demonstrate how the three variables are interrelated, and specify how exactly they combine to produce a particular intension of a term. We conclude with a general "formula" that determines what will deserve to be called "T" relative to the different values of the above variables, i.e., we come up with a calculator of intensions. Finally, we also draw some morals about rigidity.

Keywords. Natural language semantics, identity and change, formal relations

Introduction

This paper is concerned with the modal aspect of terms, i.e., with the reference of terms relative to different ways the world might be. More technically, it is concerned with intensions. One common notion of intension is that the intension of a term is a function that assigns to each possible world the term's extension relative to that world.[1] (Although there are other notions of intension, our scope will be limited to this Carnapian notion.) For example, the intension of "the fourth planet from the Sun" assigns to each possible world, the planet which occupies the fourth place from the Sun in that world (if there is such a planet there), whether it is Mars or not; whereas the

---

[1] There is by no means commitment here to intensions, thus defined, being a proper account of meaning. Ultimately, it is not: As is famously pointed out, "triangular" and "trilateral", for example, although sharing the same intension, nonetheless clearly differ in meaning. Thus sameness in intension does not guarantee sameness in meaning; yet difference in intension does entail difference in meaning. However, intensions and meanings do bear an "almost" one-one correlation to one another ("almost" due to cases like the triangular / trilateral one), and therefore sameness in intension, for the overwhelming majority of cases, does go hand in hand with sameness in meaning.

intension of "Mars" assigns Mars to each possible world in which Mars exists, whether it is the fourth planet from the Sun or not in that world. Thus while the singular terms "The fourth planet from the Sun" and "Mars" have the same extension, i.e., they designate the same object in the actual world, nonetheless they have different intensions, i.e., they designate different objects in some possible worlds. Due to this sensitivity of intensions to semantic differences, intension is widely considered a semantic concept. However, as will be demonstrated below, on top of such semantic sensitivity, intensions are no less affected by metaphysical issues, as well as by the actual state of the world. The aim of this paper is to clearly demonstrate these sensitivities, and to devise a general formula that will enable to calculate the intension of referring terms, by considering all relevant factors. More broadly, by analysing the modal aspects of our language, we will gain some insight into the nature of the interaction between semantics, metaphysics and actuality.

To achieve this goal, we consider a study case in which we are to determine the intension of a new term. To avoid presuppositions regarding the term or its referent, we shall set our study case on Mars.

1.

So we are on yet another philosophical expedition to Mars. Our host colleagues introduce us to some purple, jellylike Martian stuff called "T", and ask us to help them to identify T on other possible worlds, to which they frequently travel.[2] (Needless to say, Mars, as well as Earth, both belong to the actual world). In other words, we are asked to determine what would deserve to be called "T". Or, more technically, we are asked to assign to each possible world "T"'s extension, which is just to determine the *intension* of "T".[3] We, of course, are happy to assist. So happy, that we postpone our doubts about the possibility of travelling to other possible worlds.

2.

So we start working. Let us define a descriptive term Φ in the following manner: Φ has a sense and Φ designates, with respect to every possible world, that which fits this sense in that world (if there is such a thing there).[4] For example, "The fourth planet from the sun", would be such a descriptive term; it will designate Mars in the actual world, but other heavenly bodies in some other possible worlds. "T" may just be such a descriptive term. It may, for instance, have the sense 'jellylike purple stuff'. In such a case, the Martian stuff is designated by "T" by virtue of being jellylike purple stuff, and

---

[2] True, the task of reidentification of entities in other possible worlds is at odds with Kripke's famous contention that such identities are *stipulated* rather than discovered (S. Kripke, *Naming and Necessity*, Oxford, Blackwell, 1980, 46). Although I agree with Kripke that possible worlds *can* be thus stipulated, I am nonetheless not convinced that an alternative, *qualitative* introduction of possible worlds – i.e., in which no such stipulation of identity is involved – is not as permissible.

[3] To avoid confusion: as the Martians know what the actual world is, our mission is to determine the intension of "T" on other possible worlds *taken as counterfactual*, and not as actual. I.e., in Frank Jackson's terminology, we are after the C-intension and not after the A-intension of "T" (F.C. Jackson, *From Metaphysics to Ethics: A Defence of Conceptual Analysis*, Oxford, Oxford University Press, 1998.)

[4] Note that reference-fixing descriptions do not belong in this category, but rather in the following one.

likewise "T" will designate, with respect to every possible world, whatever is jellylike purple stuff, in that world. As there may be different stuffs that fit this sense, T on other possible worlds may be distinct from the actual Martian referent. (Thus, a descriptive "T", like "the fourth planet from the sun", need not mark a natural kind.)

Yet "T" may not be such a term; it may be something like a name – a sort of term that we shall call "nondescriptive", and define in the following way: a nondescriptive term Ψ is designed to designate, with respect to every possible world, the same stuff that it designates in the actual world (if such stuff exists in that world).[5] For example, the name "Mars" is such a nondescriptive term; it names Mars in the actual world and thus designates that same object, Mars, in every possible world in which Mars exists. If "T" is indeed such a nondescriptive term, then "T" designates, with respect to every possible world, just this very same stuff that we were introduced to a short while ago on Mars, in that world.[6] (Arguably, a nondescriptive "T" includes cases in which "T" is a proper name, or an actualised description – like "*the actual* fourth planet from the sun", or "*the actual* jellylike purple stuff", or a demonstrative – like "*that* fourth planet from the sun" or "*that* jellylike purple stuff".)

3.

So if "T" is a nondescriptive term, then in order to identify T on other possible worlds we need to be able to tell whether certain stuff that we might encounter on some such world is or is not identical to our actual stuff. This may not be so trivial, as some possible worlds contain stuffs that are similar to our stuff in certain respects but differ from it in other respects, and we need to be qualified to determine whether each stuff is or is not identical to ours. Thus before travelling to other possible worlds, we need to get a pretty good idea of what this stuff that "T" actually designates on Mars consists in. So we go and have a closer examination of that actual referent of "T". We note its manifest properties – that it is purple, jellylike, etc., and upon further examination we determine its material constitution to be P. We learn from the Martians that they in fact conceive the collection of manifest properties as one property, M. We easily manage to adapt and conclude that the actual referent of "T" has the properties P and M. So "T", if nondescriptive, designates, with respect to every possible world, that which is identical to this P+M stuff. Evidently, given that the intension of a nondescriptive "T" assigns to each possible world "T"'s reference in the actual world, had this actual referent of "T" been different from our P+M stuff, the intension of "T" would differ accordingly; it would assign to each world the alternative actual referent.

Now, with respect to these two properties, P and M, there are four kinds of stuff that may be found on other possible worlds: 1. Stuff that is P and M (P+M); 2. Stuff that although shares the manifest property M has nonetheless a different material constitution, say, Q (Q+M); 3. Stuff that has the same material constitution P but a different collection of manifest properties, say, N (P+N)[7]; and, finally, 4. Stuff that is

---

[5] Note that this definition is a description of the *semantic function* of the term, and not of its *content*, and hence does not make the term a descriptive one; as demonstrated here, such a description of function can be provided for Millian names like "Mars", which are, by definition, not descriptive.

[6] Or its counterpart, if we are persuaded by David Lewis's view on the nature of cross-worlds relations.

[7] One may object that this option violates physicalism, namely the view according to which the manifest supervenes upon the physical and hence no change in the manifest is possible without a change in the

neither P nor M, say, some Q and N stuff. (Q+N). Each of these stuffs in fact stands for a type of possible worlds; let us tag them w_1, w_2, w_3 and w_4 respectively. (We are aware, that if there is more than one alternative to P, or more than one alternative to M, there will be accordingly more candidates, and thus more types of possible worlds. Our list of possible worlds thus might not be exhaustive. This fact, however, need not currently worry us, for the argument as it stands by no means depends on a complete list of possible worlds).

4.

For a start, we consider the candidate that has the same material constitution P as the actual stuff, but different manifest property, namely, P+N, which is the stuff on w_3. Is it identical to the actual P+M stuff or not? Being heavily indoctrinated by the presuppositions of our Earthean science, we tend to believe that the universe is such that it contains various materials, such as P and Q, that merely happen to have their manifest properties, like M and N. So it seems that despite the difference in the manifest property, the stuff on w_3 (P+N), is the same stuff, P, as the actual stuff (P+M); so we are naturally drawn to conclude that that stuff is indeed identical to our actual referent of "T". Yet, to our surprise, we soon learn that the Martians have a different view on this matter; they take the universe to be such that it contains primarily manifest entities, such as M and N, that merely happen to have their material constitution, like P or Q. In other words, P+M stuff is primarily the stuff M, that merely happens to have the material constitution P, and which might have had another material constitution, like, say, Q. Thus on their view, the stuff on w_3, having the manifest property N rather than M, is in fact distinct from the stuff on actual Mars; it is, rather, the stuff on w_2, Q+M, which is identical to the actual stuff P+M, despite the difference in their material constitution.[8] What is at stake here is the identity criteria of our Martian entity, the P+M stuff, i.e., the identity criteria of "this", regardless of the way it is described, namely, regardless of calling it "stuff" or otherwise.[9] And whereas we believe that these criteria of identity are primarily material, our hosts believe that these criteria of identity are primarily manifest.

---

physical. The stuff on W_3, namely, P+N stuff, entails a change, albeit a modal one, in the manifest (from M to N) without a change in the physical (P). There are two responses to this. Firstly, physicalism in its common versions is restricted to the actual world; it is commonly accepted that, for example, there *might* have been "zombies" (same physical state but no mental state), or immaterial souls, yet there *actually* aren't any. In other words, in some possible worlds, non-physical properties may supervene in a different way on physical properties, or, indeed, may not supervene upon them at all (e.g., in worlds with different laws of nature). Hence, just as zombies exist *in other possible worlds*, so does stuff with the same physical property P as the actual stuff P+M, but with a different manifest property, N. Secondly, even if we accepted a more ambitious version of physicalism that applied to all possible worlds (and thus eliminated this type of possible world), still, this would not undermine the general argument here, for we could, in principle, choose some stuff with two *independent* dominant properties, i.e., properties that hold no supervenience relations between them. So the objection is not one of essence in this context.

[8] Note that this does not commit the Martians to deny supervenience of the manifest upon the material. For such supervenience is consistent with non-material criteria of identity; it seems perfectly consistent to assume that the universe is inhabited by, e.g., animals, that merely happen to have the material constitution they have (i.e., they might have had different material constitution), and yet at the same time to believe that these animals supervene upon their material constitution.

[9] The cost of denying that there are such independent identity criteria is enormous: it is the overall denial of intensions of nondescriptive terms, such as "T", "Mars", "Alik" etc.

After the first mutual puzzlement by our conflicting views, we soon realise how dogmatic our beliefs are, and thank the fortunate encounter that allowed us to broaden our outlook and to see both options. We both admit, however, that we have no way of determining what the universe is really like in this respect, and in particular, what "being the same" consists in when applied to the purple jellylike stuff. Indeed, for all we know, there may be no fact of the matter here at all.

Furthermore, we now appreciate that with regard to any property Ω of our stuff, it is possible, contrary to both what we or the Martians believe, that the universe is such that it primarily contains Ωs, that merely happen to have other properties, such as their material constitution P, and their manifest property M (such a property Ω may, for instance, be the object's function). So in principle, there are many more possible metaphysical backgrounds.[10]

Turning back to our job, we so far conclude that the intension of the term "T", i.e., "T"'s reference with respect to different possible worlds, is dependent upon three different factors: 1. The semantic rule of "T", i.e., whether "T" is descriptive or not; 2. The actual extension of "T", i.e., whether it is P+M, or Q+M, or P+N or Q+N; and, 3. The metaphysical background of the universe, namely, what count as objects vs. what count as properties of objects.

5.

But what *is* the intension of the term "T" then? What does in fact deserve to be called "T"? Well, surely, to determine the intension of "T" we need the *values* of each of the above three variables. We have already come to suspect that we do not know for sure the value of the third variable – the metaphysical background of the world. But as if this epistemic worry was not enough, the Martians go on to tell us that they were not even sure about the values of the other two variables as well – the semantic rule of "T", and also the true properties of the actual referent. All they are willing to commit to is the purple jellylike stuff to which the term "T" actually applies on Mars. Firstly, regarding the properties of this actual referent, although their current science told them that it had the properties P and M, still, based on their past experience, they were well aware of how fallible their science has been, and therefore were careful not to assume that it isn't failing this time as well. And secondly, as to the semantic rule of "T", some of them thought that "T" designated that stuff by virtue of simply naming it, like a label; whereas others, by contrast, contended that "T" designated the stuff by virtue of that stuff fitting the sense of the term "T", namely, by having the property M (i.e., being jellylike, purple etc.). Furthermore, they thought that other views on this matter were also possible. And there was nothing in the actual application of the term on Mars to tell them which of the views was right. Pondering about it though, we begin to suspect that our epistemic state might not be very different to theirs.

---

[10] There are various metaphysical alternatives in another sense as well. E.g., that the universe contains *both* types of objects, namely Ps and Qs as well as Ms and Ns, that simply coincide (on this view, in the case of a clay statue, there are two objects, the statue and the lump of clay, in the same place at the same time); or, that the universe contains unqualified objects, namely, an unqualified stuff that has the properties P and M, and that any further metaphysical burden is entirely theory-relative. However, such alternatives can be incorporated in the final analysis, once such an analysis is attained.

6.

The problem with this epistemic state is that without the values of the required variables, we simply cannot carry out the job. It is just impossible to determine the intension of "T" without these data, since different data, i.e., different values of the three variables, will result in different intensions. So, what do we do now? Is there a way out? Well, of course there is! We could provide the Martians with some well-defined procedure, which would enable them to calculate the intension of "T" *once* the values of the variables are determined. We could come up with some sort of a *formula*, that when filled in with the appropriate data would simply generate the exact intension. Indeed, with an appropriate re-interpretation of its variables, such a formula can be used to calculate the intension of *any* term.

We also appreciate that such a general formula would provide an understanding of the *general regularity* behind individual intensions of specific terms. After all, isn't it what drives great scientist in their pursuit for theories? Admittedly, unlike us, Newton had methods for measuring weights, speeds, forces, and other values for the variables in his formulas – whereas we, regrettably, do not seem to possess such philosophical yardsticks – yet nonetheless, what he was really after was not so much the specific outcomes of his formulas, but rather the general *rule* that would expose the *regularity* connecting such values. And in *this* respect our formula should enjoy the same merit. So it now seems that even if we knew beyond any doubt the exact values of the three variables, it would still be highly profitable to deliberately put on a "veil of ignorance", and to consider the hypothetical values of each variable, in order to find the general formula… Encouraged by these revelations about the importance of a general formula, we enthusiastically set for the task.

7.

To recall, the main values that were considered are the following: 1. The semantic rule: may be either descriptive or not; 2. The actual referent: corresponding to our apparent P+M actual referent of "T", the possibilities are that it is: indeed P+M, but also, that it may be Q+M, or P+N, or Q+N[11]; and lastly, 3. The metaphysical background may be either a material universe (that happens to have some manifest properties), or a manifest universe (that happens to have some material constitution).

True, we are aware that there are possibilities not covered by the ones mentioned – at least as far as the properties of the actual referent and the metaphysical background are concerned. For the sake of simplicity, however, we shall construct our formula by first considering these options. After arriving at the principle formula, it should be fairly straightforward to extend it to encompass the other options as well.

So apparently the logical space of possibilities here amounts to two (possibilities of the semantic rule) times four (possibilities of the actual referent) times two (possibilities of the metaphysical background), which is sixteen. Fortunately, the

---

[11] Indeed the last two possibilities are not very probable, since they suggest a different manifest property from M, and given that we seem to perceive such properties quite directly we are most likely not to be mistaken about them. However, in order for our formula to be general, we would be better off to consider those options as well, as it will make the formula applicable to cases in which the M property is not manifest and directly perceived, but rather has to be discovered.

options are considerably less than that. This is due to the fact that if "T" is descriptive, then the values of the other variables play no part in fixing the intension. Such a descriptive "T" will simply designate, with respect to every possible world, that which fits "T"'s sense (allegedly, 'being an M',) in that world – regardless of the metaphysical background, or the nature of the actual referent. Thus all eight combinations linked with a descriptive semantic rule for "T" collapse into one.

So overall we have the following nine possible combinations:

Table 1

	Semantic rule	Actual referent	Metaphysical background	W_1 P+M	W_2 Q+M	W_3 P+N	W_4 Q+N
1	Descriptive	(Whatever)	(Whatever)				
2	Nondescriptive	P+M	Material				
3			Manifest				
4		Q+M	Material				
5			Manifest				
6		P+N	Material				
7			Manifest				
8		Q+N	Material				
9			Manifest				

All we need to do now is to calculate the intension of "T", i.e., "T"'s reference with respect to the different possible worlds, for each of the nine rows. This is a fairly easy task. We shall briefly calculate the intension of the first five rows, from which it will be clear how to proceed to fill in the remaining four rows. The completed nine rows will be given in a concluding table.

In row 1, "T" is descriptive. Since, we are told, it is linked with the sense, 'have the (manifest) property M', it will designate, with respect to each type of possible world, that which M's in that type of world. Hence, the intension of "T" in that case would be the following:

Table 2

	Semantic rule	Actual referent	Metaphysical background	W_1 P+M	W_2 Q+M	W_3 P+N	W_4 Q+N
1	Descriptive	(Whatever)	(Whatever)	+	+	-	-

In all subsequent cases, "T" is nondescriptive, and therefore designates, with respect to every possible world, that which it designates in the actual world. So we need to determine what is the nature of this actual referent of "T". We can do that on the basis of the other two variables: the metaphysical background, and the properties of the actual referent. Let us demonstrate this.

In row 2, "T" designates in the actual world stuff that is P+M (as we actually believe it to be the case), and the universe is taken to be a material-universe (similar to what our current science tells us), i.e., the universe is such that it contains, among other things, Ps, that happen to have their manifest properties. Hence our actual referent is such a P that happens to have the manifest property M. So in that case, "T" will designate, with respect to every possible world, that which is P in that world. The intension is thus:

Table 3

	Semantic rule	Actual referent	Metaphysical background	W_1 P+M	W_2 Q+M	W_3 P+N	W_4 Q+N
2	Nondescriptive	P+M	Material universe	+	-	+	-

Row 3 is like Row 2, only that now we have a manifest-universe. So in that case, the same actual referent, P+M, is in fact an M that merely happens to have the material constitution P. Thus "T" will designate, with respect to every possible world, that which is M in that world. The intension of "T" in that case is therefore:

Table 4

	Semantic rule	Actual referent	Metaphysical background	W_1 P+M	W_2 Q+M	W_3 P+N	W_4 Q+N
3	Nondescriptive	P+M	Manifest universe	+	+	-	-

In rows 4 and 5, the actual referent is changed, and it is now not P+M but rather Q+M. I.e., in this row we consider the option that our actual referent has different properties than what we in fact believe it to have. Now if the universe is a material-universe, then the referent, Q+M, is primarily a Q, that merely happens to have the manifest property M. So "T" will designate, with respect to every possible world, that which Q's in that world. If, however, the universe is a manifest-universe, this actual referent is an M, and "T" will designate, with respect to every possible world, that which M's in that world:

Table 5

	Semantic rule	Actual referent	Metaphysical background	W_1 P+M	W_2 Q+M	W_3 P+N	W_4 Q+N
4	Nondescriptive	Q+M	Material universe	-	+	-	+
5			Manifest universe	+	+	-	-

Similar considerations will determine the intension for the remaining four rows.

Overall, we end up with the following complete table, that lists "T"'s intension relative to each combination of values of our three variables:

Table 6

	Semantic rule	Actual referent	Metaphysical background	W_1 P+M	W_2 Q+M	W_3 P+N	W_4 Q+N
1	Descriptive	(Whatever)	(Whatever)	+	+	-	-
2	Nondescriptive	P+M	Material	+	-	+	-
3			Manifest	+	+	-	-
4		Q+M	Material	-	+	-	+
5			Manifest	+	+	-	-
6		P+N	Material	+	-	+	-
7			Manifest	-	-	+	+
8		Q+N	Material	-	+	-	+
9			Manifest	-	-	+	+

And so we're done. Mission complete. Well, at least an outline of our task is complete (for our account to be complete we would still need to include more possible options for each variable.)

8.

Finally, we can use our newly devised formula to draw some moral about rigidity.

A *rigid* term is defined as one that designates the same referent, and only that referent, in all possible worlds in which that referent exists. A nondescriptive term was defined as a term that is designed to designate, with respect to every possible world, the same referent that it designates in the actual world (if such referent exists in that world). Thus it follows that a nondescriptive term is by definition a rigid term. A descriptive term, by contrast, carries no such entailment. To recall, a descriptive term was defined as a term that is linked with a sense, and that designates, with respect to every possible world, that which fits its sense in that term. Thus, a descriptive term might be nonrigid, e.g., "the fourth planet from the sun" designates Mars in the actual world, Venus in another possible world, etc. Yet a descriptive term might also be a rigid term, e.g., "2+2" designates 4 in every possible world, and nothing else; likewise, "stuff with atomic number 79" (arguably) designates gold in every possible world in which gold exists and nothing else. Thus, whereas nondescriptive terms are by definition rigid, descriptive terms may or may not be rigid. In other words, whereas a nondescriptive term is rigidified by the very semantic rule that is attached to it, a descriptive term is not thus rigidified. In Kripke's terms, the difference between the two kinds of rigidity is that a nondescriptive term is rigid *de jure*, i.e., by (stipulating a) law, whereas a descriptive terms is rigid, when it is rigid, *de facto*, i.e., as it happens in practice (without stipulation).[12]

Thus all nondescriptive terms are rigid, whereas only some of the descriptive terms are rigid. What is it that makes a descriptive term rigid though? Under what circumstances would a descriptive term be rigid? A rigid term is one that designates the

---

[12] S. Kripke, 1980, p. 21, n.21

same referent in all possible worlds, and only that referent. Our intensions formula enables us to determine the referent of a term with respect to every possible world; yet in order to determine rigidity, we must also know whether these referents are identical or not. For instance, the formula entails that the intension of "T" when "T" is descriptive (and has the sense "has the property M") is as follows:

Table 7

	Semantic rule	Actual referent	Metaphysical background	W_1 P+M	W_2 Q+M	W_3 P+N	W_4 Q+N
1	Descriptive	(Whatever)	(Whatever)	+	+	-	-

I.e., the referents of "T" across possible worlds are P+M and Q+M. Yet in order to determine whether "T" is rigid or not, we have to further establish whether these referents, namely, P+M and Q+M are identical or not. Now this in turn depends on the metaphysical background of the universe. The dependence works as follows. If the metaphysical background is material, i.e., the universe is such that it primarily contains material things like P and Q that merely happen to have manifest properties like M and N, then the two stuffs P+M and Q+M, one being P (that happens to have the manifest property M) and the other being Q (that happens to have the same manifest property M) are in effect distinct. If, by contrast, the metaphysical background is manifest, i.e., the universe is such that it primarily contains manifest things like M and N that merely happen to have material constitutions like P and Q, then the two stuffs P+M and Q+M, being both M, are identical (despite having different contingent material constitutions). As a consequence, a material universe will entail that a descriptive "T" (with the sense 'being an M') is nonrigid, whereas a manifest universe will entail that such a descriptive "T" is rigid, despite the identical intension in both cases:

Table 8

	Semantic rule	Actual referent	Metaphysical background	W_1 P+M	W_2 Q+M	W_3 P+N	W_4 Q+N	*Rigidity*
1a	Descriptive	(Whatever)	Material	+	+	-	-	Nonrigid
1b		(Whatever)	Manifest	+	+	-	-	Rigid

It turns out that the same term, with the same descriptive semantic function, may come out rigid or nonrigid, depending on the metaphysical background. Rigidity is thus not an exclusively semantic concept; it is no less a metaphysical concept.

To generalise, what makes a descriptive term like "T" rigid, is that its sense – in our case "being an M" – is linked with a kind of things (as opposed to a kind of properties of things), since such metaphysical background guarantees that all that fits that sense is the same stuff. Whereas when the sense is linked with a kind of a property of things rather than with a kind of things – in our case, when M is considered a kind of a property of things rather than a kind of things – then the term turns out nonrigid, since there are different kinds of things that would fit this sense.

Given that all options in which "T" is nondescriptive make "T" rigid, it follows that there is but a single case in which "T" is rendered nonrigid. This happens only when "T" is descriptive *and* its sense is linked with a kind of a property of things, rather than with a kind of things. In all other cases, "T" comes out rigid:

Table 9

	Semantic rule	Actual referent	Metaphysical background	W_1 P+M	W_2 Q+M	W_3 P+N	W_4 Q+N	Rigidity
1a	Descriptive	(Whatever)	Material	+	+	-	-	*Nonrigid*
1b		(Whatever)	Manifest	+	+	-	-	*Rigid De facto*
2	Non-descriptive	P+M	Material	+	-	+	-	*Rigid De jure*
3			Manifest	+	+	-	-	
4		Q+M	Material	-	+	-	+	
5			Manifest	+	+	-	-	
6		P+N	Material	+	-	+	-	
7			Manifest	-	-	+	+	
8		Q+N	Material	-	+	-	+	
9			Manifest	-	-	+	+	

Conclusion

We were looking for the intension of "T", i.e., the reference of "T" with respect to different possible worlds, or simply, what would deserve to be called "T". We have found the three factors upon which intensions depend. We have further considered possible values for each of these variables. We have listed the different possible combination of these values. Finally, we have calculated the resultant intension for each such combination. Thus, using the corresponding values with regard to the term "T", our Martian colleagues can now determine the intension of "T". In fact, they can do more than that. By reinterpreting "P", "M", "Q" and "N", our hosts are now in a position to determine the intension of *any* term, since the intensions given in the above table remain fixed. Finally, they can also appreciate the common general rule underlying all such intensions.

And, frankly, so can we.[13]

References

[1]　S. Kripke, *Naming and Necessity*, Oxford, Blackwell, 1980.
[2]　F.C. Jackson, From Metaphysics to Ethics: A Defence of Conceptual Analysis, Oxford, Oxford University Press, 1998

---

[13] This paper has benefited from helpful remarks made by David Papineau, Paul Snowdon, Levi Spectre, Timothy Williamson, Dror Yinon, and three anonymous referees, on earlier drafts.

Formal Ontology in Information Systems
B. Bennett and C. Fellbaum (Eds.)
IOS Press, 2006

A Dynamic Theory of Ontology

John F. SOWA
Vivomind Intelligence, Inc.

Abstract. Natural languages are easy to learn by infants, they can express any thought that any adult might ever conceive, and they accommodate the limitations of human breathing rates and short-term memory. The first property implies a finite vocabulary, the second implies infinite extensibility, and the third implies a small upper bound on the length of phrases. Together, they imply that most words in a natural language will have an open-ended number of senses — ambiguity is inevitable. Peirce and Wittgenstein are two philosophers who understood that vagueness and ambiguity are not defects in language, but essential properties that enable it to accommodate anything that people need to say. In analyzing the ambiguities, Wittgenstein developed his theory of *language games*, which allow words to have different senses in different contexts, applications, or modes of use. Recent developments in lexical semantics, which are remarkably compatible with the views of Peirce and Wittgenstein, are based on the recognition that words have an open-ended number of dynamically changing and context-dependent *microsenses*. The resulting flexibility enables natural languages to adapt to any possible subject from any perspective for any humanly conceivable purpose. To achieve a comparable level of flexibility with formal ontologies, this paper proposes an organization with a dynamically evolving collection of formal theories, systematic mappings to formal concept types and informal lexicons of natural language terms, and a modularity that allows independent distributed development and extension of all resources, formal and informal.

Keywords. Language games, ambiguity, lattice of theories, analogy, belief revision

1. Precision, Clarity, Vagueness, and Ambiguity

Formal languages, such as logic and computer programs, are precise, but what they express so precisely may have no relationship to what the author intended. Even when the author or programmer has corrected all the bugs or obvious discrepancies, the result might not satisfy the users' requirements. Engineers summarize the problem in a pithy slogan: Customers never know what they want until they see what they get.

More generally, the precision and clarity that are so admirable in the final specification of a successful system are the result of a lengthy process of discussion, analysis, and negotiation with many intermediate stages of trial, error, and revision. In most cases, the process of revision never ends until the system is obsolete, or as IBM euphemistically declares, "functionally stabilized." This predicament, which occurs in every area of science, engineering, business, and government, illustrates a universal principle: Precision and clarity are the goal, not the starting point of analysis, design, planning, or development. That principle has profound implications for ontology: A precise, finished ontology stated in a formal language is as unrealistic as a finished computer system.

Unlike formal languages, which can only express the finished result of a lengthy analysis, natural languages can express every step from an initially vague idea to the final specification. During his career as a physicist and an engineer, Peirce learned the difficulty of stating any general principle with absolute precision:

> It is easy to speak with precision upon a general theme. Only, one must commonly surrender all ambition to be certain. It is equally easy to be certain. One has only to be sufficiently vague. It is not so difficult to be pretty precise and fairly certain at once about a very narrow subject. ([1], 4.237)

This quotation summarizes the futility of any attempt to develop a precisely defined ontology of everything, but it offers two useful alternatives: an informal classification, such as a thesaurus or terminology designed for human readers; and an open-ended collection of formal theories about narrowly delimited subjects. It also raises the questions of how and whether the informal resources might be used as a bridge between informal natural language and formally defined logics and programming languages.

In his first book, Wittgenstein [2] restricted the legitimate uses of language to precisely defined mappings from sentences to configurations of objects in the world. But later, Wittgenstein [3] faced the full complexity of language as it is used in science and everyday life. For his theory of *language games*, he observed that words do not have a fixed boundary defined by necessary and sufficient conditions. As an alternative, he suggested the term *family resemblances* for the "complicated network of overlapping and criss-crossing similarities, in the large and the small" (§66), and he did not consider vagueness a defect:

> One might say that the concept 'game' is a concept with blurred edges. — "But is a blurred concept a concept at all?" — Is an indistinct photograph a picture of a person at all? Is it even always an advantage to replace an indistinct picture with a sharp one? Isn't the indistinct one often exactly what we need?
>
> Frege compares a concept to an area and says that an area with vague boundaries cannot be called an area at all. This presumably means that we cannot do anything with it. — But is it senseless to say: "Stand roughly (ungefähr) there"? (§71).

Frege's view is incompatible with natural languages and with every branch of empirical science and engineering. With their background in engineering, Peirce and Wittgenstein recognized that all measurements have a margin of error or granularity, which must be taken into account at every step from design to implementation. The option of vagueness enables language to accommodate the inevitable vagueness in observations and the plans that are based on them.

This paper takes these insights as inspiration for a *dynamic theory of ontology*, which relates the variable meanings of a finite set of words to a potentially infinite set of concept and relation types, which are used and reused in a dynamically evolving lattice of theories. Section 2 reviews related research in natural language semantics and some pioneering efforts in computational linguistics by Margaret Masterman, a former student of Wittgenstein's. To relate language to formal theories, Section 3 relates words to concept types to canonical graphs and then to a lattice of theories. Section 4 shows how that lattice can be used in both formal and informal reasoning. The concluding Section 5 discusses the implications of this approach on the design of ontologies and the interfaces to their users and developers.

2. Models of Language

During the second half of the 20th century, various models of language understanding were proposed and implemented in computer programs. All of them have been useful for processing some aspects of language, but none of them have been adequate for all aspects of language or even for full coverage of just a single aspect:

- **Statistical.** In the 1950s, Shannon's information theory and other statis-tical methods were popular in both linguistics and psychology, but the speed and storage capacity of the early computers were not adequate to process the volumes of data required. By the end of the century, the vastly increased computer power made them competitive with other methods for many purposes. Their strength is their pattern-discovery methods, but their weakness is the lack of a semantic interpretation that can be mapped to the real world or to other computational methods.

- **Syntactic.** Chomsky's transformational grammar and related methods dominated linguistic studies in the second half of the 20th century, they stimulated a great deal of theoretical and computational research, and the resulting syntactic structures can be adapted to other paradigms, including those that compete with Chomsky and his colleagues. But today, Chomsky's contention that syntax is best studied independently of semantics is at best unproven and at its worst a distraction from a more integrated approach to language.

- **Logical.** In the 1970s, the philosophical logic from Carnap and Tarski to Kripke and Montague led to formal theories with better semantic foundations and reasoning methods than any competing approach. Unfortunately, these methods can only interpret sentences that have been deliberately written in a notation that looks like a natural language, but is actually a syntactic variant of the underlying logic. None of them can take normal text that people write for the purpose of communicating with other people and translate it to logic.

- **Lexical.** In reaction to formal semantics, the methods of lexical semantics address all features of syntax and vocabulary that can cause sentences to differ in meaning. The strength of these methods is a greater descriptive adequacy and a sensitivity to more aspects of meaning than other methods. Their weakness is the lack of an agreed definition of the meaning of 'meaning' that can be related to the world and to computer systems.

- **Neural.** Many people believe that neurophysiology may someday contribute to better theories of how people generate and interpret language. That may be true, but the little that is currently known about how the brain works can hardly contribute anything to linguistic theory. Systems called *neural networks* are statistical methods that have the same strengths and weaknesses as other statistical methods, but they have almost no resemblance to the way actual neurons work.

Each of these approaches is based on a particular technology: mathematical statistics, grammar rules, dictionary formats, or networks of neurons. Each one ignores aspects of language for which the technology is ill adapted. For people, however, language is seamlessly integrated with every aspect of life, and they don't stumble over boundaries between different technologies. Wittgenstein's language games do not compartmentalize language by the kinds of technology that produce it, but by subject matter and modes of use. That approach seems more natural, but it raises the question of how a computer could recognize which game is being played, especially when aspects of multiple games are combined in the same paragraph or even the same sentence.

A novel version of lexical semantics, influenced by Wittgenstein's language games and related developments in cognitive science, is the theory of *dynamic construal of meaning* (DCM) proposed by Cruse [4] and developed further by Croft and Cruse [5]. The fundamental assumption of DCM is that the most stable aspect of a word is its spoken or written sign; its meaning is unstable and dynamically evolving as it is construed in each context in which it is used. Cruse coined the term *microsense* for each subtle variation in meaning as a word is used in different language games. That is an independent rediscovery of Peirce's view: sign types are stable, but the interpretations of a sign token in different contexts have no direct relationship to one another. The interpretation by each mind depends on the sign itself and its immediate context in a pattern of other signs, the physical environment, and each mind's memory of previous patterns of signs. Croft and Cruse showed how the DCM view of semantics could be integrated with a version of *construction grammar*, but their descriptions are not sufficiently detailed to be implemented in a computer system.

A model of language directly inspired by Wittgenstein's language games was developed by Margaret Masterman, one of six students in his course of 1933-34 whose notes were compiled as *The Blue Book* [6]. In the late 1950s, Masterman founded the Cambridge Language Research Unit (CLRU) as a discussion group, which became one of the pioneering centers of research in computational linguistics. Her collected papers from the late 1950s to 1980 [7] present a computable version with many similarities to DCM:

- A focus on semantics, not syntax, as the foundation for language: "I want to pick up the relevant basic-situation-referring habits of a language in preference to its grammar" (p. 200).

- A context-dependent classification scheme with three kinds of structures: a thesaurus with multiple groups of words organized by areas of use, a *fan* radiating from each word type to each area of the thesaurus in which it occurs, and dynamically generated combinations of fans for the word tokens of a text.

- Emphasis on images as a language-independent foundation for meaning with a small number (about 50 to 100) of combining elements represented by ideographs or monosyllables, such as IN, UP, MUCH, THING, STUFF, MAN, BEAST, PLANT, DO.

- Recognition that analogy and metaphor are fundamental to the creation of novel uses of language, especially in the most advanced areas of science. Maxwell's elegant mathematics, for example, is the final stage of a lengthy process that began with Faraday's analogies, diagrams, and vague talk about lines of force in electric and magnetic fields.

Figure 1 shows a fan for the word *bank* with links to each area in Roget's *Thesaurus* in which the word occurs (p. 288). The numbers and labels identify areas in the thesaurus, which, Masterman claimed, correspond to "Neo-Wittgensteinian families".

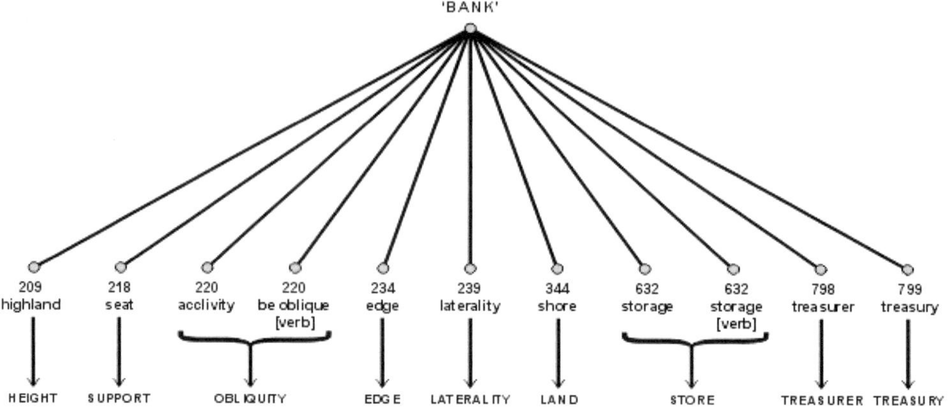

Figure 1: A fan for the word *bank*

To illustrate the use of fans, Masterman analyzed the phrases *up the steep bank* and *in the savings bank*. All the words except *the* would have similar fans, and her algorithm would "pare down" the ambiguities "by retaining only the spokes that retain ideas which occur in each." For this example, it would retain "OBLIQUITY 220 in 'steep' and 'bank'; whereas it retains as common between 'savings' and 'bank' both of the two areas STORE 632 and TREASURY 799." She went on to discuss methods of handling various exceptions and complications, but all the algorithms use only words and families of words that actually occur in English. They never use abstract or artificial markers, features, or categories. That approach suggests a plausible cognitive theory: From an infant's first words to an adult's level of competence, language learning is a continuous process of building and refining the stock of words, families of words grouped by their use in common situations, and patterns of connections among the words and families.

3. Mapping Words to Logic

Wittgenstein's language games and the related proposals by Cruse, Croft, and Masterman are more realistic models of natural language than the rigid theories of formal semantics. Yet scientists, engineers, and computer programmers routinely produce highly precise language-like structures by disciplined extensions of the methods used for ordinary language. A complete theory of language must be able to explain every level of competence from the initial vague stages to the most highly disciplined reasoning and representations of science. Furthermore, the level of precision needed to write computer programs can be acquired by school children without formal training. There is no linguistic or psychological evidence for a discontinuity in the methods of language production and interpretation.

In order to handle both formal and informal language, Masterman's approach must be extended with links to logic, but in a way that permits arbitrary revisions. Figure 2 illustrates a word fan that maps words to concept types to *canonical graphs* and finally to a lattice of theories. In this paper, the canonical graphs are represented as *conceptual graphs* (CGs), a formally defined version of logic that has the same model-theoretic foundation as Common Logic (ISO/IEC [8]). Equivalent operations may be performed with any notation, but examples shown as graphs are easier to read.

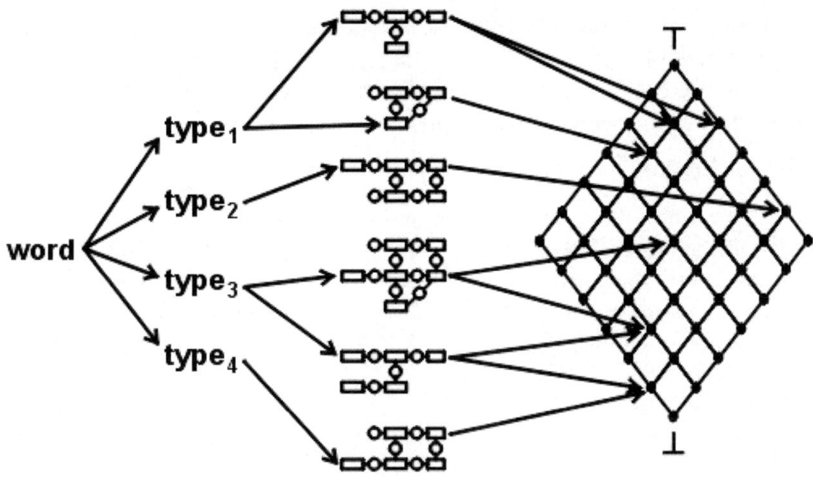

Figure 2: words → types → canonical graphs → lattice of theories

The fan on the left of Figure 2 links each word to an open-ended list of *concept types*, each of which corresponds to some area of a thesaurus in Masterman's system. The word *bank*, for example, could be linked to types with labels such as **Bank799** or **Bank_Treasury**. In various applications or language games, those types could be further subdivided into finer grained subtypes, which would correspond to Cruse's microsenses. The selection of subtypes is determined by canonical graphs, which specify the characteristic patterns of concepts and relations associated with each type or subtype. Figure 3 illustrates three canonical graphs for the types **Give**, **Easy**, and **Eager**.

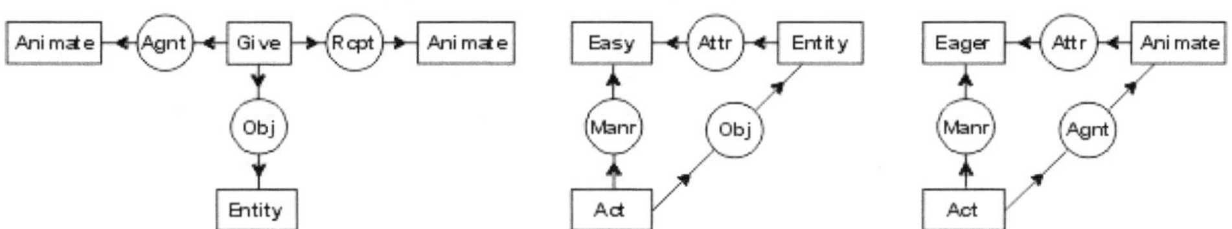

Figure 3: Canonical graphs for the types Give, Easy, and Eager

A canonical graph for a type is a conceptual graph that specifies one of the patterns characteristic of that type. On the left, the canonical graph for **Give** represents the same constraints as a typical *case frame* for a verb. It states that the agent **(Agnt)** must be **Animate**, the recipient **(Rcpt)** must be **Animate**, and the object **(Obj)** may be any **Entity**. The canonical graphs for **Easy** and **Eager**, however, illustrate the advantage of graphs over frames: a graph permits cycles, and the arcs can distinguish the directionality of the relations. Consider the following two sentences:

Bob is easy to please.   Bob is eager to please.

For both sentences, the concept **[Person: Bob]** would be linked via the attribute relation **(Attr)** to the concept **[Easy]** or **[Eager]**, and the act **[Please]** would be linked via the manner relation **(Manr)** to the same concept. But the canonical graph for **Easy** would make Bob the object of the act **Please**, and the graph for **Eager** would make Bob the agent. The first sentence below is acceptable because the object may be any entity, but the constraint that the agent of an act must be animate would make the second sentence unacceptable:

*The book is easy to read.　　　* The book is eager to read.*

Chomsky [9] used the easy/eager example to argue for different syntactic transformations associated with the two adjectives. But the canonical graphs state semantic constraints that cover a wider range of linguistic phenomena with simpler syntactic rules. A child learning a first language or an adult reading a foreign language can use semantic constraints to interpret sentences with unknown or even ungrammatical syntax. Under Chomsky's hypothesis that syntax is a prerequisite for semantics, such learning is inexplicable.

Canonical graphs with a few concept nodes are adequate to discriminate the general senses of most words, but the canonical graphs for detailed microsenses can become much more complex. For the adjective *easy*, the microsenses occur in very different patterns for a book that's easy to read, a person that's easy to please, or a car that's easy to drive. For the verb *give*, a large dictionary lists dozens of senses, and the number of microsenses is enormous. The prototypical act of giving is to hand something to someone, but a house or car can be given just by pointing to it and saying "It's yours." When the gift is an action, as in giving a kiss, a kick, or a bath, the canonical graph used to parse the sentence has a few more nodes. But the graphs required to understand the implications of each type of action are far more complex, and they're related to the graphs for taking a bath or stealing a kiss.

The canonical graph for *buy* typically has two acts of giving: money from the buyer to the seller, and some goods from the seller to the buyer. But the canonical graphs needed to understand various microsenses may require far more detail about the buyers, the sellers, the goods sold, and other people, places, and things involved. Buying a computer, for example, can be done by clicking some boxes on a screen and typing the billing and shipping information. That process may trigger a series of international transactions, which can be viewed by going to the UPS web site to check when the computer was airmailed from Hong Kong and delivered to New York. All that detail is involved in one microsense of the verb *buy*. In a successful transaction, the buyer can ignore most of it, but somebody must be able to trace the steps if something goes wrong.

4. Methods of Reasoning

The lattice of theories facilitates modularity by allowing independent agents (human or computer) to revise arbitrary aspects of the knowledge at any level of detail. The theories may be large or small, and they may be stated in any version of logic, but Common Logic is assumed for this paper. The position of each theory in the lattice shows how it is related to every other theory. If theory x is above theory y, then x is more *general* than y, and y is more *specialized* than x. If theory x is neither above nor below y, then they are siblings or cousins. New theories can be added at the top, bottom, or middle levels of the lattice at any time without affecting any application that uses other theories. The complete lattice of all possible theories is infinite, but only a finite subset is ever implemented.

A lattice of first-order theories combined with metalevel reasoning for selecting a theory is a replacement for multiplicities of special-purpose logics. Instead of non-monotonic logics, belief revision can be treated as a metalevel walk through the lattice to select an appropriate revision of the current theory (Sowa [10]). Instead of multiple logics for every modality, metalevel reasoning about the selection of laws (axioms) provides a foundation for multimodal reasoning that includes the semantics of Kripke, Montague, and many others as special cases (Sowa [11, 12]). Instead of special-purpose logics of ambiguity (van Deemter & Peters [13]), this paper proposes metalevel reasoning about the lattice as a way of simulating Wittgenstein's language games.

Formal reasoning is a disciplined application of the techniques used for informal reasoning. Analogy, the process of finding common patterns in different structures, is the foundation for both. The logical methods of reasoning by induction, deduction, and abduction are distinguished by the constraints they impose on analogy. Following is a summary of the pattern-matching operations that occur at each step of formal logic (Sowa & Majumdar [14]):

- *Deduction* applies general premises to special cases to derive their implications. The pattern-matching method of *unification* finds a common specialization of patterns found in the starting assumptions.

- *Induction* formulates general principles that may subsume a large number of special cases. It uses pattern-matching methods that determine a common generalization of all the cases.

- *Abduction* is an operation of guessing or forming hypotheses. It normally starts with an analogy that is tested by further use of induction and deduction.

Deduction can never introduce anything new that is not already implicit in a given theory. In terms of the lattice, deduction stays within the bounds of a single theory. Methods of *theory revision* move from one theory to another by deleting, adding, or modifying axioms. Figure 4 shows the four basic operators for navigating the lattice: *contraction, expansion, revision,* and *analogy* [10].

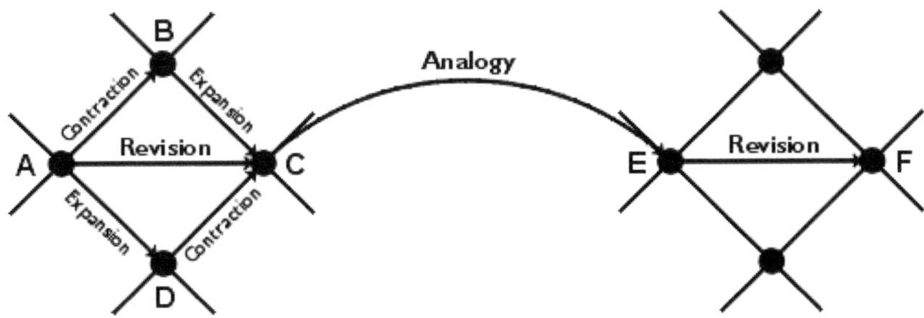

Figure 4: Four operators for navigating the lattice of theories

The operators of contraction and expansion follow the arcs of the lattice, revision makes short hops sideways, and analogy makes long-distance jumps. To illustrate the moves through the lattice, suppose that A is Newton's theory of gravitation applied to the earth revolving around the sun and F is Niels Bohr's theory about an electron revolving around the nucleus of a hydrogen atom. The path from A to F is a step-by-step transformation of the old theory to the new one. The revision step from A to C replaces the gravitational attraction between the earth and the sun with the electrical attraction between the electron and the proton. That step can be carried out in two intermediate steps:

- **Contraction.** Any theory can be contracted to a smaller, more general theory by deleting one or more axioms. In the move from A to B, axioms for the gravitational force would be deleted. Contraction has the effect of blocking proofs that depend on the deleted axioms.

- **Expansion.** Any theory can be expanded to a larger, more specialized theory by adding one or more axioms. In the move from B to C, axioms for the electrical force would be added. The result of both moves is a substitution of electrical axioms for gravitational axioms.

Unlike contraction and expansion, which move to nearby theories in the lattice, analogy jumps to a remote theory, such as C to E, by systematically renaming the types, relations, and individuals that appear in the axioms: the earth is renamed the electron; the sun is renamed the nucleus; and the solar system is renamed the atom. Finally, the revision step from E to F uses a contraction step to discard details about the earth and sun that have become irrelevant, followed by an expansion step to add new axioms for quantum mechanics.

The lattice of theories can be viewed as the theoretical background for a wide range of developments in AI, ranging from informal heuristics to the most sophisticated methods of learning and reasoning. In fact, any method of default or *nonmonotonic* reasoning can be interpreted as a strategy for walking and jumping through the infinite lattice in search of a suitable theory [10]. For vague or incomplete theories, a theorem prover can be used to check consistency. If no contradictions are found, they can be placed in the lattice, and the methods of theory revision can be used to refine and extend them to a more complete version for their intended application. Mappings specified according to Figure 2 can be used to relate any aspect of any theory in the lattice to natural language statements or queries.

5. Global Consistency vs. a Multiplicity of Modules

The lattice of theories is neutral with respect to global consistency. It does not rule out the possibility that there might exist one ideal theory of everything that could be used at every level from top to bottom, but there is no evidence that global consistency is necessary or even desirable. On the contrary, no branch of science or engineering has a globally consistent set of axioms. For the Cyc system (Lenat [15]), the largest formal ontology ever developed, the axioms are subdivided among several thousand, often inconsistent *microtheories*. Although Cyc has a single upper-level ontology, Lenat has said that the axioms at the middle levels are generally more useful and that the axioms at the lowest, task-oriented levels are the most relevant for specific problems.

The evidence from natural language use and from engineering practice indicates that a bottom-up, task-oriented approach is the way children learn language, adults use language, and scientists and engineers develop their theories and designs. In short, Wittgenstein's later theory with a multiplicity of language games is a more realistic model for language than his early unified theory of a single fixed mapping from language to the world. From their study of knowledge representation and reasoning, Bundy and McNeill [16] reached a similar conclusion: "The world is infinitely complex, so there is no end to the qualifications, ramifications and richness of detail that one could incorporate, and that you might need to incorporate for a particular application. This is not just a question of adding some additional facts or rules; it may also be necessary to modify the underlying representational language: its syntax, its representational power or even its semantics or logic."

The implications for ontology are significant: Low-level, task-oriented modules have been the most successful in science, engineering, business, and everyday life. The largest ontology project ever attempted began with a globally consistent set of axioms, but later divided it into a multiplicity of independently developed microtheories. That evidence does not prove that global consistency is impossible, but it suggests that a modular approach is easier to implement. A lattice of theories can accommodate both. It permits the development of independent modules, but it includes all possible generalizations and combinations. The recommended strategy is to support modularity, provide the lattice operators for theory revision, and allow consensus to evolve from the bottom up instead of being legislated from the top down.

References

[1] Peirce, Charles Sanders (CP) *Collected Papers of C. S. Peirce*, ed. by C. Hartshorne, P. Weiss, & A. Burks, 8 vols., Harvard University Press, Cambridge, MA, 1931-1958.

[2] Wittgenstein, Ludwig (1921) *Tractatus Logico-Philosophicus*, Routledge & Kegan Paul, London.

[3] Wittgenstein, Ludwig (1953) *Philosophical Investigations*, Basil Blackwell, Oxford.

[4] Cruse, D. Alan (2000) "Aspects of the micro-structure of word meanings," in Y. Ravin & C. Leacock, eds. (2000) *Polysemy: Theoretical and Computational Approaches*, Oxford University Press, Oxford, pp. 30-51.

[5] Croft, William, & D. Alan Cruse (2004) *Cognitive linguistics*, Cambridge University Press, Cambridge, MA.

[6] Wittgenstein, Ludwig (1958) *The Blue and Brown Books*, Basil Blackwell, Oxford.

[7] Masterman, Margaret (2005) *Language, Cohesion and Form*, edited by Yorick Wilks, Cambridge University Press, Cambridge.

[8] ISO/IEC (2006) *Common Logic: A Framework for a Family of Logic-Based Languages*, Final Committee Draft, http://cl.tamu.edu

[9] Chomsky, Noam (1965) *Aspects of the Theory of Syntax*, MIT Press, Cambridge, MA.

[10] Sowa, John F. (2000) *Knowledge Representation: Logical, Philosophical, and Computational Foundations*, Brooks/Cole Publishing Co., Pacific Grove, CA.

[11] Sowa, John F. (2003) "Laws, facts, and contexts: Foundations for multimodal reasoning," in *Knowledge Contributors*, edited by V. F. Hendricks, K. F. Jørgensen, and S. A. Pedersen, Kluwer Academic Publishers, Dordrecht, pp. 145-184. http://www.jfsowa.com/pubs/laws.htm

[12] Sowa, John F. (2006) "Worlds, Models, and Descriptions," *Studia Logica*, Special Issue, *Ways of Worlds II*, to appear in November, 2006.

[13] van Deemter, Kees, & Stanley Peters (1996) *Semantic Ambiguity and Underspecification*, CSLI, Stanford, CA.

[14] Sowa, John F., & Arun K. Majumdar (2003) "Analogical reasoning," in A. de Moor, W. Lex, & B. Ganter, eds., *Conceptual Structures for Knowledge Creation and Communication*, LNAI 2746, Springer-Verlag, Berlin, pp. 16-36. http://www.jfsowa.com/pubs/analog.htm

[15] Lenat, Douglas B. (1995) "Cyc: A large-scale investment in knowledge infrastructure," *Communications of the ACM* **38:11**, 33-38.

[16] Bundy, Alan, & Fiona McNeill (2006) "Representation as a fluent: An AI challenge for the next half century," *IEEE Intelligent Systems* **21:3**, pp 85-87.

Formal Ontology in Information Systems
B. Bennett and C. Fellbaum (Eds.)
IOS Press, 2006

Behavior of a Technical Artifact: An Ontological Perspective in Engineering

Stefano BORGO [a,1], Massimiliano CARRARA [b], Pieter E. VERMAAS [c] and
Pawel GARBACZ [d]

[a] *Laboratory for Applied Ontology, ISTC-CNR, Italy*
[b] *Department of Philosophy, University of Padua, Italy*
[c] *Department of Philosophy, Delft University of Technology, The Netherlands*
[d] *Catholic University of Lublin, Poland*

Abstract. The term 'behavior' is used ubiquitously in engineering. It refers roughly to the way technical artifacts 'behave' in a given or hypothetical situation, and plays a pivotal role in specific design methodologies since it allows connecting descriptions of the physical structure of technical artifacts to descriptions of their technical functions. However, behavior does not have a precise meaning: engineers use the term loosely and when attempting to pinpoint it, end up with incompatible characterizations. Here we formalize the different notions underlying the engineering usage by providing a uniform framework in which they can be related. This framework lays also a conceptual basis for a precise characterization of the notion of technical function in engineering. Our approach develops within the DOLCE ontology and introduces behavior as a new type of individual quality that relates a technical artifact to the event to which it participates. Starting with this assumption, one can distinguish actual, possible and general behaviors of an artifact (token). We add a few more definitions to capture more specific aspects and show their role in capturing engineering usage.

Keywords. Technical artifact, Behavior, Function, Formal Ontology, Engineering.

Introduction

Despite the central importance of *behavior* and *function* to design, it is commonplace that these terms are used in the engineering literature on engineering with various and possibly conflicting meanings. This fact mirrors the differences in the use of these terms in natural language. Talking of behavior, for instance, we point prima facie to whatever people, organisms or artificial (e.g., mechanical) systems do. But at a closer look one can distinguish, at least, four types of behavior [9]: physiological reactions and responses (e.g., salivation, increase in the blood pressure), bodily motions (e.g., walking, the motion of a robot), actions involving bodily motions (e.g., going shopping, telephoning your mother), and actions not involving overt bodily motions (e.g., reasoning, calculating).

---

[1]Corresponding Author: Stefano Borgo, Laboratory for Applied Ontology, ISTC-CNR, Italy; E-mail: borgo@loa-cnr.it.

In engineering the term behavior is used with less diverse meanings, and there is consensus that it plays a pivotal role in a number of design methodologies by allowing engineers to connect descriptions of the physical structure of technical artifacts to descriptions of their technical functions: structural descriptions should furnish a ground for behavioral descriptions, which, in turn, provide the grounds for functional and finally purposive descriptions. But notwithstanding its central role, engineers and design methodologists often use behavior without a precise meaning. The terms behavior and function are used mostly in a loose and informal way; the attempts to pinpoint their meanings highlighted their incompatible aspects. Chandrasekaran and Josephson [3] distinguish, for instance, five different meanings for the term 'behavior' (see section 2), and Chittaro and Kumar [4] mention three main approaches towards capturing functions.

Our work stems from the framework of ontological research [14] and aims at a uniform and precise characterization of the term 'behavior' to relate the different engineering meanings and to lay a conceptual basis for the notion of technical function. Our approach develops within the framework of DOLCE [11] and consists of introducing behavior as a new type of individual quality that relates an artifact (token) to the event to which it participates. Given this approach, we show that the notions we propose are well motivated and enough to formalize and relate the different engineering meanings.

1. Behavior: Some Philosophical Insights

Informally 'behavior' means whatever (publicly observable) people, organisms or artificial systems do. Some constraints of this characterization are usually adopted in philosophy. If public observablility is central, only physiological and bodily motions that are "overt" and "external" are to count as a behavior. Thus, reasoning and calculating are ruled out. Furthermore, 'doing' is to be distinguished from 'having something done'. If you grasp my arm and pull it up, the rising of my arm is not a behavior of mine. In general, it suffices that the doing is caused by some occurrence internal to the behaving system so that the motion of a robot that goes toward a table and picks out an apple is considered part of its behavior whether or not the robot 'knows' what it is doing [6]. This latter constraint corresponds to the philosophical distinction between physical and agentive behavior. With "physical behavior" we refer to any merely physical action or passion of the body; an "agential behavior" (or "behavior proper") implies a relationship with the mind. Agential behavior entails physical behavior, but not vice versa, e.g., a reflex knee jerk (physical behavior) is not agential.

Philosophical discussion about behavior is sometime associated with "behaviorism." Three main conceptions of behavior are usually distinguished in this viewpoint. Behavior is alternatively (*a*) a physical event, (*b*) a disposition, (*c*) a process.

Physical event. In this approach, behavior is simply an observable physical event or a physical state. There is no commitment to agents nor to the existence of psychological events over and above behavioral events or states.

Dispositions. Here the focus is on agential behavior. In this view behavior is something an agent does in terms of its "dispositions". One can easily specify this view to technical artifacts: the behavior of a technical artifact is the collection of its (physical) dispositions [13]. It remains open if dispositions should be analysed in terms of events, qualitive, or non qualitative properties. A qualitative property is a property that can be perceived.

Process. In this case, behavior is a process having, in the case of physical body, bodily movement as parts. It consists of a complex internal state causing a movement of the agent's body. If a movement M is brought by an internal cause C, the behavior is a process "C causing M" (cf. [6]). Behavior is so distinct from mere output in that it requires a form of explanation. Consider this analogy: an amplifier produces output and we can study such output independently of the machine itself and of the input. Note that the output itself does not tell us what the amplifier does. Therefore the behavior (C causing M) must be distinguished from the causes of the output. We may know what causes the output without knowing what causes behavior. We design, manufacture, and install the machine to do what we want it to do, i.e., we cause some C in the machine to bring about M in the desired circumstances.

2. Behavior in Engineering

In the domain of engineering design methodology 'behavior' (applied to technical artifacts) plays an important though subsidiary role. The term of 'function' is ultimately more important (and problematic): a description of the functions of a technical artifact captures how the artifact is related to the uses for which it is employed and designed; and the important and creative initial phase of designing in which engineers survey solutions to customer needs (without being immediately concerned with the nitty-gritty of the physics of the artifact to be designed), is usually taken as a phase in which engineers reason in purely functional terms. In attempts to fix the meaning of 'function', the concept 'behavior' of technical artifacts enters the central stage. Roughly speaking two approaches to function analysis can be distinguished in engineering [2]: in the first, one relates functions of artifacts to behaviors of artifacts, and then relates these behaviors to structural-physical descriptions of the artifacts; in the second approach, one models functions of artifacts in terms of inputs and outputs, and then relates these functions directly to structural-physical descriptions of artifacts (e.g., [18]). The first approach thus grants a pivotal conceptual role to the term 'behavior', and suggests a clear ontological ordering: technical artifacts have their physical structure; this structure, in interaction with a physical environment, gives rise to the artifacts' behaviors; and these behaviors then determine in some way the artifacts' functions. We call the first approach *FBS*, adopting this acronym from Gero [7], who proposed a Function-Behavior-Structure model of designing, and from Umeda et al. [16], who proposed Function-Behavior-State models of designing. The second approach is known as the *Functional Modelling* approach [12,15]. In this case behavior seems to be side-stepped and the relation between the physical structure of technical artifacts and their functions be established directly on the basis of ontologically more opaque phenomenological engineering hands-on experience as captured by technical handbooks.

With our project of giving an ontological account of behavior of technical artifacts, we position ourselves within the first *FBS* approach towards analysing functions. Ultimately this project should amount to an ontological account of artifact functions, and a first step in this direction is taken towards the end of paper. But, taking the ontological ordering suggested by the *FBS* approach seriously, we start by focussing on a solid account of behavior, built on the basis of existing ontological accounts of the physical realm.

Despite the importance of the notion of behavior in the *FBS* approach, consensus about what counts as 'behavior' has not been reached. Different authors give different characterizations, as we will see, and these are not consistent even in the works of a single author [5]. We will not attempt to survey all meanings proposed, but introduce a few examples and then focus on the survey in [3].

Starting with the two mentioned *FBS* models, [8] defines the behavior of a technical artifact (a designed object), or more precisely, its behavior variables, as describing "the attributes that are derived or expected to be derived from the structure (S) variables of the object, i.e., what it does", where the structural variables "describe the components of the object and their relationships, i.e., what it is." And they give as examples of behavioral variables of a window for instance 'thermal conduction' and 'light transmission' [8].

In [17] behavior is defined as "a transition of states along time" where "a state is represented by entities, their attributes, and their structure"; a given example of behavior is the 'electrical charging' of a drum in a photocopier.

Chandrasekaran and Josephson [3] explore the different meanings engineers attach to the term behavior and isolates five of them, which are characterised with the help of the primitive notion of state variable. These five meanings are:

1) behavior as the value of some state variable of the artifact or a relation between such values at a particular instant (example: the car rattled when the driver hit the curve).

2) behavior as the value of a property of the artifact or a relation between such values (example: a lintel distributes the load to two sides).

3) behavior as the value of some state variable of the artifact over an interval of time (example: the BHP^2 increased for a while, but then started decreasing).

4) behavior as the value of some output state variable of the artifact at a particular instant or over an interval (example: the amplifier is behaving well – the output voltage is constant).

5) behavior as the values of all the described state variables of the artifact at a particular instant or over an interval (no example is given)

Notice that for all five meanings, a behavior of a technical artifact is partially objective and partially subjective. It has an objective aspect because it eventually depends on the properties or features of the artifact. Still, the very same behavior has a subjective aspect: it depends on the designer(s) and, indirectly, on engineering practice for the choice of the state variables. The underlying intuition of Chandrasekaran and Josephson for this subjective twist, is that a state variable of an artifact represents some feature or aspect of this artifact that might be relevant only from a specific point of view [1]. Yet, in agreement with the observations of section 1, it is important to emphasise that the behavior of a technical artifact is different from the value of its state variable(s). The behavior is somehow characterised by this value(s) in a sense to be explicated. Thus, if the value of the input voltage of an amplifier is 10 mV at a particular instant, then this value (10 mV) is not identical with any behavior of this amplifier. Rather, part of the behavior of the amplifier consists of the actual situation that its input voltage is 10 mV.

---

^{2}BHP stands for Brake Horse Power and it is described as the amount of real horsepower going to the pump.

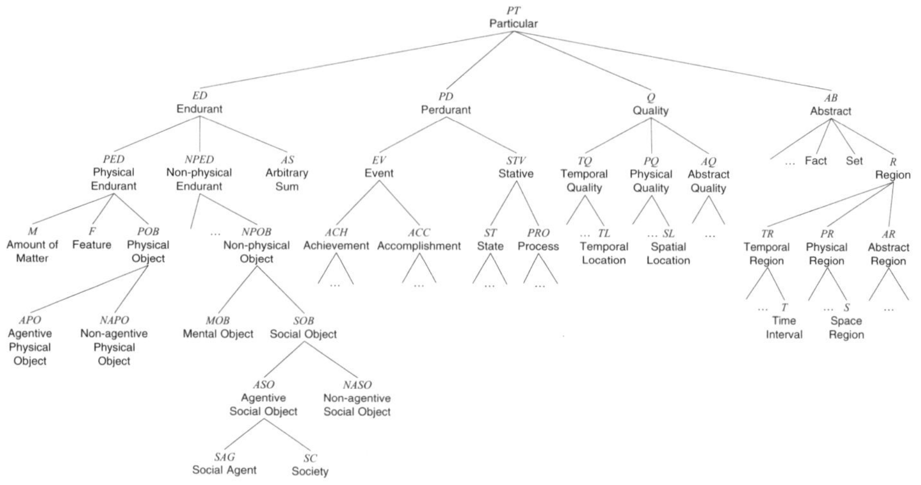

Figure 1. DOLCE basic categories (taken from [11].)

3. Scope and Adopted Framework

Our goal is to formalize a notion of *artifact behavior* that, on the one hand, captures the informal meaning this term has in engineering practice and, on the other, is ontologically motivated. In this work, we take the meanings of section 2 at face value and neither discuss their adequacy nor try to reduce or modify them. Once the characterization is posited, we will see that the relationships among these meanings becomes clear and formally expressible. The analysis is carried out within the framework of the DOLCE ontology [11] and the formal system we obtain can be considered an extension of that ontology. Our final aim is to incorporate both the notions of engineering behavior and function in DOLCE. The second notion will be only sketched in this paper by considering the notion of function as presented in [3].

The basic idea we follow to formalize behavior is to consider it as a relationship between the artifact and the event to which it participates. Since events can be actual (in the real world) or just possible, we distinguish *possible* behavior from *actual* behavior. Due to the crucial role of the notion of behavior at the design phase and at the description level, where the behavior of an artifact is (to some extent) speculative, we need to consider also events that are *believed* to be possible. To deal with these distinctions, we introduce and relate several classes of behaviors. Once these classes are formally described, one can talk of behavior according to a group of agents (typically, engineers) and of behavior descriptions. Later, we will see how this framework allows us to capture and make explicit the meanings listed in section 2.

In what remains of this section, we briefly introduce the categories of DOLCE that are relevant to our work. In parenthesis we report the formal names as used in the next sections. The full taxonomy is reported in Figure 1, while a detailed discussion of DOLCE and its categories can be found in [11]. We begin with the general notion of "endurant" (*ED*). This category collects those entities that are *wholly* present at any time they are present, for instance a car or an amount of water. Entities that take up time (a football game), that are qualities (the color of my car), or that are abstracts (the set of pens in my office) are not endurants. In DOLCE the term 'object' is used to capture a notion of wholeness and the them 'physical' to indicate entities that are located in space-time. In the next sections, we will concentrate on "non-agentive physical objects" (NAPO) which are physical objects to which one cannot ascribe intentions, beliefs or desires (like a tool or a notebook). Temporal entities like a thunderstorm, are called "perdurants" (PD). Informally, a perdurant is an entity that is only partially present at any time it is present. In this category we find football games as well as artifact productions. These entities have temporal parts (like the first half of the game) as well as spatial parts (the event restricted to a half of the football field during the game). Some perdurants, e.g., sitting, moving and drilling, are called "stative" (ST). They have two important properties: the sum of two stative perdurants is also stative and any temporal part of a stative perdurant is stative as well. A different type of entities find place in the "individual quality" category (Q). These can be seen as instantiations of basic aspects of endurants or perdurants (usually qualities can be perceived or measured like weight or energy). The term 'individual' is used to mark the essential relationship between the entity and its own qualities. Note that qualities are particulars, they should not be confused with properties (universals).

We will make use of several relationships among which *parthood*: "x is part of y", written $P(x,y)$. In DOLCE the *parthood* relation applies to pairs of endurants (e.g., to state that an object is part of another) as well as to pairs of perdurants (to state that an event is part of another). For instance, if a = 'writing paper ABC' and b = 'writing the introduction of paper ABC', then $P(b,a)$ holds. The main relation involving both endurants and perdurants is called *participation*, formally PC. This relation captures the simple fact that an endurant 'lives' in time by participating in some perdurant. For example, a person (endurant) may participate in a discussion (perdurant). A person's life is also a perdurant, in which a person participates throughout all its duration (the time spanned by the life). If endurant a participates in perdurant e at each instant of period t, we write $PC(a,e,t)$ which reads "a participates in e during all of t" (here t may be a sub-interval of the duration of e). Note that participation and parthood are distinct relations. An endurant is never part of a perdurant, only perdurants can be parts of perdurants. Also, participation is time-indexed in order to account for the varieties of participation in time (temporary participation, constant participation, etc.) Qualities are associated to quality spaces (where comparisons like "a and b have different weight" are carried out) and the position an individual quality has in a space is called a *quale*. We write $ql(r,q,t)$ to mean "r is the quale of the quality q during time t" and drop the temporal parameter for perdurant's qualities. (Our use of ql in section 5 is an obvious generalization of this relation). Finally, *sum* (symbol $+$) and *fusion* (symbol σ) are two operators. The sum of two perdurants x and y is written $x + y$ (e.g., closing a window is the sum of moving it and turning the handle), while the fusion is an extension of the binary sum to an arbitrary number of perdurants (e.g., my staying in Paris is the fusion of all the days I spent in Paris).

4. An Ontological Definition of Artifact Behavior

In DOLCE the most specific category for technical artifacts is NAPO. Let a be a non-agentive physical object, i.e., NAPO(a). Informally, the behavior b of a in a perdurant e is *the way* a *exists in* e. Formally, we take b to be a new kind of individual quality: it does not hold for a single endurant or perdurant, but for pairs of an endurant and a perdurant. In this way, it captures the special relationship between the artifact and the event in which it 'behaves'. To formalize this relationship, we introduce a ternary relation Beh(a,e,b). We talk of the behavior of a in a perdurant e if and only if a participates in e for *all the duration of* e and in the logic we impose that, for a pair endurant-perdurant satisfying this condition, the corresponding behavior b exists. A behavior b is uniquely identified by the pair endurant-perdurant, although a perdurant e may have several participants and an entity a may participate in several perdurants.

Given a perdurant e, let us write $\mathrm{tm}(e)$ for the whole period of time during which e exists. Then, we formally capture the above observations with the following axioms

$$Beh(a, e, b) \rightarrow \mathsf{PC}(a, e, \mathrm{tm}(e))$$

$$Beh(a, e, b) \wedge Beh(a, e, b') \rightarrow b = b'$$

$$Beh(a, e, b) \wedge Beh(a', e', b) \rightarrow a = a' \wedge e = e'$$

$$\mathsf{NAPO}(a) \wedge \mathsf{PC}(a, e, \mathrm{tm}(e)) \rightarrow \exists b \, Beh(a, e, b)$$

Looking at engineers activity, we need to distinguish different kinds of behavior. While an 'actual behavior' of the artifact is what it actually does during (a part of) its life, the more general notion of 'possible behavior' deals with what the artifact can possibly do. A pen may be destroyed before it happens to write, still the pen could have participated to a writing event, i.e., writing is part of its behavior although not of its 'actual' behavior. Furthermore, although a pen may not possibly write due to a design flaw, still engineers (not aware of the flaw) talk about its writing behavior. Now we see how to make room for these cases in the formalism.

Perdurants in DOLCE can be divided in **actual** (those that happen in the 'actual world', no matter when) and **possible** (those happening in a 'possible world', including the actual one). 'Impossible' perdurants, related to (designed or even constructed) artifacts that cannot perform the functionalities the designers attribute to them, are not directly isolated in DOLCE since there is no explicit constraint to contingent laws (like those of physics). Nonetheless, within the engineer domain, these perdurants are only thought but cannot possibly happen. For this reason, we assume that PD in the engineering domain collects all the physically possible perdurants, and introduce the more general category of **generalised** perdurants to account for all (actual, possible and impossible) perdurants with a proviso: a generalized perdurant cannot be describe by an inconsistency, that is, it must be believable by rational agents (namely, engineers). We write APD and GPD for the class of actual and generalised perdurants respectively. Then, APD $\subseteq$ PD $\subseteq$ GPD. We can now constrain the domain of Beh

$$Beh(a, e, b) \rightarrow \mathsf{NAPO}(a) \wedge \mathrm{GPD}(e) \wedge Q(b)$$

Some combinations of perdurants are meaningless in engineering practice. It is possible that a pen participates in a writing perdurant now (say in this world) and it is also possible that the same pen participates to a non-writing perdurant now (in another world). However, these two perdurants cannot 'physically happen' at the *same time* in the *same world*. If we sum these perdurants, the very same pen should be writing and not writing.[3]

---

[3] In principle this event could be in GPD. However, an engineer (as such) may believe wrongly that something happen or could happen, but not that something, patently known to defy physical laws, can happen.

To account for this condition, we say that two or more perdurants are **coherent** when their sum is physically meaningful and, in this case, we write a $+_c$ b. (A similar condition is set to restrict the fusion operator.) This condition depends on the laws of physics, which we assume are given. Note that actual perdurants are always coherent, i.e., their sum (fusion) is always defined.

We say that two perdurants are **co-temporal** if they occur at the same time period, e.g., "my attending Robert's talk today" and "Robert giving a talk today" are co-temporal.

Let C_a be the (non-empty) class of all generalized perdurants e such that PC(a, e, tm(e)) for some fixed a. Fix a perdurant e in it. We say that e is *minimal* in C_a if for each perdurant e' in C_a co-temporal with e, not PP(e', e). We use this notion and the previous classification of perdurants to specialize the DOLCE relation lf(x, a), which reads "perdurant x is the life of endurant a" (for lack of space, we do not report the formal expressions):

(a) Alf(x, a) stands for "perdurant x is the actual life of endurant a" and is formally defined as the fusion of the actual perdurants which are spatially minimal in C_a;

(b) Plf(x, a) stands for "perdurant x is a possible life of endurant a" and is formally defined as the fusion of a maximal class (wrt inclusion) of coherent possible perdurants which are minimal in C_a;

(c) Glf(x, a) stands for "perdurant x is the general life of endurant a" and is formally defined as the fusion of the general perdurants which are spatially minimal in C_a.

We write Alf(a) to denote the derived term "the actual life of a". Similarly for Glf(a).

Definition 1 *(Actual, Possible, Impossible, and General Behavior)*
   An actual behavior *of* a *is a* b *such that* Beh(a,e,b) *for some* e *with* APD(e).
The maximal actual behavior *of* a *is the actual behavior* b *for which* Beh(a, Alf(a),b).
   A possible behavior *of* a *is a* b *such that* Beh(a,e,b) *for some* e *with* PD(e).
A maximal possible behavior *of* a *is a* b *for which* Beh(a,e,b) *for some possible life* e *of* a, *i.e.,* Plf(e,a).
   An impossible behavior *of* a *is a* b *such that* Beh(a,e,b) *for some* e *with* GPD(e) *and not* PD(e).
   A general behavior *of* a *is a* b *such that* Beh(a,e,b) *for some* e *with* GPD(e).
The maximal general behavior *of* a *is the general behavior* b *for which* Beh(a, Glf(a),b).

Given an agent or group of agents $\mathcal{G}$, we write $\mathrm{PD}_{\mathcal{G}}$(e) to state that $\mathcal{G}$ believes that e is a possible perdurant.[4] A class C of general behaviors of a is said to be *coherent* if b, b' $\in C$ with Beh(a, e, b), Beh(a, e', b') implies that e $+_c$ e' is defined. We use these two notions to define the behavior of a technical artifact *for a group* $\mathcal{G}$.

Definition 2 *(*$\mathcal{G}$*-behavior) Let* $\mathcal{G}$ *be an agent or group of agents.*
   A $\mathcal{G}$-behavior *of* a *is a general behavior* b *such that if* Beh(a, e, b) *then* $\mathrm{PD}_{\mathcal{G}}$(e).
   A maximal $\mathcal{G}$-behavior *of* a *is a general behavior* b *such that* Beh(a, e, b) *where* e *is the fusion of all the perdurants in a coherent class* C *of* $\mathcal{G}$-behaviors *of* a *and* C *is maximal with respect to inclusion.*

---

[4] Generally speaking, this notion should include a temporal parameter since agents may change their beliefs in time. For simplicity, we disregard this issue here.

A coherent class of $\mathcal{G}$-behaviors is a collection of $\mathcal{G}$-behaviors whose perdurants are coherent. This reflects the fact that a group of engineers may believe something which is impossible (due to construction or design flaws). Nonetheless, they do not believe that incompatible things happen.

Finally, the standard distinction between device-centric and environmental-centric views of a technical artifact [3] drives the following distinction of artifact behavior.

Definition 3 *(Internal and Environmental Actual Behavior)*

An internal actual behavior *of* a *is a behavior* b *such that if* $Beh($a$,$ e$,$ b$)$ *holds, then* $\mathsf{P}($e$, \mathsf{Alf}($a$))$.

An environmental actual behavior *of* a *is a behavior* b *such that if* $Beh($a$,$e$,$b$)$ *then* $\mathrm{APD}($e$)$ *and not* $\mathsf{P}($e$, \mathsf{Alf}($a$))$.

5. Artifact Behavior In DOLCE

Now we use the above ontological framework to formalize the five meanings of section 2. Here state variables are indirectly captured through the given behavior b. Also, following the discussion in [3], we implicitly take $\mathcal{G}$ to be the designer(s) of the technical artifact a, although this is not relevant.

1. The behavior b of an artifact a from an engineering perspective of an agent $\mathcal{G}$ is a $\mathcal{G}$-behavior such that if $Beh($a$,$ e$,$ b$)$, then $\mathrm{tm}($e$)$ is an instant (a period of length zero). Example: let e $=$ "the car rattled when the driver hit the curve", then $Beh($car$,$ e$,$ b$) \wedge \mathrm{PD}_{\mathcal{G}}(e) \wedge |\mathrm{tm}(e)| = 0$

2. The behavior b of an artifact a from an engineering perspective of an agent $\mathcal{G}$ is a $\mathcal{G}$-behavior that belongs to the class of environmental actual behaviors where $Beh($a$,$ e$,$ b$)$ implies $\mathrm{ST}($e$)$. Example: let e $=$ "the lintel's distributing the load to two sides", then $Beh($lintel$,$ e$,$ b$) \wedge \mathrm{PD}_{\mathcal{G}}(e) \wedge \mathrm{ST}(e) \wedge \mathsf{P}(e, \mathsf{Alf}(a))$

3. The behavior b of an artifact a from an engineering perspective of an agent $\mathcal{G}$ is a $\mathcal{G}$-behavior such that if $Beh($a$,$ e$,$ b$)$, then $\mathrm{tm}($e$)$ is a period of positive length. Example: let e $=$ "the increasing of the BHP of the artifact for a while and its decreasing afterwards", then $Beh($artifact$,$ e$,$ b$) \wedge \mathrm{PD}_{\mathcal{G}}(e) \wedge |\mathrm{tm}(e)| > 0$

4. The behavior b of an artifact a from an engineering perspective of an agent $\mathcal{G}$ is a $\mathcal{G}$-behavior such that if $Beh($a$,$ e$,$ b$)$ and r is the quale of b during e, i.e., $ql($r$,$ b$, \mathrm{tm}($e$))$, then r satisfies the given condition during $\mathrm{tm}($e$)$ (i.e., it has some given value, it is constant, etc.) Example: let e $=$ "the amplifier performing its function", then $Beh($amplifier$,$ e$,$ b$) \wedge \mathrm{PD}_{\mathcal{G}}(e) \wedge \forall$t$,$t' $(\mathsf{P}($t$, \mathrm{tm}($e$)) \wedge \mathsf{P}($t'$, \mathrm{tm}($e$)) \rightarrow \forall$r$,$r' $(ql($r$,$ b$,$ t$) \wedge ql($r'$,$ b$,$ t'$) \rightarrow$ r $=$ r'$)$

5. The behavior b of an artifact a from an engineering perspective of an agent $\mathcal{G}$ is a maximal $\mathcal{G}$-behavior of a (restricted to the given period of time). Example: [no example given]

Admittedly, the formalization of the examples from [3] seems not very informative of our framework and its advantages. For this reason, here we formalize another example taken from [6]. Consider a mechanical thermostat in a room and suppose that the room temperature drops to 17 C°. The thermostat responds turning the furnace on. This event characterizes a behavior of the thermostat: a falling of the room's temperature causes a bimetal strip in the thermostat to bend. When the bimetal strip bends to some angle A (here 17 C°), it closes an electrical circuit which connects the furnace and the furnace ignites. The event sequence could be illustrated in the following way

(I) Temperature drops to 17 C°,   (II) Strip bends to angle A,   (III) Switch closes,
(IV) Current flows to furnace,   (V) Furnace ignites.

> "The thermostat's behavior – Dretske observes – is the bringing about of furnace ignition by events occuring in the thermosthat – in this case the closure of a switch by the movement of a temperature-sensitive strip." ([6], p.86)

In our framework we represent the thermostat behavior as Beh(thermostat, e, b) where b is the general behavior of the thermostat for the event e corresponding to the sequence (I)–(V) above. If we want to model the behavior for a sub-event e', we write Beh(thermostat, e', b') where e' is, say, event (III). Instead, the behavior of the switch itself at e' is introduced by writing Beh(switch, e', b").[5]

6. From Artifact Behaviors to Artifact Functions

Besides distinguishing different meanings of behavior, Chandrasekaran and Josephson [3] define the notion of artifact function. They presuppose a theoretical perspective in which artifact functions are construed as intended behaviors and define two concepts: device-centric function and environment-centric function. We will show in this section to what extent the ontological approach outlined above is suitable for grasping these concepts. (Note that this section wants to be as close as possible to the approach of Chandrasekaran and Josephson. Some simplifications and improvements are possibles and may make this part clearer. However, since the formalization here is tentative, we prefer to stay close to the source we consider.)

Let X be a set of non-agentive physical objects, i.e., $a \in X \to$ NAPO(a). It is said in [3] that a behavioral constraint in X is any constraint on the behaviors of the elements of X. As the examples given in [3] suggest, a behavioral constraint may be absolute, i.e., unconditional (e.g., that the value of output voltage is greater than 5 volts), or conditional (e.g., that if the input voltage is above 5 volts, the output voltage is a sinusoid.)

Following the argument in [3], we say that a behavioral constraint in X, written $Constr_{Beh}(X)$, is a set of pairs $<b_0,b_1>$, where b_0 and b_1 are behaviors of $a \in X$ such that b_0 is a condition of b_1. Write the latter as $Cond(b_0,b_1)$, then:

$$<b_0,b_1> \in Constr_{Beh}(X) \text{ iff}$$
$$\exists a \in X, e_0, e_1 \, (Beh(a, e_0,b_0) \land Beh(a, e_1,b_1) \land Cond(b_0,b_1))$$

where pair $<b_0,b_0>$ is used to represent the unconditional constraint b_0. We will say that a behavioral constraint $Constr_{Beh}(X)$ is satisfied iff for $<b_0,b_1> \in Constr_{Beh}(X)$

– if $b_0 = b_1$, then b_1 is an actual behavior,
– if $b_0 \neq b_1$ and b_0 is an actual behavior, then b_1 is an actual behavior.

We are now in a position to grasp the device-centric notion of function defined in [3]:

> "Let F be a set of behavioral constraints defined on, and satisfied by, an object D. If F is intended or desired by an agent A, then D has function F for A." ([3], p.172)

---

[5] Note that we have not characterized the relationship between behaviors b, b', and b".

In this specific sense, a function of a technical artifact a for an agent $\mathcal{G}$ is a behavioral constraint in $\{a\}$ provided that this behavioral constraint is satisfied and is desired by $\mathcal{G}$.

To define the environment-centric notion of function we need to introduce the notion of mode of deployment. By Chandrasekaran and Josephson's explanation, a mode of deployment for an artifact a consist of what they call "the specifications of the ways in the causal interactions" between a and some objects from its environment. More perspicuously speaking, a mode of deployment for an artifact a consists of the structural relations between a and these objects and the actions in which a and the objects are involved. We thus represent modes of deployment by means of perdurants. Let X be a set of physical objects. We will say that a mode of deployment for an artifact a in an environment X, written $\mathrm{MD}(a,X)$, is such set of generalized perdurants that for any of its element e, there exists $a_1 \in X$ such that $a \neq a_1$ and both a and a_1 participate in e. A mode of deployment $\mathrm{MD}(a,X)$ is said to be feasible iff all of its elements are coherent.

This is how Chandrasekaran and Josephson define environment-centric functions:

> Let F be a set of behavioral constraints that an agent, say A, desires or intends to be satisfied in some W [i.e., in some world W]. Let D be an object introduced into W, in a mode of deployment M(D, W). If D causes F to be satisfied in W, we say that D has, or performs, the function F in W. ([3], p. 171)

Here is our proposal. First, although one may represent the causal relations at stake in various ways, we will employ the theory of causality proposed in [10]. For our purposes it is important to note that by the lights of this account, the relation of causality relates perdurants. Thus, instead of saying that a technical artifact in a certain mode of deployment causes a behavioral constraint to be satisfied, we will say that a mode of deployment in which an artifact is involved causes a behavioral constraint to be satisfied.

Now let $Constr_{Beh}(X)$ be a behavioral constraint in X and $\mathrm{MD}(a,X)$ be a feasible mode of deployment for an artifact a in X. We will say that a mode of deployment $\mathrm{MD}(a,X)$ causes a behavioral constraint $Constr_{Beh}(X)$ iff

- all perdurants from $\mathrm{MD}(a,X)$ are actual,
- $Constr_{Beh}(X)$ is satisfied,
- given $<b, b> \in Constr_{Beh}(X)$, if $Beh(a, e, b)$, then there exists such perdurant $e_1 \in \mathrm{MD}(a,X)$ that e_1 causes e,
- given $<b_0,b> \in Constr_{Beh}(X)$, if $Beh(a_0,e_0,b_0)$, $Beh(a, e, b)$, and $e_0 \in \mathrm{MD}(a,X)$, then there exists such perdurant $e_1 \in \mathrm{MD}(a,X)$ that e_1 causes e.

Then, a behavioral constraint $Constr_{Beh}(X)$ is said to be a function of a technical artifact a in X relative to a mode of deployment $\mathrm{MD}(a,X)$ if $\mathrm{MD}(a,X)$ causes $Constr_{Beh}(X)$ and $Constr_{Beh}(X)$ is desired by some agent $\mathcal{G}$.

7. Results, Limits, and Future Work

We addressed the ubiquitous character of the engineering concept of the behavior of technical artifacts by providing an ontological characterization of the meanings identified in the *FBS* approach [3]. This is the first comprehensive formalization of artifact behavior that has been proposed and we showed in section 5 that it succeeds to capture and relate the given meanings. This clarifies that an ontological and uniform characterization of artifact behavior is possible.

Further extensions are needed to formalize related notions like that 'behaviors of artifact-types' (as used in design) and 'behavior-types'. We will anlyse them in the future. Moreover, we want to study the constraints between the behavior of an endurant and those of its components, and the constraints between the behavior of an endurant in an event and in its sub-events. Finally, we need to better study the engineering notion of artifact function going beyond the characterization in [3].

Acknowledgements

We thank the anonymous reviewers for their comments. Stefano Borgo was partially supported by the Provincia Autonoma di Trento (PAT), Pawel Garbacz by the Marie Curie Intra-European Fellowship (EIF-006550), and Pieter Vermaas by the Netherlands Organization for Scientific Research (NWO).

References

[1]　B. Chandrasekaran. Functional representation and causal processes. In *Advances in Computers*, pages 73–143. Academic Press, 1994.

[2]　B. Chandrasekaran. Representing function. *Artificial Intelligence for Engineering Design, Analysis and Manufacturing*, 19:65–74, 2005.

[3]　B. Chandrasekaran and J. R. Josephson. Function in device representation. *Engineering with Computers*, 16(3/4):162–177, 2000.

[4]　Luca Chittaro and Amruth N. Kumar. Reasoning about function and its applications to engineering. *Artificial Intelligence in Engineering*, 12:331–336, 1998.

[5]　K. Dorst and P. E. Vermaas. John Gero's function-behaviour-structure model of designing: A critical analysis. *Research in Engineering Design*, 16:17–26, 2005.

[6]　F. Dretske. *Explaining Behavior*. MIT Press, Cambridge, 1988.

[7]　J.S. Gero. A knowledge representation schema for design. *AI Magazine*, 11:26–36, 1990.

[8]　J.S. Gero and U. Kannengiesser. The situated function-behaviour-structure framework. *Design Studies*, 25:373–391, 2004.

[9]　J. Kim. *Philosophy of Mind*. Westview Press, Boulder Colorado, 1998.

[10]　J. Lehmann, S. Borgo, C. Masolo, and A. Gangemi. Causality and causation in dolce. In A.C. Varzi and L. Vieu, editors, *Proceedings of the Third International Conference FOIS 2004*, pages 273–284. IOS Press, 2004.

[11]　Claudio Masolo, Stefano Borgo, Aldo Gangemi, Nicola Guarino, and Alessandro Oltramari. Wonderweb deliverabled18. In *http://www.loa-cnr.it/Papers/D18.pdf*. 2003.

[12]　G. Pahl and W. Beitz. *Engineering Design*. Springer Verlag, 1998.

[13]　M.A. Rosenman and J.S. Gero. Purpose and function in design. *Design Studies*, 19:161–186, 1998.

[14]　Steffen Staab and Rudi Studer. *Handbook of ontologies*. International handbooks on information systems. Springer Verlag, Berlin (DE), 2004.

[15]　Robert B. Stone and Kristin Wood. Development of a functional basis for design. *Journal of Mechanical Design*, 122(4):359–276, 2000.

[16]　Y. Umeda, M. Ishii, M. Yoshioka, Y. Shimomura, and T. Tomiyama. Supporting conceptual design based on the function-behaviour-state modeler. *Artificial Intelligence for Engineering Design, Analysis and Manufacturing*, 10:275–288, 1996.

[17]　Y. Umeda, M. Ishii, M. Yoshioka, Y. Shimomura, and T. Tomiyama. Development of design methodology for upgradable products based on function-behavior-state modeling. *Artificial Intelligence for Engineering Design, Analysis and Manufacturing*, 10:161–182, 2005.

[18]　Michael van Wie, Cari R. Bryant, Matt R. Bohm, Daniel McAdams, and Robert B. Stone. A model of function-based representations. *Artificial Intelligence for Engineering Design, Analysis and Manufacturing*, 19:89–111, 2005.

Formal Ontology in Information Systems
B. Bennett and C. Fellbaum (Eds.)
IOS Press, 2006

A Reusable Ontology for Fluents in OWL

Chris WELTY[a,1] and Richard FIKES[b]
[a]*IBM Watson Research Center, USA*
[b]*Stanford AI Lab - Knowledge Systems, USA*

Abstract. A critical problem for practical KR is dealing with relationships that change over time. This problem is compounded by representation languages such as OWL that are biased towards binary relations; even when the relationships that vary with time are binary, the *time the relationship holds* typically requires a third argument. We discuss the standard approach to this problem, and contrast it to a new alternative based on a four-dimensionalist (perdurantist) ontology, which allows us to use more of the expressive power of description logics. The technique is usable in other logics as well.

Keywords. Ontologies, Semantic Web, Time, Fluents.

Introduction

A critical problem for practical KR is dealing with information that changes over time. In languages that are restricted to unary and binary relations, the problem is compounded by this expressive limitation. Such languages are important in practice, as they include OWL, RDF, description logics in general, and frame-based and object-oriented languages. The added problem is that, even when the relationships we wish to represent are binary (such as being a member of an organization or living at an address), the fact that they may change with time cannot be represented without some special treatment. The problem is often complicated enough that many ontologies implemented in these representation languages ignore the problem of time completely.

In this paper, we review the standard approach to representing relationships that change with time in OWL, and describe how our needs led us to adopt a four-dimensionalist approach to this problem. The approach discussed is in fact usable in systems other than OWL, but that discussion has been omitted for space considerations.

1. Background

In our work, we are using OWL to represent an ontology of entities and relations that are discussed in general news articles and may be of interest to analysts in areas such as business, finance, and government intelligence. The data that instantiates the ontology is automatically extracted through text analysis.

---

[1] Corresponding Author: IBM Watson Research Center; 19 Skyline Dr.; Hawthorne, NY. 12540; USA. E-mail: welty@us.ibm.com

Choosing OWL to represent our ontologies gave us the ability to easily build interoperable systems to produce, reason over, visualize, etc., this data. Further, the large quantity of data we are producing requires highly optimized reasoning components, which are available for several subsets of OWL DL (e.g. Racer [6] and Pellet [15]). We were also able to use off-the-shelf editors (e.g. Protégé [13]) and user-interfaces (e.g. TGViz [1]). Finally, the ability to view the resulting data as a simple graph has proven very important in demonstrating the technology because end users find such visualizations to be natural and easily understandable.

The ontologies we use are human created, and the vast amounts of information we reason with are generated automatically from news articles. Briefly, we use large-scale information extraction techniques with a specially designed integration component that maps the results of information extraction to instances in the knowledge-base. At the present stage, we generate RDF graphs of about 2M triples and 500K nodes from 50K news articles; however the technology for generating these graphs can scale at least another order of magnitude. The text extraction is fairly shallow, in particular we avoid overloading the knowledge-base with syntactic information and parse trees and map only the named entities and binary relations between them that are identified by text analysis components. For example, we would expect that text analysis of the following sentence:

> *IBM appointed a new CEO, Sam Palmisano, a graduate of The Johns Hopkins University.*

would generate the following data (we employ here the OWL abstract syntax [16]):

```
Individual(IBM type(Company))
Individual(JohnsHopkinsUniversity type(University))
Individual(SamPalmisano type(Person)
value(ceoOf IBM)
value(alumnusOf JohnsHopkinsUniversity))
```

There are a number of difficult research problems in doing such text analysis and in mapping the results to OWL that we will not address in this paper. The principle point here is that producing these binary relationships (shown as the value and type statements) is a standard practice in this community, and we make use of this existing work to populate a knowledge-base.

2. Representation Problems

The main shortcoming of the representation used in the example above is that it is *synchronic*, i.e. it refers to only one point in time. In many domains, and indeed in natural human understanding, these relationships are *diachronic*, i.e. they vary with time. For example, consider this sentence:

> *Sam Palmisano was named chief executive officer of the IBM Corporation effective March 1, 2002.*

The sentence clearly indicates that Sam Palmisano was not always the CEO of IBM, and that the relationship *ceoOf*(sam,ibm) will be true for some period of time that began on March 1, 2002.

Moving from a synchronic to a diachronic representation, however, creates a significant representation problem if we are to use RDF and OWL, even if we limit ourselves to binary relations that vary with time. In general, this problem is one of representing *fluents*. According to McCarthy and Hayes [12], a fluent is a function that maps from objects and situations to truth. We will simplify this notion slightly and consider fluents to be relations that *hold* within a certain time interval and not in others [2]. The text analysis we use is based on TimeML [10], and we map these results into the OWL-Time ontology [9] for time points and intervals. This paper remains neutral to these representations, however, and any time ontology that provides an adequate notion of time intervals will do.

The most common way to represent a binary fluent in FOL is to simply add a time argument to the binary predicate, as in McCarthy&Hayes [12], and described as a standard practice already at that time. Thus the synchronic *ceoOf*(Sam,IBM) becomes the diachronic *ceoOf*(Sam, IBM, t_1), where t_1 is a time interval that begins on March 1, 2002. This leaves us with a ternary predicate, which cannot be represented in OWL unless we move to reification, which is discussed below, or to one of the other approaches described by the W3C Semantic Web Best Practices working group [14].

In the original formulation of fluents discussed by McCarthy&Hayes, another choice presented is a meta-logical predicate to relate the relationship to a time interval. In our example, this would be *holds*(*ceoOf*(Sam, IBM), t_1). While this seems *prima facie* to be within the limits of OWL since it uses only binary predicates, RDF provides only a first-order semantics (but no syntax) for relationships over relationships [8], and as a result most tools ignore this capability. In addition, it is believed that reasoning about relations over relations is undecidable, and OWL-DL specifically disallows it [16].

Another important factor in our work is the requirement that the representation of fluents be fully round-trip transformable with a representation that uses the *holds* predicate. Within this representation, we perform more advanced temporal reasoning with a special purpose reasoner plug-in for JTP [5].

3. Fluent Reification

The problem of representing fluents in a binary-limited representation is not new. A more comprehensive survey of techniques for representing higher arity predicates in OWL can be found at [14]. Here, we discuss the standard practice, to reify the fluents.

3.1. Representation

Independent of representing change, the most common approach to dealing with predicates of higher arity than 2 in languages like OWL is to *reify* the relationships – that is, turn each tuple in the extension of a relation into an object that itself has binary relationships, typically called *roles,* identifying all the elements of the tuple. For fluents, this approach dates back at least to Davidson [4], in which an existentially quantified variable was added to all fluent predicates in order to tie the time and place of the fluent to the actors and participants, e.g.: *ceoOf*(Sam, IBM, *e*) & *holds*(*e*, t_1). This approach is used extensively in AI systems. When limited to binary predicates as in OWL, we must specifically identify the roles of the fluent predicate as binary relations themselves. For example, adding a type for the fluent itself, we would have:

```
Individual(fluent1 type(CeoOf)
   value(ceoOfCeo SamPalmisano)
```

```
    value(ceoOfCompany IBM)
    value(holds t₁))
This assumes an ontology such as:
Class(CeoOf partial Fluent)
ObjectProperty(ceoOfCeo subPropertyOf(role))
ObjectProperty(ceoOfCompany subPropertyOf(role))
ObjectProperty(holds domain(Fluent) range(time:Interval))
```

where **Fluent** and **role** are elements of a formal ontology of reified fluents, and **time:Interval** is the OWL-Time interval class [9]. We leave the presentation of the full reified fluent ontology to a longer version of the paper.

3.2. Analysis

Reification has a number of known problems that are outlined in more detail in [14]. None of these are serious, but they are important to be aware of. In brief, they are:

Proliferation of objects. For every fluent an object is created (the **fluent1** object in the example), along with a binary relationship for every role. For the type of fluents we are interested in (binary relations that change with time), we end up with an object and four relationships (two roles, holds, and the type) for every fluent. This is a mild concern as our application extracts many relationships (roughly 40, including types) per document, and we would like to scale the corpus to at least one million documents.

Redundant Objects. Since fluent reifications are objects, it is possible to have multiple objects that reify the same fluent. This is especially a problem in OWL, which has limited ability to express identity criteria. Ideally, we would want to state that any two fluents of the same type with the same values for the roles and holds relations are the same.

Confusing ontology. In our experience, it is extremely difficult to explain to users what the fluent objects are, and the user interface must present them such that they appear as binary relations.

Limited use of OWL reasoning. The use of OWL language constructs becomes severely limited with reified relationships.

The final point is of particular interest here, and deserves further discussion, as this will be the primary problem our solution will address.

3.3. Using OWL Inference

In our ontology, and the circumstances are quite common, the vast majority of our fluents are binary relations that vary with time. The relationships themselves are, again, extracted automatically through text analysis. Some examples are *ownerOf, managerOf, ceoOf, employeeOf, memberOf, locatedAt, colocatedWith*, etc. Each of these relations holds between any two individuals for some period of time, and does not hold for other periods of time.

Much of the expressiveness of OWL is devoted to describing binary relations, i.e. cardinality, inverses, domain and range, transitivity, etc. However, fluent reification treats relations as classes, and thus the ability to use OWL to describe them is limited.

For example, empirical studies have shown that simple reasoning about inverses can have the highest impact, in terms of relevance to the user, on improvements in recall [19]. For most binary relations, the inverse is potentially as important, even if it is not explicitly stated. For example, the inverse of the *ownerOf* relation is *hasOwner*. There is no *a priori* way to determine which direction may be of more use to an end user, nor which way it will be expressed in text. Reification prevents us from being able to express in OWL the relation inverses, thus we are stuck only with whatever direction is stated in text.

Reification also prevents usage of the OWL operators *transitive, symmetric, functional,* and *inverseFunctional* on the relation. The *colocatedWith* relation, for example, is typically transitive, but there is no way in any OWL dialect to express the transitivity of a reified fluent.

Local range restrictions on the roles in the fluent class must also be understood to be global restrictions on the relation expressed in the fluent. To express the equivalent of local range restrictions on the intended relation, one must use nested restrictions on the *role inverses*. For example, "A person is managed by a person at any time" would be expressed as:

```
Class(Person partial
   Restriction(managerOfManagedBy allValuesFrom(
Restriction(managerOfManager allValuesFrom(Person)))
assuming something like:
ObjectProperty(managerOfManages subPropertyOf(role)
   Domain(ManagerOf)
   inverseOf(managerOfManagedBy))
ObjectProperty(managerOfManager subPropertyOf(role)
   Domain(ManagerOf))
Class(ManagerOf partial Fluent)
```

Finally, for representing binary fluents, cardinality and value restrictions on the role inverses end up restricting the intended relation for all time. In other words, we cannot express in OWL that a person can have at most one manager *at a time*. The only thing we can say is:

```
Class(Person partial
   Restriction(managerRelManagedBy  maxCardinality(1)))
```

which says that every instance of *Person* can only ever have one manager. In most cases where such an axiom may be useful, e.g. the *hasMother* relation, it's not clear the relation should be a fluent at all. At the very least, in our ontologies we could not find a use for cardinality or value restrictions on the role inverses.

This shows that there are some things one can express in OWL about reified fluents, however in our application we were particularly interested in inverses, transitivity, and symmetry, as well as certain types of cardinality restrictions. This led us to experiment with other alternatives.

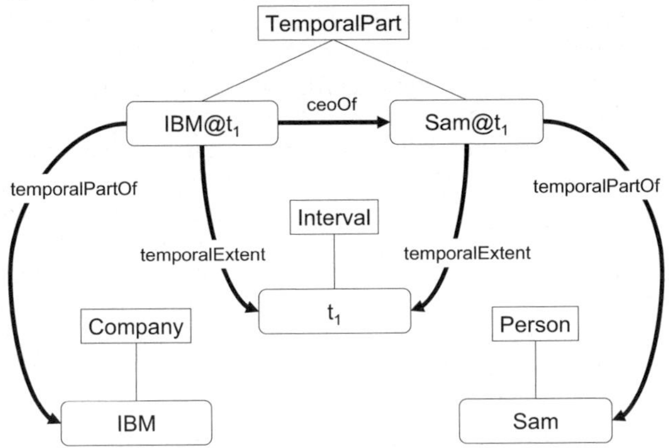

4. Four Dimensional Ontology

At the most basic level, the field of ontology is divided into two groups distinguished by their solution to the problem of diachronic identity: i.e., how do we logically account for the fact that the "same" entity appears to be "different" at different times?

The 3D view, sometimes called the endurantist view, maintains a basic distinction between *endurants* (physical objects such as people, chairs, etc.) and *perdurants* (events such as sitting on a chair or going to work). The difference between the two is that endurants are *wholly present* at all times during which they exist, while perdurants have *temporal parts* that exist during the times the entity exists. The problem of diachronic identity of endurants is addressed by establishing certain essential properties of entities through which they are identified – these properties are essential and thus must always hold. Other properties, such as having brown hair (or having hair at all), are understood to be changeable. This approach has the problem, however, that Leibniz's Law (i.e., X and Y are identical if and only if they share all and only the same properties) must be qualified with this distinction.

The 4D view, sometimes called the perdurantist view, maintains that all entities are perdurants. The idea is that, on a universal scale, even the lifetime of a planet is a simple event, and the prescription that physical objects are somehow different is a product of our own very fine-grained perspective on time and space. Thus, all entities have temporal parts and can be thought of intuitively as four dimensional "spacetime worms" whose temporal parts are slices of the worm [18]. The problem of diachronic identity becomes trivial since entities are four dimensional, and the notion of change is accounted for simply by giving different properties to different temporal parts of an entity so that Leibnitz's law always holds. This approach has the problem, however, that determining what is an entity is rather arbitrary; in fact any mere collection of matter over time can be an entity (and, in fact, *is*). However, its proponents claim that special relativity necessitates it as a correct view of reality.

The 4D approach is not something that immediately appeals to common sense, as statements such as "Joe walked into the room" must be represented as the logical equivalent of "A temporal part of Joe walked into a temporal part of the room". It was first introduced into computer science by Hayes in his seminal work on Naïve Physics [7]. Its history in philosophy dates back over a hundred years, though Willard Quine [17] is often associated with its origins, and David Lewis [11] is probably the first to have formalized it in a logical theory.

While debate rages in the ontology community about whether perdurantist ontology is "better", we have found a very practical usage for it, as one consequence of a 4D approach is that time is "bundled in" with the temporal parts themselves – they represent *entities at a time* – and binary fluents can be represented as simple binary relations between them. Returning to our example, the *ceoOf* relation between Sam Palmisano and IBM would be expressed as *ceoOf*(Sam@t_1, IBM@t_1), where the "@" sign has no special syntactic significance, merely conveying to the reader that it is not Sam or IBM but their temporal parts participating in the relation. Indeed, in a first-order syntax we can envisage replacing these temporal part objects with a function that takes the perdurant and time as arguments and returns the temporal part.

The key observation is that we can represent binary fluents in OWL as object properties between temporal parts of entities, for example:

```
Individual(IBM type(Company))
Individual(SamPalmisano type(Person))
Individual(t₁ type(time:Interval))
Individual(SamPalmisano@t₁ type(4dFluents:TemporalPart)
  value(4dFluents:temporalPartOf SamPalmisano)
  value(4dFluents:temporalExtent t₁)
  value(ceoOf IBM@t₁))
Individual(IBM@t₁ type(4dFluents:TemporalPart)
  value(4dFluents:temporalPartOf IBM)
  value(4dFluents:temporalExtent t₁))
```

Note that the "4dFluents:" namespace is intended to refer to the 4D Fluents ontology presented in the next section, and the "@" sign has no special syntactic significance and is just part of the display name. The *ceoOf* fluent is highlighted in bold. The example is shown below as an RDF graph, with unlabelled edges representing instantiation:

4.1. 4D Fluents Ontology for OWL

We present below the OWL abstract syntax for our "4D fluents" ontology. The ontology is intended to make minimal commitments outside the 4D view of fluents, such that it should be usable in any domain ontology.

```
Ontology(4dFluents
  Class(TimeInterval partial )
  Class(TemporalPart partial)
  DisjointClasses(TimeInterval TemporalPart)
  ObjectProperty(fluentProperty
    domain(TemporalPart)
    range(TemporalPart))
  ObjectProperty(temporalExtent Functional
    domain(TemporalPart)
    range(TimeInterval))
  ObjectProperty(temporalPartOf Functional
    inverseOf(hasTemporalPart)
    domain(TemporalPart)
    range(complementOf(TimeInterval)))
  )
```

While our application uses the OWL-Time ontology [9], the 4D fluents ontology is neutral with respect to this choice; as shown in the example below, one simply equates 4dFluents:TimeInterval with the equivalent class in the time ontology chosen.

As is often the case with axiomatic ontologies, there are more intended semantic constraints than can be expressed in OWL. To begin with, we intend that temporal parts be maximal with respect to the time interval of all fluents it participates in. That is, the time interval of a temporal part is defined to be the duration of the fluent holding. Thus if a temporal part participates in more than one fluent, they must hold for precisely the same interval. We also intend that two temporal parts of the same entity for the same interval are equal. In our system, it is the responsibility of the component that transforms the output of text analysis into the knowledge-base to enforce these semantics. Finally, the temporal parts participating in a fluent must have the same temporal extent.

Given this ontology, we can define a simple ontology for the classes used in our example above:

```
(Ontology example1
  (Annotation owl:imports 4dFluents)
  (Annotation owl:imports OwlTime)
  (EquivalentClasses owlTime:Interval 4dFluents:TimeInterval)
  (Class Person partial)
  (Class Company partial)
  (DisjointClasses Person Company)
  (Property ceoOf super(4dFluents:fluentProperty)
    inverseOf(hasCeo)
    (domain(restriction(4dFluents:temporalPartOf
                        allValuesFrom(Person))))
    (range (restriction(4dFluents:temporalPartOf
                        allValuesFrom(Company)))))))
```

Below we discuss the benefits and drawbacks of this approach, using the same analysis as the reified fluent approach.

4.2. Proliferation of Objects

A single fluent in the 4d approach requires two extra objects (the temporal parts) and six triples, as compared to one extra object and four triples using reification. While one imagines this would result in an overall doubling in the size of the graph, our empirical tests show rather an increase in 20% in the total number of nodes over reification for our application, and roughly 25% in the number of edges. This is due mainly to the preponderance of datatype properties in our graph, which are not impacted by the representation of fluents in our ontology. This ratio (of datatype vs. object property edges) may be an artifact of the way we generate data, but we don't have a lot of other scalable data to evaluate.

In terms of total memory, in fact, the vast bulk of memory is devoted to holding the labels, so actually the memory requirements increase by less than 10% over the same data using reification.

4.3. Redundant Objects

Like the reification approach, there is no way in OWL to express the identity condition that two temporal parts of the same object with the same temporal extent are the same, thus is it possible to have in a model two temporal parts of the same entity for the same time. Our solution, which applies to the reification approach as well, is to check identity conditions as part of the process that translates from information extraction results into OWL. This is discussed a little more in the section on OWL reasoning.

4.4. Ontology

The 4d ontology appeals to users with a scientific background, and is confusing to others. Common sense and natural language tend towards describing the world in a 3d manner, and this is the basic objection to perdurantism for common sense ontologies. Still, in our experience it is no more difficult to explain to users than reified fluents, and in some cases much easier. Further, ontologically speaking, it has a mature and stable semantics that has been studied for decades. There is no confusion in the ontology regarding what the "extra objects" being created actually represent: they are temporal parts of perdurant entities.

4.5. Use of OWL Reasoning

The most significant aspect of the 4D approach is that we can use much more of the defined capabilities of the OWL language, including the OWL-DL fragment.

To begin with, we can use the OWL inverse operator in the expected way, as shown in the example ontology. With this axiom, the data above would entail the *hasCeo* relation between *IBM@t_1* and *SamPalmisano@t_1*.

Transitivity and symmetry also have the expected meaning, allowing us to express many spatial axioms in the OWL ontology:

```
(Property colocatedWith super(4dFluents:fluentProperty) Symmetric)
(Property locatedIn super(4dFluents:fluentProperty) Transitive)
```

This allows us to use OWL reasoners rather than more computationally expensive ones to derive these relationships in the data.

Cardinality restrictions can also be expressed with this approach in a way that was useful for our domain. We had several intended relations whose semantics required temporally qualified cardinality, such as "a company has at-most one CEO at a time". This would be approximated as:

```
Class(Company partial
        restriction(hasTemporalPart
                allValuesFrom(restriction(hasCeo
                                maxCardinality(1)))))
```

This is only an approximation of the intended semantics as it does not prevent the unintended model in which a company has two temporally overlapping time slices that have a *hasCeo* relation to different people, it only eliminates the cases in which a company has two values of the *ceoOf* relation during precisely the same interval. Nevertheless, that is an improvement over any other approach to representing binary fluents in OWL, since it eliminates some unintended models. Note that this also depends on the ability to enforce the identity conditions on time slices discussed above, which cannot be represented in OWL.

Note that an interesting result of such cardinality axioms is that, in an OWL-compliant reasoner (in particular, one that is open-world) we can capture some of the semantics of our temporal part objects (that each entity has one per time interval). If there are two values of *hasCeo* for a particular temporal part of a company, an OWL reasoner should conclude that they are the same.

5. Conclusion

Representing changing information is critical to practical Knowledge Representation and Reasoning. OWL is intended to be a practical KR&R language, and its expressiveness is limited in favor of desirable computational properties. One limitation, the restriction to unary and binary predicates, creates an obstacle to representing fluents, which are relationships that change with time, even when the relationships themselves are binary. We have discussed these obstacles as well as the most common solution, reification of fluents, and shown that it further limits the use of what limited expressiveness OWL already has.

Our approach, which involves treating entities in the domain of discourse as four dimensional with temporal parts that participate in the relation, corresponds to an established ontological position in analytical metaphysics called perdurantism. The perdurantist approach offers several advantages in our case, and most importantly increases the amount of OWL expressiveness that can be utilized to practically describe the semantics of a domain in which binary relationships change with time.

We have not argued the general case of using perdurantist vs. endurantist ontologies. Rather, it should be noted that understanding both of these ontological choices and their tradeoffs gives us another tool to use when solving a practical problem, just as understanding the behavior of different sorting algorithms with respect to the distribution of data gives the software engineer choices when designing software. Without this basic knowledge of ontology, this solution would likely not have occurred to us.

Acknowledgements

This work was supported in part by the ARDA/NIMD program, and has benefited from extensive discussions with Pat Hayes.

References

[1]   Alani, H. 2003. TGVizTab: An Ontology Visualization Extension for Protégé. In *K-Cap'03 Workshop on Visualization Information in Knowledge Engineering*, Sanibel Island.

[2]   Allen, James. 1984. Towards a general theory of action and time. *Artificial Intelligence.* **23**:123-154.

[3]   Artale, Alessandro and Enrico Franconi. 2001. A Survey of Temporal Extensions of Description Logics. *Annals of Mathematics and Artificial Intelligence* (AMAI), Kluwer Academic Press, 30(1-4):171—210.

[4]   Davidson, Donald. 1967. The Logical Form of of Action Sentences. *The Logic of Decision and Action.* Pp. 81-95.

[5]   Fikes, Richard, Jessica Jenkins, and Gleb Frank. 2003. JTP: A System Architecture and Component Library for Hybrid Reasoning. *Proceedings of the Seventh World Multiconference on Systemics, Cybernetics, and Informatics.* Orlando, Florida.

[6]   Haarslev, Volker and Ralf Möller. 2001. High Performance Reasoning with Very Large Knowledge Bases: A Practical Case Study. *IJCAI-01 Proceedings.* Seattle:AAAI.

[7]   Hayes, P.J. 1985. The Second Naïve Physics Manifesto. In *Formal Theories of the Commonsense World.* Pp 1-36. Norwood, NJ: Ablex.

[8]   Hayes, P.J. 2004. *RDF Semantics.* W3C Recommendation. http://www.w3.org/TR/rdf-mt/

[9]   Hobbs, Jerry R., and Feng Pan, 2004. An Ontology of Time for the Semantic Web', *ACM Transactions on Asian Language Information Processing*: 3(1).

[10]   Ingria, Bob and James Pustejovsky. 2002. *TimeML: A Formal Specification Language for Events and Temporal Expressions* http://www.cs.brandeis.edu/~jamesp/arda/time/timeMLdocs/ TimeML12.htm.

[11]   Lewis, David. 1971, "Counterparts of Persons and their Bodies", *Journal of Philosophy*, 68: 203-211.

[12]   McCarthy, John and P.J. Hayes. 1969. Some Philosophical Problems from the Standpoint of Artificial Intelligence'. In D. Michie (ed), *Machine Intelligence:* **4**. New York: Elsevier.

[13]   Noy, N. F., W. Grosso, & M. A. Musen. 2000. Knowledge-Acquisition Interfaces for Domain Experts: An Empirical Evaluation of Protege-2000. *SEKE2000 Proceedings.* Chicago.

[14]   Noy, N.F. and Alan Rector, eds. 2005. *Defining N-ary Relations on the Semantic Web.* W3C Technical Note. http://www.w3.org/TR/swbp-n-aryRelations/

[15]   Parsia, B. and Sivrin, E. 2004. Pellet: an OWL-DL Reasoner. *ISWC 2004 Proceedings.*

[16]   Patel-Schneider, P, Ian Horrocks and Patrick Hayes. 2004. *OWL Web Ontology Language Semantics and Abstract Syntax.* W3C Recommendation. http://www.w3c.org/ TR/owl-semantics/

[17]   Quine, W.V.O. 1950, "Identity, Ostension and Hypostasis", in *From a Logical Point of View.* Pp. 65-79. Cambridge: Harvard.

[18]   Sider, Theodore. 2001. *Four-Dimensionalism.* Oxford University Press. 2001

[19]   Welty, C. 1998. Augmenting Abstract Syntax Trees for Program Understanding. *ASE-98 Proceedings.* Tahoe: IEEE CS Press.

Formal Ontology in Information Systems
B. Bennett and C. Fellbaum (Eds.)
IOS Press, 2006

PR-OWL: A Framework for Probabilistic Ontologies

Paulo C.G. COSTA, Kathryn B. LASKEY
The Volgenau School of Information Technology and Engineering
George Mason University
4444 University Drive
Fairfax, VA 22032-4444 USA
[pcosta, klaskey]@gmu.edu

Abstract. Across a wide range of domains, there is an urgent need for a well-founded approach to incorporating uncertain and incomplete knowledge into formal domain ontologies. Although this subject is receiving increasing attention from ontology researchers, there is as yet no broad consensus on the definition of a probabilistic ontology and on the most suitable approach to extending current ontology languages to support uncertainty. This paper presents two contributions to developing a coherent framework for probabilistic ontologies: (1) a formal definition of a probabilistic ontology, and (2) an extension of the OWL Web Ontology Language that is consistent with our formal definition. This extension, PR-OWL, is based on Multi-Entity Bayesian Networks (MEBN), a first-order Bayesian logic that unifies Bayesian probability with First-Order Logic. As such, PR-OWL combines the full representation power of OWL with the flexibility and inferential power of Bayesian logic.

Keywords. Probabilistic Ontologies, PR-OWL, MEBN, Bayesian networks, uncertainty, Semantic Web, knowledge sharing

Introduction

Since its adoption in the field of Information Systems, the term ontology has been given many different definitions. A common underlying assumption is that classical logic would provide the formal foundation for knowledge representation and reasoning. Until recently, theory and methods for representing and reasoning with uncertain and incomplete knowledge have been neglected almost entirely. However, as research on knowledge engineering and applications of ontologies matures, the ubiquity and importance of uncertainty across a wide array of application areas has generated consumer demand for ontology formalisms that can capture uncertainty.

Although interest in probabilistic ontologies has been growing, there is as yet no commonly accepted formal definition of the term. We demonstrate that augmenting an ontology to carry numerical and/or structural information about probabilistic relationships is not enough to deem it a probabilistic ontology. This paper proposes a formal definition based on the core notion that a probabilistic ontology formalism should provide the means to express all relevant uncertainties about the entities and relationships that exist in a domain in a logically coherent manner. This would not only provide a consistent representation of uncertain knowledge that can be reused by different probabilistic systems, but would also allow applications to perform plausible reasoning with that knowledge. We also introduce PR-OWL, an extension of the Web Ontology Language OWL that provides a consistent framework for building probabilistic ontologies. PR-OWL combines the expressive power of OWL with the flexibility and inferential power of Bayesian logic.

1. Basics of Representing and Reasoning under Uncertainty

1.1. Why should we care about uncertainty?

OWL has its roots in its own web language predecessors (i.e. XML, RDF), and in traditional knowledge representation formalisms that have historically not considered uncertainty. Examples of these formalisms include Frame systems [1] and Description Logics, which evolved from the so-called "Structured Inheritance Networks" [2]. This historical background somewhat explains the lack of support for uncertainty in OWL, a serious limitation for a language expected to support applications in uncertainty-laden domains such as biogenetics or medicine.

Although OWL itself is focused on the Semantic Web, by extending it to become a probabilistic-aware language we are tackling a problem that predates the current WWW: the quest for more efficient data exchange. Clearly, solving that problem requires more precise semantics and flexible ways to convey information. While the WWW provided a new presentation medium and technologies such as XML presented new data exchange formats, both failed to address the semantics of data being exchanged. The SW is meant to fill this gap. Realization of its goals will require major improvements in technologies for data exchange. However, since virtually all current ontology formalisms are based on classical logic, SW languages such as OWL provide no consistent support for uncertainty representation or plausible reasoning.

This lack of support for uncertainty can be justified in closed systems designed to perform well-defined tasks, for which clear and unambiguous vocabularies can be constructed. But the semantic web vision requires heterogeneous systems to interoperate in an open world. Inevitably, vocabularies that are adequate for a single stand-alone application break down when required to interoperate with systems employing different vocabularies originally tailored to different tasks. Inevitably, there is incomplete and partial overlap of terminology and concepts. Even when concepts are clearly defined, in an open-world system available inputs may be insufficient to determine which meaning is most appropriate. For example, a standard ontology might enumerate different senses for the word "Washington," such as the United States as an agent, the first President of the United States, a state in the Pacific Northwest, or a baseball team. Semantic Web applications employing the ontology must identify which of these senses is most appropriate in a given context, e.g., when the word is embedded in the sentence, "Washington voiced strong objections to the proposed policy." As another example, the developers of an ontology for military planning [3] identified over a dozen different doctrinal uses of the word "clear" within the United States Department of Defense [4]. In complex open-world problems, legislating unambiguous usage is often infeasible. Several items of evidence in combination may be required to disambiguate among different meanings of a given term. Evidential reasoners require information about the strength of association between items of evidence and the conclusions to which they point, as well as contextual factors that affect the strength of evidence.

We argue that the ontology layer is the appropriate place in the Semantic Web architecture for representing declarative knowledge about likelihood. That is, in environments in which noisy and incomplete information is the rule, likelihood information is a key aspect of domain knowledge, and should be included in formal domain ontologies. A counter-argument has been made that probability (with the possible exception of microscopic quantum phenomena) is epistemic, but formal ontology should represent phenomena and relationships as they exist in the world. Carried to its extreme, however, this philosophical stance would preclude the use of virtually every ontology that has yet been developed. To explore this idea further, we note that if computational ontologies had existed in the 17th century, Becher and his followers might well have developed an ontology of phlogiston. We may chuckle now at their naïveté, but who among our 17th century predecessors had the foresight to judge which of the many scientific theories then in circulation would stand the test of time? Researchers in medicine, biology, defense, astronomy, and other communities have developed a plethora of domain ontologies. It is virtually certain that at least some aspects of some of these ontologies will, as human knowledge progresses, turn out in retrospect to be as well founded as the theory of phlogiston. Shall we outlaw use of all these ontologies until the day we can prove they contain only that which is ontological, and nothing that is mere epistemology? We take a pragmatic stance that although our ultimate objective is to seek the truth about Reality as it is, that ultimate objective is unattainable in the lifetime of any human. Nevertheless, it is necessary and desirable to do the best we can with the knowledge we have. To pretend certainty when we are uncertain is not doing the best we can. Formal ontology provides a useful means of communicating domain knowledge in a precise and interoperable manner, and of extending and revising our descriptions as human knowledge accrues. To do this in a sound and principled manner requires a sound and principled way to represent, communicate, and reason with uncertainty. Probabilistic ontologies provide a means of doing so.

Not surprisingly, as ontology engineering research has achieved a greater level of maturity, the need for representing uncertainty in ontologies in a principled way has become more and more clear. There is increasing interest in extending traditional ontology formalisms to include sound mechanisms for representing and reasoning with uncertainty.

1.2. Probabilistic ontologies

In general, people faced with the complex challenge of representing uncertainty in languages like OWL tend to begin by writing probabilities as annotations (e.g. marked-up text describing some details related to a specific object or property). This is a palliative solution that addresses only part of the information that needs to be represented. Over the past several decades, semantically rich and computationally efficient formalisms have emerged for representing and reasoning with probabilistic knowledge (e.g., [5]-[6]). Annotating a standard ontology with numerical probabilities is just not enough, as too much information is lost to the lack of a good representational scheme that captures structural constraints and dependencies among probabilities. A true probabilistic ontology must be capable of properly representing those nuances. More formally:

Definition 1 (from [7]): A probabilistic ontology is an explicit, formal knowledge representation that expresses knowledge about a domain of application. This includes:

- Types of entities that exist in the domain;
- Properties of those entities;
- Relationships among entities;
- Processes and events that happen with those entities;
- Statistical regularities that characterize the domain;
- Inconclusive, ambiguous, incomplete, unreliable, and dissonant knowledge related to entities of the domain; and
- Uncertainty about all the above forms of knowledge;

where the term entity refers to any concept (real or fictitious, concrete or abstract) that can be described and reasoned about within the domain of application. ∎

Probabilistic Ontologies are used for the purpose of comprehensively describing knowledge about a domain and the uncertainty associated with that knowledge in a principled, structured and sharable way, ideally in a format that can be read and processed by a computer. They also expand the possibilities of standard ontologies by introducing the requirement of a proper representation of the statistical regularities and the uncertain evidence about entities in a domain of application. It is important to emphasize that a probabilistic ontology is not a probabilistic model (e.g. a model built using applications such as Netica, Hugin, or Quiddity*Suite), in the same way that an ontology is not a database application.

The differences in the in-depth underlying concepts and technologies supporting ontologies and database schemas are not easily distinguishable, as the real differentiation between the two resides in their respective intended purposes. Ontologies represent domains in a way that should facilitate interoperability with other representations of that domain (i.e. other ontologies build by different people with different views and interests) or of domains that are not directly related but share some concepts. When a database solution for a given domain is conceived, its primary focus is not in representing all concepts of a domain in a way that makes it interoperable with current or future views of that domain, but in defining the concepts of that domain which would enable storage and retrieval of the information the database stakeholders (and their customers) want to store and retrieve, in a way that best fits their requirements.

In a similar vein, when a probabilistic model is built to solve (say) a radar data fusion problem, the main interest driving its creators is not in making sure that their definitions about radar domain concepts are interoperable with other definitions that might exist for those same concepts. In contrast, interoperability would definitely be a primary focus when building a probabilistic ontology for the domain of radar data fusion. Ontology engineers would attempt to express one view of that domain in a way that others (with possibly different views) may use/understand and thus build applications (databases, decision systems, etc) that are compatible with anything built under that view.

Furthermore, it is not necessary for an ontology to be a running database, yet a database application can be built on top of an ontology. Likewise, a probabilistic ontology does not necessarily need to be a running probabilistic model, yet a running probabilistic model (i.e. an executable application built using a probabilistic package) can be built on top of a probabilistic ontology if that fits the objectives of the application at hand. A subtle difference here is that anything built on top of a traditional ontology can be built on top of a probabilistic ontology, but the converse is not always true, since the latter is an extension of the former that adds the above mentioned features of a probabilistic framework.

1.3. MEBN: The Probabilistic Logic of PR-OWL

To comply with interoperability requirements and at the same time to enable probabilistic model to be built on top of its definitions, a probabilistic ontology has to be based on a very flexible logical foundation. When searching for that framework, we realized that there will always be a trade-off between flexibility and expressiveness among the candidate probabilistic logics. After some careful research (see [7] and [8] for details) we found that MEBN logic [5] provides a particularly attractive trade-off that made our work easier when extending the OWL Semantic Web language.

MEBN is a first-order Bayesian logic that integrates classical first-order logic with probability theory. Classical first-order logic (FOL) is by far the most commonly used, studied and implemented logical system, serving as the logical basis for most current-generation AI systems and ontology languages. MEBN logic provides the basis for extending the capability of these systems by introducing a logically coherent representation for uncertainty. Because a MEBN theory represents a coherent probability distribution, Bayes Theorem provides a mathematical foundation for learning and inference, that reduces to classical logic in the case of certain knowledge (i.e., all probabilities are zero or one).

MEBN represents the world as comprised of entities that have attributes and are related to other entities. Knowledge about the attributes of entities and their relationships to each other is represented as a collection of MEBN fragments (MFrags) organized into MEBN Theories (MTheories) An MFrag represents a conditional probability distribution for instances of its resident random variables given their parents in the fragment graph and the context nodes. An MTheory is a set of MFrags that collectively satisfies consistency constraints ensuring the existence of a unique joint probability distribution over instances of the random variables represented in each of the MFrags within the set. MEBN semantics integrates the standard model-theoretic semantics of classical first-order logic with random variables as formalized in mathematical statistics.

As a full integration of first-order logic and probability, MEBN provides: (1) a means of expressing a globally consistent joint distribution over models of any consistent, finitely axiomatizable FOL theory; (2) a proof theory capable of identifying inconsistent theories in finitely many steps and converging to correct responses to probabilistic queries; and (3) a built in mechanism for adding sequences of new axioms and refining theories in the light of observations. Thus, even the most specific situations can be represented in MEBN, provided they can represented in FOL. Furthermore, because MEBN is a first order Bayesian logic, using it as the underlying semantics of PR-OWL not only guarantees a formal mathematical foundation for a probabilistic extension to the OWL language (PR-OWL), but also ensures that the advantages of Bayesian Inference (e.g. natural "Occam's Razor", support for learning from data, etc.) will accrue to PR-OWL probabilistic ontologies. A comprehensive explanation of MEBN logic is not on the scope of this work, but the interested reader is directed to [5], [9].

2. An Upper Ontology for Probabilistic Models

2.1. The Basics of PR-OWL

PR-OWL was developed as an extension enabling OWL ontologies to represent complex Bayesian probabilistic models in a way that is flexible enough to be used by diverse Bayesian probabilistic tools (e.g. Netica, Hugin, Quiddity*Suite, JavaBayes, etc.) based on different probabilistic technologies (e.g. PRMs, BNs, etc.). More specifically, OWL is an upper ontology for probabilistic systems that can be used as a framework for developing probabilistic ontologies (as defined in Section 1.2) that are expressive enough to represent even the most complex probabilistic models.

Ideally, specification of a probabilistic ontology language would follow the steps defined by the W3C [10] to issue an official standard. New tools would need to be developed to support the extended syntax and implied semantics of the probabilistic extensions. Such an effort would require commitment from diverse developers and workgroups, which falls outside our present scope. For this reason, PR-OWL was written as an upper OWL ontology. DaConta et al. define an upper ontology as a set of integrated ontologies that characterizes a set of basic commonsense knowledge notions ([11], page 230). In this preliminary work on PR-OWL as an upper ontology, these basic commonsense notions are related to representing uncertainty in a principled way using OWL syntax. If PR-OWL were to become a W3C Recommendation, this collection of notions would be formally incorporated into the OWL language as a set of constructs that can be employed to build probabilistic ontologies.

The PR-OWL upper ontology for probabilistic systems consists of a set of classes, subclasses and properties that collectively form a framework for building probabilistic ontologies. The first step toward building a probabilistic ontology in compliance with our Definition 1 is to import into any OWL editor an OWL file containing the PR-OWL classes, subclasses, and properties (one is available at http://www.pr-owl.org/pr-owl.owl). In fact, this is exactly what we did when we built the Star Trek probabilistic ontology depicted in [7]. We used the Protégé Ontology Editor (available at http://protege.stanford.edu) import feature to import the pr-owl.owl file we previously downloaded. Figure 1 shows the major elements within that file.

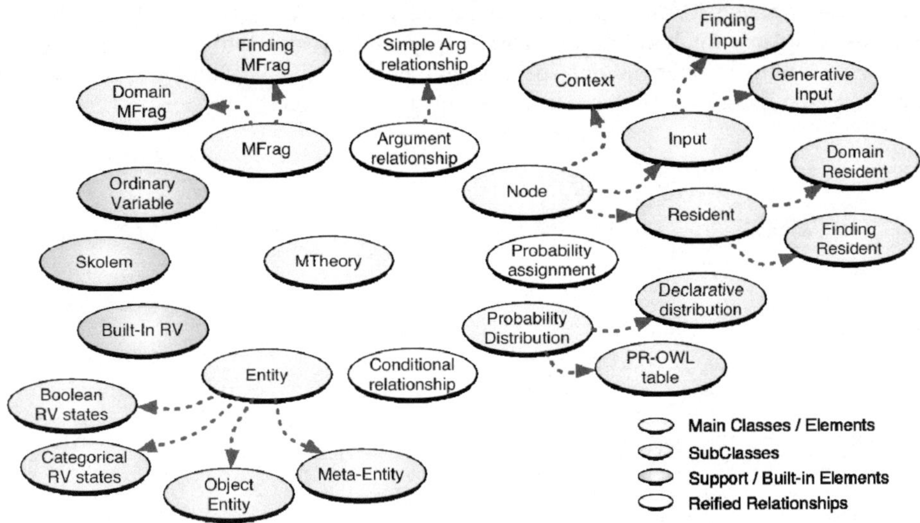

Figure 1 – Main Elements of the PR-OWL Upper Ontology

After importing the PR-OWL definitions, the next step in ontology design is to construct domain-specific concepts, using the PR-OWL definitions to represent uncertainty about their attributes and relationships. As an example, the concepts of the above-mentioned Star Trek probabilistic ontology were either subclasses or instances of the imported PR-OWL upper ontology. Using this procedure, an ontology engineer is not only able to build a coherent generative MTheory and other probabilistic ontology elements, but also make it compatible with other ontologies that use PR-OWL concepts.

Figure 2 shows the initial Protégé screen after importing the PR-OWL ontologies and defining the classes of object entities that will be part of the ontology. In Protégé, concepts of imported ontologies appear with a light colored dot icon and the namespace abbreviation at the left side of the concept's name, as it can be seen in the Asserted Hierarchy window on the left side of the picture.

The darker icons (Starship, Zone, Sensor Report, and TimeStep) correspond to the classes created as a first step in building the Starship probabilistic ontology. PR-OWL object entities correspond to frames in frame systems and to objects in object-oriented systems. The simple model used in this research contains only four object entities; so four classes were created under the PR-OWL ObjectEntity Class (i.e. Starship, Zone, SensorReport, and TimeStep). These are the user-defined classes that convey the equivalent of what a standard ontology would represent about a domain, so its individuals are the concepts and entities that would populate a non-probabilistic description of that domain. In our Starship ontology, the domain instances will be individual zones, sensor reports, starships, and time steps, all represented as individuals of the domain classes created by the user.

The other PR-OWL classes shown in the picture are directly fulfilled by individuals representing the elements of a generative MTheory. The user does not create new classes here, but individuals that convey the information necessary for performing inferences about the attributes of and relationships among instances of the entities represented in the ontology. In other words, these individuals express the probabilistic aspects of the domain MTheory. These individuals can be used by a probabilistic reasoner as templates for building a situation-specific Bayesian network (SSBN) to answer a probabilistic query about specific entities in a given situation (e.g., whether one's own starship is under attack from the starships detected by its sensors).

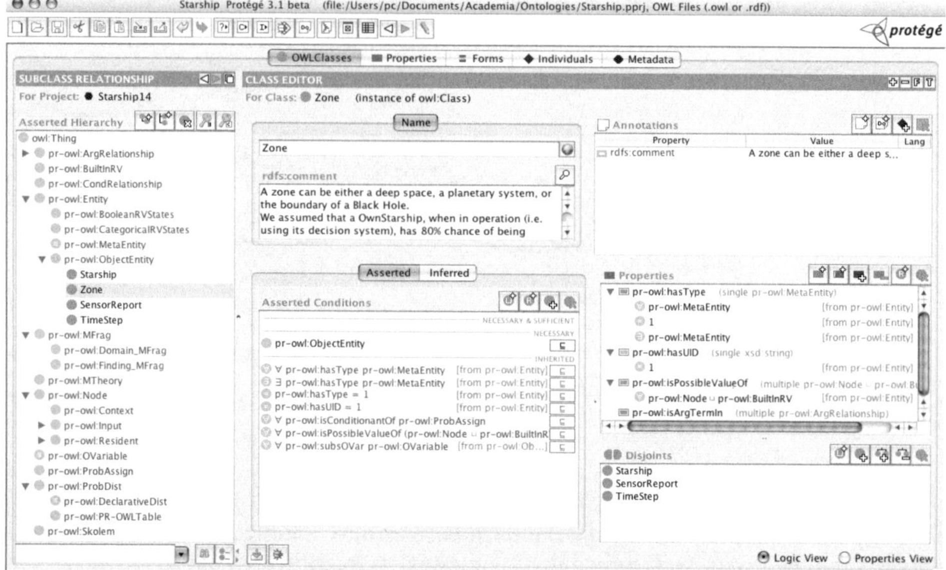

Figure 2 – Main Elements of the PR-OWL Upper Ontology

In our conceptual approach, we considered the question of whether to represent an MFrag template as a class or an instance. It is important to keep in mind that no matter what approach an ontology designer uses in the light of his/her objectives, the structural and logical constraints of MEBN logic will be inherited. Since the other elements of the ontology will also be either instances or subclasses of the imported PR-OWL upper ontology, then all will inherit the structural and logical constraints that collectively enforce the compliance with MEBN rules, thus guaranteeing that such an ontology would be a coherent, logically consistent MEBN Theory.

Although PR-OWL does not enforce a specific resolution of this issue, we considered the pros and cons of modeling our concepts as subclasses or instances of PR-OWL classes in the design of our Star Trek probabilistic ontology. Our experience leads us to conclude that the objectives and characteristics of the probabilistic ontology being built will dictate how to make this choice. Again, representing uncertainty within an ontology is not the same thing as building a probabilistic system. In our Star Trek case study, the generative MTheory was seen as the part of the system that holds the domain knowledge used in this process. In other words, the process of building, working and storing the instantiated MFrags in this case is not part of the Star Trek probabilistic ontology, but a task to be executed by a Bayesian-capable IT system that uses that ontology.

Finally, from our definition it is possible to realize that nothing prevents a probabilistic ontology from being "partially probabilistic". That is, a knowledge engineer can choose the concepts that he/she is interested to be in the "probabilistic part" of the ontology, while writing the other concepts in standard OWL.

In this specific case, the "probabilistic part" refers to the concepts written using PR-OWL definitions and that collectively form an MTheory. There is no need for all the concepts in a probabilistic ontology to be probabilistic, but at least some have to form a valid MTheory. Of course, only the concepts being part of the MTheory will be subject to the advantages of the probabilistic ontology over a deterministic one.

2.2. An Operational Concept for using PR-OWL

At its current stage of development, PR-OWL contains only the basic representation elements that provide a means of representing any MEBN theory. Such a representation could be used by a Bayesian tool (acting as a probabilistic ontology reasoner) to perform inferences to answer queries and/or to learn from newly incoming evidence via Bayesian learning.

However, building MFrags in a probabilistic ontology is a manual, error prone, and tedious process. Avoiding errors or inconsistencies requires deep knowledge of the logic and of the data structures of PR-OWL. Without considering the future paths to be followed by research on PR-OWL (i.e. whether it will be kept as an upper ontology or transformed into a semantic extension to the OWL language), the framework provided by the upper ontology on probabilistic models already enables the development of plugins to current OWL editors for building and using probabilistic ontologies.

Figure 3 illustrates a concept for a possible plugin based on the OWL Protégé editor (which is itself an OWL plugin). It shows a MFrag graphical editor that uses a concept very similar to BN construction GUIs found in graphical packages such as Netica™ (demo available at http://www.norsys.com). To build an MFrag a user has to select the icon related to the kind of node he/she wants to create (e.g. resident, input, context), connect that node with its parents and children, and enter its basic characteristics (i.e. name, probability distribution, etc.) by double-clicking on it or via another GUI-related facility. Nodes would be associated with attributes of entities or relationships among entities, either by clicking on an existing attribute or relationship to name the node, or by naming the node to automatically create the attribute or relationship.

The idea of such a plugin is to hide from users the complex constructs required to convey the many details of a probabilistic ontology, such as the reified relationships, composite RV term constructions (with or without quantifiers and Exemplar constants), and others. In the figure, the Zone MFrag was selected from the combo box in the top of the viewing area, thus information about its nodes is displayed in a graphical format that allows the user to build more nodes, edit or view the existing ones. and then chose node ZoneEShips(z) so it appears highlighted (a red box around it) and all its data is shown in the lower square.

Tedious tasks such as building a PR-OWL table with many cells could be carried out much more quickly and with fewer errors, thus providing a boost in productivity. In the probability table case, the user would only have to fill the probabilities in the correct cells of a CPT's graphical display and the plugin would build their respective PR-OWL constructs.

Another point of usage improvement is the intrinsic syntax check provided by a guided construction. As an example, when writing a composite RV term, the user would not have to actually write the complex reified relations (ArgRelationships, Skolem contants, OVariables, Inner terms, etc). Instead, a menu with the allowed connectives would be available so his/her task would be reduced to enter the arguments of the formula and embed the connectives the way he/she wants. The final result would be a valid formula that would then be transformed in PR-OWL syntax by the plugin.

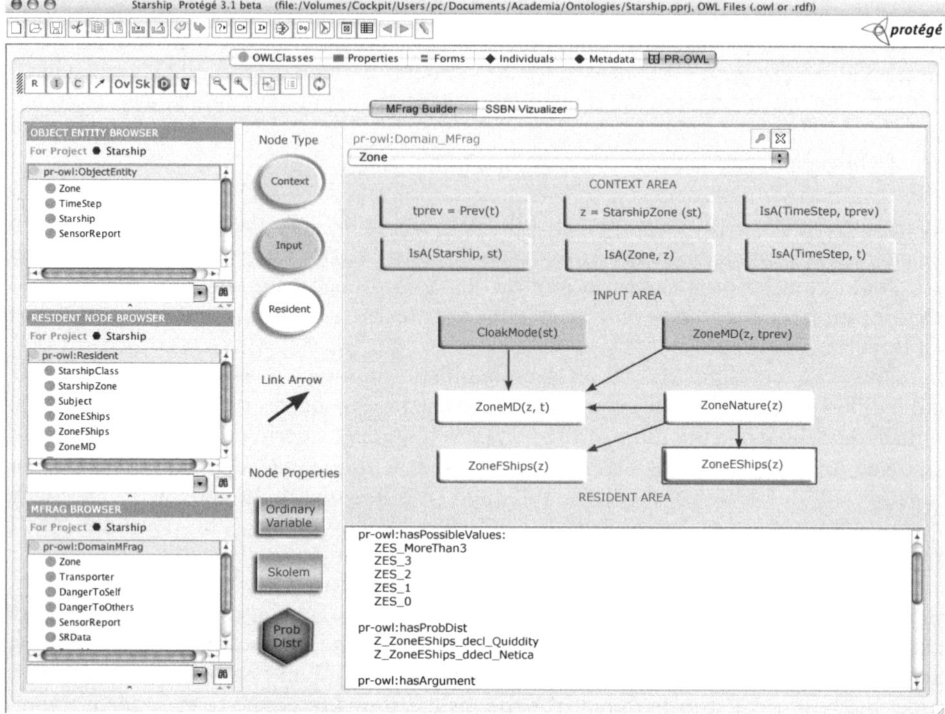

Figure 3 – Snapshot of a Graphical PR-OWL Plugin

It is important to keep in mind that this brief description of an operational concept barely scratches the surface of the many possibilities for the technology presented here, and its purpose is to point out one such possibility. Nevertheless, implementing such a plugin would be an important first step toward making probabilistic ontologies a reality, opening the door to its wide use in many domains.

3. Related Research

One of the main reasons why research in ontology languages is still focused on deterministic approaches has been the limited expressiveness of traditional probabilistic languages. There is a current line of research focused on extending OWL so it can represent probabilistic information contained in a Bayesian Network (e.g. [12]-[13].). The approach involves augmenting OWL semantics to allow probabilistic information to be represented via additional markups. The result would be a probabilistic annotated ontology that could be translated to a Bayesian network (BN). Such a translation would be based on a set of translation rules that would rely on the probabilistic information attached to individual concepts and properties within the annotated ontology. BNs provide an elegant mathematical structure for modeling complex relationships among hypotheses while keeping a relatively simple visualization of these relationships. Yet, the limited attribute-value representation of BNs makes them unsuitable for problems requiring greater expressive power.

Another option for representing uncertainty in OWL is to focus on OWL-DL, a decidable subset of OWL that is based on Description Logics [14]. Description Logics are a family of knowledge representation formalisms that represent the knowledge of an application domain (the "world") by first defining the relevant concepts of the domain (its terminology), and then using these concepts to specify properties of objects and individuals occurring in the domain (the world description). Description Logic divides a knowledge base into two components: a terminological box, or T-Box, and the assertional box, or A-Box. The first introduces the terminology (i.e. the vocabulary) of an application domain, while the latter contains assertions about instances of the concepts defined in the T-Box. Description Logic is a subset of FOL that provides a very good combination of decidability and expressiveness, and is the basis of OWL-DL. Probabilistic extensions have been developed for description logics (e.g., [15][16][17]). Description logics are highly effective and efficient for the classification and subsumption problems they were designed to address. However, their ability to represent and reason about other commonly occurring kinds of knowledge is limited. An example of a restrictive aspect of DL languages is their limited ability to represent constraints on the instances that can participate in a relationship.

Although the above approaches are promising where applicable, a definitive solution for the generic semantic mapping problem requires a general-purpose formalism that gives ontology designers a range of options to balance tractability against expressiveness. Pool and Aiken [18] developed an OWL-based interface for the relational probabilistic toolset Quiddity*Suite, developed by IET, Inc. Their constructs provide an expressive method for representing uncertainty in OWL ontologies. Their work is similar in spirit to ours, but is specialized to the Quiddity*Suite toolset. We employ MEBN as our underlying logical basis, thus providing full first-order expressiveness. Costa [7] presents rules for constructing PR-OWL ontologies in a manner that can be translated into Quiddity*Suite, and for performing the translation.

4. Discussion

Semantic interoperability is a major objective in general IT system development and a necessary ingredient for systems seeking improved knowledge sharing and reuse. In this work, we discussed the role of ontologies in general and probabilistic ontologies in particular as a means to achieve semantic interoperability. We presented a Bayesian ontology language based on MEBN logic that provides the means to express first-order probabilistic theories. We also addressed the inherent complexity of the language and the consequent need of a GUI as a means to make the development of probabilistic ontologies a less intricate task.

Probabilistic ontologies are an increasingly important topic in forums devoted to best practices in systems development. Given the nature of the domain knowledge embedded in their systems, system developers in general would profit most from the advantages of being able to convey such knowledge with a principled treatment for uncertainty. That would allow the proper use of probability information to help devise reliable, more general semantic mapping schemas by using probabilistic ontologies to represent the mappings between two or more ontologies as its instances.

References

[1]   Marvin L. Minsky. Framework for Representing Knowledge. In The Psychology of Computer Vision. P. H. Winston (Eds.), pages 211-277. New York, NY: McGraw-Hill, 1975.

[2]   Ronald J. Brachman. What's in a Concept: Structural Foundations for Semantic Networks. International Journal of Man-Machine Studies, 9(2), 127-152, 1977.

[3]   S. Carey, Martin Kleiner, Michael R. Hieb and R. Brown, Standardizing Battle Management Language – A Vital Move Towards the Army Transformation, Paper 01F-SIW-067, Fall Simulation Interoperability Workshop, 2001.

[4]   Field Manual No. FM 1-02 (FM 101-5-1) MCRP 5-12A, *Operational Terms and Graphics*, Headquarters, Department of the Army, Washington, DC, 21 September 2004.

[5]   Kathryn B. Laskey. MEBN: A Logic for Open-World Probabilistic Reasoning. The Volnegau School of Information Technology and Engineering. George Mason University, Fairfax, VA, USA. Available at http://ite.gmu.edu/~klaskey/index.html.

[6]   Heckerman, D., Meek, C., & Koller, D. (2004). *Probabilistic models for relational data*. Redmond, WA: Microsoft Corporation.

[7]   Paulo C. G. da Costa. Bayesian Semantics for the Semantic Web. Doctoral Thesis, School of Information Technology and Engineering, George Mason University. Fairfax, VA, USA, 2005. Available at http://hdl.handle.net/1920/455.

[8]   Paulo C. G. da Costa, Kathryn B. Laskey, and Kenneth J. Laskey. PR-OWL: A Bayesian Framework for the Semantic Web. Proceedings of the first workshop on Uncertainty Reasoning for the Semantic Web (URSW 2005), held at the Fourth International Semantic Web Conference (ISWC 2005). November, 6-10 2005, Galway, Ireland. Available at http://hdl.handle.net/1920/454.

[9]   Paulo C. G. da Costa, and Kathryn B. Laskey. Multi-Entity Bayesian Networks without Multi-Tears. Draft, Department of Systems Engineering and Operations Research, George Mason University: Fairfax, VA, USA, 2005. Available at http://hdl.handle.net/1920/456.

[10] Ian Jacobs, Editor. World Wide Web Consortium Process Document. June 18, 2003. Retrieved March 03, 2006, from http://www.w3.org/2003/06/Process-20030618/cover.html.

[11] Michael C. DaConta, Leo J. Obrst, and K. T. Smith. The Sematic Web: A Guide to the Future of Xml, Web Services, and Knowledge Management. Indianapolis, IN, USA: Wiley Publishing, Inc., 2003.

[12] Zhongli Ding, and Yun Peng. A Probabilistic Extension to Ontology Language OWL. in 37th Annual Hawaii International Conference on System Sciences (HICSS'04). Big Island, Hawaii, 2004.

[13] Tao Gu, Hung Keng Pung, and Da Qing Zhang. A Bayesian Approach for Dealing with Uncertainty Contexts. in Second International Conference on Pervasive Computing. Vienna, Austria: Austrian Computer Society, 2004.

[14] F. Baader, et al., Editors. The Description Logic Handbook: Theory, Implementation and Applications. First edition ed., Cambridge University Press: Cambridge, UK, 2003.

[15] Manfred Jaeger. Probabilistic Reasoning in Terminological Logics. Paper pre-

sented at the Fourth International Conference on Principles of Knowledge Representation and Reasoning (KR94), May 24-27. Bonn, Germany, 1994.

[16] Daphne Koller, A. Y. Levy, and Avi Pfeffer. P-CLASSIC: A Tractable Probabilistic Description Logic. Paper presented at the Fourteenth National Conference on Artificial Intelligence (AAAI-97), July 27-31. Providence, RI, USA, 1997.

[17] R. Giugno, and Thomas Lukasiewicz. P-SHOQ(D): A Probabilistic Extension of SHOQ(D) for Probabilistic Ontologies in the Semantic Web. in European Conference on Logics in Artificial Intelligence (JELIA 2002). Cosenza, Italy: Springer, 2002.

[18] Michael Pool, and Jeffrey Aikin. KEEPER: and Protégé: An Elicitation Environment for Bayesian Inference Tools, in Workshop on Protégé and Reasoning held at the Seventh International Protégé Conference: Bethesda, MD, USA, 2004.

Formal Ontology in Information Systems
B. Bennett and C. Fellbaum (Eds.)
IOS Press, 2006

Qualities in Possible Worlds

Stefano BORGO and Claudio MASOLO
Laboratory for Applied Ontology, ISTC-CNR, Trento, Italy

Abstract. The paper analyzes how and under which assumptions it is possible to compare (in a relationist setting and relatively to qualities) entities living in different worlds. We begin with a standard technique to construct quality kinds via an abstraction process. In the first case, the process is applied across all the possible worlds and we show that the resulting quality system has problematic consequences. Then, we focus on the alternatives that arise when the abstraction process is applied within each single world independently, i.e., assuming similarity judgments make sense only when referring to entities living in the same world. This situation leads to worlds with unrelated quality systems and we look at the problem of quality comparison across worlds. We analyze under which assumptions this comparison is possible and discuss its limits by considering the structural information that one can infer from the elements shared by (two or more) overlapping worlds. Exploiting the use of such information and comparing this situation with the construction of time in branching worlds, it becomes possible to relate and (in a sense to be explained) to 'tune' the quality systems of different worlds.

Motivations for this work come from epistemological considerations. Consider a possible world as a context or an information system. The framework we develop helps to understand whether the quality systems of the two contexts (information systems) can be related and, if so, it provides a basic methodology to formally link them.

Keywords. Theory of properties, Theory of qualities, Modal Logic

Introduction

There are two traditional and alternative views about time and they are often identified with the two philosophers that most contributed to them, namely, Newton and Leibniz. The Newtonian position or *substantiavalism* claims that time *flows equably without relation to anything external*, that is, time is a container-like manifold and what happens occupies it only *contingently*. Leibniz contrasted this position for its ontological import and pushed forward what is also known as *relationism*, i.e., the view that time is derived from relationships between events. Analogous distinctions arise when dealing with the notion of space since the view of space as an independent *container* and the view of space as a conceptual *construction* are both consistent and philosophically sound.

One can establish a parallelism between this philosophical contraposition about time and the main philosophical alternatives about *properties*: universalism, trope theory, and resemblance nominalism (see [2] for a good overview). *Universalism* assumes properties (called *universals*) as primitive entities of which *particulars* (specific events, objects, etc.) are instances. Since the nature of universals and their relationships are independent from the instances, universalism mirrors the substantivalist approach. *Trope theory* assumes properties as classes of *exactly resembling* tropes, the latter being individualized properties that inhere in particulars. That is, properties are constructed from tropes by recognizing that some particulars possess resembling tropes. Finally, *resemblance nominalism* rejects the existence both of tropes and of universals and constructs properties as classes of *resembling* particulars. In this case, only one resemblance relation is admitted and, it is well known, in this approach co-extensional properties are identified (attempts to overcome this consequence make the construction of properties quite complex [11]).

Both trope theory and resemblance nominalism are interesting theories for comparing particulars in a relationist setting. However, to directly connect our approach to the relationist view of time and space where tropes are not considered, here we take a weaker position than trope theory but, to avoid complicated constructions, stronger than resemblance nominalism. More specifically, we assume that particulars are comparable only with respect to a fixed number of properties. Because we are interested in lengths, weights, volumes, masses, shapes, colors, etc., we call these properties *quality kinds*. In addition, we say that two particulars share the same *quality* if they are indistinguishable with respect to a quality kind, for example, they have exactly the same weight. In terms of trope theory, this presupposes a system of type $\langle O, T^1, \ldots, T^n, i, \equiv \rangle$, where O is the set of particulars (also called objects), $T^1, \ldots, T^n$ are disjoint sets of tropes corresponding to the quality kinds, i is the inherence relation between tropes and particulars, and $\equiv$ is the exact resemblance relation holding only between tropes of the same kind. In this system, the fact that two particulars x and y share a quality of kind i can be stated by $\exists t, s \in T^i (i(t, x) \wedge i(s, y) \wedge t \equiv s)$, i.e. qualities can be understood as equivalence classes of exactly resembling tropes. To avoid tropes we associate to each quality kind a resemblance relation directly holding between particulars, i.e. we consider a system of type $\langle O, \equiv_O^1, \ldots, \equiv_O^n \rangle$. The sharing of a quality of kind i is here represented by $x \equiv_O^i y$, i.e. qualities can be associated to equivalence classes of exactly resembling particulars. This system is stronger than resemblance nominalism because of the presence of n different resemblance relations. On the other hand, it is weaker than trope theory because tropes themselves cannot be reconstructed in it. Note that, those committing to tropes are not left out. They can rephrase our formalization adopting the definition of the i-resemblance between particulars proposed above in the system of tropes.

When modeling time (and space) it is standard to introduce *structural constraints*. For example, a precedence relation can force time to be linear or branching, a congruence relation can constrain the metric, etc. Even though less usual, these structural constraints are not uncommon for quality kinds. For example, a RGB structure can be assumed for colors, and weights are usually linearly arranged. Clearly different quality kinds have different structures, therefore, in general, we will apply structural constraints separately for each quality kind.

The paper starts (section 1) with a basic structure in a single world and develops to consider more complex structures as well as different possible worlds. The idea is to look at the construction of time from an event structure as a guideline and to extend it to possible worlds. The second part (section 2) looks at the different ways to introduce quality kinds in possible worlds and to relate quality systems of different worlds. Our motivation is twofold: on the one hand we want to see what needs to be assumed (and for which reason) in a relationist framework for qualities. On the other hand we want to understand how and when epistemological considerations should enter to complete the overall system. If a possible world is seen as a context or an information system, one can rephrase our work as a theoretical study on how these contexts or systems can be formally related with a strong emphasis on the principles that may help in setting their relationships.

1. From events to time, from objects to quality kinds

Following the relationist approach, this section begins defining an *abstraction process* and looks at the construction of time in an event structure to later implement it for the construction of quality kinds. Toward the end of the section, we see how to deal with structural constraints for quality kinds.

1.1. Abstraction process

Fix a generic structure $S = \langle D, \equiv \rangle$ where D is a non-empty set (the domain) and $\equiv$ is a reflexive, symmetric and transitive binary relation (an equivalence relation) on D. One obtains a new structure $S^e = \langle D^e, =^e \rangle$ where D^e is the set of (non-empty) equivalence classes[1] of D and $=^e$ is the equality on D^e. The process that leads to the new structure S^e is quite standard and is known as *abstraction*. In the case of time, the above structure is called an event structure $\mathcal{E} = \langle E, \equiv_E \rangle$: E is a non-empty set of *events* and $\equiv_E$ is the *temporal coincidence* relation between them. The abstract structure of $\mathcal{E}$, called *time structure*, is $\mathcal{T} = \langle T, =^e \rangle$ where T is informally the set of *times* (temporally indiscernible events)[2]. The intuition behind this construction is that different events can be temporally co-localized, 'they happen at the same time' one would say. Times, then, are the result of abstracting from events by considering their temporal aspect only.

Theories of properties constructed from the *resemblence* relation are the result of a similar process applied on other aspects of the entities in the domain. First, these entities are grouped via the relation of *exact resemblance* which is associated to a quality kind. For example, the property 'being scarlet' is abstracted from entities that resemble with respect to the color quality kind. Formally, given $O = \langle O, \equiv_O^c \rangle$ (where O is a non-empty set of *objects* and $\equiv_O^c$ is the equivalence relation of *color exact resemblance in O*), it is possible to build the color abstract structure $C = \langle C, =_C \rangle$ where C is the set of equivalence classes representing *color properties*. In presence of different quality kinds, we consider several resemblance relations, one for each quality kind. Therefore, the general structure has form $O = \langle O, \equiv_O^1, \dots, \equiv_O^n \rangle$.[3] From this, we can abstract n different structures: $\langle D^1, =_{D^1} \rangle, \dots, \langle D^n, =_{D^n} \rangle$ where D^i is the equivalence class of objects resembling each other with respect to $\equiv_O^i$ (*i-resembling*, for short), i.e. qualities of kind i.

---

[1]That is, $x^e \in D^e$ if (*i*) $x^e \subseteq D$ is non-empty and (*ii*) whenever $a \in x^e$, then $b \in x^e$ if and only if $a \equiv b$.

[2]Following standard practice, 'times' is used as generic term. Here the events can be extended or punctual. The construction is exactly the same in both cases although extended events generate extended times, while punctual events generate punctual times.

[3]In practice, some $\equiv_O^i$ could be defined on a subset of O only. This is quite common in knowledge representation and can be captured introducing these subsets of O as separate domains or introducing sorts. These technicalities are largely irrelevant: they make the formalism more complicated without affecting the general argument. We disregard them here.

1.2. Structuring

Our next goal is to introduce structural information on the system(s) obtained by abstraction. We do this by considering further relations in the structures and studying the constraints they impose on the quality kinds. Let us go back to the general structure $S = \langle D, \equiv \rangle$ and its abstraction structure $S^e = \langle D^e, =^e \rangle$. Structuring relations can be introduced directly at the level of the domain (the set of events in the case of times, the set of objects in the case of qualities). Let us add the structuring relation R to S and put $S' = \langle D, \equiv, R \rangle$. On the basis of R, a new relation R^e (the abstraction of R) can be defined in the abstraction structure. Let R be binary, then we put: $x^e R^e y^e \triangleq \exists a \in x^e, b \in y^e\ a R b$. The abstraction structure of S' is then $S'^e = \langle D^e, =^e, R^e \rangle$.

Given an event structure, one can induce an ordering on the abstract structure of times by using a precedence relation $\lhd_E$ (asymmetric and transitive, i.e., a strict order) for R. Let $\mathcal{E}_{pre} = \langle E, \equiv_E, \lhd_E \rangle$ be the event structure $\langle E, \equiv_E \rangle$ augmented with the new relation. The idea is to use $\lhd_E$ to further *structure* times. The structure we obtain with the technique described earlier is an *ordered time structure* $\mathcal{T}_{pre} = \langle T, \equiv_T, \lhd_T \rangle$ where $\langle T, =^e \rangle$ is a time structure and $\lhd_T$ is the abstraction of $\lhd_E$. Further constraints arise by considering a quaternary relation between events: $e_1 e_2 \leq_E e_3 e_4$ stands for "the distance between e_1 and e_2 is less or equal to the distance between e_3 and e_4". This relation induces metric constraints on events and, indirectly, on times. Let $\mathcal{E}_{cg} = \langle E, \equiv_E, \lhd_E, \leq_E \rangle$ be the previous event structure augmented with $\leq_E$. The associated time structure is $\mathcal{T}_{cg} = \langle T, =^e, \lhd_T, \leq_T \rangle$ where $\leq_T$ is the abstraction of $\leq_E$.

All the constructions we have just implemented on event structures can be applied to structures for qualities $O = \langle O, \equiv_O^1, \ldots, \equiv_O^n \rangle$ when expanded with structuring relations. For example, quality kind i can be enriched with m structuring relations $R_1^i, \ldots R_m^i$ on objects that induce corresponding abstraction relations $R_1^{i,e}, \ldots R_m^{i,e}$ on qualities.

Digression 1. Instead of $S = \langle D, \equiv \rangle$, one can start from a structure $S_p = \langle D, \sqsubseteq \rangle$ where $\sqsubseteq$ is a reflexive and transitive binary relation (a pre-order) on D. A new relation $\approx$ on D is defined by $x \approx y \triangleq x \sqsubseteq y \wedge y \sqsubseteq x$, which turns out to be an equivalence relation. At this point, one applies the previous abstraction process on $S' = \langle D, \approx \rangle$. The relation $\sqsubseteq^e$ (the abstraction of $\sqsubseteq$) turns out to be an order. One sees that relations $\sqsubseteq$ and $\sqsubseteq^e$ are more expressive than $\equiv$ and $=^e$, they include some (weak) structuring constraint. In temporal structures with *extended* events, the relation $\sqsubseteq_E$ is usually interpreted as *temporal inclusion*. In the case of qualities, the relation $\sqsubseteq_O$ can be the *ordered inexact resemblance* that induces a relation of *specialization* between qualities. When we pair $\sqsubseteq_E$ with a precedence relation as in structure $\langle E, \sqsubseteq_E, \lhd_E \rangle$, a different abstraction process, known as *filtering*, can be defined (see [7,14]). The abstraction process based on filters is stronger than the one based on equivalence relations since it may generate times that do not correspond to (the temporal extension of) events in the domain E. We do not discuss further this alternative since the specific abstraction methods are marginal to our goal. Also, note that the number of primitive relations in the structures is not very informative since it may be reduced without loss of expressivity. For example, both a pre-order and a precedence relations can be defined in a structure $\langle E, \| \rangle$, where $\|$ is the *meets* relation between extended events as defined in [1].

Digression 2. The abstraction R^e of a relation R has been defined using an existential quantifier: $x^e R^e y^e$ was defined by $\exists a \in x^e, b \in y^e$ such that $a R b$. It follows that there might be entities $c \in x^e$ and $d \in y^e$ that are not in relation R, i.e., c is equivalent to a, d is equivalent to b, $a \, R \, b$ and $\neg c \, R \, d$. It may look strange that the same relationship can be true for some entities and false for others since these very entities are all indistinguishable with respect to the quality kind related to that relationship. The situation does not change if R^e is defined using a universal quantification: the same problem arises considering 'negative' statements. One can force a sort of homogeneity by adding specific constraints on relations R like, e.g., $x \equiv y \rightarrow \forall z (z \, R \, x \leftrightarrow z \, R \, y)$.

We have seen that *both* times (qualities) and their structure are built from events (objects, respectively) and their relations; nothing else is needed. Technically, it is possible to introduce the structuring relations directly in the abstract structure and to define the corresponding relations on events or objects. For example, let us introduce the relation R^e in $\mathcal{S}^e$ (the abstraction structure of $\mathcal{S}$). Given R^e, in $\mathcal{S}$ it is possible to define R as: $a \, R \, b$ iff there exist $x^e, y^e \in D^e$ such that $x^e \, R^e \, y^e$ and $a \in x^e, b \in y^e$. Once the abstraction process is fixed, it is possible to introduce the structuring relations in $\mathcal{S}^e$ or in $\mathcal{S}$. External motivations may drive this choice, like the objective vs. the subjective *nature* of these relations. The philosophical construction of time from events seems to commit to the ontological nature of relations, but this is hardly the case for qualities like color or shape. For example, it is widely accepted that colors can be structured in different ways (e.g., RGB, CMYK, HSB), that is, the colors themselves do not isolate a unique structure. In [9], it has been shown that, given a quality kind, a single *ontological* exact resemblance relation can generate *all* the qualities (called *qualia* in [9]) relative to this kind. In such approach, structuring relations are introduced directly on qualia and different structural constraints can be applied to the same set of qualia.

In this paper, we assume a weaker position (that gives also a direct parallelism with the construction of time) and introduce relations directly on the elements of the domain. This does not prevent us from considering them as ontological or as epistemological relations, and allows for a direct connection with the approach in [9]. Given this assumption and the analogy between the construction of time and the construction of quality kinds, in the next section we proceed by looking at *quality structures* QS of form $\langle D, \equiv^1, \ldots, \equiv^n, R_1^1, \ldots, R_{m_1}^1, \ldots, R_1^n, \ldots, R_{m_n}^n \rangle$. Note that we concentrate on sets D of generic objects. Thus, D may contain both objects and events, so that some classes represent the temporal quality, others physical qualities, etc. However, we look at qualities in general and the analysis of the particular commonsense relationship between different types of qualities is out of the scope of this paper.

2. Quality Change through Worlds

In the previous sections we motivated the use of a unique quality structure QS and explained the role of the relations in generating and structuring qualities. In particular, we have seen that the *exact i-resemblance* for an entity $a \in D$ is given by the equivalence class built from $\equiv^i$ to which a belongs. *Similarity* notions, generally of qualitative or metrical nature, can be expressed via (combinations of) the structural relations $R_1^i, \ldots, R_{m_i}^i$.

In this section, we study how to compare entities living in *different* worlds. In a sense, QS gives us all the tools to compare entities living in the same world, since the quality structure encodes all the types of comparisons we are interested in. Things get more complicated when there are different worlds. Let us add to QS a set of possible worlds W and the relation *being in a world*. Writing $a\downarrow_w$ for "$a \in D$ is in the world w", we consider $QS = \langle D, W, \downarrow, \equiv^1, \ldots, \equiv^n, R^1_1, \ldots, R^1_{m_1}, \ldots, R^1_1, \ldots, R^n_{m_n} \rangle$ and use this structure to analyze different technical and philosophical positions.

A first approach is characterized by *cross-world* equivalence which consists in assuming that the $\equiv^i$ relations are independent from $\downarrow$, i.e., they apply to entities no matter in which world they live. Although this setting seems to arise naturally from the one-world case, it suffers from a puzzling problem. Note first that it must be possible that some entity changes (at least some of) its qualities in different worlds. (If not, all the worlds would look the same and we loose the reason for introducing them.) Now, if entity a 'persists' through worlds (i.e. a exists in different worlds) and a's quality of kind i changes in two worlds where a persists, then to which equivalent class of $\equiv^i$ does a belong? For example, let $w \neq w'$ with $a\downarrow_w$, $a\downarrow_{w'}$ and assume a is red in w and yellow in w'. Assuming $\equiv^c$ is a cross-world relation for the color quality kind, we get a contradiction if we include a in the class of the red entities as well as if we put it in the class of the yellow ones. Different solutions have been provided to this problem (and to the analogous problem arising in the case of change through time). Here we sketch the more relevant and focus on the *endurantist* solution.

On one side of the spectrum we find David Lewis [8] who claims, analogously to the *stage theory* [5], that entities cannot be in different worlds, they must be *world bound*. Lewis introduces a new relation, *counterpart* (C), to link similar entities in different worlds and uses it to formally interpret the modal operators. Going back to the previous example: if $a\downarrow_w$, then not $a\downarrow_{w'}$ but there is a counterpart entity a', i.e. an entity for which $C(a', a)$, such that $a'\downarrow_{w'}$ and a is (say) red while a' is yellow. Therefore, with respect to $\equiv^c$, a belongs to the class of red entities while a' belongs to the class of yellow entities. The weakness of this solution is that the counterpart relation must be taken as primitive and why a' (and not, say, a'') is the counterpart of a is not explained by the theory.

The *intensional* interpretation of the modality [3] matches up with the *perdurantist* position with respect to change through time [13]. Here an entity a has a *world stage* $a_{/w}$ in each world w to which it belongs, also $a_{/w}\downarrow_{w'}$ is false whenever $w \neq w'$. To formalize the color example, one now has three entities, a, $a_{/w}$, and $a_{/w'}$, and the $\equiv^c$ applies to world stages only: $a_{/w}$ belongs to the class of red stages while $a_{/w'}$ belongs to the class of yellow stages. Then, we can say that a is red *at* w, because it has a world stage $a_{/w}$ that it is red (for criticisms of this reduction of predication to a world see [12,15]).

The *endurantist* solution [16,10] to cross-world change requires the introduction of a world argument in the properties: entity x is not red in general, it can be red relatively to a world which must be specified. The principal criticism to this solution regards the *de facto* negation of *intrinsic properties*: all the properties become relations with the worlds.

Our approach stems from this latter position. Assume the set of quality kinds is fixed across possible worlds,[4] and that equivalence and structuring relations are *localized* to single worlds, i.e. qualities are word dependent. Let a, b be both in w, then $a \equiv^i_w b$ means that a i-resembles b in the world w. Maybe, in another world, a and b do not resemble each other with respect to the quality kind i. This means that the equivalence classes themselves are local: the class of entities that are red in w could be completely different from the class of entities that are red in w'. This approach weakens the standard endurantist position. While endurantists are able to link the class of (say) red objects

---

[4]This assumption is not necessary but simplifies the comparison.

in w with the class of red objects in w' (because they use a single red property with an additional world-index), this move is not possible in our approach. All we know is which quality kind the localized qualities refer to. Instead, the correspondence between a quality in w and a quality in w' is not given to us: given the class of red objects in one world, one has no way to infer which class corresponds to it in a different world. A new equivalence at the level of the qualities in the two worlds is needed. One way to obtain it is by iterating the abstraction process. Alternatively, one could introduce an additional primitive playing a role similar to the counterpart relation (here over qualities). However, we are interested in understanding whether and on which assumptions such a link can be derived without additional primitives. Once again a look at the construction of time becomes helpful.

2.1. *The construction of times in branching-worlds*

Graeme Forbes [4] describes the construction of time-series from event-series via an abstraction process. In his approach, the construction is localized to worlds: in each world he constructs a separate set of times on the basis of the events present in that world. Similarly to the case of qualities, Forbes has to face the problem of relating across worlds the result of the localized abstractions. Before analyzing the solution proposed by Forbes, let us clarify the framework he adopts. The only entities he considers are events, in particular punctual events.[5] The notion of *branching worlds* plays a central role in the construction and he characterizes it in this way: "two worlds may share an initial segment of their courses of history, diverging from each other only after a certain point. Such worlds are called branching worlds." ([4]. p.86). Two worlds share those events that lay in the shared course of history while events in different branches (that is, after the worlds separate) are necessarily different. Worlds that do not share an initial segment of their course of history are totally apart and Forbes argues that no interrelationship between them should be sought. In this setting, a single equivalence relation on events is enough to construct (localized) times by independently applying it to the set of events present in each world. Additional *precedence* ($\lhd_T$) and *distance* (d) relations between events are introduced, we will see below their roles.

Forbes' proposal consists in reiterating the abstraction process. Once localized times are obtained, he focuses on the branching relationship among worlds. Since this is an equivalence relation, one can apply the abstraction process to worlds to obtain equivalence classes of branching worlds: worlds are in the same branching class if and only if they share some initial segment of their courses of history. The time relationship across worlds is obtained by a new abstraction process that applies to the (localized) times of all the worlds belonging to the same branching class. (Times in worlds belonging to different branching class remain unrelated.) The abstraction that leads to equivalence classes among localized times becomes possible because of the order and the distance relationships and because any pair of worlds in the same branching class share a segment, i.e., at least two punctual *times*. Two times t_1 and t_2 in two different branches are said to be equivalent if they have same distance from a time t shared by the two worlds: $t_1 \equiv_T t_2$ iff

---

[5]According to Forbes, punctual events are considered because they simplify the construction.

$d_T(t_1, t) = d_T(t_2, t)^6$ and $t \lhd_T t_1, t \lhd_T t_2$. The class of times given by $\equiv_T$ is the time-series for the whole branching class. Before proposing a generalization of this construction for qualities, some observations are needed.

As we have seen, the assumption of a 'shared segment' of events in two branching worlds plays a key role in the construction since it grants the alignment of the measurement systems. Since most quality kinds are organised neither in one dimension nor linearly, the reference system needed to relate qualities in different worlds might be much more complex than that used by Forbes. As a consequence, the required shared component between two worlds might be much richer if it has to ensure that the quality kinds can be compared and aligned. Also, we must be clear on the meaning of the term 'shared segment'. One might mean to say that there is (at least) an event that is in both worlds. A stronger reading would imply that the worlds share (at least) one time, i.e., an equivalence class of events. In Forbes' work these two notions collapse because the equivalence relation is defined in a whole branching class. However, when localized equivalences are adopted, the two readings have different imports. Furthermore, in our localized environment if we use x, for which $x\downarrow_w$ and $x\downarrow_{w'}$, to align worlds w and w' on quality i, how can we ensure that x remains 'the same' in the two worlds at least with respect to the quality kind i? We face a sort of circularity: we need a common reference system to compare entities in different worlds and we need common entities to establish a shared reference system. Forbes solution goes even further. He does not assume that there are different segments sharing all the entities they contain. He actually claims that exactly *the same* segment is in the two worlds. With this stronger assumption, Forbes forces all the other relations between entities to be shared as well.

2.2. Tuning the System with Epistemological Considerations

Our final goal is to find a way to align qualities in different possible worlds. The goal is trivial if one has some external condition relating the qualities in one world to the qualities in the others. Following Forbes, a more interesting case arises if one assumes that some objects are invariant across worlds so that these furnish exact correspondences between the equivalence classes to which they belong. We believe it is instructive (and in some cases necessary) to start from a much weaker position. We will see that the overall procedure we develop, which we dub *tuning*, often requires considerations that go beyond the information contained in the given world structures. In these cases, we discuss epistemological considerations that allow the procedure to go through. For this reason, we call this an *epistemological tuning*.

In general, we make the overall assumption that there is a one-to-one correspondence between the quality kinds in the worlds and that, for each i, each world has the same number of i-qualities.[7] This correspondence is given beforehand. We illustrate the basic idea by considering two worlds and a single quality kind. The abstraction process we apply is local, that is, $x \equiv_w y \rightarrow (x\downarrow_w \wedge y\downarrow_w)$. Let w, w' be the worlds and $\equiv_w, \equiv_{w'}$ the two relations. The tuning process consists in establishing a (motivated) correspon-

---

[6]Here the distance between times is not directly induced by the distance between events. Forbes assumes that in the shared segment of the worlds there exist at least two events e_1 and e_2 and uses these to fix a common *origin* and *unit* of measure. Thus, one can define a unique d_T for the two worlds.

[7]An interesting complication (useful in applications) arises if we drop this assumption taking into account worlds where quality kinds have different granularities.

dence between the qualities in w and the qualities in w' which, in turn, makes possible a comparison (with respect to the given quality kind) of objects in the two worlds. We write $q_w \multimap q_{w'}$ to state that quality q_w (an equivalence class in w) corresponds to quality $q_{w'}$ (an equivalence class in w'). For instance, if q_w is the class of red objects in w, then $q_w \multimap q_{w'}$ tells us that q_w is the class of red objects in w'.

We have seen that Forbes uses the 'shared segment' between two worlds w and w' to synchronize the events occurring in these branches. This segment designates what w and w' have in common, their overlapping part so to speak. Our goal is to extend this notion of 'shared segment' to general worlds (that is, to worlds where a branching relationship is not defined) to make it applicable for objects and qualities. Given a quality, we want to collect the elements the two worlds have in common with respect to this quality. In other words, we want to isolate what remains constant through w and w' with respect to the given quality.

We start from the objects that exist in both w and w'. Since the objects can change through worlds, we do not know if two entities equivalent in w are equivalent in w' also; it is possible that an entity is red in both w and w' while another changes from red in w to, say, brown in w', or that all entities are red in w and brown in w'. This situation is expressed formally by saying that from $x \equiv_w y \wedge x\downarrow_{w'} \wedge y\downarrow_{w'}$ one can infer neither $x \equiv_{w'} y$ nor $q_w \multimap q_{w'}$. To gather more information, we now investigate the information conveyed by the relations compared in the structure. Let D_w be the set of entities in w, R_w the relation R restricted to D_w, and $\varepsilon(R)$ the extension of R. Formally, $D_w = \{x \in D \mid x \downarrow_w\}$, $R_w(x_1, \ldots, x_n)$ if $R(x_1, \ldots, x_n)$ and $x_j \downarrow_w$ for all relevant j, and $\varepsilon(R) = \{\langle x_1, \ldots, x_n \rangle \mid R(x_1, \ldots, x_n)\}$. We write $F^i_{w,w'}$ for the set of common facts in w and w' with respect to a quality kind i, that is,

$$F^i_{w,w'} = \bigcup_{j=1}^{n_i} (\varepsilon(R^i_{j,w}) \cap \varepsilon(R^i_{j,w'})).$$

In our simplified case, the set of facts reduces to $F_{w,w'} = \varepsilon(\equiv_w) \cap \varepsilon(\equiv_{w'})$.

We now look at particular cases to exemplify how one can use this information to tune qualities and to show when there is need for further constraints.

Let $F_{w,w'} = \{\langle a_1, a_2 \rangle, \langle a_2, a_3 \rangle, \langle a_1, a_3 \rangle\}$.[8] Then, the three objects a_1, a_2, and a_3 are indiscernible in both the worlds w and w'. Let q^1_w be the quality in w to which a_1, a_2, and a_3 belong, and similarly let $q^1_{w'}$ be the quality in w'. Now, are q^1_w and $q^1_{w'}$ corresponding qualities? To all effects, it is compatible with the available information to assume that the three objects have not changed (with respect the given quality kind) in the two worlds so that one can posit the equivalence $q^1_w \multimap q^1_{w'}$. This choice is depicted in figure 1.a where an equivalence class is graphically represented by a closed line (with its elements listed inside) and the segment connecting the two classes shows that they correspond. Still, it is possible that all three object changes "in the same way". Things may be more complex. Consider the situation depicted in figure 1.b in which $F_{w,w'} = \{\langle a_1, a_2 \rangle\}$, $a_3 \equiv_w a_1$, and $\neg a_3 \equiv_{w'} a_1$. Here only a_1 and a_2 are equivalent in both w and w'. This figure represents the choice of taking $q^1_w \multimap q^1_{w'}$ and a_3 as changing object. However, we do not have enough information to rule out other cases. For instance, it might be that both a_1 and a_2 actually change in the same way while $q^1_w \multimap q^2_{w'}$. Finally, nothing stops us from the more radical reading: all the objects actually change, two of which change in the same

---

[8]To simplify the notation, we omit all pairs $\langle a_i, a_i \rangle$ (reflexivity) as well $\langle a_j, a_i \rangle$ if $\langle a_i, a_j \rangle$ is listed (symmetry).

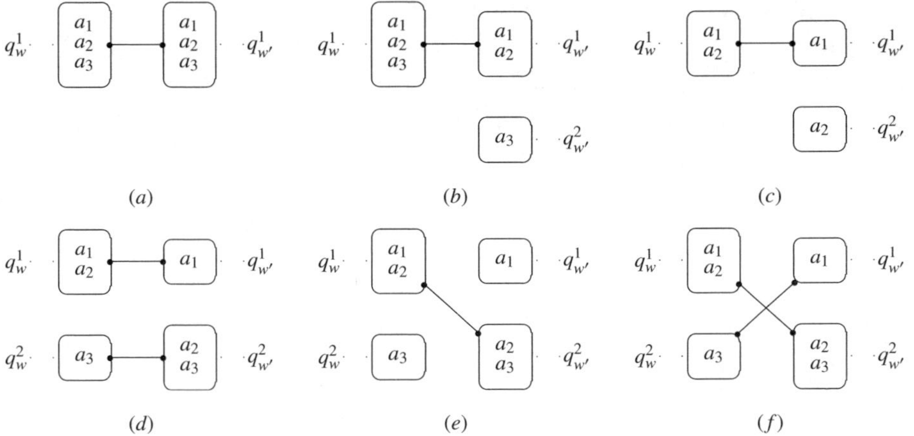

Figure 1. Possible equivalences between qualities in local abstraction processes.

way. These considerations show that additional assumptions need to be taken to justify the correspondence between qualities.

In applications, one can often determine if the two worlds are really apart. For example, consider two satellites and suppose we want to tune their color measurement systems. Let us say that we are given two sets of data about the same piece of land. In tuning the systems, there is a spectrum of options to choose from. If we can assume that the piece of land did not change to a considerable point during the interval in which the data were collected (e.g., if the two sets are collected instantaneously and at exactly the same time), then it is sensible to apply the *minimal object change hypothesis* (mOCH), that is, the systems should be tuned taking the reading that forces the minimal number of changes in the objects as illustrated in figures 1.a, 1.b, and 1.d. Figure 1.c shows that this hypothesis might not be enough. In this figure, one object must change and yet we have two alternatives: $q_w^1 \circ\!\!-\!\!\circ q_{w'}^1$ (i.e., a_2 changes) and $q_w^1 \circ\!\!-\!\!\circ q_{w'}^2$ (i.e., a_1 changes).

Suppose now that the satellites are two equivalent copies of the same satellite model. The measurement systems they use are similar and, although they may not give exactly the same values, they are *qualitatively* compatible. Cases like this push us to consider a condition here called *minimal structural change hypothesis* (mSCH). In this reading, structural relations become relevant because a strong structural similarity can be assumed. If a local precedence relation $\lhd_w$ is available, the number of possible correspondences between qualities may decrease considerably. We show this with an example. Consider figure 1.c and add a new object (namely, a_3) to obtain figure 2.a. Both the situations in the figures 2.b and 2.c are compatible with mOCH. In the case of figure 2.c both a_2 and a_3 do not change, but while $a_3 \lhd_w a_2$, we have $a_2 \lhd_{w'} a_3$. Instead, the case in figure 2.b gives us two unchanging objects (a_1 and a_3) while preserving their order as well ($a_3 \lhd_w a_1$ and $a_3 \lhd_{w'} a_1$). Therefore, if we have reasons to assume a strong correspondence between $\lhd_w$ and $\lhd_{w'}$, we have a criterion to prefer the tuning of figure 2.b to that of figure 2.c.

It is easy to construct some other example in which mOCH and mSCH do not individuate a unique correspondence between qualities. But the real issue is that the two hypotheses are independent: their interaction may lead to inconsistent results and they

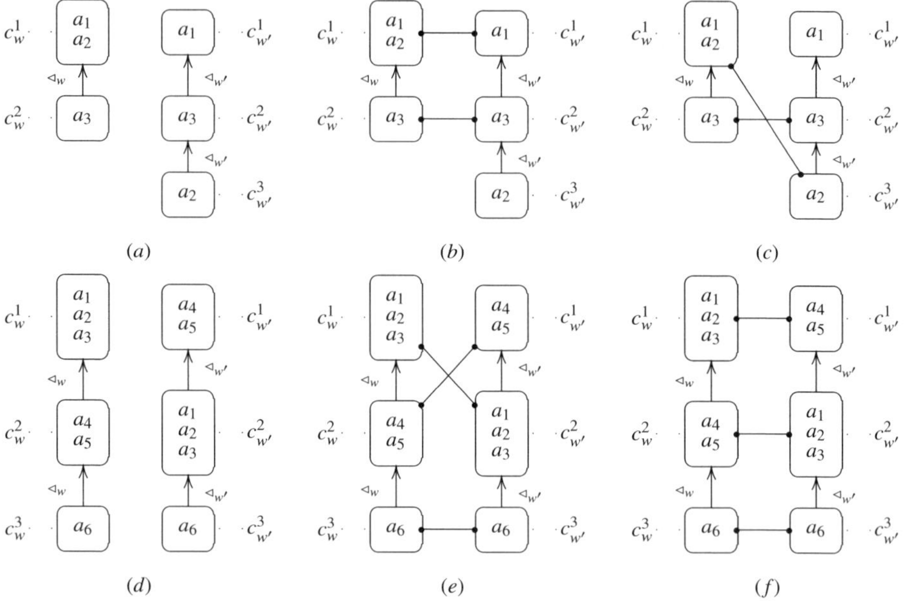

Figure 2. Possible equivalences between local qualities in the presence of local structuring relations.

must be used with some care. Take the situation in figure 2.d. A possible correspondence is shown in figure 2.e where no change in objects is presupposed. However, here the precedence relationships in the two worlds are incompatible. The correspondence in figure 2.f complies with the precedence constraints but presupposes the change of two (or more) objects. One can verify that there is no way to satisfy both mOCH and mSCH. If a choice has to be made (among which we include the choice of adopting weakened versions of the two hypotheses), it should be based on further information. For example, if we know that there is just one satellite that collected the two sets of data about a piece of land with an interval of six months, then hypothesis mSCH becomes more reliable and we can favor the correspondence of figure 2.f over that of figure 2.e.

Once we have reached a motivated correspondence between qualites in w and qualities in w', we should be able to say how and in which cases the correspondence can be used to compare objects in the two worlds. From the abstraction processes, one can define a cross-world equivalence relation between objects in w and objects in w':

$$x \equiv_{w,w'} y \triangleq x \in q_w \wedge y \in q_{w'} \wedge q_w \circ\!\!-\!\!\circ q_{w'}$$

This allows us to compare those objects that belong to qualities connected by the correspondence and the information we have gathered so far is not enough to relate other objects or qualities. The situation changes when structural relations are added. Let us go back to the familiar case of the precedence relation. Suppose that we have motivated (or inferred) a correspondence for which $q_w^1 \circ\!\!-\!\!\circ q_{w'}^1$ and $q_w^3 \circ\!\!-\!\!\circ q_{w'}^3$. Also, let us say that $q_w^1 \lhd_w q_w^2 \lhd_w q_w^3$, and $q_{w'}^1 \lhd_{w'} q_{w'}^2 \lhd_{w'} q_{w'}^3$ and no direct correspondence has been posited between q_w^2 and $q_{w'}^2$. If there is only one quality between classes q_w^1 and q_w^3, and so between classes $q_{w'}^1$ and $q_{w'}^3$, then statements that hold for objects in q_w^2 can be rephrased for objects in $q^2_{w'}$ and vice versa. We can then extend the correspondence between qualia in the two worlds with $q^2_w \multimap q^2_{w'}$. Furthermore, if the two systems are based on the same metric (the strategy adopted by Forbes), all we need is a minimal correspondence that fixes the reference system and the measurement unit in the two worlds.[9] From this information, the correspondence extends naturally to all the qualities in these worlds.

Finally, what can we say if $F^i_{w,w'} = \emptyset$? We can look for a sequence of worlds $w, w_1, \ldots, w_n, w'$ such that $F^i_{w,w_1} \neq \emptyset$, $F^i_{w_n,w'} \neq \emptyset$, and $F^i_{w_r,w_{r+1}} \neq \emptyset$, for $1 \leq r < n$, and obtain an indirect tuning of w and w'. If such a sequence does not exists, our procedure cannot provide a correspondence and further assumptions must be taken into account.

Acknowledgements

The research for this work by Stefano Borgo has been supported by the Provincia Autonoma di Trento (PAT).

References

[1] James F. Allen and Patrick J. Hayes. A common-sense theory of time. In *International Joint Conference on Artificial Intelligence (IJCAI85)*, pages 528–538, Los Angeles, 1985.

[2] D.M. Armstrong. *Universals. An Opinionated Introduction*. Focus Series. Westview Press, San Francisco, 1989.

[3] Melvin Fitting. First-order intensional logic. *Annals of Pure and Applied Logic*, 127(1-3):171–193, 2004.

[4] Graeme Forbes. Time, events, and modality. In Robin Le Poidevin and Murray MacBeath, editors, *The Philosophy of Time*, pages 80–95. Oxford University Press, 1993.

[5] K. Hawley. *How Thing Persist*. Clarendon Press, Oxford, UK, 2001.

[6] Ingvar Johansson. Determinables as universals. *The Monist*, 83(1):101–121, 2000.

[7] H. Kamp. Events, istants and temporal reference. In R. Baerle, U. Egli, and A von Stechow, editors, *Semantics from Different Points of View*, pages 376–417. Springer, Berlin, 1979.

[8] D.K. Lewis. Counterpart theory and quantified modal logic. *The Journal of Philosophy*, 65:113–126, 1968.

[9] C Masolo and S. Borgo. Qualities in formal ontology. In P. Hitzler, C. Lutz, and G. Stumme, editors, *Foundational Aspects of Ontologies (FOnt 2005) Workshop at KI 2005*, pages 2–16, Koblenz, Germany, 2005.

[10] Trenton Merricks. Endurance and indiscernibility. *Journal of Philosophy*, 91:165–184, 1994.

[11] G. Rodriguez-Pereyra. *Resemblance Nominalism. A Solution to the Problem of Universals*. Clarendon Press, Oxford, 2002.

[12] Thomas Sattig. Temporal predication with temporal parts and temporal counterparts. *Australian Journal of Philosophy*, 81(3):355–368, 2003.

[13] T. Sider. *Four-Dimensionalism. An Ontology of Persistence and Time*. Clarendon Press, Oxford, 2001.

[14] J. Van Benthem. *The Logic of Time*. Kluwer, Dordrecht, 1983.

[15] A. Varzi. Perdurantism, universalism, and quantifiers. *Australian Journal of Philosophy*, 81(2):208–215, 2003.

[16] D. Wiggins. *Sameness and Substance*. Blackwell, Oxford, 1980.

---

[9]It would be useful to analyze the minimal initial correspondence (at least for important sets of structural relations) needed to formally derive an overall correspondence between worlds.

6. Linking and Merging Ontologies

Formal Ontology in Information Systems
B. Bennett and C. Fellbaum (Eds.)
IOS Press, 2006

An Algebra for Composing Ontologies[1]

Saket KAUSHIK [a] Csilla FARKAS [b] Duminda WIJESEKERA [a] and Paul AMMANN [a]
[a] *Department of Information & Software Engineering*
George Mason University
Fairfax, VA 22030, U.S.A
{skaushik\dwijesek\pammann}@gmu.edu
[b] *Department of Computer Science and Engineering*
University of South Carolina
Columbia, SC 29208 USA
farkas@cse.sc.edu

Abstract.
Ontologies are used as a means of expressing agreements to a vocabulary shared by a community in a coherent and consistent manner. As it happens in the Internet, ontologies are created by community members in a decentralized manner, requiring that they be merged before being used by the community. We develop an algebra to do so in the Resource Description Framework (RDF). To provide formal semantics of the proposed algebraic operators, we type a fragment of the RDF syntax.

Keywords. Ontology composition, Ontology merging, Ontology alignment, Ontology Mapping, Ontology translation

1. Introduction

Ontologies, considered as specifications of conceptualizations are designed for the purpose of enabling knowledge sharing and reuse [13]. Rooted in Philosophy as a systematic theory of *existence* they specify the entities that *exist* and relationships among existing objects, and are used in artificial intelligence and the world wide web to describe of domains of discourse. With the hope of having self describing, machine understandable and operable data, the Semantic Web uses on ontologies to describe its resources, referred to as the *Resource Description Framework* (RDF), to be summarized shortly. Because the world wide web is a collection of independently maintained web sites without centralized control or agreement, their domain knowledge, captured by various domain experts, need to be combined, compared, contrasted and operated upon during web-based computations. Therefore, one of the core challenges identified for the Semantic Web involves decentralization and reuse of ontological conceptualization [19]

Several approaches exist to *combine* independently-developed ontologies, as surveyed by Klein and Kalfoglou *et al.* [19,16]. Differences in syntax, expressivity, and semantics of the representation are common among ontologies [19]. Other problems include structural similarities [10], *equality*, consistent combination, and subsumption.

We define precise syntax and semantics for a limited version of RDF and define some algebraic operations including products, quotients and homomorphisms for them

---

[1] This project funded in part by the National Science Foundation under grant CCR-0208848

in this paper. Because RDF allows considerable freedom of expression prompting many higher level languages to restrict features that it doesn't support. In our case, we model all RDF features except collections as will be shown shortly, making our semantics a higher order version of RDFS(FA) [25].

In order to formalize the algebra of combinators, we first present a recursive finite typing of RDF without collections for expressing ontologies expressed in heterogenous languages. Next, we construct an well-founded algebraic scheme over a universe of ontologies that respects well known algebraic operations and identities.

The rest of the paper is organized as follows. In Section 2 and 3 we formalize RDF as a collection of higher typed objects and their properties. Section 4 defines homomorphisms between ontologies; in Section 5 we show how homomorphisms can be represented as ontologies in the same universe. In Section 6 we define basic algebraic operations and give their properties. We conclude in Section 7.

2. The Resource Description Framework

The Semantic Web consists of a layered architecture [6] of web languages. The lowest layer of this stack is Unicode/URI layer on which the XML and `xmlschema` are built. The next layer has RDF(S), which defines both the syntax and semantics of subsequent layers. Consequently, languages above the layer of RDF, such as OWL *etc.*, are built on top of RDF(S).

RDF specifies meta-information about *resources, i.e.*, entities that can be uniquely identified, where the objectives of providing them are to enable machine processing and sharing meta-information about resources. Such meta information about resources are specified in RDF using binary properties between resources. RDF does so by using the syntax of *triples* where the subject (the first component of the triple) is related by the property (the second component of the triple) to the object (the third component). An RDF schema can be extended further through *reification,* that specify binary properties between triples. RDF(S) or RDF Schema is RDF's vocabulary description language. It has syntax to describe concepts and resources through meta-classes such as `rdfs:Class`, `rdf:type`, *etc.*, and relationships between resources through `rdf:property`. These meta classes are used to specify properties of user defined schema. RDF(S) vocabulary descriptions are written in RDF using a set of language primitives, described in [5].

3. Formalizing RDF

We formalize RDF as a collection of higher typed objects and binary relations among them, subjected to the restriction that containers and collections of RDF like `rdf:bag`, `rdf:alt`, *etc.* are not interpreted.

In our semantics, we interpret classes and properties as well founded sets in ZF set theory [20] with a name. Consequently, as in imperative programming languages, a class has a name, a location – given by its URI an universal address space, and elements. As a result, syntactic elements that are equal by name are also equal by location.

Definition 1 (Ontology [5]).

Primitive classes and properties: *Suppose U be a universe of objects. Let $C_0 \subseteq \mathcal{P}(U)$ and $P_0 \subseteq (C_0 \times C_0)$. Then any $c \in C_0$ is said to be a primitive class and any $p \in P_0$ said to be a primitive binary property over U.*

Classes and properties of finite type: *Suppose C_n and P_n are respectively classes and properties of type n. Then, classes and properties of type $(n + 1)$ are those that satisfy $C_{n+1} \subseteq \mathcal{P}(C_n) \cup P_n$, and $P_{n+1} \subseteq (C_{n+1} \times C_{n+1})$. That is, in addition to classes of type n, classes of type $(n + 1)$ may include properties of type n as elements. Collectively, the sequence of sets, i.e., $\bigcup_{i \geq 0} C_i$ is called a schema.*

Schema Naming: *We use a set of class names $\mathcal{CNAMES}$ for schema, and a function $\mathcal{CN}$: $\bigcup_{n \geq 0} (C_n \cup P_n) \mapsto \mathcal{CNAMES}$ - a naming function from $\bigcup_{n \geq 0} (C_n \cup P_n)$ to the name set $\mathcal{CNAMES}$. Also, $\mathcal{CNAMES} = \bigcup_{i \geq 0} CNAME_i$ where $CNAME_i$ is the set $C_i \cup P_i$ elements are mapped to.*

Instances: *A class c belonging to type C_n is represented $c :: C_n$ and a property p of type P_n is represented as $p :: P_n$. For any such class c and property p of type C_n, P_n (resp.), any member x being a member of $c :: C_n$ is represented as $x \in c :: C_n$ and pair of instances (y, z) related through the property $p :: P_n$ is represented as $(y, z) \in p :: P_n$. The set of instances of type n is named I_n and the set of all instances is named $\mathcal{I}$. Note that whenever the type is apparent, we drop '::' from the representation.*

Instance Naming: *We use a set of names $\mathcal{INAMES}$ for instances, and a function $\mathcal{IN} : \mathcal{I} \mapsto \mathcal{INAMES}$ said to be a naming function from $\mathcal{I}$ to $\mathcal{INAMES}$. Also, $\mathcal{INAMES} = \bigcup_{i \geq 0} INAME_i$ where elements in $I_i \cup P_i$ are mapped to the set $INAME_i$.*

Ontology *An ontology $\mathcal{O}$ is a tuple $\langle \mathcal{C}, \mathcal{P}, \mathcal{CN}, \mathcal{I}, \mathcal{IN} \rangle$ where $\mathcal{C} = \bigcup_{n \geq 0} C_n$ is a set of classes, $\mathcal{P} = \bigcup_{n \geq 0} P_n$ are the properties and $\mathcal{I}$ is the set of instances.*

Definition 1 defines Ontologies consisting of entities and relationships among them as recursively defined classes and relationships, respectively. The base case of the recursion defines the *base* class and their *properties*. In that base case of the recursive definition the collection of base classes C_0 are given axiomatically. That is, they can be chosen without any other restrictions, and have to be given a name in some arbitrarily chosen, but fixed thereafter, collection of symbols referred to as $\mathcal{CNAME}$. In case of RDF, these are chosen to be the collection of URIs. Every class in C_0 has the semantics as some collection of named objects chosen out of a universe U with a name chosen from a class of instances $\mathcal{INAME}$. Relationships between classes in C_0 are defined as a collection of axiomatically chosen binary relationships given by P_0. That is, properties of P_0 are chosen binary relationships between objects of C_0 with names chosen from $\mathcal{CNAMES}$.

The inductive step of definition 1 chooses next class of objects - that is C_1 named subsets - to be all objects of C_0 and all named binary properties of P_0. That makes every property of P_0 an object of the next class C_1. The properties of second stage - that is P_1 - are defined as suitably chosen named binary relations among C_1. This application of the inductive step follows the same pattern for all stages.

This definition has several desirable properties. The first is that, because properties of a (lower) level become classes of the immediately higher class, properties among such properties - i.e. higher level properties - can be specified in the next level. Secondly, because RDF does not explicitly define classes and properties, and allows the user to define them, the type definition does not provide type constructors. Thirdly, when a class c of C_n becomes a class of C_{n+1}, the name that c is assigned is carried over to the next level. Similarly, a property p at level P_n is also on object in C_{n+1} and therefore has a name assigned at P_n that we take at the next level as well. Fourthly, due to the relationships $C_n \subset C_{n+1}$ and $P_n \subset C_{n+1}$, any class c of C_n and a property p of P_n are also classes of C_{n+1}. (For further explanation and examples see [17].)

Our definition of an ontology may appear to be different from RDF specification [14] of an ontology. However, by allowing the set of instances, *i.e.*, $\mathcal{I}$ to be empty, the two definitions can be made to converge. Thus, ontologies are named nested unary and binary schema [23] sans *keys*. Because ontologies are sometimes modeled as connected graphs with $c :: C_i, i \geq 0$ elements as nodes, $p :: P_i$ as edges and $\mathcal{I}$ as the set of instances, paths in ontologies have been defined. Next, we define (typed) paths as follows.

Definition 2 (Path).

Directed Typed Path *An n-edged directed typed path is a triple $\langle u_1, \pi_t, u_{n+1} \rangle$ where $u_i ::$ C_j (for some $j \geq 0$), $i \in [1, n + 1]$ and π_t is a sequence of n edges given by $\langle \mathcal{CN}(e_1), \ldots, \mathcal{CN}(e_n) \rangle$, where $e_k :: P_j, k \in [1, n]$ and $e_1 = u_1 \mapsto u_2, \ldots, e_n = u_n \mapsto u_{n+1}$. Each property in a path is related through $\prec$ relation, i.e., $e_i \prec e_{i+1}$. The reflexive transitive closure of $\prec$ ($\prec^*$) arranges every pair of properties in π_t in a partial order.*

Directed path *An n-edged directed path is a triple $\langle u_1, \pi_d, u_{n+1} \rangle$ where $u_i \in \bigcup_j c :: C_j, i \in$ $[1, n + 1]$ and π_d is a sequence of n edges given by $\langle \mathcal{CN}(e_1), \ldots, \mathcal{CN}(e_n) \rangle$, where $e_k \in$ $p :: P_j, k \in [1, n]$ and $e_1 = u_1 \mapsto u_2, \ldots, e_n = u_n \mapsto u_{n+1}$*
We abuse the syntax at times by relating paths as $\langle \mathcal{CN}(u_1), \pi, \mathcal{CN}(u_{n+1}) \rangle$ instead of $\langle u_1, \pi, u_{n+1} \rangle$.

3.1. Limited RDF Semantics

In this section we briefly describe our semantics for named ontologies of finite types. Our semantics is closest to those of RDFS(FA) [25], where we build a hierarchy of named sets. In order to do so we start with a universe, *i.e.*, a set of URI's (denoted URI) and other constants, say B as *urelements, i.e.*, those atomic elements that do not have any further set theoretical structure to them)[1,20]. Hierarchical universe is built as follows:

C_0 and P_0:

$$C_0 = \{(u, b) : u \in URI \text{ and } b \in B\}$$

$$P_0 = \{(u, (b, b')) : u \in URI \text{ and } b, b' \subseteq B\}$$

C_{n+1} and P_{n+1}: Suppose $\mathbf{C_n}$ and $\mathbf{P_n}$ have been defined. Let $U_n = \{x : \exists u \in URI (u, x) \in C_n\}$. Then define

$$C_{n+1} = \{(u, B) : u \in URI \text{ and } B \subseteq \mathcal{P}(U_n)\}$$

$$P_{n+1} = \{(u, (B, B')) : u \in URI \text{ and } B, B' \subseteq \mathcal{P}(U_n)\}$$

Notice that every strata of the universe consists of ordered pairs, where the first component is a URI, denoting the name, and the second component is a set. Consequently, in the inductive step U_n recreates the base elements from the previous step. The level of the nestings in the construction of the set indicates the level of the universe. That is, a set with n nesting is at level n. Also notice that, stripped out of the name, a class at level n becomes an element at level $n + 1$. The main reason for introducing names (somewhat artificially, we agree) is to make the distinction between name (intensional) equality and extensional equality, because in ZF set theory, set equality is extensional. We use this stratified named universe to interpret our ontology and RDF syntax as follows:

Definition 3 (Semantic mapping $[\![\ ]\!]$).

Universe:

1. *Suppose U is the universe as defined in definition 1.*
2. *Let $[\![\ ]\!]_u : U \mapsto B$ be the surjective mapping that maps the constants in the syntax to a set B of urelements over which the syntax is interpreted.*

3. *Let* $[\![\,]\!]_{Iname} : \mathcal{INAMES} \mapsto URI$ *be a mapping of RDF names to URIs.*
4. *Let* $[\![\,]\!]_{Iname} : \mathcal{CNAMES} \mapsto URI$ *be a mapping of RDF names to URIs.*

Mapping instances: *Every instance i with name a is mapped as* $[\![(a,i)]\!] = ([\![i]\!]_{INAMES}, [\![i]\!]_u)$.

Mapping classes: *For every class $c :: C_n$ named a is mapped as* $[\![(a,c)]\!] = ([\![a]\!]_{CNAMES}, [\![c]\!])$
   where $[\![c]\!]$ is constructed by replacing every $u \in U$ in c with $[\![u]\!]$.

Mapping properties: *For every property $p :: P_n$ named a is mapped as* $[\![(a,p)]\!] = ([\![a]\!]_{CNAMES},$
   $[\![p]\!])$ *where $[\![p]\!]$ is constructed by substituting every $u \in U$ in p with $[\![u]\!]$.*

Interpreting `rdf:type`: *We say that $[\![\,rdf\!:type\ x = y]\!]$ iff $x = (a,b)$, $y = (p,q)$ and $[\![b]\!] \in [\![q]\!]$.*

Interpreting `rdfs:subClassOf`: *We say that $[\![x\ rdfs\!:subClassOf\ y]\!]$ iff $x = (a,b)$, $y = (p,q)$
   and $[\![b]\!] \subseteq [\![q]\!]$.*

Interpreting names: *The name of an object or a property x is defined as the first coordinate of
   $[\![x]\!]$.*

Interpreting intensional equality: *x is said to be intensionally equal to y (written $x =_{int} y$) iff
   $[\![x]\!] = [\![y]\!]$*

Interpreting schema equality: *x is said to be structurally equal to y, written $x = y$ iff $(a,b) =
   [\![x]\!]$, $(p,q) = [\![y]\!]$ and $b = q$.*

The reason we say that our interpretation of RDF is limited because, as [11], stratified RDF semantics is more restrictive than RDF MT [25].

4. Homomorphisms

This section defines homomorphisms between ontologies. That is, structure preserving mapping between ontologies. We do so in order to analyze various existing definitions of *connections* in the literature in light of structure preserving mappings, and calibrate them against the latter with respect to preserving structure. For example $\mathcal{E}$-connections [12], that introduce subsumption relationships between ontologies do not preserve all structural properties, although commonly used functional mappings such as alignment, translation, *etc.*, preserve some structure. Our definition follows.

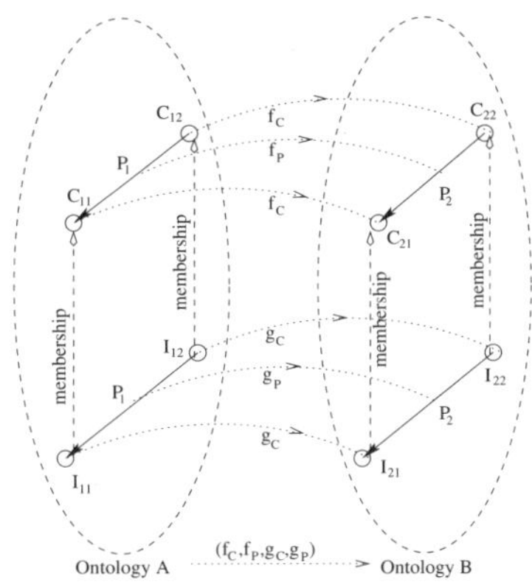

Figure 1. Schema and instance homomorphisms

Definition 4 (Ontological homomorphism).

Schema homomorphism *An ontological schema homomorphism from ontology $A = (\mathcal{C}^A, \mathcal{P}^A,$
   $\mathcal{CN}^A, \mathcal{I}^A, \mathcal{IN}^A)$ to ontology $B = (\mathcal{C}^B, \mathcal{P}^B, \mathcal{CN}^B, \mathcal{I}^B, \mathcal{IN}^B)$ is a pair of mappings
   (f_C, f_P) that satisfy:*

1. $f_C(C_n^A) \subseteq C_n^B$ and
2. $f_P(P_n^A) \subseteq P_n^B$ satisfy
3. If $p^A :: (c^A, c'^A)$ then $f_P(p^A) :: (f_C(c^A), f_C(c'^A))$.

Furthermore, if $\mathcal{CN}(c^a) = \mathcal{CN}(f_C(c^a))$ for every $c^a \in C^A$ and $\mathcal{CN}(p^a) = \mathcal{CN}(f_P(p^a))$ for every $p^a \in P^A$, then we say that it is a name preserving homomorphism, or an intensional schema homomorphism.

Furthermore, if (f_C, f_P) is an intensional schema homomorphism that satisfy $\mathcal{IN}(x^a) = \mathcal{IN}(g_C(x^a))$ for every $x^a \in c^a :: C^A$, then we say that it is a name preserving homomorphism or an intensional instance homomorphism.

Using standard terminology, we say that a schema homomorphism is class-wise, property-wise or completely injective iff f_C, f_P or both f_C and f_P are injective mappings, respectively. An analogous notation is used for surjective homomorphisms. A homomorphism to itself is referred to as an endomorphism. As stated in definition 4, an ontological schema homomorphism maps classes and properties of a source ontology to classes and properties of the target ontology with the same type. Notice that intensional or name preserving homomorphisms are also homomorphisms that preserve the names in addition. As an explanation of the definition of homomorphism, the homomorphism sketched in Figure 1 maps the classes and properties of the source ontology A to those of the the target ontology B using the function f_C, f_P respectively and their instances using functions g_C, g_P respectively., where $f_C(C_{11}) = C_{21}$, $f_C(C_{12}) = C_{22}$, $f_P(P_1) = P_2$, etc., holds.

We now consider equality between ontologies.

Definition 5 (Equality).

Schema equality *Two ontologies $A = (C^A, P^A, \mathcal{CN}^A, \mathcal{I}^A, \mathcal{IN}^A)$ and $B = (C^B, P^B, \mathcal{CN}^B, \mathcal{I}^B, \mathcal{IN}^B)$ are said to be structurally equal - expressed $A \equiv_s B$ - iff there is a schema isomorphism (f_C, f_P) from A to B.*

Name equality *Two structurally equal ontologies $A = (C^A, P^A, \mathcal{CN}^A, \mathcal{I}^A, \mathcal{IN}^A)$ and $B = (C^B, P^B, \mathcal{CN}^B, \mathcal{I}^B, \mathcal{IN}^B)$ through the isomorphism (f_C, f_P) are said to be equal by name - expressed $A \equiv_N B$ - iff for every class $c \in C^A$, $\mathcal{CN}(c) = \mathcal{CN}(f_C(c))$.*

As stated, two ontologies are schema equal if classes and properties between them are isomorphic. If a schema isomorphism between two ontologies preserve names, the they are said to be name equal.

5. Homomorphisms as ontologies

Ontological homomorphisms capture knowledge about similarities between concepts, properties and instances across ontologies within a universe. Consequently, they specify or express relationships between existing ontologies or concepts and properties between them, and therefore can be represented in ontologies [13]. In this section we show how this can be achieved by constructing homomorphisms as ontologies.

Definition 6 (Homomorphic ontology). *Given ontologies $A = (C^A, P^A, \mathcal{CN}^A, \mathcal{I}^A, \mathcal{IN}^A)$, $B = (C^A, P^B, \mathcal{CN}^B, \mathcal{I}^B, \mathcal{IN}^B)$, and an instance homomorphism (f_C, f_P, g_C, g_P) between them, their homomorphic ontology $H^{AB} = (C, P, CN, I, IN)$ is defined as:*

C_0: *The set of primitive concepts is given by $(domain(f_C \cup f_P) \cap (C_{0,A} \cup P_{0,A})) \cup (range(f_C \cup f_P) \cap (C_{0,B} \cup P_{0,B}))$*

P$_0$: *The set of primitive properties $P_0 \subseteq (C_0 \times C_0)$ where*

$$P_0 = \begin{cases} \{p | p \in (f_C \cup f_P) \wedge p \subset C_0 \times C_0\} \\ \cup \{\pi_A | \exists \langle a, \pi_A, b \rangle \in A \wedge a, b \in C_0\} \\ \cup \{\pi_B | \exists \langle a, \pi_B, b \rangle \in B \wedge a, b \in C_0\} \end{cases}$$

C$_{n+1}$: $C_{n+1} \subseteq \mathcal{P}(C_n) \cup P_n$

P$_{n+1}$: $P_{n+1} \subseteq (C_{n+1} \times C_{n+1})$

CN *Schema naming function is defined as CN: $\mathcal{CN}^A \cup \mathcal{CN}^B \cup \{(f_C \cup f_P) \mapsto sameAs, \pi \mapsto related, p :: P_n \ (n > 0) \mapsto samePath\}$*

I: *Instances of classes and properties are provided by the original ontologies, i.e., $x \in c :: C_{0,A} \wedge c :: C_0 \to x \in c :: C_0$. Similarly, B contributes instances for C_0. Property instances are then defined in the standard manner.*

IN: *Instance naming is the union of the respective instance naming function and new property name mappings, i.e., IN: $\mathcal{IN}^A \cup \mathcal{IN}^B \cup \{(g_C \cup g_P) \mapsto sameAs, \pi \mapsto related, p :: P_n \ (n > 0) \mapsto samePath\}$*

Definition 6 precisely captures the knowledge regarding *alignment* of ontologies, as discussed in the literature [19,21,22,24]. Elements of ontology A are mapped to elements in ontology B are cast as type C_0 classes in the homomorphic ontology H^{AB}. Mappings (f_C, f_P) (resp. (g_C, g_P) for instances) constitute the level 0 binary properties between these level 0 concepts. Note that the information that pairs of type C_0 classes in ontology A (resp. B) that are connected through a path π_A (resp. π_B) are connected in H^{AB}. This captures structure from the original ontology into the homomorphic ontology, allowing us to mark the classes as 'related'. Paths need not traverse only through classes that are mapped. Further, similar paths, *i.e.*, π_A, π_B may be related through a binary property, named 'samePath' – a P_1 level property, and so on.

6. Algebraic operators and their properties

For web-based computations; independently developed and maintained ontologies may need to be suitably merged, composed, compared and contrasted in many ways. In this section, we define these operations and show their utility.

The first kind of operations we explore are the set theoretical ones such as union, intersection, complement, *etc.* This is because ontologies consist of classes with relationships among them and elements that populate the aforementioned. However, due to the fact that classes and properties have instances, above operations exist at the schema and instance levels. Another difference is the distinction between extensional and intensional equality, because RDF uses the latter, and set theory uses the former, any set theoretical interpretation of algebraic operations need to find suitable encodings to account for both.

Definition 7 (Set-based intensional operations). *Suppose $A = (\mathcal{C}^A, \mathcal{P}^A, \mathcal{CN}^A, \mathcal{I}^A, \mathcal{IN}^A)$ and $B = (\mathcal{C}^B, \mathcal{P}^B, \mathcal{CN}^B, \mathcal{I}^B, \mathcal{IN}^B)$ are two ontologies. Then define the*

Intensional union of (A $\cup$ B) as:

1. $\mathcal{C}_i^{A \cup B} = \mathcal{C}_i^A \cup \mathcal{C}_i^B$ *for every type i. That is, for every type i, all classes in $\mathcal{C}_i^A$ and $\mathcal{C}_i^B$ are taken together for $\mathcal{C}_i^{A \cup B}$*
2. $\mathcal{P}_i^{A \cup B} = \mathcal{P}_i^A \cup \mathcal{P}_i^B$ *for every type i. That is, for every type i, all properties in $\mathcal{P}_i^A$ or $\mathcal{P}_i^B$ are taken together for $\mathcal{P}_i^{A \cup B}$*
3. $\mathcal{CN}^{A \cup B} = \mathcal{CN}^A \cup \mathcal{CN}^B$. *That is, the names of the classes and properties given from the components A and B are the same taken to be the names assigned in the ontology $A \cup B$.*

4. $x \in c :: C_n^{A \cup B}$ *iff* $x \in c :: C_n^A$ *or* $x \in c :: C_n^B$. *That is, an element belongs to a class* c *in* $C_n^{A \cup B}$ *iff it belongs to a constituent class of* c *in* C_n^A *or* C_n^B.
5. $(x,y) \in p :: P_n^{A \cup B}$ *iff* $(x,y) \in p :: P_n^A$ *or* $(x,y) \in p :: P_n^B$ *That is, a subject object pair* (x,y) *satisfy a property* p *in* $\mathcal{P}_n^{A \cup B}$ *iff* (x,y) *satisfy the same property in either* $\mathcal{P}_n^A$ *or* $\mathcal{P}_n^B$.

Intensional intersection (A ∩ B) as:

1. $C_i^{A \cap B} = C_i^A \cap C_i^B$ *for every type* i. *That is, for every type* i, *all classes common to* C_i^A *and* C_i^B *are in* $C_i^{A \cup B}$
2. $\mathcal{P}_i^{A \cap B} = \mathcal{P}_i^A \cap \mathcal{P}_i^B$ *for every type* i. *That is, for every type* i, *properties common to* $\mathcal{P}_i^A$ *and* $\mathcal{P}_i^B$ *are in* $\mathcal{P}_i^{A \cup B}$.
3. $\mathcal{CN}^{A \cup B} = \mathcal{CN}^A \cap \mathcal{CN}^B$. *That is, the names of the classes and properties given from the components* A *and* B *are taken as the names in* $A \cap B$.
4. $x \in c :: C_n^{A \cap B}$ *iff* $x \in c :: C_n^A$ *and* $x \in c :: C_n^B$. *That is, an element belongs to a class* c *in* $C_n^{A \cap B}$ *iff it belongs to the same class* c *in* C_n^A *and* C_n^B.
5. $(x,y) \in p :: P_n^{A \cup B}$ *iff* $(x,y) \in p :: P_n^A$ *and* $(x,y) \in p :: P_n^B$ *That is, a subject object pair* (x,y) *satisfy a property* p *in* $\mathcal{P}_n^{A \cap B}$ *iff* (x,y) *satisfy the same property in both ontologies* $\mathcal{P}_n^A$ *and* $\mathcal{P}_n^B$.

Definition 7 defines intensional union and intersection. They mimic the basic set theoretical operations of union and intersection, interpreted as a class or a property belonging to the union or the intersection iff they belong to either or both constituents, but with a difference. The difference is that two classes in the constituents are considered the same iff they are name-wise equal according to definition 5. The same holds for properties and instances of classes and properties. This is the reason that step (3) of definition 7 does not create a name clash in using the same name of classes/ properties that exists in both constituent classes/properties. A similar definition can be given for the difference of two ontologies that we omit here. Next we define the notion of substructure among ontologies, that we refer to as a *sub-ontology* as follows.

Definition 8 (Sub-ontologies).

Substructures: *An ontology* $A = (\mathcal{C}^A, \mathcal{P}^A, \mathcal{CN}^A, \mathcal{I}^A, \mathcal{IN}^A)$ *is said to be a schema subontology of an ontology* $B = (\mathcal{C}^B, \mathcal{P}^B, \mathcal{CN}^B, \mathcal{I}^B, \mathcal{IN}^B)$, *denoted by* $A \sqsubseteq_S B$ *iff* $\mathcal{C}^A \subseteq \mathcal{C}^B$, $\mathcal{P}^A \subseteq \mathcal{P}^B$, $\mathcal{CN}^A = \mathcal{CN}^B \upharpoonright \mathcal{C}^A$.
Intensional substructures: *In addition, if* $x \in c :: \mathcal{C}^A$ *implies* $x \in c :: \mathcal{C}^B$ *and* $(x,y) \in p :: \mathcal{P}^A$ *implies* $(x,y) \in p :: \mathcal{P}^B$, *we say that* B *is an intensional sub ontology of* A, *and is denoted* $A \sqsubseteq_I B$.

Clearly, the relations $\sqsubseteq_S$ and $\sqsubseteq_I$ are partial orders. Consequently, any sub ontology of an ontology is itself an ontology, implying that all its paths originating in the sub ontology only reach entities within the sub ontology.

We now use the sub ontologies to define *quotient* ontologies that are obtained by abstracting an entire sub ontology of a a super ontology to a single entity. This concept is the same as the contraction of a graph [9], and has the same meaning in the graph semantics of RDF.

Definition 9 (Quotient ontology). *Suppose* $B = (\mathcal{C}^B, \mathcal{P}^B, \mathcal{CN}^B, \mathcal{I}^B, \mathcal{IN}^B)$ *is a schema sub ontology of* $A = (\mathcal{C}^A, \mathcal{P}^A, \mathcal{CN}^A, \mathcal{I}^A, \mathcal{IN}^A)$. *Then we define the quotient ontology* A/B, *say* (C, P, CN, I, IN) *as follows.*

$$C = \mathcal{C}^A \setminus \mathcal{C}^B \cup \{c^*\} \text{ where } c^* \notin \mathcal{C}^A$$

$$P = \begin{cases} \mathcal{P}^A \setminus \mathcal{P}^B \cup \{p^* :: c_1 \times c^* \mid p :: c_1 \times c_2 \text{ and } c_2 \in \mathcal{C}^B\} \\ \cup\{p^* :: c^* \times c_2 \mid p :: c_1 \times c_2 \text{ and } c_1 \in \mathcal{C}^B\} \end{cases}$$

$$CN(x) = \begin{cases} \mathcal{CN}^A(x) & \text{if } x \in \mathcal{C}^A \setminus \mathcal{C}^B, \\ n \text{ if } x=c^* & \text{where } n \notin \mathcal{CN}(\mathcal{C}^B) \text{ is a new name} \end{cases}$$

The intuition captured in definition 9 is that the entire sub ontology B is shrunk to a single entity in the quotient ontology, and therefore the properties that relates any entity in $\mathcal{C}^A \setminus \mathcal{C}^B$ relates to this single (shrunk) entity in the quotient ontology A/B. This construction directly mirrors the contraction operation in graphs, and captures the intent of quotients they are defined in algebra or topology.

We now follow this trend and define *products* of ontologies, where the intent is to invert the contraction induced by taking a quotient, and therefore *expand* the original ontology. Towards that end taking a quotient resulted in two things: first, all entities in the sub ontology were identified as one *new* entity, and all properties that involved those entities were now associated with this *new* entity. Thus, to reverse the effect of a quotient, we select a point - called a pivot point - that we substitute with an ontology and re-direct all properties associated with the selected pivot point to all other entities of the substituting ontology. Our formal definition follows.

Definition 10 (Pivoted product of ontologies). *Suppose $A = (C^A, P^A, CN^A, I^A, IN^A)$ and $B = (C^B, P^B, CN^B, I^B, IN^B)$ are schema ontologies and $c^* \in C^A$ a class in A. Then we define the product of A and B pivoted around c^*, say (C, P, CN, I, IN), denoted by $A\lfloor c^* \rfloor B$ as follows.*

$$C = C^A \setminus \{c^*\} \cup C^B$$

$$P = \begin{cases} P^A \setminus \{p \in P^A \mid domain(p) = c^* \ \vee \ range(p) = c^*\} \cup \\ \bigcup\{p_{c'} \mid \exists p \in P^A, domain(p) = c^*, domain(p_{c'}) = c' \text{ and } c' \in C^B\} \cup \\ \bigcup\{p_{c'} \mid \exists p \in P^A, range(p) = c^*, range(p_{c'}) = c' \text{ and } c' \in C^B\} \end{cases}$$

$$CN(x) = \begin{cases} CN^B(x) \text{ if } x \in P^B \\ CN^A(x) \text{ if } x \in P^A, dom(x) \neq c^*, range(x) \neq c^* \\ n_{c'} \text{ where } n_{c'} \text{ is a new name for } c' \in C^B \end{cases}$$

Thus, the pivoted cartesian product of two ontologies collects the entities *sans* the pivot point of its two constituents as the entities of the pivot product. Then it replaces every property that has the pivot point with a set of *new* relations that relates the entity that is not the pivot point to every entity in the second ontology. The objective here is to ensure that the pivoted product produces the maximal possible properties between the entities that are not the pivot and the elements replacing the pivot, stated and proved next.

Lemma 6.1 (Quotient-Product theorem). *Suppose $B = (C^B, P^B, CN^B, I^B, IN^B)$ is a schema sub ontology of the ontology $A = (C^A, P^A, CN^A, I^A, IN^A)$, $A/B = (C, P, CN, I, IN)$ is their quotient and $c \in C$ is some entity in C, $c \notin C^A$. Then $A \sqsubseteq_S (A/B)\lfloor c \rfloor B$ holds.*

Proof Sketch: See [17].

Next we define merge operation to construct a new ontology from the image and co-image of a homomorphism. Due to space constraints we restrict to intensional merge operation using fused elements, defined next (see [17] for extensional merge).

Definition 11 (Fused Elements). *Suppose $A = (C^A, P^A, CN^A, I^A, IN^A)$ and $B = (C^B, P^B, CN^B, I^B, IN^B)$ are schema ontologies and (f_C, f_P, g_C, g_P) be a morphism from A to B. Then for every pair of classes, properties or instances related through the homomorphism we say that they are intensionally equal up to the homomorphism, i.e., $c::C^A =_{mrph} f_C(c)$, $p::P^A =_{mrph} f_P(p)$, etc. (In the following, we omit subscript of = symbol to reduce clutter). Each component of the pair can be mapped to a fused set as follows.*

Fused Class F_C**:** If $c::C^A = f_C(c) = d::C^B$, then $F_C(c) = F_C(d) = \{c,d\}$ and $CN(F_C(c)) = CN(F_C(d)) = \{CN^A(c), CN^B(d)\}$

Fused Property F_P**:** If $p::P^A = f_C(p) = q::P^B$, then $F_P(c) = F_P(d) = \{p,q\}$ and $CN(F_P(p)) = CN(F_P(q)) = \{CN^A(p), CN^B(q)\}$

Fused Instance F_I**:** If $x \in c :: C^A$ (resp $p :: P^A$) $= g_C(c)$ (resp $g_P(p)$)$= y \in d :: C^B$ (resp $q :: P^B$), then $F_I(x) = F_I(y) = \{x,y\}$ and $CN(F_I(x)) = CN(F_I(y)) = \{CN^A(x), CN^B(y)\}$

Definition 12 (Intensional merge).

Schema Merge *Suppose $A = (C^A, P^A, CN^A, I^A, IN^A)$ and $B = (C^B, P^B, CN^B, I^B, IN^B)$ are schema ontologies and (f_C, f_P) be a schema morphism from A to B. Then we define the intensional schema merge of A and B, say (C, P, CN, I, IN), denoted $A \oplus B$, as follows:*

$$C_1 = \{c :: C^A | \exists d :: C^B, d = f_C(c)\}$$

$$C = (C^A \cup C^B \setminus C_1)) \cup F_C(C_1)$$

$$P_1 = \{p | p = c_1 \times c_2, (c_1 \vee c_2 \in dom(f_C) \cup ran(f_C))\}$$

$$P_2 = \{p | \begin{cases} p = c_1 \times c_2^* \wedge \exists p = c_1 \times c_2 \wedge c_2 \in dom(f_C) \cup ran(f_C) \text{ and } c_2^* = F_C(c_2) \\ p = c_1^* \times c_2 \wedge \exists p = c_1 \times c_2 \wedge c_1 \in dom(f_C) \cup ran(f_C) \text{ and } c_1^* = F_C(c_1) \\ p = c_1^* \times c_2^* \wedge \exists p = c_1 \times c_2 \wedge c_1, c_2 \in dom(f_C) \cup ran(f_C) \text{ and } c_1^* = F_C(c_1) \\ \quad c_2^* = F_C(c_2) \end{cases}$$

$$P_3 = \{p | p \in (dom(f_P) \cup ran(f_P))\}$$

$$P_4 = \{F_P(p) | p \in (dom(f_P) \cup ran(f_P))\}$$

$$P = (P^A \cup P^B \cup P_2 \cup P_4) \setminus (P_1 \cup P_3)$$

$$CN(x) = \begin{cases} CN^A(x) \text{ if } x \in C^A \wedge x \notin dom(f_C) \\ CN^B(x) \text{ if } x \in C^B \wedge x \notin ran(f_C) \\ CN^A(x) \text{ if } x \in P^A \wedge x \notin dom(f_P) \\ CN^B(x) \text{ if } x \in P^B \wedge x \notin ran(f_P) \\ CN(F_C(x)) \text{ if } x \in (dom(f_C) \cup ran(f_C)) \\ CN(F_P(x)) \text{ if } x \in (dom(f_P) \cup ran(f_P)) \end{cases}$$

$$I = \begin{cases} x \in c :: C^A \text{ if } x \in c :: C^A \wedge x \notin dom(f_C) \\ x \in c :: C^B \text{ if } x \in c :: C^B \wedge x \notin ran(f_C) \\ x \in F(c) \text{ if } x \in c :: C^A \wedge x \in dom(f_C) \\ x \in F(c) \text{ if } x \in c :: C^B \wedge x \in ran(f_C) \end{cases}$$

$$IN = IN$$

Definition 12 captures the cases where homomorphisms or mappings are used to identify 'similar' elements across ontologies and then fused together to yield a single ontology. Essentially, this involves replacing a class in either ontology by its fused class, a property by its fused property and an instance by its fused instance. Also, all the properties that were earlier connecting classes that are now fused have to be reconnected to the fused class in the merged ontology. The above definition achieves this by identifying those properties and replacing them.

6.1. Algebraic properties

In this section we explore simple algebraic properties of the operations introduced in the previous section.

Lemma 6.2. *For all ontologies A, B and C $\in$ U, the following statements hold:*

1. *commutative union:* $A \cup B = B \cup A$
2. *associative union:* $A \cup (B \cup C) = (A \cup B) \cup C$
3. *commutative intersection:* $A \cap B = B \cap A$, *associative intersection:* $A \cap (B \cap C) = (A \cap B) \cap C$
4. *distributive union:* $A \cup (B \cap C) = (A \cup B) \cap (A \cup C)$, *distributive intersection:* $A \cap (B \cup C) = (A \cap B) \cup (A \cap C)$
5. *Absorption:* $A \cap (A \cup B) = A$, $A \cup (A \cap B) = A$
6. *If homomorphisms are injective then,* $A \oplus B = B \oplus A$ *and* $A \otimes B = B \otimes A$ *hold.*
7. *Idempotence:* $A \oplus A = A$, $A \otimes A = A$
8. *Subontology: If* $A \sqsubseteq B$ *then* $A \oplus C \sqsubseteq B \oplus C$ *and If* $A \sqsubseteq B$ *then* $A \otimes C \sqsubseteq B \otimes C$

Proof Sketch: See [17]

7. Conclusion

In this paper we develop an algebra for composing ontologies. With our basic operations, like, intensional union/intersection, quotients, intensional/extensional merge, pivot products, *etc.*, readers can reduce any operation in the literature to the combination of these basic operations. In addition, we formally define countably reified RDF statements through a recursive countable type representation for reified statements that assigns them layered semantics – more general than the stratified semantics presented by Pan and Horrocks [25]. Thus we enhance the state of the art in formalizing RDF. It is our hope that these contributions will help remove ambiguities that currently exist in the field.

Acknowledgments

Our sincerest thanks to the (anonymous) reviewers who provided extremely helpful insights. We greatly appreciate their help.

References

[1] P. Aczel. *Non-well-founded sets*, volume 14 of *Lecture Notes*. CSLI, 1988. (See page 11).

[2] J. Barwise and J. Seligman. *Information flow: the logic of distributed systems*. Cambridge University Press, 1997.

[3] T. Bench-Capon and G. Malcolm. Semantics for interoperability. In V. Marik, W. Retscitzegger, and O. Stepankova, editors, *Proceedings of DEXA 2003*, number 2736 in Lecture Notes in Computer Science, pages 703–712. Springer: Berlin.

[4]   Y. Breitbart, P. L. Olson, and G. R. Thompson. Database integration in a distributed heterogeneous database system. In *Proceedings of the Second International Conference on Data Engineering, February 5-7, 1986, Los Angeles, California, USA*, pages 301–310. IEEE Computer Society, 1986.

[5]   D. Brickley and R. Guha. Resource Description Framework (RDF) Schema Specification 1.0: RDF schema. W3C workding Draft, 2003.

[6]   T. Burners-Lee, J. Hendler, and O. Lassila. The semantic web. *Scientific American*, May 2001.

[7]   P. P. Chen. The Entity-Relationship Model - Toward a Unified View of Data. *ACM Transactions on Database Systems (TODS)*, 1(1):9–36, 1976.

[8]   U. Dayal and H.-Y. Hwang. View definition and generalization for database integration in a multi-database system. *IEEE Transactions on Software Engineering*, SE(10):628–645, Nov 1984.

[9]   R. Diestel. *Graph Theory*. Springer-Varlag, 1997. Graduate texts in Mathamatics 173.

[10] J. Geller, Y. Perl, P.Cannata, A. Sheth, and E. Neuhold. A case study of structural integration. In *Proceedings of the 1st Intl. Conference on Information and Knowledge Systems*, Baltimore, MD, November 1992.

[11] B. C. Grau. A possible simplification of the semantic web architecture. In *WWW 2004*, pages 17–22. ACM, May 2004.

[12] B. C. Grau, B. Parsia, and E. Sirin. Working with multiple ontologies on the semantic web. In *Proceedings of the Third Internatonal Semantic Web Conference (ISWC2004). Volume 3298 Lecture Notes in Computer Science.*, 2004.

[13] T. Gruber. What is an ontology. available at http://www-ksl.stanford.edu/kst/what-is-an-ontology.html.

[14] P. Hayes. RDF semantics. W3C workding Draft, February 2003.

[15] Y. Kalfoglou and M. Schorlemmer. IF-Map: an ontology mapping method based on information flow theory. *Journal on Data Semantics*, 1(1):98–127, Oct. 2003.

[16] Y. Kalfoglou and M. Schorlemmer. Ontology mapping: the state of the art. *The Knowledge Engineering Review*, 18(1):1–31, 2003.

[17] S. Kaushik, C. Farkas, D. Wijesekera, and P. Ammann. An algebra for composing ontologies. Technical Report ISE-TR-06-07, ISE Department, George Mason University, July 2006.

[18] R. Kent. The IFF foundation for ontological knowledge organization. *Knowledge organization and classification in international information retrieval*, 37(1), 2003.

[19] M. Klein. Combining and relating ontologies: an analysis of problems and solutions. In A. Gomez-Perez, M. Gruninger, H. Stuckenschmidt, and M. Uschold, editors, *Workshop on Ontologies and Information Sharing, IJCAI'01*, Seattle, USA, Aug. 4–5, 2001.

[20] K. J. Kunen. *Set Theory*. North Holland, Reprint edition, December 1983.

[21] D. L. McGuinness, R. Fikes, J. P. Rice, and S. Wilder. An environment for merging and testing large ontologies. In *KR2000: Principles of Knowledge representation and reasoning*, pages 483–493, 2000.

[22] P. Mitra and G. Wiederhold. *An Ontology-Composition Algebra*, pages 93–117. International Handbooks on Information Systems. Springer-Verlag, handbook on ontologies edition, 2004.

[23] W. Y. Mok. A comparative study of various nested normal forms. *Knowledge and Data Engineering*, 14(2):369–385, 2002.

[24] N. F. Noy, M. A. Musen, and E. Shortliffe. PROMPT: algorithm and tool for automated ontology merging and alignment. In *17th National conference on artificial intelligence (AAAI-2000)*, 2000.

[25] J. Pan and I. Horrocks. RDFS(FA) and RDF MT: Two semantics for RDFS. In *2003 International Semantic Web Conference (ISWC 2003)*, pages 30–46, 2003.

[26] C. Parent and S. Spaccapietra. Issues and approaches of database integration. *Communications of the ACM*, 41(5es):166–178, May 1998.

[27] A. Sheth and J. Larson. Federated database systems for managing distributed, heterogeneous, and autonomous databases. *ACM Computing Surveys*, 22(3):183–236, September 1990.

Formalizing Ontology Alignment and its Operations with Category Theory[1]

Antoine ZIMMERMANN [a], Markus KRÖTZSCH [b], Jérôme EUZENAT [a] and
Pascal HITZLER [b]

[a] *INRIA Rhône-Alpes, 655 avenue de l'Europe, 38330 Montbonnot (France)*
[b] *AIFB, Universität Karlsruhe, D-76128 Karlsruhe (Germany)*

Abstract. An ontology alignment is the expression of relations between different
ontologies. In order to view alignments independently from the language expressing ontologies and from the techniques used for finding the alignments, we use a
category-theoretical model in which ontologies are the objects. We introduce a categorical structure, called V-alignment, made of a pair of morphisms with a common domain having the ontologies as codomain. This structure serves to design
an algebra that describes formally what are ontology merging, alignment composition, union and intersection using categorical constructions. This enables combining alignments of various provenance. Although the desirable properties of this
algebra make such abstract manipulation of V-alignments very simple, it is practically not well fitted for expressing complex alignments: expressing subsumption
between entities of two different ontologies demands the definition of non-standard
categories of ontologies. We consider two approaches to solve this problem. The
first one extends the notion of V-alignments to a more complex structure called
W-alignments: a formalization of alignments relying on "bridge axioms." The second one relies on an elaborate concrete category of ontologies that offers high expressive power. We show that these two extensions have different advantages that
may be exploited in different contexts (*viz.*, merging, composing, joining or meeting): the first one efficiently processes ontology merging thanks to the possible use
of categorical institution theory, while the second one benefits from the simplicity
of the algebra of V-alignments.

Keywords. Ontology alignment, category theory

Introduction

In its most general form, the term "ontology alignment" can refer to almost any formal
description of the (semantic) relationship between ontologies. A more restricted conception of the term is used in surveys [6,23] or alignment API [7], that conceive alignments
as pairs of elements of the ontologies[2], together with information on the type of the relation and the confidence in its correctness. An alignment is thus given a set-theoretic defi-

---

[1]This work has been partly supported by the European Knowledge Web network of excellence (IST-2004-
507482), by the German Ministry for Education and research (BMBF) under the SmartWeb project, and by the
European Commission under contract IST-2003-506826 SEKT.

[2]We speak of "elements of an ontology" to refer to arbitrary semantic entities of a given ontology language,
e.g., concepts, relations, or instances.

nition as a set of correspondences. Though perfectly acceptable in applications, it has the disadvantage of using entities—something local—as the basis of ontology alignment—something global.

Here we present a complementary approach that treats alignments as first class citizens where locally defined elements are not needed. Our main goal is to build a formal theory of ontology alignments and their associated operations that is independent of the internal representation language. To achieve this objective, we start from a category-theoretic definition of ontology alignment that was already sketched in [24,4,15,12,14]: a pair of *morphisms** with a common domain. However, none of these works provided in-depth investigations of this abstract formulation of the alignment problem.

Based on this related work, we build up a framework around the notion of *V-alignments*, with an abstract definition of the merge of two ontologies and an algebra allowing composition, intersection and union of alignments (§2). Then, disposing of a well-behaved, language-independent infrastructure, concrete alignments must be embedded into it as an example of the generality of our approach. A critical issue is the ability to express non-symmetrical relations (*e.g.*, a class in one ontology being subsumed by another class in another ontology) within such theoretical framework. No solution is given to this problem in all cited papers. The difficulty does not reside in the theoretical ability to express such relations, but in the manner we should instantiate the abstract formulation. In §3, we propose two solutions to this problem:

- define a more complex structure for the definition of category theoretic alignments, while reusing already existing categories of ontologies;
- design a category—or rather a class of categories—with elaborate morphisms enabling the expression of complex, non-symmetrical relations.

The former approach, presented in §4, is a re-construction of the framework with the new notion of *W-alignments*. The latter solution presents a home-made category of ontologies that increases the expressivity of morphisms, in comparison to previously published categories of ontologies (§5). Both approaches have interesting advantages and constraining drawbacks that we consider in §6.

1. Related work

In [24], a similar categorical approach is mentioned but not rigorously formalized. [4] uses morphisms of algebraic specifications[3] to define morphisms between ontologies and say a relation (an alignment in their sense) between ontologies O_1 and O_2 consists of an ontology O and a pair of morphisms $\chi_1 : O \rightarrow O_1$ and $\chi_2 : O \rightarrow O_2$. This is precisely the definition of V-alignment given below, but it does not provide any means of representing complex alignments as we do. In [15], a category-theoretic approach using the information flow theory of Barwise and Seligman [3] is given, with no concrete representation of alignments. Kent also gives an intuition of the bridge ontology idea in [16] but he does not formalize it within category theory and only describes the merge of two ontologies. Information Flow is also the basis of an implemented system called IF-

---

*Words marked with a * are category-theoretic terms. Their definition can be found in, *e.g.*, [20,1,19].

[3] Algebraic specifications are closely related to specifications in institution theory, which we often refer to, without using it explicitly.

Map [13] designed for automated ontology mapping, but they do not have a categorical representation for rich alignments. [12] gives a concrete example of a representation of an alignment in category theory, but since it is so simplistic, it is hard to see the generality of the approach. Joseph Goguen's work on *institution** theory [10], especially [9,8], advertises the use of *colimits** for ontology integration. This theory, though not sufficient to model complex alignments with a V-alignment structure, can be used as a grounding for our so-called W-alignments. More details on the categorical approach are given in a survey on ontology mapping [14]. Finally, ontology alignment and schema matching are closely related. In particular, [5] describes a schema matching algebra that we partially generalize with our approach. See [21,14,23] for surveys on ontology and schema mappings in general.

2. Simple alignments

This part presents a categorical formulation of various operations employed when manipulating different ontologies and alignments. These operations are ontology merging, alignment composition, alignment union and intersection. They are presented in more details in [11]. They are but mere application of common categorical constructions to the abstract alignment structure and will only be sketched here.

Remark: In the remainder, some familiarity with category theory would be useful. For more details on the basics of category theory, see [20] for an easy yet good introduction. [1,19] give something more elaborated.

2.1. Category-theoretic alignments

As said before, an ontology alignment is a description of the relationship between two ontologies. Category theory generalizes the set-theoretic notion of relation, and offers a definition for a (generalized) relation between two arbitrary objects in a *category**. An alignment thus corresponds to the diagram given below, where *objects** O_1, O_2 and A are ontologies and π_1 and π_2 are ontology *morphisms**. In categorical terminology, such diagram is called a *span*.

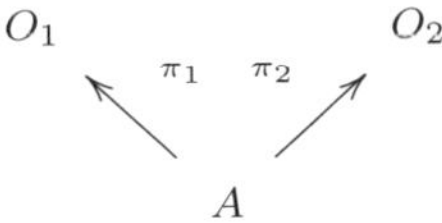

When the objects O_1, O_2, A are ontologies and π_1, π_2 are ontology morphisms, we call this structure a V-alignment due to the shape of the associated diagram and in order not to confuse it with the informal notion of alignment. The very same definition is used in [4,12,14] with different names (ontology relation, ontology alignment, ontology articulation).

2.2. Merging with V-alignments

Once a V-alignment between two ontologies is known, it is desirable to integrate the aligned ontologies into a single ontology. This operation, called *ontology merging*, aims at uniting heterogeneous specifications into a larger, more precise one which allows more information sharing. The categorical formalization of V-alignments allows for a simple description of the merge, and this can be described in terms of the category-theoretic *pushout** construction. [15,13,12] give more details about this construction, and the present paper also discusses this point in §3.

2.3. Algebra for V-alignments

The need for ontology alignment naturally arises when information from many ontologies is relevant to a given task. However, since the task of constructing alignments is not an easy one and can hardly be accomplished in a fully automatic fashion, it is reasonable to store and reuse known alignments. The purpose of this section is to introduce a sound algebra of V-alignments that allows for essential operations that enable us to compose, join, and intersect alignments.

These operations are application of general operations over categorical *spans*, so interested readers shall refer to [19] for their general properties. They are also more detailed in [11]. This is why here we present them briefly.

2.3.1. Composing alignments

Composition is a central operation for the reuse of alignments: if we have alignments between ontologies O_1 and O_2, and between O_2 and O_3, then it should be possible to obtain an alignment of O_1 and O_3. The definition is the same as the composition of spans in category theory (see [19]). So it is obtained by the use of the categorical construction called *pullback**.

The following *commutative diagram** shows two V-alignments $\langle A, \alpha_1, \alpha_2 \rangle$ and $\langle B, \beta_2, \beta_3 \rangle$. The composition is the alignment $\langle C, \alpha_1 \circ f_A, \beta_3 \circ f_B \rangle$, where $\langle C, f_A, f_B \rangle$ is the pullback of α_2 and β_2.

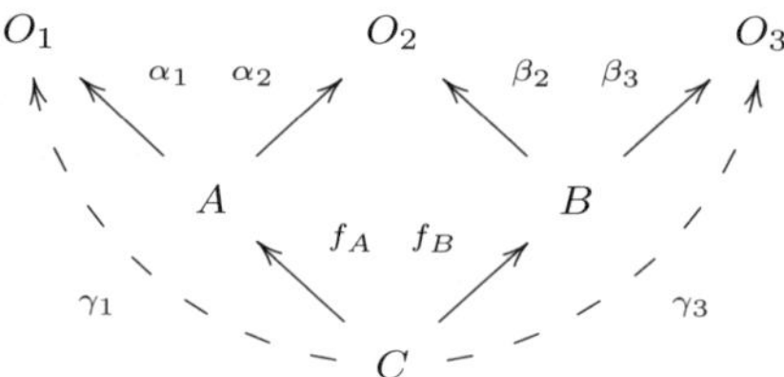

Composition is associative and identity exists, which confirms that the proposed operation is well-behaved as a composition of alignments.

2.3.2. Intersection and union of alignments

Intersection gives the mutually agreed correspondences of two alignments. Union gathers all asserted relations specified in two alignments. These operations are indeed very useful in the context of the Semantic Web since they allow a modularization of alignments. In this respect, one can give a partial alignment with only part of the relevant correspondences and expect to retrieve more on the Web when needed.

Figure 1 **a.** gives the diagram of intersected alignments $\langle A, f_1, f_2 \rangle$ and $\langle B, g_1, g_2 \rangle$. Object C together with morphisms k_A, k_B, h_1 and h_2 make the *limit** of the diagram composed of the two alignments. The resulting alignment is $\langle C, h_1, h_2 \rangle$.

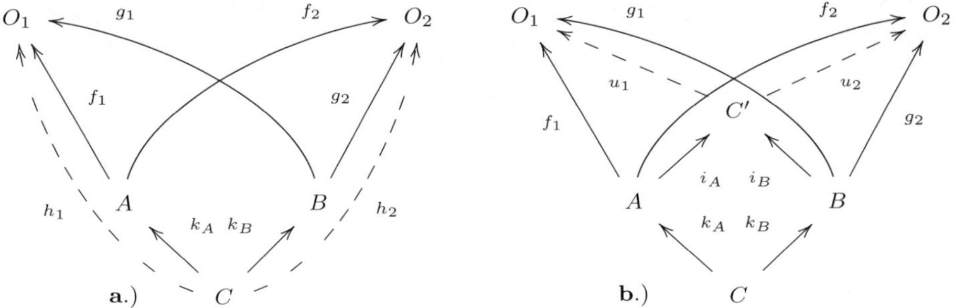

Figure 1. Intersection and union of alignments.

Union is defined via intersection. In order to unify two alignments, one has to know what is common to both of them. Then the union is the disjoint union of this common part and the non-common parts. In Figure 1 **b.**, this is done by way of a categorical *pushout*[*] of $\langle k_A, k_B \rangle$. Morphisms u_1 (resp. u_2) is obtained by *factorizing*[*] f_1 (resp. f_2) through i_A (resp. i_B). So informally, we say that union is the pushout of intersection.

These operations are, as expected, commutative and associative.

This algebra concisely formalizes operations combining two or more alignments provided by different alignment algorithms or experts, either by composing (when there is no alignment between two related ontologies), joining (union of alignments: if both algorithms take into account different aspects of ontologies) or meeting them (intersection of alignments: if on the contrary they should agree for considering correspondences to be correct).

3. Concretizing V-alignments

In order to apply the previous framework to real cases, it is necessary to instantiate it with concrete categories. For instance, one can consider the most basic way to describe relationships between two ontologies: identifying those elements which represent the same semantic entities. This can be adequately described by a binary relation between the sets of elements, that is, consider morphisms as functions.

In the literature, the most adapted categories of ontologies are found in institution theory [10], where *specifications*[*] (*i.e.*, ontologies in our terms) are mapped with truth-preserving functions. Notably the language OWL can be described as an institution [17]. Unfortunately, a pair of functions (even structure-preserving), is only adequate to express equivalence of entities. In many cases, though, the two ontologies to align were designed in such way that some concepts do not have their equivalent in the other ontology, although several concepts are closely related. For instance, one may find that concept *Woman* in ontology O_1 is a subclass of *Person* in ontology O_2. In this case, the merge should contain concepts *Person* and *Woman* with a subsumption relation between them (see Figure 2). However, assuming this is the result of a pushout operation, it is not clear what the alignment should be.

A pair of functions cannot lead to such a pushout. So the problem of expressing complex alignments requires investigation, and we therefore propose the following solutions to work out this issue:

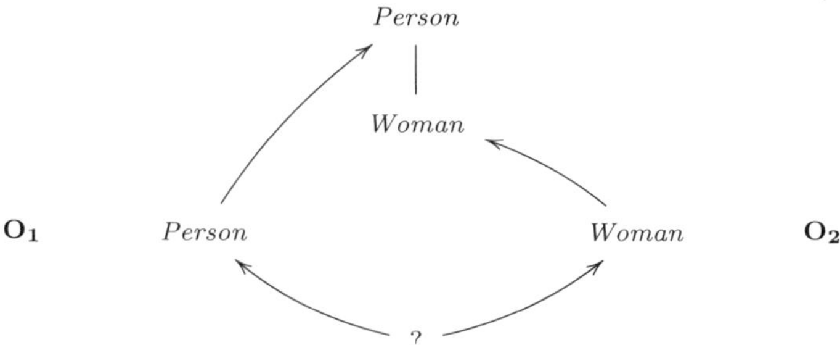

Figure 2. Expressing non-symmetrical relations with V-alignments.

1. Find more complex categories, where objects still are ontologies, but with morphisms able to express other relations;
2. Keep the category simple, and complexify the definition of an alignment using more elaborate structure;
3. Change the definition of the merge, for example by using different type of *colimit**.

The last item implies that the operations defined in §2 are to be abandoned. Since they are built on well established work, we will not challenge this idea. We first discuss item (2) in §4, where a new alignment structure is defined on top of the previous one and leads to an upgrade of the associated infrastructure. Item (1) is considered in §5, which defines a new category of ontologies where morphisms are family of relations instead of functions.

4. W-alignments

In this section, we combine existing material into an extended formulation of alignments that we will suggestively name W-alignments. It corresponds to a categorization of the notion of bridge axioms. Merging and composing are defined in this framework, but the algebra suffers from defects.

4.1. Categorical formulation of bridge axioms

Let us start with the example from §3: consider two OWL-ontologies O_1 and O_2 that contain the atomic concepts *Woman* and *Person*, respectively. Assuming that none of the ontologies contains both concepts, it is not possible to express the intended subsumption of *Woman* and *Person* with V-alignments in a common category of ontologies where concepts are mapped to equivalent concepts.

In such cases, the relation is nonetheless expressible in the ontology language but cannot be represented with the vocabulary of any of the two ontologies. So the idea is to externalize the assertion "*Woman* $\sqsubseteq$ *Person*" in another ontology. These external assertions are called *bridge axioms* (described from a logical point of view in *e.g.*, [18]). As observed in the introduction, alignments described as sets of bridge axioms give a local description of the correspondences between two ontologies. In order to conform to the categorical paradigm, we must first give a globalized definition of these axioms.

We do this by representing bridge axioms in form of an additional *bridge ontology*. The fact that certain concepts of the aligned ontologies occur within the bridge ontology is captured by V-alignments between the bridge and each of the aligned ontologies. We thus arrive at the following definition:

Definition 4.1 (W-alignment) *A* W-alignment *between two ontologies O_1 and O_2 is a triple $\langle B, A_1, A_2 \rangle$ where B is a* bridge ontology *and A_1 and A_2 are two V-alignments between O_1 and B and between O_2 and B, respectively.*

The following diagram depicts the situation, which also serves to illustrate why the above terminology was chosen. Note also that we do not impose any restrictions on the bridge ontology B. In particular B could contain axioms that are related to neither O_1 nor O_2.

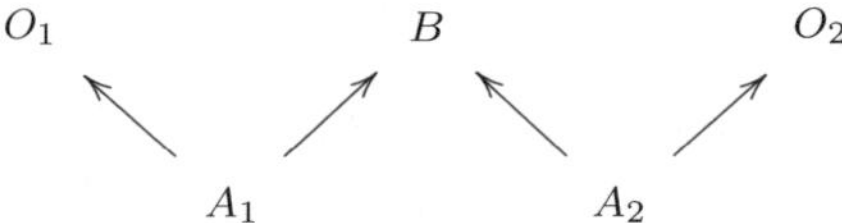

Based on this categorical formulation, here we give a suitable definition for merging of ontologies that are aligned with a W-alignment.

Definition 4.2 *Given two ontologies O_1 and O_2 and a W-alignment between them, the merge of O_1 and O_2 is defined to be the* colimit* *of the alignment diagram. More explicitly, this colimit M is computed by successive pushouts as in Figure 3.*

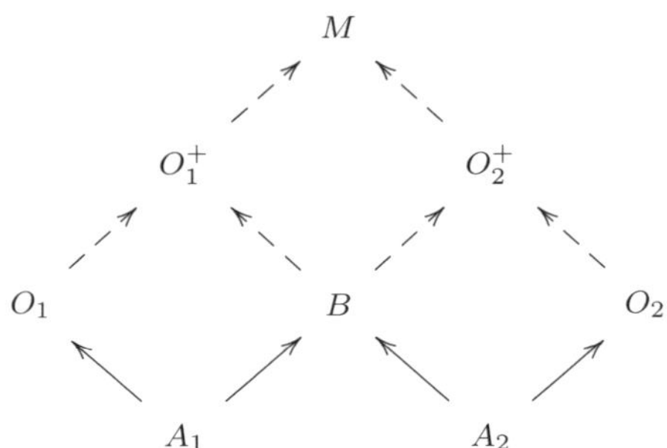

Figure 3. Merging with W-alignments.

Intuitively, O_1^+ and O_2^+ represent the original ontologies O_1 and O_2 extended with axioms and elements that enable us to express their alignment as a simple V-alignment. This idea is not entirely new, and in [16] O_1^+ and O_2^+ have been called *portal ontologies*, referring to their specific role in making the knowledge of each of the ontologies accessible to the other one.

Since this merge is obtained by successive pushouts, this operation for W-alignments is in the same class of complexity as merging with V-alignments.

Example 4.3 *A more demonstrative example consists in expressing the semantic connection between a n-ary relation and its reification with only binary relations. For instance, property "sells" relates a seller to a buyer and to an object (3-ary relation) in the first ontology. The second ontology has a class "Sale" that has three properties "hasSeller", "hasBuyer" and "hasObject". The bridge ontology will contain the axiom* $R(x, y, z) \Leftrightarrow \exists t S(t) \wedge r_1(t, x) \wedge r_2(t, y) \wedge r_3(t, z)$. *The first V-alignment matches* R *with "sells" and the second matches* S, r_1, r_2, r_3 *with "Sale", "hasSeller", "hasBuyer", "hasObject", respectively. The merge will contain both the relation and its reification, together with the axiom.*

4.2. Composing W-alignments

A full-featured algebra for W-alignments, along the lines of §2.3, would be complicated and unintuitive. However, we can easily describe a useful operation for composing W-alignments.

Definition 4.4 *Consider ontologies* O_1, O_2, *and* O_3 *with W-alignments as in Figure 4. The composition of the W-alignments of Figure 4 is described as follows:*

- *The bridge ontology* B *is obtained as the merge of the bridge ontologies* B_1 *and* B_2, *according to the W-alignment* $\langle O_2, A_2, A_3 \rangle$,
- *the V-alignment of* O_1 *and* B *is* $\langle A_1, f_1, b_1 \circ g_1 \rangle$, *and*
- *the V-alignment of* O_3 *and* B *is* $\langle A_4, g_4, b_3 \circ f_4 \rangle$.

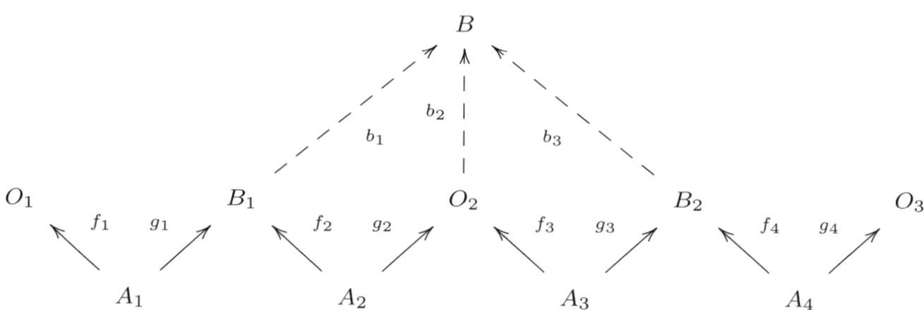

Figure 4. Composing W-alignments.

This definition formalizes the fact that we know there is a relation of O_1 and O_3, given by means of an intermediate ontology O_2. In order to describe this with a single bridge ontology, we integrate both of the involved bridges with O_2. This construction has the advantage that it faithfully captures all information that is available about the composed alignment.

However, there is a major problem with the above definition: by deriving bridge axioms from the ontologies B_1, B_2, and O_2, we incorporate all their embedded information into the new bridge ontology. But this set of bridge axioms might be highly redundant for the given purpose: it may involve axioms of O_2 that are neither related to O_1 nor to O_3. Another pathological case is when O_2 is the disjoint union of O_1 and O_3, while O_1 and O_3 are not related at all. In this case, we would rather wish the composed bridge ontology to be empty, instead of containing the whole information of all involved ontologies.

Overcoming this difficulty at the concrete level relates to the problem of finding a minimal non-redundant set of axioms that yields a given set of desired (or relevant) conclusions. Unfortunately, logical languages tend to be highly non-local in this respect.

Other operations like intersection and union suffer from the same kind of deficiency: there is neither canonical nor intuitive definition that satisfies the notion they are supposed to cover. We therefore omit their mentioning in this paper, and prefer to focus on a different approach that relies on a newly proposed category of ontology.

5. Improved category of ontologies

The other possible solution consists in using elaborate morphisms capable of expressing complex alignments with V-alignments alone. We describe here an enhanced category of ontologies, that we name $\mathfrak{Ont}^+$, which has ontologies as objects and particularly elaborate morphisms.

Definition 5.1 (Morphisms) *A morphism $f : O_1 \rightarrow O_2$ in $\mathfrak{Ont}^+$ is a set of triples $\langle e_1, e_2, R \rangle$ such that:*

- *e_1 and e_2 are syntactic entities (concepts, relations, individuals, etc.) from ontologies O_1 and O_2 respectively,*
- *R denotes a relationship that holds between e_1 and e_2 (e.g., subsumption, equivalence, temporal relations, etc.). The set of available relations will be denoted $\mathcal{R}$.*

This category is defined modulo the set of available relations $\mathcal{R}$. So, there is a category of ontologies with relations such as *subClass*, *superClass*, *equivalentClass*, *disjointClass*, *partiallyOverlappingClass*. Besides, the set of relations *startsString*, *endsString*, *startedByString*, etc. forms another category. Moreover, the types of entities that can appear in the triples is very dependent on the kind of relations in $\mathcal{R}$.

Example 5.2 *In order to envision the possibilities of such morphisms, we can give the following examples of correspondences, were the syntactical entities are compound entities:* $\langle A_1 \sqcup B_1, C_2 \sqcap D_2, subClass \rangle$ *or* $\langle \text{concat}(\text{name}, \text{surname}), \text{fullname}, eqString \rangle$.

The categorical composition operation associated to these morphisms is thus defined:

Definition 5.3 (Composition) *Let $f : O_1 \rightarrow O_2$ and $g : O_2 \rightarrow O_3$ be two morphisms in $\mathfrak{Ont}^+$. The composition of f and g, noted $g \circ f$ is the set of triples $\langle e_1, e_3, R \rangle$ such that there exist e_2, R_1, R_2 such that $\langle e_1, e_2, R_1 \rangle \in f$, $\langle e_2, e_3, R_2 \rangle \in g$ and $R = \phi(R_1, R_2)$ with $\phi : \mathcal{R} \times \mathcal{R} \rightarrow \mathcal{R}$ given by a composition table, such as the one given in Example 5.4.*

The small figure below gives the intuition of this definition: if an entity e_2 is related to entities in ontologies O_1 and O_3, then there should be some kind of relation between e_1 and e_3. This relation depends on the relationship between e_2 and the other entities, and is expressed by the function ϕ. It corresponds to the composition of relational constraints, as found in temporal [2] or spatial algebras [22].

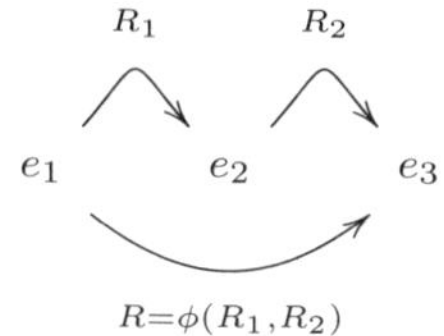

$$R = \phi(R_1, R_2)$$

Example 5.4 *In the following composition table, $=$ is equality, $\subset$ is strict inclusion, $\supset$ is strict containment, $\perp$ is disjointness and $\lozenge$ is overlapping with partial disjointness.*

$\mathbf{R_1}$ \ $\mathbf{R_2}$	$=$	$\subset$	$\supset$	$\perp$	$\lozenge$
$=$	$\{=\}$	$\{\subset\}$	$\{\supset\}$	$\{\perp\}$	$\{\lozenge\}$
$\subset$	$\{\subset\}$	$\{\subset\}$	$\{=, \subset, \supset, \perp, \lozenge\}$	$\{\perp\}$	$\{\subset, \perp, \lozenge\}$
$\supset$	$\{\supset\}$	$\{=, \subset, \supset, \lozenge\}$	$\{\supset\}$	$\{\supset, \perp, \lozenge\}$	$\{\supset, \lozenge\}$
$\perp$	$\{\perp\}$	$\{\subset, \perp, \lozenge\}$	$\{\perp\}$	$\{=, \subset, \supset, \perp, \lozenge\}$	$\{\subset, \perp, \lozenge\}$
$\lozenge$	$\{\lozenge\}$	$\{\subset, \lozenge\}$	$\{\supset, \perp, \lozenge\}$	$\{\supset, \perp, \lozenge\}$	$\{=, \subset, \supset, \perp, \lozenge\}$

Table 1. Table of composition for Example 5.4.

Property 5.5 *The composition is associative iff ϕ is associative.*

The associativity of ϕ is not a severe constraint because all usual relations in description logics, temporal and spatial reasoning have associative composition tables. Moreover, in order to have the identity morphism, $\mathcal{R}$ must contain equality. Given these somewhat reasonable constraints, $\mathfrak{Ont}^+$-morphisms together with ontologies as objects form a category. Relations in $\mathcal{R}$ are not restricted to the ontology language. So, for example, two OWL[4] ontologies can be related with temporal or spatial relations, as well as fuzzy ones.

This category has strong advantages with regard to its expressivity and the elegance of the V-alignment algebra that can still be applied here. Additionally, independently from V-alignments, they are, alone, composable and tunable. However, they have a major drawback: pushouts does not generally coincide with the expected merge. In next section, we further discuss advantages, drawbacks and potential interest of both approaches.

6. Discussion

Both of the two solutions proposed have pros and cons. On the one hand, the representation of W-alignments is less intuitive as V-alignments and demands a prior understanding of V-alignments. Moreover, manipulating W-alignments necessitates a reconstruction of the infrastructure available with V-alignments. This infrastructure has a defective algebra: no identity alignment, no canonical union and intersection. Another counter-intuitive property of W-alignments is the capability to use axioms in the bridge ontology that do not relate to any of the aligned ontologies. These drawbacks make W-alignments inappropriate to build new alignments out of existing ones, so they do not fit for highly

---

[4]http://www.w3.org/TR/owl/

distributed semantic applications. On the other hand, W-alignments can express very rich alignments, such as relations between a n-ary property and its reification. Moreover, it is built upon the same principle as simple alignment: colimits serve for ontology integration. This is a strong advantage because, for instance, the category of OWL ontologies is cocomplete [17], *i.e.*, all pushouts exist in this category. So they are well-suited for the merging of ontologies.

Working at the concrete category level leads to different and complementary results. Certain correspondences are hard to express (*e.g.*, reification of n-ary relation), but the enhanced category has the advantage of separating the alignment language—which appears in the morphisms—from the ontology language—which appears in the objects. As long as the relations verify loose constraints, the complexity of relations can be arbitrarily increased, offering possibilities like fuzzy relations or other uncommon relations, without interfering with the ontology language. Besides, they benefit from the algebra described in §2, which makes them easy to manipulate at an abstract level. But when the category gets more complex, allowing expression of non-symmetrical relations, the merge does not always coincide with the pushout. However, the alignment algebra is adequate for abstracting modular ontology alignment applications thanks to the operation of composition, intersection and union. Finally, complicated structure similar to W-alignments could also be constructed on top of them.

7. Conclusion

Finding suitable categorical representations of alignments is the ultimate goal of our work.

To address this issue, the present paper (1) provides a formalization of several operations on ontologies and ontology alignments relying on simple category-theoretic constructions that is consistent with previous published category-theoretic representation of ontology alignment and integration; (2) shows that this simple formalization does not allow to account for expressive alignments; (3) proposes two attempts to repair this, which can represent complex semantic relationships within category theory: (3.a) a categorical formulation of the notion of bridge axioms and (3.b) a proposal for a concrete category of ontologies improving the expressivity of formerly proposed categories. In both cases, we study the repercussion of each contribution to the original algebra mentioned in (1) above.

Both approaches show the lack of expressivity in existing work with respect to semantic relationship. They offer partial solutions to the problem. We presented the advantages of each solution. Though both approaches have interesting benefits, we are leaning toward the second one because we think it can lead to a more general theory of ontology alignment and coordination. Of course, the morphisms we presented have to be connected to the semantics of the ontologies. Our future investigation aims at providing an abstract model theory with such complex morphisms, along the line of institution theory which encompasses both syntax and semantics. Doing this, we will be able to design a legitimate semantics for ontology alignment and distributed systems, while so far, no common agreement exists on such a semantics.

References

[1]   Jiří Adámek, Horst Herrlich, and George E. Strecker. *Abstract and Concrete Categories (The Joy of Cats)*. web published, 2004.

[2]   James F. Allen. Maintaining knowledge about temporal intervals. *Communications of the ACM*, 26(11):832–843, 1983.

[3]   John Barwise and Jerry Seligman. *Information flow: the logic of distributed systems*. Number 44. Cambridge University Press, Cambridge, United Kingdom, 1997.

[4]   Trevor J. M. Bench-Capon and Grant Malcolm. Formalising ontologies and their relations. In *Proc. 10th Database and Expert Systems Applications (DEXA'99)*, pages 250–259, 1999.

[5]   Philip A. Bernstein. Applying model management to classical meta data problems. In *Proc. First Biennial Conference on Innovative Data Systems Research (CIDR'03)*, January 2003.

[6]   Paolo Bouquet, Jérôme Euzenat, Enrico Franconi, Luciano Serafini, Giorgos Stamou, and Sergio Tessaris. Specification of a common framework for characterizing alignment. Deliverable 2.2.1, Knowledge Web NoE, August 2004.

[7]   Jérôme Euzenat. An API for ontology alignment. In *Proc. Third International Semantic Web Conference (ISWC)*, volume 3298 of *LNCS*, pages 698–712, Hiroshima, Japan, 2004. Springer-Verlag GmbH.

[8]   Joseph A. Goguen. Information integration in institutions. Paper for Jon Barwise memorial volume.

[9]   Joseph A. Goguen. Data, schema and ontology integration. In *Workshop on Combination of Logics: Theory and Applications (CombLog'04)*, July 2004.

[10]   Joseph A. Goguen and Rod M. Burstall. Institutions: abstract model theory for specification and programming. *Journal of the ACM*, 39(1):95–146, 1992.

[11]   Pascal Hitzler, Jérôme Euzenat, Markus Krötzsch, Luciano Serafini, Heiner Stuckenschmidt, Holger Wache, and Antoine Zimmermann. Integrated view and comparison of alignment semantics. Deliverable, Knowledge Web NoE, August 2005.

[12]   Pascal Hitzler, Markus Krötzsch, Marc Ehrig, and York Sure. What is ontology merging? - a category-theoretic perspective using pushouts. In *Proc. First International Workshop on Contexts and Ontologies: Theory, Practice and Applications (C&O)*, pages 104–107. AAAI Press, July 2005.

[13]   Yannis Kalfoglou and Marco Schorlemmer. Information flow based ontology mapping. In *On the Move to Meaningful Internet Systems 2002: CoopIS, DOA, and ODBASE : Confederated International Conferences 2002*, volume 2519 of *LNCS*, pages 1132–1151. Springer-Verlag GmbH, 2002.

[14]   Yannis Kalfoglou and Marco Schorlemmer. Ontology mapping: The state of the art. In *Semantic Interoperability and Integration*, number 04391 in Dagstuhl Seminar Proceedings, Dagstuhl, Germany, 2005. Internationales Begegnungs und Forschungszentrum.

[15]   Robert E. Kent. The information flow foundation for conceptual knowledge organization. In *Proc. 6th International Conference of the International Society for Knowledge Organization (ISKO)*, 2000.

[16]   Robert E. Kent. The IFF foundation for ontological knowledge organization. *Cataloging and Classification Quarterly*, 37(1):187–203, 2003.

[17]   Dorel Lucanu. A logical foundation for the OWL languages. In *Proc. First International Symposium on Leveraging Applications of Formal Methods (ISoLA)*, 2004.

[18]   Christopher Menzel. Basic semantic integration. In *Semantic Interoperability and Integration*, number 04391 in Dagstuhl Seminar Proceedings. Internationales Begegnungs und Forschungszentrum, 2005.

[19]   Maria Cristina Pedicchio and Walter Tholen, editors. *Categorical Foundations: Special Topics in Order, Topology, Algebra, and Sheaf Theory*, volume 97 of *Encyclopedia of Mathematics and its Applications*. Cambridge University Press, 2004.

[20]   Benjamin C. Pierce. *Basic Category Theory for Computer Scientists*. Foundations of Computing. The MIT Press, Cambridge, MA, 1991.

[21]   Erhard Rahm and Philip A. Bernstein. A survey of approaches for automatic schema matching. *The Very Large Data Base Journal*, 10(4):334–350, December 2001.

[22]   David A. Randell, Zhan Cui, and Anthony Cohn. A spatial logic based on regions and connection. In *Proc. Third International Conference on Principles of Knowledge Representation and Reasoning (KR'92)*, pages 165–176. Morgan Kaufmann, 1992.

[23]   Pavel Shvaiko and Jérôme Euzenat. A survey of schema-based matching approaches. *Journal on Data Semantics*, 4:146–171, 2005.

[24]   Danladi Verheijen, Gio Wiederhold, Jan Jannink, and Srinivasan Pichai. Encapsulation and composition of ontologies. In *Proc. 15th National Conference on Artificial Intelligence (AAAI'98)*, July 1998.

Formal Ontology in Information Systems
B. Bennett and C. Fellbaum (Eds.)
IOS Press, 2006

Linking FrameNet to the Suggested Upper Merged Ontology

Jan SCHEFFCZYK [a,1] Adam PEASE [b] Michael ELLSWORTH [a]

[a] *International Computer Science Institute*
1947 Center St., Suite 600, Berkeley, CA, 94704
{jan,infinity}@icsi.berkeley.edu
[b] *Articulate Software*
420 College Ave., Angwin, CA 94508
apease@articulatesoftware.com

Abstract. Deductive reasoning with natural language requires combining lexical resources with the world knowledge provided by ontologies. In this paper we describe the connection of FrameNet – a lexicon for English – to the Suggested Upper Merged Ontology (SUMO). We align FrameNet Semantic Types (ST) with SUMO classes, which we express in SUO-KIF, the language of SUMO. Based on this general-domain alignment, we have developed a semi-automatic, domain-specific approach for linking FrameNet Frame Elements (FE) to SUMO classes that is based on typical fillers of FEs in a particular domain. We thus provide restricted, ontology-based types on the fillers of FEs. We are confident that our basic work can improve semantic parsing and ontology lexicalization.

Keywords. FrameNet, SUMO, Ontologies, Lexicons

Introduction

Deductive reasoning with natural language requires combining semantically rich lexical resources with world knowledge provided by ontologies and databases. Concrete applications include semantic parsing and question answering. While great progress has been made in natural-language retrieval tasks, using natural language to support deep, automatic reasoning has progressed more slowly. The lack of large lexicons, large formal ontologies and linguistic Frames, and most importantly, interrelationships among these products is a major obstacle. Ontologies like the Suggested Upper Merged Ontology [2] (SUMO) [1] or Cyc [2] can be used for reasoning but do not have adequate linguistic components. Linguistic resources like WordNet [3] or FrameNet [3] [4] provide means for syntactic and semantic analysis of natural language but are not intended for general reasoning. Given the maturity of these resources, combining them should result in significant benefits to natural-language processing (NLP).

---

[1] Part of this work was supported by the German Academic Exchange Service.
[2] For more information and downloads see http://www.ontologyportal.org.
[3] For more information and downloads see http://framenet.icsi.berkeley.edu.

There have not, to our knowledge, been other mapping efforts like ours to integrate SUMO with FrameNet and WordNet. Other efforts have combined formal ontologies with linguistic resources (mainly WordNet) but in each case lose some of the power of the ontology or linguistic resource. For Omega [5] – a lightweight lexical merging effort – the authors state 'Omega contains no formal concept definitions . . .'. Cyc [2] has been mapped to a small portion of WordNet and has not released their results. DOLCE [6] has also mapped to an even smaller portion of WordNet.

SUMO, WordNet, and FrameNet all have their inherent weaknesses and strengths: SUMO lacks lexical information but formally defines concepts in the world. WordNet lacks formal definitions of concepts but has very good lexical coverage. FrameNet has lower lexical coverage than WordNet but has a uniquely rich level of semantic detail, especially predicate-argument structure. Part of the semantics of FrameNet is defined in OWL DL [7], but lacks the axiomatization of SUMO. Although this is beyond the scope of this paper, a promising next step would be the integration of all three products.

Our primary goal is to provide an improved foundation for NLP tasks, e.g., semantic parsing and ontology lexicalization. We proceed by combining lexical Frame semantics [8] (as provided by FrameNet) and formal world knowledge (as provided by SUMO). Frame semantics encodes language as interrelated semantic Frames (types of predication) with Frame Element (FE) arguments. SUMO is a large formal ontology coded in first-order logic. A secondary goal is the improvement of both resources as a result of comparing and linking them.

Compared to other lexicon-ontology bindings [9,10], our bindings offer a range of advantages due to specific characteristics of FrameNet and SUMO: FrameNet, in contrast to WordNet, models semantic and syntactic valences and exemplifies them with many high-quality annotations. Frame semantics naturally provides cross-linguistic abstraction and normalization of paraphrases. We have chosen SUMO as the formal ontology to map to for a number of reasons. Unlike Cyc and DOLCE [6], SUMO has been mapped to all of WordNet. SUMO is much larger than DOLCE. Unlike Cyc, all of SUMO and its domain ontologies are open source.

In this paper, we report on the first steps toward our goals. We aligned the FrameNet Semantic Types (STs) with SUMO, thus asserting SUMO axioms on STs for free. Based on this general-domain alignment, we have developed a semi-automatic approach to link FrameNet Frame Elements (FEs) to SUMO classes, taking advantage of pre-existing mappings from WordNet to SUMO [9]. This allows us to develop restricted, domain-specific, and ontology-based types on the fillers of FEs, which should help semantic parsers.

This paper proceeds as follows: We introduce FrameNet in Sect. 1 and SUMO in Sect. 2. We present our design decisions for linking FrameNet to SUMO in Sect. 3. Sect. 4 shows how we aligned the FrameNet STs with SUMO for the general domain. In Sect. 5 we illustrate our semi-automatic approach to linking FrameNet FEs to SUMO in a domain-specific way. In Sect. 6 we show how SUMO and FrameNet themselves have benefited and discuss further impacts of our work. Sect. 7 concludes.

1. The FrameNet Lexicon

FrameNet [4] is a lexical resource for English, based on Frame semantics [8]. A semantic Frame (hereafter simply Frame) represents a set of concepts associated with an event or

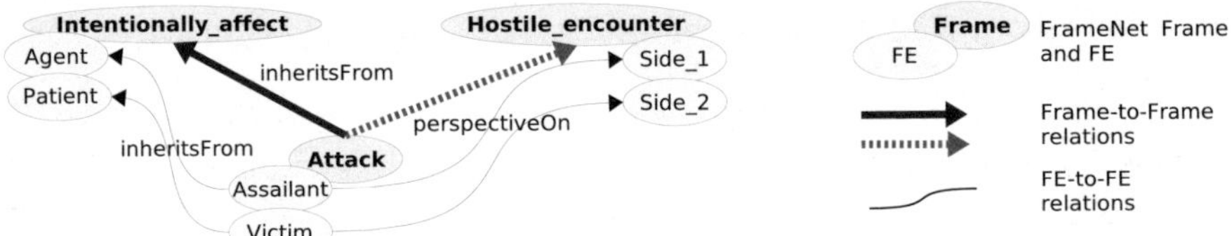

Figure 1. Abridged example Frame Attack and some connected Frames.

a state, ranging from simple (Arriving, Attack) to complex (Revenge, Criminal_process). For each Frame, a set of roles (or arguments), called Frame Elements (FEs), is defined, about 10 per Frame. We say that a word can *evoke* a Frame, and its syntactic dependents can *fill* the FE slots. Semantic relations between Frames are captured in Frame relations, each with corresponding FE-to-FE mappings. FrameNet currently contains more than 790 Frames, covering more than 10,000 Lexical Units (LUs) = word senses; these are supported by more than 135,000 FrameNet-annotated example sentences used as training data for Frame and FE recognizing systems [11,12].

Fig. 1 shows a portion of the Attack Frame, which *inherits* from the more general Frame Intentionally_affect. In addition, Attack has a *perspectiveOn* relation to the Frame Hostile_encounter. The FEs of the Attack Frame are mapped to the corresponding FEs in the related Frames. For example, the FE Assailant in the Attack Frame is mapped to the FE Agent in the Intentionally_act Frame.

2. The Suggested Upper Merged Ontology

SUMO [1] is an open source, formal ontology of about 1000 terms and 4000 definitional statements. It is provided in first-order logic (SUO-KIF), and also translated into OWL. It is now in its 75th version, having undergone five years of development, review by a community of hundreds of people, and application in expert reasoning and linguistics. The ontology has been subjected to formal verification with an automated theorem prover and has been extended with a number of domain ontologies, also open-source, that together number some 20,000 terms and 60,000 axioms. SUMO has also been mapped to the WordNet lexicon of 100,000 noun, verb, adjective, and adverb word senses [9], which not only acts as a check on coverage and completeness, but also provides a basis for its use in NLP tasks. Most importantly, SUMO employs *rules*. These formal descriptions make explicit the meaning of terms in the ontology, unlike a simple taxonomy, or controlled keyword list. SUMO has an open-source ontology management system called Sigma [13], which incorporates a version of the Vampire theorem prover [14].

3. Toward Linking FrameNet to SUMO

FrameNet and SUMO are both relatively mature resources, but their strengths must be combined in order to reach their full potential for NLP. In particular, NLP applications using FrameNet require knowledge about the possible fillers for FEs. For example, a semantic Frame parser needs to know whether a certain piece of text (or a named entity) might be a proper filler for an FE – so it will check whether the *filler type* of the FE is compatible with the type of the named entity. Therefore, we want to provide Semantic Types (STs) as constraints on fillers of FEs.

FrameNet has defined about 40 STs that are ordered by a type hierarchy. For example, the Assailant FE in the Attack Frame has the ST Sentient. Compared to SUMO classes, STs are much shallower, have fewer relations between them (only subtyping), and lack axiomatization. Therefore, we want FrameNet to refer to SUMO classes directly as STs, thereby realizing a number of advantages almost for free:

- AI applications can use the knowledge provided by SUMO.
- We can provide domain-specific STs by bindings to SUMO domain ontologies.
- From the SUMO axioms, parts of FrameNet gain axiomatization.
- FrameNet supplements SUMO's ontological knowledge with a Frame-based lexicon and annotated sentences.

We have expressed all bindings from FrameNet to SUMO in SUO-KIF, permitting the use of SUMO tools without any intermediate steps. Also, we have used SUO-KIF to define axioms and ad-hoc classes if no equivalent class could be found in SUMO. In our experience this is often needed because FrameNet STs are motivated by lexicographic concerns, rather than the knowledge engineering concerns that drive ontologies. Thus, our bindings are more flexible than the SUMO-WordNet mappings, which include only instance, equivalent, and subsuming relations to SUMO classes (or their complements).

In order to simplify the linking of FEs and to preserve the FE hierarchy, we have taken the following approach:

1. We have aligned STs with SUMO classes by hand, which asserts SUMO axioms on STs. Moreover, we gain an initial indication of how FEs that have STs associated should be linked in a hierarchy-preserving way (Sect. 4).
2. We have developed a semi-automatic approach to linking FEs to SUMO classes. For an FE f, we take into account how f was annotated in a particular domain, how the STs of f were linked to SUMO, and how other FEs that are connected to f (and their STs) were linked to SUMO (Sect. 5).

For each ST we want to find high-level SUMO classes that express its meaning across all domains. For FEs, however, our links should express the most specific meaning possible for a particular domain, so that we get a very constrained meaning, which is most useful for semantic parsing. Moreover, our links to SUMO express the literal meaning of FE fillers. In natural language almost everything can be construed as something completely different.[4]

4. Linking Semantic Types to SUMO

Fig. 2 shows the alignment of a portion of the FrameNet ST hierarchy to SUMO.[5] The SUMO class hierarchy is slightly different from the ST hierarchy because it follows knowledge engineering principles rather than linguistic principles. For example, SUMO

---

[4]The obvious cases involve metaphor and metonymy [15], but many other more subtle cases exist. For example, almost everything is interpretable as a literal container – people, houses, planets, most artifacts – since they are physically existent, three-dimensional entities with an interior that can be filled.

[5]Other STs – including Event and State – are linked straightforwardly to SUMO.

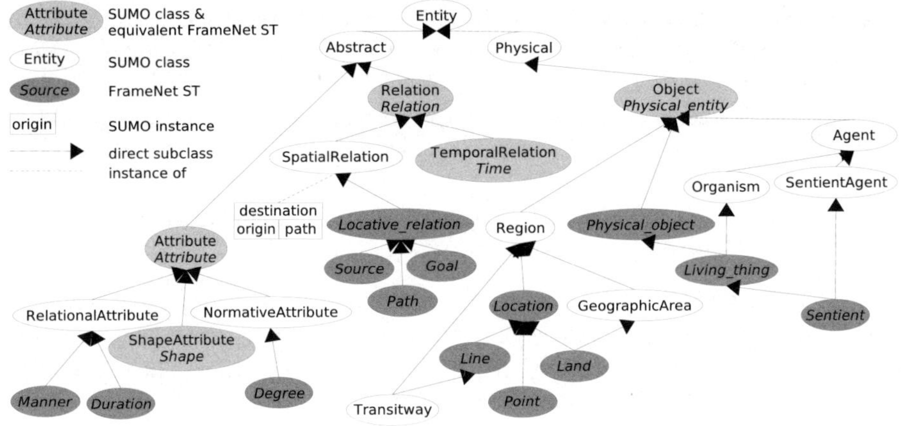

Figure 2. Bindings of a portion of the FrameNet STs to SUMO

distinguishes between physical and abstract entities. Also, the level of detail is different between SUMO classes and STs.

FrameNet has defined STs that best cover the most general and common FE fillers. STs are not intended to correspond to WordNet synsets or SUMO classes, but many of the STs we formed do, in fact, correspond naturally. The most important STs that do *not* correspond to SUMO classes are Source, Path, and Goal. We use Source to mark FEs whose fillers relate themes of processes to their origins. Similarly, Goal relates to destination relations and Path to path relations. We distinguish between Locative_relations and Locations; Locations are often used as the range of Locative_relations. Relations in the Source and Goal class have Point as their range. Relations in the Path class have Line as their range. Point and Line do *not* mean geometric figures but locations construable as geometric figures.

Our alignment preserves the hierarchies of both SUMO and STs. The bindings are, however, of various kinds:

- Some STs have equivalent SUMO classes, such as Shape, Time, Relation, or Physical_entity. In such cases, we identify the ST with its corresponding SUMO class.
- Some STs, e.g., Sentient, correspond to the intersection of multiple SUMO classes. A Sentient being is something alive that is able to reason. In SUMO a SentientAgent does not need to be alive; e.g., organizations are also SentientAgents. So we use multiple inheritance to SentientAgent and Organism.
- Some STs, such as Line, have a broader meaning than the corresponding SUMO classes. Line is an arbitrary linear region, whereas Transitway is used for transportation. Therefore, we make Transitway a subclass of Line.
- For some STs we find classes in SUMO with a broader meaning, but instances of them are closely related. For example, for the ST *classes* Source, Path, and Goal, we find closely related relation *instances* like origin, path, and destination. (We show axiomatization of these facts below.)

If we do not find an equivalent SUMO class for an ST, we refine its semantics, i.e., we express in SUO-KIF what distinguishes the ST from its SUMO superclass. Also, we define relations between STs themselves.

For example, a Locative_relation r is a SpatialRelation relating at least two physical objects:

$$r : \texttt{Locative\_relation} \Rightarrow \texttt{domain}(r, 1, \texttt{Physical}) \ \wedge \ \texttt{domain}(r, 2, \texttt{Physical})$$

Given a Goal relation rel as filler of an FE of some process p, we can conclude the following: The relation rel relates some patient thm of the Motion process p to its destination $dest$, which also is a filler of rel. The destination $dest$ itself will be of type Point. Finally, rel invokes a Locative_relation lr at the end of p:

$$
\begin{array}{l}
rel : \texttt{Goal} \ \wedge \\
\texttt{feFiller}(p, rel)
\end{array}
\ \Rightarrow \
\begin{array}{l}
\exists \ dest, thm, lr \ \bullet \\
p : \texttt{Motion} \ \wedge \ dest : \texttt{Point} \ \wedge \ lr : \texttt{Locative\_relation} \ \wedge \\
\texttt{feFiller}(lr, dest) \ \wedge \ \texttt{feFiller}(lr, thm) \ \wedge \\
lr(thm, dest, (\texttt{EndFn}(\texttt{WhenFn} \ p))) \ \wedge \\
rel(thm, dest, p) \ \wedge \\
\texttt{patient}(p, thm) \ \wedge \ \texttt{destination}(p, dest) \ \wedge
\end{array}
$$

The semantics of Source and Path relations are expressed similarly. Notice that these fairly complex alignments between FrameNet and SUMO do not point out flaws or errors. Rather, they reveal modeling choices taken due to different methodologies.

The ST Manner describes the manner attribute of a process. Therefore, given such an attribute for some process, the manner of the process must be defined:

$$attr : \texttt{Manner} \ \wedge \ \texttt{attribute}(attr, pr) \ \Rightarrow \ \exists m \bullet \texttt{manner}(pr, m)$$

In FrameNet we distinguish countable entities (Physical_object) from non-countable entities (Material). Therefore, for every Physical_object, a Counting process has the capability to count the Physical_object and vice versa. Similarly, for every Material, a Measuring process has the capability to measure the Material and vice versa.

$$
\begin{array}{lcl}
o : \texttt{Physical\_object} & \Leftrightarrow & \texttt{capability}(\texttt{Counting}, \texttt{patient}, o) \\
m : \texttt{Material} & \Leftrightarrow & \texttt{capability}(\texttt{Measuring}, \texttt{patient}, m)
\end{array}
$$

5. Linking Frame Elements to SUMO

In this section we introduce and demonstrate our semi-automatic approach to linking FEs to SUMO classes, which is based on our general-domain alignment of STs with SUMO. Since the links from FEs to SUMO are highly domain-specific we will end up with many different bindings. Therefore, we want to automatize the linking process as much as possible.

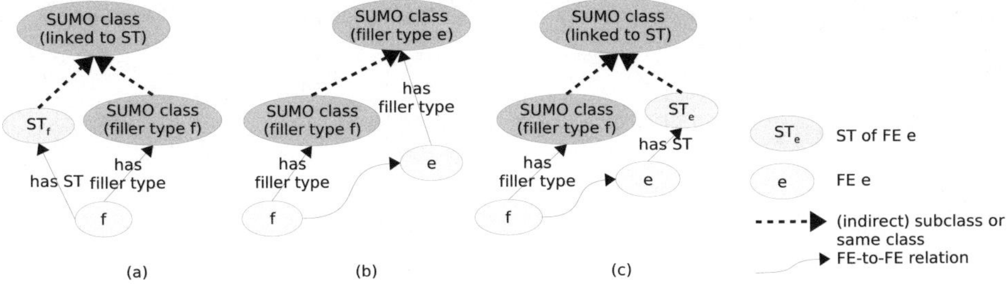

Figure 3. Conditions for linking FEs in a hierarchy-preserving way.

5.1. A Semi-automatic Approach

Our approach finds candidate classes in SUMO (or any of its domain ontologies) that a particular FE can be linked to, respecting both hierarchy preservation and the use of the FE in a particular domain. The filler type of an FE is represented as a SUMO class. For restricting the possible SUMO superclasses, we use the following automated procedure, which is similar to the WordNet detour to FrameNet [16]:

1. Determine all fillers of the FE from annotations of a particular domain.
2. Look up all WordNet synsets of the headword[6] of each filler.
3. Determine SUMO classes associated with the WordNet synsets from the SUMO-WordNet mappings.

Finally, we manually analyze *frequency* (how often a SUMO class is evoked by the fillers) and *coverage* (how many fillers a SUMO class covers), both of which should be high for "good" candidate classes.

We subject these candidate classes to the following conditions in order to preserve the associations of FEs to STs and the hierarchy of FE mappings in FrameNet:

- If an FE has associated STs then the filler type should be a subclass[7] of each of the classes the STs are linked to (see Fig. 3a).
- If in FrameNet an FE f is a subtype of another FE e, then the SUMO classes associated with f should be subclasses of the SUMO classes associated with e; i.e., f is more restricted than e (see Fig. 3b).
- If in FrameNet an FE f is a subtype of another FE e, which has STs, linked to some SUMO classes cs then f should be linked to subclasses of cs (see Fig. 3c).

If there are conflicts (at least) one of the following conditions must hold: (1) There is a metonymic or metaphorical mapping from the typical fillers in this particular domain to a subclass of the FE's ST. (2) We have found an error in the FE annotations, the ST-SUMO alignment, the association of an FE to an ST, the FrameNet mappings between FEs, the SUMO-WordNet mapping, or WordNet itself.

For a particular domain, we suggest beginning by linking those FEs that are most frequently annotated.

---

[6]For this we employ the minipar parser, which claims to have a 88% precision and 80% recall. See http://www.cs.umanitoba.ca/~lindek/minipar.htm.

[7]By "subclass" we mean the reflexive transitive closure of the subclass relation.

Filler	Headword	Frequency		SUMO Class or Instance	Frequency
it	it	3		Nation	4
its	its	3		UnitedStates : Nation	4
Iraqi	Iraqi	2		ViolentContest	4
Iran	Iran	2		SubjectiveAssessmentAttribute	4
terrorist	terrorist	2		GroupOfPeople	2
the US	US	2		SocialRole	2
Iraq	Iraq	1		Human	2
Al-Qaida	Al-Qaida	1		Group	2
his forces	force	1		FunctionQuantity	2
by Iraq	Iraq	1		NormativeAttribute	2
US	US	1		EthnicGroup	2
U.S.	U.S.	1		MilitaryUnit	2
Chadian forces	force	1		Newton	2
				TerroristOrganization	1
(a)				(b)	

Table 1. (a) Fillers of the Assailant FE; (b) SUMO classes associated to corresponding WordNet synsets.

5.2. Example

We exemplify our approach with the Assailant FE of the Attack Frame, comparing attestations in a special domain with those in the general domain. For the domain of Weapons of Mass Destruction (WMD) and terrorism, we examine sentences from the Nuclear Threat Initiative Country Profiles[8] and a separate smaller corpus with 21 text annotations overall for the Assailant FE. For the general domain, we examine the main corpus of FrameNet examples, which come from the (open-domain) British National Corpus[9] with 27 annotations for the Assailant FE.

Fillers for the Assailant FE in the example domain-specific corpora, their headwords, and frequencies are shown in Tab. 1.a. Tab. 1.b shows the SUMO classes associated with WordNet synsets of these headwords. Some fuzziness results from the headword "terrorist" whose synset is mapped to SocialRole. For our experiments we added SUMO-WordNet bindings from synsets like terrorist to the SUMO class Human to reflect the intended interpretation of SocialRole in SUMO. Additional fuzziness is introduced by words like "force" with many synsets. Note, e.g., "Newton" as a unit of measure in Tab. 1.b.

Fig. 4 shows part of the SUMO class hierarchy for the Assailant FE, which we generate from Tab. 1.b and the corresponding table for the general domain. Each SUMO class has two associated numbers, showing the percentage of fillers that are covered by this class and its subclasses: The first number is for our example domain; the second number is for the general domain. For example, the class Agent (and its subclasses) cover 71% of all fillers of the Assailant FE in our example domain and 52% of all fillers in the general domain.[10]

First, we discuss the results for our example domain. Good candidate classes are low-level classes with coverage equal to the coverage of their superclasses. Whenever we

---

[8]See http://www.nti.org/e_research/profiles/.
[9]See http://www.natcorp.ox.ac.uk/.
[10]Due to pronouns and parsing errors we do not find SUMO classes for all FE fillers.

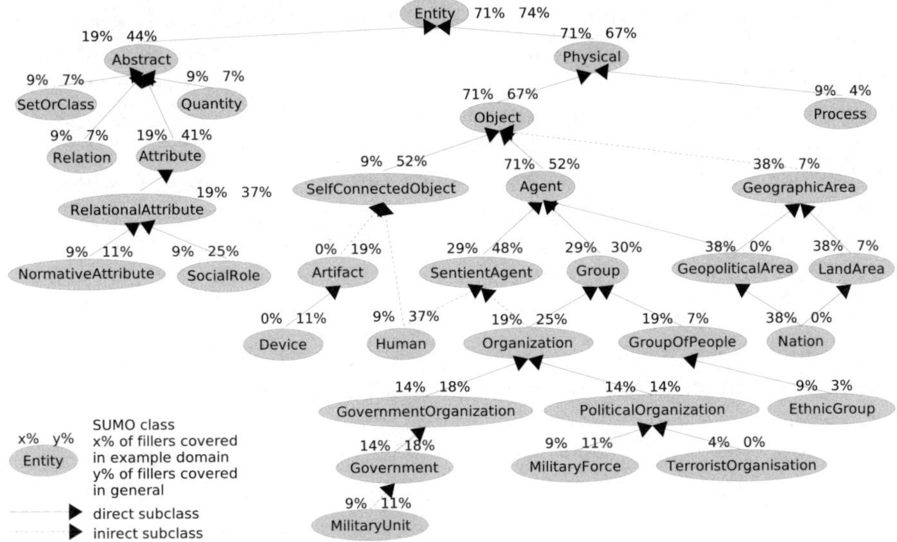

Figure 4. Generated partial SUMO class hierarchy for the Assailant FE

hypothesize a superclass S of such a candidate class, we also take into account other subclasses of S, which may or may not be appropriate for the domain at hand. This results in a few restricted classes with high individual coverage. Nation, e.g., is a one of the best candidates – it has the same coverage as its superclasses GeopoliticalArea, GeographicArea, and LandArea. We discard these superclasses because: (1) GeopoliticalArea also has subclasses like StateOrProvince and City, which are observed to be unlikely fillers of the Assailant FE in our domain, (2) LandArea has subclasses including ShoreArea, Field, or Campground and thus is an even worse candidate. Another good candidate is PoliticalOrganization because it only has subclasses MilitaryForce and TerroristOrganization. GovernmentOrganization is a mixed candidate – it has ill-fitting subclasses like PublicLibrary and PublicSchool but also the fitting subclass MilitaryOrganization. Agent covers all mapped fillers. It has, however, many ill-fitting subclasses and is, therefore, not preferred. In summary, we link the Assailant FE to the union of the SUMO classes Nation, PoliticalOrganization, Government, MilitaryOrganization, and EthnicGroup:

$$\texttt{Assailant} \subseteq \frac{\texttt{Nation} \cup \texttt{Government} \cup \texttt{PoliticalOrganization} \cup}{\texttt{EthnicGroup} \cup \texttt{MilitaryOrganization}}$$

Nation and EthnicGroup are *not* subclasses of SentientAgent, which is, however, a necessary condition because the Assailant FE has the ST Sentient, which in turn is linked to SentientAgent (see Sect. 5.1). Strictly speaking, this would imply that they are impossible filler types. In our example domain, however, nations and ethnic groups are *construed* as sentient agents via a standard and commonly understood metonymy.[11]

For the general-domain fuzziness increases, as seen by the 44% coverage of abstract classes. Again, this is due to words like "soldier" (evoking the class Soldier – a subclass

---

[11] We propose that metonymy be detected by the fact that a metonymic filler always implies the existence of a specific non-metonymic filler. For example, from a Nation filler, one can construe the actual SentientAgents who are the Assailants. This is, however, beyond the scope of this paper.

of SocialRole). 52% of the fillers are classified as SelfConnectedObject, resulting from fillers like "man" (evoking Human) and "tank" (evoking Device). The class Nation is not evoked at all in the general domain. Finally, SentientAgent covers a greater proportion of fillers than in the WMD and terrorism domain (48% vs. 29%).

The main differences follow straightforwardly from the nature of the corpora: In the special domain Nations are valid Assailants because they are the major actors in this domain, whereas Humans are unlikely (and vice versa for the general domain).

Our semi-automatic approach points us to appropriate filler types, providing a constrained semantics of FEs in a particular domain. A lot of human judgment is still required, e.g., for

- deciding whether the superclass of an evoked class should be considered,
- determining proper candidate classes that are *not* evoked by the data,
- determining sources of error or abstracting from errors (like eliminating the class Abstract although it covers 44% of the fillers in the general domain).

6. Lessons Learned and Impact of Our Work

We found that the hierarchies of SUMO and the FrameNet STs can be aligned. Therefore, we can confirm that the SUMO ontology relates well to natural language, a fact already indicated by the SUMO-WordNet mappings. For specifying the alignment of the two hierarchies, we need, however, a fairly complex formal language like first-order logic. This is due to fundamental differences in methodology between ontological and linguistic resources.

In addition, our research has helped us to find a number of issues both in FrameNet and SUMO and resolve them, as shown below.

Through our research we identified some deficiencies with the FrameNet STs:

- STs were described by natural language, which was ambiguous. Now, we have a clear axiomatization of STs and improved formal definitions.
- The STs Source, Path, and Goal were subtypes of Location. We now have a clear distinction between Location and Locative_relation the new supertype of Source, Path, and Goal.
- Some STs like Aktionsarten and Animate_being described meta information or were indistinguishable and never used. So we removed these STs from FrameNet and put their subtypes elsewhere.

We also identified some issues in SUMO version 75 (April 2006):

- Some SUMO relations like knows relate a CognitiveAgent and a Formula. Formula is, however, the *representation* of knowledge and not the knowledge itself. So we will change knows and similar relations to take a Proposition as range, which is an arbitrary bit of knowledge.
- The class CorpuscularObject should have an axiom stating that its instances are countable things. SUMO lacks this formal axiom, which will now be added.
- The relation capacity should not allow a TimePoint as an argument. TimePoint is a subclass of TimePosition, which in turn is a subclass of TimeMeasure and then ConstantQuantity. A point in time is, however, not a quantity.

- Other additions to SUMO are the creation of a Line class, which would cover linear regions such as the earth's equator, and LivingThing which would be SUMO Organisms that have the AnimacyAttribute of Living.

We conjecture that our work has immediate impact on semantic parsing and reasoning about natural language.

A Frame parser [11,12] that analyzes a sentence like "Iraq attacked Kuwait" could use a named entity recognizer, which asserts that "Iraq" invokes an instance of the SUMO class Nation. In order for "Iraq" to be a proper Assailant, the Nation class must be a subclass of the SUMO class, the Assailant FE is linked to for the domain of discourse. A more sophisticated approach could involve reasoning in order to figure out proper FE fillers.

Through our work, FrameNet data receive a greater level of ontologization. For example, in the Placing frame, we have annotation such as the following:

[AGENT She] PUT [THEME two pieces] [GOAL under the grill] [PURPOSE to toast].

Leaving aside the Agent, Theme, and Purpose FEs, the ST on the Goal FE is specified as Goal. by definitions of the FrameNet concepts we can conclude w.r.t. a Putting process P and a Goal relation `rel`:

$$\texttt{rel:Goal} \;\wedge\; \texttt{feFiller(P,rel)} \;\wedge\; \texttt{P:Putting}$$

Our axiom for Goal relations yields:

$$\exists\, dest, thm, lr \;\bullet\; dest\texttt{:Point} \;\wedge\; lr\texttt{:Locative\_relation} \;\wedge$$
$$\texttt{feFiller}(lr, dest) \;\wedge\; \texttt{feFiller}(lr, thm) \;\wedge$$
$$lr(thm, dest, (\texttt{EndFn}(\texttt{WhenFn P}))) \;\wedge\; \texttt{rel}(thm, dest, \texttt{P}) \;\wedge$$
$$\texttt{patient}(\texttt{P}, thm) \;\wedge\; \texttt{destination}(\texttt{P}, dest)$$

Thus there must be a Locative_relation lr in the context that relates thm and $dest$, which should be given as a second annotation. Given such an annotation, the existentially quantified variables lr, thm, and $dest$ can be instantiated with the locative relation, theme, and destination mentioned in the sentence thus concluding that "two pieces" were located "under the grill" after the Putting P. Otherwise, this should instruct a Frame parser to create a proper Locative_relation annotation. Even without this annotation for the Locative_relation lr, one could instantiate the filler for thm via the $\texttt{patient}(\texttt{P}, thm)$ assertion above, given a link from the Motion Frame (which the Putting Frame uses) to the Translocation Process in SUMO.

7. Conclusion and Outlook

Our goal has been to link FrameNet to SUMO in order to provide a foundation for further experimentation in NLP, e.g., semantic parsing and ontology lexicalization. A particularly important subgoal is to constrain the filler types of FEs for specific domains. This work relies on our manual alignment of FrameNet STs with SUMO classes for the general domain. We use SUO-KIF to specify this alignment, which allows us to express complex, axiom-based, formal interrelations and gives us a homogeneous representation featuring good tool support. Based on our alignment, we have developed a semi-automatic approach that suggests SUMO classes as filler types for FEs. Suggestions are based on (1) typical fillers of FEs for a particular domain, (2) FE-to-FE relations in FrameNet, and (3) STs associated with FEs. We thus provide restricted, domain-specific, ontology-based types on the fillers of FEs, which we anticipate will help semantic parsers.

We are currently investigating ways to use SUMO classes directly as STs. In the future, we will put forward our axiomatization of FrameNet STs like the Degree attributes, which calls for an ontological treatment of gradable attributes. Also, bindings from Frames to Processes in SUMO are crucial for reasoning about natural language as well as a proper ontological treatment of metonymy and metaphor. We plan further to continue to link FEs to SUMO and refine our semi-automatic approach by including additional heuristics. Finally, we envision further integration of WordNet, FrameNet, and SUMO in order to foster reasoning over natural language resources.

References

[1] I. Niles and A. Pease. Towards a standard upper ontology. In *Proc. of the 2nd Int. Conf. on Formal Ontology in Information Systems (FOIS-2001)*, Ogunquit, Maine, 2001.

[2] D. B. Lenat. Cyc: a large-scale investment in knowledge infrastructure. *Commun. ACM*, 38(11):33–38, 1995.

[3] Christiane Fellbaum, editor. *WordNet: An Electronic Lexical Database*. The MIT Press, 1998.

[4] J. Ruppenhofer, M. Ellsworth, M. R. Petruck, and C. R. Johnson. *FrameNet: Theory and Practice*. ICSI Berkeley, 2005. http://framenet.icsi.berkeley.edu.

[5] A. Philpot, E.H. Hovy, and P. Pantel. The omega ontology. In *Proc. of the ONTOLEX Wkshp. at the Int. Conf. on Natural Language Processing (IJCNLP)*, Jeju Island, Korea, 2005.

[6] A. Gangemi et al. Sweetening ontologies with dolce. In *13th Int. Conf. on Knowledge Engineering and Knowledge Management*, volume 2473 of *LNCS*, page 166 ff, Sig uenza, Spain, 2002.

[7] J. Scheffczyk, C. F. Baker, and S. Narayanan. Ontology-based reasoning about lexical resources. In *Proc. of OntoLex 2006*, pages 1–8, Genoa, Italy, 2006.

[8] C. J. Fillmore. Frame semantics and the nature of language. *Annals of the New York Academy of Sciences*, (280):20–32, 1976.

[9] I. Niles and A. Pease. Linking lexicons and ontologies: Mapping wordnet to the suggested upper merged ontology. In *Proc. of the 2003 Int. Conf. on Information and Knowledge Engineering*, 2003.

[10] K. J. Burns and A. R. Davis. Building and maintaining a semantically adequate lexicon using cyc. In Evelyne Viegas, editor, *Breadth and Depth of Semantic Lexicons*. Kluwer, 1999.

[11] K. Litkowski. Senseval-3 task: Automatic labeling of semantic roles. In *Senseval-3: Third Int. Wkshp. on the Evaluation of Systems for the Semantic Analysis of Text*, pages 9–12. Association for Computational Linguistics, 2004.

[12] K. Erk and S. Padó. Shalmaneser – a toolchain for shallow semantic parsing. In *Proceedings of LREC-06*, Genova, Italy, 2006. to appear.

[13] A. Pease. The sigma ontology development environment. In *working notes of the IJCAI-2003 Wkshp. on Ontologies and Distributed System*, Acapulco, Mexico, 2003. URL http://sigmakee.sourceforge.net.

[14] A. Riazanov and A. Voronkov. The design and implementation of vampire. *AI Communications*, 15(2-3):91–110, 2002.

[15] G. Lakoff and M. Johnson. *Metaphors we live by*. University of Chicago Press, Chicago, IL, 1980.

[16] A. Burchardt, K. Erk, and A. Frank. A WordNet detour to FrameNet. In *Proceedings of the GLDV 2005 Workshop GermaNet II*, Bonn, 2005.

Formal Ontology in Information Systems
B. Bennett and C. Fellbaum (Eds.)
IOS Press, 2006

301

Linking the Gene Ontology with Social Ontology: A Prolegomena to the Ontology of Personhood

David R. KOEPSELL[1]
SUNY Buffalo/Yale Center for Bioethics

Abstract. The Gene Ontology captures information at a very small scale, namely: molecular function, biological process, and cellular components. At this level, the Gene Ontology project should be capable of developing a semantics for every relation of genomic data to protein synthesis to the biological processes that result. In essence, the Gene Ontology should be able to describe the complete biomechanical functioning of an organism. But what of the social ontological statuses of organisms, and the relations of individuals to their higher level functions? Can the Gene Ontology account for higher level activities of an organism (such as intentionality, rights, property relations, etc)? Without leaping to conclusions about whether higher level functions are in fact naturalistically based, we should develop a semantics to serve as a hypothetical bridge should genomics lead us in that direction.

Keywords: genome, Gene Ontology, social ontology, bridge ontology, organism, legal ontology

1. Introduction

Genomes carry the instructions for the complete functioning of organisms. The human genome, for instance, contains about 3 billion base pairs, which coordinate, through a variety of molecular, cellular and biological processes, the development, functioning and reproduction of individual humans. Describing the relations between the genome and its expression is

---

[1] drkoepsell@gmail.com ; home page: http://www.davidkoepsell.com. Presently Research Assistant Professor at SUNY Buffalo Dept. of Philosophy -- coordinator of Graduate Research Ethics; Donaghue Visiting Scholar in Research Ethics at the Yale Center for Bioethics, 2006-2007.

clearly a challenging ontological puzzle. The data architecture for the genome evolved, and is not necessarily plainly visible nor elegant. The genome itself carries apparently large chunks of junk that does not seem to play any practical role – at least not any more. Moreover, the useful data is not always coded in generally transparent ways, and useful units of information come in various sizes, places on the chromosomes, and not always contiguously. Thus, while the working definition of a gene (the largest of which is nearly 2.3 million base pairs long) is still the unit of information involved in making a particular protein, units of useful, or at least "effective," information come in packets as small as a single base pair. Moreover, the old notion of "one gene, one polypeptide" has been challenged with the completion of the human genome project, which helped scientists conclude that individual genes may in fact code for as many as three proteins.

To decipher the relation of the information contained in an individual's genome, and the individual himself, clearly requires ontology. The Gene Ontology (GO) is aimed at attempting to gather data from gene discovery and correlate it in a useful ontology in order to fully describe an organism's phenotype based on its genotype. Yet, lacking from this is any form of bridge to describe the individual beyond its phenotype. Because human *persons* appear to be more complex than the biomechanical processes that compose them, a complete Gene Ontology will only describe individuals at one level. Ontologies developed in fields such as law, sociology, psychology, and at the level of social institutions, all consider *persons* as complex, intentional, thinking beings imbued with features such as rights, duties, and relations to subjects and objects above the biomechanical level. Can a bridge ontology be developed that will tie the Gene Ontology together with ontologies of persons, and allow for semantic links among future ontologies in the biological, social, and especially legal domains?

2. The Gene Ontology: Overbroad and Insufficient

The Gene Ontology does not describe persons, nor is it limited even to human beings. Rather, because genes often direct the same biochemical processes from one species to another, their ontologies capture relations among genes, proteins and biological processes across domains. As it turns out, for instance, the gene responsible for color vision exists in species as diverse as humans and *drosophila melanogaster* (the fruit fly). This information is tremendously helpful in identifying the evolutionary basis of inherited genetic traits among and within species, as well as diseases. The culmination of the Gene Ontology project, if there ever is one, will be a generic description of all genes and resulting proteins as well as biological processes, not restricted to any one species. Onto this, one could superimpose just the human genome, and acquire a general understanding of the functioning of a generic human organism, or a particular human's genome, and understand fully the functioning of that individual at least on a biomechanical level. However, such an understanding, while perhaps biomechanically describing the functional basis of a *person,* fails to account for essential, higher order features of personhood. The Gene Ontology is thus both overbroad and insufficient on its own to incorporate or account for social ontologies that describe or involve persons as objects.

At one level, then, the Gene Ontology describes a common set of phenotypes expressed by genes among all species, but also describes (ideally) some generic member of a species. Imagine then that we can sequence an individual's genome, and have the complete Gene Ontology before us. That complete ontology will give us a snapshot of the biomechanical processes involved in that person, but will it describe the *person per se*? There are some heady philosophical issues tied up with a complete description of a person which we need not delve into for the moment, but a couple of criteria not already described by the GO are worth mentioning. Persons are complex continuants, whereas the most complex objects described by the Gene Ontology are simple chemical processes (occurrents). Even assuming a completely naturalistic basis for complex person-processes (like intending, bearing rights, reasoning, etc.) the sum of all the pysio-chemical processes described in the Gene Ontology still does not amount to a description of the continuant "person." Intentionality is at most an emergent phenomenon, dependant on biomechanical processes, but in itself much more. It is at least a computationally highly complex neurochemical process, as yet uncontemplated by any of the categories or relations exiting in the current Gene Ontology.

Another way to consider this is to ask: to what degree is an individual the sum of the entities expressed by his genomic data? Certainly, genomic data encodes something very important in describing a particular *human*, but it seems unlikely that it can fully describe an individual adult *person*. One reason is that the genomic data, while it codes for many, if not every, trait of an individual (including hair color, eye color, intelligence, and perhaps even preferences and tastes), fails to capture other historical factors that go into forming an adult person. On the other hand, infant persons are legally and socially relevant, and for a time, at least, little more than the sum of the entities expressed phenotypically by their genomic data.

A complete ontology of *personhood* will necessarily include the human Gene Ontology and the other necessary and sufficient conditions of personhood. A complete ontology of personhood is necessary for other social ontologies. Since the Gene Ontology seeks to capture useful descriptions of much of what composes a human, and science shows that a good many features of personhood (e.g. behaviors, predilections, intelligence) are hereditable and many of them are genetically based. There is a dilemma: extend the Gene Ontology to capture relations and features of personhood, or develop a bridge ontology? As discussed below, one or the other is necessary for existing and future social ontologies.

3. The Necessity and Use of an Ontology of Personhood

The necessity for linking the Gene Ontology with social ontologies is most apparent considering legal ontologies, in which nearly every legal category contemplates some right or duty owed among *persons*, rather than simply humans. Increasingly, new ethical and legal issues regarding the relations between persons and either a generic *human* genome or an individual's particular genome (or some portion thereof) require ontological clarity regarding the statuses of those relations. The Gene Ontology describes the expression of the genome in the phenotype, and ultimately seeks to do so completely and comprehensively. Legal ontologies describe the relationships of persons to property and other persons. One glaring gap common to medical, biological, and social ontologies is a coherent description of the relations among individuals, their particular genomes, and the generic "map" of the human genome. The Gene Ontology does not presently have sufficient categories to deal with those sorts of relations, though it could conceivably at some level of complexity. Thus, while the Gene Ontology describes cellular components and biological functions, it does not yet encompass things like "mental states or processes" composed of the former, or the potentiality thereof, either of which is generally considered necessary for *personhood* in legal ontologies.

Genes account for a number of persistent and legally relevant mental states that are considered to negate legal intentionality. A genetic link has been found between Aph-1b and mental illnesses such as schizophrenia. Genetic links seem likely with other mental illnesses and certain forms of mental retardation (such as defects on the FMR-1 gene), any of which may create the legally and socially relevant state of lacking capacity for sufficient intentionality for legal or social accountability. Genes seem also to be responsible for severe conditions such as microencephalia and Lissencephaly both of which may also diminish or negate the legal status of personhood. While cognitive defects may have a number of other possible causes, the potential for firm genetic links to persistent states that interfere with personhood suggests that other necessary "healthy" genetic bases exist for the presence in a human of the mental states considered to be relevant to personhood, or upon which personhood may necessarily depend.

As a further example, the legal class "disabled" person" encompasses those who are congenitally disabled, as well as those who may acquire a disability. Defining a class of genomic disabilities, in other words -- finding genetic causes for a range of known disabilities, could have significant legal implications for those covered by such acts as the Americans with Disabilities Act (ADA). The benefits, and potential complications, of being able to determine with certainty the genomic existence of a particular individual's disability are obvious. Linking legal and biomedical ontologies, and having access at some point to an individual's genomic data, will clarify issues regarding the status of a particular "disabled person," and potentially streamline processes under the ADA as well as insurance and medical schemes.

Distinctions among racial "classes" or "races" have been used both legally and socially to broadly define ethnic classes, generally based on phenotype, and to legitimize and then later remunerate for disparate treatment of individuals and groups. Genomic research has cast doubt on the entire notion of "race" but has also shown some use for ethnic/geographic distinctions among groups in drug development. The nascent field of pharmacogenomics is aimed at targeting populations (which seem in some instances to fall along classical racial lines) with more appropriate drugs. It seems that certain ethnic groups respond in empirically different ways due to minor differences in genotype. [1] Genomic data, which can map these relevant genomic differences, will have significant legal and ethical repercussions. Remuneration or affirmative action schemes meant to provide relief to a historically oppressed class may be bolstered or hindered, depending upon how we treat discoveries regarding classical notions of race, and how we class individuals among various ethnic groups.

What is clear is that as we refine the GO and other biomedical ontologies, some accommodation, either by new categories in those ontologies, or in bridge ontologies of persons and subclasses of persons, will add significant value to both legal and biomedical ontologies.

Indeed, Barry Smith and others have done much to fix the errors and gaps in the GO and other biomedical ontologies through refinements in the GO and Open Biomedical Ontology (OBO) semantics and logic. [2], [3], and [4]. However, little has been done to link legal and biomedical ontologies, despite the obvious necessity and potential benefits. For instance, criminal liability attaches only to sane, adult persons. Only persons may be held criminally liable for wrongdoing. If biological and genetic conditions are responsible for certain forms of legal insanity or other incapacity, then it will be considerably helpful for those accessing legal ontologies to have all relevant evidence of biomedical or genetic determinants of various incapacities. As well, larger "philosophical" issues such as the ethics and legality of abortion or euthanasia depend on definitions of personhood that could be further clarified by access to a GO that accounts for all the necessary features of personhood and not mere human-ness.

A rights-bearing person and a fresh human corpse are socially and legally distinct, although, at least momentarily, biologically and biomechanically (on the cellular level) indistinguishable. The law and culture, however, distinguish between the two by punishing, for instance, the fatal stabbing of one differently than the impalement of the other. The distinction is the same as the ontological distinction between mere humans and persons. The complete ontology of a person will include all relevant genomic features (i.e. those responsible for the requisite mental and physical states) and descriptions of whatever emergent features might be necessary to describe a person (e.g., a "soul" if naturalistic bases for personhood are ever deemed insufficient by the relevant empirical sciences). The legal class "person" already exists and is utilized in every legal ontology, whether explicitly or implicitly, but linkage with the GO and other biomedical ontologies requires further clarification and expansion, as well as incorporation of certain features of the GO.

The gap noted is not necessarily a failure in the meta-ontology of the GO or other biological ontologies. It could conceivably be accommodated for by a comprehensive ontology of personhood, which belongs somewhere between biomedical and social ontologies. In fact, implicit in most existing social ontologies is a notion of personhood, to which rights, duties, obligations, etc. attach, but the relations and features of the entity "person" should be clarified and expanded to include relevant relations and features from the GO and other biomedical ontologies. Assuming, as empirical science does, a naturalistic basis for all relevant human behaviors (intentionality, rationality, etc.) then a bridge to legal and other social ontologies could be built into layers of the GO and other biomedical ontologies, or a bridge ontology of personhood could be developed. Either way, the GO and biomedical ontologies need to have a common entity at some level to facilitate interaction at the levels discussed in this paper. Even assuming that consciousness and other complex personhood-features are emergent or irreducible, they are nonetheless ontologically dependant upon genetic, molecular, biological processes which, when fully described, should encompass those emergent phenomena. Either approach should make clear that, given a certain set of preconditions, a genomic string plus X is a person, and thus has a certain legal and social status, and absent such, no person yet exists.

4. The Genome, Particular Genomes, Persons and Possessory Interests

One important but tricky problem posed by the discovery of the sequence of the generic human genome, and the ability to sequence an individual's *particular* genome, is the problem of defining the relationships among those entities. To what extent, for example, is your genome part of you, or is it in fact another expression of you? [5]. It turns out that answers to these and similar questions are both legally and socially significant as more aspects of the genome, and particular SNPs, haplotypes and alleles come to be "owned" through schemes such as patent and copyright.

Ordinarily, expressions are productions of human intentionality. [6]. Humans, however, are "expressions" of particular genomes. Persons, finally, are a result of both genome and perhaps other factors (for instance, X + [occurrent] *life of X*). Whatever the ultimate ontological status of persons, there is currently no good account of the nature of the relations between humans, persons, the human genome, and particular genomes. Do persons stand in the relation of "owners" of their genome, given their arguably possessory interest in the data? Does the human species stand in the role of possessor of the generic human genome, as against, say, some alien species wishing to utilize the genome for evil (or profit). [7].

The human — person — genome relation, whether one of ownership, or otherwise, needs resolving to deal with a number of weighty and unresolved ethical and legal issues, such as: patenting of genes, cloning, stem cell research, etc. [8], [9]. The GO's current ontology, because it does not extend to social ontological terms, cannot capture these relations. A bridge ontology of *personhood*, extending from the GO, can link this and other important biomedical concepts to legal and ethical concepts.

5. Conclusion

The GO and other biomedical ontologies capture important data and relations within and among species and members of species. Missing from these ontologies is any ready manner to link these important concepts with legal and other social ontologies, specifically regarding the critical concept of personhood. Complex and timely ethical and legal issues are emerging from genomic and bioinformatics research, and central to most of these is the ontology of *personhood* which, if formally described, and linked to GO and OBO concepts, could do much to clarify emerging legal and ethical issues. Such a bridge ontology should be developed.

References

[1]　Van Delden, J., I. Bolt, et al. (2004). "Tailor-Made Pharmacotherapy: Future Developments and Ethical Challenges in the Field of Pharmacogenomics." <u>Bioethics</u> **18**(4): 303-321.

[2]　Anand Kumar, B. S. "The Ontology of Processes and Functions: A Study of the　International Classification of Functioning, Disability and Health ".

[3]　Barry Smith, e. a. (2005). "Relations in biomedical ontologies." <u>Genome Biology</u> **6**(46).

[4]　Olivier Bodenreider, A. B. (2005). Linking the Gene Ontology to other biological ontologies. <u>Proceedings of the ISMB'2005 SIG meeting on Bio-ontologies</u> 17-18.

[5]　Guenin, L. M. (2003). "Dialogue Concerning Natural Appropriation." <u>Synthese</u> **136**(3): 321-336.

[6]   Koepsell, D. (2000). The Ontology of Cyberspace. Chicago, Open Court.

[7]   Berry, R. M. (2003). "Genetic Information and Research: Emerging Legal Issues." HealthCare Ethics Committee Forum **15**(1): 70-99.

[8]   Strydom, H. (2003). "The human rights side of the human genome. [Summ. in Afrikaans]." Tydskrif vir die Suid Afrikaanse Reg/Journal of South African Law; T35 2003:37 55.

[9]   Spinello, R. A. (2004). "Property Rights in Genetic Information." Ethics and Information Technology **6**(1): 29-42.

Formal Ontology in Information Systems
B. Bennett and C. Fellbaum (Eds.)
IOS Press, 2006

Principles for the Development of Upper Ontologies in Higher-level Information Fusion Applications

Eric LITTLE[a1], Ph.D., Lowell VIZENOR[b], Ph.D.
*aDoctoral Programs, Center for Ontology and Interdisciplinary Research,
D'Youville College, Buffalo, NY*
bMedical Ontology Research, National Library of Medicine, Bethesda, MD

Abstract. The use of ontologies within many information science communities is growing at an ever-increasing rate. This is especially true of higher-level multisource information fusion applications, where there is a genuine need for an improved understanding of the complex relational items (e.g. intentions, capabilities, opportunities and vulnerabilities) typically associated with situation and threat assessment (STA). Still, most current ontology development tools lack the resources to support the sorts of ontological distinctions necessary to provide a sufficiently scalable and reusable ontology product for STA purposes. In this paper we analyze the types of complex relations typically involved in STA ontology and discuss how these distinctions can serve as a theoretical framework for the enhancement of existing ontology development tools, especially as these relate to STA ontology.

Keywords: Ontology, Relations, Relation-types, Higher Level Fusion, Threat Ontology, STA Ontology

1. Introduction

Multisource information fusion is the process of utilizing data from various sources to produce accurate descriptions of the world with respect to a given area of interest. Information sources might include (among other things) any combination of the following: legacy databases, electronic signals from sonar or radar, human intelligence reports, webpages, photos, and domain expertise and knowledge. The goal of higher-level multisensor fusion is to effectively combine all these sundry bits of information into a meaningful representation of the world. As a consequence, the knowledge gained from fusion processing can be used to improve the inferential and predictive abilities of decision-makers operating within a given area of interest.

Although multisource information fusion originated in defense research [1, 2] it is by no means limited to it. Recently, it has been extended to a variety of non-military applications such as robotics, transportation, remote sensing, optical character recognition, medical decision-making, and crisis management [3-6, 12-15]. So, the general approach discussed here can be extended beyond ontology development for higher level information fusion related to situation and threat assessment as described

---

[1] corresponding author: little@dyc.edu

in [14, 15]. One such area is healthcare, where decision-making is a key component to providing services associated with medical diagnosis, treatment, emergency service monitoring, etc.

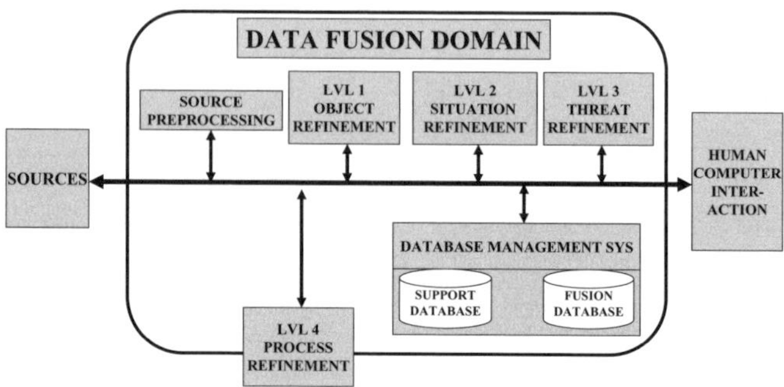

Figure 1: Joint Directors of Laboratories (JDL) Fusion Model [7,8]

The process of information fusion is broken down into several interrelated, abstract levels (see Fig. 1) [7]. The most commonly used fusion processing model is the Joint Directors of Laboratories (JDL) Fusion Model [7, 8]. There exists other (albeit less widely used) fusion processing models such as the Endsley model for situation awareness [9] and Blasch & Plano's Level 5 fusion [10]). The JDL model shows that processes at the lower levels of abstraction (Levels 0/1) operate with numerical data (measurements, features) and employ numerical, algorithm-oriented methods free of contextual significance. These processes produce information about location, kinematics, and the identity of single objects. At higher levels of abstraction (JDL Levels 2 and 3), the information obtained at the lower levels is used to provide decision-makers with a contextual understanding and interpretation of current and future events as well as behaviors of interest. At this higher level of abstraction, the process of information fusion operates with symbols or belief values for context processing and employs both numeric and symbolic techniques such as Real-Time Knowledge-Based Systems, Evidence Theory, Logic, Belief Networks, and Neural Networks. The results of the fusion process, at any level of abstraction, must be continually evaluated to define the needs for additional sources or the modification of the process itself (Level 4). The product of information fusion is a stored representation of dynamic objects and events, as well as their corresponding spatio-temporal relations, which are obtained through fusion processing, enabling effective action in a corresponding domain [11].

Level 1 (L1) fusion processing focuses on providing information about individual concrete objects. By contrast, the objects treated by higher-level fusion processing (L2-L3) are often aggregations of various objects. These aggregates are not singular, discreet units, but rather collections of such items unified under a given relation or set of relations. Understanding the items of higher-level fusion amounts to accurately identifying, and systematically capturing, the complexities associated with relational items at various levels of granularity [16]. For this reason, it is important to analyze from an ontological point of view the kinds of entities, attributes, events, behaviors, and settings which comprise L2/L3 items. These analyses should be metaphysically-driven, meaning they should be guided by formal-ontological principles that can provide the following kinds of ontological distinctions:

- Distinguish between summative wholes, which are identical to their parts, and non-summative wholes, which have an identity over and above their parts.
- Distinguish between dispersed wholes, which are spatially or temporally discontinuous, and compact wholes, which are physically connected.
- Distinguish between those relations that are directly perceivable via sensing capabilities (e.g., external spatial relations such as, *x IsNextTo y*, *x IsInRangeOf y*) and those relations that must be inferred from those direct sensing capabilities (e.g., complex relations such as, *x DependsOn y*, *x IsCausedBy y*, where such information results from further processing of the sensor data) [14,15].

Recognizing these sorts of distinctions facilitates the construction of powerful, large-scale upper ontologies, which can structure information about the most abstract levels of reality. This upper-level framework provides fusion scientists with information about the kinds of abstract categories and relations that comprise various complex states of affairs, especially those associated with situation and threat assessment (STA).

2. The Role of Ontologies in STA

The purpose of STA processing in higher-level fusion applications is to infer and approximate the critical characteristics of an uncertain environment, especially as these relate to the particular goals and information requirements of decision-makers [13, 20]. In order to build current and predicted situational pictures, it is necessary to reason about various relationships between objects of interest within a particular context. Some of these relations can be directly obtained by processing sensor information (e.g., external spatial relations such as 'is located at', 'has physical property of', 'is traveling at speed x'). As a consequence, they can be handled by L1 techniques for object identification, location, tracking, etc. Generally L1 items are restricted to discrete perceivable units. Other relations, however, are structurally more complicated and, therefore, resist being captured by current L1 techniques. These relations can exist as situated, relational (i.e., abstract) items, embedded within a contextual surrounding [11, 13].

Many current techniques for ontology construction in STA applications fail to provide an adequate ontological analysis of these relations. In fact, they are primarily designed with a particular ontology tool/language in mind (e.g., description logics such as OWL-DL and frame-based systems such as Protégé). These tools are, in most cases, limited with respect to the ways in which they can represent complex relation-types [17, 18]. In such cases, the ontology inherits a number of syntactic/semantic constraints that severely limit the sorts of relations that can be expressed in the ontology.

Consider the Situation Awareness (SAW) Ontology designed for higher-level fusion applications [19]. The SAW Ontology provides a tool for decomposing the types of objects, attributes and relations which are of interest to decision-makers in processing information in a battlefield environment (see Fig. 2). This model represents a human-centric view of the ontology's categorical structure, which can then be utilized by computational ontology development tools such as OWL to provide a formal description of the battlefield domain. However, in many fusion applications, insufficient attention is paid to the nature of relation-types. In the case of the SAW Ontology as well as OWL ontologies that employ a description logic, a relation is understood as the subset of a Cartesian product that is derived from the number of objects/concepts represented in the domain. Furthermore, in these systems only binary relations are considered [17, 18].

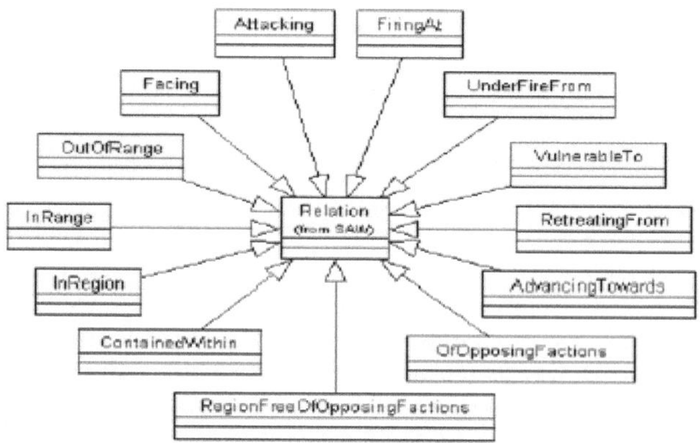

Figure 2: Battlefield Relations Represented in the Situation Awareness (SAW) Ontology [19]

In the final analysis, the SAW Ontology does not provide an adequate decomposition of relation-types needed for proper situational awareness. Purely spatial relations such as *InRange* or *InRegion* are represented in the same way as spatio-temporal relations such as *FiringAt* or *Attacking*, where some object(s) is participating in a process which is unfolding over time. In SAW, the ontological distinction between spatial and spatio-temporal relations is passed over in silence (see Figure 2). These distinctions are important. Purely spatial relations such as *x InRegion y* exist in full at a given time and can exist and maintain their identity over a period of time in spite of changes to either *x* or *y*. For example, a group of militants may establish a post in a geographic region and remain their over an extended period of time, despite losing members to death, desertion, and other factors over time. However, spatio-temporal relations such as *FiringAt* or *Attacking* are processes that unfold over time. They do not exist in full at any given moment, but rather exist only as successive temporal phases. The act of *FiringAt* breaks down into any number of sub-activities and sub-processes which themselves extend over a given duration. In the case of a purely spatial relation, all of its parts exist at a time; in the case of a spatio-temporal relation, the parts unfold over time.

A further criticism of ontologies such as SAW is that no distinction is drawn between one-sided and reciprocal relations (i.e., symmetric vs. asymmetric). One-sided (or asymmetric) relations include: *x* hitting *y*, *y* lying to *x*, or *x* existentially depending on *y* (e.g., the color of a car depends on there being a car). Reciprocal (or symmetric) relations include: *x* being married to *y* (where *y* is, by definition, also married to *x*), or *x* and *y* depending on each other (e.g., positive and negative charges that result in cellular homeostasis, a teacher-pupil relationship). The relation *FiringAt* is a one-sided (asymmetric) relation, where *a* fires at *b*; but it is not antisymmetric, since *a* and *b* can exchanging fire (i.e., *b* fires back at *a*). These distinction need to be accurately captured within an ontology to ensure effective modeling of complex spatio-temporal phenomena.

Finally, as is apparent from Figure 2, the SAW ontology does not capture *nested relations* (with the exception of a singe subsumption relation). A relation-type such as *InRange* can be represented as a necessary sub-relation of a broader relation-type such as *VulnerableTo* [16].   In these cases, important internal relationships that exist *between* various relata can be captured. Consider the case of *a FiringAt b* (which is an action that occurs *in* space and *over* time). Typically, this action would occur only if *b* were *InRange* of *a* (as a purely spatial consideration *at* some time). But the converse is not the case. We have little reason to infer from the fact that *b InRange* of *a* that it is the case that *a FiringAt b*. The SAW Ontology diagram, however, only shows two levels of relation-types, where subsumption (isa) relations exist between the singular most basic category of 'Relation' and all of its constitutive sub-relations are taken together at the same level of granularity.

3. Exemplary Metaphysical Relations Necessary for Higher-level Fusion in STA

It has been argued in [14, 15] that STA ontologies need to be constructed using both a metaphysically-driven upper-ontology capable of treating numerous kinds of relation-types including *causal relations*, *intentional relations*, and *dependence relations* and an empirically-driven domain-specific ontology, capable of treating the particular tokens of those relation-types (i.e., the domain-specific relations and relata particular to a given place, time or set of events). A metaphysically-driven set of upper relation-types would provide a means for overcoming some of the limits of current ontological models such as the SAW Ontology, since a careful consideration of metaphysically-structured relation-types would be able to improve upon the distinctions between spatial and temporal relations, one-sided and reciprocal relations and hierarchically-nested relations. Such improvements would in turn provide for better reasoning about situations and threat in the following ways:

- Capture the dependence relations between components of intent, capability and opportunity.
- Capture the distinction between *viable* (i.e., real, immediate) and *non-viable* (e.g. potential, non-immediate) threats.
- Capture how relations between intentions, capabilities and opportunities shed light on other kinds of complex relational items such as *vulnerabilities*.

3.1 Design Principles for an STA Upper-Level Ontology

3.1.1 SNAP/SPAN

The threat ontology presented here represents a modified version of the Basic Formal Ontology (BFO) [14, 15, 21-24]. (There are a number of upper-level ontologies such as DOLCE[2] and SUMO[3] that could also be used as a framework for the development of an STA upper-level ontology. That said, BFO is more consistent with

---

[2] http://www.loa-cnr.it/index.html
[3] http://www.ontologyportal.org/

our general philosophical outlook.) BFO embraces the view that all real world entities fall into one of two exclusive categories of *continuant* and *occurrent*. Think of the difference between a human being and the event of losing weight. Informally, what changes (the human) is the continuant and the change itself (the weight-loss event) is the occurrent. More precisely, continuants are entities which continue to exist through time; they preserve their identity from one moment to the next even while undergoing a variety of different sorts of changes [21, 23]. Examples include individual soldiers and battalions, landmines, T-72s and structures such as buildings and bunkers. Occurrents differ from continuants in several important respects. Most importantly, though, whereas continuants exist fully at a given time—i.e. all their parts are present at a time—occurrents never exist in full at a time; instead, they unfold through successive phases. Occurrents have a beginning, middle and end [21]. Examples include the process of securing an enemy area, a battle or skirmish, and the issuing of a command.

One of the basic principles of BFO is that there is no single ontological perspective in which to view both continuants and occurrents. Instead, there are two distinct yet complementary types of ontologies, namely, SNAP and SPAN ontologies. A SNAP ontology is a catalog of continuants at a given point in time, and a SPAN ontology is a catalogue of temporal entities. The SNAP/SPAN division provides a basis for constructing principled ontologies and makes it possible to define trans-ontological relations that transcend the SNAP/SPAN divide.

In addition to the distinction between continuants and occurrents, there is also a distinction between *independent* and *dependent* continuants. Independent continuants (also sometimes called substances) are entities such as humans, which do not require the existence of any other entity in order to exist. Dependent continuants (sometimes called accidents) are entities such as capacities, dispositions, functions, properties, qualities, roles and states. A dependent continuant is such as to be fully present at a given time, but nevertheless requires ultimately the existence of some independent continuant in order to exist.

The ontological categories of continuant and occurrent provide a basis for the distinction between intra-ontological relations and trans-ontological relations [21]. Examples of intra-ontological relations are subsumption (the relation of one class being wholly included in another) and the part-whole relation. These relations are always restricted to a given ontological category. A sound ontological principle for the construction of hierarchies is that all the classes employed should belong to one and only one of the categories: independent continuant, dependent continuant or occurrent. So, no continuant has an occurrent as a part and vice versa. Similarly, no continuant class is subsumed under an occurrent class and conversely. Trans-ontological relations are those sorts of relations that transcend the ontological divide between the formal ontological categories of continuant and occurrent. For example, there exists a participation relation, which is a trans-ontological relation, between the act of issuing a command (an occurrent) and the person who issues the command (a continuant). By adhering to these principles we get a clean partition of ontological types and the possible relations that exist between them.

3.1.2 Mereotopology

Of particular interest to STA ontology design is *mereotopology*, which is a theory that extends mereology (the theory of part-relations) with concepts from topology (the theory of spatial connectedness and extension). Mereotopology is a powerful formal tool for characterizing many L2/L3 threat items. In fact, [14, 15] have shown that it is possible to obtain useful ontological categories specific to higher-level fusion applications from basic mereotopological relations. Important here is the ability to characterize not only singular objects (maximally connected wholes), but also groups of such objects such as a casualty clusters or ambulatory services. Fig. 3 represents a number of relation-types that are used in constructing an ontology for earthquake disaster management. This ontology is designed to deal with the problems related to identifying and servicing casualty clusters of various sizes, dispersed across large urban regions. Mereotopology provides a useful framework for understanding many of these relations by providing ways of modeling relations such as 'casualty cluster x is larger than before,' 'casualty x inside ambulance y is close to a hospital,' or 'casualty cluster x overlaps with building cluster y.'

Table 1. SPAN relations

Relation between time points	Before, At the same time, Start, Finish, Soon, Very soon, Resulting in, Initiating, value of time interval
Relation between time intervals	Disjoint, Joint, Overlap, Inside, Equal

Table 2. SNAP relations

Topology/ mereology	Direction	Size	Distance
Disjoint Joint Overlap Cover Reachable Unreachable Contain A part of	Along Towards East West South North Similar Opposite	Smaller Larger size difference	Not far Far Very far Close Very close distance between clusters centroids

Figure 3: Categories Used in Higher-level Fusion Processing of Casualty Clusters in Post-Earthquake Disaster Areas [see 13, 15]

3.1.3 Trans-Ontological Relations

In many cases, L2/L3 threat items involve any number of what we have referred to as trans-ontological relations. This means that these items involve a complex of SNAP and SPAN elements. Consider an improvised explosive device (IED). An IED is an independent continuant. It is a physical object that is composed of numerous physical components (e.g., an explosive charge, a triggering devise, a container/shell) — which are also independent continuants. The part-relation of an IED's components is an intra-ontological relation. An IED is also involved in a variety of trans-ontological relations. Examples include: 'IED x HasLocation y' where there is a trans-ontological relation between an independent continuant, x, and the dependent continuant, y, a spatial region into which it has been inserted. There are also an array of trans-ontological relations between an independent continuant and an occurrent. In the case of an IED, it is related to a number of events and processes such as the acts of assembling, concealing and triggering the IED.

If an STA ontology is designed in compliance with BFO, then these sorts of relational complexes can be captured simply by identifying the trans-ontological relations that exist between the SNAP/SPAN elements. In other words, the description of complex situational items found in L2/L3 processing models can be formally

     E. Little and L. Vizenor / Principles for the Development of Upper Ontologies

captured in the BFO by arranging SNAP /SPAN items into distinct ontological categories (e.g. independent continuants, dependent continuants, spatial regions and temporal regions, processual entities, etc.) and then drawing out the hosts of relations between those categories. These ontologies provide a basis for identifying complex SNAP-SPAN trans-ontological relations such as *IsIntendedBy, IsVulnerableTo, IsCapableOf, ProvidesOpportunityFor, IsParticipantIn* [21], which stand between a range of objects, attributes and processes.

The ability to provide for trans-ontological relations between distinct ontological categories is an important theoretical step in ontology construction, since most ontology tools are constrained by their general taxonomic structure, where only limited hierarchical relations are represented. It is important to be able to build a high level ontology that can overcome these limitations. Upper-level ontologies can be thought of as a group of inter-related robust taxonomies (e.g., SNAP and SPAN), where complex relations such as dependence or causality are modeled by drawing trans-taxonomic relations between different taxonomic elements (see Fig. 4). For example, one may wish to provide independent SNAP and SPAN taxonomies for various items within a domain (e.g., urban environments containing items such as buildings, roads, bridges, population densities; various IED's and their components such as triggers, charges, implantation methods; and various other threat items such as dirty bomb materials, which include radioactive items like Cobalt-60 or Cesium-137, and known places for their procurement). By drawing these taxonomies together into an ontology for STA, one can show relations between various structures within the environment and threatening activities associated with things such as IED insertion or dirty bomb detonation, and the resulting damage that could ensue from such attacks [11].

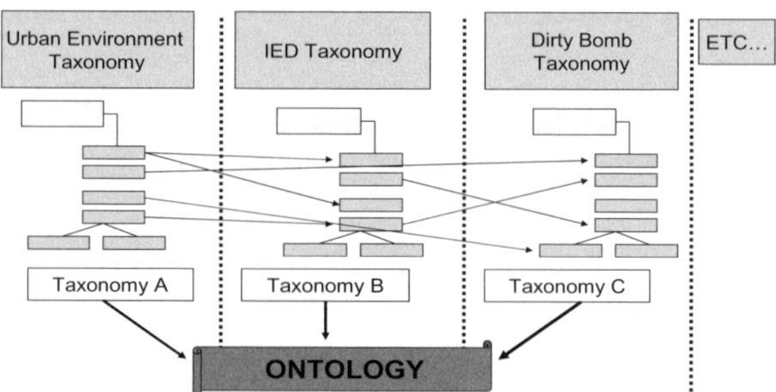

Figure 4: Higher-ordered Ontologies As Inter-related Taxonomies

3.2 The Importance of Formal-Ontological Relations to STA Ontologies

A robust framework of formal-ontological relations is essential for the development of sound STA ontologies, since it will help identify numerous relation-types that are currently not available to many higher-level fusion ontologies (e.g., the SAW Ontology). Within the JDL Model, L2/L3 items have historically been characterized as *aggregations* (or *sets*) of L1 items [1, 2, 7, 8]. There are a number of criticisms of set theory as an ontological tool for the analysis of complex entities [26, 27]. For one, set theory cannot do justice to non-summative wholes such as a platoon, which can preserve its identity over time even as it gains and loses members. A proper analysis of L2/L3 items requires that we not only identify the constituent elements of

L2/L3 items but that we also identify the relations that exist between these elements. For example, the notion of ontological dependence as discussed in [28] is useful notion for the analysis of a number of distinct kinds of wholes based on the strength of their unity.

We argue, in accordance with [14, 31], that a threat is composed of three basic elements: intent, capability and opportunity. An intention is a plan or goal directed state. A capability is a feature (e.g. projectile, explosive) that is associated with a certain type of object such as a particular weapons system. Generally, these are restricted to those features that can inflict an effective level of harm, disruption or lethality on a target. An opportunity is a state of affairs that makes it possible to carry out a given intent when supplied with sufficient capabilities (e.g., a line of sight to the target, access to a person or facility). A viable (i.e., immanent) threat exists only if all three elements are present. But there are also a number of important relations that exist between these elements. For instance, is it possible for *a* to have an opportunity to do *b* if there does not exist an intention on the part of *a* to do *b* or if *a* lacks the capability to do *b*? An understanding of the sorts of relations that exist between the three elements of threat will not only help clarify the threat phenomenon itself, but also a host of related phenomena such as the difference between an actual threat and a potential threat.

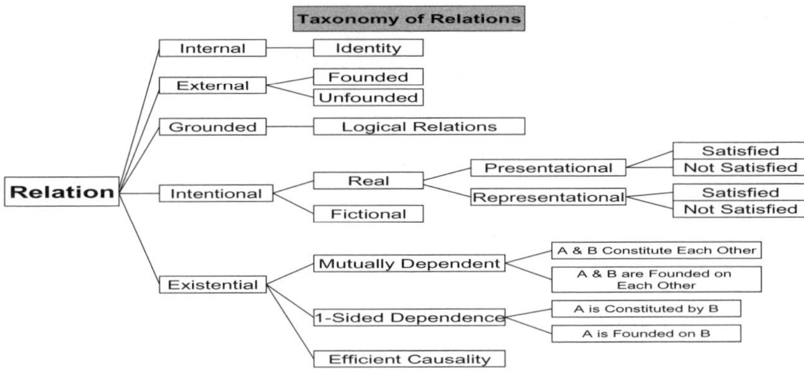

Figure 5: Exemplary Metaphysical Relations for Use in STA Ontologies [15]

The authors of [15] have developed an initial taxonomy of relation-types to offer insight into the kinds of relations relevant for higher-level fusion (See Fig. 5). The relation-types depicted in Fig. 6 represent a mixture of the formal-ontological relations discussed in [29, 30]. These relations can exist between, ontologically speaking, heterogeneous entities at different levels of granularity. For example, these formal relations can hold between physical and non-physical entities, spatial and temporal entities, and object-specific and group-specific as well as be applied to different kinds of sensing/reasoning capabilities (e.g. directly perceived vs. inferred kinds of relations).

Because the relations described in Figure 6 possess a hierarchical structure, they provide a means for representing nested relational items found in threat conditions where one must model complex items associated with command structures, communications, materials procurement, etc. Nested hierarchies can be used to derive the ontological structure of various relational states such as: relations between various intentional agents, inter- and intra-relations between items at different levels of granularity, and wholes/aggregates that contain various sorts of parts/members [29]. A formal ontological model of threat items, considered at different levels of granularity, can in turn be used as the basis for such things as the formulation of a situational calculus or similar computational approaches which require robust ontological decompositions of reality, currently lacking in many ontology development tools for higher-level fusion [31].

3.3 Distinguishing Between Viable and Non-Viable Threats

If an ontology is to be used for threat analysis/mitigation within STA applications, it must also be able to model the ontological distinction between a viable and non-viable threat. One place to start is to analyze the sorts of entities that are derived when we modify one of the three elements of threat. Viable threats exist when all three threat elements (intent, capability, opportunity) are present and relate to one another in the appropriate way (as in Figure 5). A non-viable (or potential) threat is one that involves only two of the three elements of threat. For example, *a* may represent a non-viable threat to *b* if 1) *a* has the intent to inflict harm on *b* but lacks an *opportunity* to do so or 2) *a* has the intent to inflict harm on *b* but lacks the *capability* to do so (see Figure 6). The greater our ability to understand the formal-ontological relations that exist between the elements of threat the greater will be our capacity to represent the difference between a viable and non-viable threat in an information system.

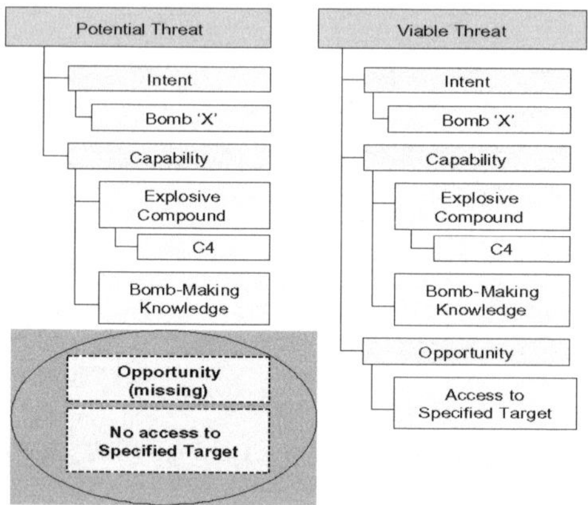

Figure 6: Non-Viable (Potential) vs. Viable Threats [from 14]

4. Conclusion

This paper provides a theory of relation-types for STA to be used for enhancing current ontology development tools. STA ontologies could more accurately capture important contextual features of reality, if designed in accordance with a metaphysically-driven theory of relations that allows for a clearer understanding of the dynamic characteristics of situations and threats. By providing an upper-level formal framework for formally describing items such as differences between potential and viable threats, hierarchically-nested relations, and relations between threat components, ontologists can design improved STA ontologies that are re-usable and scalable across numerous particular domains of interest.

Acknowledgements

This research was supported in part by Development & Research for the Defense of Canada (DRDC) under Contract No. W7701-011616/001/QCA, MIT-Lincoln Laboratories under Air Force Contract FA8721-05-C-0002 and Air Force Office of Scientific Research grant # F49620-01-1-0371, and in part by the Intramural Research Program of the National Institutes of Health, National Library of Medicine.

References

[1]   Llinas, J. & Waltz, E. (1990) *Multisensor Data Fusion*, Boston: Artech House.

[2]   Hall, D & Llinas, J. (eds.). (2001) *Handbook of Multisensor Data Fusion*, Boca Raton: CRC Press.

[3]   Shimshoni Y. and Intrator N. (1998) "Classification of Seismic Signals by Integrating Ensembles of Neural Networks," *IEEE Trans. on Signal Processing*, 46(5), 1194-1201.

[4]   Rogova, G.. Stomper P. (2002) "Information Fusion Approach to Microcalcification Characterization," *International Journal on Multi-Sensor, Multi-Source Information Fusion,* 3 (2), 91-102.

[5]   Rogova, G. Llinas, J. (1996) "Data Fusion For Real-Time Dynamic Traffic Assignment," in *Proceedings of the Sixth Annual IEEE Dual-Use Technologies and Applications Conference*, 1-5.

[6]   Scott, P. and Rogova, G. (2004) "Crisis Management in a Data Fusion Synthetic Task Environment," in *Proceedings of FUSION 2004*, Stockholm, Sweden.

[7]   White, F. (1998) "A Model for Data Fusion," in: *Proc. 1ˢᵗ National Symposium on Sensor Fusion*.

[8]   Steinberg, A.N., Bowman, C.L., and White F.E., (1999) "Revisions to the JDL Data Fusion Model," *NSSDF*, pp. 235-51.

[9]   Endsley, M. (1995) "Toward a Theory of Situation Awareness in Dynamic Systems," *Human Factors*, 37 (1), 32-64.

[10]   Blasch, E and Plano, S. (2002) "JDL Level 5 Fusion Model: User Refinement Issues and Applications in Group Tracking," *SPIE* Vol 4729, *Aerosense*, pp. 270 – 279.

[11]   Lambert, D. (2003) "Grand Challenges of Information Fusion," in *Proceedings of Sixth Inernational. Conference on Information Fusion*, pages 570-574, Cairns, Australia, 213-220, 8 July–10 July.

[12]   Llinas, J. (2002) "Information Fusion for Natural and Man-Made Disasters," in *Proceedings of the Fifth International Conference on Information Fusion*, pages 570-574, Annapolis, MD, USA, 8 July–11 July.

[13]   Rogova, G., Scott, P., Lollett, C. (2005) "Higher Level Fusion for Post-disaster Casualty Mitigation Operations," in *Proceedings of the 8th International Conference on Multisource Information Fusion*, July 25-29, Philadelphia, PA.

[14] Little, E., Rogova, G., Boury-Brisset, A.C., (2005) "Theoretical Foundations of Threat Ontology (ThrO) for Data Fusion Applications", *TR-2005 -269*, Nov. 2005.

[15] Little, E. & Rogova, G. (2005) "Ontology Meta-Model for Building A Situational Picture of Catastrophic Events," in *Proceedings of the 8th International Conference on Multisource Information Fusion*, July 25-29, Philadelphia, PA.

[16] Bittner, T. and Smith, B. (2003) "A Theory of Granular Partitions," in *Foundations of Geographic Information Science*, M. Duckham, M. F. Goodchild and M. F. Worboys, (eds.), London: Taylor & Francis, 117-151.

[17] Kokar, M.M. (2005) Tutorial PM7: "Ontology Based High Level Fusion: Methods and Tools," presented at *8th International Conference on Multisource Information Fusion*, July 25-29, Philadelphia, PA.

[18] Kokar, M., (2004) "Choices in Ontological Languages and Implications for Inferencing", Presented at Fusion 2004 Workshop III, *Critical Issues in Information Fusion*, Java Center, NY, September.

[19] C. J. Matheus, M. M. Kokar, and K. Baclawski. (2003) "A Core Ontology for Situation Awareness," in *Proceedings of the Sixth International Conference on Information Fusion*, pages 545 –552.

[20] M. M. Kokar. (2004) "Situation Awareness: Issues and Challenges," in *Proceedings of the Seventh International Conference on Information Fusion*, pages 533–534.

[21] Smith B. and Grenon, P. (2004) "The Cornucopia of Formal-Ontological Relations," *Dialectica* 58, No. 3, pp. 279-296.

[22] Grenon, P. (2003) "Knowledge Management From the Ontological Standpoint," in *Proceedings of WM 2003 Workshop on Knowledge Management and Philosophy*, April, Luzern Switzerland.

[23] Grenon, P. (2003) "Spatiotemporality in Basic Formal Ontology: SNAP and SPAN, Upper-Level Ontology and Framework for Formalization," *IFOMIS Technical Report Series*, (http://ifomis.de).

[24] Grenon, P. & Smith, B. (2003) "SNAP and SPAN: Towards Dynamic Spatial Ontology," in *Spatial Cognition and Computation*, 4(1), 69-104.

[25] Smith, B. (1996) "Mereotopology: A Theory of Parts and Boundaries," *Data and Knowledge Engineering*, 20 (1996), 287–303.

[26] Simons, P. (1987) *Parts: A Study in Ontology*, Oxford: Oxford Univ. Press.

[27] Smith, B. (2005) "Against Fantology," in M. E. Reicher, J. C. Marek (Eds.), *Experience and Analysis.* 153-170.

[28] Husserl, E. (1900-01) *Logische Untersuchungen*, 2 Bde, Husserliana, Band XIX, Den Haag: Martinus Nijoff, 1985 ed.

[29] Johansson, I. (2004) *Ontological Investigations.* (2nd ed.) Ontos-Verlag, Frankfurt.

[30] Campbell, K. (1990) *Abstract Particulars*, Cambridge, MA: Basil Blackwell.

[31] Steinberg, A. (2005) "An Approach to Threat Assessment," in *Proceedings of the 8th International Conference on Multisource Information Fusion*, July 25-29, Philadelphia, PA.

Formal Ontology in Information Systems
B. Bennett and C. Fellbaum (Eds.)
IOS Press, 2006

Towards A Realism-Based Metric for Quality Assurance in Ontology Matching

Werner CEUSTERS [1]
Center of Excellence in Bioinformatics and Life Sciences,
University at Buffalo, NY, USA

Abstract: Ontology matching is commonly defined as a matter of dealing with semantic correspondences between terms in ontologies and thus refers to more specific activities such as mapping or aligning, possibly with ontology merging in mind. However, it has been pointed out that there still prevails no common understanding of what such 'semantic correspondences' are supposed to be, and that in consequence "human experts do not agree on how ontologies should be merged, and we do not yet have a good enough metric for comparing ontologies." In what follows we define such a metric, which is designed to allow assessment of the degree to which the integration of two ontologies yields improvements over either of the input ontologies. We start out from the thesis that if two or more ontologies are to be considered for matching, then, however much they may reflect distinct views of reality on the part of their authors, the portions of reality to which they refer must be such as to overlap. Our approach takes account of the fact that both authors and users of ontologies may make mistakes (the former in their interpretation of reality and in the formulation of their views, the latter in misinterpreting the former's intentions).To do justice to such factors, we need to draw a distinction between three levels of: (1) reality; (2) cognitive representations; and (3) publicly accessible concretizations of these representations. We can then define 'semantic correspondence' not, as is usual, in terms of (horizontal) relations of 'association' or 'synonymy' between the terms within the ontologies to be matched, but rather in terms of the (vertical) relation of reference: terms correspond semantically if they refer to the same entities in reality. One conclusion of our argument is that, when ontology matching has been used as the first step towards ontology merging, then the merged ontology can contain inconsistencies only if there are already inconsistencies in at least one of the source ontologies.

Keywords: ontology matching, quality assurance, realism

1. Introduction

An ontology is commonly defined as '*a shared and agreed upon conceptualization of a domain*'. Often, an ontology so conceived takes the form of a graph, whose nodes are seen as referring to what are called 'concepts.' The combinations of nodes and edges in such a graph provide *concept descriptions*, and sometimes, in the best case, can be used to generate *concept definitions*. Unfortunately, the documentation of such concept-

---

[1] Corresponding author: Werner Ceusters, Center of Excellence in Bioinformatics and Life Sciences, Ontology Research Group, 701, Ellicott Street, Buffalo NY, 14203, USA. Email: ceusters@buffalo.edu.

based ontologies leaves unspecified what *concepts* actually are, and to what, if anything, they might correspond in reality [1]. We have argued elsewhere that this lack of specification leaves so much free play for ontology developers that a series of mismatches are created both within and between ontologies, with consequences which can be compared to the consequences of creating an international railway system in which it is left unspecified what gauge should be used by the separate national systems. The many different kinds of mistakes detected in existing terminologies and ontologies have a variety of sources (including, increasingly, the unjustified belief in the quality assurance capacities of Description Logic-based languages [2]). We believe, however, that the uncertainty as to what is meant by 'concept' is still the main reason why such mistakes arise [3, 4, 5].

Increasingly, however, and especially in the domain of biomedicine, ontologies are being built that are not based on 'concepts' but on philosophical realism. Here the nodes and edges in the ontology graph are required to correspond not to concepts but rather to entities in reality, for example to molecules, or tumors, or diseases on the side of patients. More precisely, they are required to refer to *universals* (such as person, organ, liver, tumor). It is universals which form the objects of scientific research. Where we acquire knowledge about 'concepts' by examining ideas or thoughts or meanings, universals are directly accessible through their instances in reality, for example as they appear in the lab or clinic: they are entities that are multiply located in space and time through their particular instances and they are identified by discovering that particular families of instances share in common certain corresponding intrinsic features and dispositions.

On the realist paradigm, the nodes in an ontology graph correspond to universals and the edges in the graph to relations between such universals, as expressed in assertions such as: *liver is_a organ, liver part_of mammal*, and so on – relations which are themselves defined in turn in terms of further relations obtaining among the underlying instances. Thus when we say that universal *A* stands in the *part_of* relation to universal *B*, then what we mean is that every instance of *A* stands to some instance of *B* in that instance-level parthood relation which is defined through the standard axioms of mereology [6].

The use of relations so defined allows us to ensure that ontologies have a direct relation to instances in reality, so that they may be used in association with realism-based *inventories* of such instances, built out of assertions such as: patient #324 *instance_of person*, meningitis #4612 *instance_of disease_of_nervous_system* in the construction of an electronic health record system that is designed to support instance-based reasoning. Instances in reality can hereby provide a benchmark of correctness for the assertions in an ontology [7], and instance information can also be used to help solve some of the problems of ontology merging to be addressed in what follows.

2. Terminological Conventions

Following a recently proposed terminology [8], we will use the expression '*portion of reality*' to denote instances, universals, and the simple and complex combinations they form when combined through relations of the mentioned sorts. By 'instance-level portion of reality' we mean: individuals and collections thereof: you, your digestive system, your family, your favorite hospital.

The terminology used by practitioners of ontology matching is not consistent, but we believe that it is best conceived as an operation on pairs of ontologies yielding an input to support further operations such as *merging, fusion,* or *integration* of ontologies designed to yield new single artifacts out of the ontologies with which we begin. Matching consists in dealing with what are called 'semantic correspondences' between the representational units (the single terms) of the individual ontologies. It involves activities such as *'ontology mapping'*, which is mostly concerned with the *representation* of correspondences between ontologies, and *'ontology alignment'*, which is concerned with the (semi-)automatic discovery of such correspondences [9].

This task of identification is still normally addressed from the concept-based point of view; thus ontology representational units or terms are 'matched' when, as it is said, they express, refer to, or represent the *same concepts*. Ehrig and Sure for example describe ontology mapping as follows: "*given two ontologies A and B, mapping one ontology with another means that for each concept (node) in ontology A, we try to find a corresponding concept (node), which has the same or similar semantics, in ontology B and vice verse.*" [10] To say that two concepts have similar semantics, on this account, means roughly that they occupy similar places in the associated graphs (called 'concept lattices').

An analogous approach is advanced by Kalfoglou and Schorlemmer, who define an ontology as "*a pair O = (S, A), where S is the (ontological) signature – the vocabulary – and A is a set of (ontological) axioms – specifying the intended interpretation of the vocabulary in some domain of discourse*". The ontological signature itself they see as "*a hierarchy of concept symbols together with a set of relations symbols* [sic] *whose arguments are defined over the concepts of the concept hierarchy*". Ontology mapping is then: "*the task of relating the vocabulary of two ontologies in such a way that the mathematical structure of ontological signatures and their intended interpretations, as specified by the ontological axioms, are respected*" [11].

Bouquet *et al.* define ontology mapping in similar vein as "*a formal expression that states the semantic relation between two entities belonging to different ontologies*", and they continue: "*Simple examples are: concept c1 in ontology O1 is equivalent to concept c2 in ontology O2; concept c1 in ontology O1 is similar to concept c2 in ontology O2; individual i1 in ontology O1 is the same as individual i2 in ontology O2*", and so on [12].

Based on this same point of view, Kotis *et al.* define ontology merging as follows: "*Given two source ontologies O1 and O2* [we can] *find an alignment between them by mapping them to an intermediate ontology, and then, get the minimal union of their (translated) vocabularies and axioms with respect to their alignment.*" [13].

The problems with all of the above are however clear: ontology matching is defined in terms of the correspondence (equivalence, sameness, similarity) of concepts. But how, precisely, do we gain access to these concepts in order to determine whether they stand in a relation of correspondence (presupposing that we have already solved the prior problem of working out what 'concept' means in any given context). One option is via definitions, but then these definitions themselves, as they are supplied by the different ontologies to be matched, will likely employ different terms (or 'concepts'), so that the problem of matching has merely been shifted to another place. The Ehrig and Sure suggestion of establishing correspondence by looking at the positions of given concepts in their surrounding concept lattices is subject to a similar difficulty. For how, unless we have already matched (some) single concepts, can we compare 'places' in distinct lattices (which as experience shows will likely still – if they are lattices at all – have very different mathematical forms). This leaves only a series of more or less statistically-based algorithms involving lexical term-matching, the results of whose application have thus far proved uneven, to say the least [14].

When Euzénat *et al.* carried out a survey of ontology alignment methods, they did indeed find that the majority are based on analyzing either the vocabulary used to label concepts or the structure in terms of which the latter are organized [15]. But more interesting was their statement that *"there is no common understanding of what to align, how to provide the results and what is important"*, a conclusion which echoes that of Noy and Musen, according to whom *"human experts do not agree on how ontologies should be merged, and we do not yet have a good enough metric for comparing ontologies."* [16]

3. Objectives

Our goal is to define such a metric, based on what the expressions in ontologies are intended to refer to in reality. That is, we hold that ontology matching is possible only if we view expressions in terms of that in reality to which they are believed to refer. In the case of realism-based ontologies such as the Foundational Model of Anatomy [17] the resultant methodology can be applied directly. However it can also be extended quite easily to the analysis of concept-based ontologies, since the expressions of the latter can in many cases be viewed from the realist perspective.

Central to our approach is the claim that expressions (terms in natural language or expressions constructed by means of a formal language) from two or more ontologies can be considered from the point of view of matching only if they are built out of representational units which refer to instance-level portions of reality which overlap. The referents of two expressions are said to overlap if either they or the referents of expressions from out of which they are composed are such that the portions of reality referred to by these expressions share parts. Thus the coverage of an ontology of anatomy will likely overlap with that of an ontology of disease since many diseases are associated with specific bodily locations, as is marked by the use of expressions like 'lung cancer' or 'spinal fracture'. Note that the ontologies in these domains do not overlap *because* they contain expressions of the given sorts. Rather, such expressions are included, and associated relations posited, *because of the relationships that obtain in reality* between the corresponding entities (between spinal fractures and spines, between lung cancers and lungs).

An adequate metric for comparing ontologies and the quality of the matching between them must be able to deal with a variety of problems by which ontology matching endeavors thus far have been affected:

(a) different ontology authors may have different though still veridical views on the same reality,

(b) ontology authors may make mistakes, either when interpreting reality or when formulating their interpretations in their chosen ontology language,

(c) an agent – whether human or machine – who is charged with carrying out the matching (and who from this point forward we will be calling *the assessor*) can never be sure to what the expressions in an ontology actually refer (for this, he would need to be able to adopt a God's eye perspective),

(d) if two ontologies are developed at different times, reality itself may have changed in the intervening period.

Each of these factors represents a dimension of unknowns in the ontology matching exercise, and we provide the resources to solve for each of these unknowns in the discussion which follows below.

One (expensive) way to create a metric for the quality of ontology matching would be to have experts manually prepare for each given matching problem a gold standard 'ideal' solution, to which matching efforts to be evaluated could be compared [18]. Our solution is of a different sort. It relies on the idea that one can measure what has been gained – which means: that we can count the improvements that have been effected – when the results of a given matching are compared to the ontologies as they had existed earlier. With this type of metric, we are able to assess whether the integration of two ontologies is an *improvement* over either of the input ontologies.

4. Material and methods

We base our method on the same distinction between three levels that we introduced as part of the methodology for the measurement of quality improvements in single ontologies advanced in [19]. These levels are:

- Level 1: *reality*, consisting of both instances and universals, as well as the various relations that obtain between them;

- Level 2: the *cognitive representations* of this reality embodied in observations and interpretations;

- Level 3: the *publicly accessible concretizations* of such cognitive representations in *representational artifacts* of various sorts, of which ontologies are examples.

For adepts of the concept-based approach, ontologies are representational artifacts which are intended to mirror the cognitive representations shared by domain experts. From the realist perspective, ontologies (independently of the paradigm on the basis of which they were constructed) are to be interpreted as if their expressions are intended to refer to entities in reality. This then gives us the possibility of using objective reality as a benchmark for the correctness of ontologies and of ontology matching efforts.

We have talked thus far of the 'expressions' in an ontology. In line with the theory of granular partitions [20], however, we prefer to talk more precisely of ontologies as being composed in modular fashion out of sub-representations which are built ultimately out of minimal (syntactically non-decomposable) *representational units* (including alphanumeric identifiers to uniquely identify universals), each of which is assumed by its author to correspond to some portion of reality (POR).

We are interested primarily in ontologies created for clinical or research purposes. The representational units of such ontologies are marked by the following characteristics:

1) each such unit is assumed by the authors, on the basis of their best current understanding of reality (which may, of course, rest on errors), to be veridical, i.e. to refer to some relevant POR;

2) several units may correspond to the same POR by representing distinct though still veridical views or perspectives on this POR, for instance at different levels of granularity (one thing may be described both as being brown and as reflecting light of a certain wavelength; one event as being both an act of buying and an act of selling).

In addition we take it that ontologies in general are characterized by the fact that the choice of what is to be represented by their representational units depends on the purposes which a given ontology is designed to serve (for example: to provide domain knowledge to a software application). And because reasoning with ontologies requires efficiency from a computational point of view, we argue that an optimal ontology should constitute a representation of *all and only* those portions of reality that are relevant to the purpose for which the ontology was built.

Clearly, things may go wrong on the way to achieving such an optimal representation. First, ontology developers may be in error as to what is the case in their target domain, leading to *assertion errors*. Second, they may be in error as to what is objectively relevant to a given purpose, leading to *relevance errors*. Third, they may be in error because their ontologies do not successfully encode the underlying cognitive representations, so that particular representational units fail to point to the intended PORs because of errors of syntax, leading to *encoding errors*.

The ideal (optimal) ontology, now, would be marked by containing no errors of the three just-mentioned types. This means that each representational unit in such an ontology would designate (1) a single POR, that is (2) relevant to the purposes of the ontology, and such that (3) the authors of the ontology intended to use this term to designate this POR. In addition, (4) there would be no PORs objectively relevant to these purposes that are not referred to in the ontology.

Table 1 shows this ideal case and the possible types of departure therefrom divided into two groups, which we have labeled 'P' and 'A', respectively, to denote the *presence* or *absence* of an expression in or from an ontology. These cases reflect the different kinds of mismatch between what the ontology author believes to exist (BE) or to be relevant (BRV) on the one hand, and matters of objective existence (OE) and objective relevance-to-purpose (ORV) on the other. The encoding of a belief can be either correct (R+) or incorrect, either (a) because the encoding does not refer (¬R) or (b) because it does refer, but to a POR other than the one which was intended (R–).

Table 1 presents a second-order view of how expressions and reality are related together. Thus it allows us to assert for example that certain expressions ought to be in an ontology because there are relevant PORs that need to be referred to.

To see how the table works, consider the second and fourth columns in its main body. We can there distinguish four OE/BE value pairs, as follows:

- Y/Y: correct assertion of the existence of a POR;
- Y/N: lack of awareness of a POR, reflecting an assertion error;
- N/N: correct assertion that some putative POR does not exist (for example: 'there is no one-horned mammal');
- N/Y: the false belief that some putative POR exists (another kind of assertion error).

As concerns the ORV and BRV columns in the table, these do not receive a value (cases marked '–') whenever either OE or BE, respectively, has the value N.. An expression is included in an ontology only when BRV has the value Y. Wherever ORV has a value different from that of BRV, a relevancy error has been committed.

Out of the 15 alternative types of included and excluded expressions, only 3 are desirable: P+1, A+1, and A+2. P+1 consists in the presence in an ontology of an expression that correctly refers to a relevant POR; A+1 and A+2 consist in the correct exclusion of an expression from an ontology, either because there is no POR to be referred to, or because this POR is not relevant to the ontology's purpose. A-3 and A-4

Table 1: Typology of expressions included in and excluded from an ontology in light of relevance and relation to external reality

	Reality		Under-standing		Encoding		E
	OE	ORV	BE	BRV	Int.	Ref.	
P+1	Y	Y	Y	Y	Y	R+	0
A+1	N	–	N	–	–	–	0
A+2	Y	N	Y	N	–	–	0
P-1	N	–	Y	Y	Y	¬R	3
P-2	N	–	Y	Y	N	¬R	4
P-3	N	–	Y	Y	N	R–	5
P-4	Y	Y	Y	Y	N	¬R	1
P-5	Y	Y	Y	Y	N	R–	2
P-6	Y	N	Y	Y	Y	R+	1
P-7	Y	N	Y	Y	N	¬R	2
P-8	Y	N	Y	Y	N	R–	3
A-1	Y	Y	Y	N	–	–	1
A-2	Y	Y	N	–	–	–	1
A-3	N	–	Y	N	–	–	1
A-4	Y	N	N	–	–	–	1

Legend: **OE:** objective existence; **ORV:** objective relevance; **BE:** belief in existence; **BRV:** belief in relevance; **Int.:** intended encoding; **Ref.:** manner in which the expression refers; **E:** number of errors when measured against the benchmark of reality. **P/A:** presence/absence of term. (See text for details.)

are borderline cases, in which errors made by ontology authors are without deleterious effect, either because something that is erroneously assumed to exist is deemed irrelevant, or because something that is truly irrelevant is overlooked. There are 9 different types of P cases, i.e. of cases which arise where an expression is present in an ontology. Of these, interestingly, only expressions of types P+1 and P-6 refer correctly to a corresponding POR: the former reflects our ideal case referred to above; the latter is marred by an inclusion that is incorrect because the included expression lacks relevance.

The last column of Table 1 shows for each type the numbers of mistakes committed with respect to the corresponding baseline 'best case'. These baselines are P+1 for P-4, P-5, A-1 and A-2; A+1 for P-1, P-2, P-3 and A-3; and A+2 for all the others.

5. Ontology matching and merging

The minimal requirement for releasing an ontology, on the realist paradigm, is that the authors assume in good faith that all its constituent expressions are of the P+1 type. A stronger requirement would be that the authors advance the ontology as complete, i.e. as containing expressions designating all the PORs deemed relevant to its purpose. In reality, of course, any single ontology will contain expressions of the various P-*n* types. It will typically also lack expressions for PORs which are relevant to its purposes. This is certainly the case when ontologies are candidates for merging, since this presupposes at least an incompleteness on the side of both ontologies.

The matching of expressions in ontologies O^1 and O^2 now comes down in our view to assessing which expressions EO^1_i present in the first ontology stand in a relationship of reference to the same PORs as expressions EO^2_j in the second.

If two distinct expressions are judged to refer to the same POR, then the expressions can be counted as synonymous (a case which is taken to include the relation between expressions drawn from different languages which are translations of each other).

Trivially, something has thereby been gained, and this gain can be quantified. For the purposes of this communication, however, we will not take this trivial case further into account. Our attentions are focused rather on the more challenging sort of case, where for an expression in ontology O^1 no co-designating expression is found in ontology O^2. Our methodology then requires that the assessor needs to document what, in his mind, is the reason for this mismatch using the typology described in Table 1. The latter enables him to quantify the seriousness of the mismatch in terms of the number of errors associated which each deviation from the baseline (P+1, A+1 or A+2) cases.

A P-8 configuration for example deviates from its baseline (A+2) in three respects: (1) the POR is falsely believed to be relevant, (2) the expression does not encode what its author intends it to encode, and (3) the expression refers to a POR different from that to which it is intended to refer.

The possibilities for co-reference are restricted by the following principles (which can be incorporated into the software support for the assessor's work):

- there is only one reality to which expressions in O^1 and O^2 may refer;
- the relevance of a POR is to be assessed in light of the purposes for which the resultant mapped or merged ontology is being created, not in terms of the original purposes of the individual ontologies;
- everything that exists or has existed can be referred to (where necessary by using appropriate temporal indices).

6. Dealing with differences in coverage

There are various ways an assessor can deal with differences in the ontologies he is called upon to match. A first option would be to assume that there are no mistakes in the source ontologies, and that any difference is to be accounted for in terms of their different *purposes*. (We use 'pO' in what follows to refer to the purpose of an ontology O.) On this option, if a POR is referred to in O^1 but not in O^2, then this does not mean that the authors of O^2 did not believe in the existence of that POR, but rather that they did not consider the POR to be relevant for pO^2. Another option would be to assume (perhaps because one has evidence for the thesis) that these purposes are identical, so that any difference is to be explained on the basis of a false assumption as to the relevance of that POR underlying one or other of the source ontologies. The assessor must then apply some strategy to resolve conflicting information in ways which will allow him to identify the false belief. Here information reflecting quality improvements over successive versions of the ontologies under scrutiny (compiled along the lines developed in [19]) can provide important clues.

Table 2 demonstrates the application of our metric to a case in which two ontologies are to be matched in which the purposes of the input ontologies themselves and of the sought for merged ontology do not need to be the same. Rows 1 and 2 depict situations where expressions in O^1 and O^2 have been mapped to the same POR, and rows 3 and 4 situations in which a POR is referred to in only one ontology. Rows 5 and 6 reflect situations where both source ontologies lack reference to a POR that is either relevant (C5) or irrelevant (C6) for the purposes of the matching.

Table 2 reflects a situation in which the assessor, during the matching process, is assumed to have some procedure which enables him to assess PORs as relevant or not relevant for the purposes of the ontology which is to result from matching or merging (since it will typically not be the case that everything relevant to the source ontologies will also be relevant to the merged result). The assessment of relevance will then yield one or other of: correct presence (P+1), justified absence because of lack of relevance (A+2), or unjustified absence because of missed relevance (A-1) (shown in column (9) of Table 2).

The 'objective relevance' of a POR, and thus of a corresponding expression in an ontology, is something that becomes at least indirectly measurable whenever the ontology is used to solve the problems for which it was designed. To this end we need to measure improvements in the performance of applications after they have started to use the merged ontology. If the postulation of some POR as relevant leads to improvements in such performance, then it is likely that that the POR in question (or something very like it) is indeed relevant.

But even where we have no knowledge as to the objective relevance of a given POR, it is still possible to measure the quality of the source ontologies relative to the matching result. Consider for example row 3 in Table 2: if it is believed that for purpose pO^m of a merged ontology O^m a certain POR is relevant, and that for purpose pO^2 it is not, then one must also believe that if O^2 would be used for pO^m then there is an unjustified absence of an expression, namely one characterized as being of type A-1.

To have a quantitative assessment of the relative quality of the ontologies with respect to pO^m, it suffices to use the number of errors that are involved in an expression of a certain type as indicated in the column labeled 'E' in Table 1 and to use them in appropriate formulas for dealing with errors. Under the assumptions used for Table 2, a simple tally of the percentage of error-free expressions relative to the total number of expressions may suffice, since the number of errors for expressions of types P-6 and A-1 equals 1 in both cases. For more complex cases, in which the number of errors per expression type might be higher than 1 (in the worst case, if all expressions would be of type P-3, there would be 5 times more errors than expressions), error percentage formulas that include adjustments for the number of expressions would yield more adequate results. These calculations may seem at first difficult to master; however, they soon prove themselves to have a high degree of intuitiveness, as is seen in the fact that they can easily by carried out by means of simple software embedded in ontology matching tools. They do however require some additional effort on the part of those involved in ontology matching, in that they are required to assess (through checklists or similar technology) the relevance of each expression in the input ontologies in light of the purposes involved in the intended merger.

7. Reality as benchmark

When two or more source ontologies are mapped or merged, then it may happen that inconsistencies are discovered. In [21], a distinction is made between inconsistency and

Table 2: Possible combinations of the believed relevance of a POR in source ontologies (O^1 and O^2) and resulting merger (O^m)

(1)	(2)	(3)	(4)	(5)	(6)	(7)	(8)	(9)
	O^1			O^2			O^m	
	BRV	ET		BRV	ET		BRV	ET
	pO^1	pO^1	pO^m	pO^2	pO^2	pO^m	pO^m	pO^m
1	Y	P+1	P+1	Y	P+1	P+1	Y	P+1
2	Y	P+1	P-6	Y	P+1	P-6	N	A+2
3	Y	P+1	P+1	N	A+2	A-1	Y	P+1
4	Y	P+1	P-6	N	A+2	A+2	N	A+2
5	N	A+2	A-1	N	A+2	A-1	Y	A-1
6	N	A+2	A+2	N	A+2	A+2	N	A+2

<u>Legend</u>: **BRV:** believed relevance; **ET:** expression type (see Table 1); columns (2), (5) and (8): relevance of the POR for the purposes of O^1, O^2 and O^m respectively; columns (3), (6) and (9): expression types according to pO^1, pO^2 and pO^m respectively; columns (4) and (7): expression types if O^1 or O^2 would be used without any modification in pO^m.

incoherence: *"An ontology will be called inconsistent iff there is no interpretation satisfying all the DL axioms in the ontology; it will be called incoherent iff it does not satisfy certain predefined constraints or invariants related to efficient ontology design."* Thus it is claimed that the ontology with the axioms (1) birds fly, (2) penguins are birds, and (3) penguins don't fly, is incoherent. Only when an assertion is added to the effect that a particular individual is an instance of *penguin*, we are told, does the ontology become inconsistent. Yet, so the authors continue, an ontology of exactly the same structure consisting of the axioms: (1) horses don't have horns, (2) unicorns are horses, and (3) unicorns have horns, is also incoherent, but will become never inconsistent because *"To the authors' knowledge, there are no unicorns"*. This difference (perhaps) makes sense from a concept-based view; not however from a realist perspective. For when reality is taken as benchmark, then it becomes clear that *both* ontologies contained mistakes from the very beginning. Thus, if ontology O^1, with expressions (1) birds fly and (2) penguins are birds, becomes merged with ontology O^2, which contains (3) penguins don't fly, then it is not such that only the merged ontology *became* wrong; O^1 was *already* wrong!

Mistakes of this kind do not *arise* because of merging; rather, they are *discovered* thereby. To find out which of the three axioms is (or are) the source of error is a matter not of applying logic, but rather of looking carefully at reality in light of what the axioms assert. It might be that the ontology authors' understanding of reality was erroneous from the start, so that an assertion error was made; or it might be that the intended representational unit was erroneously encoded. Indeed, it might also be that reality has changed between the times that O^1 and O^2 were published, perhaps because penguins lost the ability to fly. In each such case, the complete range of possible types of mistakes as shown in Table 1 must be taken into account.

Of course, Table 1 alone is not able to inform an assessor which of the expressions to be mapped or merged are wrong: to find out whether penguins fly or whether they are birds is a matter of scientific discovery. It does however inform an assessor of the improvement in quality which will result from a given merger according to the position that is taken as to the reasons for mistakes which this merger corrects. In [19], we argued that while revising ontologies, authors should keep track of the reasons for any changes made by registering whether or not the changes are believed to be dictated by changes in (1) the underlying reality, (2) the objective relevance of an included expression to the purposes of the ontology, (3) the ontology authors' understanding of each of these, and (4) the correction of encoding errors. Of course, authors will always assume that changes are *towards* the P+1, A+1, or A+2 cases. But this does not prevent the assessor from measuring how much the ontology is believed to have been improved as compared to its predecessor (and it does not prevent him, either from evaluating the skills of ontology authors by tracking the history of their earlier revisions).

8. Conclusion

We presented a novel methodology for assessing the quality of ontologies that are mapped upon each other, or that result from merging two or more source ontologies. We concluded that differences between the ontologies should be resolved by resorting to (1) the ontology authors' beliefs in what is the case in the underlying reality, (2) their belief in the relevance of an included expression to the purposes of the ontology, and (3) the possible presence of encoding errors. Differences between these beliefs and what is the case in reality are quantifiable and can be used to assess the adequateness of both the original ontologies and the resultant matching or merging. The methodology for quality measurement thereby provides a pathway by which ontology matching and merging can be transformed from art into science.

References

[1] B. Smith, Beyond concepts: Ontology as reality representation. Varzi A, Vieu L (eds.), Proc FOIS 2004. International Conference on Formal Onto-logy and Information Systems, Turin, p. 73-84.

[2] W. Ceusters, B. Smith, Ontology and Medical Terminology: why Descriptions Logics are not enough. Proceedings of the conference Towards an Electronic Patient Record (TEPR 2003), San Antonio, 10-14 May 2003 (electronic publication 5pp)

[3] W. Ceusters, B. Smith, A. Kumar, C. Dhaen, Mistakes in medical ontologies: where do they come from and how can they be detected? in Pisanelli DM (ed) Ontologies in Medicine. Proceedings of the Workshop on Medical Ontologies, Rome October 2003, IOS Press, Studies in Health Technology and Informatics, 2004;102: 145-63.

[4] W. Ceusters, B. Smith, A. Kumar, C. Dhaen, Ontology-based error detection in SNOMED-CT. Proceedings of MEDINFO 2004;:482-6.

[5] W. Ceusters and B. Smith, A Terminological and Ontological Analysis of the NCI Thesaurus. Methods of Information in Medicine 2005; 44: 498-507

[6] B. Smith, W. Ceusters, B. Klagges, J. Köhler, A. Kumar, J. Lomax, C. Mungall, F. Neuhaus, A. Rector and C. Rosse, Relations in biomedical ontologies, Genome Biology (2005), 6 (5), R46.

[7] B. Smith, From Concepts to Clinical Reality: An Essay on the Benchmarking of Biomedical Terminologies, J Biomed Inform, 2006 Jun;39(3):288-98.

[8] B. Smith, W. Ceusters, Towards a Coherent Terminology for Principle-Based Ontologies. (under review).

[9] J. de Bruijn, M. Ehrig, C. Feier, F. Martín-Recuerda, F. Scharffe, M. Weiten, Ontology mediation, merging and aligning. In Davies J, Studer R, Warren P (eds), Semantic Web Technologies: Trends and Research in Ontology-based Systems, Wiley, UK, 2006.

[10] M. Ehrig M and Y. Sure, Ontology mapping - an integrated approach. In Proceedings of the First European Semantic Web Symposium, ESWS 2004, volume 3053 of Lecture Notes in Computer Science, pages 76–91, Heraklion, Greece, May 2004. Springer Verlag.

[11] Y. Kalfoglou and M. Schorlemmer, Ontology mapping: the state of the art. Knowl. Eng. Rev., 18(1):1--31, 2003.

[12] P. Bouquet *et al.* KnowledgeWeb deliverable D2.2.1. Specification of a common framework for characterizing alignment.
http://www.inrialpes.fr/exmo/cooperation/kweb/heterogeneity/deli/kweb-221.pdf

[13] K; Kotis, G. Vouros, K. Stergiou, Towards Automatic Merging of Domain Ontologies: The HCONE-merge approach. Elsevier's Journal of Web Semantics (JWS), vol. 4:1, pp. 60-79, January 2006.

[14] S. Staab and A. Maedche. Measuring similarity between ontologies. Lecture notes in artificial intelligence, 2473:251--263, 2002.

[15] J. Euzénat *et al.* KnowledgeWeb Deliverable D2.2.3: State of the art on ontology alignment. V1.2, August 2004.
http://www.starlab.vub.ac.be/research/projects/knowledgeweb/kweb-223.pdf

[16] N.F. Noy and M.A. Musen, Evaluating Ontology-Mapping Tools: Requirements and Experience. Workshop on Evaluation of Ontology Tools at EKAW'02 (EON2002). 2002, p1-14.

[17] C. Rosse and J.L.V. Mejino, A reference ontology for bioinformatics: the Foundational Model of Anatomy. J Biomed Inform, 36: 478-500, 2003.

[18] M. Ehrig and J. Euzenat, Relaxed Precision and Recall for Ontology Matching, in: Proc. K-Cap 2005 workshop on Integrating ontology, Banff (CA), p. 25-32, 2005.

[19] W. Ceusters and B. Smith, A Realism-Based Approach to the Evolution of Biomedical Ontologies. Forthcoming in Proceedings of AMIA 2006, Washington DC, November 11-15, 2006.
http://ontology.buffalo.edu/bfo/Versioning.pdf

[20] T. Bittner and B. Smith, A theory of granular partitions. In: Foundations of Geographic Information Science, M Duckham, MF Goodchild and MF Worboys (eds.), London: Taylor & Francis, 2003, 117–151

[21] G. Flouris and D. Plexousakis, Handling Ontology Change: Survey and Proposal for a Future Research Direction, Technical Report 362, ICS-FORTH, Heraklion, Crete, Greece, September 2005.

7. Maintaining and Exploiting Ontologies

Formal Ontology in Information Systems
B. Bennett and C. Fellbaum (Eds.)
IOS Press, 2006

Approximation of Ontologies in CASL

Klaus Lüttich

SFB/TR8 – FB3, Universität Bremen, P.O.B. 33 04 40, 28334 Bremen, Germany
e-mail: luettich@informatik.uni-bremen.de

Abstract. In this paper we present methods to generate a Description Logic (DL) theory from a given First Order Logic (FOL) theory, such that each DL axiom is entailed by the given FOL theory. This is obtained by transforming the given FOL formulas. If this method is applied to an ontology specification in FOL, the resulting DL specification is still grounded on the same semantics but clearly weaker than the FOL specification. The benefit of specification in DL is that efficient reasoning procedures are available as implemented in tools such as Racer, Fact++ or Pellet. Such ontologies in DL could be used for knowledge representation systems and the semantic web where efficient reasoning plays a major role. This method can be used to compile a foundational ontology formalized in FOL, like DOLCE (Descriptive Ontology for Linguistic and Cognitive Engineering), into DL for use with domain ontologies formalized in DL, or for the development of domain ontologies based on the compiled foundational ontology. These weakening strategies are described using CASL (Common Algebraic Specification Language) and CASL-DL, and will be integrated into HETS (Heterogeneous Tool Set). Furthermore, this paper includes examples from DOLCE.

Keywords. Theory Approximation, Knowledge Compilation, CASL, Description Logic

1. Introduction

Traditionally, Description Logics (DL) [1] or other less expressive formalisms have been used to describe and reason about knowledge in an efficient way. This is clearly needed for applications such as the Semantic Web [2] and natural language processing. However, on the other hand DLs are too weak to formalize a rich axiomatized foundational ontology such as DOLCE (Descriptive Ontology for Linguistic and Cognitive Engineering) [3,4]. Therefore CASL [5] (Common Algebraic Specification Language) and even ModalCASL (an extension of CASL with multi-modalities) will be used for the formalization of DOLCE. That this offers great potential has been previously presented in [6]. One advantage of CASL is the associated tool HETS [7] (Heterogeneous Tool Set). It allows syntax and type checking of CASL and is connected to the semi-automatic theorem prover Isabelle [8] as well as the automatic first-order reasoner SPASS [9].

This paper offers a bridge between rich axiomatizations in FOL and tractable theories in DL. It describes an approximation of FOL theories to DL preserving the semantics. This idea is also called knowledge compilation as the knowledge or semantics of a theory should be kept while the tractability is improved [10,11].

This paper is structured as follows: First we introduce description logic, CASL and CASL-DL, the languages used in the examples. Then we present the idea of knowledge compilation in general, and further we present our approach to approximate FOL with DL. This section is accompanied by an informative example illustrating the method. The paper ends with a perspective on future work.

2. Logical Foundations

In this section we introduce the logical foundations for our approach: First we briefly present Description Logics, then we describe the formal languages Casl and Casl-DL.

2.1. Description Logic

Description Logic (DL) has been developed for efficient knowledge representation and reasoning. Its principle is the distinction between so-called TBoxes and ABoxes. TBoxes provide the terminology of the knowledge base such as hierarchies of concepts and roles, and axioms describing which individuals belong to a concept based on relations to other individuals. These descriptions are formulas with a restricted flow of variables. Furthermore, some predefined datatypes like strings and numbers are available to attach data to individuals with data-valued roles. ABoxes, on the other hand, represent facts about the world and the individuals, by axioms with constants (individuals) [1].

DLs have the benefit that the tractability, decidability, and the complexity of the reasoning systems has been studied very well by now [1]. Another advantage is the great number of automatic reasoners available, such as Racer [12], FaCT++ [13] or Pellet [14].

2.2. Casl

Casl, the *Common Algebraic Specification Language* [5], has been designed by CoFI, the *Common Framework Initiative* for algebraic specification and development. It has been designed by a large number of experts from different groups, and serves as a de-facto standard. The design of Casl has been approved by the IFIP WG 1.3 "Foundations of System Specification". Originally Casl was designed for specifying software requirements and design, but this paper goes further to explore the use of Casl for the specification of ontologies [6,15].

Casl consists of two major *levels*, which are quite independent: *basic specifications* and *structured specifications*. This paper focuses on the basic specification level where theories are defined in terms of FOL axioms. These axioms are based on signatures introduced by the user. A signature is the declaration of symbols for sorts, predicates, total and partial functions. Sorts are to be interpreted as non-empty sets and are used for the types of predicates and functions. Subsort hierarchies are available and axioms can be formed by the usual first order logical connectives. A sort can be declared to consist only of values reachable by terms (generated types) or to be isomorphic to a term algebra (free types). Casl offers loose specification and design specification, where loose specification covers only requirements, but leaves representation issues unspecified. For design specifications it is possible to describe representations of datatypes in great detail.

The present approach uses Casl in a limited way; only predicates with one or two arguments, functions (operations) with one argument and constants are used. The specification of subsorting is not limited. Casl datatype definitions must not contain constructors with arguments; hence only datatypes consisting of subsort embeddings or constant constructors are allowed. We refer to this sublanguage of CASL as *2-FOL* in the rest of this paper.

2.3. CASL-DL

CASL-DL is a sublanguage of CASL, which is equivalent to the description logic $\mathcal{SHOIN}(\mathbf{D})$ [15,16,1]. Basically, this is a DL with concepts (unary predicates) and roles (binary predicates), which allows to specify a hierarchy of concepts and a hierarchy of roles. For roles, only specific axioms are allowed: they can be specified as functional, inverse functional, transitive or symmetric, and they can be related to other roles as inverse, equivalent or as subrole. Also, the range and domain of a role can be specified. Concepts can be fully defined by, or just imply, certain descriptions. Descriptions either allow us to describe the negation, union and intersection of descriptions, or they are just another concept. Further descriptions are role restrictions, which allow limited introduction of one new variable and either demand the existence of certain relations between members of two descriptions or restrict the second argument of a role to be in the specified description. The following paragraph gives a detailed list of CASL constructs allowed in CASL-DL which can be used for the specification of a $\mathcal{SHOIN}(\mathbf{D})$ theory.

Explicitly, the following CASL constructs are allowed in CASL-DL:

- sorts and subsorts, but limited to those having a common maximal supersort called *Thing*, used for classes / concepts;
- free types with only the subsort alternative used to define the disjoint union of concepts;
- subsort definitions;
- a free or generated type with constant constructors is used to define enumerated concepts where all members are known; a free type implies that all constants have distinct values;
- predefined datatypes are allowed which have *DATA* as maximal supersort and form a hierarchy separate from the concept hierarchy below *Thing*;
- predicates with an arity of one (possibly empty concepts / classes) or two (roles / properties) arguments;
- partial functions restricted to one argument (functional roles / properties) and total constants (individuals);
- types for predicates and functions are only *Thing* or subsorts of it as subject (first or only argument position); the object position (second argument or result) is either typed with *Thing* or *DATA* or a subsort of one of these; except for constants which are typed with *Thing* or a subsort of it;
- formulas defining predicates and functions with types *Thing* × *Thing* and *Thing* → *Thing*, which are restricted to implication, equivalence, symmetry, transitivity, functional and inverse functional axioms with the further restriction that functional predicates cannot be transitive; for predicates and functions which relate to *DATA* only equivalence and implication axioms are allowed; additionally, so-called argument restriction axioms are allowed which allow the implication of a conjunction of two descriptions (see below) each restricting the arguments of the role which forms the premise;

- description axioms characterize either named concepts (sorts or unary predicates) or relate two descriptions via implication (partial definition) or equivalence (complete definition);
- descriptions are the logical constants *true* and *false*, concept membership axioms, negation, union and intersection of descriptions ($\neg$, $\wedge$, $\vee$), existential quantifications stating the existence of a relation to some object (or data value) described by a description, all-value restrictions stating that all fillers (second argument of predicate or result of partial function) fall into the given description, and has-value restrictions stating the relation to a particular individual or data value and cardinality restrictions;
- facts are axioms involving only constants and stating the relation among them (the ABox).

Further details on the expressiveness of CASL-DL and its relation to OWL DL and $\mathcal{SHOIN}(\mathbf{D})$ can be obtained from [15].

3. Approximating FOL Theories

In [17] a method is described to derive tractable Horn clauses from arbitrary propositional theories. This method (called *knowledge compilation*) uses Horn approximation to obtain a tractable form of the theory for automated reasoning. The approximation produces a stronger and a weaker set of Horn clauses, which is used in the reasoning process. Furthermore, [17] shows a sketch for the approximation of arbitrary FOL theories by Horn clauses. Alvaro del Val studies in [18,11] a general algorithm for FOL Knowledge Compilation into various sublanguages of FOL, but he mainly focuses on variants of Horn-languages. Del Val shows that only a weaker theory (which is maximally strong, s. Sect. 3.2) is needed if only a sublanguage of the target language is allowed for query answering from the compiled theory [18].

3.1. Approximating 2-FOL by DL Formulas

Inspired by this Horn approximation we have developed a DL approximation of 2-FOL. Our method tries to find a weaker DL theory that is entailed by the 2-FOL theory. In terms of CASL structured specifications this is a *view*:

view ENTAILMENT_OF_DL : EXMPLTHY_DL **to** EXMPLTHY_FOL

that gives a proof obligation that all axioms in EXMPLTHY_DL are entailed by EXMPLTHY_FOL. The model theoretic semantics of this view is

$$Mod(\text{EXMPLTHY\_FOL}) \subseteq Mod(\text{EXMPLTHY\_DL}).$$

Hence we generate a DL theory that is logically weaker than the original theory and that has a larger set of models.

The signature of the 2-FOL theory is translated by newly introducing one maximal sort which subsumes all sorts which are concepts and not datatypes in the DL sense if such is a sort is not available before. This sort is then mapped to the sort *Thing*. All sorts

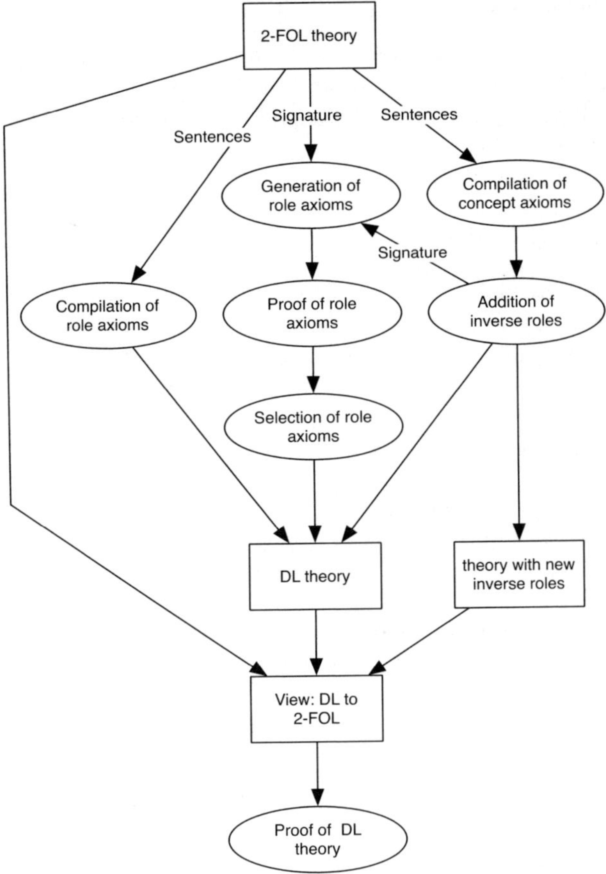

Figure 1. Flow of data during the generation of DL sentences

not subsumed by this topsort have to be mapped to one of the predefined datatypes in CASL-DL or must be hidden.

For the generation of the sentences of the approximated theory we distinguish two cases: (i) generation of axioms for each role (binary predicate) (ii) selection of formulas by patterns for argument restrictions, implications, equivalence and inverse axioms of roles and for descriptions of concepts (sorts and unary predicates). These patterns are derived from the allowed constructs in $\mathcal{SHIF}$ with reflexive relations, which is a sublogic of CASL-DL ($\mathcal{SHOIN}(\mathbf{D})$). $\mathcal{SHIF}$ has EXPTIME complexity but there exist DL reasoners that are highly optimized for this DL, e.g. Racer [12] and FaCT++ [13]. Although the DL variant we use is theoretically intractable, it is still tractable for practical purposes [19,20].

Figure 1 shows the schema of the following algorithm. Unlabeled edges transport a whole theory consisting of signature and sentences to the next node, labeled edges transport only signatures or sentences, respectively.

3.1.1. Generating role axioms

First we generate for each binary relation symbol in the theory transitive, symmetric, functional and inverse functional axioms and we try to prove all these axioms within the original theory. All proved axioms are included in the new theory except for those which are simultaneously prohibited by $\mathcal{SHIF}$. Here the user has to decide for each role which of the conflicting axioms should be kept.

3.1.2. Selection of role axioms by patterns

Here only those axioms are considered which involve binary predicates (roles) as premise or on one side of an equivalence axiom and are quantified over two variables. For the implications the consequent should either describe a concept for one or both arguments which yields an argument restriction or is a role application to the same argument variables (with the same order) as in the premise or is a conjunction of such constructs. Schematic template of these implications:

$$\forall x,y\colon s \ \bullet\ Rel_1(x,y) \Rightarrow \phi(x,y) \text{ and}$$
$$\phi(x,y) \equiv C_1(x) \mid C_2(y) \mid Rel_2(x,y) \mid \phi_1(x,y) \wedge \phi_2(x,y)$$
$$\text{where } C_i \text{ are descriptions of concepts and } \phi_i \text{ are constructed by the same rules as } \phi$$

Equivalences where role applications occur on both sides either state that the two roles are equivalent or that one role is the inverse of the other one. These axioms are allowed in CASL-DL, hence they are just kept. Other equivalences are checked for conjunctions with binary predicates (having the same argument order) where each conjunct with a role yields a consequence of an implication.

Here are some examples of axioms concerning roles:

$$\forall x,y\colon s \ \bullet\ PP(x,y) \Leftrightarrow P(x,y) \wedge \neg P(y,x) \qquad \%(\text{Dd1\_Proper\_Part})\%$$

where s is either the maximal topsort or a subsort of it. Here $PP(x,y)$ implies the conjunction and the conjunction has one conjunct that is allowed in DL. So the weak semantics that is compiled to DL is this

$$\forall x,y\colon s \ \bullet\ PP(x,y) \Rightarrow P(x,y) \qquad \%(\text{Dd1\_Proper\_Part\_Impl})\%$$

Clearly more than one implication could be derived from such a defining equivalence if more positive conjuncts are available. If P is transitive then PP is transitive, which can be proved. Further the symmetry of O can be proved directly from

$$\forall x,y\colon s \ \bullet\ O(x,y) \Leftrightarrow (\exists y\colon s \ \bullet\ P(z,x) \wedge P(z,y)) \qquad \%(\text{Dd2\_Overlap})\%$$

All the above proof obligations can be discharged automatically with SPASS [9].

3.1.3. Selection of concept axioms by patterns

The abstraction of formulas describing sorts or unary predicates is slightly more difficult than for binary predicates as there are recursive constructs of descriptions in CASL-DL. We focus on the cases where a formula is given as an implication or equivalence and respectively the premise or one of the equivalent formulas is a sort membership or unary predicate application. The formula must have only one outer free variable used in the left and right hand side of the logical connective. The consequent or other side of the equivalence must match a so-called role restriction: restrictions allow the introduction of a new variable only together with relation to the outer variable, where the outer variable is the first argument and the newly introduced variable is the second argument of the binary predicate. Here is the schema of such formulas where x is the outer variable and y the newly introduced one: $\phi(x) \equiv \forall y \bullet R(x, y) \Rightarrow \psi(y)$ In case that a predicate application fails to fall into this pattern, the inverse predicate is tried and introduced into the new theory if needed. Thus the axiom can be rewritten with the inverse predicate (formula %(Ad18_rw)% below in Section 3.3 is an example). Furthermore, a formula which is not universally quantified can be turned in such an implication as required above, with the sort membership as antecedent.

In summary, a view between the DL theory and the original theory plus inverse predicate definitions (introduced by the compilation) holds:

spec THY_FOL$^+$ =
   THY_FOL
then %**def**
   <inverse-predicate-definitions>

view THEORY_IN_DL_TO_FOL : THY_DL **to** THY_FOL$^+$

This method abstracts via approximation some 2-FOL theory into a semantically weaker but tractable DL theory such that for the model classes $Mod(\text{THY\_FOL}^+) \subseteq Mod(\text{THY\_DL})$ holds. Such a view and its symbol mapping are constructed as the last step of the approximation and its proof obligations must be discharged with SPASS (or Isabelle).

3.2. Is the resulting theory maximally strong?

One important question is not addressed in the above algorithm: Is the resulting DL-theory maximally strong with respect to the original theory? A DL-theory T_{DL} is maximally strong with respect to a FOL-theory T_{FOL} iff T_{DL} is weaker than T_{FOL} and equally strong as every DL-Theory between T_{DL} and T_{FOL}. A maximally strong theory is also called a minimal upper bound with respect to the original theory [17].

This paper will not give a complete answer to this question. But for roles (binary predicates) all possible formulas which can be generated with the given signature and are allowed (together) within a DL theory are kept if they can be proved. Thus, it is not possible to add further role axioms without leaving the restriction to DL, i.e. for formulas on roles this approach finds the maximal theory up to equivalence. For concept descriptions, only very few formulas are selected by patterns for inclusion into the DL theory. Here it is an open question, how close the approach in this paper comes to a maximal theory. Further ways of keeping more knowledge of the original theory in the DL theory and possibly finding a maximal DL theory with respect to the original theory are the subject of ongoing work.

3.3. Example: Mereology in FOL and CASL-DL

First a 2-FOL theory of mereology is presented which is the 2-FOL part of the FOL fragment of DOLCE (Descriptive Ontology for Linguistic and Cognitive Engineering) [3,4] as library MEREOFOL. A mereology provides the basic parthood relations for base concepts (categories) like *time interval (T)*, *space region (S)* and *perdurant (PD)*. We omit all ternary predicates (or two argument functions) like sum, product and difference which are present in the original FOL fragment of DOLCE. The specification PRIMITIVES gives a subset of the taxonomy with concepts named *particular (PT)*, *physical endurant (PED)*, *spatial location (SL)* and *temporal location (TL)*. All subconcepts (subsorts) of *PT* are pairwise disjoint, as specified by the free type construct.

library MEREOFOL **version** 0.1

```
%{This library is based on "A fragment of DOLCE for CASL"
    by Stefano Borgo, Claudio Masolo
    LOA-CNR
    March 5, 2004}%
```

spec PRIMITIVES =
    sorts *PD, PED, S, SL, T, TL*
    free type *PT* = *sorts PD, PED, S, SL, T, TL*
end

spec GENPARTHOOD [**sort** *s*] =
    pred $P : s \times s$
    $\forall\, x, y, z : s$
    • $P(x, x)$ %(Ad11)%
    • $P(x, y) \wedge P(y, x) \Rightarrow x = y$ %(Ad12)%
    • $P(x, y) \wedge P(y, z) \Rightarrow P(x, z)$ %(Ad13)%
end

spec GENMEREOLOGY [**sort** *s*] =
    GENPARTHOOD [**sort** *s*]
then preds $PP(x, y : s) \Leftrightarrow P(x, y) \wedge \neg P(y, x);$ %(Dd1_Proper_Part)%
        $O(x, y : s) \Leftrightarrow \exists z : s \bullet P(z, x) \wedge P(z, y);$ %(Dd2_Overlap)%
        $At(x : s) \Leftrightarrow \neg\, (\exists y : s \bullet PP(y, x));$ %(Dd3_Atom)%
    $\forall\, x, y : s$
    • $\neg\, P(x, y) \Rightarrow \exists z : s \bullet P(z, x) \wedge \neg\, O(z, y)$ %(Ad14)%
    • $\exists z : s \bullet At(z) \wedge P(z, x)$ %(Ad18)%
then %**implies**
%% Probable Theorems (1)
    $\forall\, x, y, su, su', p, p', d, d' : s$
    • $(\forall z' : s \bullet At(z') \Rightarrow P(z', x) \Rightarrow P(z', y)) \Rightarrow P(x, y)$ %(Td1)%
    • $At(x) \Leftrightarrow (\forall y' : s \bullet P(y', x) \Rightarrow x = y')$ %(Td2)%
    • $(\forall z : s \bullet O(z, x) \Leftrightarrow O(z, y)) \Rightarrow x = y$ %(Td3)%
end

spec MEREOLOGY =
    PRIMITIVES **and** GENMEREOLOGY [**sort** *T*] **and**
    GENMEREOLOGY [**sort** *S*] **and** GENMEREOLOGY [**sort** *PD*]
end

Library MEREODL shows the DL theory by applying the rules above to the library MEREOFOL. The inverse predicates of *PP* and *P* marked with *_i* are introduced to rewrite axioms %(Dd3_Atom)% and %(Ad18)%. Rewritten axioms are marked with _rw and axioms for inverse predicates are named either with the label of the original predicate definition or with the predicate name, and are marked with _inv. Derived implication, symmetry and transitivity axioms are named like the originating axiom and marked with respectively _impl, _sym and _trans. For the disambiguation of names they would be just numbered. Note that generic specifications are just kept in the resulting library of DL theories. So the structuring and grouping of the original theories is preserved and aids the readability of the result in this example. The real algorithm will just look at the theory of the specification to be compiled, but it can be extended to keep the structuring.

library MEREODL **version** 0.1

%{This library is based on "A fragment of DOLCE for CASL"
    by Stefano Borgo, Claudio Masolo
    LOA-CNR
    March 5, 2004
    further it is translated to CASL-DL}%

spec PRIMITIVES_DL =
    sorts *PD, PED, S, SL, T, TL*
    free type *Thing* = **sorts** *PD, PED, S, SL, T, TL*
end

spec GENPARTHOOD_DL [**sort** *s*] =
    pred *P* : *s* × *s*
    $\forall\, x, y, z$: *s*
    • $P(x, y) \wedge P(y, z) \Rightarrow P(x, z)$ %(Ad13)%
end

spec GENMEREOLOGY_DL [**sort** *s*] =
    GENPARTHOOD_DL [**sort** *s*]
then preds *PP* : *s* × *s*;
        $PP\_i(x, y: s) \Leftrightarrow PP(y, x)$;   %(Dd1_Proper_Part_inv)%
        $O(x, y: s) \Leftrightarrow O(y, x)$;   %(Dd2_Overlap_sym)%
        $At(x: s) \Leftrightarrow \neg\, (\exists\, y: s \bullet PP\_i(x, y))$;   %(Dd3_Atom_rw)%
        $P\_i(x, y: s) \Leftrightarrow P(y, x)$ %(P_inv)%
    $\forall\, x, y, z$: *s*
    • $\exists\, z': s \bullet P\_i(x, z') \wedge At(z')$ %(Ad18_rw)%
    • $PP(x, y) \Rightarrow P(x, y)$ %(Dd1_Proper_Part_impl)%
    • $PP(x, y) \wedge PP(y, z) \Rightarrow PP(x, z)$ %(Dd1_Proper_Part_trans)%
end

spec MEREOLOGY_DL =
    PRIMITIVES_DL **and** GENMEREOLOGY_DL [**sort** *T*] **and**
    GENMEREOLOGY_DL [**sort** *S*] **and** GENMEREOLOGY_DL [**sort** *PD*]
end

The view from MEREOLOGY_DL to MEREOLOGY that we proved to show the correctness of the approximation is presented below. For the inverse predicate definitions again a generic specification INVPP_P is used as the original axioms were defined in a generic specification. The instantiations are also derived from the instantiations of GEN-MEREOLOGY used in MEREOLOGY.

from MEREOFOL **get** MEREOLOGY
from MEREODL **get** MEREOLOGY_DL

spec INVPP_P [**sort** s
　　　　　　　preds $PP, P : s \times s$] =
　　preds $PP\_i(x, y: s) \Leftrightarrow PP(y, x)$;
　　　　$P\_i(x, y: s) \Leftrightarrow P(y, x)$
end

spec MEREOLOGY_INV =
　　MEREOLOGY
and INVPP_P [**sort** T
　　　　　　　preds $PP, P : T \times T$]
and INVPP_P [**sort** S
　　　　　　　preds $PP, P : S \times S$]
and INVPP_P [**sort** PD
　　　　　　　preds $PP, P : PD \times PD$]
end

view MEREOLOGY_DL_TO_FOL :
　　MEREOLOGY_DL **to** MEREOLOGY_INV =
　　sorts $Thing \mapsto PT, T \mapsto T, S \mapsto S, PD \mapsto PD, TL \mapsto TL,$
　　$SL \mapsto SL, PED \mapsto PED$
end

4. Conclusion

We have presented a method for compiling the knowledge of a 2-FOL theory into a tractable DL theory. Further, we have given a method for deriving proof obligations to ensure that the approximated theory subsumes the FOL theory. This is done by constructing a view that shows the refinement from the approximated DL theory to the original theory. Also the derived proof obligations written as views can be structured along the original theory, so that the user easily finds the originating specifications. This method of approximation generates only a weaker approximation (rather than also a stronger one). This is sufficient if the query language is a sublanguage of the target language [18]. Thus, with this method a formal underpinning for applied ontologies can be generated that is based on a foundational ontology and approximates its semantics. Such a foundational ontology can be formalized in a very expressive language without losing the connection to tractable application ontologies.

4.1. Future Work

Further extensions to this approach should be investigated such as the encoding of n-ary predicates into binary predicates while not cluttering the whole theory with complicated formulas. It should be investigated how to preserve the structuring of the original theory such that the resulting DL theory will be more readable.

In addition we can examine the quality of the compiled theory, i.e. check whether it is maximally strong with respect to the original (or as close as possible, but stronger and in DL). The generation of the DL theory and the proof of the generated view will be implemented within the HETS framework, using SPASS (or if necessary Isabelle). We expect that the approximated theory can in any case be proved to be a logical consequence of the original automatically with SPASS.

Moreover it is worth studying an application to the entire theory of DOLCE and to develop rich domain ontologies based on this, e.g. for Spatial Cognition. Furthermore, one should have a look at keeping some concrete domains such as integers which could be expressed in CASL (with axiomatization) and CASL-DL (only as literals). This would compile into $\mathcal{SHIF}(\mathbf{D})$, which is a DL that is still practically tractable and a sublogic of CASL-DL.

Acknowledgments

This paper has been supported by Deutsche Forschungsgemeinschaft (DFG) in the SFB/TR8 "Spatial Cognition". We thank Stefano Borgo, Nino Trainito, Till Mossakowski, Claudio Masolo, John Bateman, Stefan Wölfl, Scott Farrar, Lutz Schröder, Robert Ross, Wencke Lüttich and Nicola Guarino for discussions and ideas. Finally we thank two anonymous referees for their advice and comments.

References

[1]   F. Baader, D. Calvanese, D. McGuinness, D. Nardi, and P. F. Patel-Schneider, editors. *The Description Logic Handbook*. Cambridge University Press, 2003.

[2]   T. Berners-Lee, J. Hendler, and O. Lassila. The Semantic Web. *Scientific American*, May 2001.

[3]   A. Gangemi, N. Guarino, C. Masolo, A. Oltramari, and L. Schneider. Sweetening Ontologies with DOLCE. In A. Gómez-Pérez and V. R. Benjamins, editors, *EKAW*, volume 2473 of *LNCS*, pages 166–181. Springer Verlag; Berlin; http://www.springer.de, 2002.

[4]   C. Masolo, S. Borgo, A. Gangemi, N. Guarino, A. Oltramari, and L. Schneider. WonderWeb deliverable D17. The wonderWeb Library of Foundational Ontologies and the DOLCE ontology. Preliminary Report (ver. 2.0, 15-08-2002).

[5]   CoFI (The Common Framework Initiative). CASL *Reference Manual*. LNCS 2960 (IFIP Series). Springer Verlag; Berlin; http://www.springer.de, 2004.

[6]   K. Lüttich and T. Mossakowski. Specification of Ontologies in CASL. In A. C. Varci and L. Vieu, editors, *Formal Ontology in Information Systems – Proceedings of the Third International Conference (FOIS-2004)*, volume 114 of *Frontiers in Artificial Intelligence and Applications*, pages 140–150. IOS Press; Amsterdam; http://www.iospress.nl, 2004.

[7]   T. Mossakowski. The Heterogeneous Tool Set. Available at www.tzi.de/cofi/hets, University of Bremen.

[8]   T. Nipkow, L. C. Paulson, and M. Wenzel. *Isabelle/HOL — A Proof Assistant for Higher-Order Logic*. Springer Verlag; Berlin; http://www.springer.de, 2002.

[9]   C. Weidenbach, U. Brahm, T. Hillenbrand, E. Keen, C. Theobalt, and D. Topic. SPASS version 2.0. In A. Voronkov, editor, *Automated Deduction – CADE-18*, volume 2392 of *Lecture Notes in Computer Science*, pages 275–279. Springer Verlag; Berlin; http://www.springer.de, July 27-30 2002.

[10]   B. Selman and H. Kautz. Knowledge Compilation Using Horn Approximation. In *Proceedings of the Ninth National Conference on Artificial Intelligence (AAAI-91)*, pages 904–909, 1991.

[11]   A. del Val. First order LUB approximations: characterization and algorithms. *Artif. Intell.*, 162(1-2):7–48, 2005.

[12]   V. Haarslev and R. Möller. Racer System Description. In R. Goré, A. Leitsch, and T. Nipkow, editors, *IJCAR*, volume 2083 of *Lecture Notes in Computer Science*, pages 701–706. Springer Verlag; Berlin; `http://www.springer.de`, 2001.

[13]   I. Horrocks. FaCT++. Available at `http://owl.man.ac.uk/factplusplus/`.

[14]   E. Sirin, M. Grove, B. Parsia, and R. Alford. Pellet OWL reasoner. `http://www.mindswap.org/2003/pellet/index.shtml`, May 2004.

[15]   K. Lüttich, T. Mossakowski, and B. Krieg-Brückner. Ontologies for the Semantic Web in CASL. In J. Fiadeiro, editor, *Recent Trends in Algebraic Development Techniques, 17th International Workshop (WADT 2004)*, volume 3423 of *Lecture Notes in Computer Science*, pages 106–125. Springer Verlag; Berlin; `http://www.springer.de`, 2005.

[16]   I. Horrocks and P. F. Patel-Schneider. Reducing OWL Entailment to Description Logic Satisfiability. In D. Fensel, K. Sycara, and J. Mylopoulos, editors, *Proc. of the 2003 International Semantic Web Conference (ISWC 2003)*, number 2870 in Lecture Notes in Computer Science, pages 17–29. Springer Verlag; Berlin; `http://www.springer.de`, 2003.

[17]   B. Selman and H. A. Kautz. Knowledge Compilation and Theory Approximation. *J. ACM*, 43(2):193–224, 1996.

[18]   A. del Val. An Analysis of Approximate Knowledge Compilation. In *IJCAI (1)*, pages 830–836, 1995.

[19]   I. Horrocks and U. Sattler. A description logic with transitive and inverse roles and role hierarchies. *J. Log. Comput.*, 9(3):385–410, 1999.

[20]   S. Tobies. *Complexity Results and Practical Algorithms for Logics in Knowledge Representation*. PhD thesis, RWTH Aachen, 2001.

Formal Ontology in Information Systems
B. Bennett and C. Fellbaum (Eds.)
IOS Press, 2006

OntOWLClean: Cleaning OWL ontologies with OWL

Chris WELTY[1]
IBM Watson Research Center, NY, USA

Abstract. OWL is now very widely used for ontology development and several attempts have been made at incorporating OntoClean analysis into an OWL-based tool. I present here an OWL ontology representing the basic OntoClean distinctions, and a tool and methodology for applying it to OWL ontologies. I briefly touch on the semantic issues implied by using OWL Full syntax to characterize the OntoClean meta-properties as properties of OWL Classes, and how that was solved to employ an off-the-shelf OWL DL reasoner to check the OntoClean constraints on the taxonomy.

Keywords. OWL, OntoClean.

Introduction

OWL is now by far the most common language used to encode formal ontologies for information systems, and after two years is still the only standard. While adoption has been somewhat slow, open-source and free tool support is now available for reasoners, editors, browsers, syntax checkers, viewers, explanation, and numerous others. In some cases the ontologies being developed in OWL are extremely lightweight and scruffy, and do not need extensive analysis or maintenance. In other cases, however, correctly conveying the meaning of terms in an ontology is important and the demand for ontology quality is high, and this has led people to analysis tools such as OntoClean.

OntoClean was first published in a series of papers in 2000 [10,11,12,13]. Since them it has been widely cited, used, and criticized. One of the most common criticisms of OntoClean as a tool for analyzing ontologies is that it is too complicated. Indeed, the semantics of the OntoClean meta-properties were presented using S5 Modal Logic, and many ontology authors are unable to penetrate the axioms. Another, likely consequent, criticism has been that it is not always clear how to assign the meta-properties, and that agreement between even experienced ontology designers is quite low. The most common question we receive by email is, "Is X rigid?" Finally, the use of S5 modal logic for expressing the semantics of OntoClean has led some to conclude, incorrectly, that the computational complexity of any OntoClean analysis tool is too high. I will address each of these issues in this paper.

---

[1] Corresponding Author: IBM Watson Research Center; 19 Skyline Dr.; Hawthorne, NY. 12540; USA. E-mail: welty@us.ibm.com

1. Understanding the meta-properties

In one recent article, it was claimed that "multiple ontologists assign different meta-properties to the same concept" [1], based on the interesting evaluation work done by Völker et al [2]. This is impossible, of course, the same concept cannot have different meta-properties, in reality the disagreement is due to the same term representing different concepts to different people. In fact, this is precisely the main value of OntoClean, to expose subtle differences in different people's understanding of concepts represented in an ontology. This is the very crux of the issue, a class cannot be both rigid and non-rigid, cannot be both a sortal and non-sortal, etc. If two different analysts adopt conflicting meta-property assignments then they have different interpretations. It is critical to expose such differences as ontologies are supposed to capture a "common understanding" or "shared meaning" of terms.

In our own experience, we have encountered this phenomenon every time we applied the OntoClean analysis, including the very first OntoClean example, which is reproduced in OWL below. We had developed the example drawing specific poorly chosen subsumption relations from existing ontologies and lexical resources, adding a few of our own. The major objective was for the taxonomy to appear reasonable *prima facie*, but to break down under the close scrutiny of the meta-properties. Once we had chosen our classes and taxonomy, we set out to independently to assign the meta-properties. For the class Food, I had chosen Rigid, Independent, Sortal, and Unity. Nicola chose Anti-Rigid, Dependent, Sortal, and Anti-Unity. In the ensuing discussion, I held up a piece of chocolate as an instance of Food and suggested that the only way it could cease to be food would be if it ceased to exist, which I then demonstrated. Nicola's position was that the chocolate was not Food until I ate it.

The key here is not to try and determine who is right – we were both right in the sense that we had applied the meta-properties correctly to reflect what we each thought Food meant – we had to recognize that there are (at least) two ways of thinking about what Food means. I had thought of Food as basically the class of all human edible objects, whereas Nicola thought of Food as a role in a relation, anything can in that sense be Food if it is eaten.

The next step in ontology design would be to determine if both the possible meanings are needed and select one or distinguish them as different classes. In this case we agreed to use Nicola's meaning and dropped the other.

Finally, note that OntoClean doesn't tell us what the class Food means, it allows us to clarify some part of the meaning. Some people have come away from the papers thinking the example ontology is supposed to be authoritative, and that "according to OntoClean" the Person class is Rigid. Thus we so often get questions from people about whether some class in their ontology is rigid or not. The answer is always that *it depends on what you mean*. It's rather a frustrating misunderstanding as the papers repeat the point often: the examples are only examples and it is certainly possible to have an ontology with a class called Person that is not rigid, or (as above) a class called Food that is. What OntoClean does tell us is that these classes mean something different, despite having the same names, because they have different meta-properties.

What has become clear from our experiences is that people need a standard and reusable way to share the meta-property assignments in order to communicate them, discover their disagreements, and take appropriate action.

2. Previous OntoClean Implementations

The semantics of OntoClean were such that a few simple constraints on taxonomic organization fell out:

- A rigid class cannot be a subclass of an anti-rigid class
- A class with unity cannot be a subclass of a class with anti-unity
- All subclasses of a sortal are sortals (sortals are classes that have an identity criterion)
- All subclasses of a dependent class are dependent

The primary challenge in implementing any tool to support OntoClean is that it requires reasoning about the classes and their taxonomic relationships. In logical systems, the taxonomic relationship is often not expressed as a relation but by using implication. In OWL-DL, it *is* expressed as a relation (`rdfs:subClassOf`), but the formal semantics do not treat it as such. Thus the relation (in OWL DL) is privileged and cannot be further refined or restricted (as we would like).

The full version of OWL does allow one to further refine the axiomatization of the subClassOf relation, but such reasoning in general is undecidable [3] and experience with reasoners that implement it is that they are very slow.

In two particular implementations of OntoClean support, the OntoClean constraints were simply encoded in systems that treated the classes as instances and did not consider the instances of the classes themselves: the tools merely pointed out inconsistencies in the taxonomic structure implied by the constraints (e.g. a rigid class subsumed by an anti-rigid class). Thus each class was represented by an individual that "stood in" for it in order to support the OntoClean reasoning. This is analogous to "punning", a technique in logic in which objects are given multiple interpretations depending on certain syntactic or semantic contexts. In a possible new OWL dialect that supports "meta modeling" (i.e. the ability to reason about classes of classes), punning has been proposed as a way to keep the semantic domains of classes and individuals disjoint [4], which is a well understood way to promote decidability, and is a requirement in all OWL-DL reasoners today.

The first OntoClean implementation [5], used LISP-Classic and has not survived. It required generating an a-box version of an ontology which was in no way connected to the original (other than having visibly similar names).

The second implementation [6] uses Protégé PAL constraints and works well within the Protégé system, but the meta-property annotations can not be shared with others who don't use Protégé. Also, it does not work seamlessly with OWL Ontologies, being designed more for use with the built-in OKBC language Protégé was originally designed for.

3. Implementing the OntoClean Constraints in OWL

In order to develop a standard representation of the OntoClean meta-properties and their constraints, and furthermore to enable today's tools to process those constraints in a standard way, I have developed an OWL-DL ontology of the OntoClean meta-properties and constraints, and a simple tool that creates an instance view of an OWL class hierarchy.

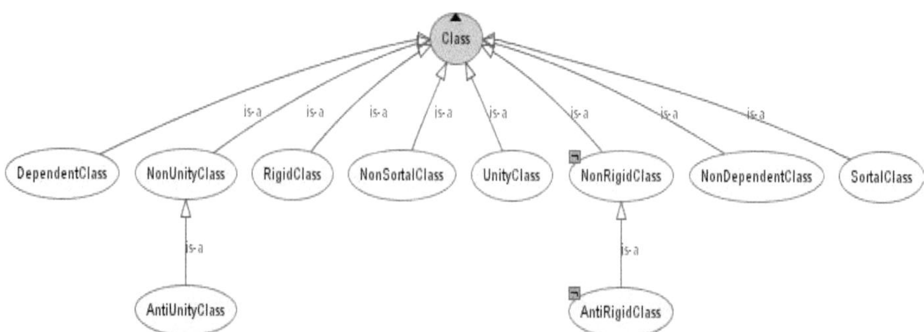

Figure 1. The OntoClean taxonomy of Classes

The OntoClean ontology is shown in Figure 1 and listed below in the OWL abstract syntax (this and the other OWL ontologies shown in this paper are available at the URLs referenced in the Ontology element, with added information like comments):

```
Namespace(rdfs = <http://www.w3.org/2000/01/rdf-schema#>)
Namespace(owl  = <http://www.w3.org/2002/07/owl#>)
Namespace(oc = <http://www.ontoclean.org/ontoclean-dl-v1.1.owl#>)

Ontology( <http://www.ontoclean.org/ontoclean-dl-v1.1.owl>

 Annotation(owl:versionInfo "1.1"@en)

 ObjectProperty(hasSubClass inverseOf(oc:subClassOf)
              domain(Class) range(Class))
 ObjectProperty(oc:subClassOf Transitive inverseOf(hasSubClass)
              domain(Class) range(Class))

 Class(oc:Class complete
   intersectionOf(unionOf(NonSortalClass SortalClass)
              unionOf(RigidClass NonRigidClass)
              unionOf(UnityClass NonUnityClass)
              unionOf(NonDependentClass DependentClass)))

 Class(RigidClass partial oc:Class
    restriction(oc:subClassOf
              allValuesFrom(complementOf(AntiRigidClass))))
 Class(NonRigidClass partial oc:Class)
 Class(AntiRigidClass partial NonRigidClass)
 DisjointClasses(RigidClass NonRigidClass)

 Class(SortalClass partial oc:Class
    restriction(hasSubClass allValuesFrom(SortalClass)))
 Class(NonSortalClass partial oc:Class)
 DisjointClasses(SortalClass NonSortalClass)

 Class(UnityClass partial oc:Class
    restriction(oc:subClassOf
              allValuesFrom(complementOf(AntiUnityClass))))
 Class(NonUnityClass partial oc:Class)
 Class(AntiUnityClass partial NonUnityClass)
 DisjointClasses(UnityClass NonUnityClass)

 Class(DependentClass partial oc:Class
    restriction(hasSubClass allValuesFrom(DependentClass)))
```

```
Class(NonDependentClass partial oc:Class)
DisjointClasses(DependentClass NonDependentClass)
)
```

The ontology is quite simple and well within the expressive limitations of OWL-DL and any reasoner I have tried. Pellet [8] lists the ontology as requiring *ALCR+* expressivity. Note that it is not necessary to encode the modal axioms, just the meta-properties as classes with proper disjointness and constraints on the `oc:subClassOf` relation. In particular, the `oc:subClassOf` relation is defined to be transitive and have an inverse, and the four OntoClean constraints above are expressed as "local range constraints" on the `oc:subClassOf` relation.

The semantics of OntoClean, however, are not expressed in this ontology alone, as one must understand to use it that the domain of the ontology is another ontology; the instances of these classes are OWL classes themselves. To complete the semantics of OntoClean, I have defined a separate ontology that contains two mapping axioms, shown below, that equate `oc:Class` and `oc:subClassOf` to their OWL equivalents:

```
Namespace(rdfs = <http://www.w3.org/2000/01/rdf-schema#>)
Namespace(owl  = <http://www.w3.org/2002/07/owl#>)
Namespace(oc = <http://www.ontoclean.org/ontoclean-dl-v1.1.owl#>)

Ontology( <http://www.ontoclean.org/ontoclean-full-v1.owl>

 Annotation( owl:imports
             <http://www.ontoclean.org/ontoclean-dl-v1.1.owl>)

 SameIndividual(oc:Class owl:Class)
 SameIndividual(oc:subClassOf rdfs:subClassOf)
)
```

This ontology is kept separate for several reasons: I have not yet found a tool that handles it properly (since it uses the OWL and RDFS vocabulary which these tools treat as immutable), and more importantly keeping the basic ontology within DL enables use of existing reasoners to check the OntoClean constraints.

Without support for this kind of meta-modeling, it was necessary to create a simple tool that takes as input an OWL ontology and generates a "view" of that ontology in which all classes are individuals and all `rdfs:subClassOf` relations are `oc:subClassOf` relations, again rather like punning except done explicitly. An important and perhaps subtle point here is that the generated view does not contain new objects, it uses the URIs of the classes in the original ontology as the identifiers for the individuals. The trick is not to import the ontology in which these URIs are labeled as classes, and thus any tool, including reasoners, will load and reason about the data.

Figure 2 shows the infamous OntoClean example, before cleaning, and it is listed below in the OWL abstract syntax:

```
Namespace(rdf  = <http://www.w3.org/1999/02/22-rdf-syntax-ns#>)
Namespace(xsd  = <http://www.w3.org/2001/XMLSchema#>)
Namespace(rdfs = <http://www.w3.org/2000/01/rdf-schema#>)

Ontology( <http://www.ontoclean.org/example-dirty-v1.owl>

 Class(Agent partial Entity)
 Class(AmountOfMatter partial Entity)
 Class(Animal partial Agent PhysicalObject LivingBeing)
 Class(Apple partial Fruit Food)
```

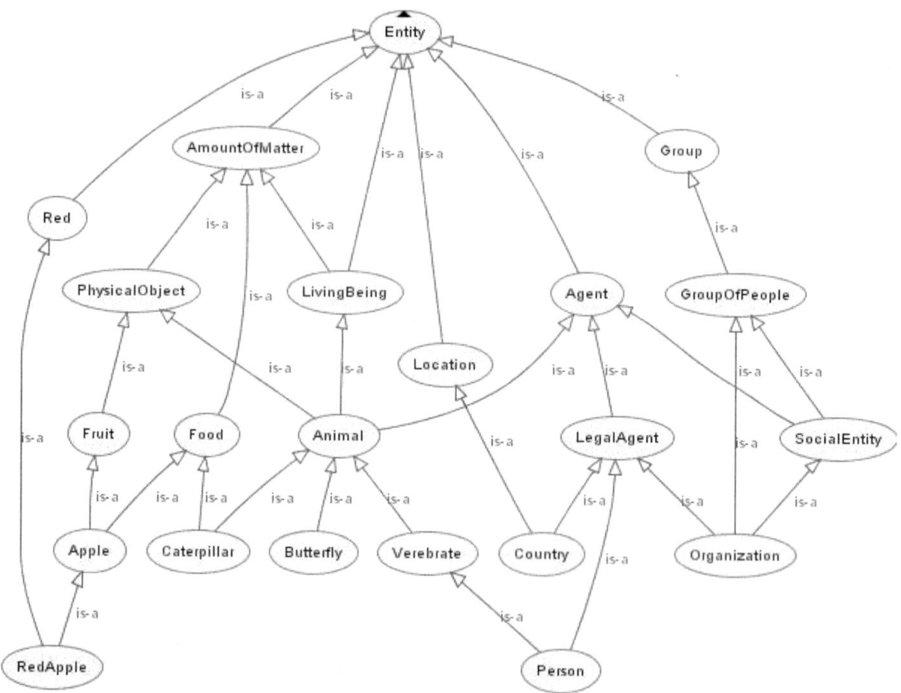

Figure 2. The example before cleaning.

```
Class(Butterfly partial Animal)
Class(Caterpillar partial Animal Food)
Class(Country partial LegalAgent Location)
Class(Entity partial)
Class(Food partial AmountOfMatter)
Class(Fruit partial PhysicalObject)
Class(Group partial Entity)
Class(GroupOfPeople partial Group)
Class(LegalAgent partial Agent)
Class(LivingBeing partial Entity AmountOfMatter)
Class(Location partial Entity)
Class(Organization partial GroupOfPeople SocialEntity LegalAgent)
Class(Person partial LegalAgent Verebrate)
Class(PhysicalObject partial AmountOfMatter)
Class(Red partial Entity)
Class(RedApple partial Apple Red)
Class(SocialEntity partial Agent GroupOfPeople)
Class(Verebrate partial Animal)
)
```

The result of generating the instance view of the example is shown below:

```
Namespace(ont = <http://www.ontoclean.org/example-dirty-v1.owl#>)
Namespace(oc = <http://www.ontoclean.org/ontoclean-dl-v1.1.owl#>)

Ontology( <http://www.ontoclean.org/example-dirty-v1-punned.owl>

   Annotation( owl:imports
            <http://www.ontoclean.org/ontoclean-dl-v1.1.owl>)

Individual(ont:Agent type(oc:Class) value(oc:subClassOf ont:Entity))
Individual(ont:AmountOfMatter type(oc:Class)
          value(oc:subClassOf ont:Entity))
Individual(ont:Animal type(oc:Class)
```

```
                value(oc:subClassOf ont:PhysicalObject))
  Individual(ont:Apple type(oc:Class) value(oc:subClassOf ont:Fruit))
  Individual(ont:Butterfly type(oc:Class)
                value(oc:subClassOf ont:Animal))
  Individual(ont:Caterpillar type(oc:Class)
                value(oc:subClassOf ont:Animal))
  Individual(ont:Country type(oc:Class)
                value(oc:subClassOf ont:LegalAgent))
  Individual(ont:Entity type(oc:Class))
  Individual(ont:Food type(oc:Class)
                value(oc:subClassOf ont:AmountOfMatter))
  Individual(ont:Fruit type(oc:Class)
                value(oc:subClassOf ont:PhysicalObject))
  Individual(ont:Group type(oc:Class) value(oc:subClassOf ont:Entity))
  Individual(ont:GroupOfPeople type(oc:Class)
                value(oc:subClassOf ont:Group))
  Individual(ont:LegalAgent type(oc:Class)
                value(oc:subClassOf ont:Agent))
  Individual(ont:LivingBeing type(oc:Class)
                value(oc:subClassOf ont:AmountOfMatter))
  Individual(ont:Location type(oc:Class)
                value(oc:subClassOf ont:Entity))
  Individual(ont:Organization type(oc:Class)
                value(oc:subClassOf ont:LegalAgent))
  Individual(ont:Person type(oc:Class)
                value(oc:subClassOf ont:LegalAgent))
  Individual(ont:PhysicalObject type(oc:Class)
                value(oc:subClassOf ont:AmountOfMatter))
  Individual(ont:Red type(oc:Class) value(oc:subClassOf ont:Entity))
  Individual(ont:RedApple type(oc:Class) value(oc:subClassOf ont:Red))
  Individual(ont:SocialEntity type(oc:Class)
                value(oc:subClassOf ont:Agent))
  Individual(ont:Verebrate type(oc:Class)
                value(oc:subClassOf ont:Animal))
)
```

Again, take specific note that the ontology does not define any identifiers of its own, each individual is labeled with tags from other ontologies. In the context of FOIS it is worth commenting that, strictly speaking, this is not an ontology at all, just a collection of axioms. However the OWL definition of ontology is a syntactic one – an RDF file that has the `owl:ontology` element in it. In addition, from a semantic web perspective it is not really well-defined what this ontology "means" – should the meaning include the complete definitions of the objects referenced? In practice, most OWL tools do not "follow hyperlinks" to external URIs, and take the "import" annotation to be the only such directive. In this case, every tool I tested will load only the individual view and the imported OntoClean ontology.

4. OntoCleaning using existing tools

The most prominent tools for OWL are Protégé [9] and Swoop [7]. This section provides an informal evaluation of each for the purposes of supporting OntoClean.

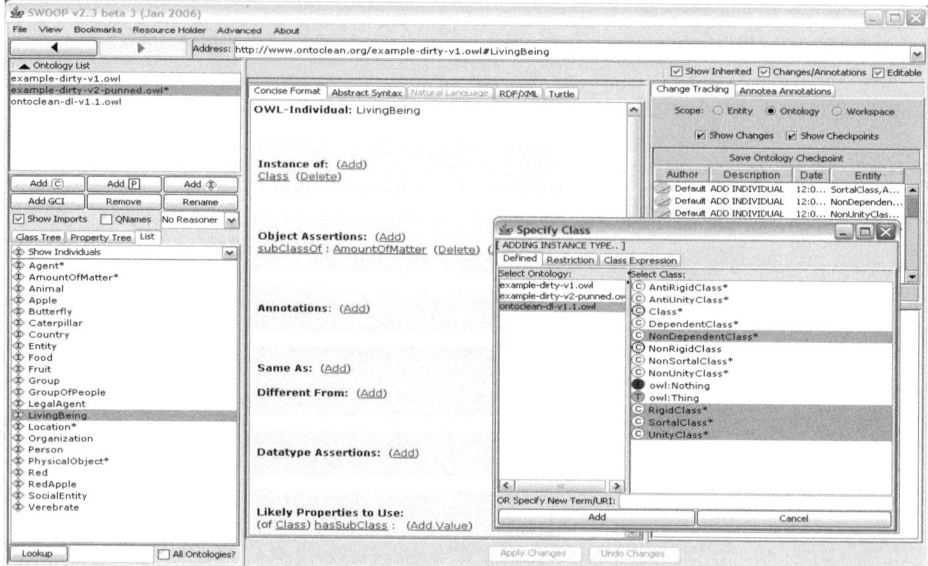

Figure 3. Assigning meta-properties in SWOOP.

4.1. Assigning and Checking the MetaProperties

When the individual view is loaded into SWOOP, assigning the meta-properties is done by going to the instance list tab in the left pane and selecting an individual view of one of the classes. Then, in the individual description, click on the "Add" link next to the "Instance Of" heading, which brings up a dialog that lets you select as many classes as desired. Figure 3 shows assigning meta-properties in SWOOP.

When the individual view is loaded into Protégé, the meta-properties can be assigned by switching to the "Individuals" Tab and then selecting one of the inviduals. On the bottom of the individual list is a pane that allows you to add "Asserted Types". Protégé supports dragging an individual from the middle individual list pane to a class on the left class list pane, however this moves the individual rather than copying it so you can only assign one meta-property this way. The rest must be done using the add operation. Figure 4 shows assigning of meta-properties in Protégé.

The individual view in the OWL abstract syntax with all the meta-properties assigned for the example is shown in the appendix.

Both SWOOP and Protégé seem to assume that individuals are defined within an ontology, and do not let you "browse" the individuals in the case where their URIs are external. Protégé is general does not appear to be particularly web-savvy, and does not provide this functionality in general, but SWOOP typically provides clickable links for any URI referenced in an ontology that allows you to, at the least, open up a browser with the URI. This capability is not, however, provided for individuals.

Protégé displays the names of individuals with their full namespaces, but in Pellet they are shown with the namespace stripped off. So rather than `ont:Agent` in Pellet we see just `Agent`. This would be a problem if the analysis was being done on a merge between two ontologies that used the same short name for a class, and visually the namespace prefix helps reinforce that these are externally defined objects.

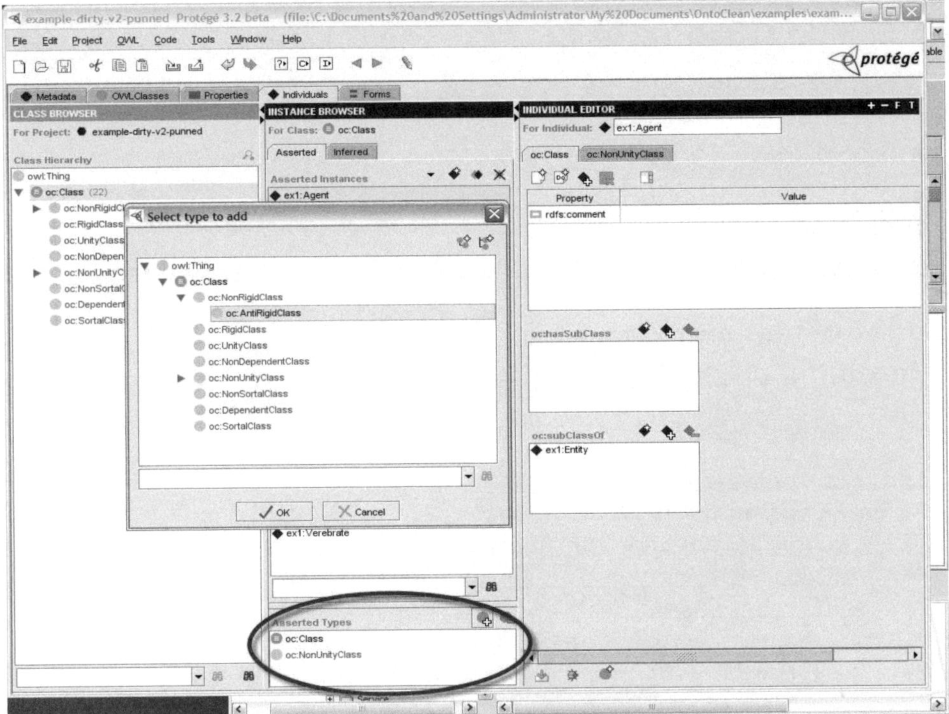

Figure 4. Assigning meta-properties in Protégé.

In general, the SWOOP interface is easier to use for the assignment of meta-properties because it allows you to add all four at once, whereas Protégé requires you assign each meta-property for each individual separately. Dragging seemed a more convenient way to do the assignment, if it could have been used for all four.

In either system, one can assign all the meta-properties and then check the constraints, or turn on a reasoner (Pellet for SWOOP and Racer for Protégé) and have it check as you assign them. There are basically two kinds of violations to be checked for, disjointness (e.g. assigning both Dependent and non-Dependent to a single class) and constraints on the subclass relation (e.g. an anti-rigid class subsuming a rigid one). Technically, all constraints end up being disjointness violations, the distinction is whether the violation arose from the class hierarchy or a primitive assignment.

The interface in Protégé is far better at indicating a meta-property violation, in SWOOP there is no visual indication of a problem, one must know to click on the ontology in the "Ontology List" pane to see if there is a problem. However, in Protégé (really, in Racer) the explanation of the problem is of no use at all, it basically tells you that something is wrong, but not where. Thus you are forced to assign the meta-properties one at a time and run the check after each.

In SWOOP, when you discover a problem the explanation tells you precisely the problem. One can imagine the explanations running rather long if there is a deep taxonomy and a violation occurs between two classes that are very distant, but in general the explanation facility in SWOOP does precisely what is needed, with very little extraneous information. An example of an explanation is shown in Figure 5.

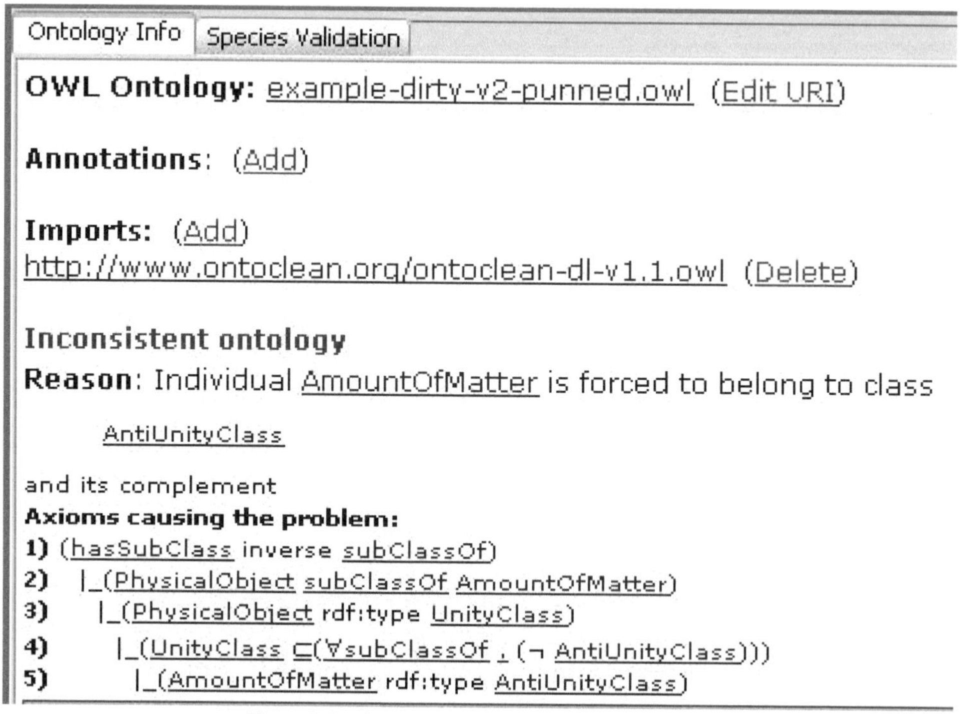

Ontology Info | Species Validation

OWL Ontology: example-dirty-v2-punned.owl (Edit URI)

Annotations: (Add)

Imports: (Add)
http://www.ontoclean.org/ontoclean-dl-v1.1.owl (Delete)

Inconsistent ontology
Reason: Individual AmountOfMatter is forced to belong to class

     AntiUnityClass

and its complement
Axioms causing the problem:
1) (hasSubClass inverse subClassOf)
2) |_(PhysicalObject subClassOf AmountOfMatter)
3) |_(PhysicalObject rdf:type UnityClass)
4) |_(UnityClass ⊑ (∀subClassOf . (¬ AntiUnityClass)))
5) |_(AmountOfMatter rdf:type AntiUnityClass)

Figure 5. Explaining constraint violations in SWOOP.

4.2. Fixing the Taxonomy

When a violation of the OntoClean constraints is found, the user should either reconsider the meaning of the class and reassign the meta-properties to be consistent, or change the class hierarchy. One can easily experiment with reassignment of the meta-properties in the tools, but if the taxonomy is to be changed the process is somewhat roundabout.

One can experiment in the view to get the hierarchy right by changing the values of the `oc:subClassOf` relation, however the user must keep track of these changes and then manually change them in the original ontology. It would seem that the simple tool used to generate the individual view should be able to "go the other way", i.e. generate the `rdfs:subClassOf` relations from the `oc:subClassOf` relations in the view, but this does not work in general. The problem is twofold:

The generated individual view is a view in a very real sense, it is a monotonic *addition* to the original ontology, it simply adds rdf:type axioms. Any changes to this view must be interpreted the same way, and there is no way to "retract" an assertion in OWL by adding axioms. One can make it inconsistent, but not retract.

The view file itself is not the original ontology in a different form, in particular it does not include properties, nor any axioms on properties, etc., thus a new version of the ontology generated from a modified view would have only the class names and the new subClassOf values.

The simplest way to make changes is to keep an editor open on the original ontology while working in the view. Make changes in the original and regenerate the view. This does not take very many extra steps than if the changes were made in the view directly, and in theory either Protégé or SWOOP could add buttons that run the view generator to make it even easier.

In SWOOP one can have multiple ontologies open (in the ontology List) so switching between them is easier than in Protégé, which needs to be "run" separately for each ontology open. One can run Pellet separately for each ontology as well, obviously, and this makes it possible to actually view both ontologies on the screen at the same time.

5. Conclusion

One of the obstacles to successfully using OntoClean today is the lack of ability to communicate the meta-property assignments in a standard way, and the lack of tooling to support this assignment and validation of the constraints. I have presented here an OWL ontology of the OntoClean meta-properties that, along with a simple view generator, can be used along with existing off-the-shelf OWL tools to assign the meta-properties and validate the taxonomy. I also briefly surveyed the use of SWOOP and Protégé for meta-property assignment with this ontology, and Pellet and Racer to validate the constraints. The ontology and examples are available on the web.

References

[1]   Sleeman, Derek. and Quentin Reul. 2006. CleanONTO: Evaluating Taxonomic Relationships in Ontologies. *2006 Workshop on Evaluating Ontologies* (EON 2006). Edinburgh.

[2]   Völker, Johanna , Denny Vrandecic, and York Sure. 2005. Automatic Evaluation of Ontologies (AEON). *International Semantic Web Conference 2005* (ISWC-05): 716-731. Galway.

[3]   Motik, Boris. 2005. On the Properties of Metamodeling in OWL. *International Semantic Web Conference 2005* (ISWC-05). Galway.

[4]   Patel-Schneider, Peter. 2005. *The OWL 1.1 Extension to the W3C OWL Web Ontology Language.* http://www-db.research.bell-labs.com/user/pfps/owl/overview.html

[5]   Welty, Chris and Nicola Guarino. 2001. Support for Ontological Analysis of Taxonomic Relationships. *J. Data and Knowledge Engineering.* **39**(1):51-74. October, 2001.

[6]   Noy, Natasha. 2003. *The OntoClean Ontology in Protégé.* http://protege.stanford.edu/ontologies/ontoClean/ontoCleanOntology.html

[7]   Kalyanpur, Aditya, Bijan Parsia, Evren Sirin, Bernardo Cuenca-Grau, and James Hendler. 2005. Swoop - a web ontology editing browser. *Journal of Web Semantics*, 4(1).

[8]   Sirin, Evren, Bijan Parsia, Bernardo Cuenca Grau, Aditya Kalyanpur, and Yarden Katz. In Press. Pellet: A practical owl-dl reasoner. Submitted for publication to *Journal of Web Semantics.*

[9]   Knaublock, Holger. 2003. *Protégé-OWL.* http://protege.stanford.edu/overview/protege-owl.html

[10] Guarino, Nicola and Chris Welty. 2000. A Formal Ontology of Properties. In, Dieng, R., and Corby, O., eds, *Proceedings of EKAW-2000: The 12th International Conference on Knowledge Engineering and Knowledge Management.* Spring-Verlag LNCS Vol. 1937:97-112. October, 2000.

[11] Guarino, Nicola and Chris Welty. 2000. Identity, Unity, and Individuality: Towards a formal toolkit for ontological analysis. *In, Horn, W. ed., Proceedings of ECAI-2000: The European Conference on Artificial Intelligence.* Pp. 219-223. Berlin: IOS Press. August, 2000.

[12] Guarino, Nicola and Chris Welty. 2002. Identity and Subsumption. In Rebecca Green, Carol A. Bean, & Sung Hyon Myaeng (Eds.), *The Semantics of Relationships: An Interdisciplinary Perspective.* Pp. 111-125. Dordrecht: Kluwer.

[13] Guarino, Nicola and Chris Welty. 2004. An Overview of OntoClean. In Steffen Staab and Rudi Studer, eds., *The Handbook on Ontologies.* Pp. 151-172. Berlin:Springer-Verlag.

Appendix

```
Namespace(ont  = <http://www.ontoclean.org/example-dirty-v1.owl#>)
Namespace(oc = <http://www.ontoclean.org/ontoclean-dl-v1.1.owl#>)
Ontology( <http://www.ontoclean.org/example-dirty-v1-punned.owl>

  Annotation(imports <http://www.ontoclean.org/ontoclean-dl-v1.1.owl>)

  Individual(ont:Agent type(oc:NonSortalClass) type(oc:AntiRigidClass)
    type(oc:NonUnityClass) type(oc:DependentClass)
    value(oc:subClassOf ont:Entity))
  Individual(ont:AmountOfMatter type(oc:AntiUnityClass)
    type(oc:NonDependentClass) type(oc:SortalClass)
    type(oc:RigidClass) value(oc:subClassOf ont:Entity))
  Individual(ont:Animal type(oc:UnityClass) type(oc:NonDependentClass)
    type(oc:SortalClass) type(oc:RigidClass)
    value(oc:subClassOf ont:PhysicalObject))
  Individual(ont:Apple type(oc:UnityClass) type(oc:NonDependentClass)
    type(oc:SortalClass) type(oc:RigidClass)
    value(oc:subClassOf ont:Fruit))
  Individual(ont:Butterfly type(oc:AntiRigidClass) type(oc:UnityClass)
    type(oc:NonDependentClass) type(oc:SortalClass)
    value(oc:subClassOf ont:Animal))
  Individual(ont:Caterpillar type(oc:AntiRigidClass)
    type(oc:UnityClass) type(oc:NonDependentClass) type(oc:SortalClass)
    value(oc:subClassOf ont:Animal))
  Individual(ont:Country type(oc:AntiRigidClass) type(oc:UnityClass)
    type(oc:NonDependentClass) type(oc:SortalClass)
    value(oc:subClassOf ont:LegalAgent))
  Individual(ont:Entity type(oc:Class))
  Individual(ont:Food type(oc:AntiRigidClass) type(oc:AntiUnityClass)
    type(oc:SortalClass) type(oc:DependentClass)
    value(oc:subClassOf ont:AmountOfMatter))
  Individual(ont:Fruit type(oc:UnityClass) type(oc:NonDependentClass)
    type(oc:SortalClass) type(oc:RigidClass)
    value(oc:subClassOf ont:PhysicalObject))
  Individual(ont:Group type(oc:AntiUnityClass)
    type(oc:NonDependentClass) type(oc:SortalClass) type(oc:RigidClass)
    value(oc:subClassOf ont:Entity))
  Individual(ont:GroupOfPeople type(oc:AntiUnityClass)
    type(oc:NonDependentClass) type(oc:SortalClass) type(oc:RigidClass)
    value(oc:subClassOf ont:Group))
  Individual(ont:LegalAgent type(oc:AntiRigidClass)
    type(oc:SortalClass) type(oc:NonUnityClass) type(oc:DependentClass)
    value(oc:subClassOf ont:Agent))
  Individual(ont:LivingBeing type(oc:UnityClass)
    type(oc:NonDependentClass) type(oc:SortalClass) type(oc:RigidClass)
    value(oc:subClassOf ont:AmountOfMatter))
  Individual(ont:Location type(oc:NonDependentClass)
    type(oc:SortalClass) type(oc:NonUnityClass) type(oc:RigidClass)
    value(oc:subClassOf ont:Entity))
  Individual(ont:Organization type(oc:UnityClass)
    type(oc:NonDependentClass) type(oc:SortalClass) type(oc:RigidClass)
    value(oc:subClassOf ont:LegalAgent))
  Individual(ont:Person type(oc:UnityClass) type(oc:NonDependentClass)
    type(oc:SortalClass) type(oc:RigidClass) value(oc:subClassOf
    ont:LegalAgent))
  Individual(ont:PhysicalObject type(oc:UnityClass)
    type(oc:NonDependentClass) type(oc:SortalClass) type(oc:RigidClass)
    value(oc:subClassOf ont:AmountOfMatter))
  Individual(ont:Red type(oc:NonSortalClass) type(oc:NonDependentClass)
```

```
      type(oc:NonUnityClass) type(oc:NonRigidClass)    value(oc:subClassOf
      ont:Entity))
   Individual(ont:RedApple type(oc:AntiRigidClass) type(oc:UnityClass)
      type(oc:NonDependentClass) type(oc:SortalClass)
      value(oc:subClassOf ont:Red))
   Individual(ont:SocialEntity type(oc:NonSortalClass)
      type(oc:UnityClass) type(oc:NonDependentClass) type(oc:RigidClass)
      value(oc:subClassOf ont:Agent))
   Individual(ont:Verebrate type(oc:UnityClass)
      type(oc:NonDependentClass) type(oc:SortalClass) type(oc:RigidClass)
      value(oc:subClassOf ont:Animal))
)
```

Formal Ontology in Information Systems
B. Bennett and C. Fellbaum (Eds.)
IOS Press, 2006

Using Selectional Restrictions to Query an OWL Ontology

Leila KOSSEIM [a,1], Reda SIBLINI [a], Christopher J. O. BAKER [a] and
Sabine BERGLER [a]

[a] *CLaC Laboratory*
Department of Computer Science and Software Engineering
Concordia University
1400 de Maisonneuve Blvd. West
Montreal, Quebec, Canada H3G 1M8
{kosseim, r_sibl, baker, bergler}@cse.concordia.ca

Abstract. This paper discusses the linguistic module of an Ontology Natural Language Interaction System that is based on semantic restrictions. The system, called ONLI, takes as input questions in unrestricted natural language, translates them into nRQL, an extension to the RACER ontology query language, then generates answers as returned by the RACER ontology reasoning server. Translation into nRQL is done through a syntactic analysis (with Minipar), followed by the use of semantic restrictions imposed by the roles stored in the ontology to map terms in the question to concepts and roles in the ontology. The system was evaluated on the FungalWeb ontology using the mean reciprocal rank (MRR) measure used in question-answering. With a test set of 36 questions, the systems achieved an MRR of 0.72.

Keywords. Natural Language, Ontology Interface, Selectional Restrictions, Semantic Web

1. Introduction

The query of knowledge representation formalisms such as ontologies is a central requirement of the Semantic Web. Increasingly we are forced to recognize the importance of providing simple query access to such knowledge repositories. Existing tools that allow users to query and reason over ontologies [1,2,3] use custom designed query languages [4] with complex syntax which are reportedly difficult for domain experts to master [5]. With this in mind, we sought to develop a question-answering (QA) system as a front-end to RACER, the Renamed ABox and Concept Expression Reasoner [1]. The intended users are experts who are knowledgeable in the domain, but may have little or no knowledge of the structure of the ontology. By providing a QA interface, experts can formulate their queries using natural language prose. This allows for a seemingly transparent search environment, where the users do not need to formulate different syntaxes depending on the collection they are searching. Searching a document collection (such as the Web) or searching an ontology can be seen by the user as the same task.

---

[1]Corresponding author

In this paper, we present a novel approach to building a natural language front-end to an ontology that uses the semantic restrictions imposed by the ontology design to map terms in the questions to the content of the ontology. The question, formulated in unrestricted natural language, is mapped into the new RACER Query language syntax and presented to the description logic automated reasoner RACER which returns the query results.

1.1. nRQL as a Knowledge Representation Query Language

Since the recent establishment of the Ontology Web Language (OWL), design specifications for Description Logic (DL) based query languages have been proposed and existing languages contrasted, highlighting their advantages and limitations [6]. nRQL emerges as a prominent and highly expressive DL-query language and extends the existing capabilities of RACER with a series of query atoms. nRQL uses a Lisp based syntax and the general structure of a query is composed of a query head e.g. `retrieve(?x)` upon which variables used in the body are projected e.g. `(?x Fungi)`, where `(retrieve (?x)(?x Fungi))` queries for instances of the concept `Fungi`. In this paper, we employ conjunctive queries where the atoms are simple concept or role assertions and where the variables in the body of the query match the corresponding individuals in the ontology that satisfy all query conditions. A detailed description of nRQL is given in [7] and verbose examples are outlined in [8].

1.2. The FungalWeb Ontology

The NL interface was developed and tested on the FungalWeb Ontology [9]. The FungalWeb Ontology is a prototype bio-ontology, scripted in the OWL formalism. It is an integrated conceptualization of multiple scientific domains. These overlapping domains include taxonomies of fungi and enzyme reaction mechanisms as well as enzyme substrates and industrial specifications describing the applications and benefits of enzymes. The FungalWeb Ontology is a large scale ontology comprising 3616 concepts and 11,163 instances related by 142 roles. The conceptualization was designed so that fungal species, enzyme names, enzyme product names, enzyme vendor names and chemical names are modeled as instances. Free text segments describing enzyme applications, industrial benefits of enzymes were also modeled as instances. The following example illustrates the query capability of the conceptualization e.g. if the user is looking for vendors selling enzyme products that contain Xylanase, the user composes the nRQL syntax below:

```
(retrieve (?x) (AND (AND
  (?x ?y <http://a.com/ontology#Sells>)
  (?y ?z <http://a.com/ontology#Contains>))
  (?z <http://a.com/ontology#Xylanase>))))
```

The scope of the ontology has been further illustrated in a series of application scenarios [10,11] demonstrating the range of query capabilities afforded by the conceptualization.

During the development of the FungalWeb Ontology there was a need for domain experts to interact directly with the conceptualisation. The Ontoligent Interactive Query

Tool (OntoIQ) [12] was subsequently developed to provide browse and click query functionality to the ontology using nRQL. OntoIQ is useful in the context of ontology development and has been able to identify challenges in the ontology query paradigm that could be overcome by Natural Language Query access to nRQL.

2. Previous Work on querying ontologies

Natural language interfaces to databases have been a significant research focus, especially during the 70s and 80s (e.g, [13,14,15]). However, only recently has the topic of natural language interfaces to ontologies been seriously investigated. Earlier work has been on restricted language or simplified English (e.g. [16]) where constraints are imposed on the expressiveness of the user's prose. For example, [17,18] use the Attempto Controlled English (ACE) to query the Semantic Web. The interface imposes some structure on the user's input to guide the entry but does not restrict the user with an excessively formal language. Each ACE query is translated into a discourse representation structure that is then translated into an N3-based semantic web querying language (RDQL), which allows their execution. Their work shows that these kinds of interfaces are simple to use and provide superior retrieval performance to traditional logic-based approaches when used by a casual user. However, to provide an easier to use interface, unrestricted language seems more *natural*, especially for the occasional user.

Few systems however allow questions in unrestricted English. AquaLog [19] and its successor PowerAqua [20], for example, are ontology-driven QA systems, which take an ontology and a natural language question as an input and return answers drawn from semantic data compliant with the input ontology. AquaLog was tested on the KMi ontology on academic life. Its linguistic module makes use of the Gate package [21] and uses several metrics to compute the similarity between terms in the question and terms in the ontology based on string-based algorithms and WordNet. This paper presents a system similar to AquaLog and PowerAqua, but relies on semantic restrictions to improve its linguistic module.

3. The ONLI Natural Language Interface

3.1. Overview

The system consists of 3 main modules in addition to a web user interface that allows the user to interact with the system. The question is first processed by the Minipar [22] general purpose syntactic parser. The resulting dependency parse tree is then analysed to extract all predicate-argument structures that will be mapped to the concepts and roles of the selected ontology. The mapping is done using the selectional restrictions imposed by the ontology. The result is a set of mappings along with their confidence score. The next module of the system then generates nRQL queries using hand-made transformation rules, and executes the highest scoring query over the ontology. Let us now describe each module in detail.

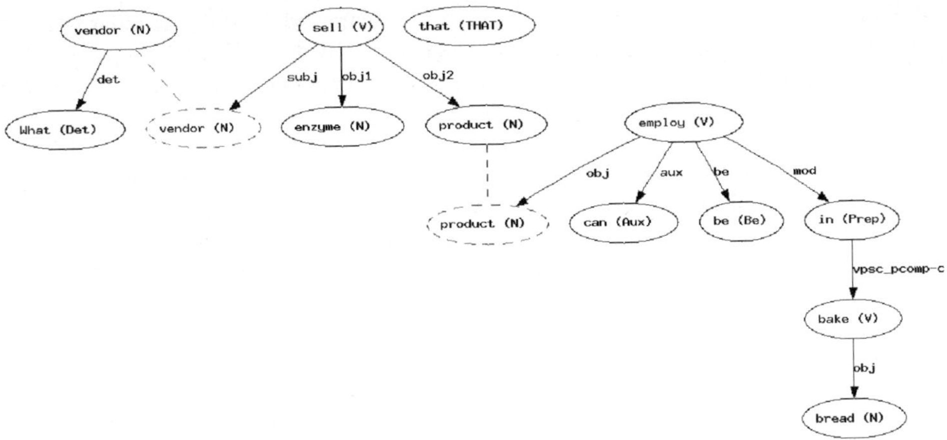

Figure 1. Minipar parse tree for the sentence *What vendors sell enzyme products that can be employed in baking bread?*

3.2. Syntactic Analysis

Initially, the user's question is parsed to identify its syntactic constituents. For this, we use the general purpose an freely available Minipar parser [22].

Predicates and noun phrases contain the main semantic information of the question. These will thus be extracted from the question and mapped to roles, concepts or instances in the ontology. Roles in the FungalWeb ontology can be binary, relating two concepts to each other; or unary, relating one instance to a concept. Therefore, from the parse tree of a question, all sets of predicates along their arguments are extracted and represented into a predicate structure made of the triplet argument-predicate-argument.

In the parse tree, these predicate structures may be realized by many grammatical relations: a verb with its subject (deep or surface) and object (direct or not), an adjective modifying a noun, a noun-noun compound, a passive verb modifying a noun ...or may need to be extracted from more complex verb phrases (e.g. an inverted auxiliary *is it sold?*). To be more concrete, consider the question:

What vendors sell enzyme products that can be employed in baking bread?

Minipar will generate the dependency tree shown in Figure 1. From this structure, two predicate structures must be extracted: the predicate *sell* and its arguments *enzyme product* and *vendors*, and the predicate *employ* and its arguments *enzyme products* and *baking bread*. These 2 predicate structures are shown below:

arg1	pred	arg2
vendor	sell	enzyme product
enzyme product	employ	baking bread

Although not shown in Figure 1, in the parse tree, the predicate *sell* introduces an `i` relation (a relation between the main clause and the inflectional phrase). Similarly, the predicate *employ* also introduces an `i` relation. Arguments can participate in different types of grammatical relations; for example, *vendor* is a subject, the argument *enzyme* is an `obj1`, while *product* is an `obj2` and *bread* is an `obj`. Given this variety of syntactic realisations, we analysed the output of Minipar on a set of 144 questions (see section 4), and developped 20 extraction rules to cover them. These rules take into account the grammatical category and relation of each word as extracted from the Minipar tree. To select the relations to consider, we were inspired by the work of [23] who devised a list of common relations accross parsers in order to normalise their output for comparative evaluation. For example, extraction rule #7 states:

Rule 7: If a noun is being modified by a relative clause, then this relative clause is treated as a new predicate structure with the noun as one of its arguments.

For example, in the sentence: *Find a fungus that has Pectinase.*, the noun *fungus* is modified by a relative clause. This creates a new predicate structure, as illustrated below.

Word	Category	Relation	
Find	V		$\Rightarrow$ a verb in first position creates an empty predicate (Rule 20)
a	Det		$\Rightarrow$ determiners are ignored (Rule 1)
fungus	N	object of *find*	$\Rightarrow$ *fungus* is arg2 of *find*
that	THAT	subject of *has* antecedent: *fungus*	$\Rightarrow$ *fungus* is arg2 of *has*
has	V		$\Rightarrow$ new predicate
Pectinase	N	object of *has*	$\Rightarrow$ *Pectinase* is arg2 of *has*

and will produce 2 predicate structures:

```
arg1:⊘ pred:⊘ arg2:fungus
arg1:fungus pred:have arg2:Pectinase
```

The rules are applied recursively to embedded structures to find all predicate structures from the question. These rules form by no means an exhaustive list, but they cover all our 144 training questions and our 32 randomly selected testing questions (see section 4).

The argument slot of a predicate structure may be left empty if the argument was elided in the question or if a relative determiner was used and Minipar could not identify its antecedent. An empty argument slot will be replaced by a variable name in the final nRQL query (see section 3.4). The predicate slot may also be empty. Such empty predicates occur if the predicate is in the first position in the question (e.g. *Find enzymes, Give enzymes.*) or is a verb *to-be*. Such predicates are treated differently, because they will map to a unary concept rather than to a binary role.

Table 1 shows other examples of questions along with their predicate structures. In the first question in Table 1, the first argument *enzyme* will be mapped to a concept or an actual instance. When mapped to an actual instance, the query created will not include a variable. On the other hand, if mapped to a concept the query created will have a variable that is restricted to the mapped concept.

3.3. Ontology Matching

Once all predicate structures have been extracted from the question, we attempt to match each constituent of the structure to variables, concepts, instances or roles in the ontology. This can be seen as a classical categorization problem, in particular, Word Sense Disambiguation. Indeed, the task here is to find a function to map the linguistic expressions to particular senses (concepts, instances or roles in the ontology).

Question	Predicate Structure
What enzyme can be used in baking bread?	`(arg1:`*`enzyme`*`, pred:`*`use`*`, arg2:`*`baking bread`*`)`
Find an enzyme that can be used in baking bread.	`(arg1:∅, pred:∅, arg2:`*`enzyme`*`)` `(arg1:∅, pred:`*`use`*`, arg2:`*`baking bread`*`)`
Is protease an enzyme?	`(arg1:`*`protease`*`, pred:∅, arg2:`*`enzyme`*`)`
What is used in baking bread?	`(arg1:∅, pred:`*`use`*`, arg2:`*`baking bread`*`)`

Table 1. Examples of predicate structures

Domain Concept	Role	Range Concept
`substrate`	`is activated by enzyme`	`enzyme`
`enzyme`	`can be found in`	`commercial enzyme product`
`fungi`	`grows on substrate`	`substrate`
`industrial and environmental process`	`is using`	`commercial enzyme product`
`industrial and environmental process`	`is using`	`fungi`
`industrial and environmental process`	`is using`	`enzyme`
...	...	...

Table 2. Examples of roles and their domain and range in the FungalWeb ontology

To select the correct mapping we were inspired by the selectional restriction-based disambiguation approach used in word-sense disambiguation [24]. Indeed, in a text, a predicate often imposes semantic constraints on its arguments which allow one to disambiguate its sense, and in turn, the sense of its arguments. For example, in its transitive form, the verb *drink* imposes that its direct object be a *liquid*. The correct sense of an ambiguous direct object can therefore be identified through this semantic constraint. With an ontology, this same strategy can be used as the roles in the ontology impose constraints on the domain and range of the concepts they can relate. In turn, correctly identifying the concepts or instances involved in the question can help us identify an ambiguous role.

For example, Table 2 shows selected roles in the FungalWeb ontology along with their corresponding domain and range concepts. As the table shows, a concept for an argument may not be semantically compatible with all roles. For example, if the predicate has been mapped to the role `grows on substrate`, then the arguments must map to either the concepts (or instances of) `fungi` or `substrate`. In the FungalWeb ontology, on average, a role is used to relate 2.4 different pairs of concepts. Since roles are not heavily overloaded, we can expect semantic restrictions to be quite useful.

For each predicate structure, the result of the semantic analysis is a list of possible roles, concepts, and instances in the ontology along with a confidence measure. For efficiency reasons, predicates are only mapped to roles, while the arguments are mapped to concepts and instances. Empty arguments in the predicate structure are mapped to variables.

3.3.1. Mapping predicates

Because predicates do not exhibit much domain terminology, we can use general purpose lexical resources to match them to roles in the ontology. To map a predicate of the question to a role in the ontology, we try to unify its stem (identified by Minipar) with a role of the ontology. For this, we use a measure of semantic similarity.

To compute the semantic distance between a predicate and a candidate role, we use WordNet::Similarity [25,26]. This package uses WordNet and, by default, the path length between 2 words to compute their semantic relatedness. The predicate in the sentence should be a correct English term, however, the name of the role in the ontology is not restricted to be available in WordNet. In fact, many role names in the FungalWeb ontology do not correspond to English verbs, they are often mult1i-word terms (e.g. `is activated by enzyme`). In the case of multi-word terms, we add the appropriate words to the role to form a complete sentence If a role name is given, then we parse the sentence and use the head of the sentence to be compared using WordNet similarity to the retrieved predicate.

If the semantic similarity returns zero, then a default small value (ϵ) of 0.001 is used, so as not to rule out any mapping. The ϵ value is in fact rarely used. It is meant as a smoothing technique so that so that no match is completly ruled out just because the mapping returned zero (WordNet may not contain the term, for example).

The result of this step is that each role is mapped to each predicate, with a different confidence level.

3.3.2. Mapping arguments

Once the predicate is matched to a set of possible roles, we try to match its arguments to a variable, or a concept or an instance in the domain and range of this role. This is where semantic restrictions come into play.

If the argument is empty, then a new variable is created as a placeholder, but the domain and range of the role already mapped are kept as constraints to the variable. If the argument is not empty, then we need to map it to a concept or an actual instance. Because NPs tend to be much more domain specific (e.g. enzyme names, substrate names, ...), general purpose lexical resources such as WordNet cannot be used to match NPs. Instead, we use a measure of lexical similarity.

To score the lexical relatedness between an argument and a concept or an instance, we use the inverse of the edit distance – the minimal number of characters needed to make the 2 strings identical. The lexical score is also normalized to be within 0 and 1. If the argument matches a concept and an instance we give the matched instance a slightly higher score over the matched concept. If the lexical similarity returns zero, then we use the same ϵ value.

The Cartesian product of all possible mappings for the predicate and all possible mappings for the arguments is then computed. The overall score of the final mapping is computed as the product of the individual mappings. Table 3 shows an example, where the predicate structure arg1: *vendor* pred: *sell* arg2: *enzyme product* is mapped to two different ontological structures with different mapping scores.

predicate structure	mapping	score
pred:*sell*	role:`sells`	1
arg1:*vendor*	concept:`vendor name`	× 0.498
arg2:*enzyme product*	concept:`commercial enzyme product`	× 0.66
		0.328
pred:*sell*	role:`producing enzyme for`	0.333
arg1:*vendor*	concept:`vendor name`	× 0.498
arg2:*enzyme product*	concept:`industrial processes`	× 0.01
		0.001

Table 3. Examples of semantic mapping for the predicate structure `arg1:`*vendor* `pred:`*sell* `arg2:`*enzyme product*

3.3.3. Variable Co-referencing

Once a set of possible mapping is built for each predicate structure of the question, we need to make sure that variables that should refer to the same entities actually do. This, in effect, allows us to process the predicate structures of a question as a single semantic unit, rather than a conjunction of unrelated predicate structures.

To identify which variables should co-refer to the same entities, we use the semantic constraints we set when we used the semantic relations to bound our variables (see section 3.3.2). If the constraints of two variables can be unified, then we consider the variables to co-refer. Since we already know the possible concepts that this variable could belong to, we gave the variable name the concept id, so referring to the same variable and thus the same id leads us to create the relationship between the predicate structures.

This strategy seems to work with the FungalWeb ontology, but may not scale up to other ontologies with a larger role "overloading". By that, we mean that if the roles in the ontology are used to relate a large number of concepts or instances, then the selectional restrictions may not be enough to perform variable co-referencing effectively. In this case, a deeper analysis of the question is probably needed.

For each question, the list of the possible mappings is finally ranked according to the overall confidence score and the best 10^2 are sent to be translated to nRQL.

3.4. Querying with a Reasoner

The reasoner query module is responsible for creating the nRQL queries and sending them to the RACER reasoner. In the current state of the project, only two types of nRQL queries have been considered: unary concept queries and binary role queries.

A unary concept query tries to find instances of a particular concept (e.g. *Find all enzymes* ⇒ `(retrieve (?x) (?x enzyme))`) or to determine if an entity is an instance of a concept (e.g. *Is Protease an Enzyme?* ⇒ `(retrieve () (Protease Enzyme))`). A unary concept query can therefore have one of the two forms:

```
1.   (retrieve (?x) (?x <concept>))
2.   (retrieve () (<instance> <concept>))
```

---

[2] This threshold was set arbitrarily.

concept1 role concept2	`(?x <concept1>) (?y <concept2>) (?y ?x <role>)`
variable1 role variable2	`(retrieve (?y ?x) (?y ?x <Role>))`
variable ⊘ concept	`(retrieve (?x) (?x <concept>))`

Table 4. Examples of predicate structure patterns and corresponding nRQL queries

A binary role query searches for the binding between variables representing concepts or instances (e.g. *What can be used in what?* ⇒ `(retrieve (?y ?x) (?y ?x can be used in))`). A binary role can also specify particular concepts or instances instead of specifying a variable. For example, *What can be used in baking?* ⇒ `(retrieve (?x) (?x <Baking> can be used in))`, or *Can Protease be used in baking?* ⇒ `(retrieve () (<Protease> <Baking> can be used in))`. A binary role query can therefore take the 4 following forms:

```
3.    (retrieve (?y ?x)(?y ?x <role>))
4.    (retrieve (?x)(?x <instance> <role>))
5.    (retrieve (?x)(<instance> ?x <role>))
6.    (retrieve ()(<instance> <instance> <role>))
```

In order to create the nRQL queries from the mappings, we created cases for all possible combinations of the argument-predicate-argument triplet. An argument could have a variable, an instance, or a concept and the predicate could be a empty or not. That leads us to 18 different combinations, and for each combination, a hand made rule is created to produce one or more appropriate nRQL statements. Table 4 shows a sample of these patterns and the corresponding nRQL expression.

For example, from the question in section 3.2 *What vendors sell enzyme products that can be employed in baking bread?*, 2 predicate structures were extracted:

```
arg1:vendor pred:sell arg2:enzyme product
arg1:vendor pred:sell arg2:enzyme product
```

The corresponding highest ranking ontological matches are:

```
concept:vendor name role:sells concept:commercial enzyme product
concept:commercial enzyme product role:can be used in instance:baking
```

The first triplet corresponds to the case of `concept1 role concept2` shown in Table 4 which creates 3 nRQL statements:

```
1. (?x <vendor name>))
2. (?y <commercial enzyme product>))
3. (?y ?x <sells>)
```

The second triplet corresponds to the case of `concept role instance` which creates 2 nRQL statements:

```
1. (?y <commercial enzyme product>))
2. (?y <baking> <can be used in>))
```

Notice how the two triplets are related using the variable y, which co-refer to the same concept *commercial enzyme product*). Individual nRQL expressions are then connected with an AND operator.

4. Evaluation

To develop and test the system, we used a corpus of 206 pairs of questions and their associated nRQL queries. The material was created by 4 different casual users in order not to be influenced by the writing style of one particular person. The users were all knowledgeable in the domain and the content of the ontology, but did not necessarily know its structure and role names.

From the original 206 question-query pairs, 26 were discarded because they involved issues we do not consider (e.g. quantifiers, see section 5). From the 180 remaining, 80% randomly selected pairs were used to develop the system (develop the syntactic rules, ...) and the 20% remaining were used for the evaluation.

We thus evaluated the prototype using 36 questions and compared the system-generated results with the human composed queries as gold-standard. The comparison was based on query equivalence. If the generated query was not equivalent to the one in the gold-standard, it was considered wrong. For each question, the system generates a set of possible queries ranked in order for confidence. For each question q, we therefore computed the final score as the reciprocal rank of their first correct answer. If none of the generated queries was equivalent to the gold-standard, a score of 0 was given. Otherwise, the score is equal to the reciprocal of its rank. For example, if a question generated 4 ranked queries, and the 3rd one is correct, the question received a score of $\frac{1}{3}$. The overall system score is the average $RR(q)$ for all questions q. This methodology is called the mean-reciprocal rank (MRR) score as used in question-answering [27].

For all 36 questions, the MRR was 0.72. Out of the 36 questions, 24 were found at rank 1; 6 questions ranked between 2 and 10, and 6 were not found in the top 10 answers. Out of the 6 questions that were not translated properly, 3 were not parsed correctly by Minipar, 2 did not match correctly the actual instance in the ontology, and 1 contained a hidden relation.

Hidden relationships involve deeper reasoning, For example, in *Which proteins are known to act on p-aminophenol?* the relation act on relates a substrate to an enzyme, but the question is looking for a protein, so we need to recognise that an enzyme is a protein, which means we must also check the subsumption hierarchy of the ontology for *is a* relations. Hidden relationships were not considered in the system analysis.

5. Conclusion and Future Work

In this paper we have described a system that acts as natural language interface system for a domain ontology. The interface takes as input questions in unrestricted language and translates them into nRQL queries that are then run over the RACER reasoner. The linguistic analysis of the questions is based on a syntactic parse from which a set of predicate structures is extracted, which are mapped to the correct ontology entities using semantic restrictions imposed by the ontology structure. We tested the interface on the

FungalWeb ontology, with real questions composed by four different casual users, and obtained an MRR of 0.72.

Further work includes a more robust evaluation of the system with larger, more diverse ontologies and a larger test collection. We presume that the semantic restrictions approach worked well in our case because each role was not used in many contexts, but as roles can relate a larger number of domains and ranges, the approach may not scale up if the semantic and lexical mappings do not hold. The use of semantic restrictions derived from the ontology are pretty effective in determining the correct mapping to formal queries. However we need to evaluate that this strategy works with more diverse ontologies. The system should scale up with ontologies with a larger number of roles, but we anticipate a drop in performance if these roles are heavily overloaded; the selection restrictions may not be able to discriminate what sense is referred to.

In addition, several linguistic phenomena are not taken into account. For example, conjunctions and disjunctions within noun phrases, as well as quantifiers (*some, three, ...*) are simply ignored. For example, *Find three fungi that have been reported to have Pectinase* will be considered equivalent to *Find all fungi that have been reported to have Pectinase*. In the case of conjunctions or disjunctions (e.g *What fungi have been reported to have Pectinase and/or Cellulase?*), the system will not be able to recognize and deal appropriately with the issue. In the case of quantifiers, the system will ignore the quantifier and will search for all possible answers.

Another drawback is our limitation to use noun phrases that are lexically close to the vocabulary used in the ontology for concepts and instances. Mapping of noun phrases can only be performed at the lexical level because a general purpose semantic lexicon for general English is not helpful for domain specific terminology. In the biology domain, terminology plays a central role, and several domain-dependant synonyms are typically used to refer, for example, to enzymes or proteins. Without a dictionary of the domain, only lexical matches can be made. In our experiment, this did not cost a lower performance, but if we use a larger ontology or a larger pool of users, the lexical similarity alone may not scale up.

Acknowledgments

This project was financially supported by Genome Québec. Many thanks to Mike Carrick for this help in building the question set. The authors would also like to thank the anonymous referees for their valuable comments.

References

[1] Haarslev, V., Möller, R.: RACER System Description. In Goré, R., Leitsch, A., Nipkow, T., eds.: Proceedings of International Joint Conference on Automated Reasoning (IJCAR-2001), Sienna, Italy, Springer-Verlag, Berlin (2001) 701–705

[2] Pellet: http://www.mindswap.org/2003/pellet/. (last accessed 2006-01-16)

[3] FaCT: http://www.cs.man.ac.uk/ horrocks/fact/. (last accessed 2006-01-16)

[4] Wessel, M., Molle, R.: A high performance semantic web query answering engine. In: Proceedings of the 2005 International Workshop on Description Logics (DL2005), Whistler, Canada (2005)

[5] Smith, B., Ceusters, W., Klagges, B., Kohler, J., Kumar, A., Lomax, J., Mungall, C., Neuhaus, F., Rector, A., Rosse, C.: Relations in biomedical ontologies. Genome Biology **6** (2005)

[6]   Glimm, B., Horrocks, I.R.: Query answering systems in the semantic web. In Bechhofer, S., Haarslev, V., Lutz, C., Moeller, R., eds.: CEUR Workshop Proceedings of KI-2004 Workshop on Applications of Description Logics (ADL 04), Ulm, Germany (2004)

[7]   Haarslev, V., Moeller, R., Wessel, M.: Querying the semantic web with racer + nrql. In Bechhofer, S., Haarslev, V., Lutz, C., Moeller, R., eds.: CEUR Workshop Proceedings of KI-2004 Workshop on Applications of Description Logics (ADL 04), Ulm, Germany (2004)

[8]   nRQL: The new racer query language. (www.cs.concordia.ca/haarslev/racer/racer-queries.pdf)

[9]   Shaban-Nejad, A., Baker, C.J., Butler, G., Haarslev, V.: The FungalWeb Ontology: Semantic Web Challenges in Bioinformatics and Genomics. In: 4th International Semantic Web Conference (ISWC). Lecture Notes in Computer Science 3729, Galway, Ireland (2004) 1063–1066

[10]   Baker, C., Witte, R., Shaban-Nejad, A., Butler, G., Haarslev, V.: The fungalweb ontology: Application scenarios. In: Eighth Annual Bio-Ontologies Meeting, co-located with ISMB 2005, Detroit, Michigan (2005)

[11]   Baker, C., Shaban-Nejad, A., Xu, S., Haarslev, V., Butler, G.: Semantic web infrastructure for fungal enzyme biotechnologists. Journal of Web Semantics: Special Edition on Semantic Web for the Life Sciences (2006) in press.

[12]   Baker, C., Xu, S., Butler, G., Haarslev, V.: Ontoligent interactive query tool. In: Proceedings of Canadian Semantic Web Working Symposium. (2006) in press.

[13]   Androutsopoulos, I., Ritchie, G., Thanisch, P.: Natural language interfaces to databases–an introduction. Journal of Language Engineering 1 (1995) 29–81

[14]   Copestake, A., Sparck-Jones, K.: Natural language interfaces to databases. Knowledge engineering Review 5 (1990) 225–249

[15]   Clifford, J.: Natural language querying of historical databases. Computational Linguistics 14 (1988) 10–34

[16]   Decker, S., Erdmann, M., Fensel, D., Studer, R.: ONTOBROKER: Ontology Based Access to Distributed and Semi-Structured Information. In Meersman, R., ed.: Database Semantics: Semantic Issues in Multimedia Systems, Proceedings TC2/WG 2.6 8th Working Conference on Database Semantics (DS-8), Rotorua, New Zealand, Kluwer Academic Publishers (1999) 351–369

[17]   Bernstein, A., Kaufmann, E., Fuchs, N.E.: Talking to the Semantic Web - A Controlled English Query Interface for Ontologies. AIS SIGSEMIS Bulletin 2 (2005) 42–47

[18]   Bernstein, A., Kaufmann, E., Gohring, A., Kiefer, C.: Querying ontologies: A controlled english interface for end-users. In: Proceedings of the 4th International Semantic Web Conference. (2005) 112–126

[19]   Lopez, V., Pasin, M., Motta, E.: Aqualog: An ontology-portable question answering system for the semantic web. In: Proceedings European Semantic Web Conference (ESWC), Crete (2005) 546–562

[20]   Lopez, V., Motta, E., Uren, V.: Poweraqua: Fishing the semantic web. In: Proceedings European Semantic Web Conference (ESWC), Montenegro (2006)

[21]   Cunningham, H.: GATE, a General Architecture for Text Engineering. Computers and the Humanities 36 (2002) 223–254

[22]   Lin, D.: Dependency-based evaluation of MINIPAR. In: Proceedings of the Workshop on the Evaluation of Parsing Systems, Granada, Spain (1998)

[23]   Carroll, J., Briscoe, T., Sanlippo, A.: Parser evaluation : A survey and a new proposal. In: LREC-98, Granada (1998) 447–455

[24]   Resnik, P., Yarowsky, D.: A perspective on word sense disambiguation methods and their evaluation (1997)

[25]   Pedersen, T., Patwardhan, S., Michelizzi, J.: Wordnet::similarity - measuring the relatedness of concepts. In: Proceedings of the Nineteenth National Conference on Artificial Intelligence (AAAI-04), San Jose, California (2004)

[26]   Patwardhan, S., Banerjee, S., Pedersen, T.: Using measures of semantic relatedness for word sense disambiguation. In: Proceedings of the Fourth International Conference on Intelligent Text Processing and Computational Linguistics (CICLING-2003). (2003)

[27]   Voorhees, E.: Overview of the TREC 2001 Question Answering Track. In: Proceedings of The Tenth Text REtrieval Conference (TREC-X), Gaithersburg, Maryland (2001) 157–165

Formal Ontology in Information Systems
B. Bennett and C. Fellbaum (Eds.)
IOS Press, 2006

Author Index